*"EDUCATION IS NOT
THE FILLING OF A PAIL,
BUT THE LIGHTING OF A FIRE"*

WILLIAM BUTLER YEATS

AURORA BOREALICE

JOAN STEACY

First Edition
Printed by Gauvin Press in Gatineau, Quebec

Library and Archives Canada Cataloguing in Publication

Steacy, Joan, author, illustrator
Aurora Borealice / Joan Steacy.

ISBN 978-1-77262-037-5 (softcover)

1. Comics (Graphic works). I. Title.

PN6733.S72A97 2019 741.5'971 C2018-905607-X

Conundrum Press
Wolfville, Nova Scotia, Canada
www.conundrumpress.com

Conundrum Press acknowledges the financial assistance of the Canada Council for the Arts, the Government of Canada, and the Nova Scotia Creative Industries Fund toward this publication.

Canada Council for the Arts | Conseil des Arts du Canada

Canada

NOVA SCOTIA

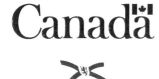

INTRODUCTION

We're told we're stupid, we're told we have a lousy voice so can't sing, are clumsy so we can't dance, don't colour within the lines so we can't draw - and we believe. The Alice of *Aurora Borealice* is brilliant, talented, and a functional illiterate who believes what she's been told all her life, until with the aid of a supportive boyfriend and a healthy dose of Marshall McLuhan, she breaks free of her labels. It helps that she, and said supportive boyfriend, have good senses of humor.

I'm reminded of Dale Messick, creator of the comic strip *Brenda Starr*. As if being dyslexic wasn't enough, Dale was also nearsighted. She couldn't see the blackboard, and so spent her time in the back row drawing pictures. She was left-handed back in the days when the teacher whacked you on the palm if she caught you drawing with your left hand. As a result, Dale graduated from high school at the age of twenty, but she drew all the illustrations for her high school yearbook, and went on to create one of the most famous comic strips in America. Who cares if she also remained the world's worst speller?

Did I mention that *Aurora Borealice* is wittily written and charmingly drawn? Roar, Alice!

Trina Robbins
Writer and Herstorian

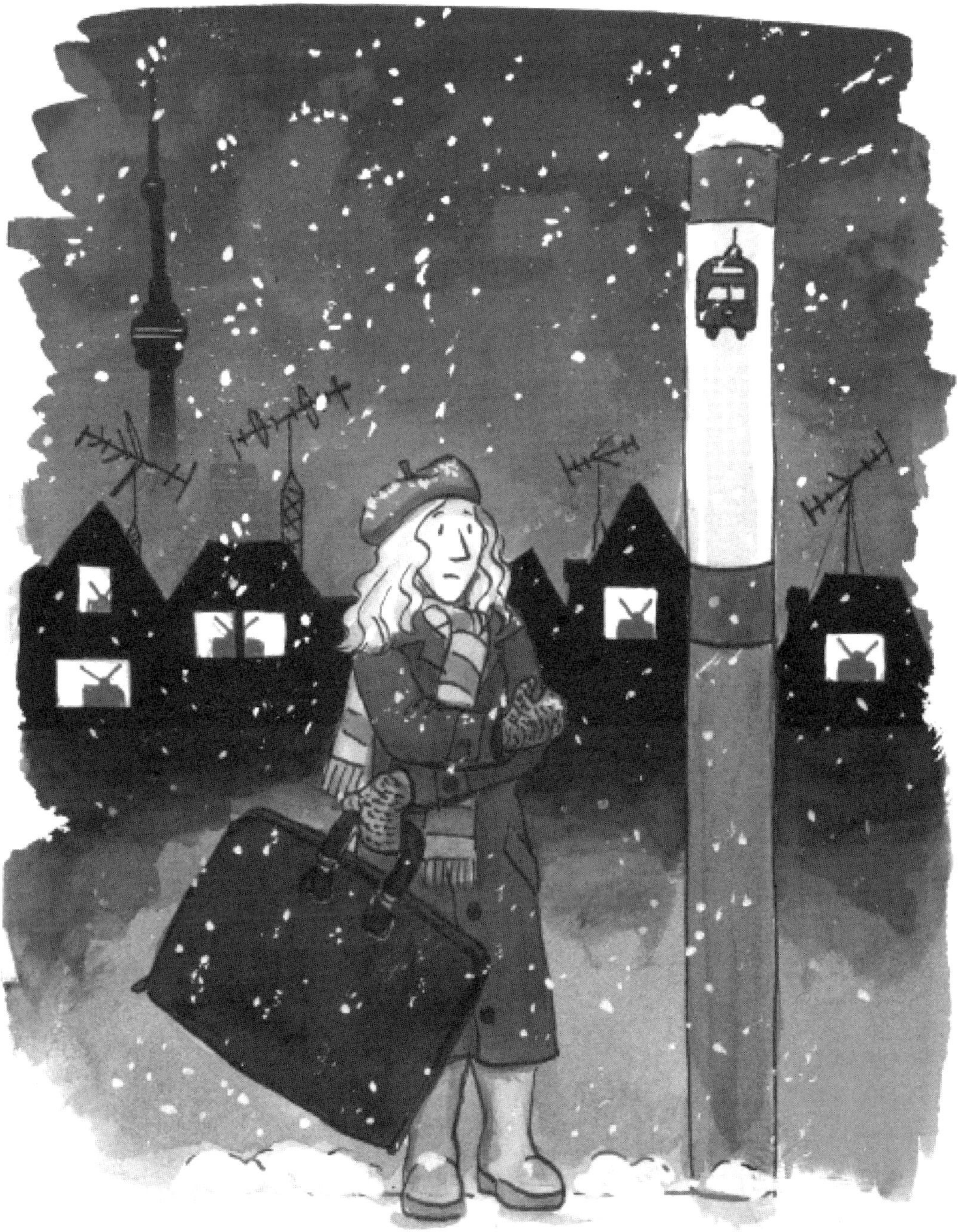

CHAPTER 1

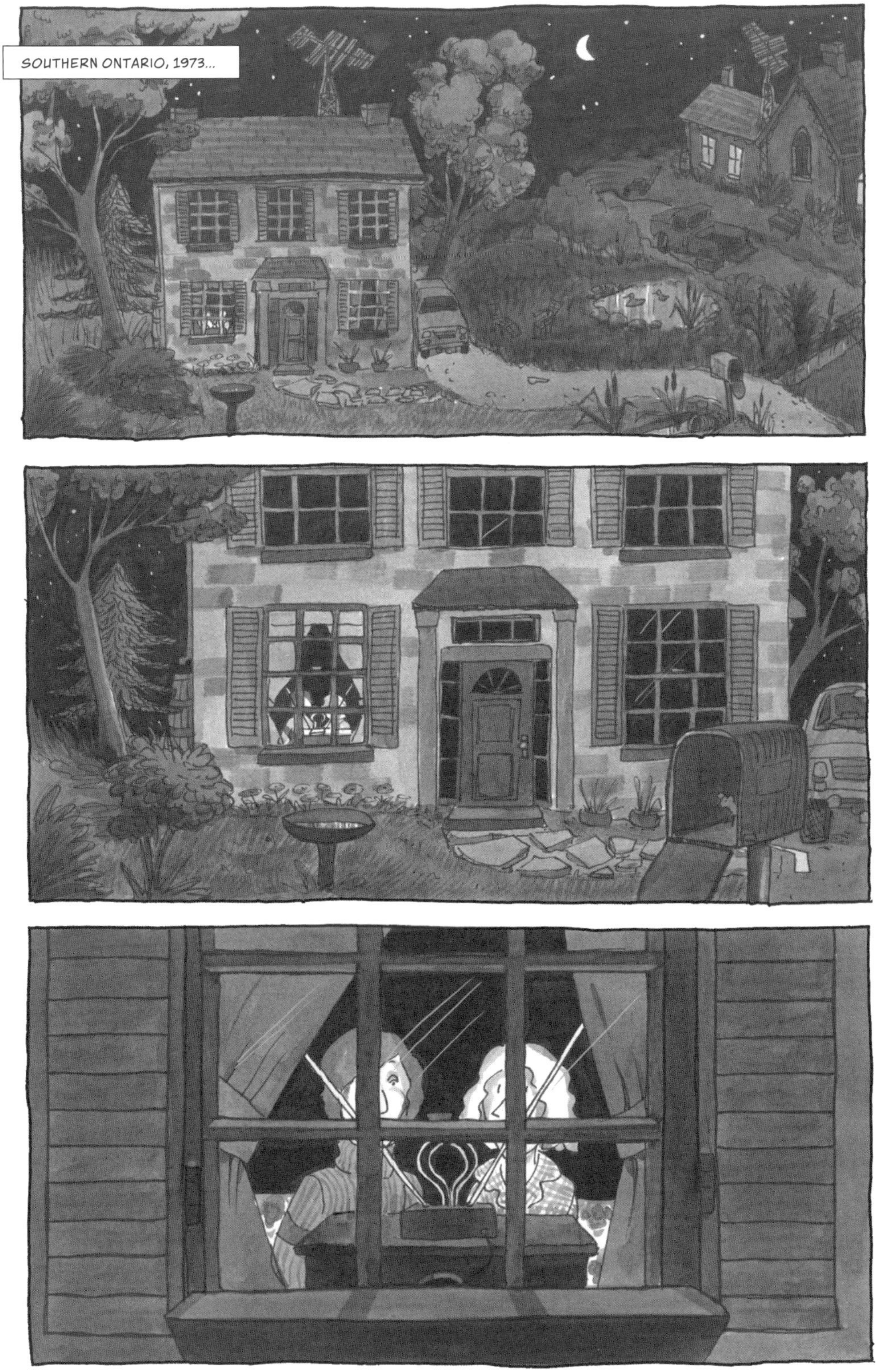
SOUTHERN ONTARIO, 1973...

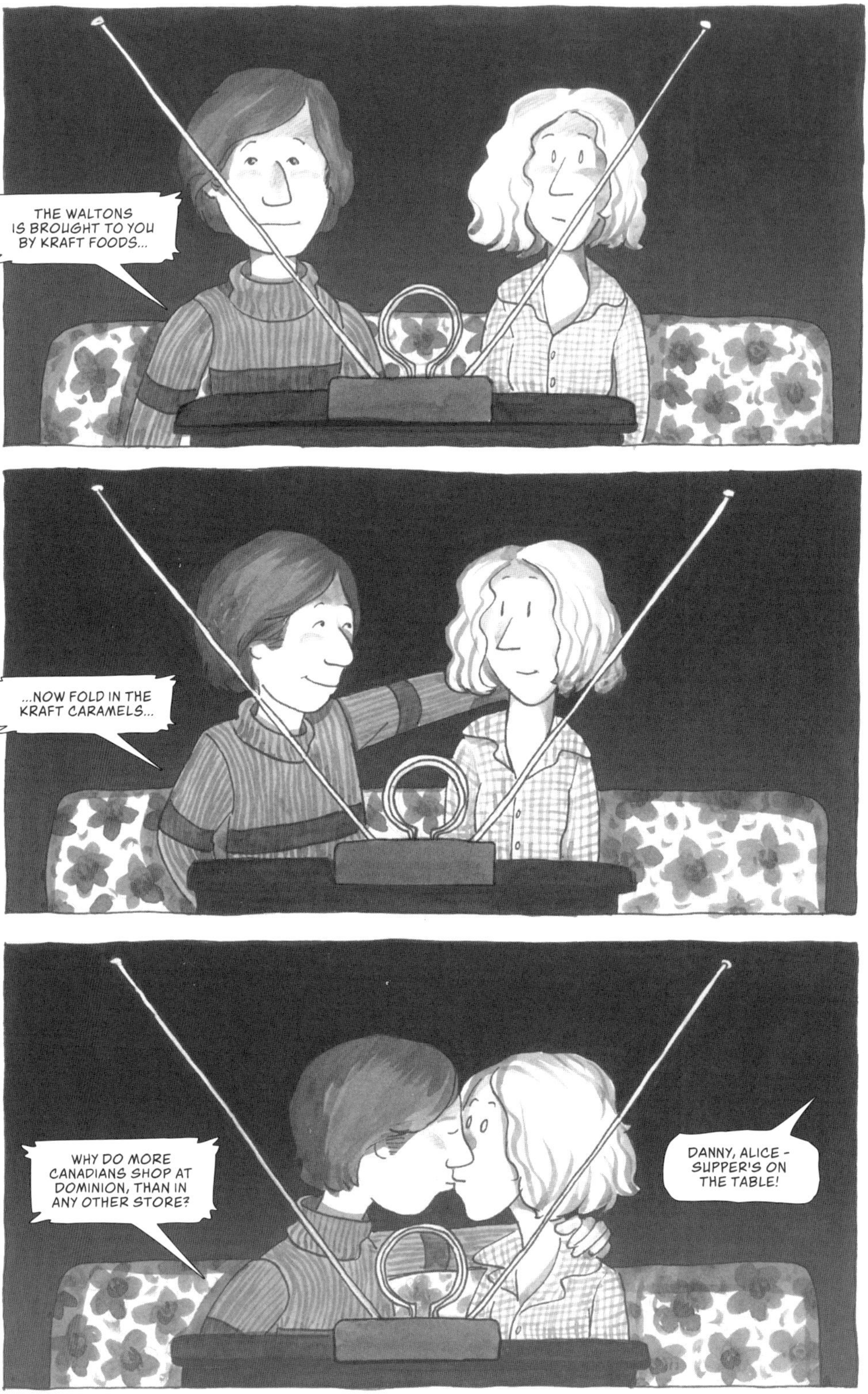
THE WALTONS IS BROUGHT TO YOU BY KRAFT FOODS...
...NOW FOLD IN THE KRAFT CARAMELS...
WHY DO MORE CANADIANS SHOP AT DOMINION, THAN IN ANY OTHER STORE?
DANNY, ALICE - SUPPER'S ON THE TABLE!

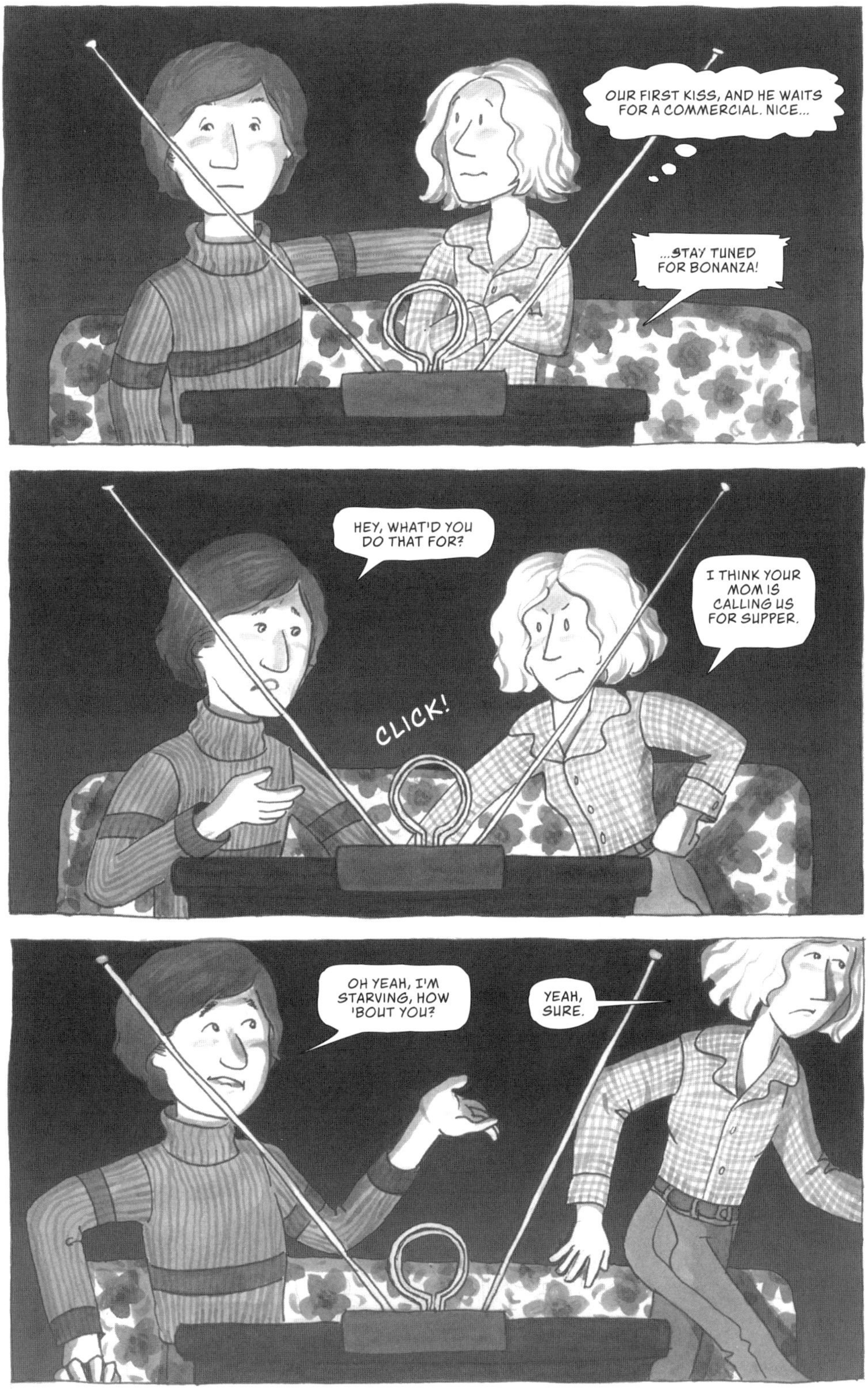

OUR FIRST KISS, AND HE WAITS FOR A COMMERCIAL. NICE...
...STAY TUNED FOR BONANZA!
HEY, WHAT'D YOU DO THAT FOR?
I THINK YOUR MOM IS CALLING US FOR SUPPER.
CLICK!
OH YEAH, I'M STARVING, HOW 'BOUT YOU?
YEAH, SURE.

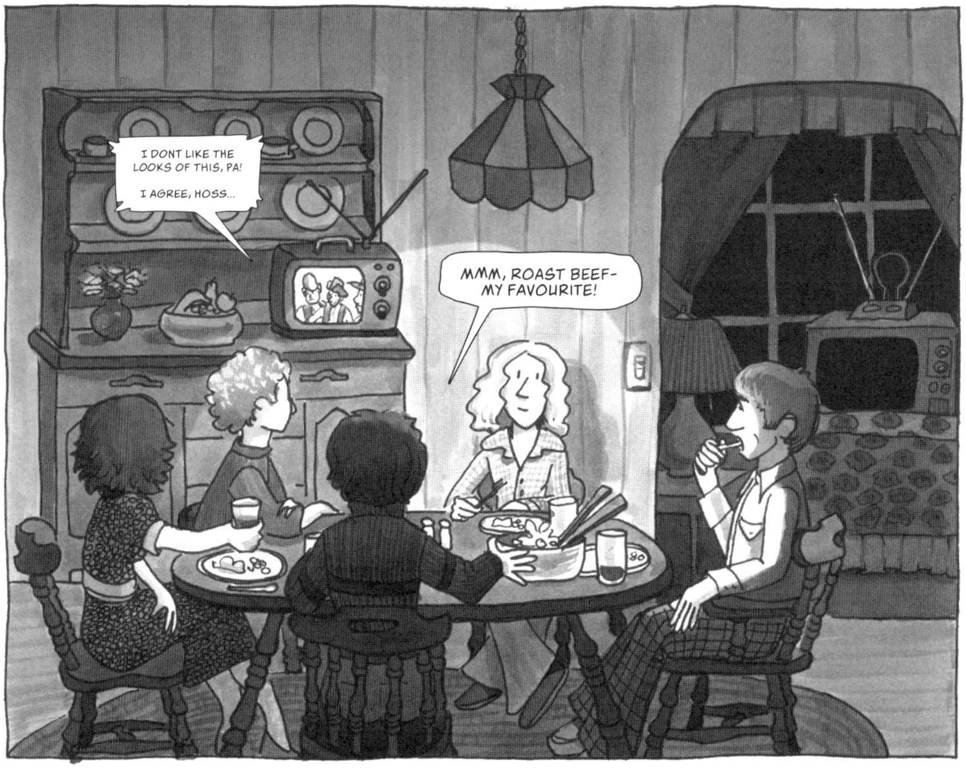
I DONT LIKE THE LOOKS OF THIS, PA!
I AGREE, HOSS...
MMM, ROAST BEEF- MY FAVOURITE!

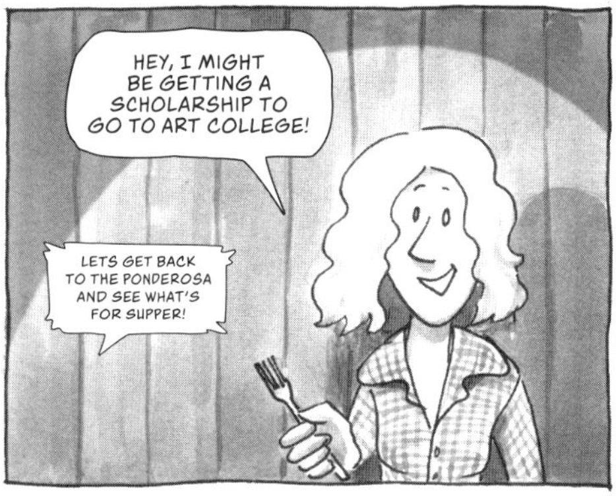
HEY, I MIGHT BE GETTING A SCHOLARSHIP TO GO TO ART COLLEGE!
LETS GET BACK TO THE PONDEROSA AND SEE WHAT'S FOR SUPPER!

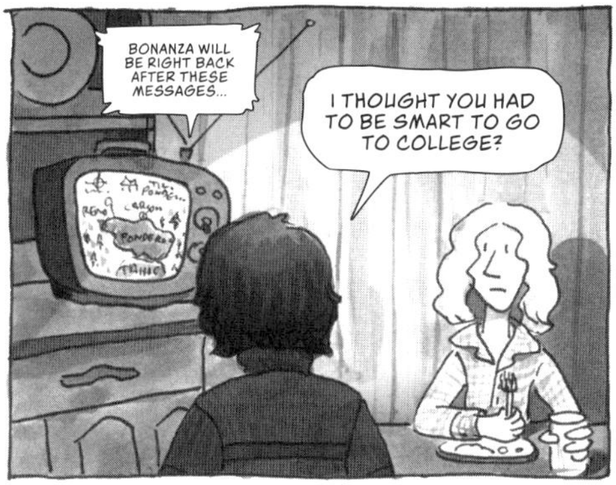
BONANZA WILL BE RIGHT BACK AFTER THESE MESSAGES...
I THOUGHT YOU HAD TO BE SMART TO GO TO COLLEGE?

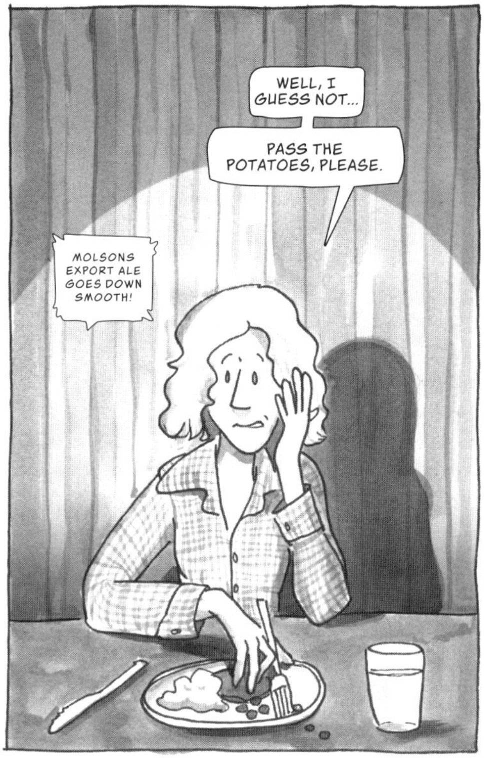
WELL, I GUESS NOT...
PASS THE POTATOES, PLEASE.
MOLSONS EXPORT ALE GOES DOWN SMOOTH!

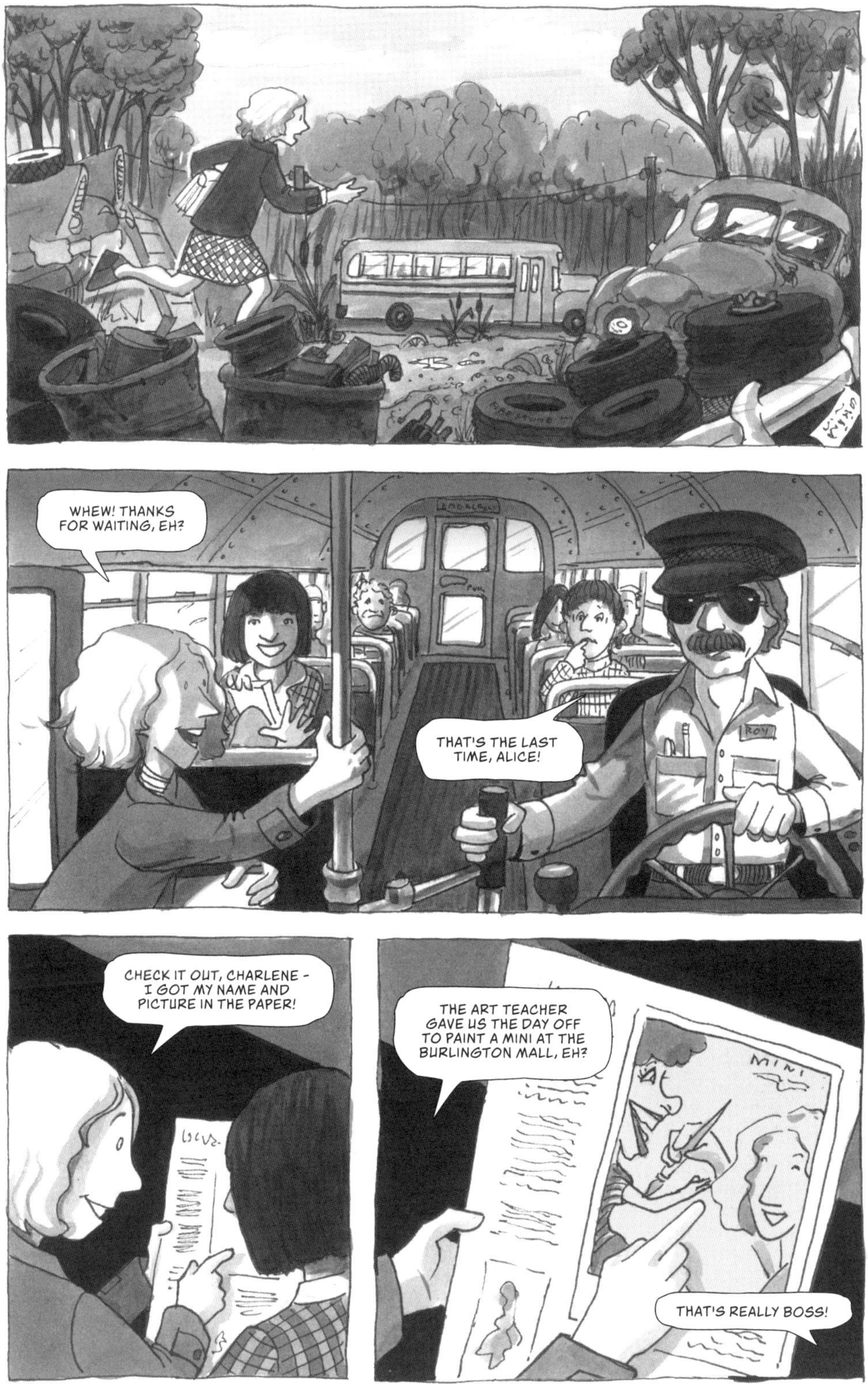
WHEW! THANKS FOR WAITING, EH?
THAT'S THE LAST TIME, ALICE!
ROY
CHECK IT OUT, CHARLENE - I GOT MY NAME AND PICTURE IN THE PAPER!
THE ART TEACHER GAVE US THE DAY OFF TO PAINT A MINI AT THE BURLINGTON MALL, EH?
MINI
THAT'S REALLY BOSS!

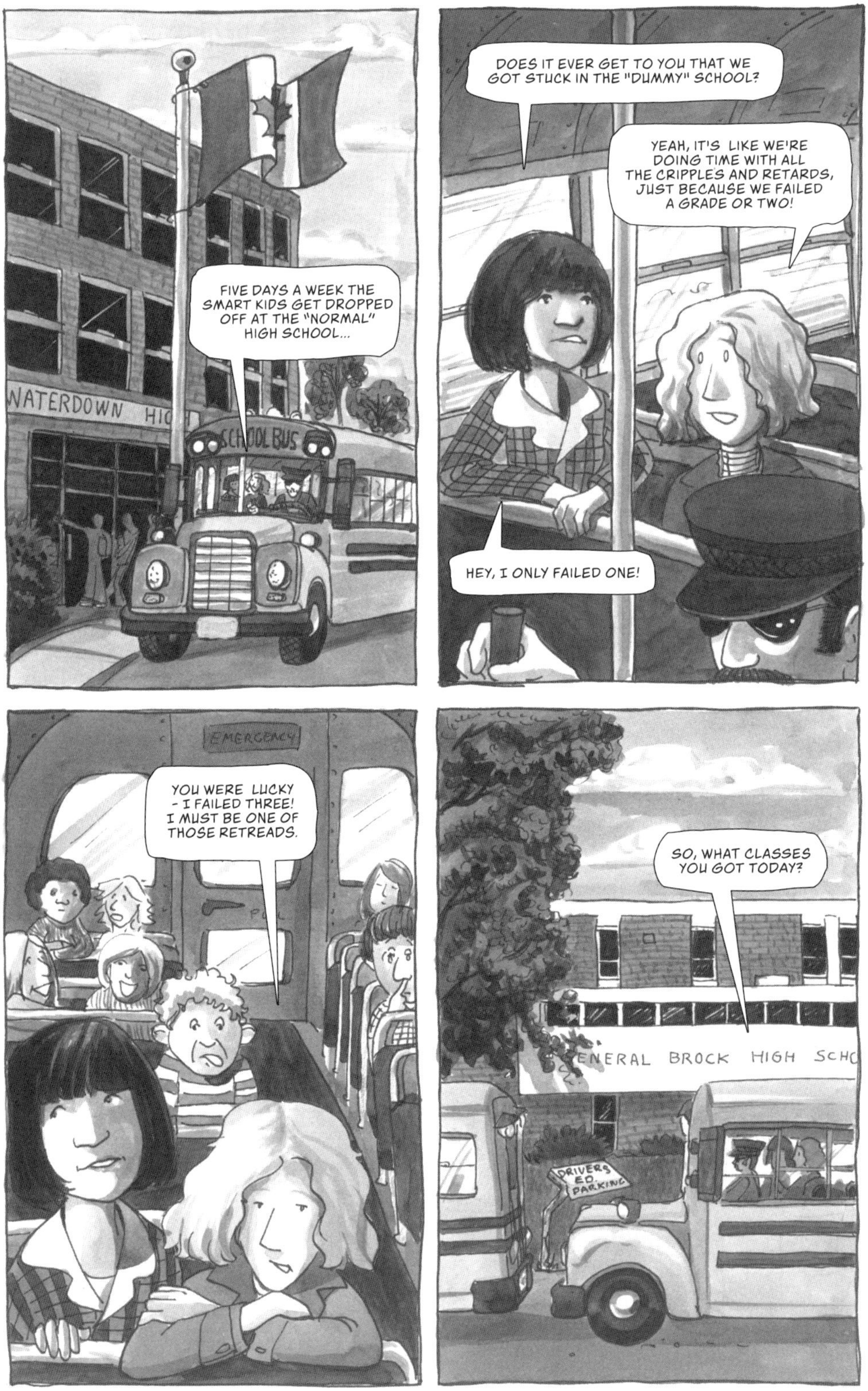
FIVE DAYS A WEEK THE SMART KIDS GET DROPPED OFF AT THE "NORMAL" HIGH SCHOOL...
SCHOOL BUS
DOES IT EVER GET TO YOU THAT WE GOT STUCK IN THE "DUMMY" SCHOOL?
YEAH, IT'S LIKE WE'RE DOING TIME WITH ALL THE CRIPPLES AND RETARDS, JUST BECAUSE WE FAILED A GRADE OR TWO!
HEY, I ONLY FAILED ONE!
EMERGENCY
YOU WERE LUCKY - I FAILED THREE! I MUST BE ONE OF THOSE RETREADS.
SO, WHAT CLASSES YOU GOT TODAY?
DRIVERS ED. PARKING

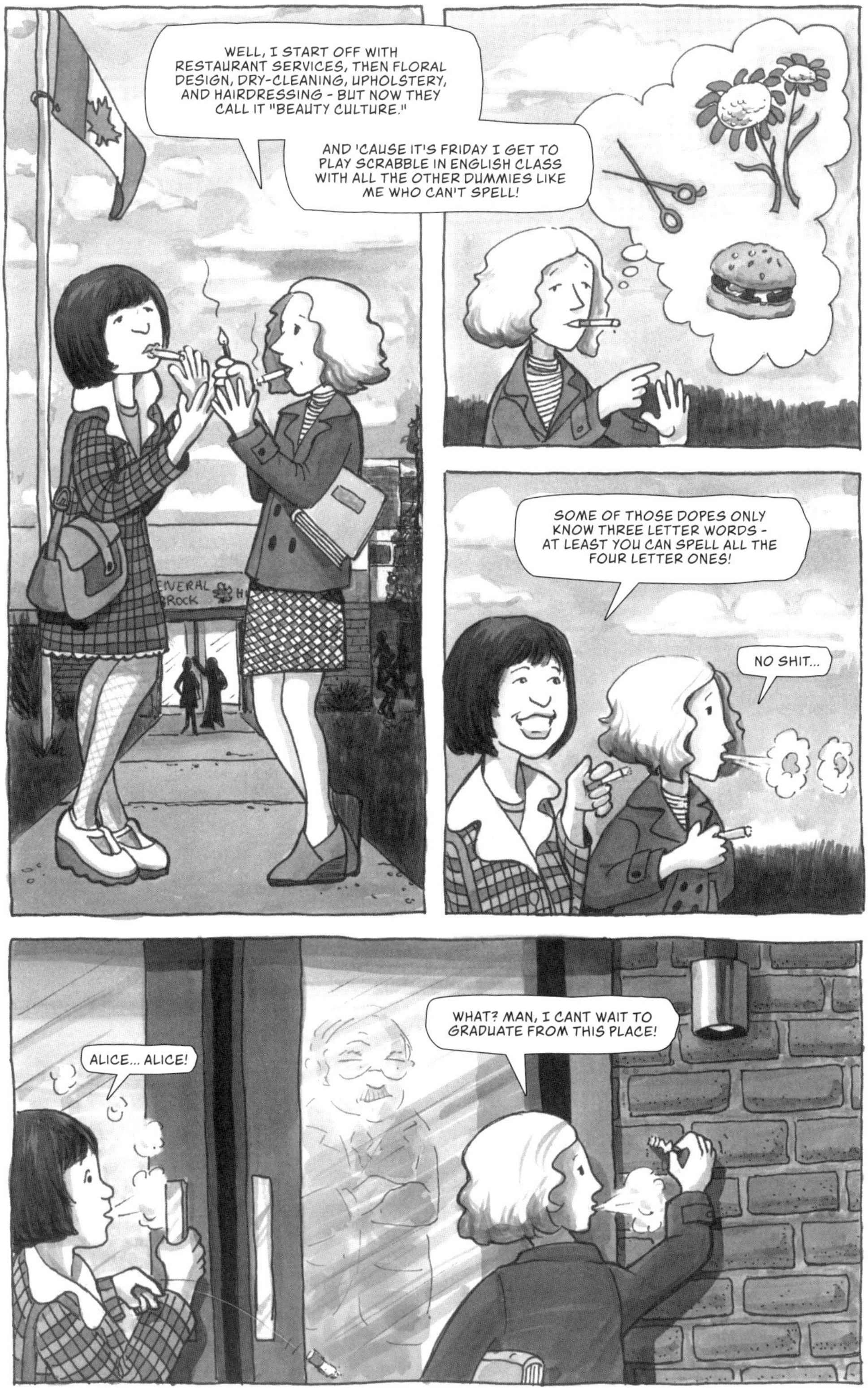

WELL, I START OFF WITH RESTAURANT SERVICES, THEN FLORAL DESIGN, DRY-CLEANING, UPHOLSTERY, AND HAIRDRESSING - BUT NOW THEY CALL IT "BEAUTY CULTURE."
AND 'CAUSE IT'S FRIDAY I GET TO PLAY SCRABBLE IN ENGLISH CLASS WITH ALL THE OTHER DUMMIES LIKE ME WHO CAN'T SPELL!
SOME OF THOSE DOPES ONLY KNOW THREE LETTER WORDS - AT LEAST YOU CAN SPELL ALL THE FOUR LETTER ONES!
NO SHIT...
ALICE... ALICE!
WHAT? MAN, I CANT WAIT TO GRADUATE FROM THIS PLACE!

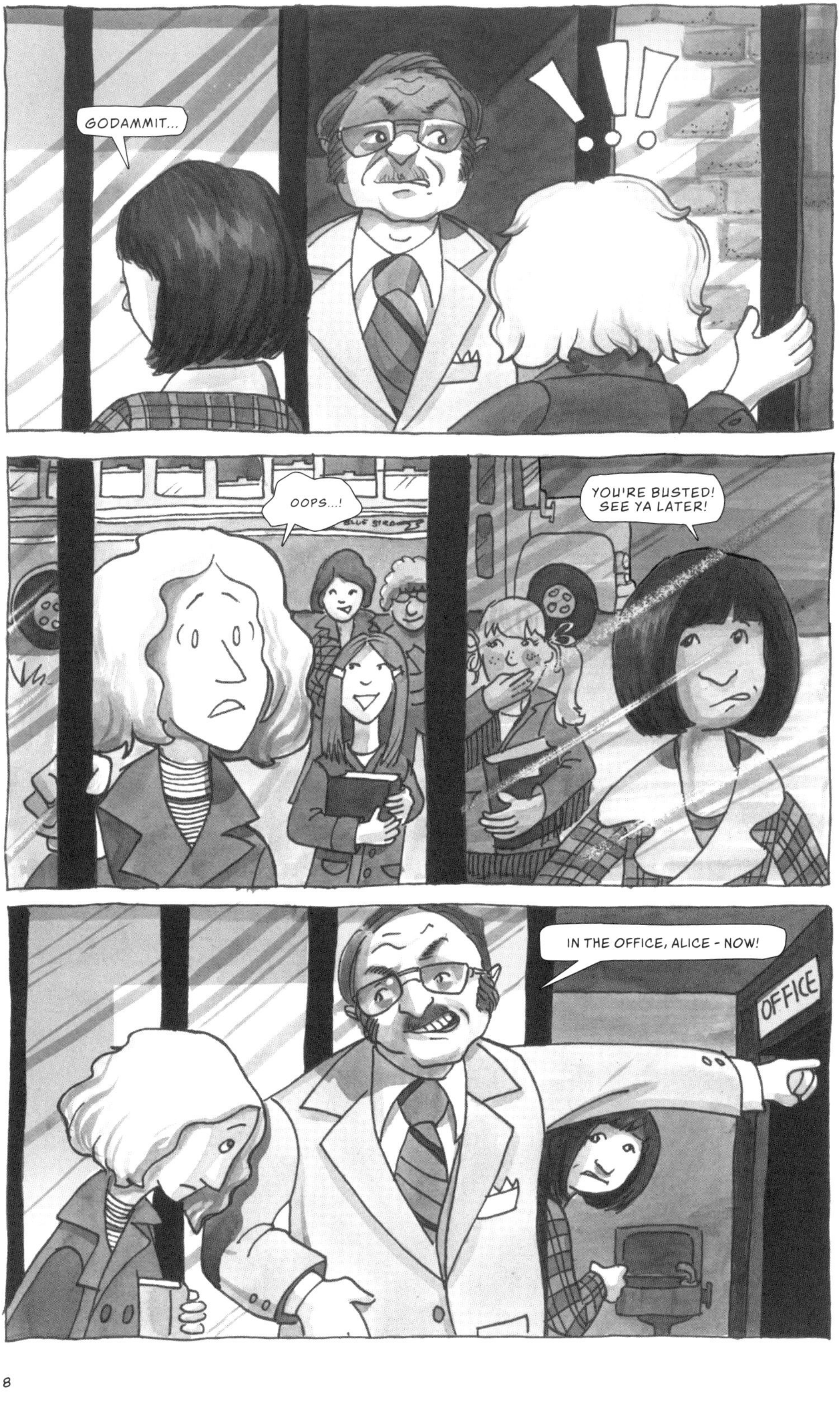
GODAMMIT...
OOPS...!
YOU'RE BUSTED! SEE YA LATER!
IN THE OFFICE, ALICE - NOW!
OFFICE

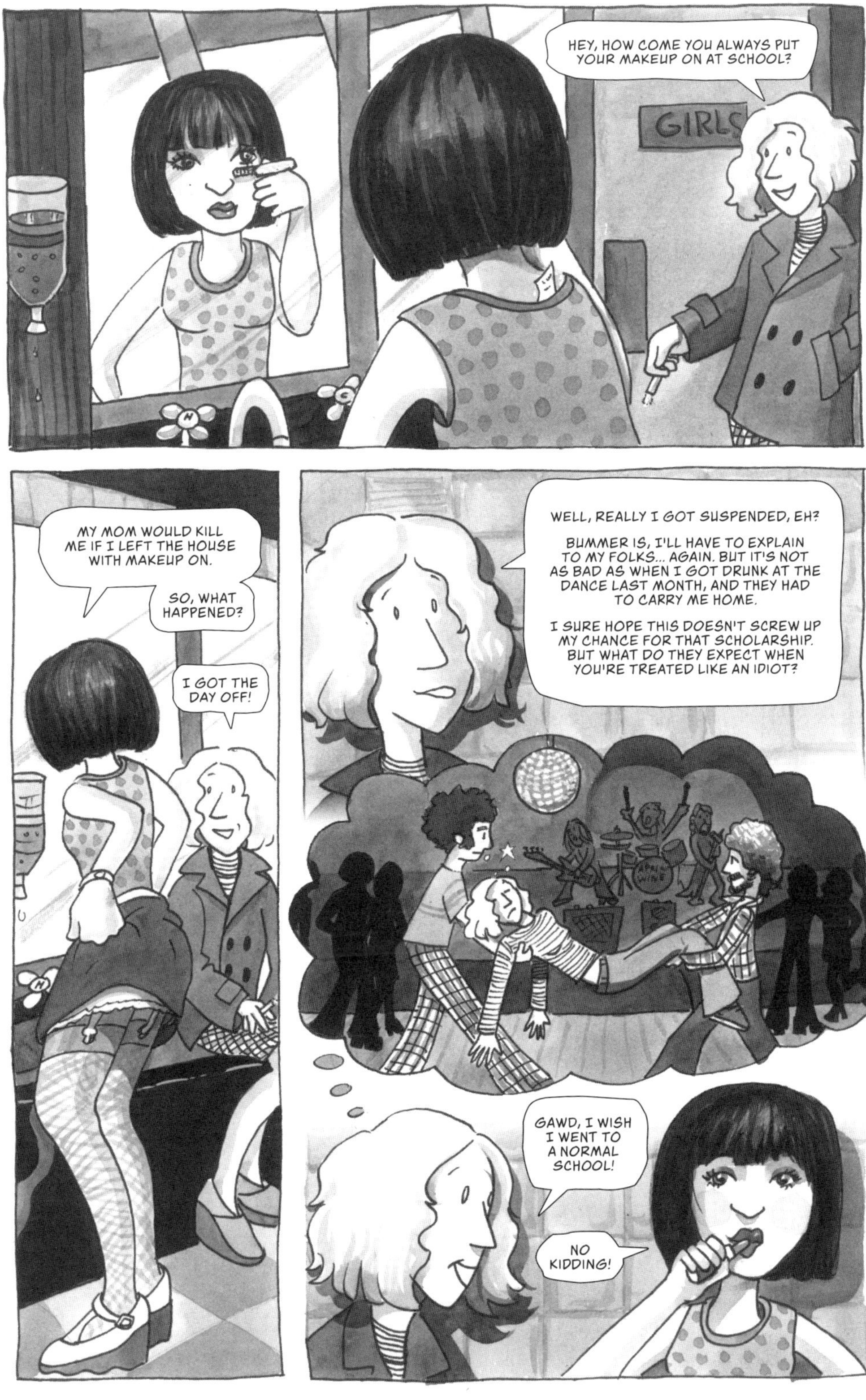

HEY, HOW COME YOU ALWAYS PUT YOUR MAKEUP ON AT SCHOOL?
GIRLS
MY MOM WOULD KILL ME IF I LEFT THE HOUSE WITH MAKEUP ON.
SO, WHAT HAPPENED?
I GOT THE DAY OFF!
WELL, REALLY I GOT SUSPENDED, EH?
BUMMER IS, I'LL HAVE TO EXPLAIN TO MY FOLKS... AGAIN. BUT IT'S NOT AS BAD AS WHEN I GOT DRUNK AT THE DANCE LAST MONTH, AND THEY HAD TO CARRY ME HOME.
I SURE HOPE THIS DOESN'T SCREW UP MY CHANCE FOR THAT SCHOLARSHIP. BUT WHAT DO THEY EXPECT WHEN YOU'RE TREATED LIKE AN IDIOT?
GAWD, I WISH I WENT TO A NORMAL SCHOOL!
NO KIDDING!

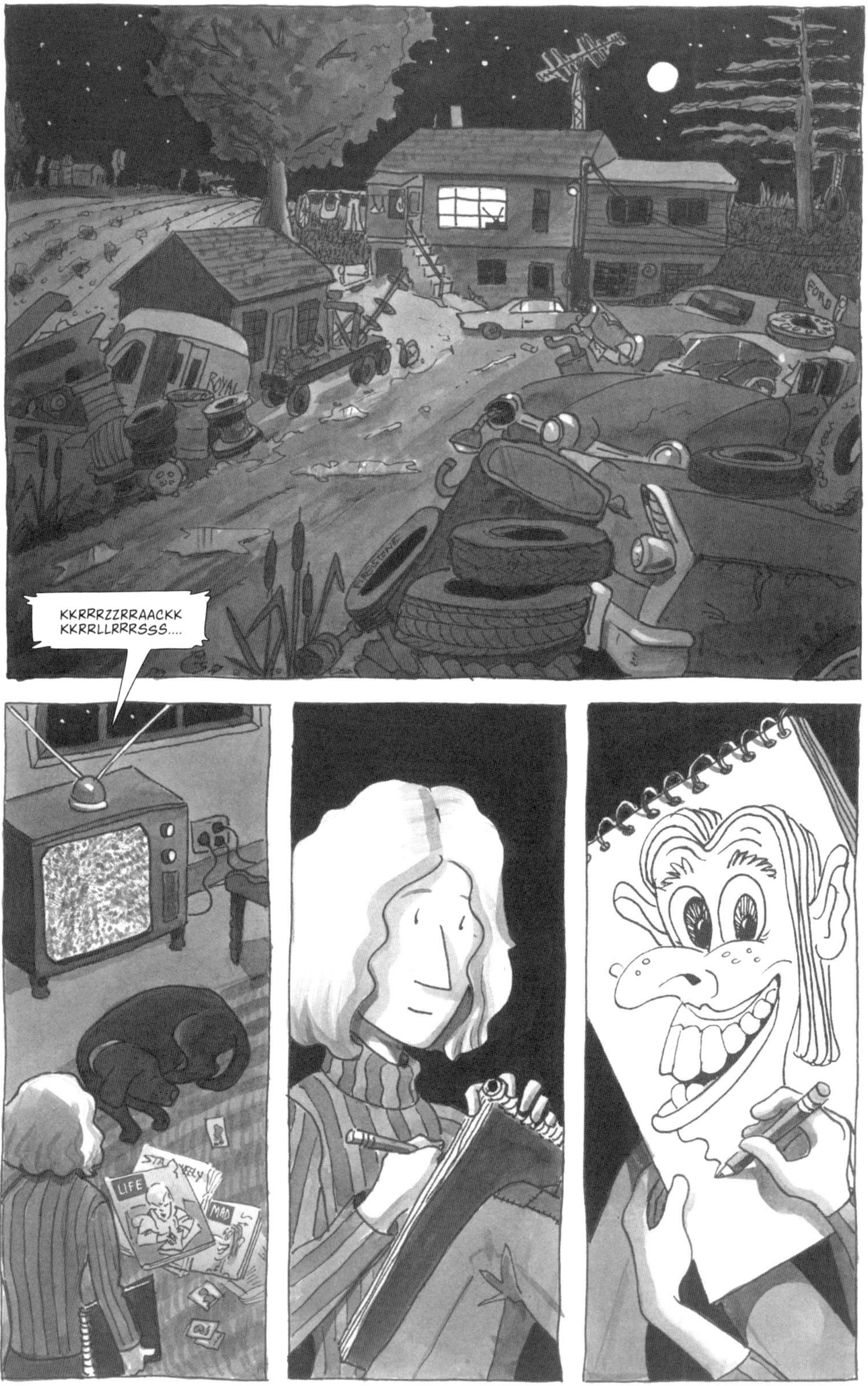
ROYAL
FORD
KKRRRZZRRAACKK
KKRRLLRRRSSS....
LIFE
MAD

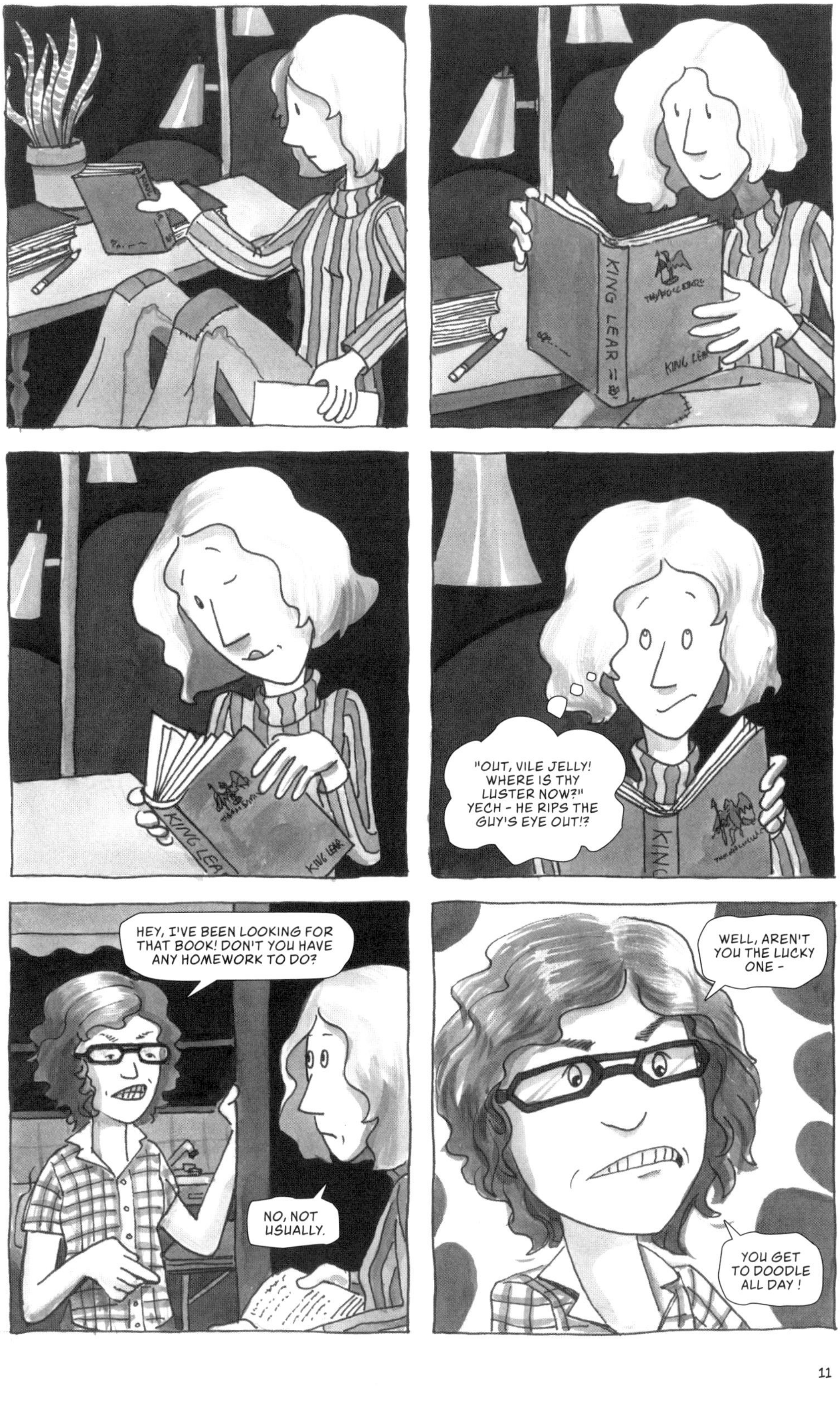
KING LEAR
KING LEAR
KING LEAR
KING LEAR
"OUT, VILE JELLY! WHERE IS THY LUSTER NOW?" YECH - HE RIPS THE GUY'S EYE OUT!?
KING
HEY, I'VE BEEN LOOKING FOR THAT BOOK! DON'T YOU HAVE ANY HOMEWORK TO DO?
NO, NOT USUALLY.
WELL, AREN'T YOU THE LUCKY ONE -
YOU GET TO DOODLE ALL DAY !

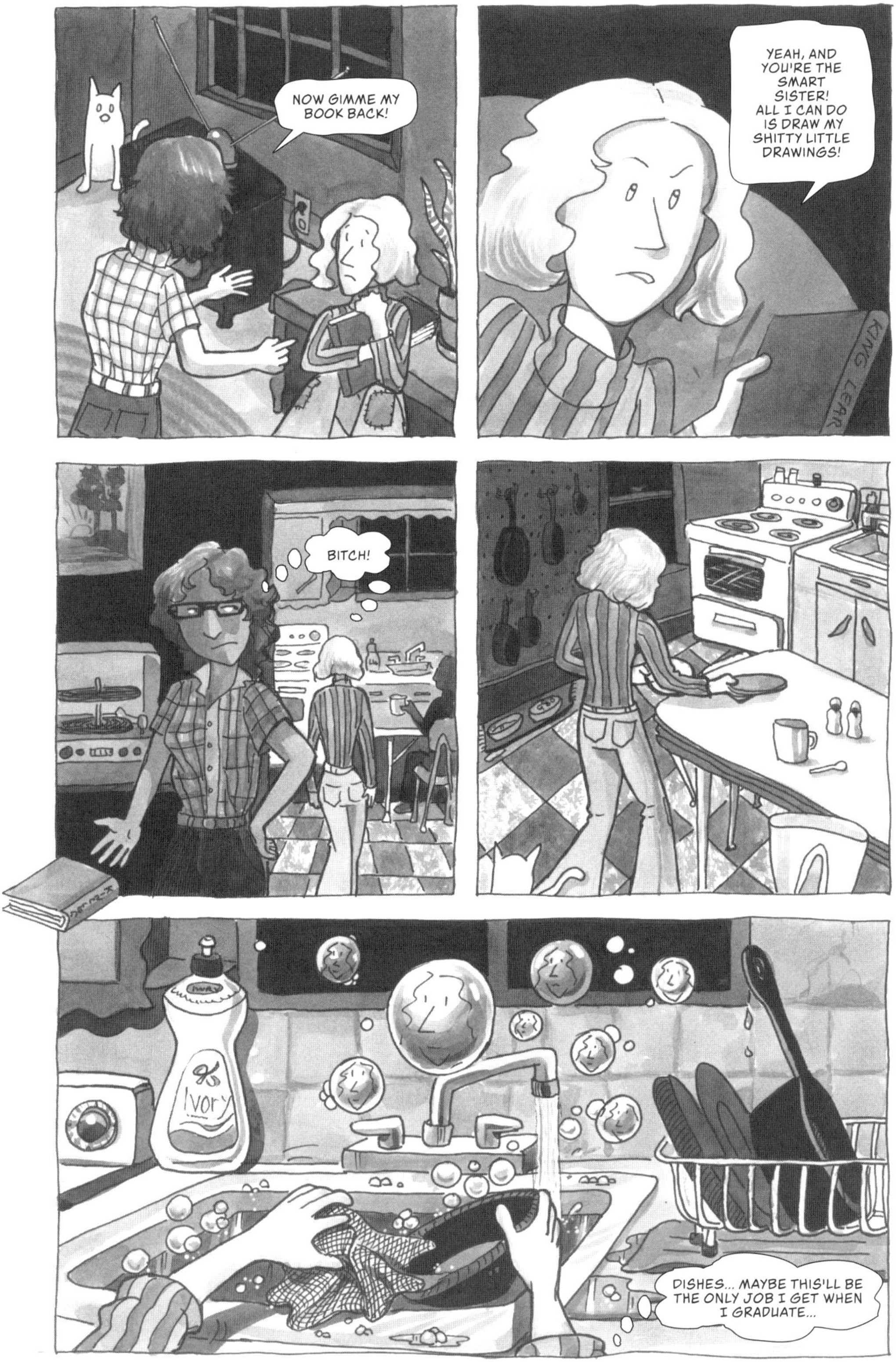
NOW GIMME MY BOOK BACK!
YEAH, AND YOU'RE THE SMART SISTER! ALL I CAN DO IS DRAW MY SHITTY LITTLE DRAWINGS!
KING LEAR
BITCH!
Ivory
DISHES... MAYBE THIS'LL BE THE ONLY JOB I GET WHEN I GRADUATE...

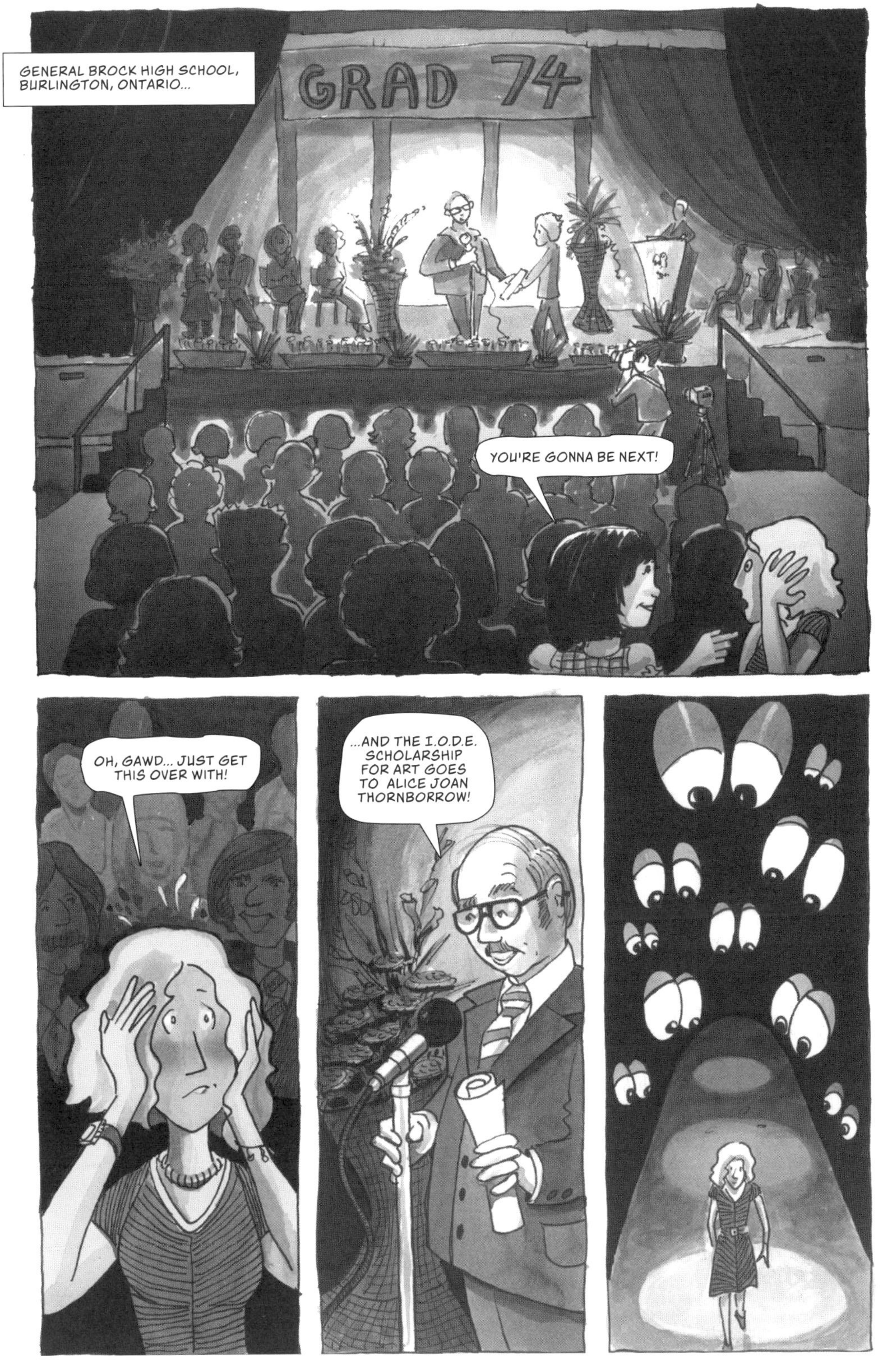
GENERAL BROCK HIGH SCHOOL, BURLINGTON, ONTARIO...
GRAD 74
YOU'RE GONNA BE NEXT!
OH, GAWD... JUST GET THIS OVER WITH!
...AND THE I.O.D.E. SCHOLARSHIP FOR ART GOES TO ALICE JOAN THORNBORROW!

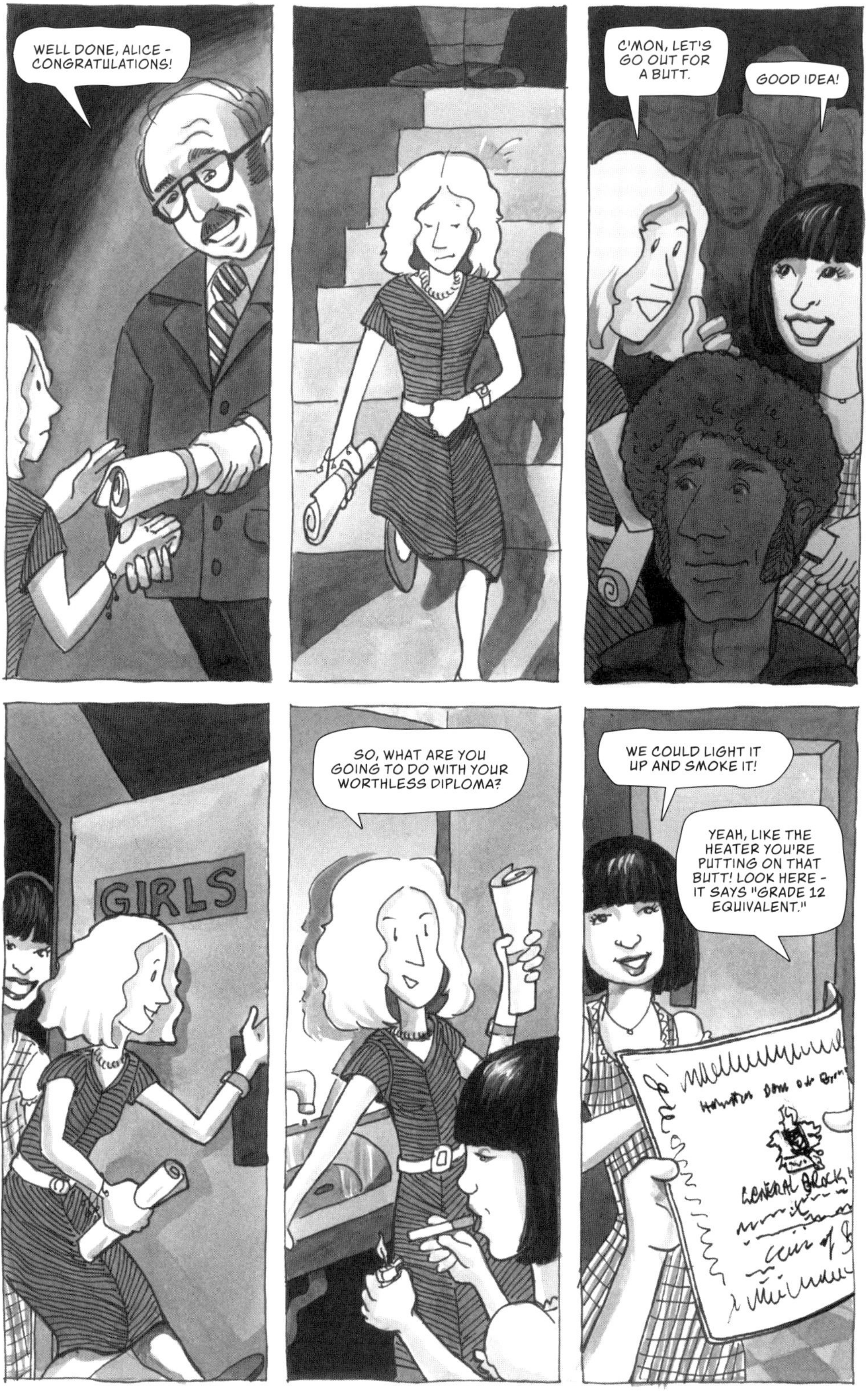
WELL DONE, ALICE - CONGRATULATIONS!
C'MON, LET'S GO OUT FOR A BUTT.
GOOD IDEA!
GIRLS
SO, WHAT ARE YOU GOING TO DO WITH YOUR WORTHLESS DIPLOMA?
WE COULD LIGHT IT UP AND SMOKE IT!
YEAH, LIKE THE HEATER YOU'RE PUTTING ON THAT BUTT! LOOK HERE - IT SAYS "GRADE 12 EQUIVALENT."

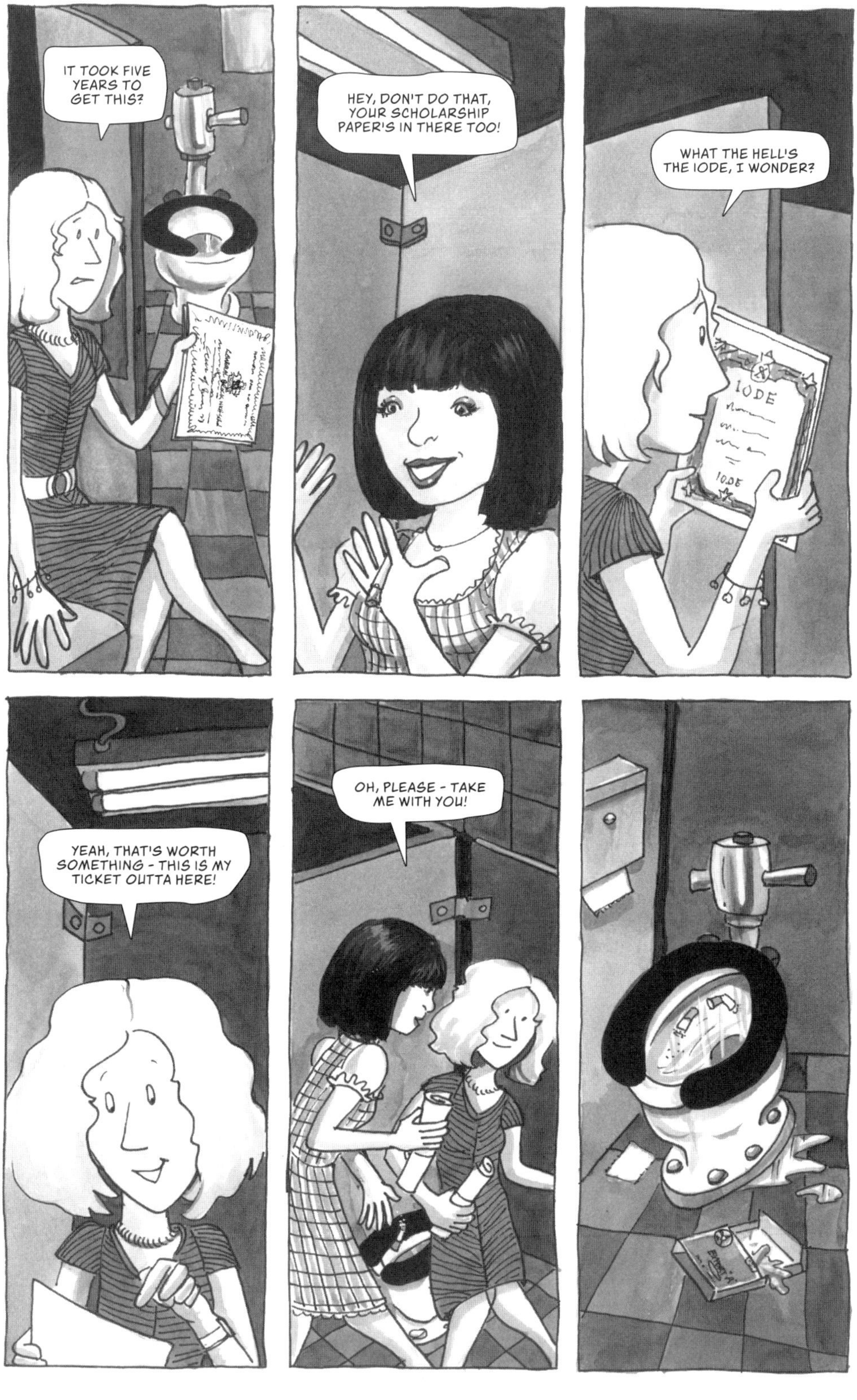
IT TOOK FIVE YEARS TO GET THIS?
HEY, DON'T DO THAT, YOUR SCHOLARSHIP PAPER'S IN THERE TOO!
WHAT THE HELL'S THE IODE, I WONDER?
IODE
YEAH, THAT'S WORTH SOMETHING - THIS IS MY TICKET OUTTA HERE!
OH, PLEASE - TAKE ME WITH YOU!

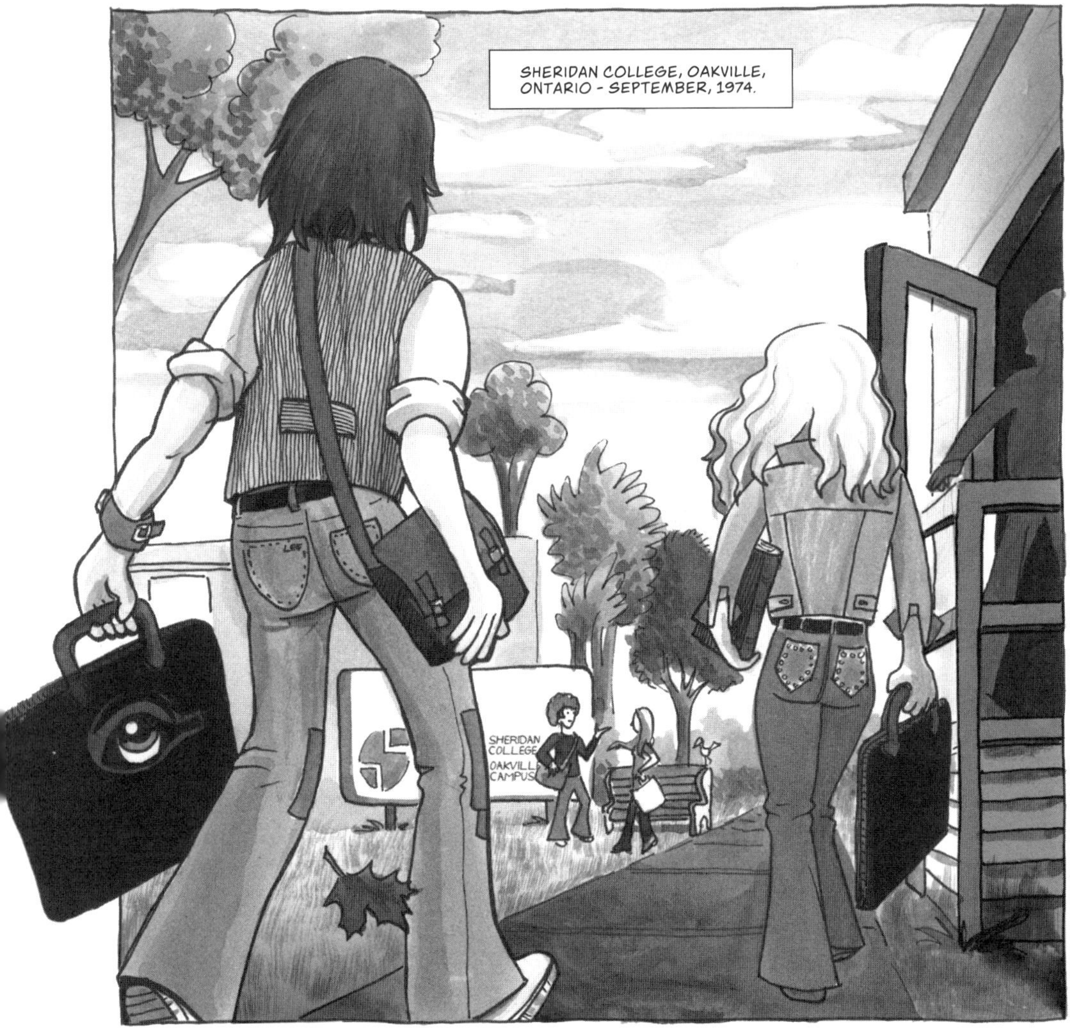
SHERIDAN COLLEGE, OAKVILLE, ONTARIO - SEPTEMBER, 1974.
SHERIDAN COLLEGE
OAKVILL
CAMPUS

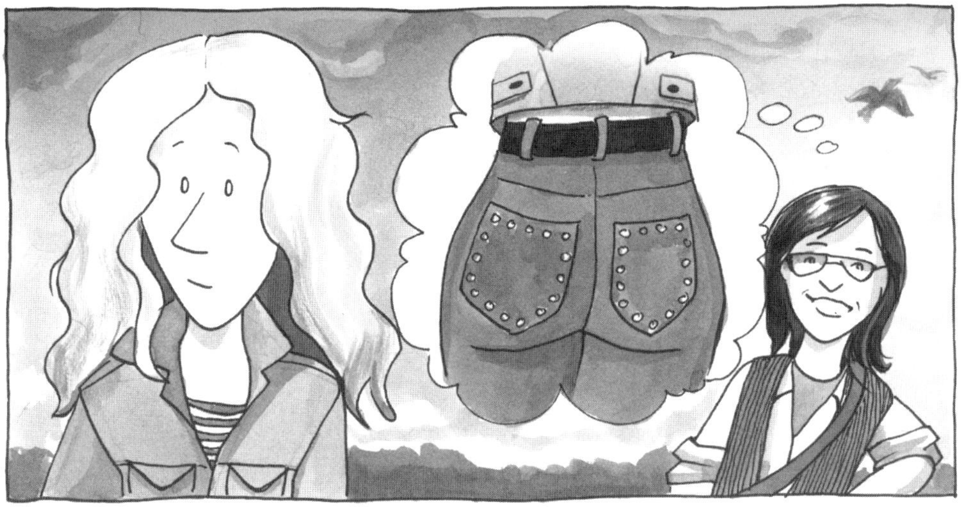

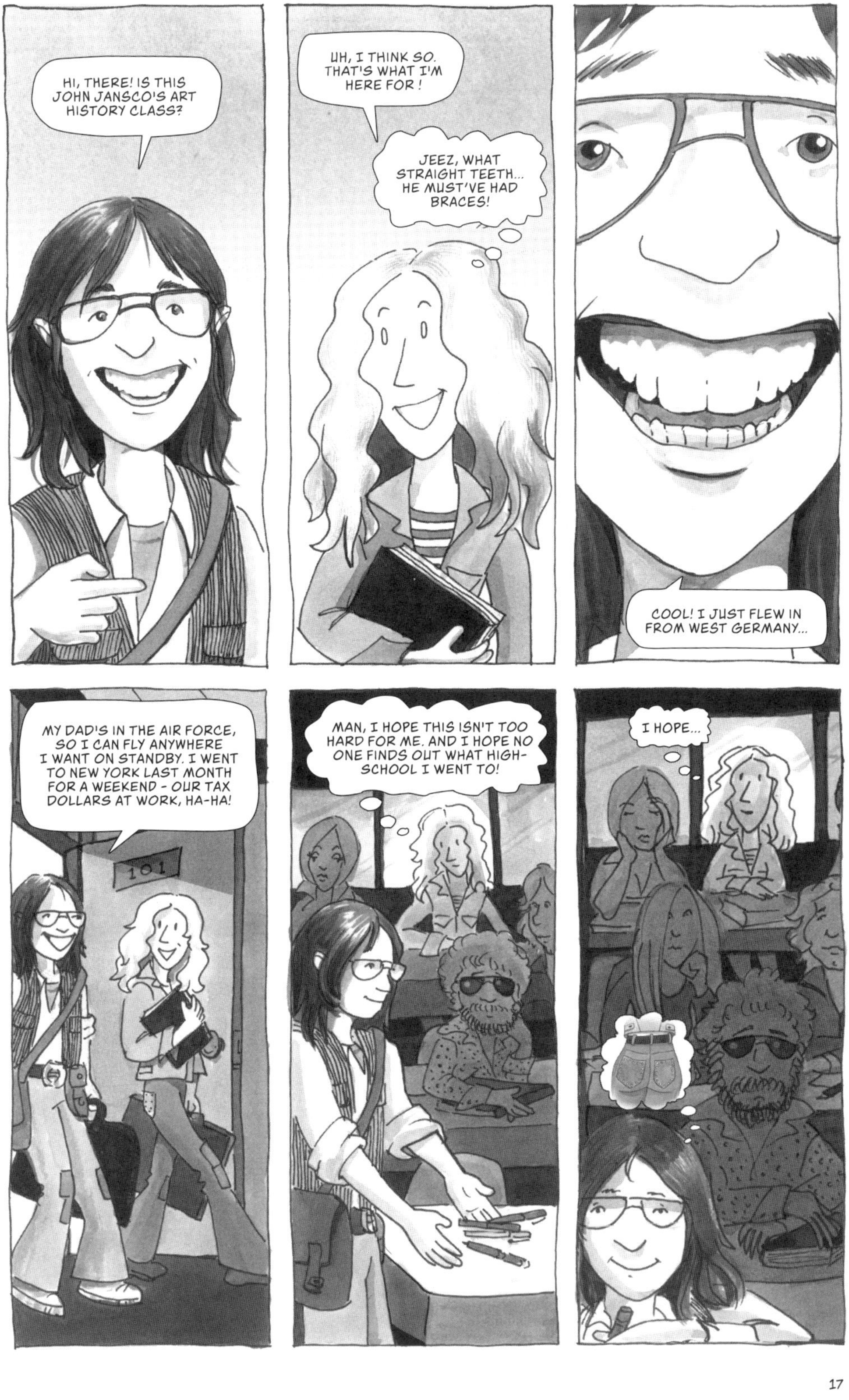
HI, THERE! IS THIS JOHN JANSCO'S ART HISTORY CLASS?
UH, I THINK SO. THAT'S WHAT I'M HERE FOR !
JEEZ, WHAT STRAIGHT TEETH... HE MUST'VE HAD BRACES!
COOL! I JUST FLEW IN FROM WEST GERMANY...
MY DAD'S IN THE AIR FORCE, SO I CAN FLY ANYWHERE I WANT ON STANDBY. I WENT TO NEW YORK LAST MONTH FOR A WEEKEND - OUR TAX DOLLARS AT WORK, HA-HA!
101
MAN, I HOPE THIS ISN'T TOO HARD FOR ME. AND I HOPE NO ONE FINDS OUT WHAT HIGH-SCHOOL I WENT TO!
I HOPE...

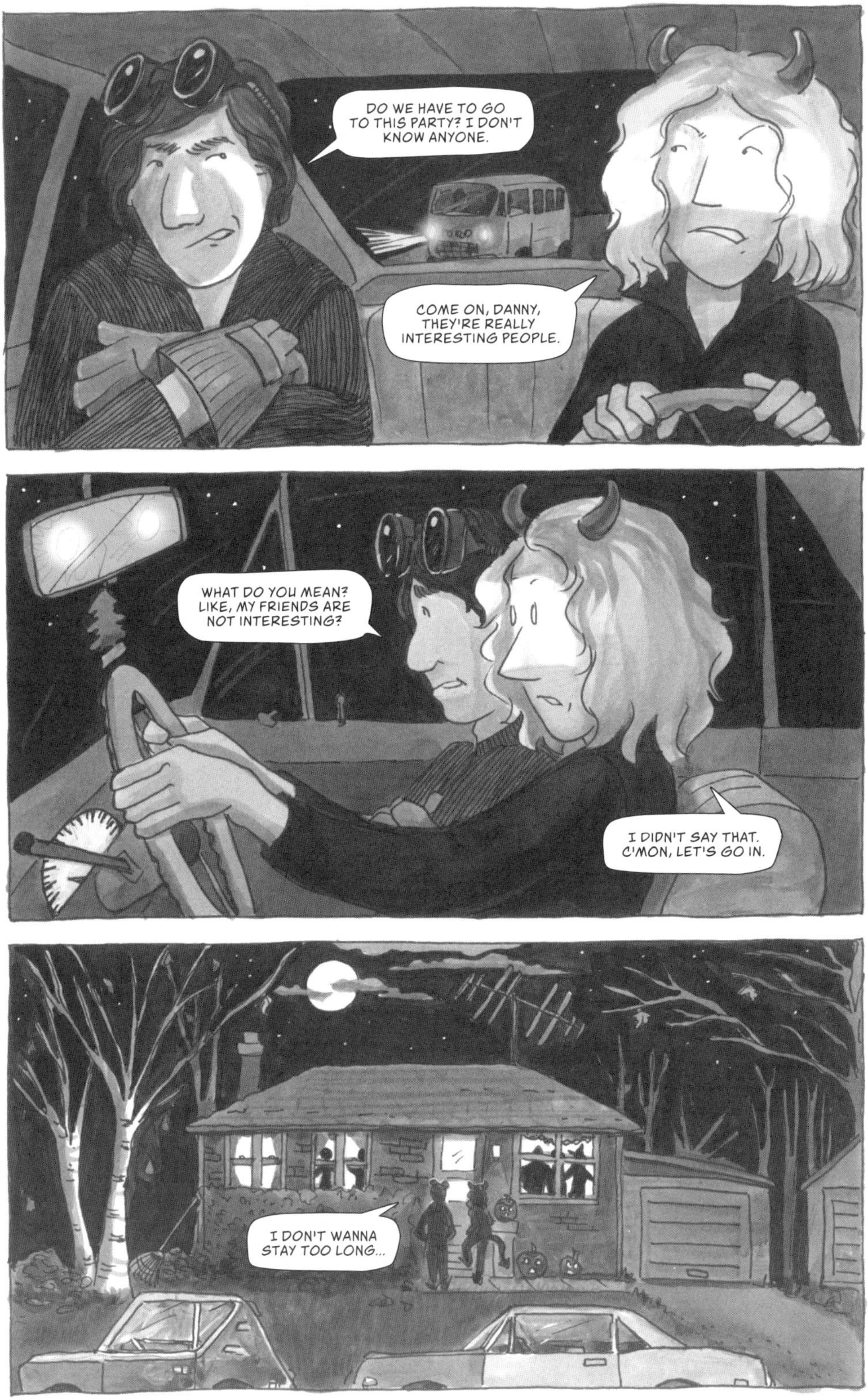
DO WE HAVE TO GO TO THIS PARTY? I DON'T KNOW ANYONE.
COME ON, DANNY, THEY'RE REALLY INTERESTING PEOPLE.
WHAT DO YOU MEAN? LIKE, MY FRIENDS ARE NOT INTERESTING?
I DIDN'T SAY THAT. C'MON, LET'S GO IN.
I DON'T WANNA STAY TOO LONG...

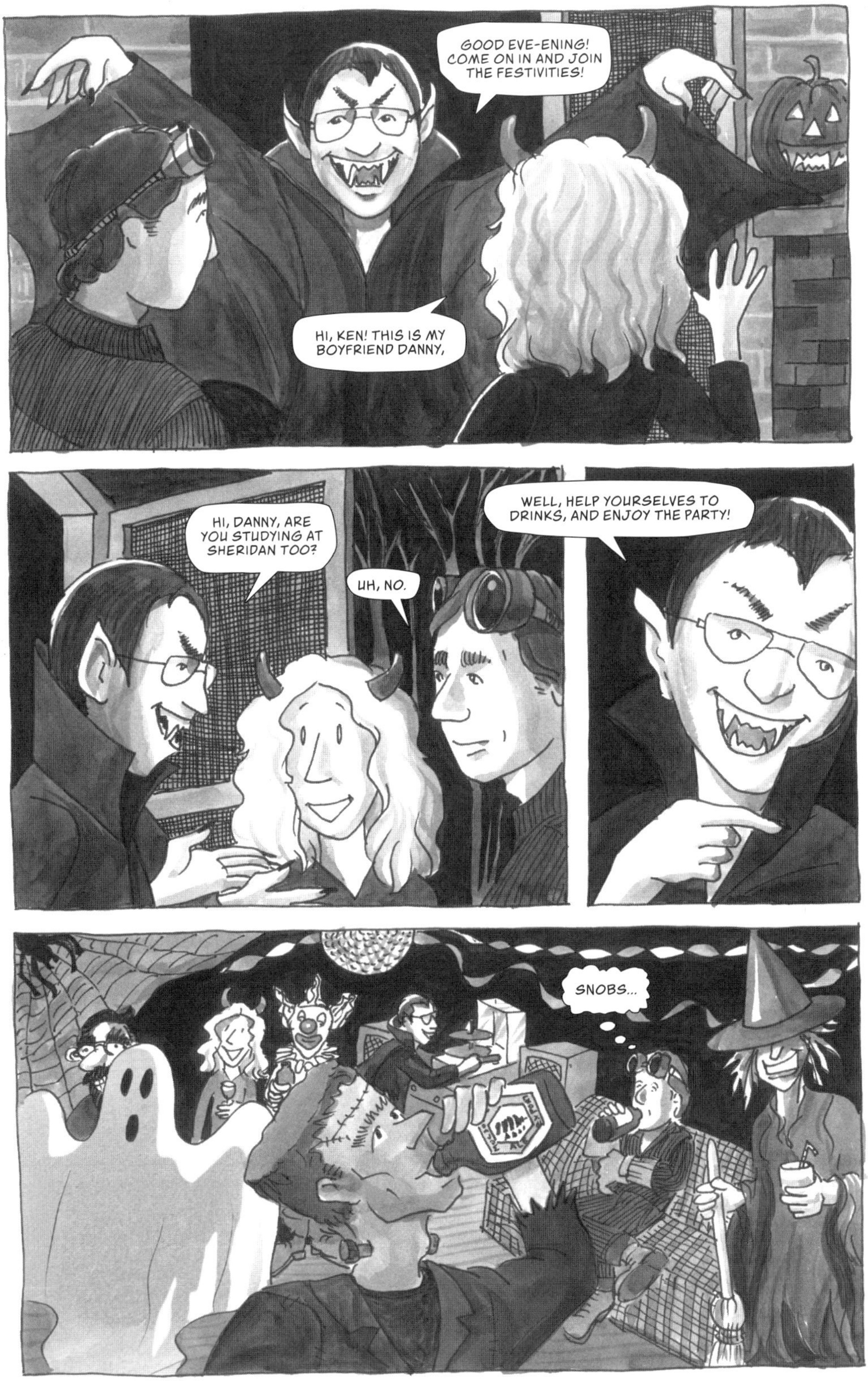
GOOD EVE-ENING! COME ON IN AND JOIN THE FESTIVITIES!
HI, KEN! THIS IS MY BOYFRIEND DANNY,
HI, DANNY, ARE YOU STUDYING AT SHERIDAN TOO?
UH, NO.
WELL, HELP YOURSELVES TO DRINKS, AND ENJOY THE PARTY!
SNOBS...

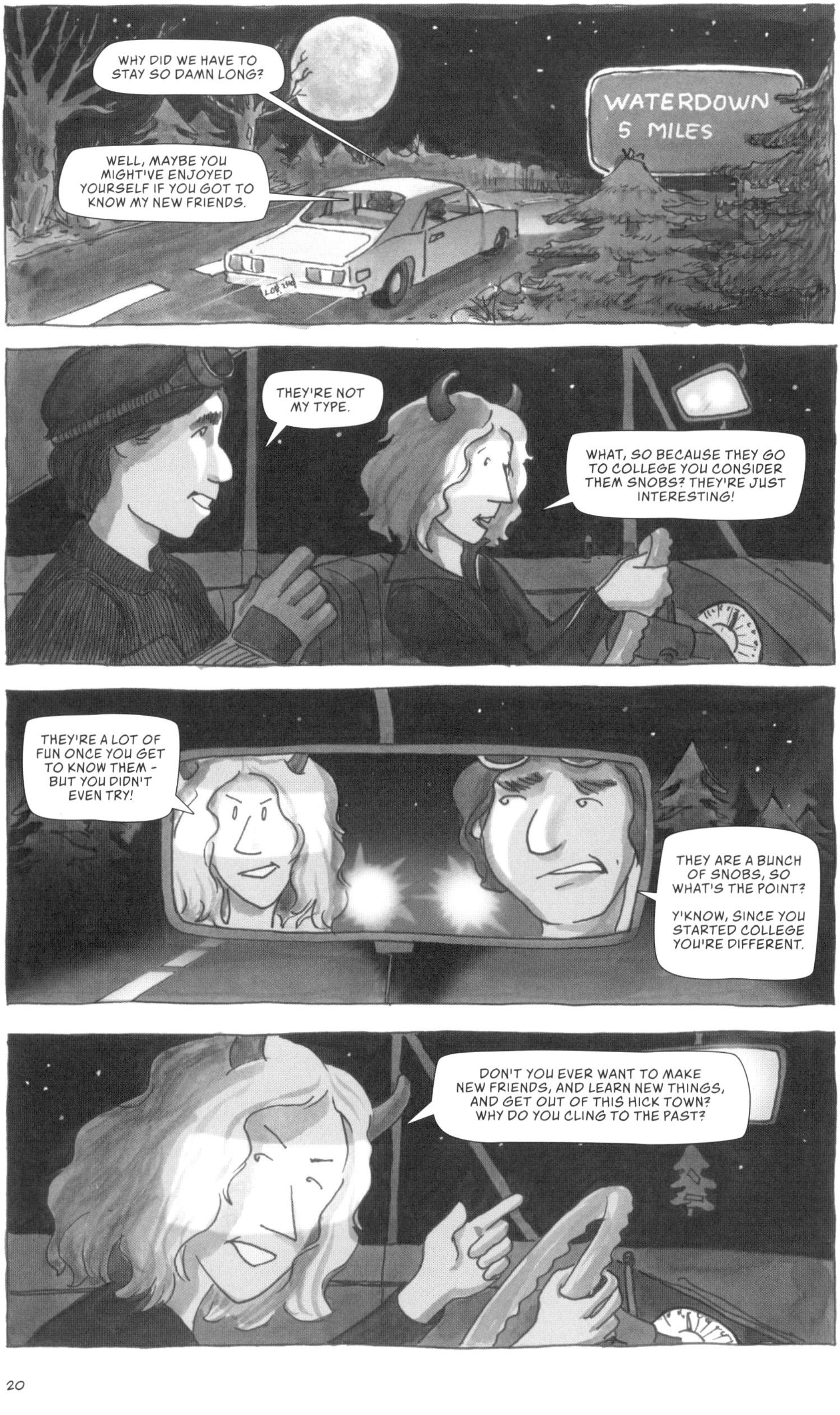
WHY DID WE HAVE TO STAY SO DAMN LONG?
WATERDOWN 5 MILES
WELL, MAYBE YOU MIGHT'VE ENJOYED YOURSELF IF YOU GOT TO KNOW MY NEW FRIENDS.
THEY'RE NOT MY TYPE.
WHAT, SO BECAUSE THEY GO TO COLLEGE YOU CONSIDER THEM SNOBS? THEY'RE JUST INTERESTING!
THEY'RE A LOT OF FUN ONCE YOU GET TO KNOW THEM - BUT YOU DIDN'T EVEN TRY!
THEY ARE A BUNCH OF SNOBS, SO WHAT'S THE POINT?
Y'KNOW, SINCE YOU STARTED COLLEGE YOU'RE DIFFERENT.
DON'T YOU EVER WANT TO MAKE NEW FRIENDS, AND LEARN NEW THINGS, AND GET OUT OF THIS HICK TOWN? WHY DO YOU CLING TO THE PAST?

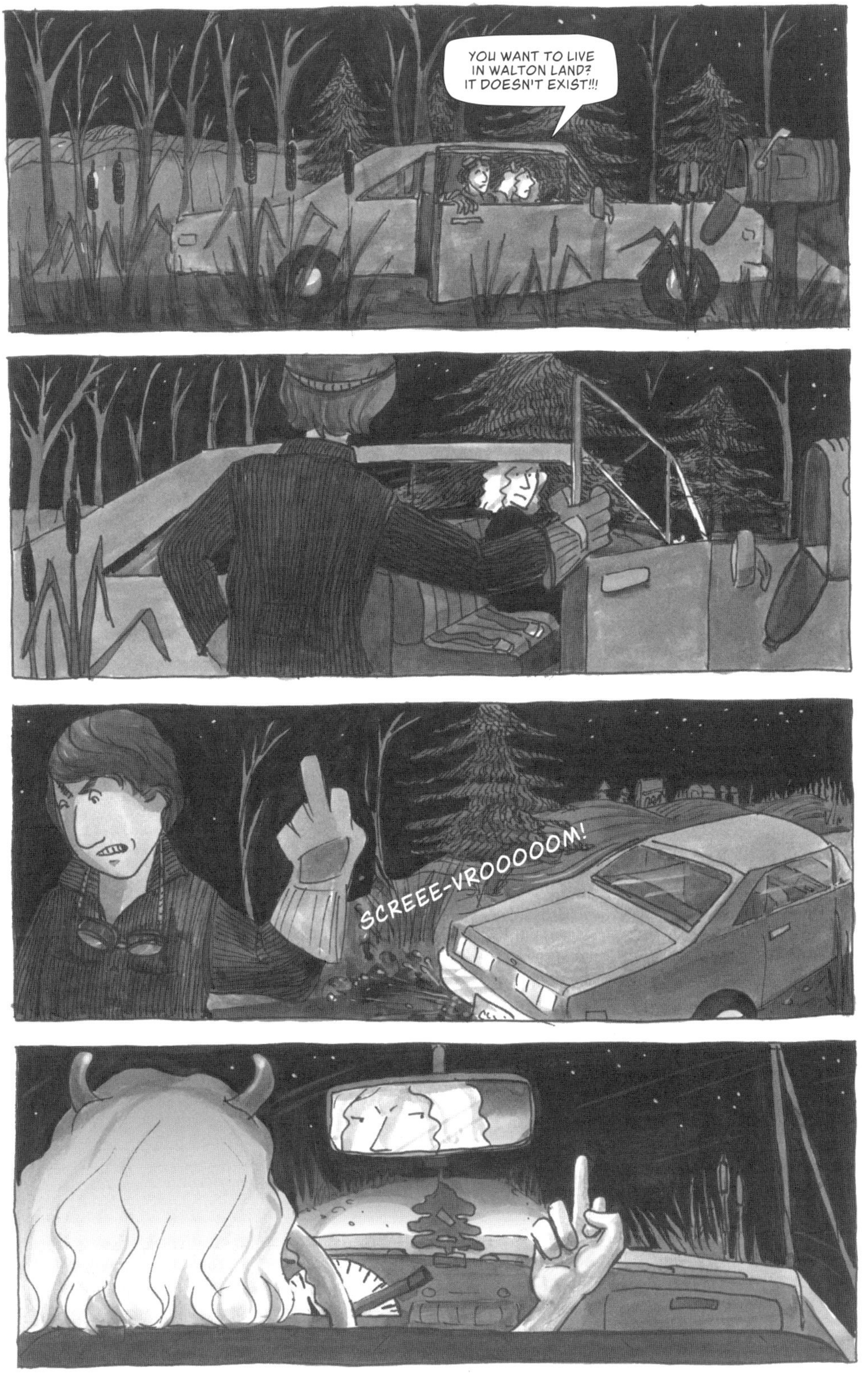
YOU WANT TO LIVE IN WALTON LAND? IT DOESN'T EXIST!!!
SCREEE-VROOOOOM!

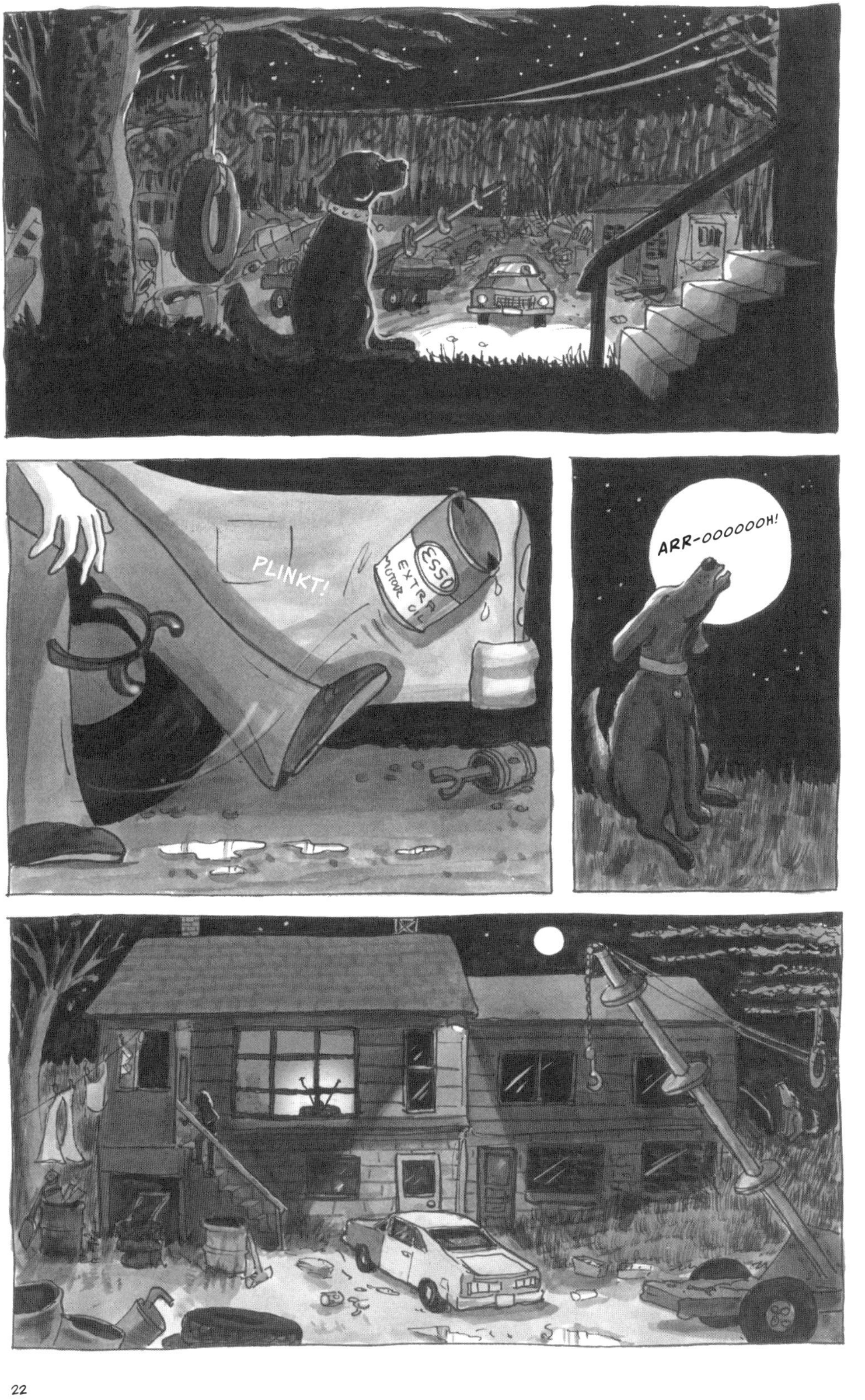
PLINKT!
ESSO EXTRA MOTOR OIL
ARR-OOOOOOH!

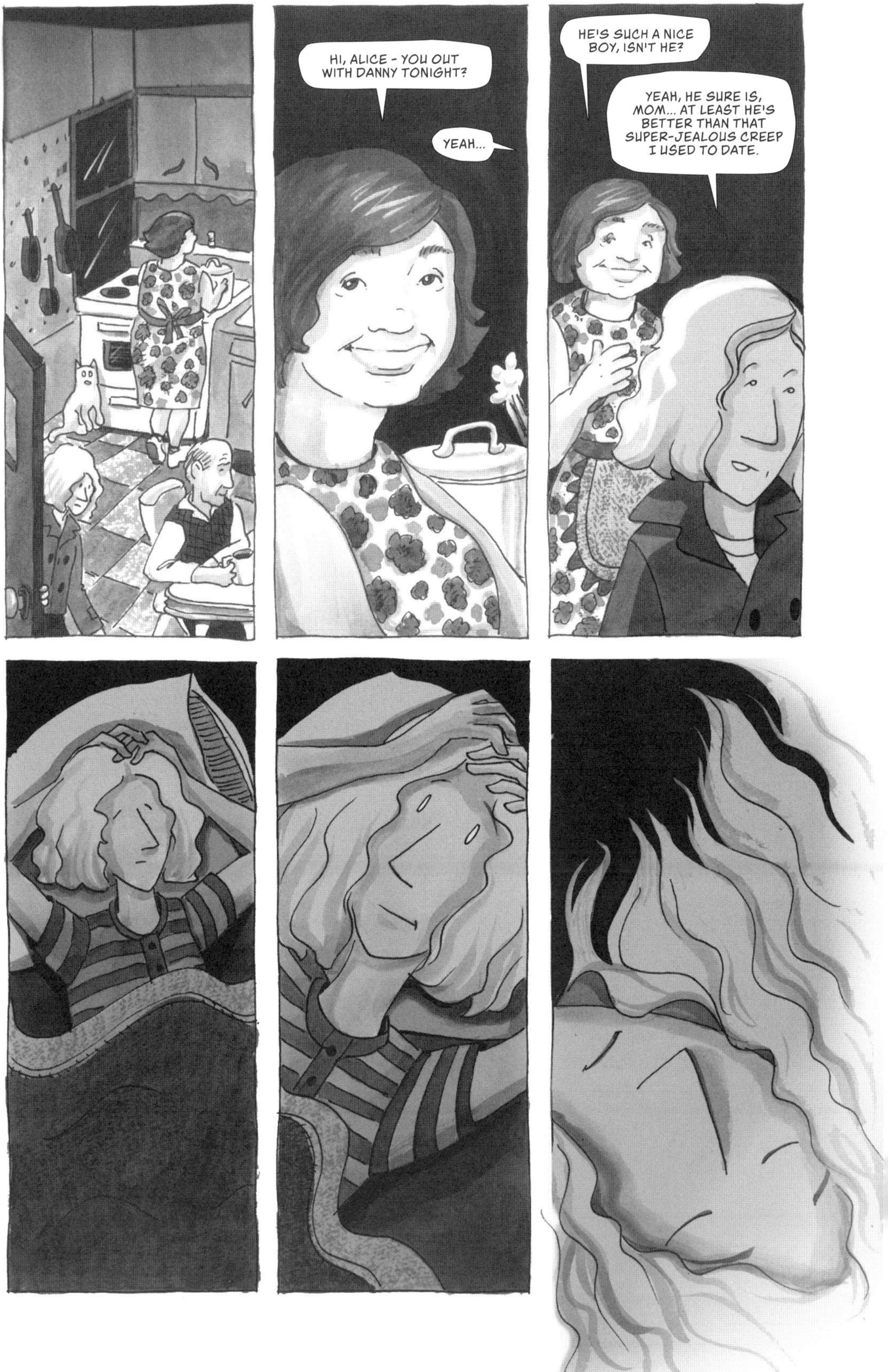
HI, ALICE - YOU OUT WITH DANNY TONIGHT?
YEAH...
HE'S SUCH A NICE BOY, ISN'T HE?
YEAH, HE SURE IS, MOM... AT LEAST HE'S BETTER THAN THAT SUPER-JEALOUS CREEP I USED TO DATE.

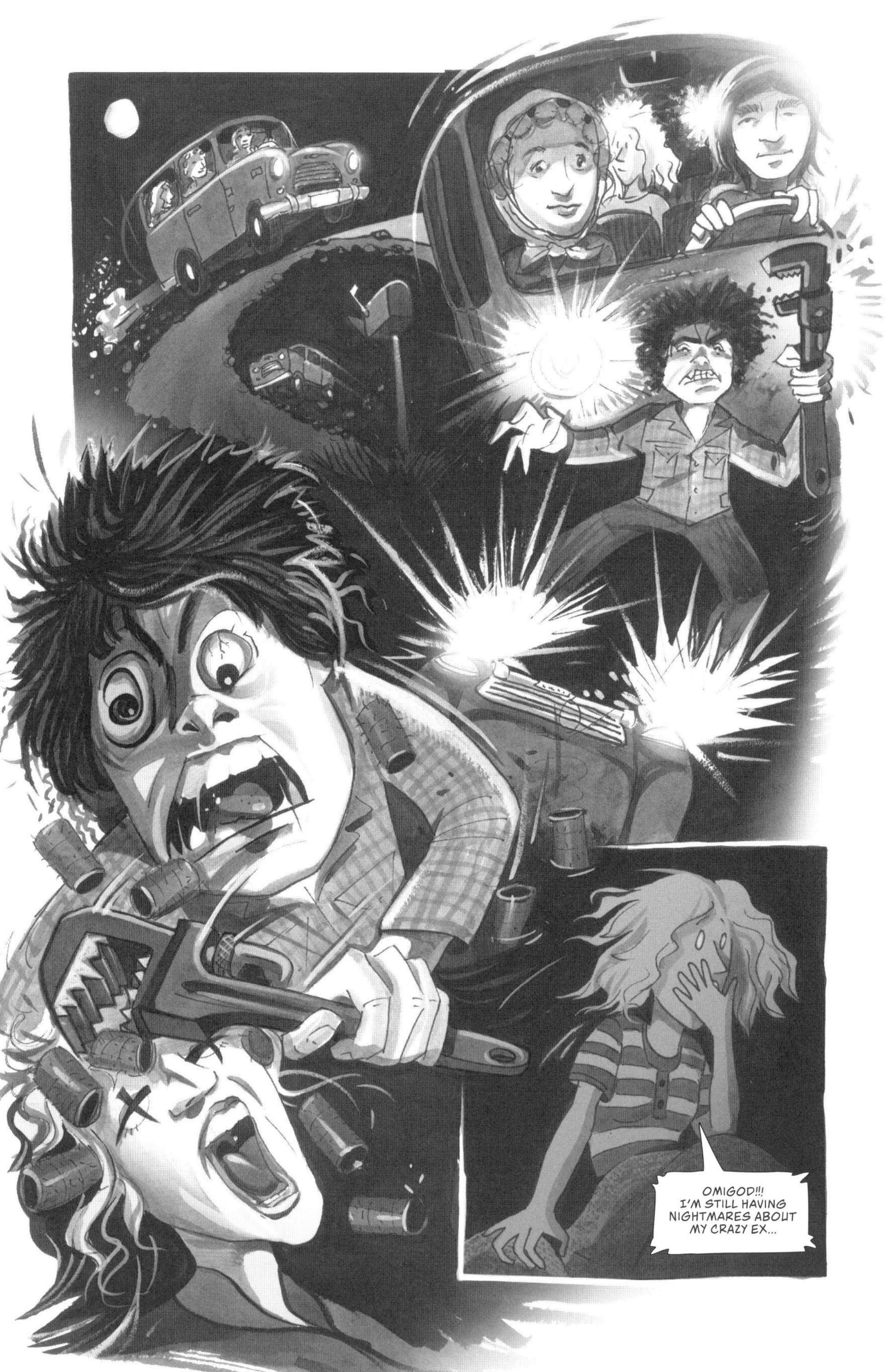
OMIGOD!!! I'M STILL HAVING NIGHTMARES ABOUT MY CRAZY EX...

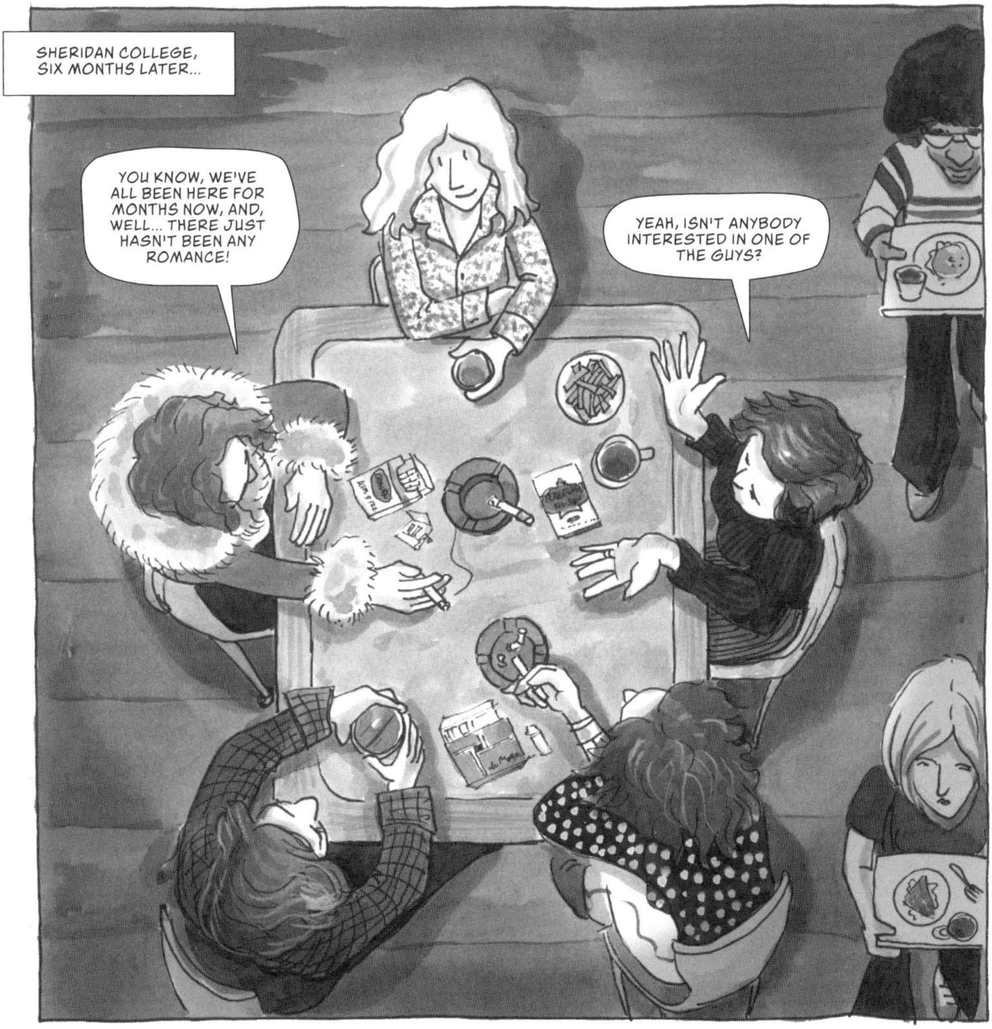
SHERIDAN COLLEGE, SIX MONTHS LATER...
YOU KNOW, WE'VE ALL BEEN HERE FOR MONTHS NOW, AND, WELL... THERE JUST HASN'T BEEN ANY ROMANCE!
YEAH, ISN'T ANYBODY INTERESTED IN ONE OF THE GUYS?

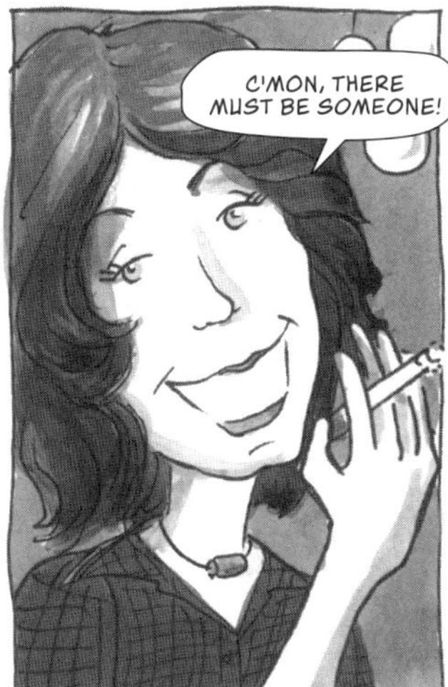
C'MON, THERE MUST BE SOMEONE!

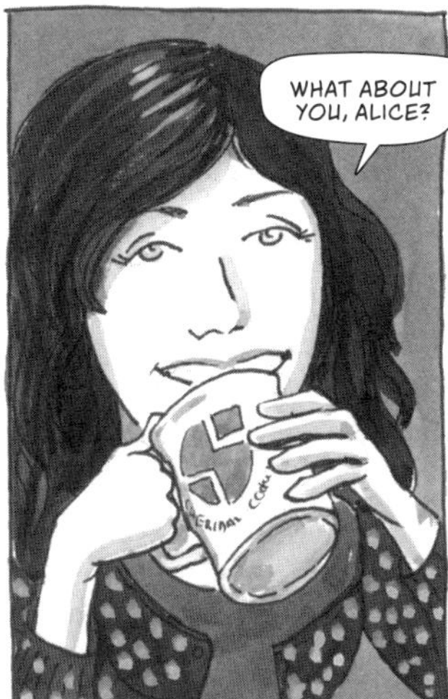
WHAT ABOUT YOU, ALICE?

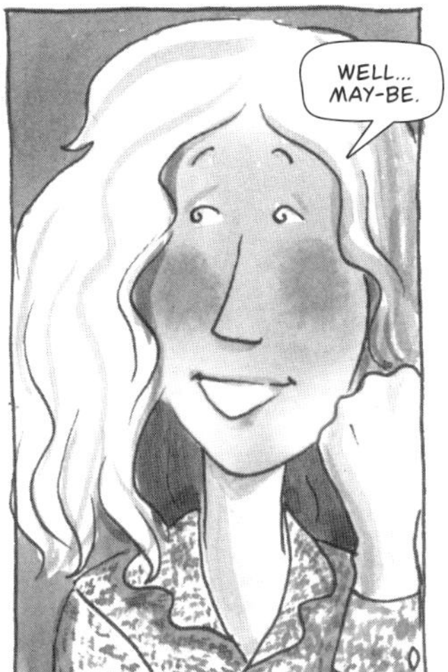
WELL... MAY-BE.

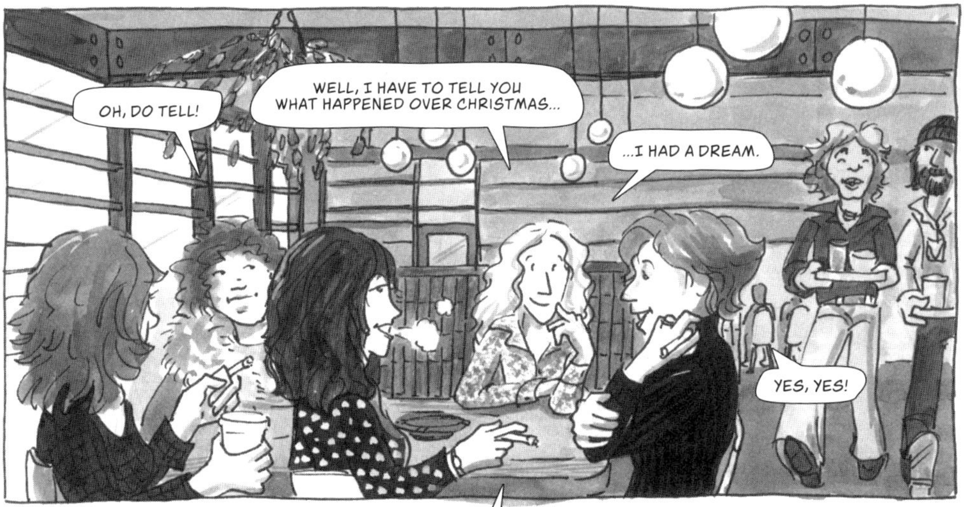
OH, DO TELL!
WELL, I HAVE TO TELL YOU WHAT HAPPENED OVER CHRISTMAS...
...I HAD A DREAM.
YES, YES!

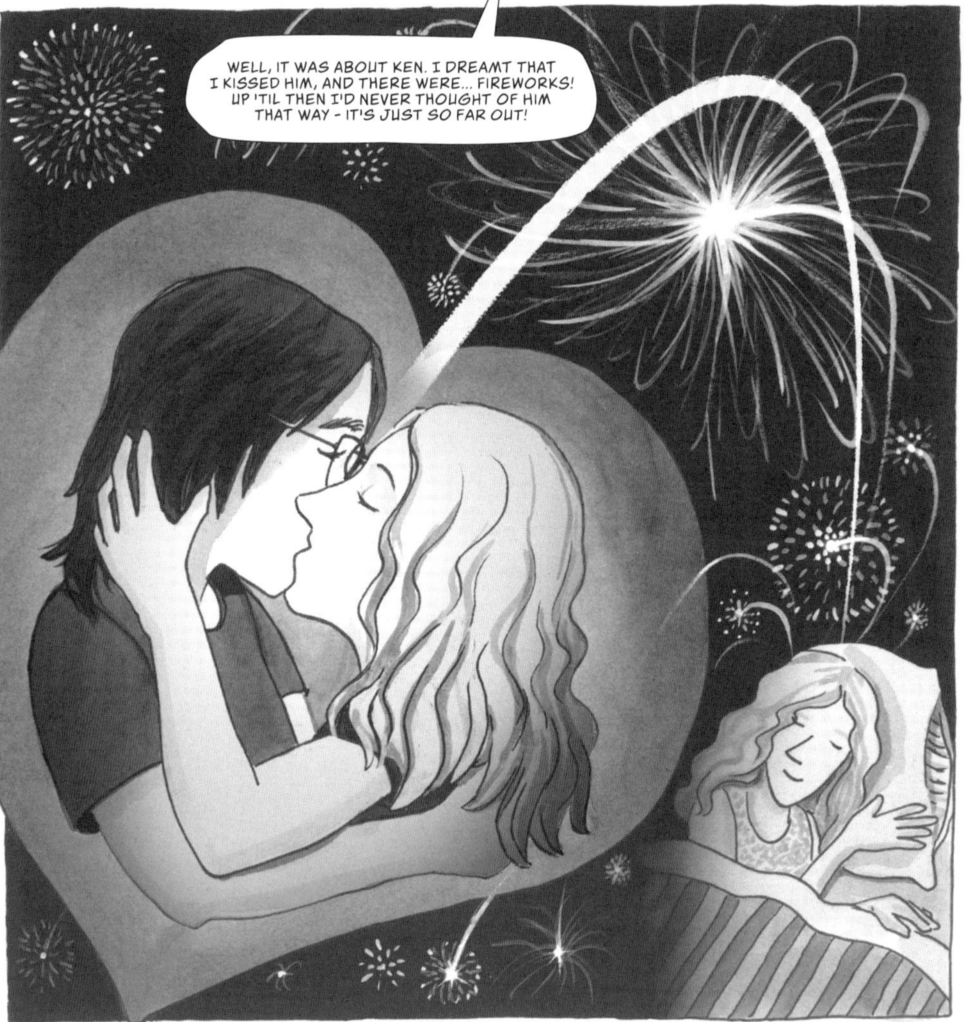
WELL, IT WAS ABOUT KEN. I DREAMT THAT I KISSED HIM, AND THERE WERE... FIREWORKS! UP 'TIL THEN I'D NEVER THOUGHT OF HIM THAT WAY - IT'S JUST SO FAR OUT!

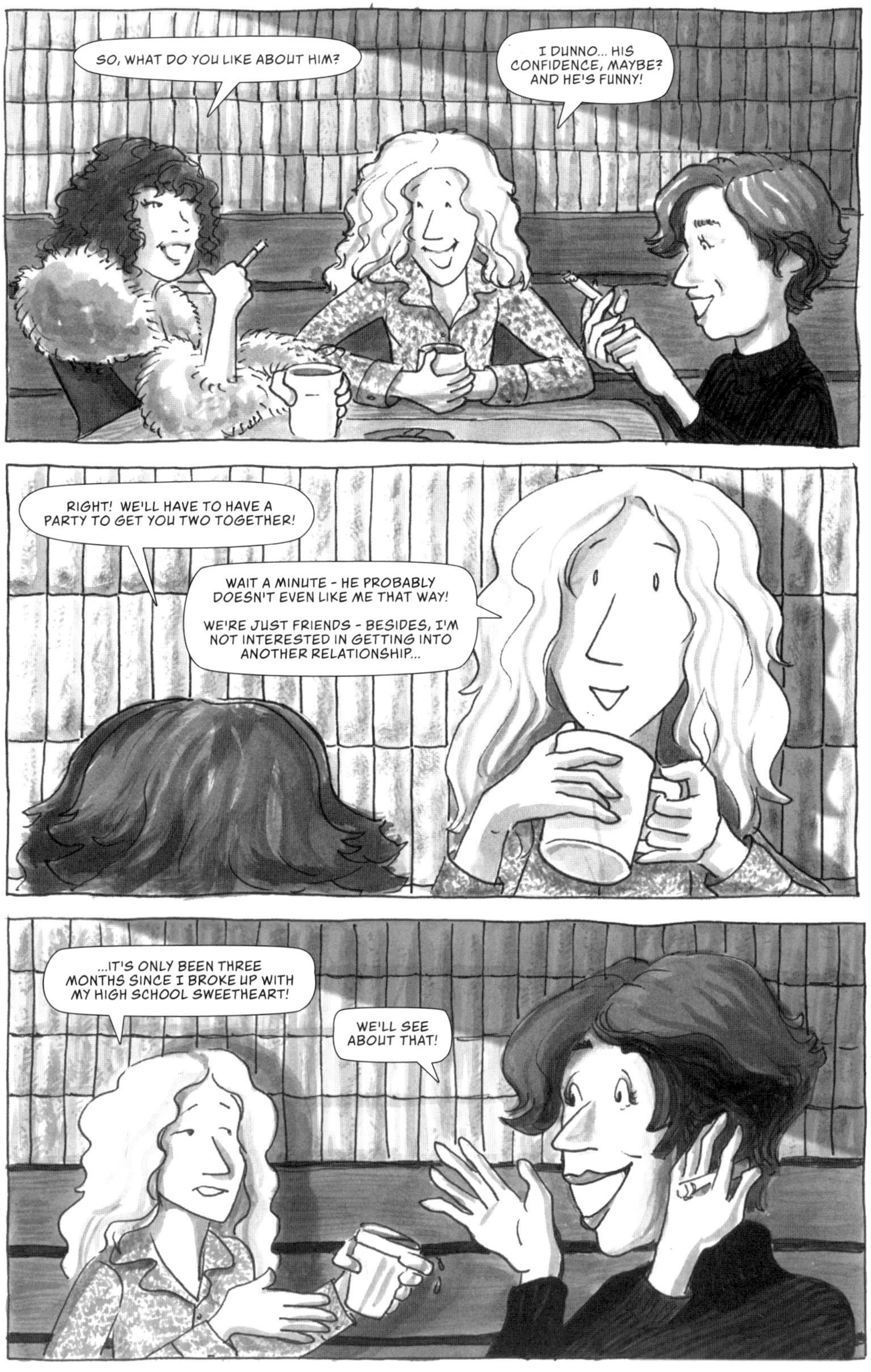
SO, WHAT DO YOU LIKE ABOUT HIM?
I DUNNO... HIS CONFIDENCE, MAYBE? AND HE'S FUNNY!
RIGHT! WE'LL HAVE TO HAVE A PARTY TO GET YOU TWO TOGETHER!
WAIT A MINUTE - HE PROBABLY DOESN'T EVEN LIKE ME THAT WAY!
WE'RE JUST FRIENDS - BESIDES, I'M NOT INTERESTED IN GETTING INTO ANOTHER RELATIONSHIP...
...IT'S ONLY BEEN THREE MONTHS SINCE I BROKE UP WITH MY HIGH SCHOOL SWEETHEART!
WE'LL SEE ABOUT THAT!

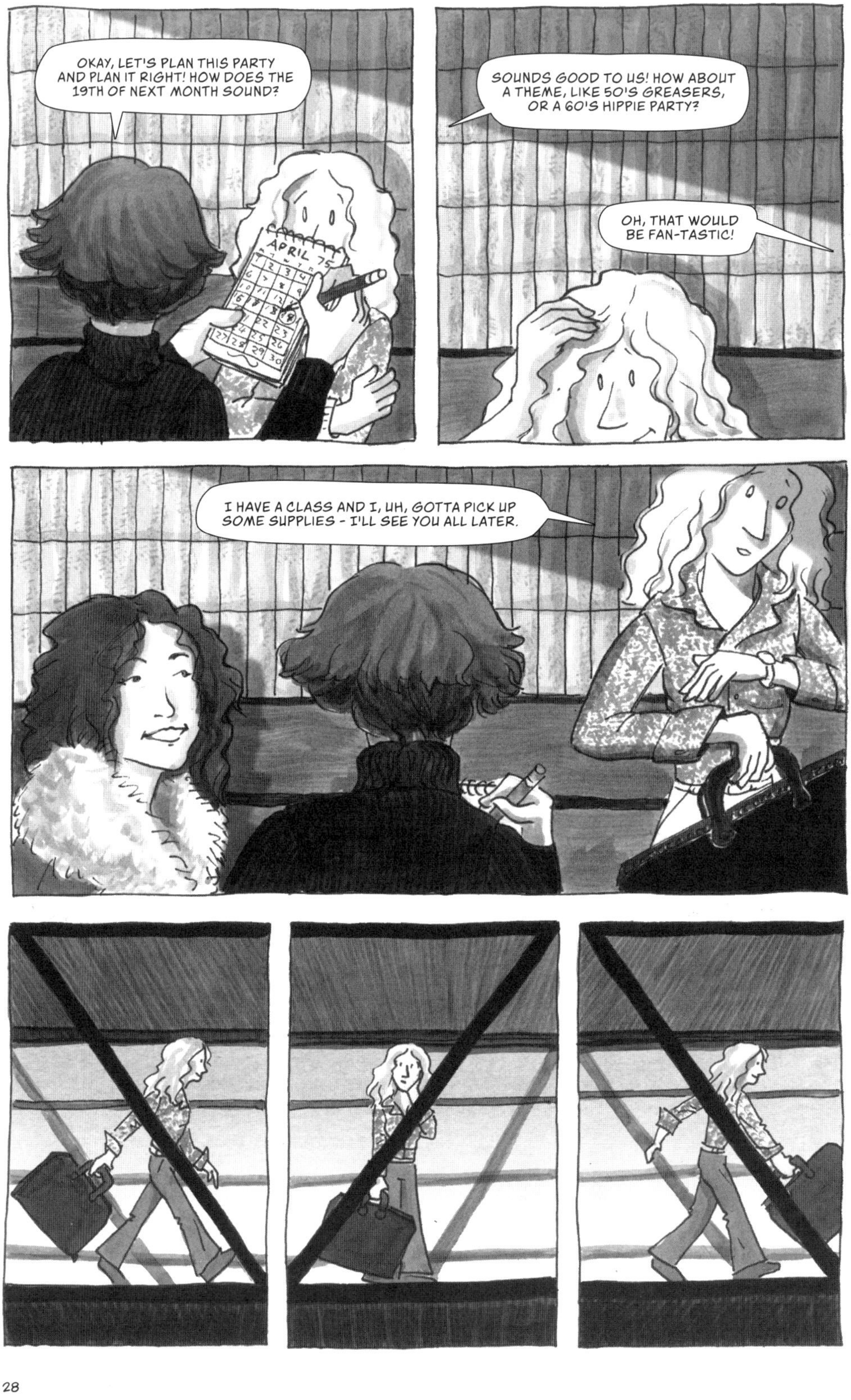
OKAY, LET'S PLAN THIS PARTY AND PLAN IT RIGHT! HOW DOES THE 19TH OF NEXT MONTH SOUND?
APRIL 75
SOUNDS GOOD TO US! HOW ABOUT A THEME, LIKE 50'S GREASERS, OR A 60'S HIPPIE PARTY?
OH, THAT WOULD BE FAN-TASTIC!
I HAVE A CLASS AND I, UH, GOTTA PICK UP SOME SUPPLIES - I'LL SEE YOU ALL LATER.

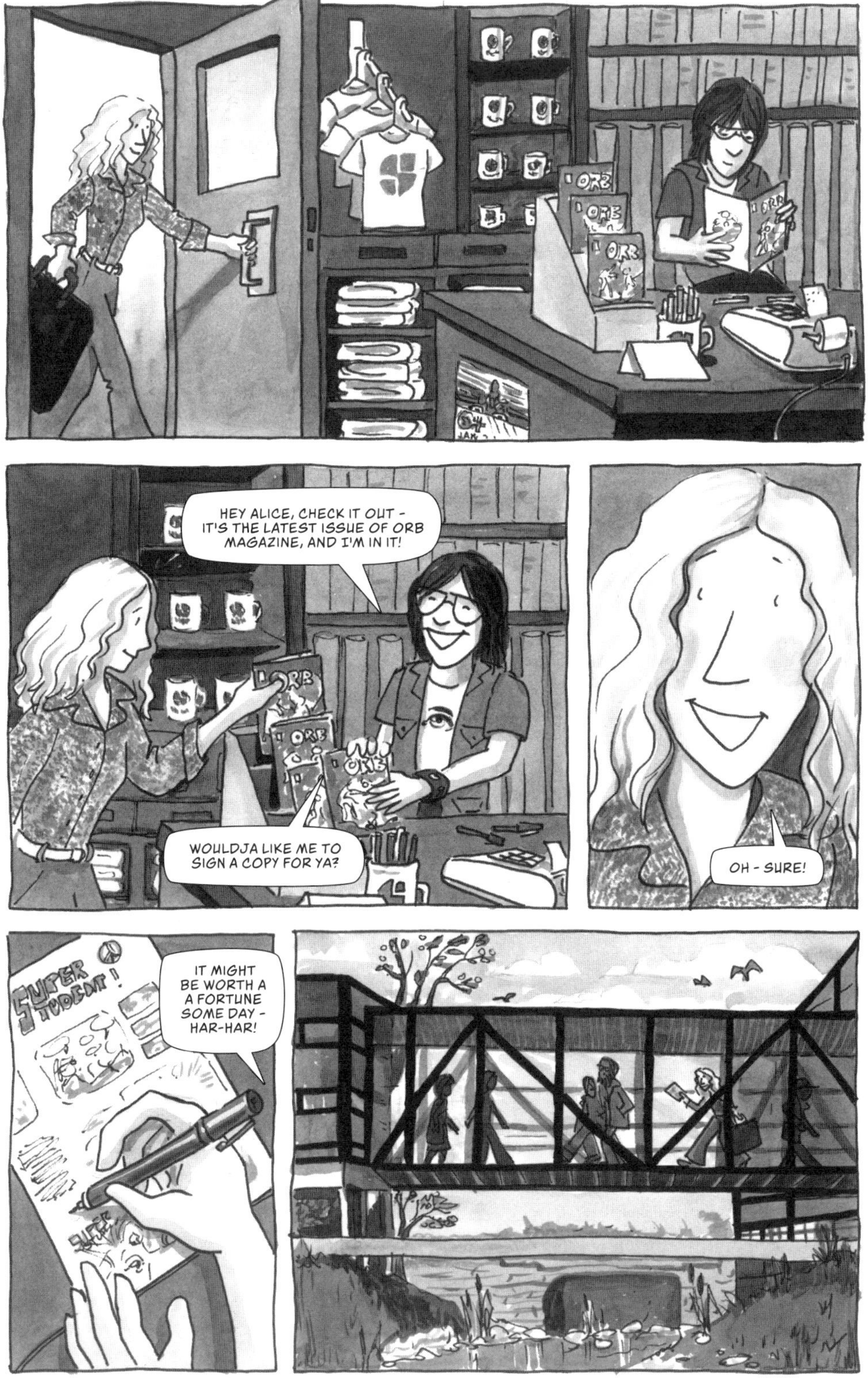
HEY ALICE, CHECK IT OUT - IT'S THE LATEST ISSUE OF ORB MAGAZINE, AND I'M IN IT!
WOULDJA LIKE ME TO SIGN A COPY FOR YA?
OH - SURE!
SUPER STUDENT!
IT MIGHT BE WORTH A A FORTUNE SOME DAY - HAR-HAR!

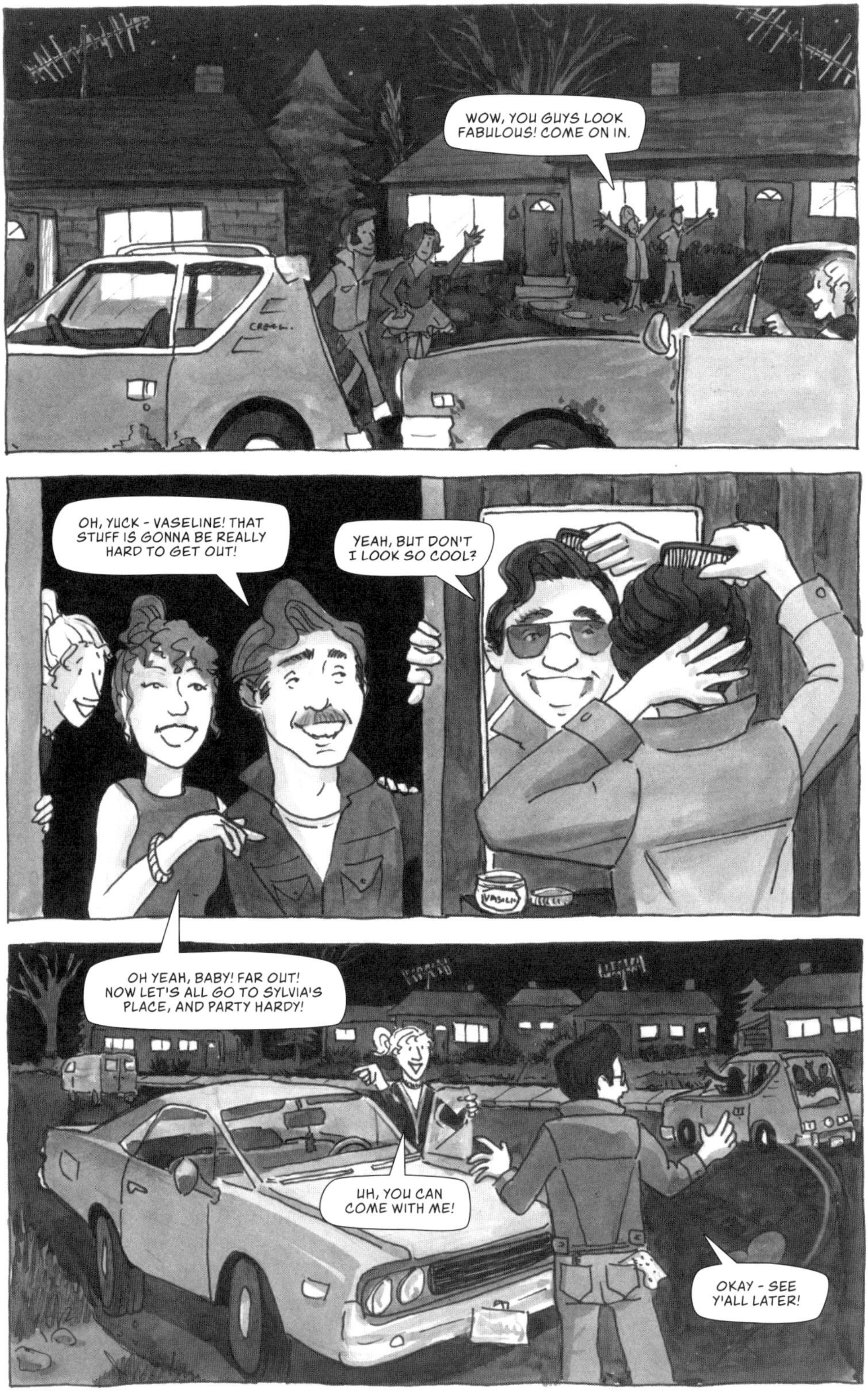
WOW, YOU GUYS LOOK FABULOUS! COME ON IN.
OH, YUCK - VASELINE! THAT STUFF IS GONNA BE REALLY HARD TO GET OUT!
YEAH, BUT DON'T I LOOK SO COOL?
OH YEAH, BABY! FAR OUT! NOW LET'S ALL GO TO SYLVIA'S PLACE, AND PARTY HARDY!
UH, YOU CAN COME WITH ME!
OKAY - SEE Y'ALL LATER!

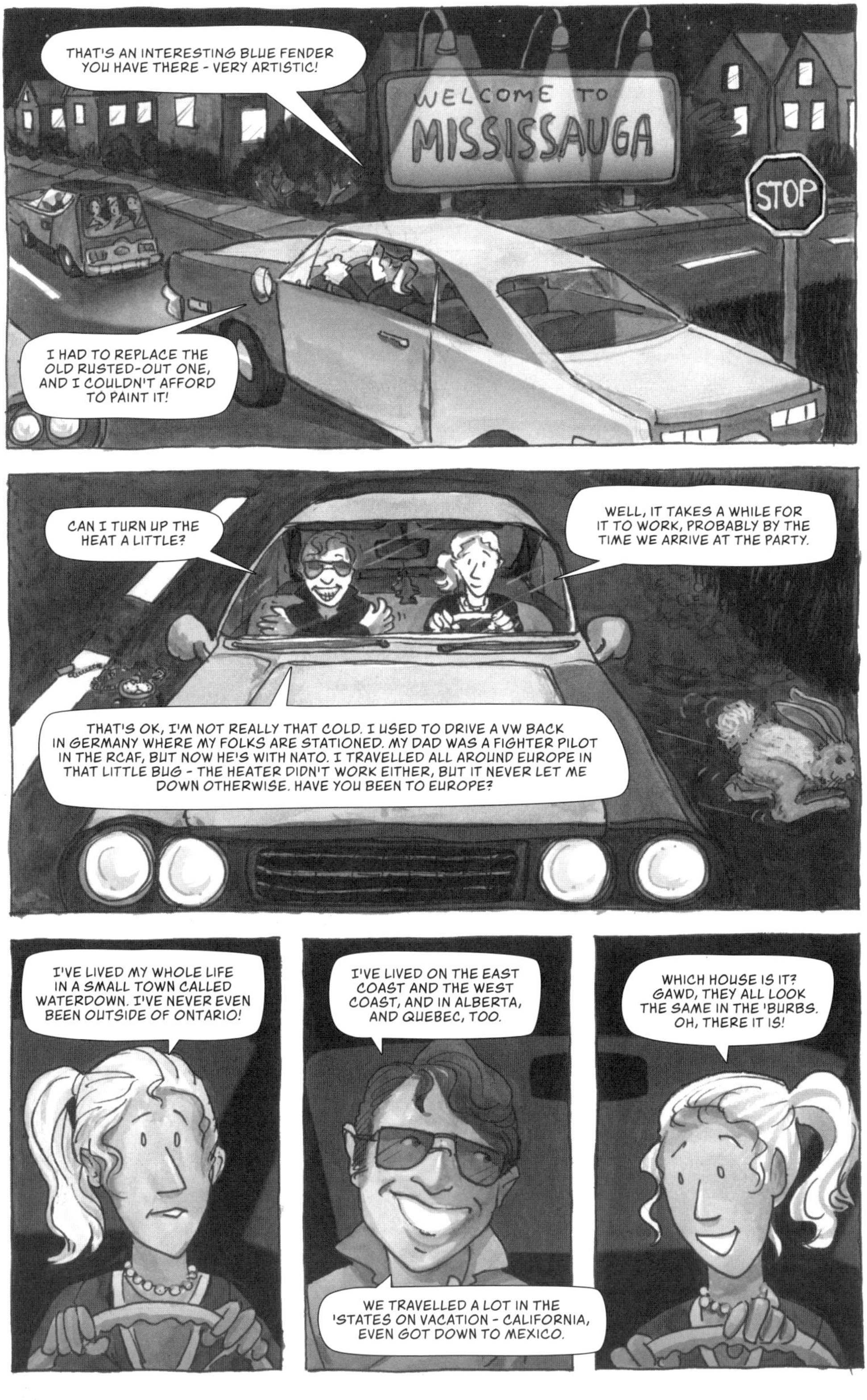
THAT'S AN INTERESTING BLUE FENDER YOU HAVE THERE - VERY ARTISTIC!
WELCOME TO MISSISSAUGA
STOP
I HAD TO REPLACE THE OLD RUSTED-OUT ONE, AND I COULDN'T AFFORD TO PAINT IT!
CAN I TURN UP THE HEAT A LITTLE?
WELL, IT TAKES A WHILE FOR IT TO WORK, PROBABLY BY THE TIME WE ARRIVE AT THE PARTY.
THAT'S OK, I'M NOT REALLY THAT COLD. I USED TO DRIVE A VW BACK IN GERMANY WHERE MY FOLKS ARE STATIONED. MY DAD WAS A FIGHTER PILOT IN THE RCAF, BUT NOW HE'S WITH NATO. I TRAVELLED ALL AROUND EUROPE IN THAT LITTLE BUG - THE HEATER DIDN'T WORK EITHER, BUT IT NEVER LET ME DOWN OTHERWISE. HAVE YOU BEEN TO EUROPE?
I'VE LIVED MY WHOLE LIFE IN A SMALL TOWN CALLED WATERDOWN. I'VE NEVER EVEN BEEN OUTSIDE OF ONTARIO!
I'VE LIVED ON THE EAST COAST AND THE WEST COAST, AND IN ALBERTA, AND QUEBEC, TOO.
WE TRAVELLED A LOT IN THE 'STATES ON VACATION - CALIFORNIA, EVEN GOT DOWN TO MEXICO.
WHICH HOUSE IS IT? GAWD, THEY ALL LOOK THE SAME IN THE 'BURBS. OH, THERE IT IS!

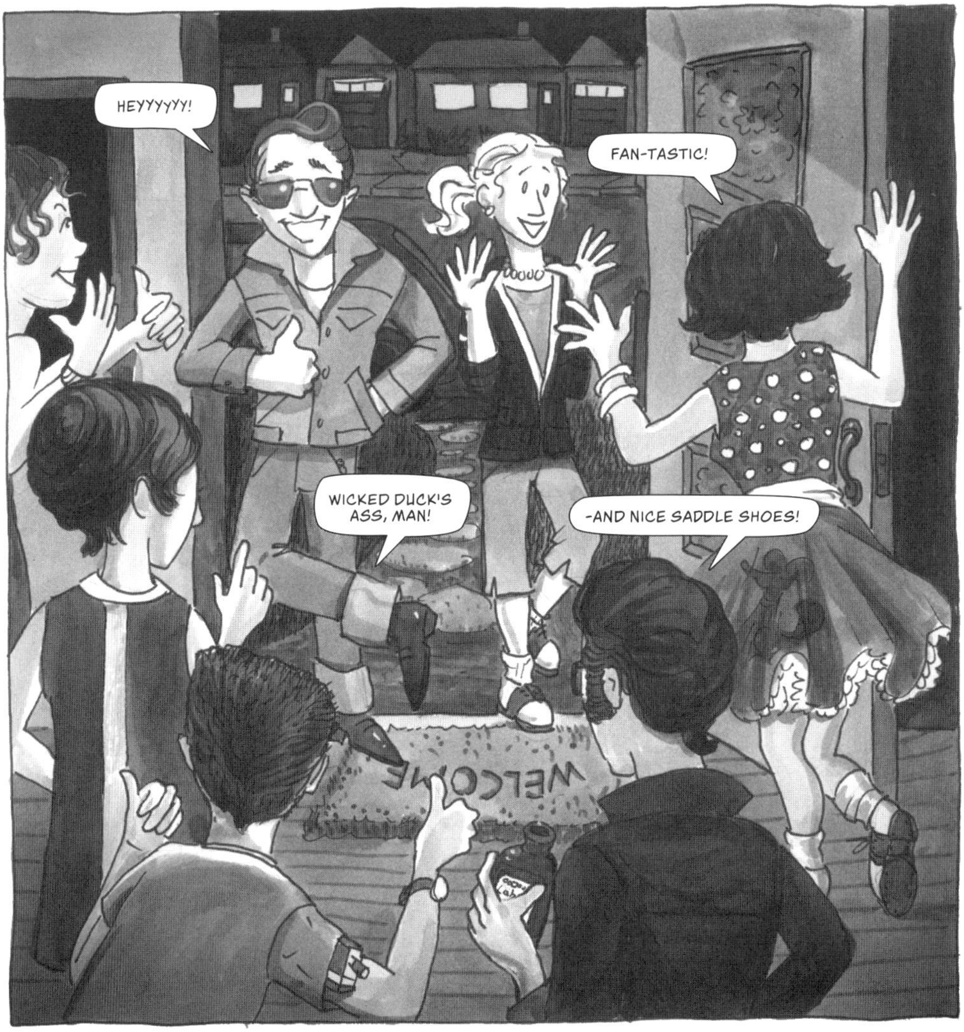
HEYYYYYY!
FAN-TASTIC!
WICKED DUCK'S ASS, MAN!
-AND NICE SADDLE SHOES!
WELCOME

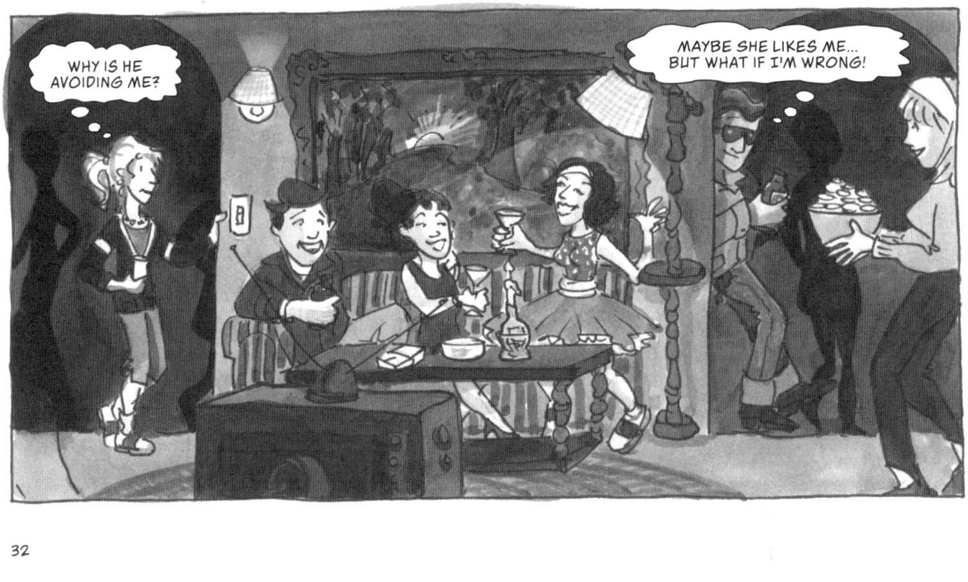
WHY IS HE AVOIDING ME?
MAYBE SHE LIKES ME... BUT WHAT IF I'M WRONG!

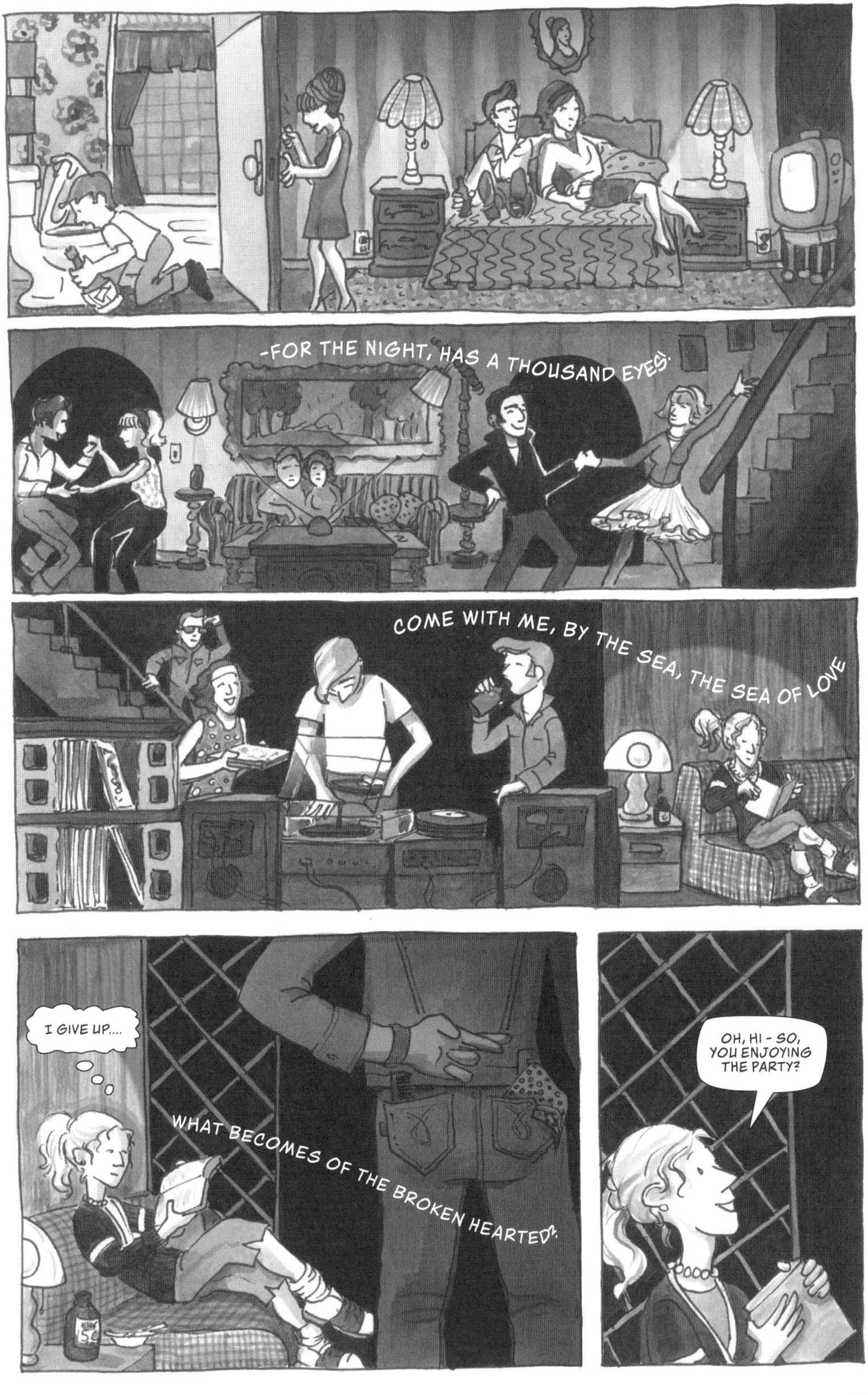
-FOR THE NIGHT, HAS A THOUSAND EYES♫
COME WITH ME, BY THE SEA, THE SEA OF LOVE
I GIVE UP....
WHAT BECOMES OF THE BROKEN HEARTED♫
OH, HI - SO, YOU ENJOYING THE PARTY?

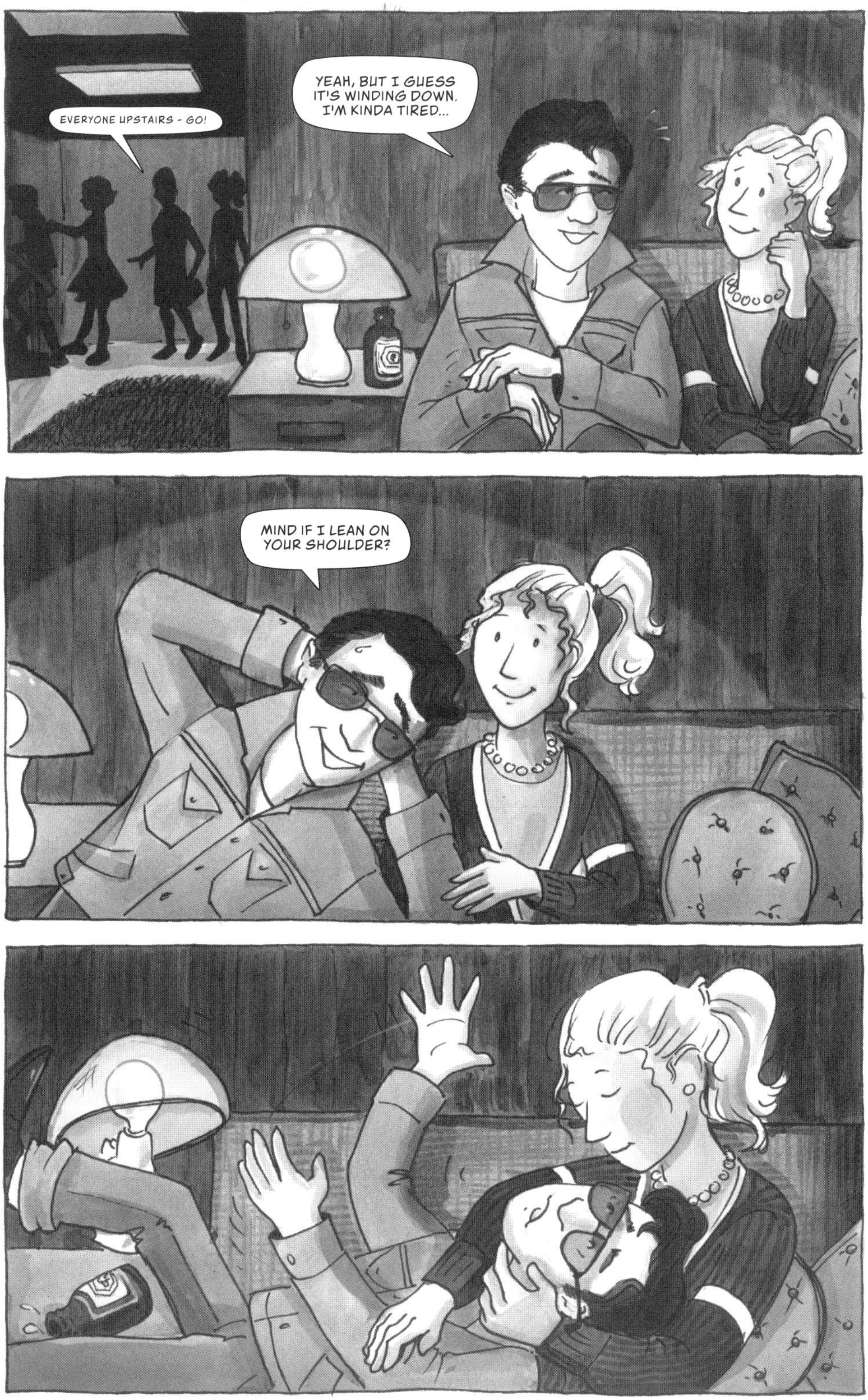
EVERYONE UPSTAIRS - GO!
YEAH, BUT I GUESS IT'S WINDING DOWN. I'M KINDA TIRED...
MIND IF I LEAN ON YOUR SHOULDER?

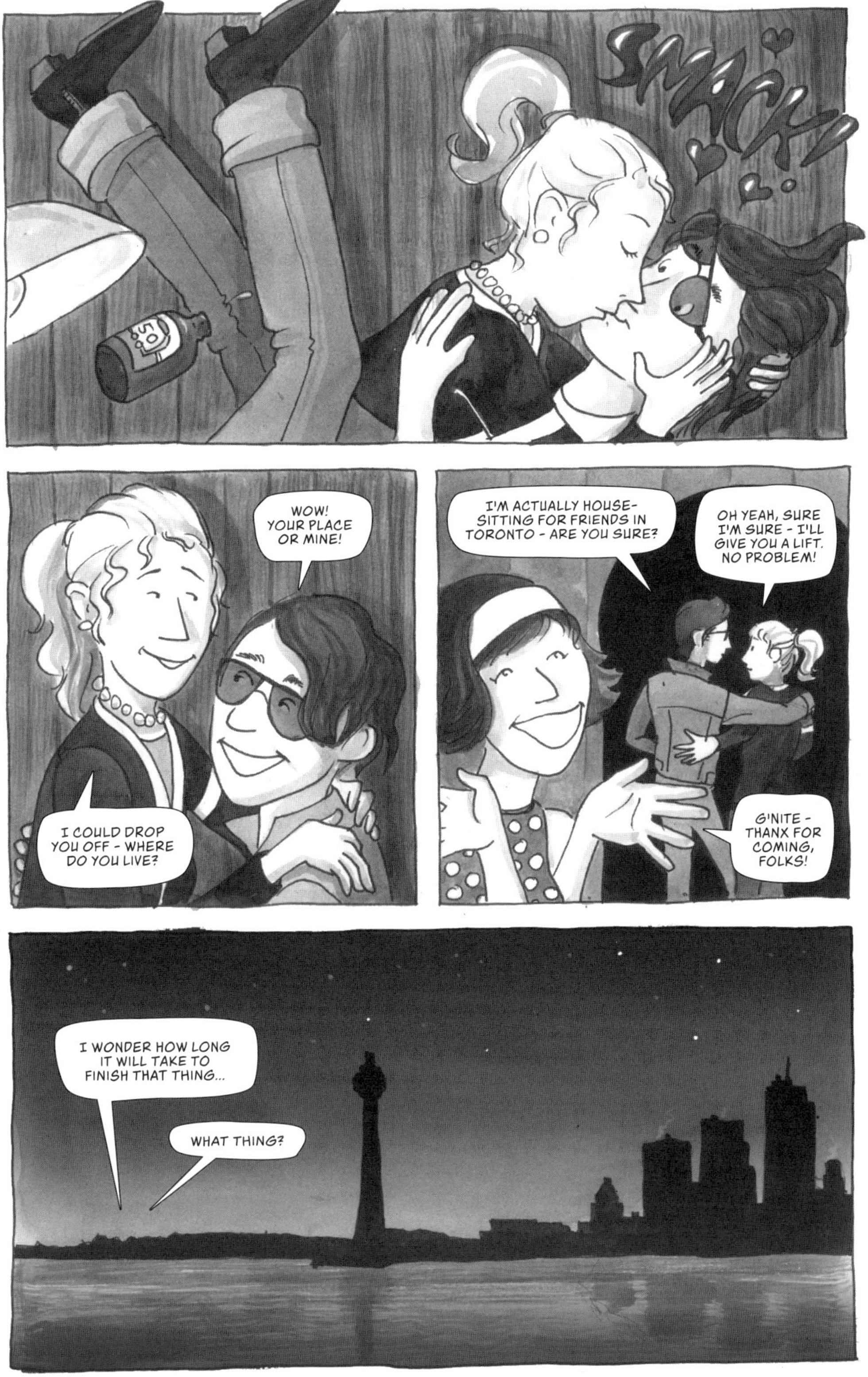
SMACK!
WOW! YOUR PLACE OR MINE!
I COULD DROP YOU OFF - WHERE DO YOU LIVE?
I'M ACTUALLY HOUSE-SITTING FOR FRIENDS IN TORONTO - ARE YOU SURE?
OH YEAH, SURE I'M SURE - I'LL GIVE YOU A LIFT. NO PROBLEM!
G'NITE - THANX FOR COMING, FOLKS!
I WONDER HOW LONG IT WILL TAKE TO FINISH THAT THING...
WHAT THING?

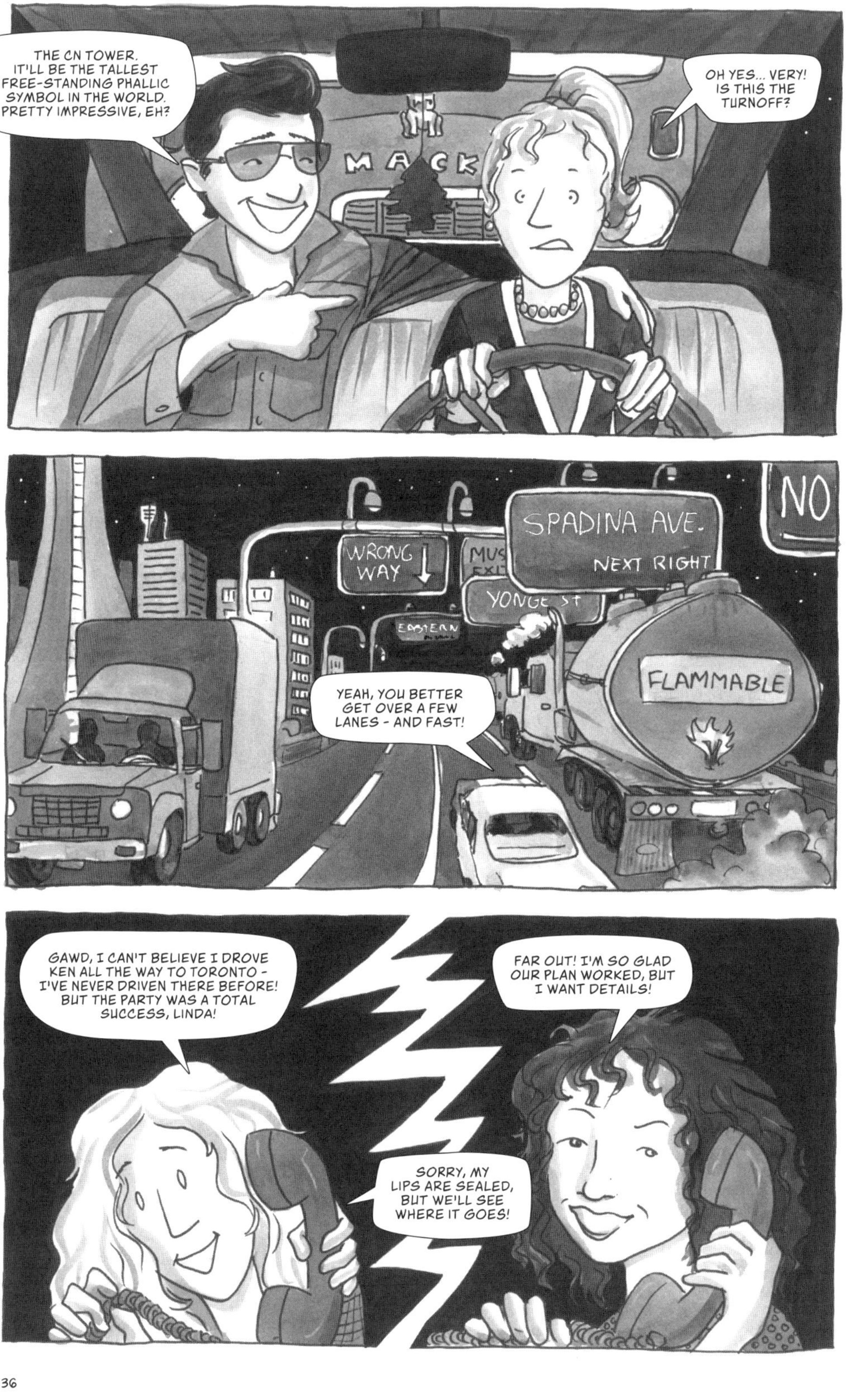
THE CN TOWER. IT'LL BE THE TALLEST FREE-STANDING PHALLIC SYMBOL IN THE WORLD. PRETTY IMPRESSIVE, EH?
MACK
OH YES... VERY! IS THIS THE TURNOFF?
WRONG WAY
SPADINA AVE. NEXT RIGHT
NO
YONGE ST
EASTERN
FLAMMABLE
YEAH, YOU BETTER GET OVER A FEW LANES - AND FAST!
GAWD, I CAN'T BELIEVE I DROVE KEN ALL THE WAY TO TORONTO - I'VE NEVER DRIVEN THERE BEFORE! BUT THE PARTY WAS A TOTAL SUCCESS, LINDA!
FAR OUT! I'M SO GLAD OUR PLAN WORKED, BUT I WANT DETAILS!
SORRY, MY LIPS ARE SEALED, BUT WE'LL SEE WHERE IT GOES!

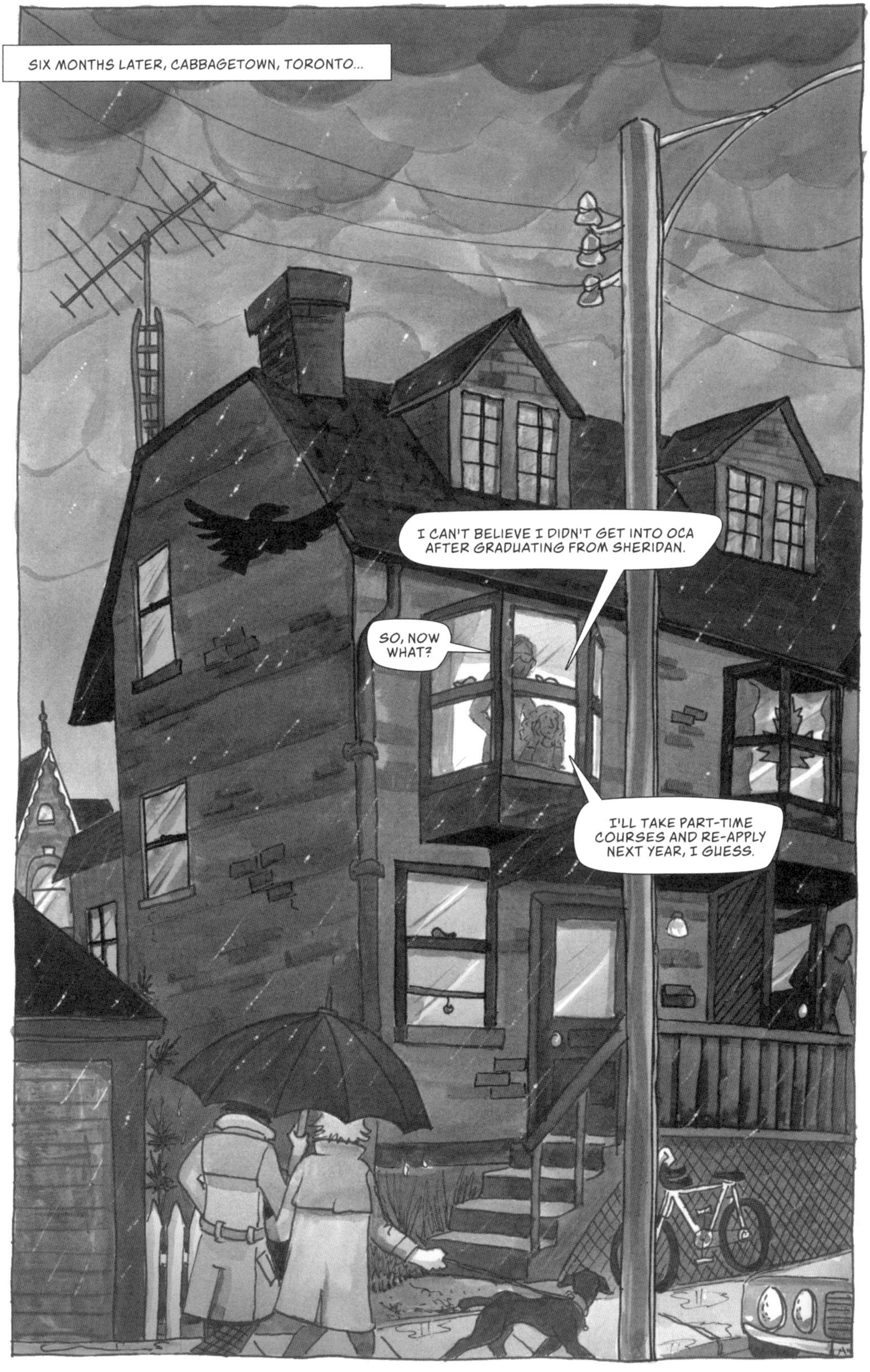
SIX MONTHS LATER, CABBAGETOWN, TORONTO...
I CAN'T BELIEVE I DIDN'T GET INTO OCA AFTER GRADUATING FROM SHERIDAN.
SO, NOW WHAT?
I'LL TAKE PART-TIME COURSES AND RE-APPLY NEXT YEAR, I GUESS.

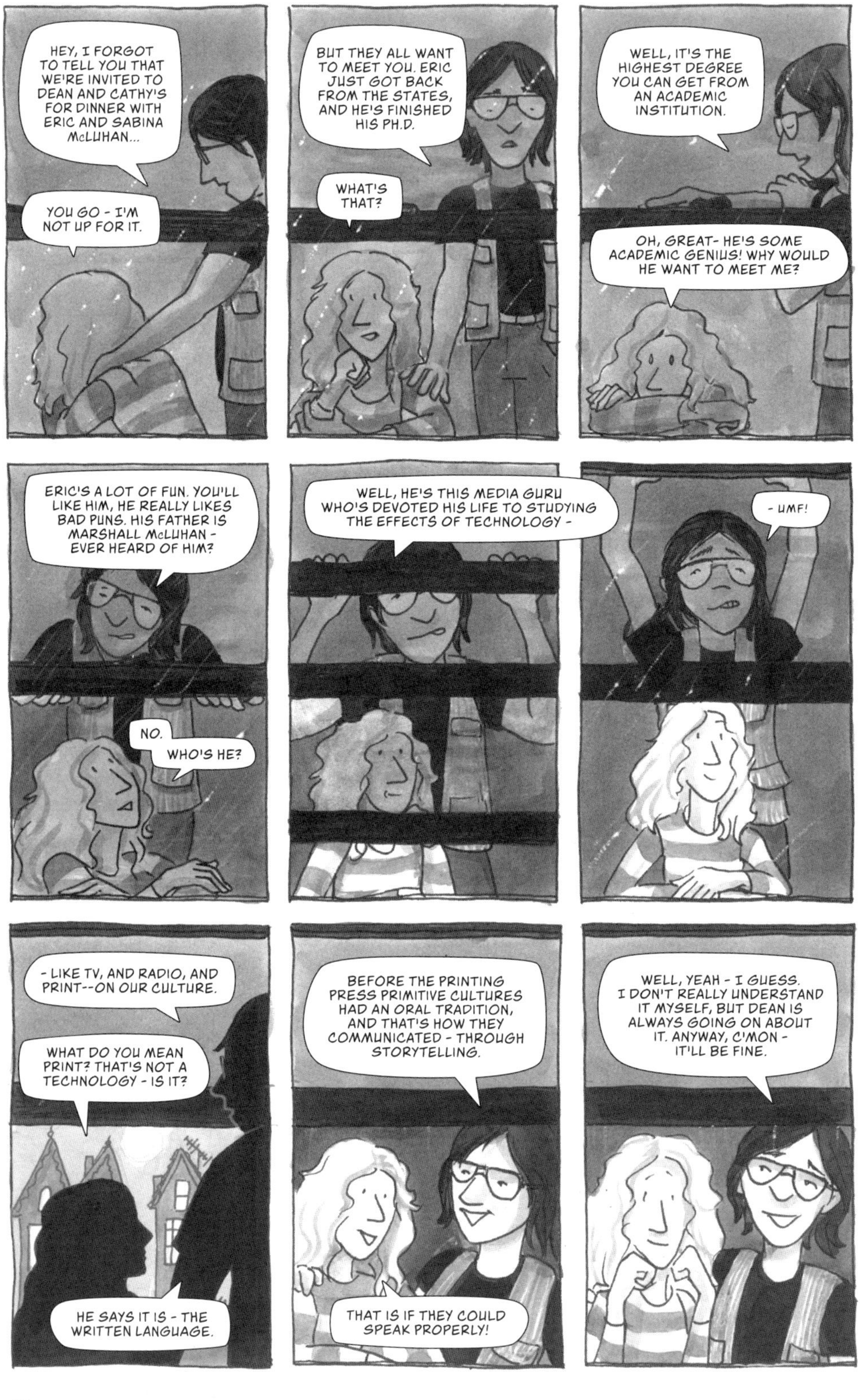
HEY, I FORGOT TO TELL YOU THAT WE'RE INVITED TO DEAN AND CATHY'S FOR DINNER WITH ERIC AND SABINA McLUHAN...
YOU GO - I'M NOT UP FOR IT.
BUT THEY ALL WANT TO MEET YOU. ERIC JUST GOT BACK FROM THE STATES, AND HE'S FINISHED HIS PH.D.
WHAT'S THAT?
WELL, IT'S THE HIGHEST DEGREE YOU CAN GET FROM AN ACADEMIC INSTITUTION.
OH, GREAT- HE'S SOME ACADEMIC GENIUS! WHY WOULD HE WANT TO MEET ME?
ERIC'S A LOT OF FUN. YOU'LL LIKE HIM, HE REALLY LIKES BAD PUNS. HIS FATHER IS MARSHALL McLUHAN - EVER HEARD OF HIM?
NO.
WHO'S HE?
WELL, HE'S THIS MEDIA GURU WHO'S DEVOTED HIS LIFE TO STUDYING THE EFFECTS OF TECHNOLOGY -
- UMF!
- LIKE TV, AND RADIO, AND PRINT--ON OUR CULTURE.
WHAT DO YOU MEAN PRINT? THAT'S NOT A TECHNOLOGY - IS IT?
HE SAYS IT IS - THE WRITTEN LANGUAGE.
BEFORE THE PRINTING PRESS PRIMITIVE CULTURES HAD AN ORAL TRADITION, AND THAT'S HOW THEY COMMUNICATED - THROUGH STORYTELLING.
THAT IS IF THEY COULD SPEAK PROPERLY!
WELL, YEAH - I GUESS. I DON'T REALLY UNDERSTAND IT MYSELF, BUT DEAN IS ALWAYS GOING ON ABOUT IT. ANYWAY, C'MON - IT'LL BE FINE.

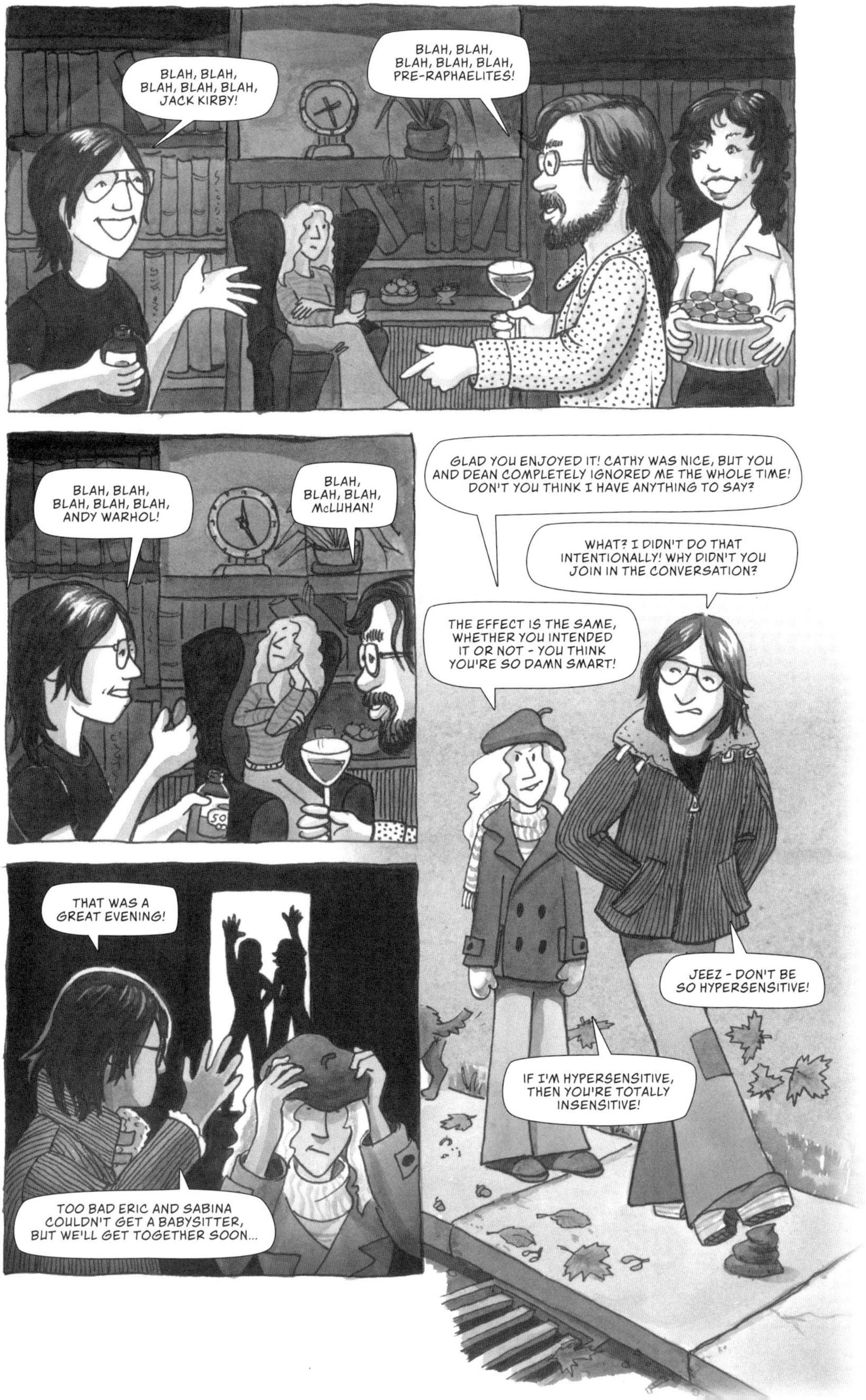
BLAH, BLAH, BLAH, BLAH, BLAH, JACK KIRBY!
BLAH, BLAH, BLAH, BLAH, BLAH, PRE-RAPHAELITES!
BLAH, BLAH, BLAH, BLAH, BLAH, ANDY WARHOL!
BLAH, BLAH, BLAH, McLUHAN!
THAT WAS A GREAT EVENING!
TOO BAD ERIC AND SABINA COULDN'T GET A BABYSITTER, BUT WE'LL GET TOGETHER SOON...
GLAD YOU ENJOYED IT! CATHY WAS NICE, BUT YOU AND DEAN COMPLETELY IGNORED ME THE WHOLE TIME! DON'T YOU THINK I HAVE ANYTHING TO SAY?
WHAT? I DIDN'T DO THAT INTENTIONALLY! WHY DIDN'T YOU JOIN IN THE CONVERSATION?
THE EFFECT IS THE SAME, WHETHER YOU INTENDED IT OR NOT - YOU THINK YOU'RE SO DAMN SMART!
JEEZ - DON'T BE SO HYPERSENSITIVE!
IF I'M HYPERSENSITIVE, THEN YOU'RE TOTALLY INSENSITIVE!

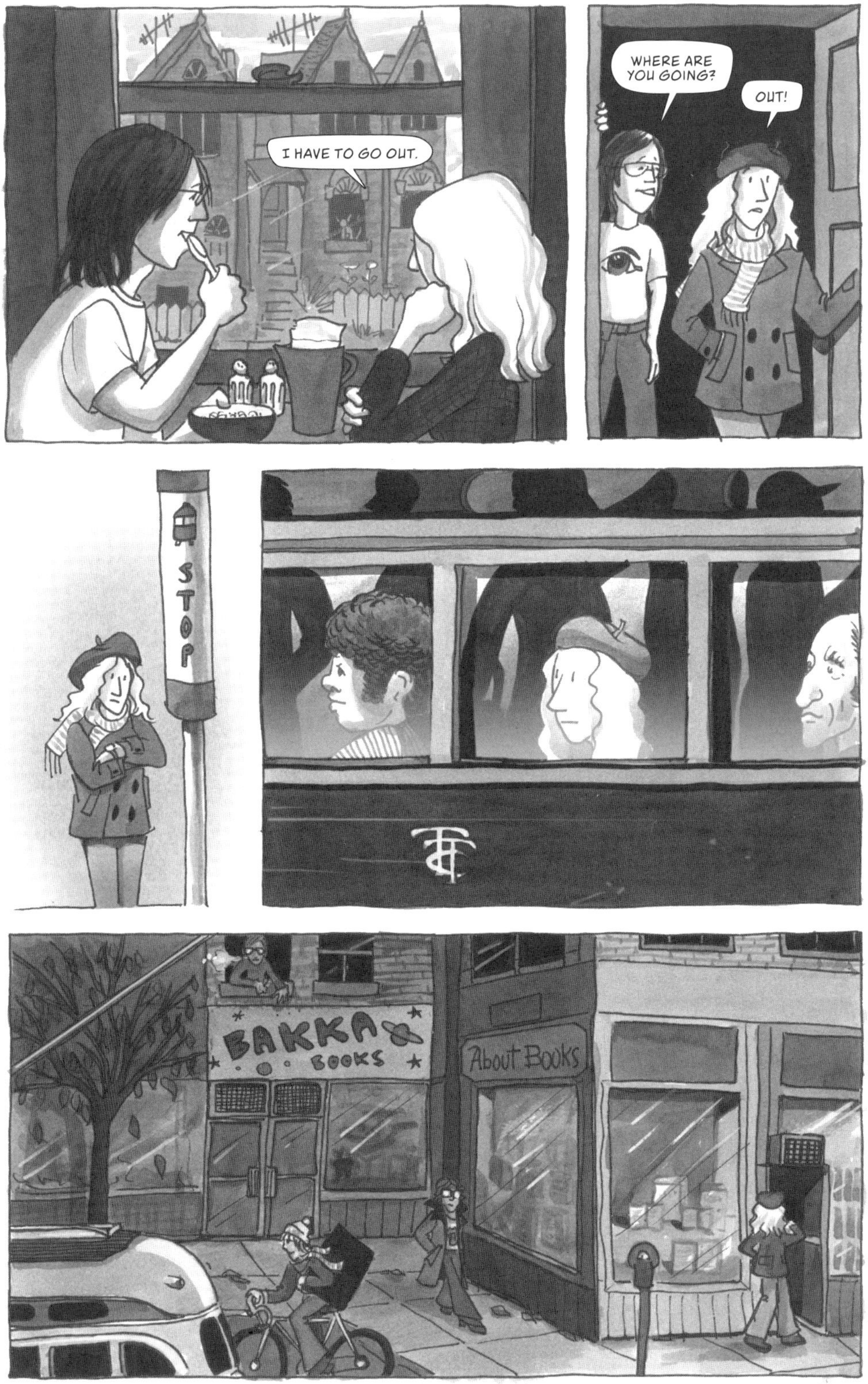
I HAVE TO GO OUT.
WHERE ARE YOU GOING?
OUT!
STOP
BAKKA BOOKS
About Books

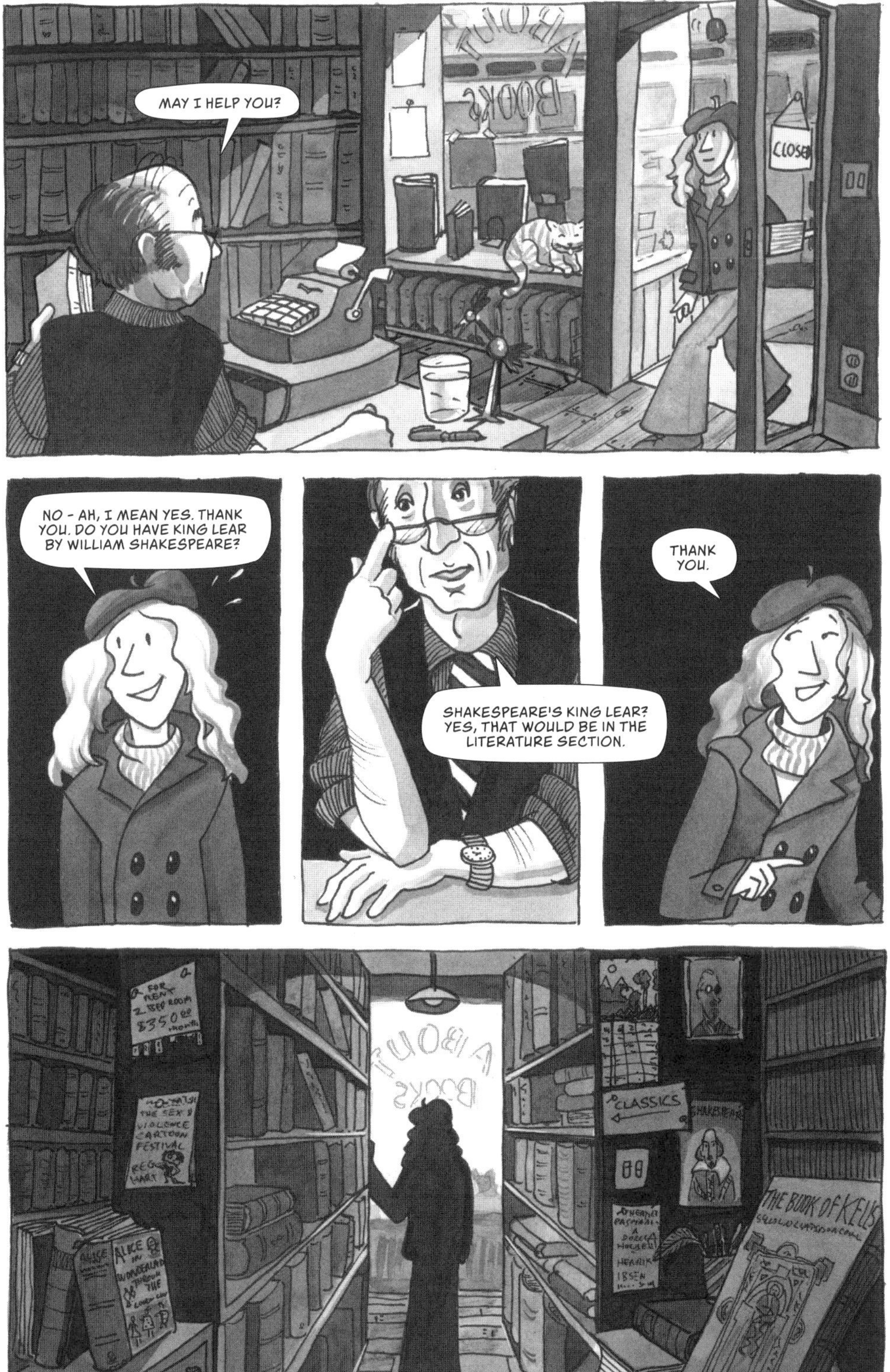
MAY I HELP YOU?
CLOSED
NO - AH, I MEAN YES. THANK YOU. DO YOU HAVE KING LEAR BY WILLIAM SHAKESPEARE?
SHAKESPEARE'S KING LEAR? YES, THAT WOULD BE IN THE LITERATURE SECTION.
THANK YOU.
CLASSICS
THE BOOK OF KELLS
ALICE IN WONDERLAND

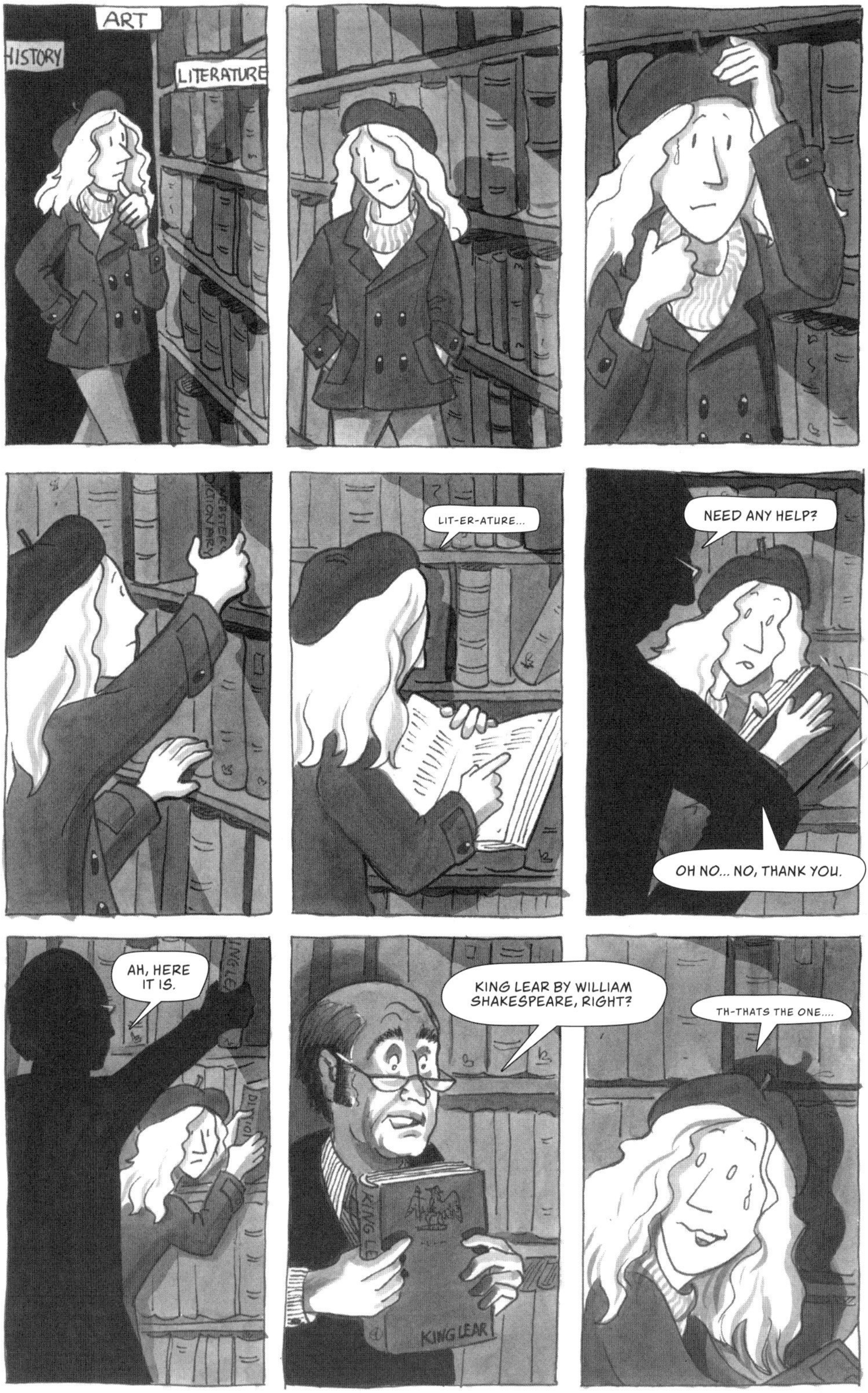
ART
HISTORY
LITERATURE
WEBSTER DICTIONARY
LIT-ER-ATURE...
NEED ANY HELP?
OH NO... NO, THANK YOU.
AH, HERE IT IS.
KING LEAR BY WILLIAM SHAKESPEARE, RIGHT?
KING LEAR
TH-THATS THE ONE....

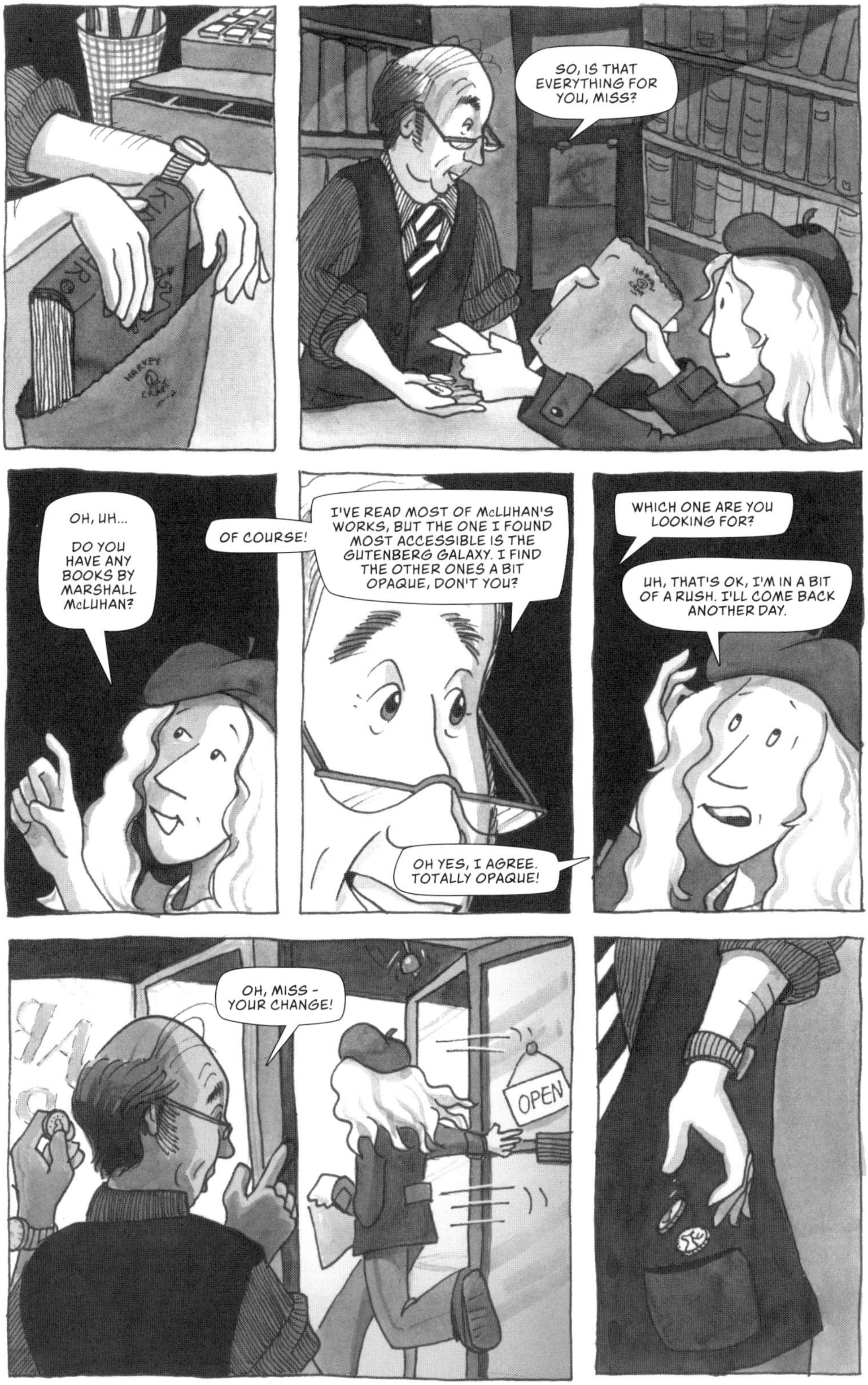
SO, IS THAT EVERYTHING FOR YOU, MISS?
OH, UH... DO YOU HAVE ANY BOOKS BY MARSHALL McLUHAN?
OF COURSE!
I'VE READ MOST OF McLUHAN'S WORKS, BUT THE ONE I FOUND MOST ACCESSIBLE IS THE GUTENBERG GALAXY. I FIND THE OTHER ONES A BIT OPAQUE, DON'T YOU?
OH YES, I AGREE. TOTALLY OPAQUE!
WHICH ONE ARE YOU LOOKING FOR?
UH, THAT'S OK, I'M IN A BIT OF A RUSH. I'LL COME BACK ANOTHER DAY.
OH, MISS - YOUR CHANGE!
OPEN

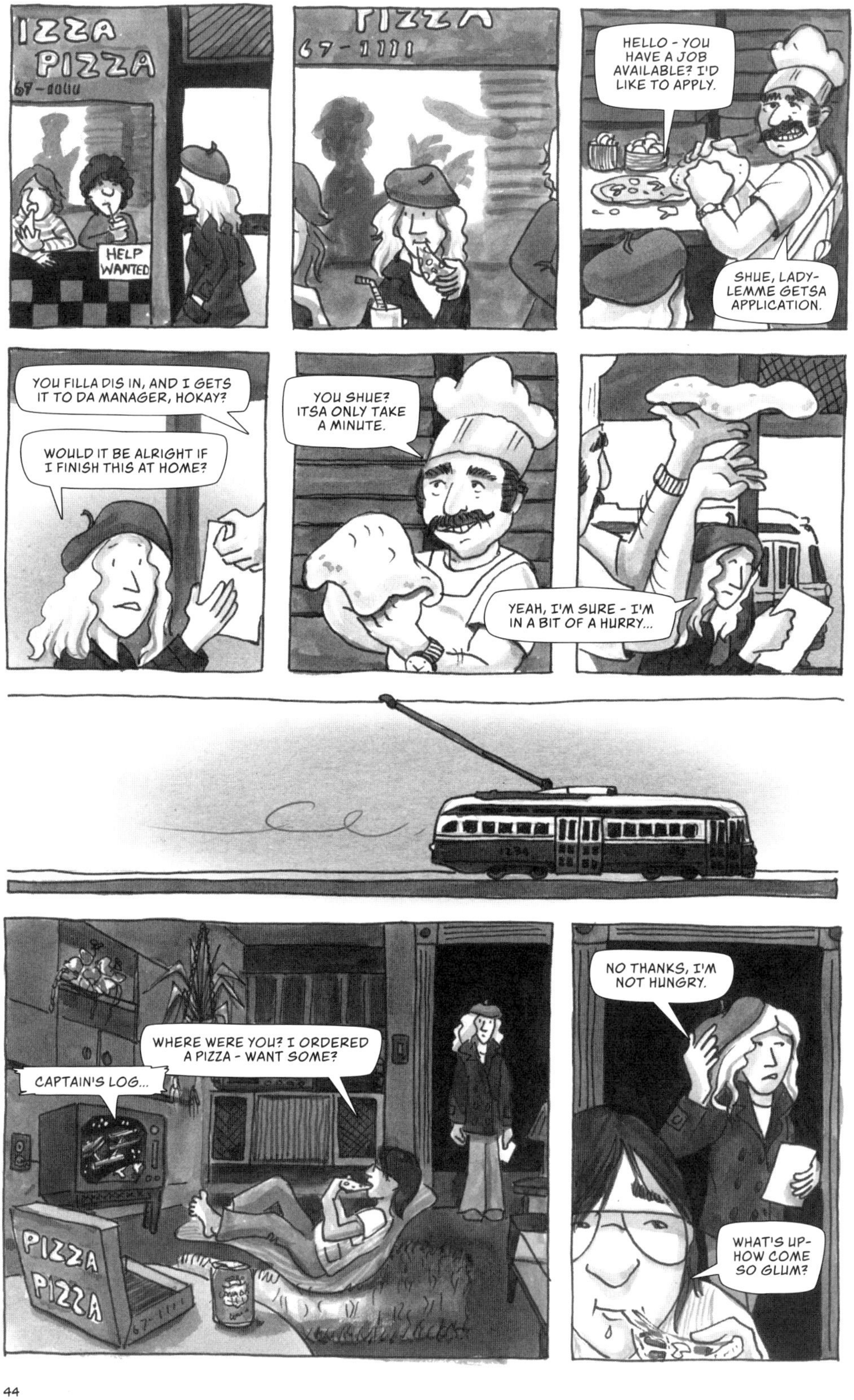
IZZA
PIZZA
67-1111
HELP WANTED
PIZZA
67-1111
HELLO - YOU HAVE A JOB AVAILABLE? I'D LIKE TO APPLY.
SHUE, LADY- LEMME GETSA APPLICATION.
YOU FILLA DIS IN, AND I GETS IT TO DA MANAGER, HOKAY?
WOULD IT BE ALRIGHT IF I FINISH THIS AT HOME?
YOU SHUE? ITSA ONLY TAKE A MINUTE.
YEAH, I'M SURE - I'M IN A BIT OF A HURRY...
1234
CAPTAIN'S LOG...
WHERE WERE YOU? I ORDERED A PIZZA - WANT SOME?
PIZZA
PIZZA
67-1111
NO THANKS, I'M NOT HUNGRY.
WHAT'S UP- HOW COME SO GLUM?

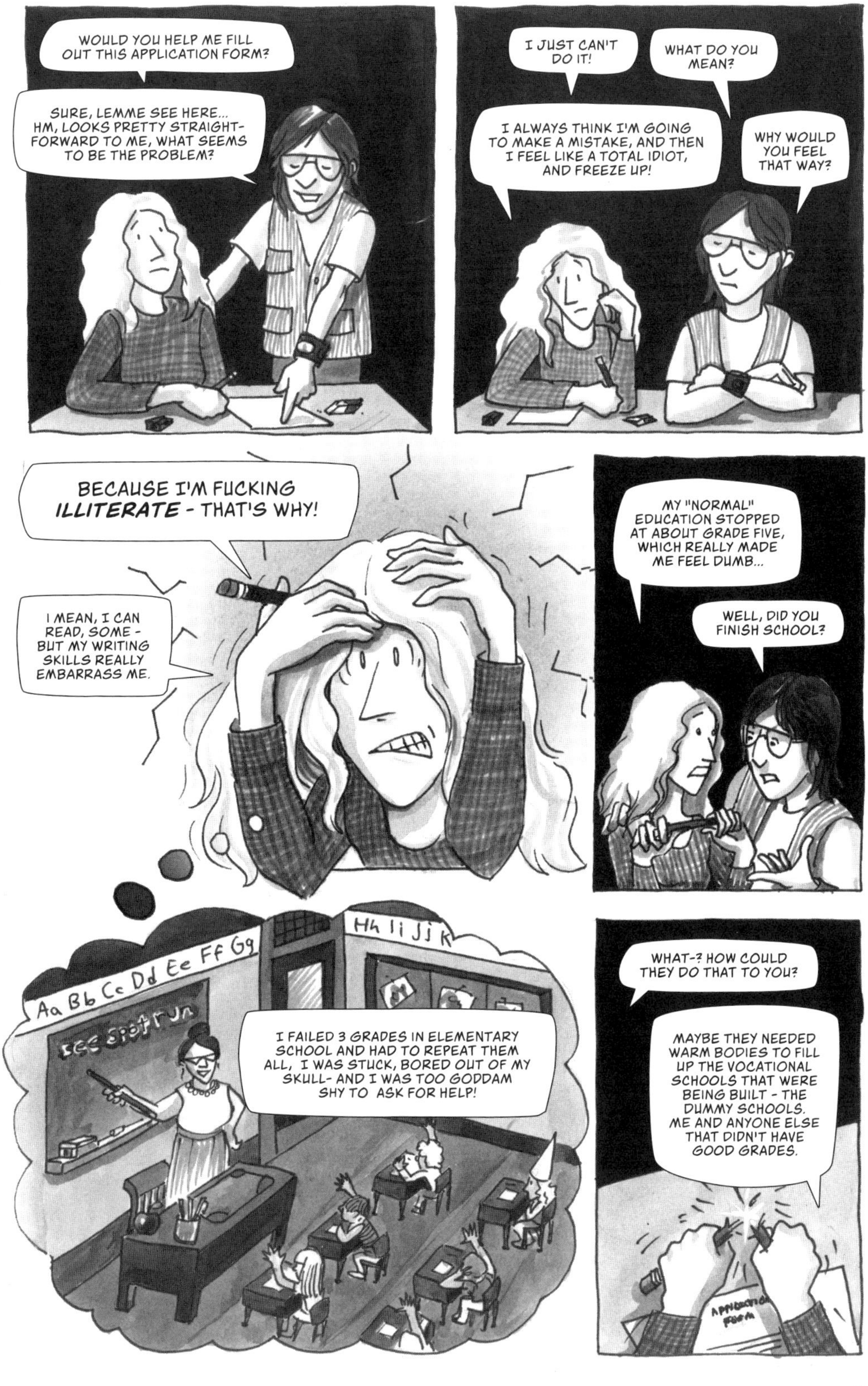
WOULD YOU HELP ME FILL OUT THIS APPLICATION FORM?
SURE, LEMME SEE HERE... HM, LOOKS PRETTY STRAIGHT-FORWARD TO ME, WHAT SEEMS TO BE THE PROBLEM?
I JUST CAN'T DO IT!
WHAT DO YOU MEAN?
I ALWAYS THINK I'M GOING TO MAKE A MISTAKE, AND THEN I FEEL LIKE A TOTAL IDIOT, AND FREEZE UP!
WHY WOULD YOU FEEL THAT WAY?
BECAUSE I'M FUCKING *ILLITERATE* - THAT'S WHY!
I MEAN, I CAN READ, SOME - BUT MY WRITING SKILLS REALLY EMBARRASS ME.
MY "NORMAL" EDUCATION STOPPED AT ABOUT GRADE FIVE, WHICH REALLY MADE ME FEEL DUMB...
WELL, DID YOU FINISH SCHOOL?
Aa Bb Cc Dd Ee Ff Gg
Hh Ii Jj K
I FAILED 3 GRADES IN ELEMENTARY SCHOOL AND HAD TO REPEAT THEM ALL, I WAS STUCK, BORED OUT OF MY SKULL- AND I WAS TOO GODDAM SHY TO ASK FOR HELP!
WHAT-? HOW COULD THEY DO THAT TO YOU?
MAYBE THEY NEEDED WARM BODIES TO FILL UP THE VOCATIONAL SCHOOLS THAT WERE BEING BUILT - THE DUMMY SCHOOLS. ME AND ANYONE ELSE THAT DIDN'T HAVE GOOD GRADES.

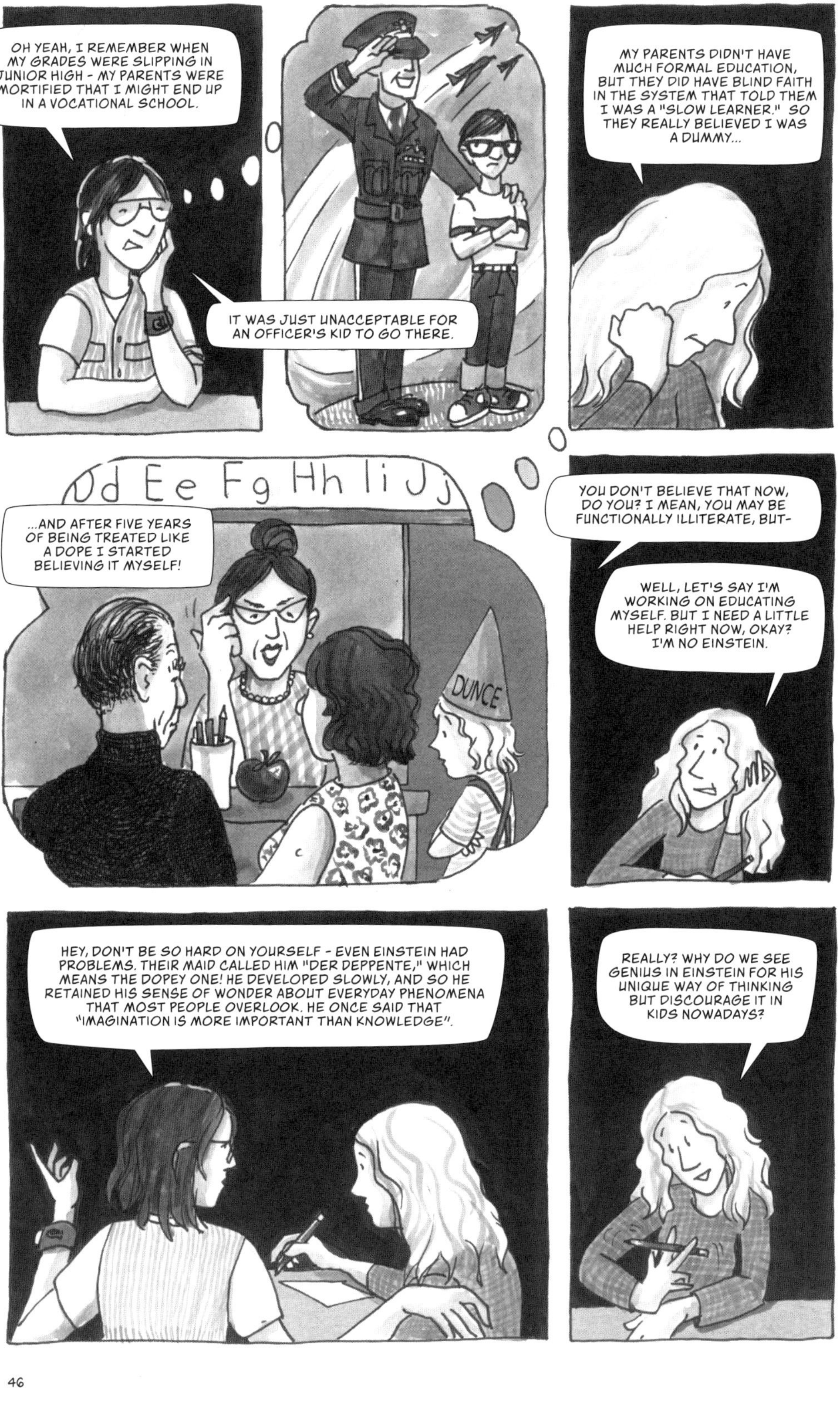
OH YEAH, I REMEMBER WHEN MY GRADES WERE SLIPPING IN JUNIOR HIGH - MY PARENTS WERE MORTIFIED THAT I MIGHT END UP IN A VOCATIONAL SCHOOL.
IT WAS JUST UNACCEPTABLE FOR AN OFFICER'S KID TO GO THERE.
MY PARENTS DIDN'T HAVE MUCH FORMAL EDUCATION, BUT THEY DID HAVE BLIND FAITH IN THE SYSTEM THAT TOLD THEM I WAS A "SLOW LEARNER." SO THEY REALLY BELIEVED I WAS A DUMMY...
...AND AFTER FIVE YEARS OF BEING TREATED LIKE A DOPE I STARTED BELIEVING IT MYSELF!
DUNCE
YOU DON'T BELIEVE THAT NOW, DO YOU? I MEAN, YOU MAY BE FUNCTIONALLY ILLITERATE, BUT-
WELL, LET'S SAY I'M WORKING ON EDUCATING MYSELF. BUT I NEED A LITTLE HELP RIGHT NOW, OKAY? I'M NO EINSTEIN.
HEY, DON'T BE SO HARD ON YOURSELF - EVEN EINSTEIN HAD PROBLEMS. THEIR MAID CALLED HIM "DER DEPPENTE," WHICH MEANS THE DOPEY ONE! HE DEVELOPED SLOWLY, AND SO HE RETAINED HIS SENSE OF WONDER ABOUT EVERYDAY PHENOMENA THAT MOST PEOPLE OVERLOOK. HE ONCE SAID THAT "IMAGINATION IS MORE IMPORTANT THAN KNOWLEDGE".
REALLY? WHY DO WE SEE GENIUS IN EINSTEIN FOR HIS UNIQUE WAY OF THINKING BUT DISCOURAGE IT IN KIDS NOWADAYS?

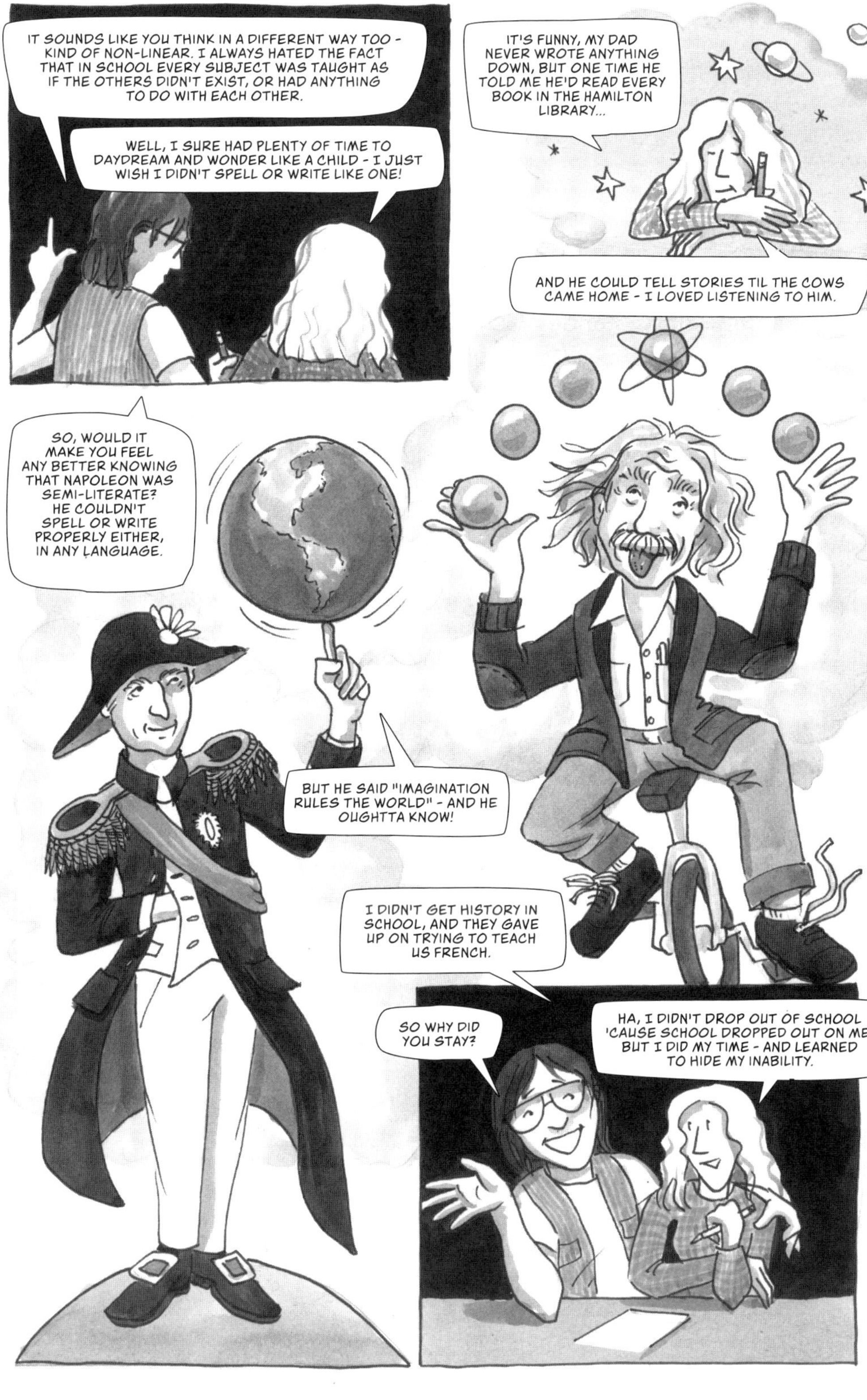

IT SOUNDS LIKE YOU THINK IN A DIFFERENT WAY TOO - KIND OF NON-LINEAR. I ALWAYS HATED THE FACT THAT IN SCHOOL EVERY SUBJECT WAS TAUGHT AS IF THE OTHERS DIDN'T EXIST, OR HAD ANYTHING TO DO WITH EACH OTHER.
WELL, I SURE HAD PLENTY OF TIME TO DAYDREAM AND WONDER LIKE A CHILD - I JUST WISH I DIDN'T SPELL OR WRITE LIKE ONE!
IT'S FUNNY, MY DAD NEVER WROTE ANYTHING DOWN, BUT ONE TIME HE TOLD ME HE'D READ EVERY BOOK IN THE HAMILTON LIBRARY...
AND HE COULD TELL STORIES TIL THE COWS CAME HOME - I LOVED LISTENING TO HIM.
SO, WOULD IT MAKE YOU FEEL ANY BETTER KNOWING THAT NAPOLEON WAS SEMI-LITERATE? HE COULDN'T SPELL OR WRITE PROPERLY EITHER, IN ANY LANGUAGE.
BUT HE SAID "IMAGINATION RULES THE WORLD" - AND HE OUGHTTA KNOW!
I DIDN'T GET HISTORY IN SCHOOL, AND THEY GAVE UP ON TRYING TO TEACH US FRENCH.
SO WHY DID YOU STAY?
HA, I DIDN'T DROP OUT OF SCHOOL 'CAUSE SCHOOL DROPPED OUT ON ME! BUT I DID MY TIME - AND LEARNED TO HIDE MY INABILITY.

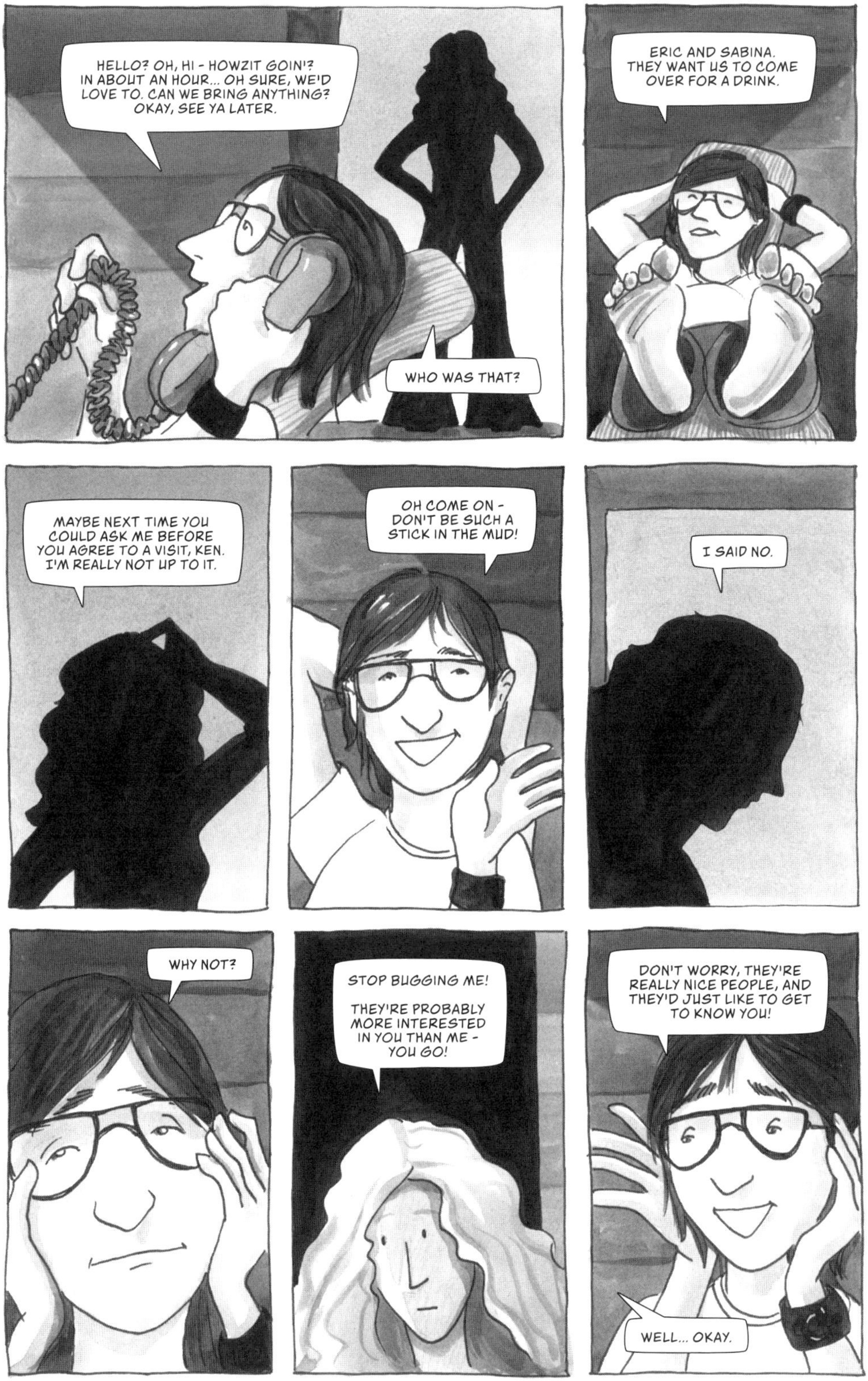
HELLO? OH, HI - HOWZIT GOIN'? IN ABOUT AN HOUR... OH SURE, WE'D LOVE TO. CAN WE BRING ANYTHING? OKAY, SEE YA LATER.
WHO WAS THAT?
ERIC AND SABINA. THEY WANT US TO COME OVER FOR A DRINK.
MAYBE NEXT TIME YOU COULD ASK ME BEFORE YOU AGREE TO A VISIT, KEN. I'M REALLY NOT UP TO IT.
OH COME ON - DON'T BE SUCH A STICK IN THE MUD!
I SAID NO.
WHY NOT?
STOP BUGGING ME!
THEY'RE PROBABLY MORE INTERESTED IN YOU THAN ME - YOU GO!
DON'T WORRY, THEY'RE REALLY NICE PEOPLE, AND THEY'D JUST LIKE TO GET TO KNOW YOU!
WELL... OKAY.

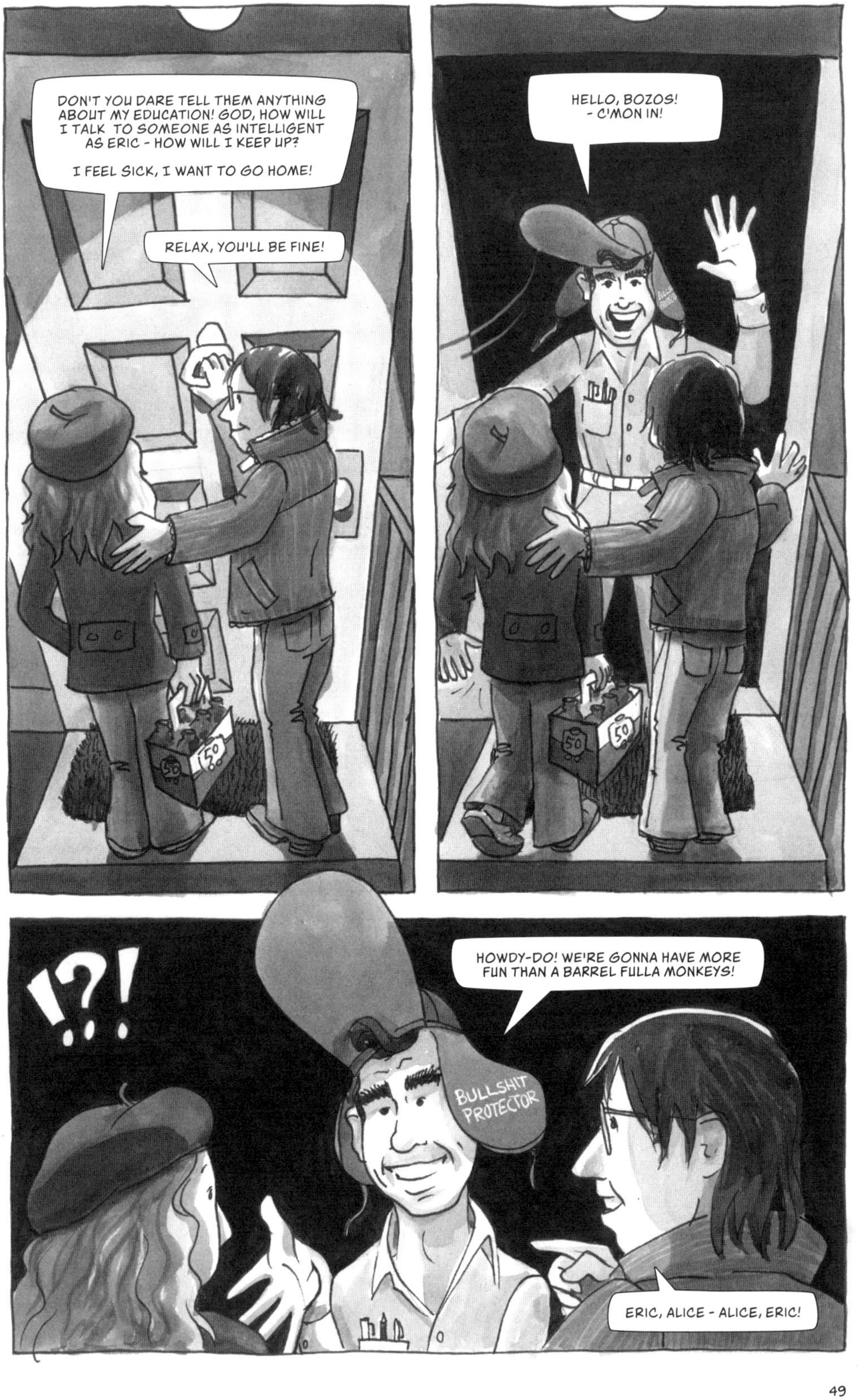
DON'T YOU DARE TELL THEM ANYTHING ABOUT MY EDUCATION! GOD, HOW WILL I TALK TO SOMEONE AS INTELLIGENT AS ERIC - HOW WILL I KEEP UP?
I FEEL SICK, I WANT TO GO HOME!
RELAX, YOU'LL BE FINE!
50
HELLO, BOZOS! - C'MON IN!
50
!?!
HOWDY-DO! WE'RE GONNA HAVE MORE FUN THAN A BARREL FULLA MONKEYS!
BULLSHIT PROTECTOR
ERIC, ALICE - ALICE, ERIC!

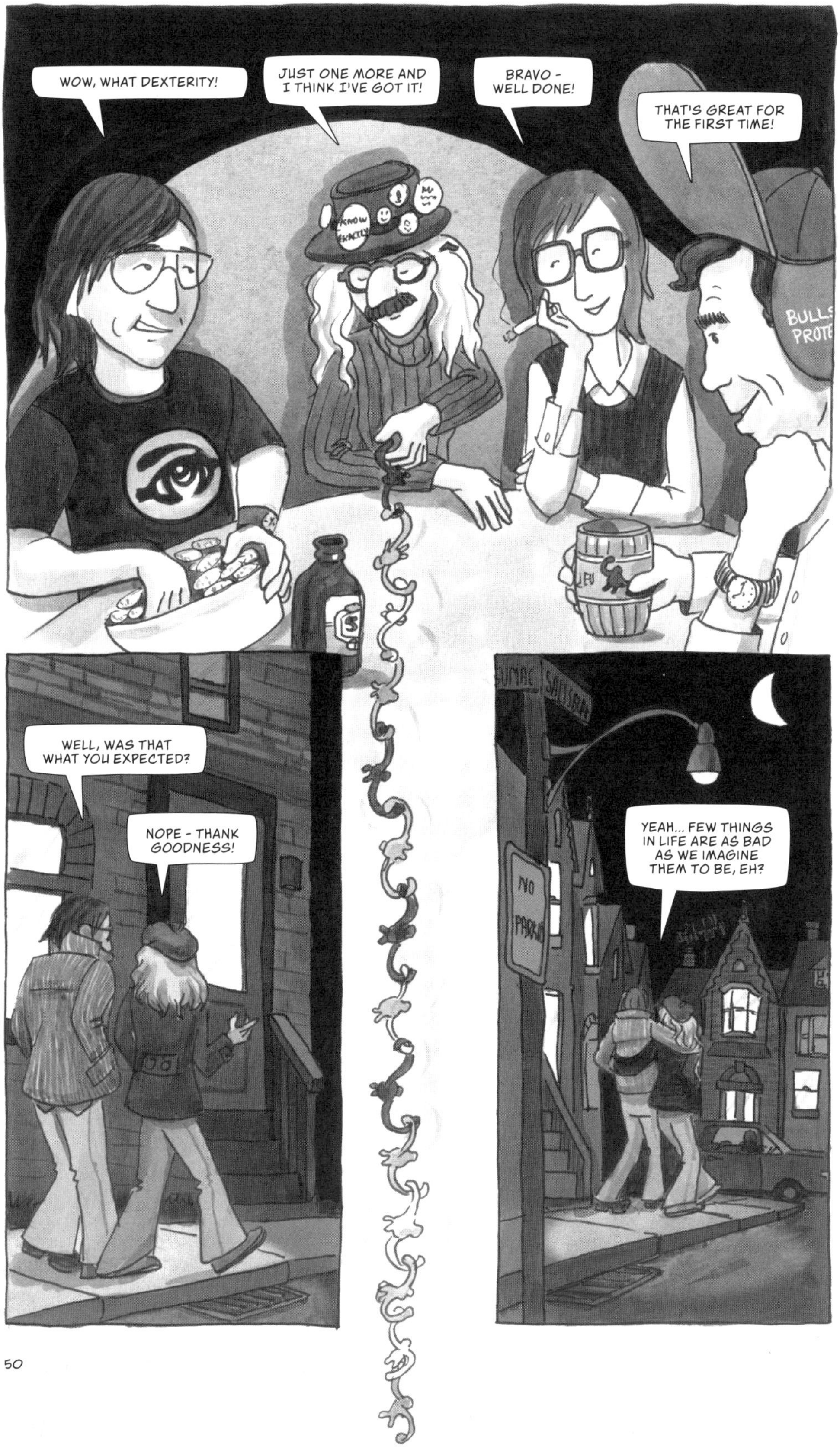
WOW, WHAT DEXTERITY!
JUST ONE MORE AND I THINK I'VE GOT IT!
BRAVO - WELL DONE!
THAT'S GREAT FOR THE FIRST TIME!
WELL, WAS THAT WHAT YOU EXPECTED?
NOPE - THANK GOODNESS!
YEAH... FEW THINGS IN LIFE ARE AS BAD AS WE IMAGINE THEM TO BE, EH?

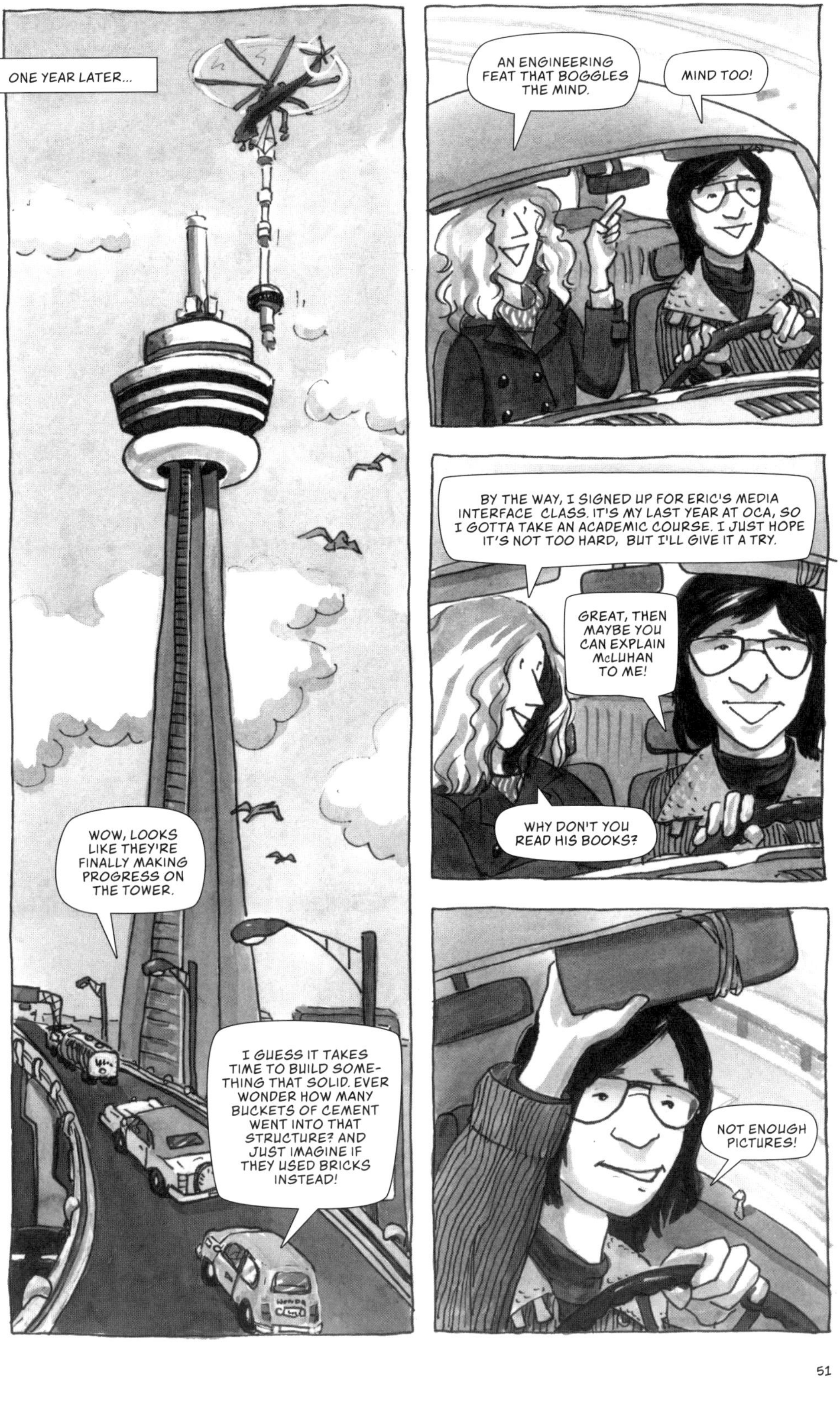
ONE YEAR LATER...
WOW, LOOKS LIKE THEY'RE FINALLY MAKING PROGRESS ON THE TOWER.
I GUESS IT TAKES TIME TO BUILD SOME-THING THAT SOLID. EVER WONDER HOW MANY BUCKETS OF CEMENT WENT INTO THAT STRUCTURE? AND JUST IMAGINE IF THEY USED BRICKS INSTEAD!
AN ENGINEERING FEAT THAT BOGGLES THE MIND.
MIND TOO!
BY THE WAY, I SIGNED UP FOR ERIC'S MEDIA INTERFACE CLASS. IT'S MY LAST YEAR AT OCA, SO I GOTTA TAKE AN ACADEMIC COURSE. I JUST HOPE IT'S NOT TOO HARD, BUT I'LL GIVE IT A TRY.
GREAT, THEN MAYBE YOU CAN EXPLAIN McLUHAN TO ME!
WHY DON'T YOU READ HIS BOOKS?
NOT ENOUGH PICTURES!

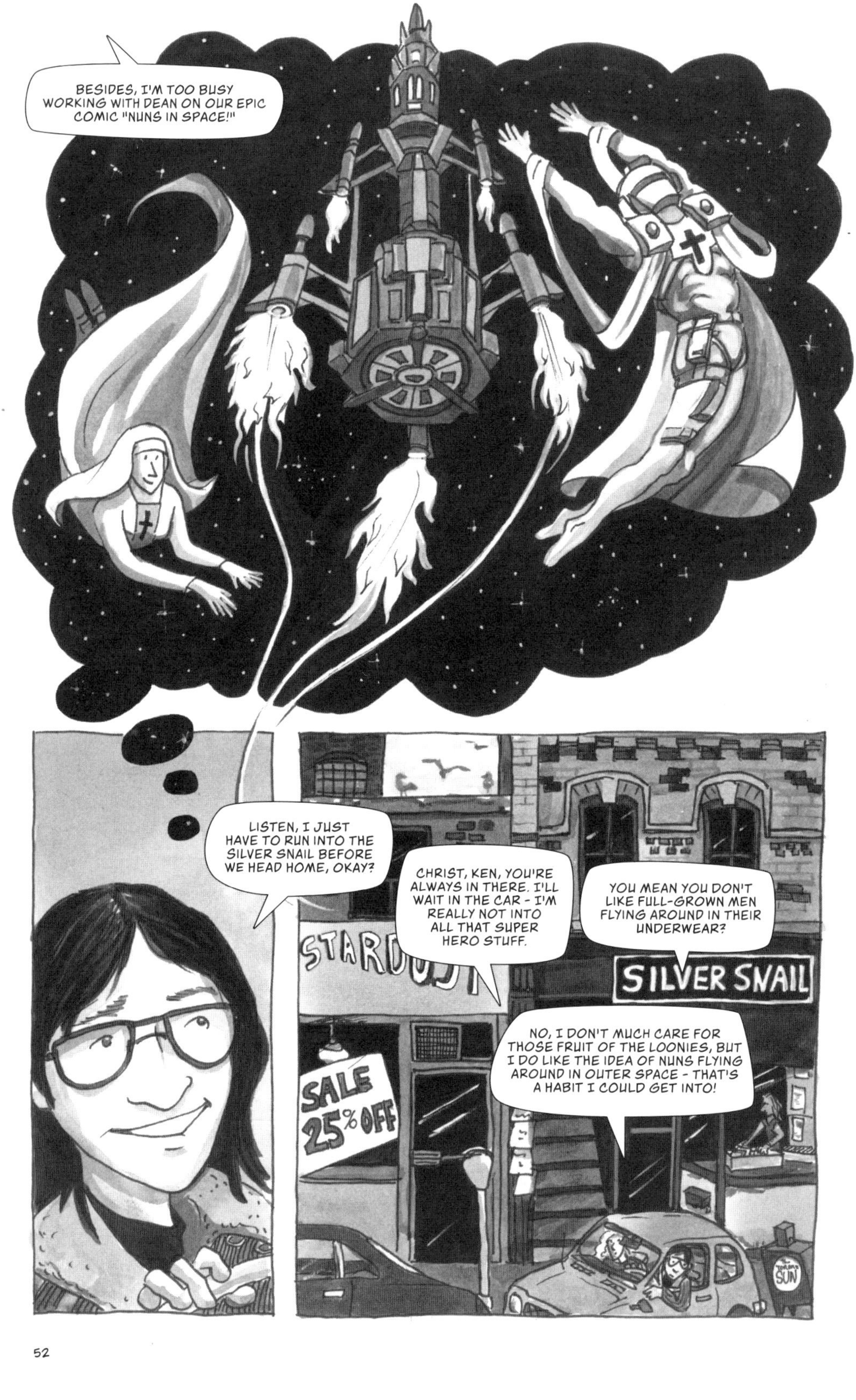
BESIDES, I'M TOO BUSY WORKING WITH DEAN ON OUR EPIC COMIC "NUNS IN SPACE!"
LISTEN, I JUST HAVE TO RUN INTO THE SILVER SNAIL BEFORE WE HEAD HOME, OKAY?
CHRIST, KEN, YOU'RE ALWAYS IN THERE. I'LL WAIT IN THE CAR - I'M REALLY NOT INTO ALL THAT SUPER HERO STUFF.
YOU MEAN YOU DON'T LIKE FULL-GROWN MEN FLYING AROUND IN THEIR UNDERWEAR?
NO, I DON'T MUCH CARE FOR THOSE FRUIT OF THE LOONIES, BUT I DO LIKE THE IDEA OF NUNS FLYING AROUND IN OUTER SPACE - THAT'S A HABIT I COULD GET INTO!
SILVER SNAIL
SALE 25% OFF
SUN

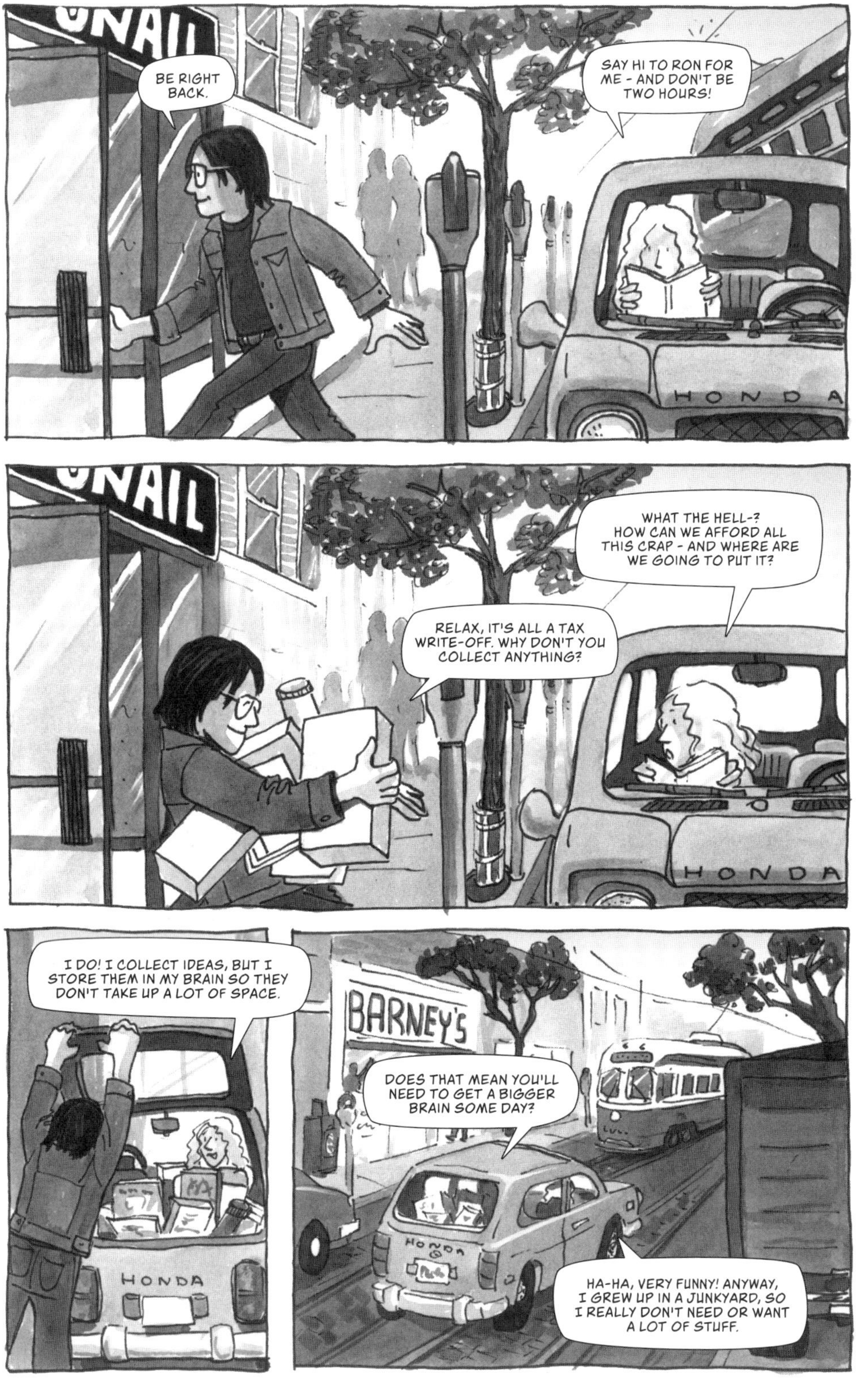
BE RIGHT BACK.
SAY HI TO RON FOR ME - AND DON'T BE TWO HOURS!
HONDA
WHAT THE HELL-? HOW CAN WE AFFORD ALL THIS CRAP - AND WHERE ARE WE GOING TO PUT IT?
RELAX, IT'S ALL A TAX WRITE-OFF. WHY DON'T YOU COLLECT ANYTHING?
HONDA
I DO! I COLLECT IDEAS, BUT I STORE THEM IN MY BRAIN SO THEY DON'T TAKE UP A LOT OF SPACE.
HONDA
BARNEY'S
DOES THAT MEAN YOU'LL NEED TO GET A BIGGER BRAIN SOME DAY?
HA-HA, VERY FUNNY! ANYWAY, I GREW UP IN A JUNKYARD, SO I REALLY DON'T NEED OR WANT A LOT OF STUFF.

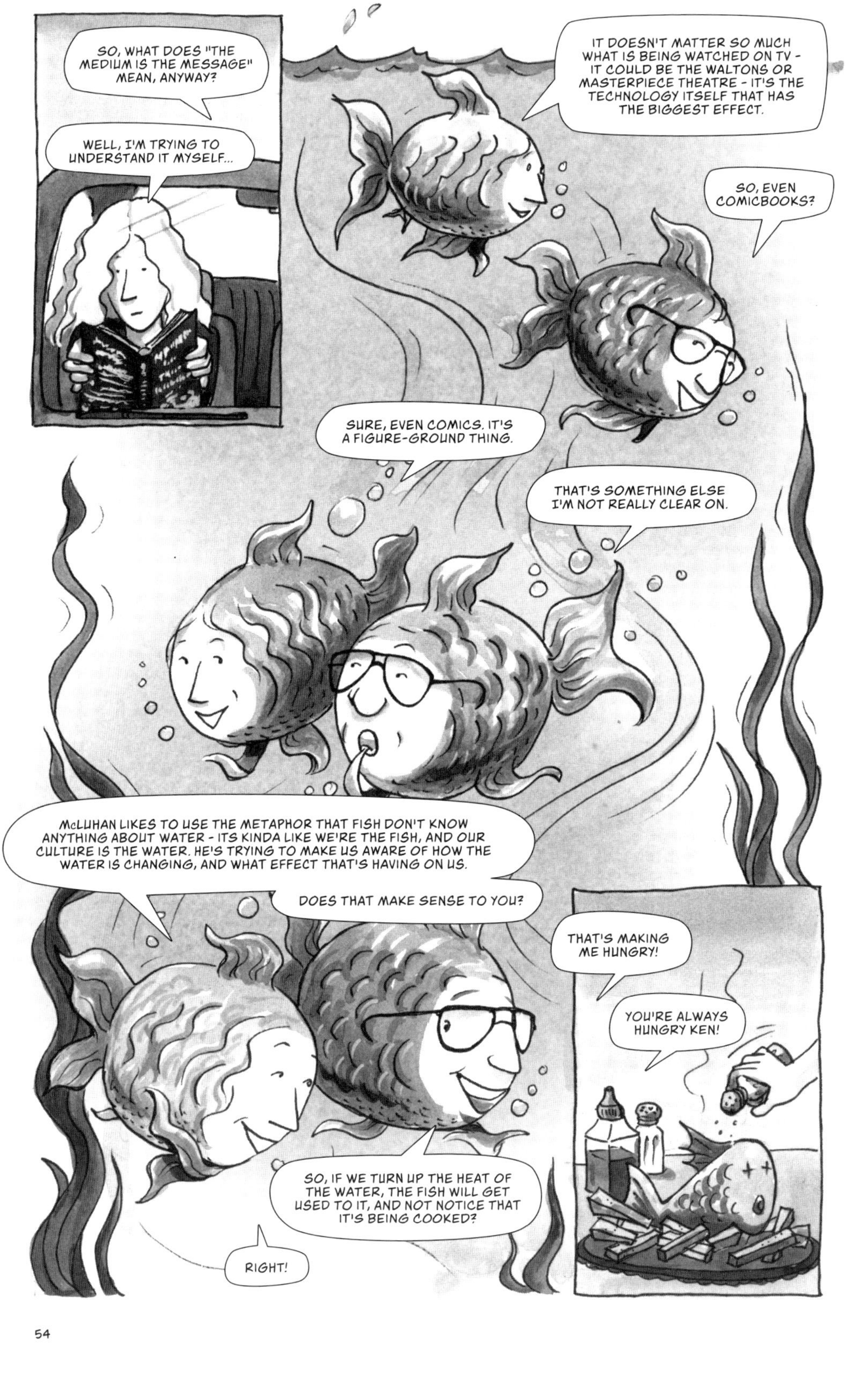
SO, WHAT DOES "THE MEDIUM IS THE MESSAGE" MEAN, ANYWAY?
WELL, I'M TRYING TO UNDERSTAND IT MYSELF...
IT DOESN'T MATTER SO MUCH WHAT IS BEING WATCHED ON TV - IT COULD BE THE WALTONS OR MASTERPIECE THEATRE - IT'S THE TECHNOLOGY ITSELF THAT HAS THE BIGGEST EFFECT.
SO, EVEN COMICBOOKS?
SURE, EVEN COMICS. IT'S A FIGURE-GROUND THING.
THAT'S SOMETHING ELSE I'M NOT REALLY CLEAR ON.
McLUHAN LIKES TO USE THE METAPHOR THAT FISH DON'T KNOW ANYTHING ABOUT WATER - ITS KINDA LIKE WE'RE THE FISH, AND OUR CULTURE IS THE WATER. HE'S TRYING TO MAKE US AWARE OF HOW THE WATER IS CHANGING, AND WHAT EFFECT THAT'S HAVING ON US.
DOES THAT MAKE SENSE TO YOU?
SO, IF WE TURN UP THE HEAT OF THE WATER, THE FISH WILL GET USED TO IT, AND NOT NOTICE THAT IT'S BEING COOKED?
RIGHT!
THAT'S MAKING ME HUNGRY!
YOU'RE ALWAYS HUNGRY KEN!

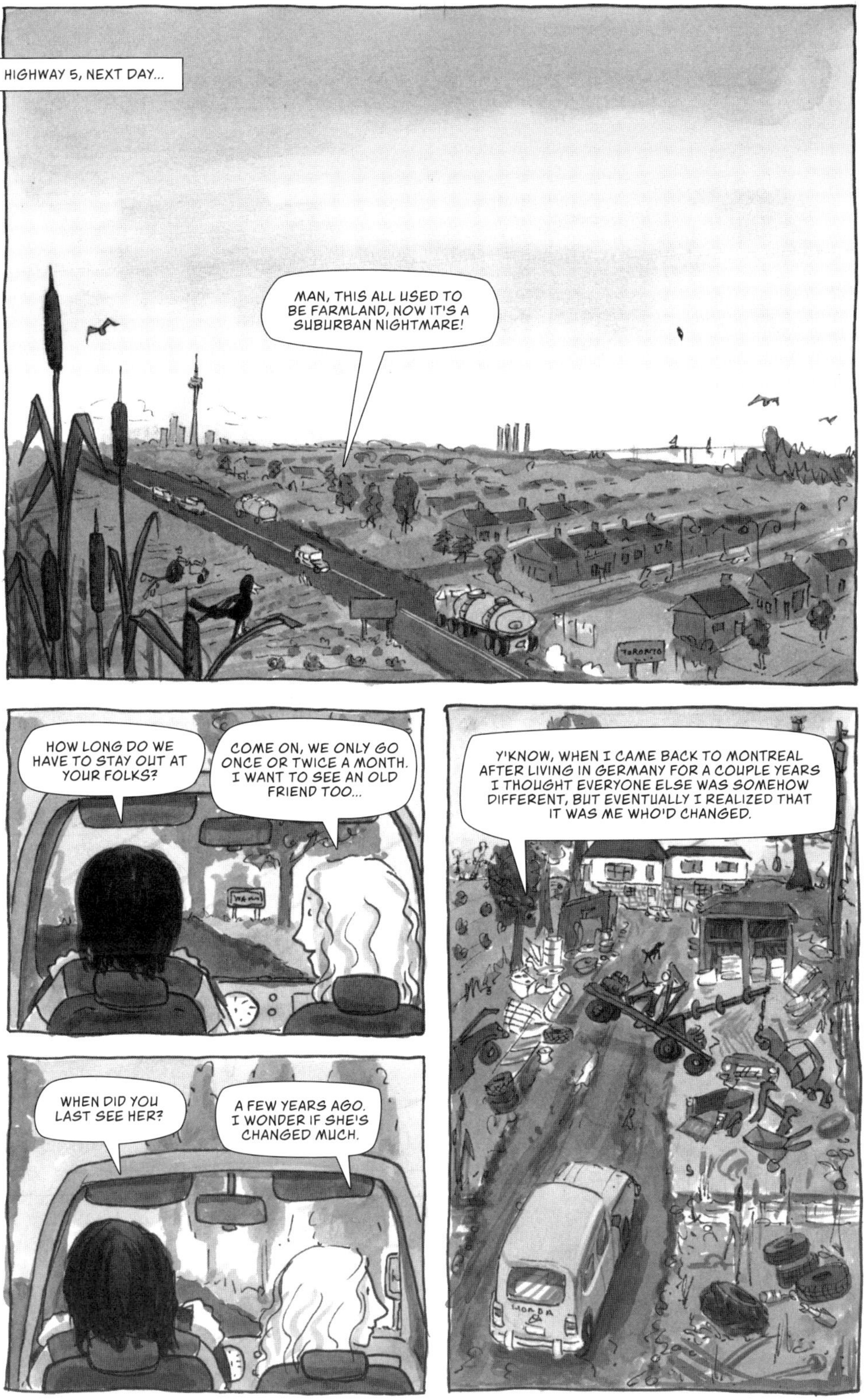
HIGHWAY 5, NEXT DAY...
MAN, THIS ALL USED TO BE FARMLAND, NOW IT'S A SUBURBAN NIGHTMARE!
TORONTO
HOW LONG DO WE HAVE TO STAY OUT AT YOUR FOLKS?
COME ON, WE ONLY GO ONCE OR TWICE A MONTH. I WANT TO SEE AN OLD FRIEND TOO...
WHEN DID YOU LAST SEE HER?
A FEW YEARS AGO. I WONDER IF SHE'S CHANGED MUCH.
Y'KNOW, WHEN I CAME BACK TO MONTREAL AFTER LIVING IN GERMANY FOR A COUPLE YEARS I THOUGHT EVERYONE ELSE WAS SOMEHOW DIFFERENT, BUT EVENTUALLY I REALIZED THAT IT WAS ME WHO'D CHANGED.

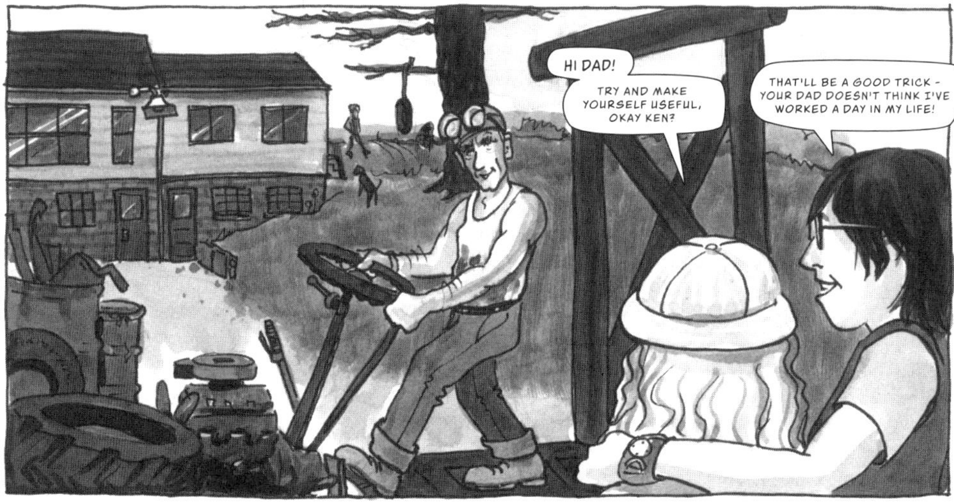
HI DAD!
TRY AND MAKE YOURSELF USEFUL, OKAY KEN?
THAT'LL BE A GOOD TRICK - YOUR DAD DOESN'T THINK I'VE WORKED A DAY IN MY LIFE!

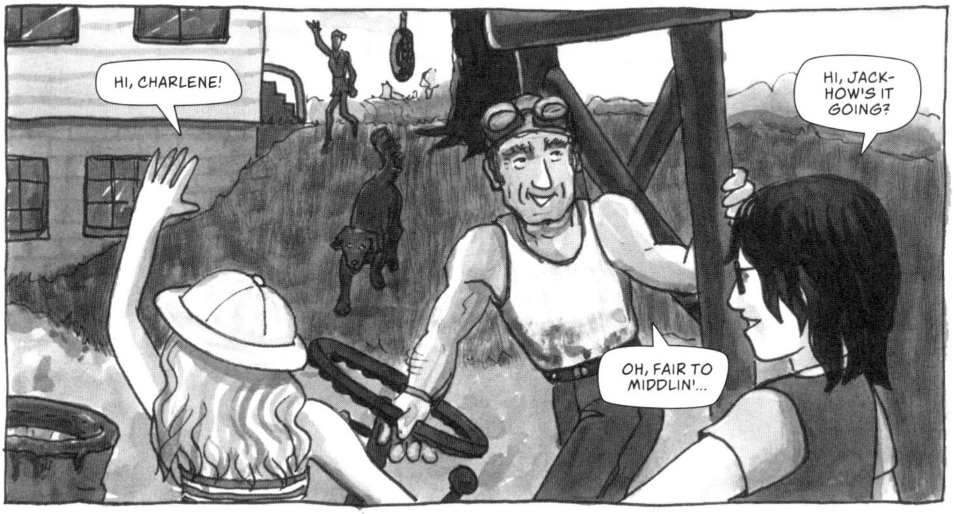
HI, CHARLENE!
HI, JACK- HOW'S IT GOING?
OH, FAIR TO MIDDLIN'...

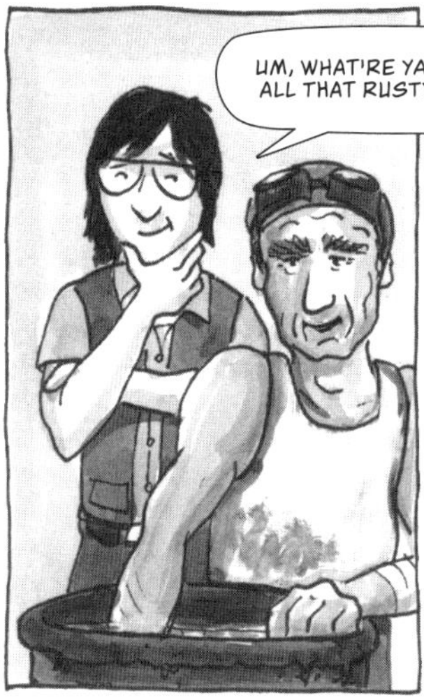
UM, WHAT'RE YA DOING WITH ALL THAT RUSTY OLD JUNK?

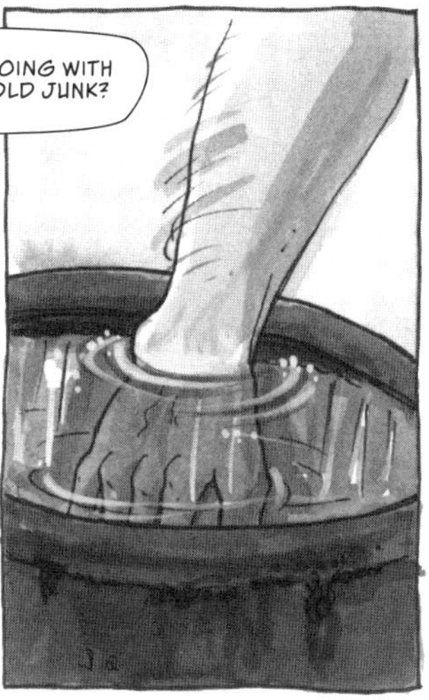

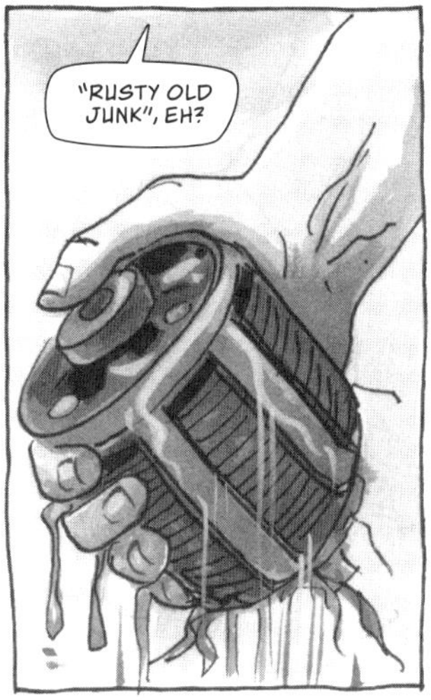
"RUSTY OLD JUNK", EH?

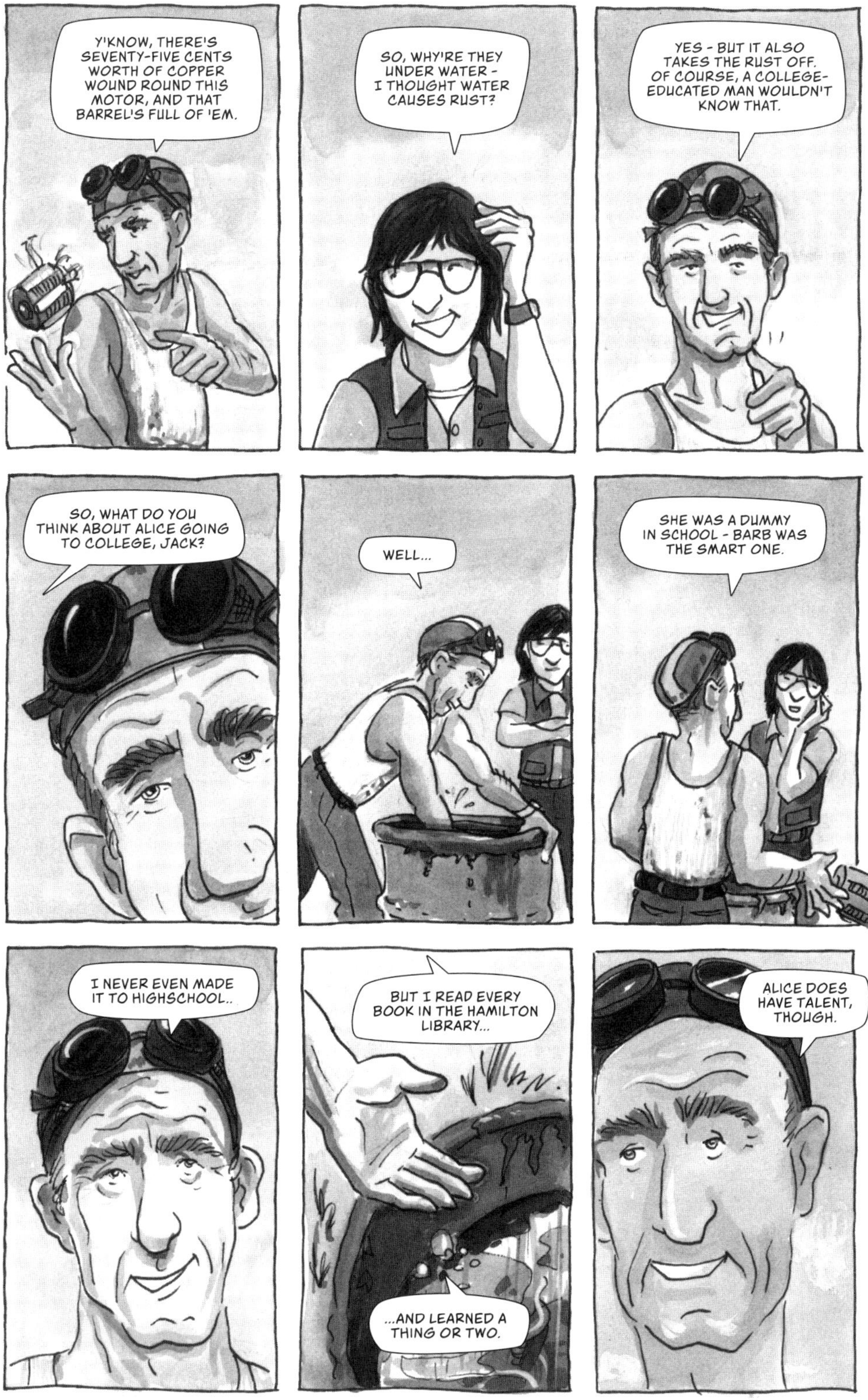
Y'KNOW, THERE'S SEVENTY-FIVE CENTS WORTH OF COPPER WOUND ROUND THIS MOTOR, AND THAT BARREL'S FULL OF 'EM.
SO, WHY'RE THEY UNDER WATER - I THOUGHT WATER CAUSES RUST?
YES - BUT IT ALSO TAKES THE RUST OFF. OF COURSE, A COLLEGE-EDUCATED MAN WOULDN'T KNOW THAT.
SO, WHAT DO YOU THINK ABOUT ALICE GOING TO COLLEGE, JACK?
WELL...
SHE WAS A DUMMY IN SCHOOL - BARB WAS THE SMART ONE.
I NEVER EVEN MADE IT TO HIGHSCHOOL..
BUT I READ EVERY BOOK IN THE HAMILTON LIBRARY...
...AND LEARNED A THING OR TWO.
ALICE DOES HAVE TALENT, THOUGH.

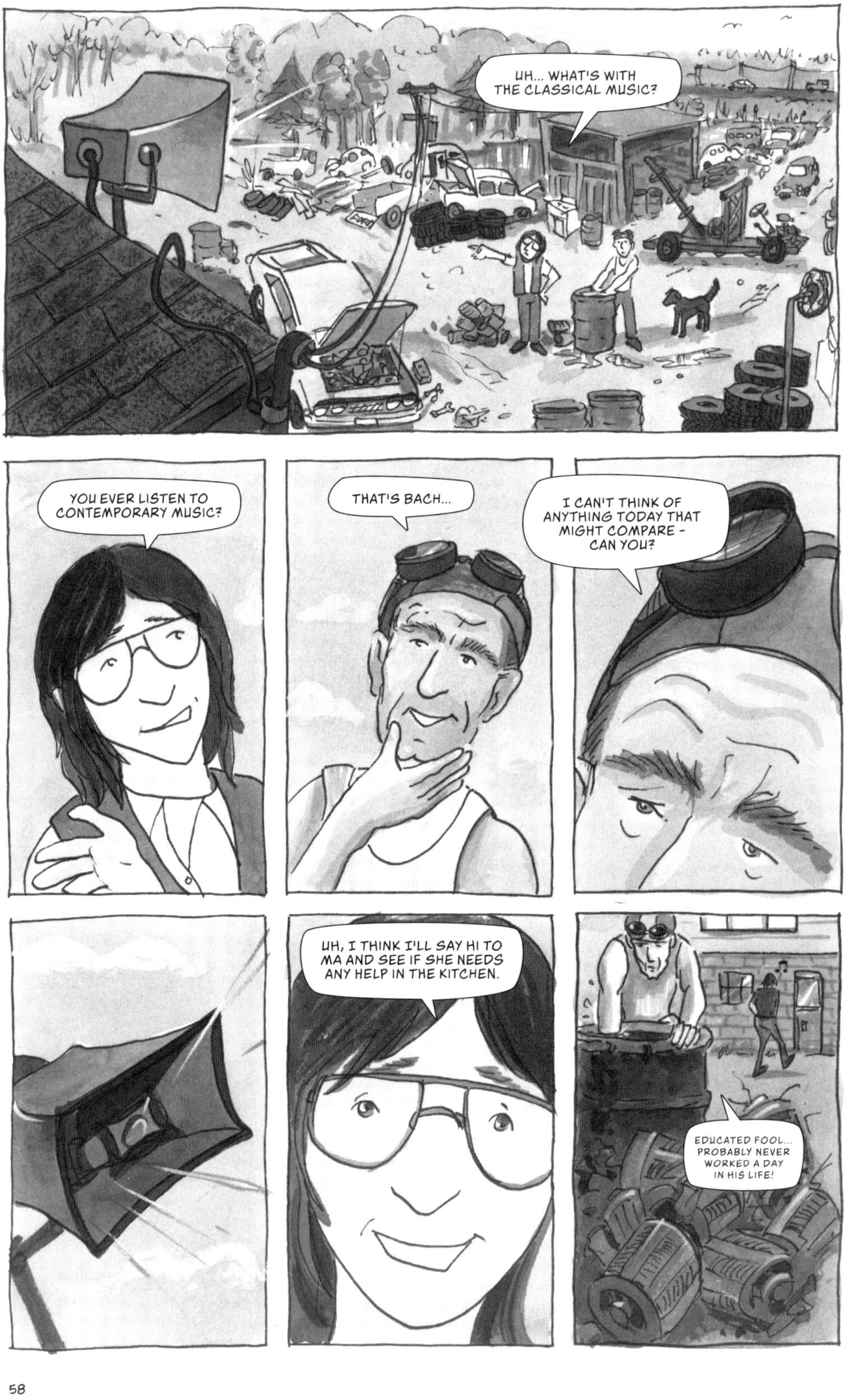
UH... WHAT'S WITH THE CLASSICAL MUSIC?
YOU EVER LISTEN TO CONTEMPORARY MUSIC?
THAT'S BACH...
I CAN'T THINK OF ANYTHING TODAY THAT MIGHT COMPARE - CAN YOU?
UH, I THINK I'LL SAY HI TO MA AND SEE IF SHE NEEDS ANY HELP IN THE KITCHEN.
EDUCATED FOOL... PROBABLY NEVER WORKED A DAY IN HIS LIFE!

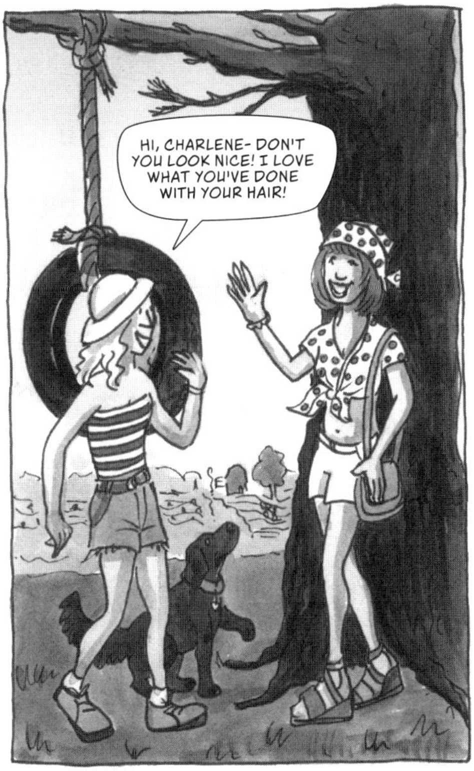
HI, CHARLENE- DON'T YOU LOOK NICE! I LOVE WHAT YOU'VE DONE WITH YOUR HAIR!

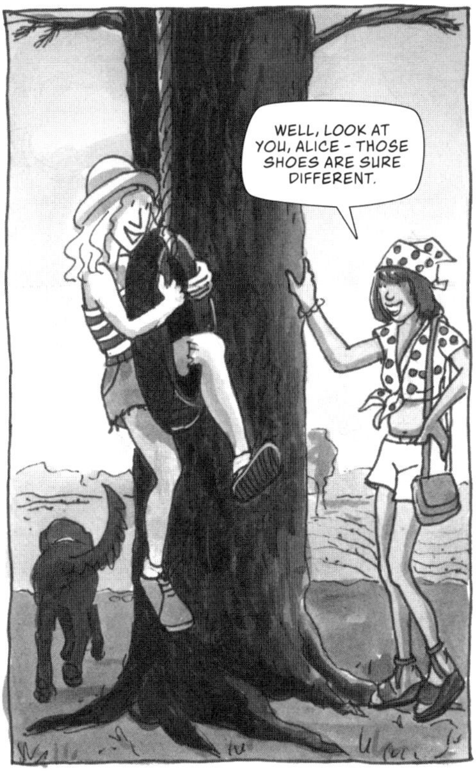
WELL, LOOK AT YOU, ALICE - THOSE SHOES ARE SURE DIFFERENT.

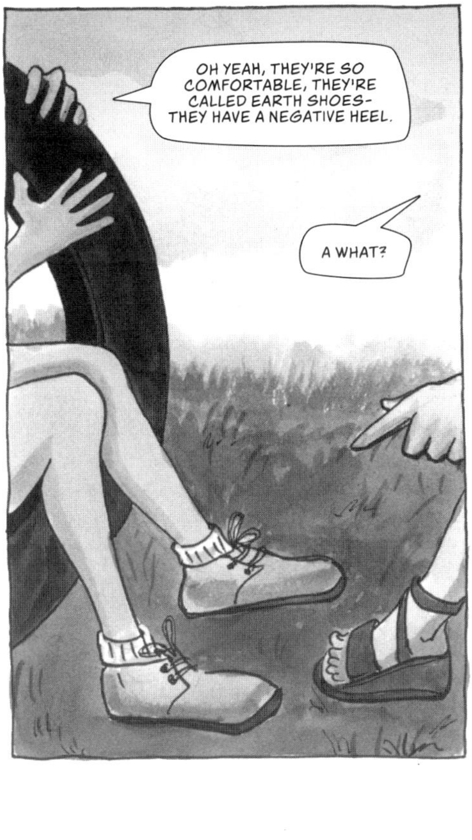
OH YEAH, THEY'RE SO COMFORTABLE, THEY'RE CALLED EARTH SHOES- THEY HAVE A NEGATIVE HEEL.
A WHAT?

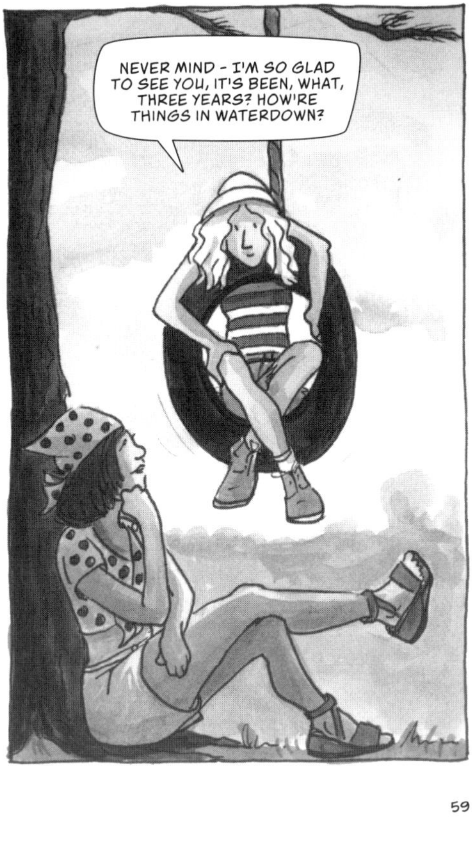
NEVER MIND - I'M SO GLAD TO SEE YOU, IT'S BEEN, WHAT, THREE YEARS? HOW'RE THINGS IN WATERDOWN?

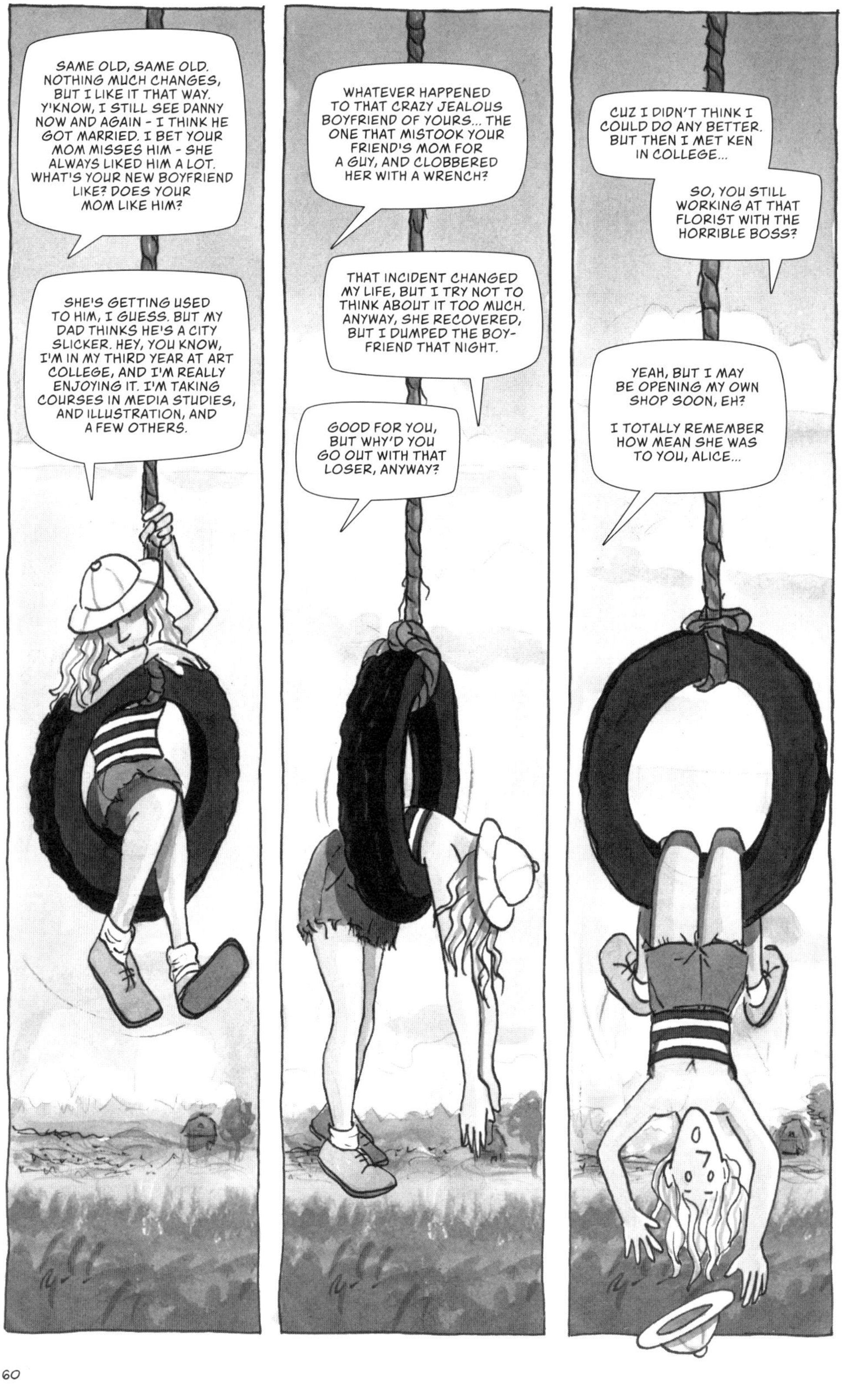
SAME OLD, SAME OLD. NOTHING MUCH CHANGES, BUT I LIKE IT THAT WAY. Y'KNOW, I STILL SEE DANNY NOW AND AGAIN - I THINK HE GOT MARRIED. I BET YOUR MOM MISSES HIM - SHE ALWAYS LIKED HIM A LOT. WHAT'S YOUR NEW BOYFRIEND LIKE? DOES YOUR MOM LIKE HIM?
SHE'S GETTING USED TO HIM, I GUESS. BUT MY DAD THINKS HE'S A CITY SLICKER. HEY, YOU KNOW, I'M IN MY THIRD YEAR AT ART COLLEGE, AND I'M REALLY ENJOYING IT. I'M TAKING COURSES IN MEDIA STUDIES, AND ILLUSTRATION, AND A FEW OTHERS.
WHATEVER HAPPENED TO THAT CRAZY JEALOUS BOYFRIEND OF YOURS... THE ONE THAT MISTOOK YOUR FRIEND'S MOM FOR A GUY, AND CLOBBERED HER WITH A WRENCH?
THAT INCIDENT CHANGED MY LIFE, BUT I TRY NOT TO THINK ABOUT IT TOO MUCH. ANYWAY, SHE RECOVERED, BUT I DUMPED THE BOY-FRIEND THAT NIGHT.
GOOD FOR YOU, BUT WHY'D YOU GO OUT WITH THAT LOSER, ANYWAY?
CUZ I DIDN'T THINK I COULD DO ANY BETTER. BUT THEN I MET KEN IN COLLEGE...
SO, YOU STILL WORKING AT THAT FLORIST WITH THE HORRIBLE BOSS?
YEAH, BUT I MAY BE OPENING MY OWN SHOP SOON, EH?
I TOTALLY REMEMBER HOW MEAN SHE WAS TO YOU, ALICE...

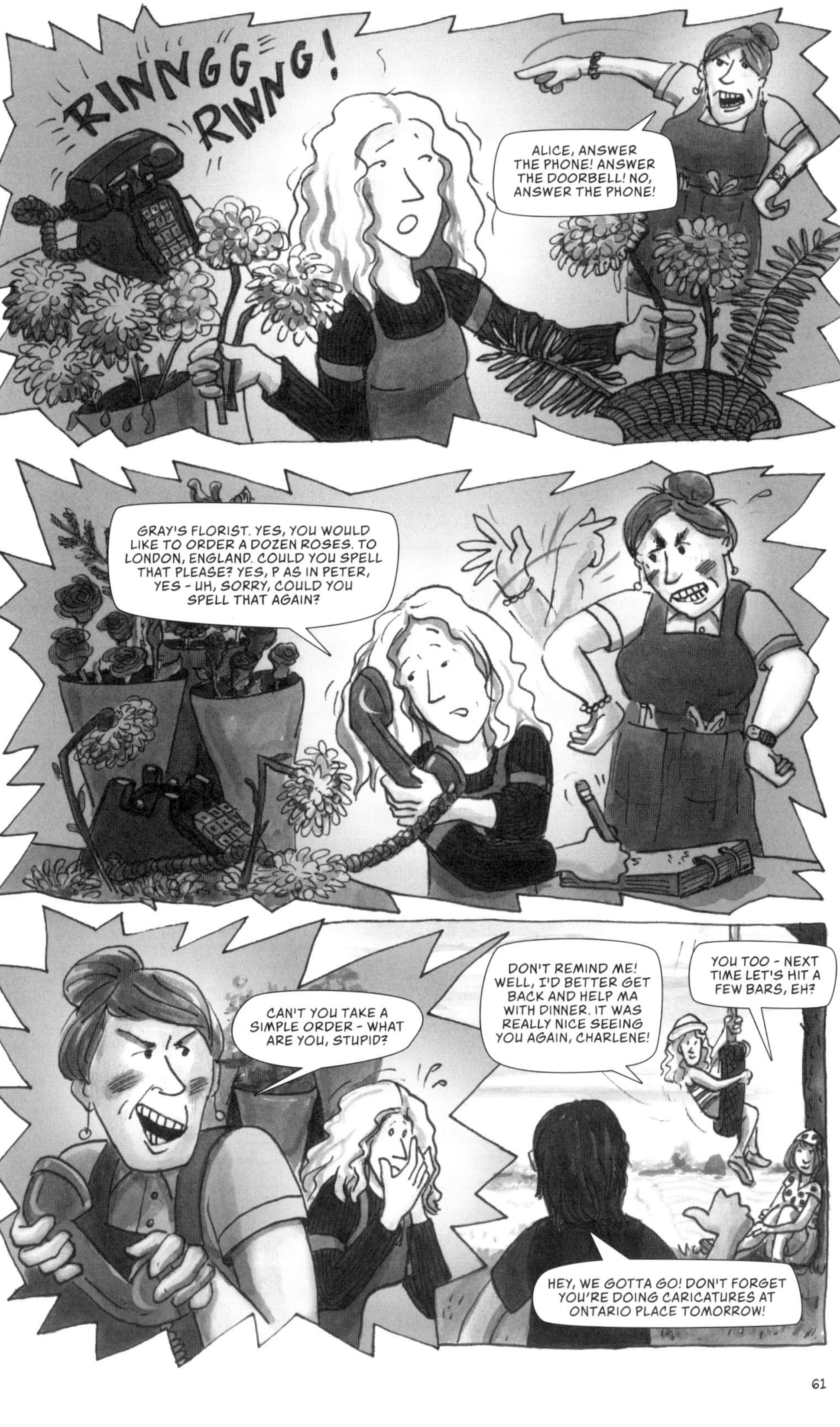
RINNGG RINNG!
ALICE, ANSWER THE PHONE! ANSWER THE DOORBELL! NO, ANSWER THE PHONE!
GRAY'S FLORIST. YES, YOU WOULD LIKE TO ORDER A DOZEN ROSES. TO LONDON, ENGLAND. COULD YOU SPELL THAT PLEASE? YES, P AS IN PETER, YES - UH, SORRY, COULD YOU SPELL THAT AGAIN?
CAN'T YOU TAKE A SIMPLE ORDER - WHAT ARE YOU, STUPID?
DON'T REMIND ME! WELL, I'D BETTER GET BACK AND HELP MA WITH DINNER. IT WAS REALLY NICE SEEING YOU AGAIN, CHARLENE!
YOU TOO - NEXT TIME LET'S HIT A FEW BARS, EH?
HEY, WE GOTTA GO! DON'T FORGET YOU'RE DOING CARICATURES AT ONTARIO PLACE TOMORROW!

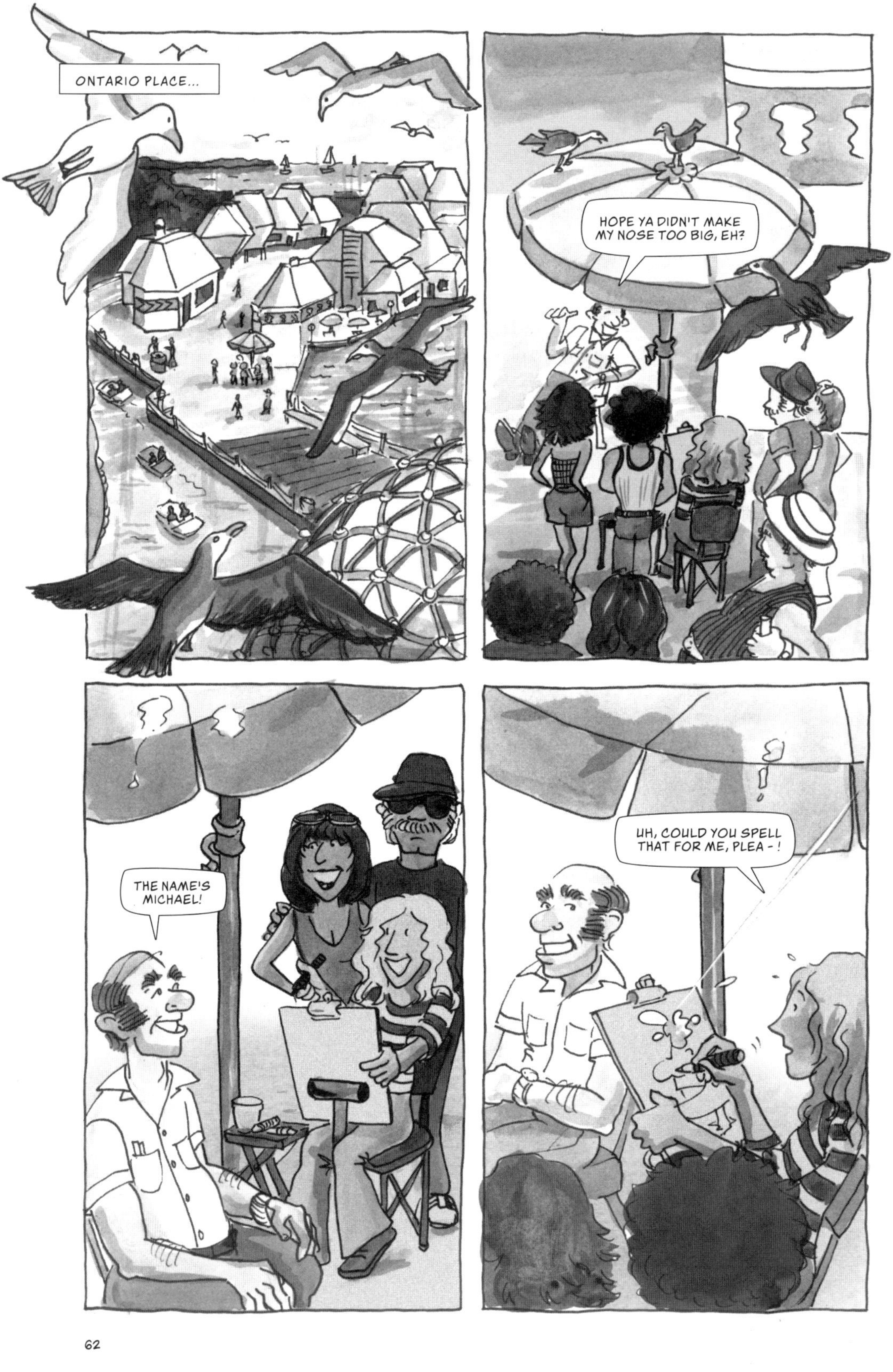
ONTARIO PLACE...
HOPE YA DIDN'T MAKE MY NOSE TOO BIG, EH?
THE NAME'S MICHAEL!
UH, COULD YOU SPELL THAT FOR ME, PLEA - !

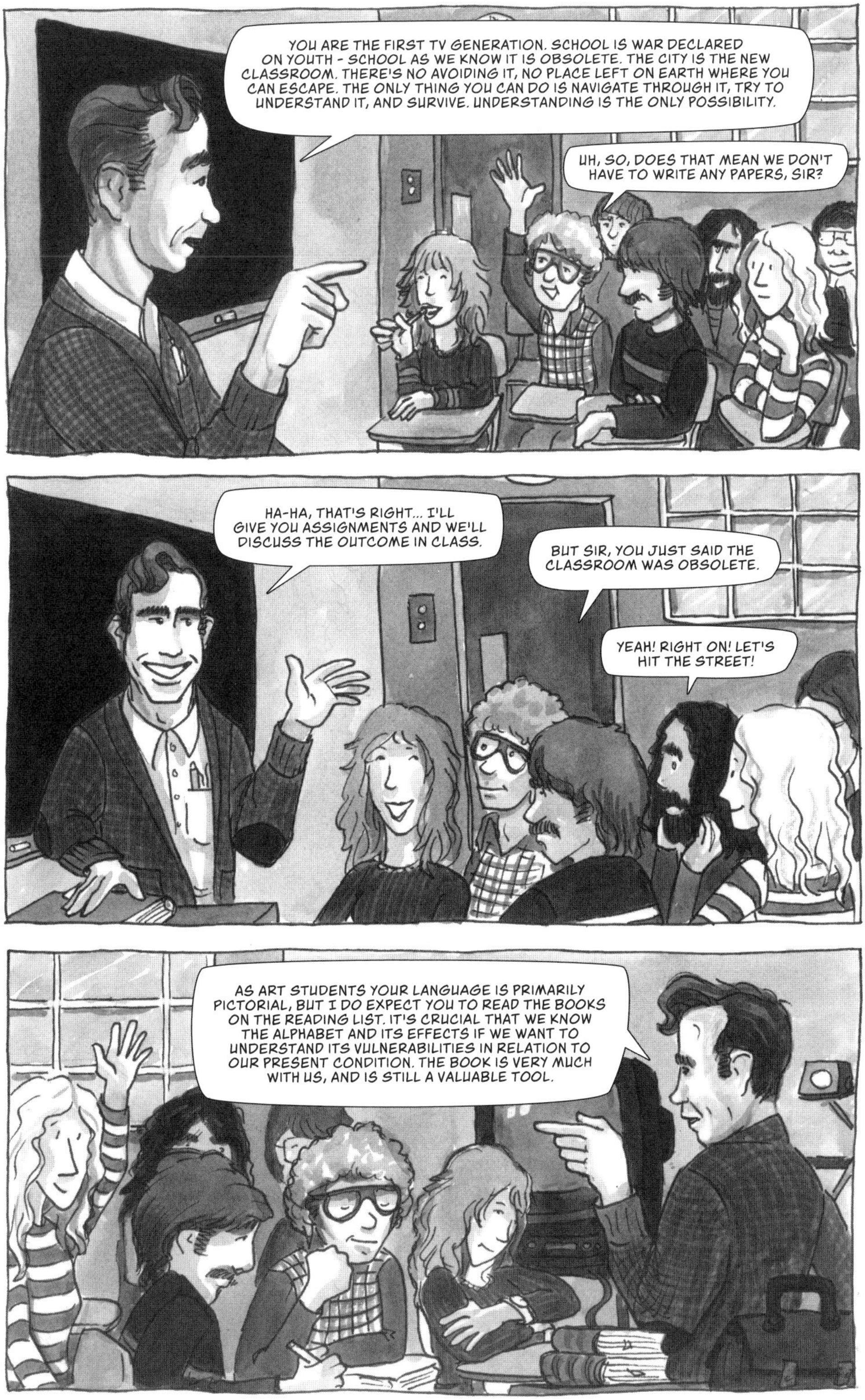
YOU ARE THE FIRST TV GENERATION. SCHOOL IS WAR DECLARED ON YOUTH - SCHOOL AS WE KNOW IT IS OBSOLETE. THE CITY IS THE NEW CLASSROOM. THERE'S NO AVOIDING IT, NO PLACE LEFT ON EARTH WHERE YOU CAN ESCAPE. THE ONLY THING YOU CAN DO IS NAVIGATE THROUGH IT, TRY TO UNDERSTAND IT, AND SURVIVE. UNDERSTANDING IS THE ONLY POSSIBILITY.
UH, SO, DOES THAT MEAN WE DON'T HAVE TO WRITE ANY PAPERS, SIR?
HA-HA, THAT'S RIGHT... I'LL GIVE YOU ASSIGNMENTS AND WE'LL DISCUSS THE OUTCOME IN CLASS.
BUT SIR, YOU JUST SAID THE CLASSROOM WAS OBSOLETE.
YEAH! RIGHT ON! LET'S HIT THE STREET!
AS ART STUDENTS YOUR LANGUAGE IS PRIMARILY PICTORIAL, BUT I DO EXPECT YOU TO READ THE BOOKS ON THE READING LIST. IT'S CRUCIAL THAT WE KNOW THE ALPHABET AND ITS EFFECTS IF WE WANT TO UNDERSTAND ITS VULNERABILITIES IN RELATION TO OUR PRESENT CONDITION. THE BOOK IS VERY MUCH WITH US, AND IS STILL A VALUABLE TOOL.

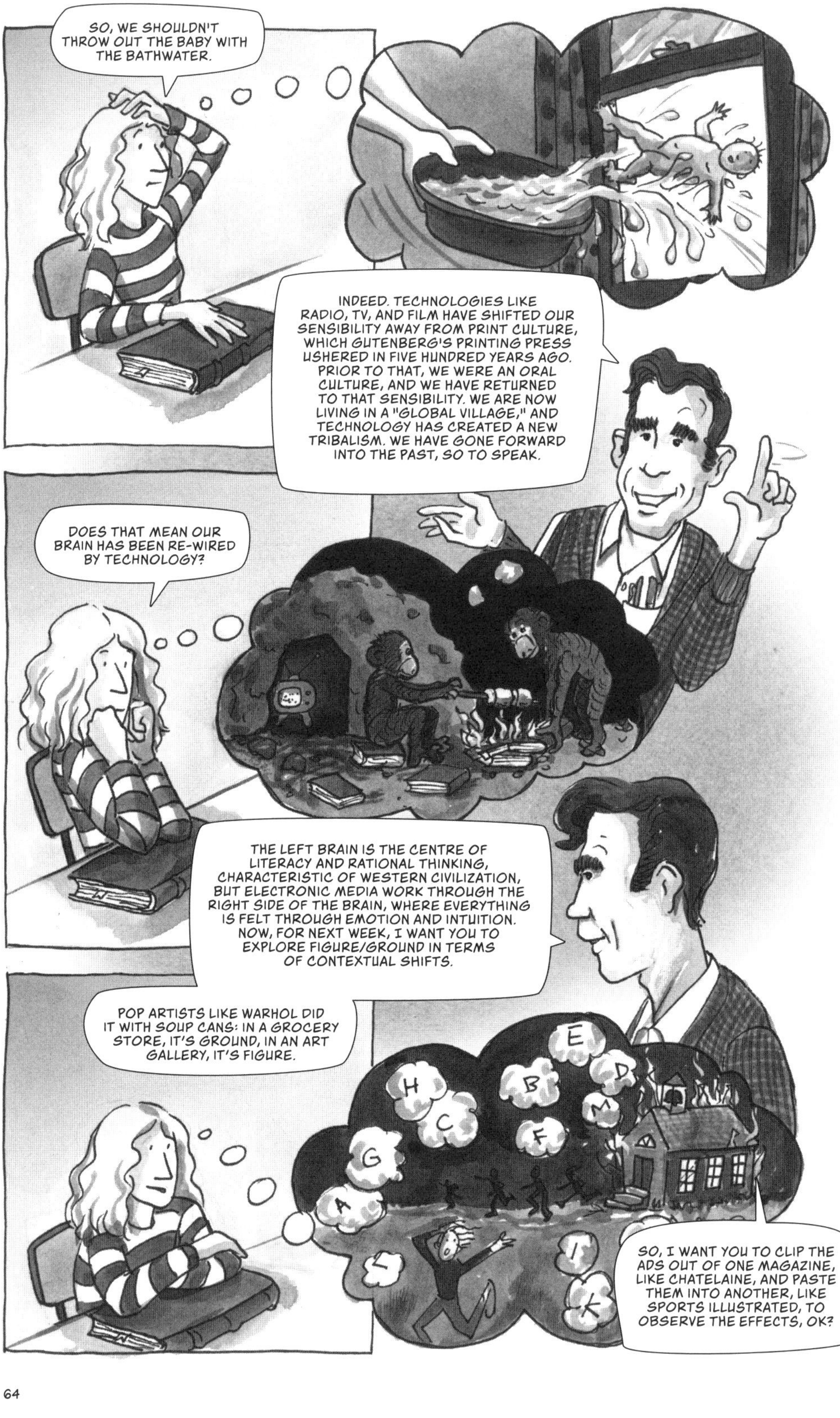
SO, WE SHOULDN'T THROW OUT THE BABY WITH THE BATHWATER.
INDEED. TECHNOLOGIES LIKE RADIO, TV, AND FILM HAVE SHIFTED OUR SENSIBILITY AWAY FROM PRINT CULTURE, WHICH GUTENBERG'S PRINTING PRESS USHERED IN FIVE HUNDRED YEARS AGO. PRIOR TO THAT, WE WERE AN ORAL CULTURE, AND WE HAVE RETURNED TO THAT SENSIBILITY. WE ARE NOW LIVING IN A "GLOBAL VILLAGE," AND TECHNOLOGY HAS CREATED A NEW TRIBALISM. WE HAVE GONE FORWARD INTO THE PAST, SO TO SPEAK.
DOES THAT MEAN OUR BRAIN HAS BEEN RE-WIRED BY TECHNOLOGY?
THE LEFT BRAIN IS THE CENTRE OF LITERACY AND RATIONAL THINKING, CHARACTERISTIC OF WESTERN CIVILIZATION, BUT ELECTRONIC MEDIA WORK THROUGH THE RIGHT SIDE OF THE BRAIN, WHERE EVERYTHING IS FELT THROUGH EMOTION AND INTUITION. NOW, FOR NEXT WEEK, I WANT YOU TO EXPLORE FIGURE/GROUND IN TERMS OF CONTEXTUAL SHIFTS.
POP ARTISTS LIKE WARHOL DID IT WITH SOUP CANS: IN A GROCERY STORE, IT'S GROUND, IN AN ART GALLERY, IT'S FIGURE.
E
D
H
B
M
C
F
G
A
L
I
K
SO, I WANT YOU TO CLIP THE ADS OUT OF ONE MAGAZINE, LIKE CHATELAINE, AND PASTE THEM INTO ANOTHER, LIKE SPORTS ILLUSTRATED, TO OBSERVE THE EFFECTS, OK?

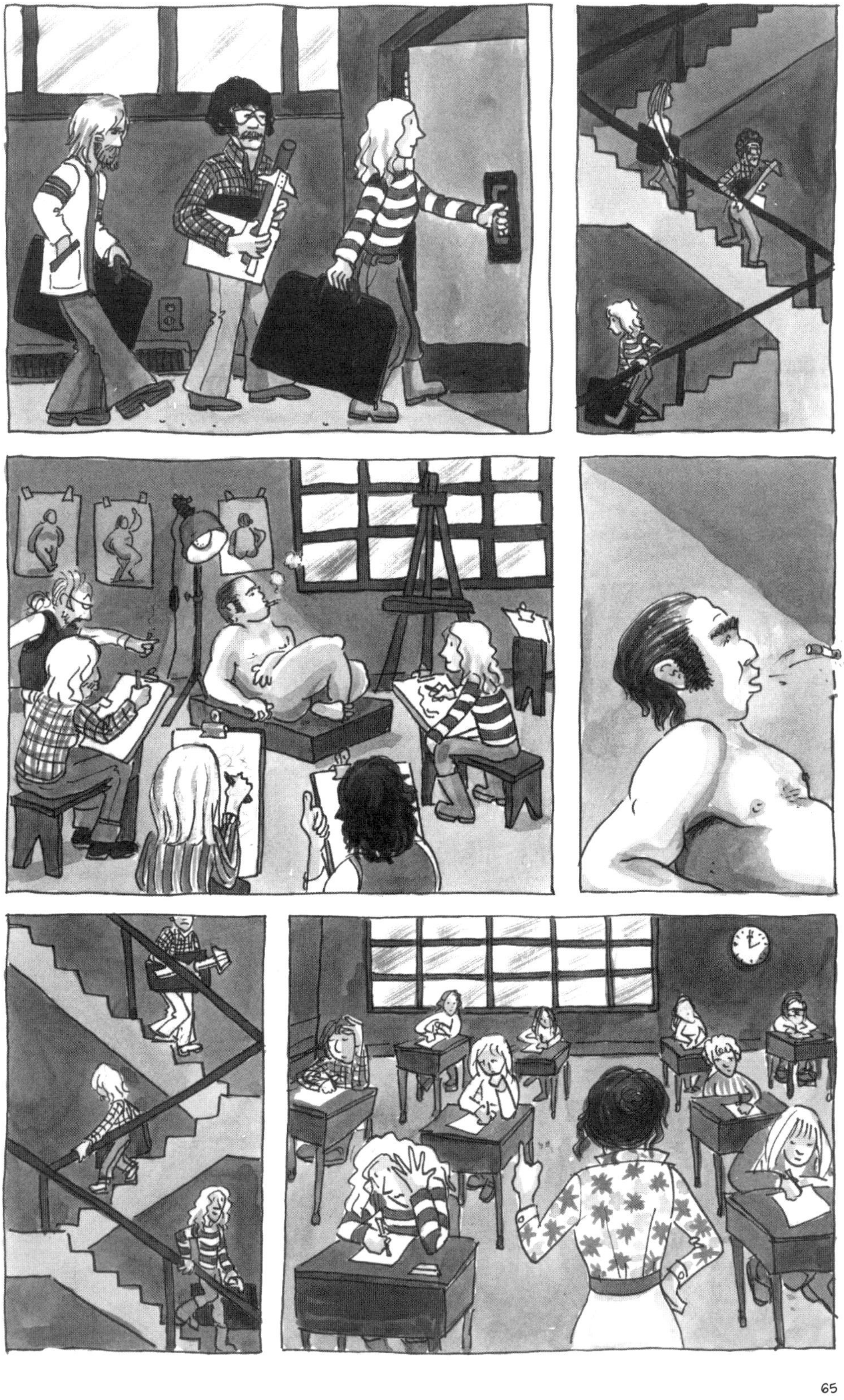

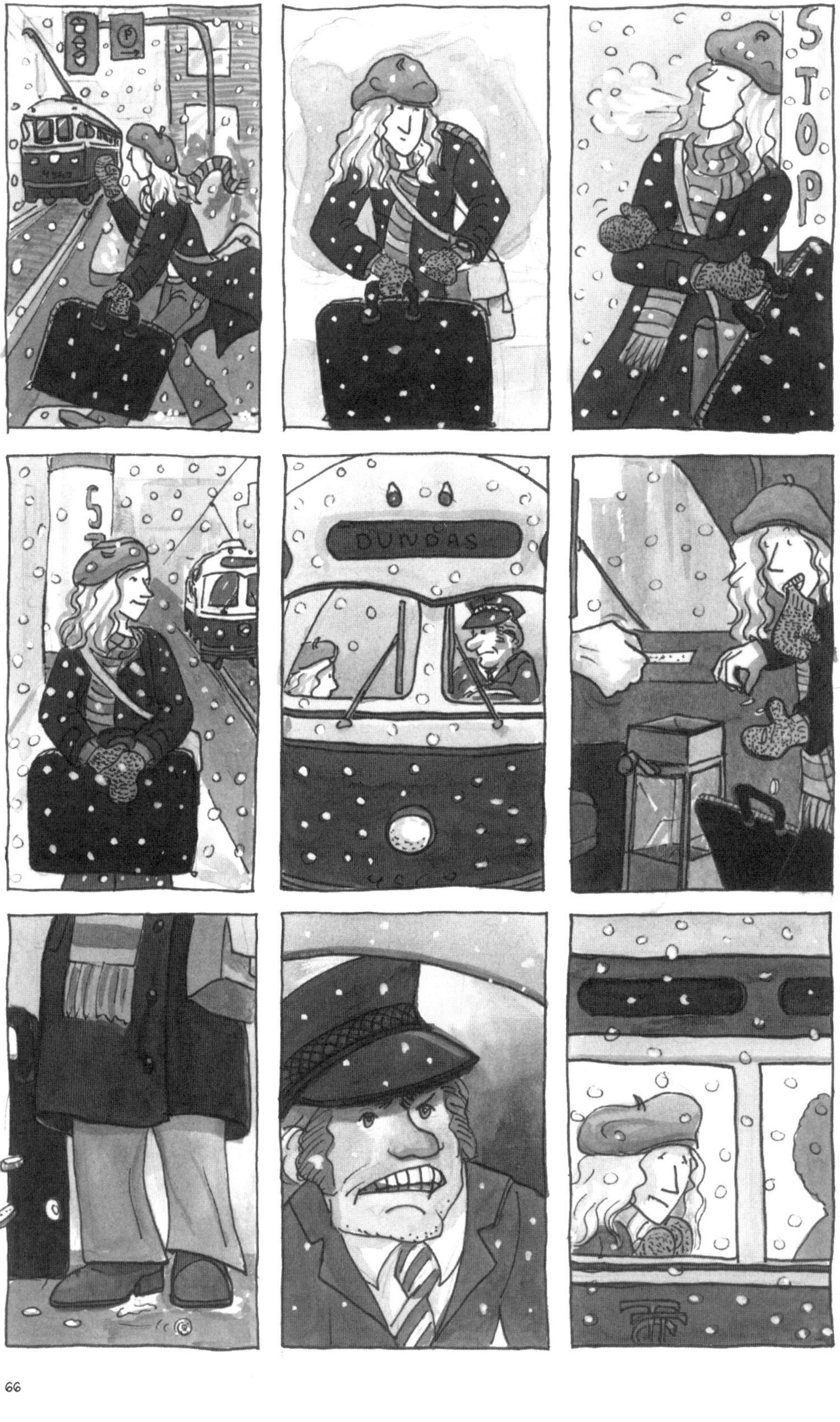
STOP
DUNDAS

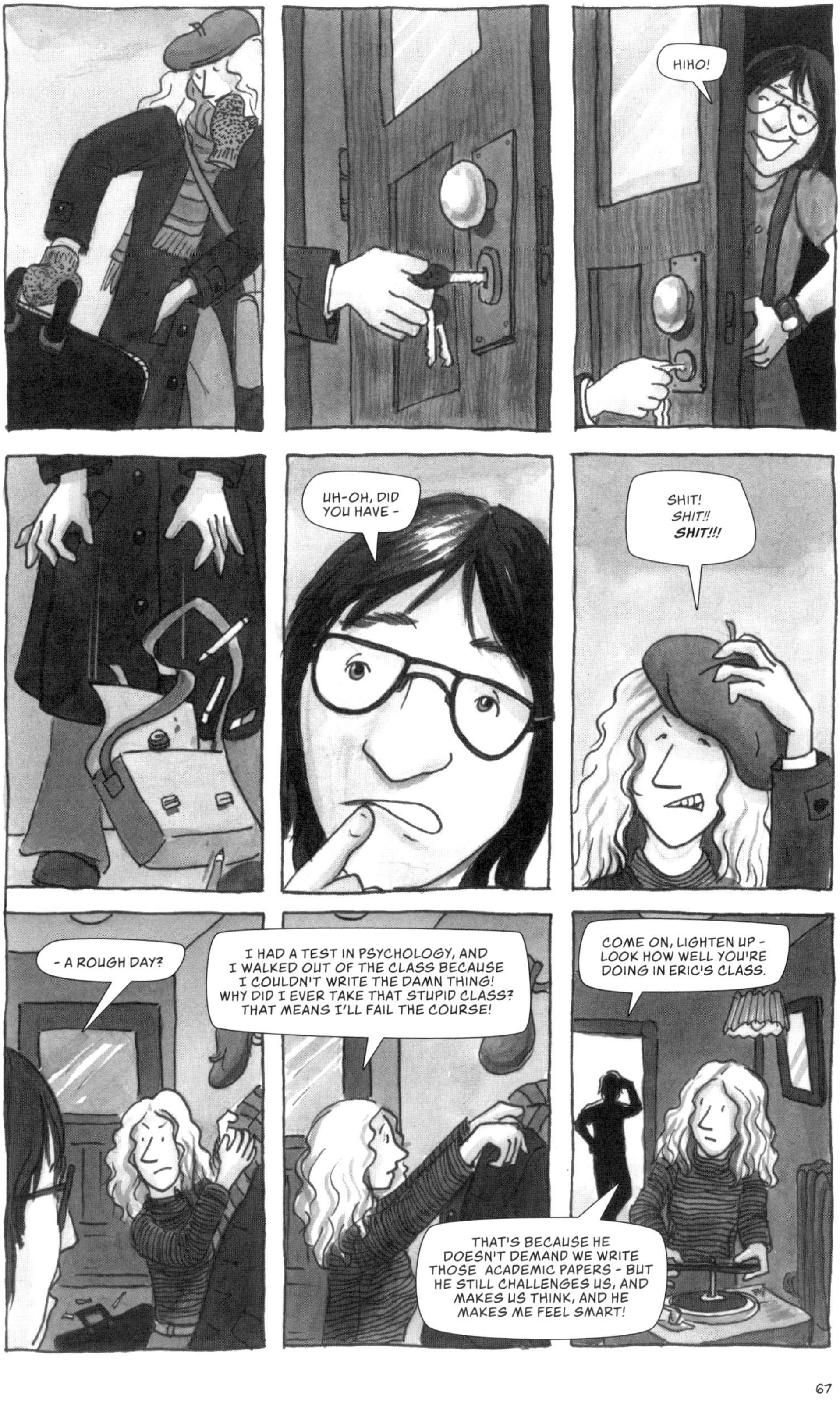
HIHO!
UH-OH, DID YOU HAVE -
SHIT! SHIT!! SHIT!!!
- A ROUGH DAY?
I HAD A TEST IN PSYCHOLOGY, AND I WALKED OUT OF THE CLASS BECAUSE I COULDN'T WRITE THE DAMN THING! WHY DID I EVER TAKE THAT STUPID CLASS? THAT MEANS I'LL FAIL THE COURSE!
COME ON, LIGHTEN UP - LOOK HOW WELL YOU'RE DOING IN ERIC'S CLASS.
THAT'S BECAUSE HE DOESN'T DEMAND WE WRITE THOSE ACADEMIC PAPERS - BUT HE STILL CHALLENGES US, AND MAKES US THINK, AND HE MAKES ME FEEL SMART!

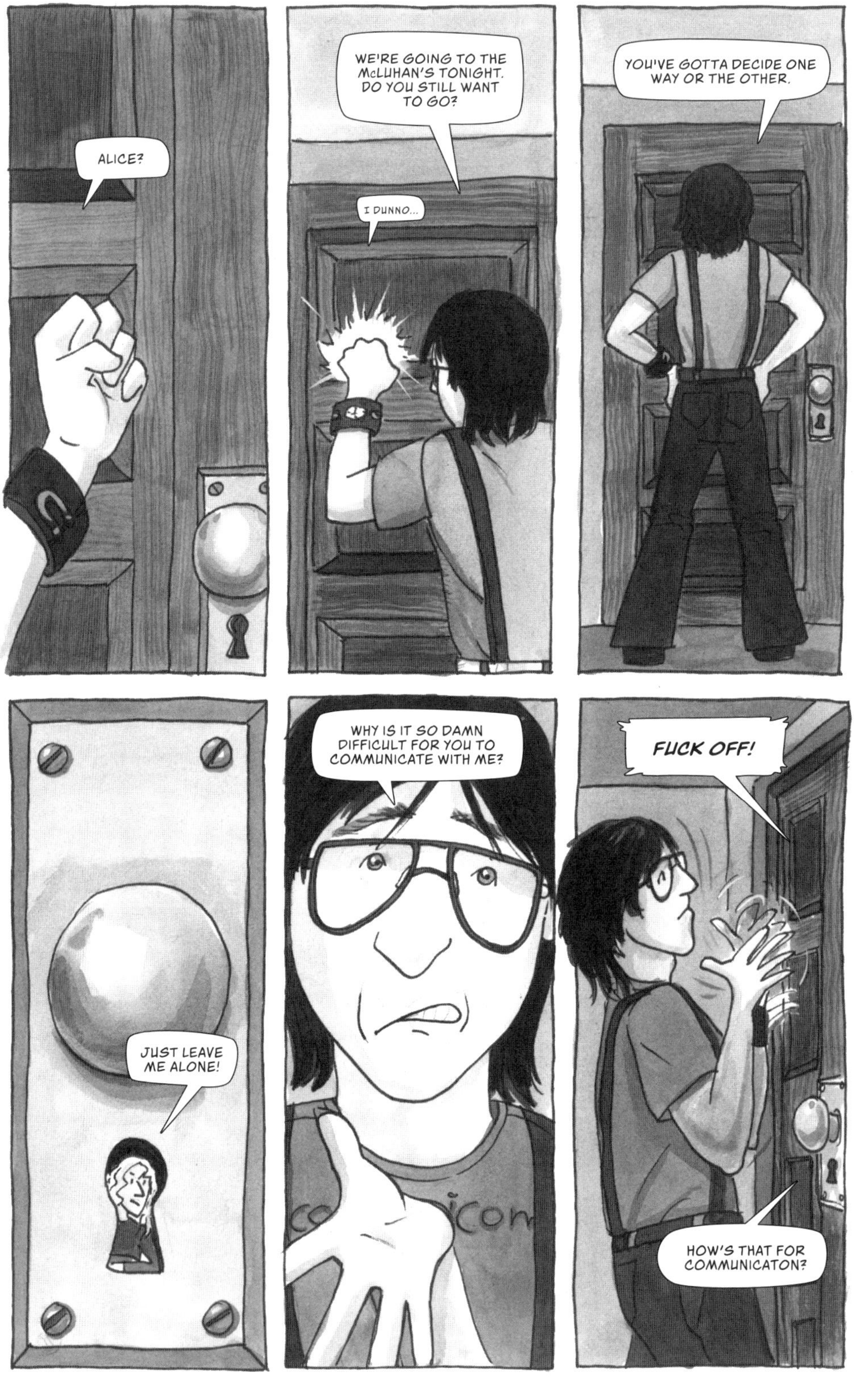
ALICE?
WE'RE GOING TO THE McLUHAN'S TONIGHT. DO YOU STILL WANT TO GO?
I DUNNO...
YOU'VE GOTTA DECIDE ONE WAY OR THE OTHER.
JUST LEAVE ME ALONE!
WHY IS IT SO DAMN DIFFICULT FOR YOU TO COMMUNICATE WITH ME?
FUCK OFF!
HOW'S THAT FOR COMMUNICATON?

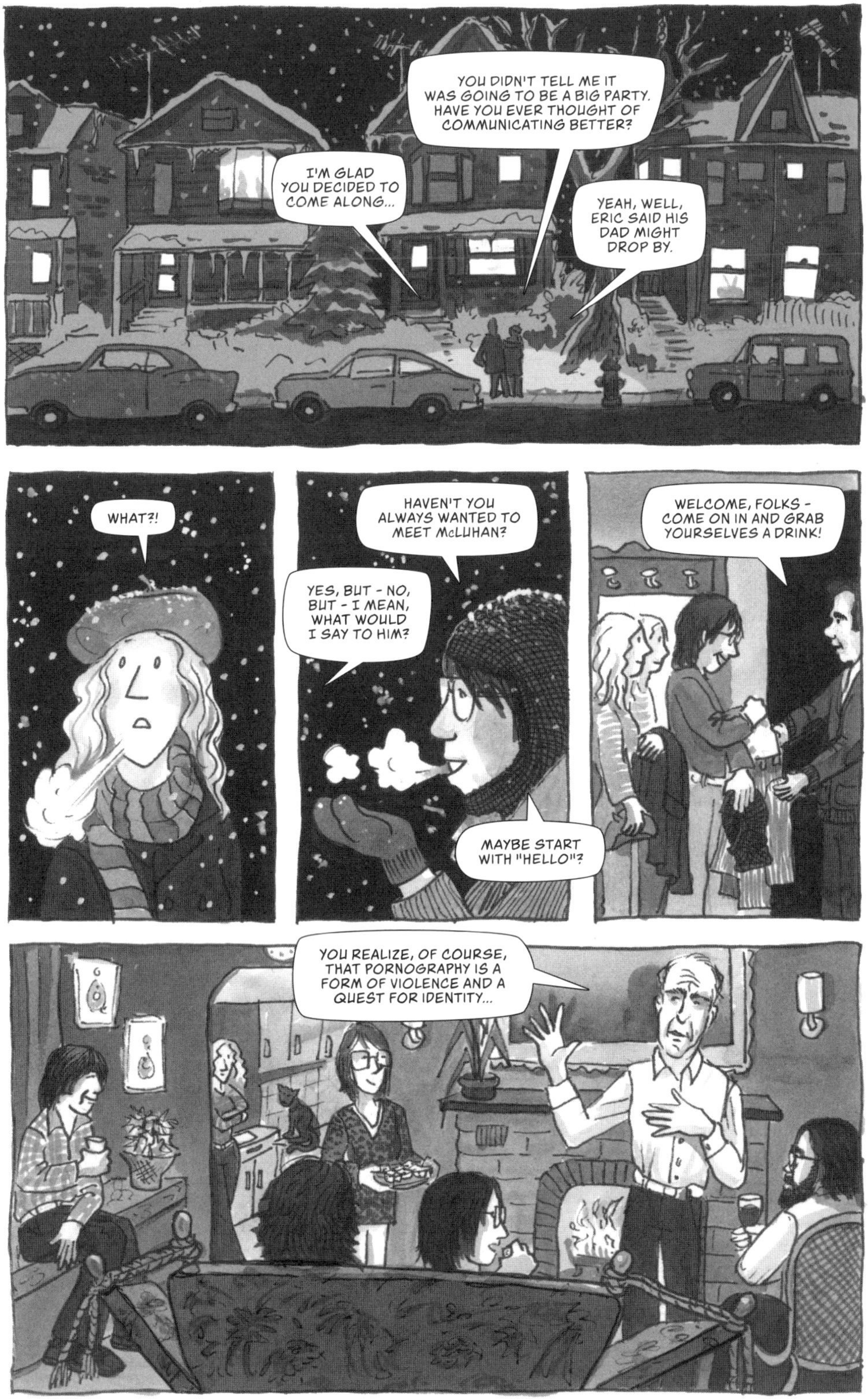

YOU DIDN'T TELL ME IT WAS GOING TO BE A BIG PARTY. HAVE YOU EVER THOUGHT OF COMMUNICATING BETTER?
I'M GLAD YOU DECIDED TO COME ALONG...
YEAH, WELL, ERIC SAID HIS DAD MIGHT DROP BY.
WHAT?!
HAVEN'T YOU ALWAYS WANTED TO MEET McLUHAN?
YES, BUT - NO, BUT - I MEAN, WHAT WOULD I SAY TO HIM?
MAYBE START WITH "HELLO"?
WELCOME, FOLKS - COME ON IN AND GRAB YOURSELVES A DRINK!
YOU REALIZE, OF COURSE, THAT PORNOGRAPHY IS A FORM OF VIOLENCE AND A QUEST FOR IDENTITY...

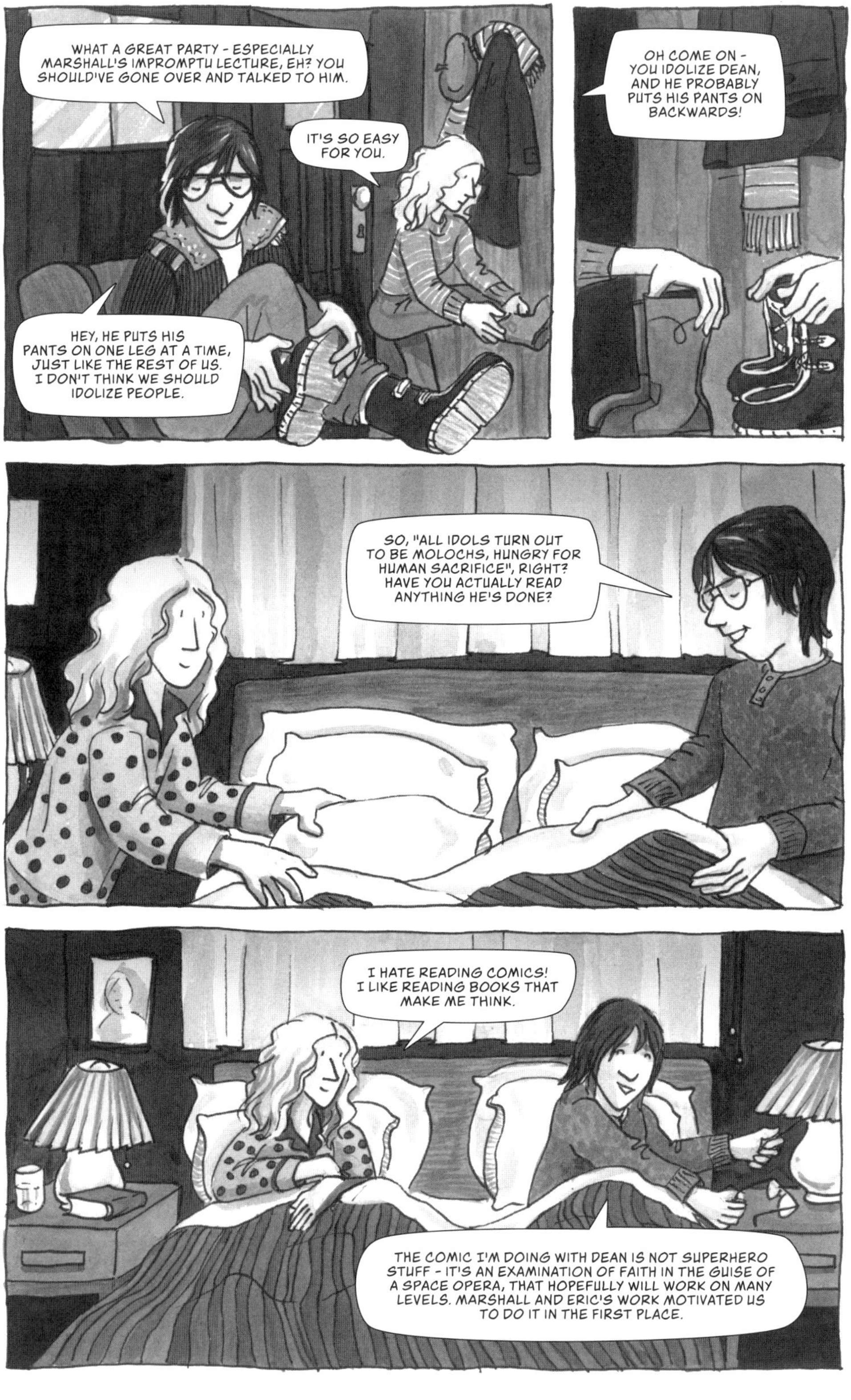

WHAT A GREAT PARTY - ESPECIALLY MARSHALL'S IMPROMPTU LECTURE, EH? YOU SHOULD'VE GONE OVER AND TALKED TO HIM.
IT'S SO EASY FOR YOU.
HEY, HE PUTS HIS PANTS ON ONE LEG AT A TIME, JUST LIKE THE REST OF US. I DON'T THINK WE SHOULD IDOLIZE PEOPLE.
OH COME ON - YOU IDOLIZE DEAN, AND HE PROBABLY PUTS HIS PANTS ON BACKWARDS!
SO, "ALL IDOLS TURN OUT TO BE MOLOCHS, HUNGRY FOR HUMAN SACRIFICE", RIGHT? HAVE YOU ACTUALLY READ ANYTHING HE'S DONE?
I HATE READING COMICS! I LIKE READING BOOKS THAT MAKE ME THINK.
THE COMIC I'M DOING WITH DEAN IS NOT SUPERHERO STUFF - IT'S AN EXAMINATION OF FAITH IN THE GUISE OF A SPACE OPERA, THAT HOPEFULLY WILL WORK ON MANY LEVELS. MARSHALL AND ERIC'S WORK MOTIVATED US TO DO IT IN THE FIRST PLACE.

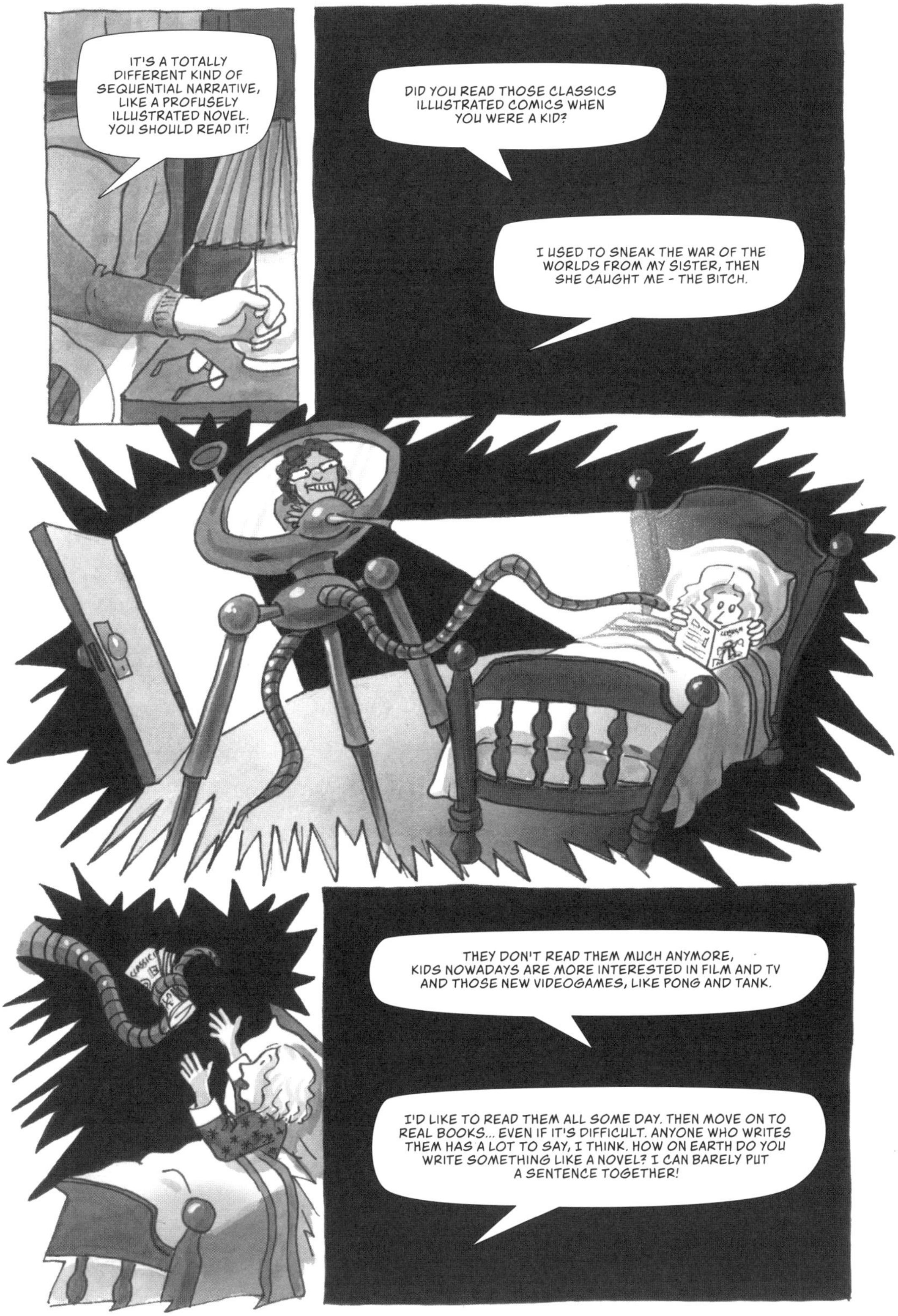
IT'S A TOTALLY DIFFERENT KIND OF SEQUENTIAL NARRATIVE, LIKE A PROFUSELY ILLUSTRATED NOVEL. YOU SHOULD READ IT!
DID YOU READ THOSE CLASSICS ILLUSTRATED COMICS WHEN YOU WERE A KID?
I USED TO SNEAK THE WAR OF THE WORLDS FROM MY SISTER, THEN SHE CAUGHT ME - THE BITCH.
THEY DON'T READ THEM MUCH ANYMORE, KIDS NOWADAYS ARE MORE INTERESTED IN FILM AND TV AND THOSE NEW VIDEOGAMES, LIKE PONG AND TANK.
I'D LIKE TO READ THEM ALL SOME DAY. THEN MOVE ON TO REAL BOOKS... EVEN IF IT'S DIFFICULT. ANYONE WHO WRITES THEM HAS A LOT TO SAY, I THINK. HOW ON EARTH DO YOU WRITE SOMETHING LIKE A NOVEL? I CAN BARELY PUT A SENTENCE TOGETHER!

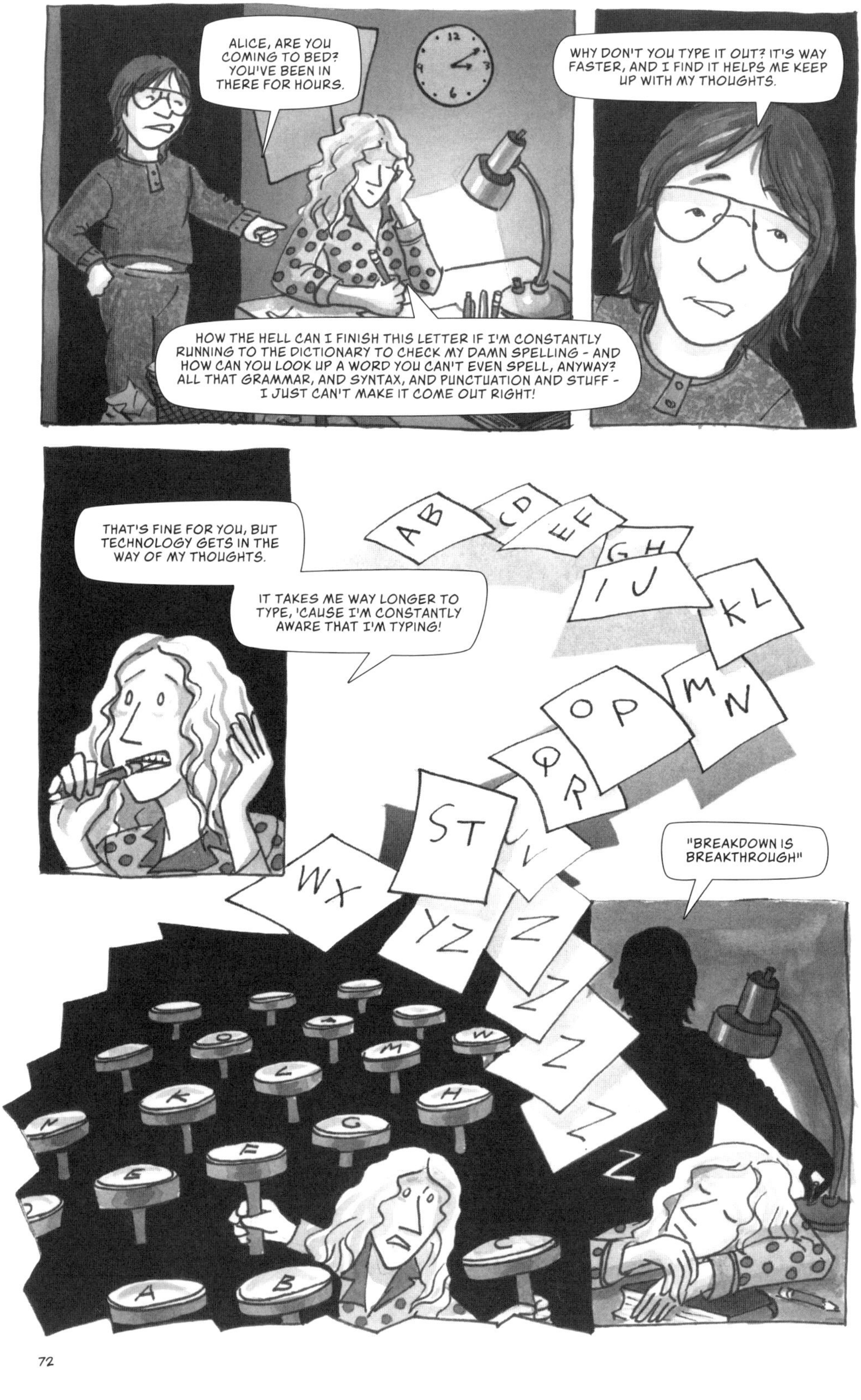
ALICE, ARE YOU COMING TO BED? YOU'VE BEEN IN THERE FOR HOURS.
HOW THE HELL CAN I FINISH THIS LETTER IF I'M CONSTANTLY RUNNING TO THE DICTIONARY TO CHECK MY DAMN SPELLING - AND HOW CAN YOU LOOK UP A WORD YOU CAN'T EVEN SPELL, ANYWAY? ALL THAT GRAMMAR, AND SYNTAX, AND PUNCTUATION AND STUFF - I JUST CAN'T MAKE IT COME OUT RIGHT!
WHY DON'T YOU TYPE IT OUT? IT'S WAY FASTER, AND I FIND IT HELPS ME KEEP UP WITH MY THOUGHTS.
THAT'S FINE FOR YOU, BUT TECHNOLOGY GETS IN THE WAY OF MY THOUGHTS.
IT TAKES ME WAY LONGER TO TYPE, 'CAUSE I'M CONSTANTLY AWARE THAT I'M TYPING!
AB
CD
EF
GH
IJ
KL
MN
OP
QR
ST
UV
WX
YZ
"BREAKDOWN IS BREAKTHROUGH"

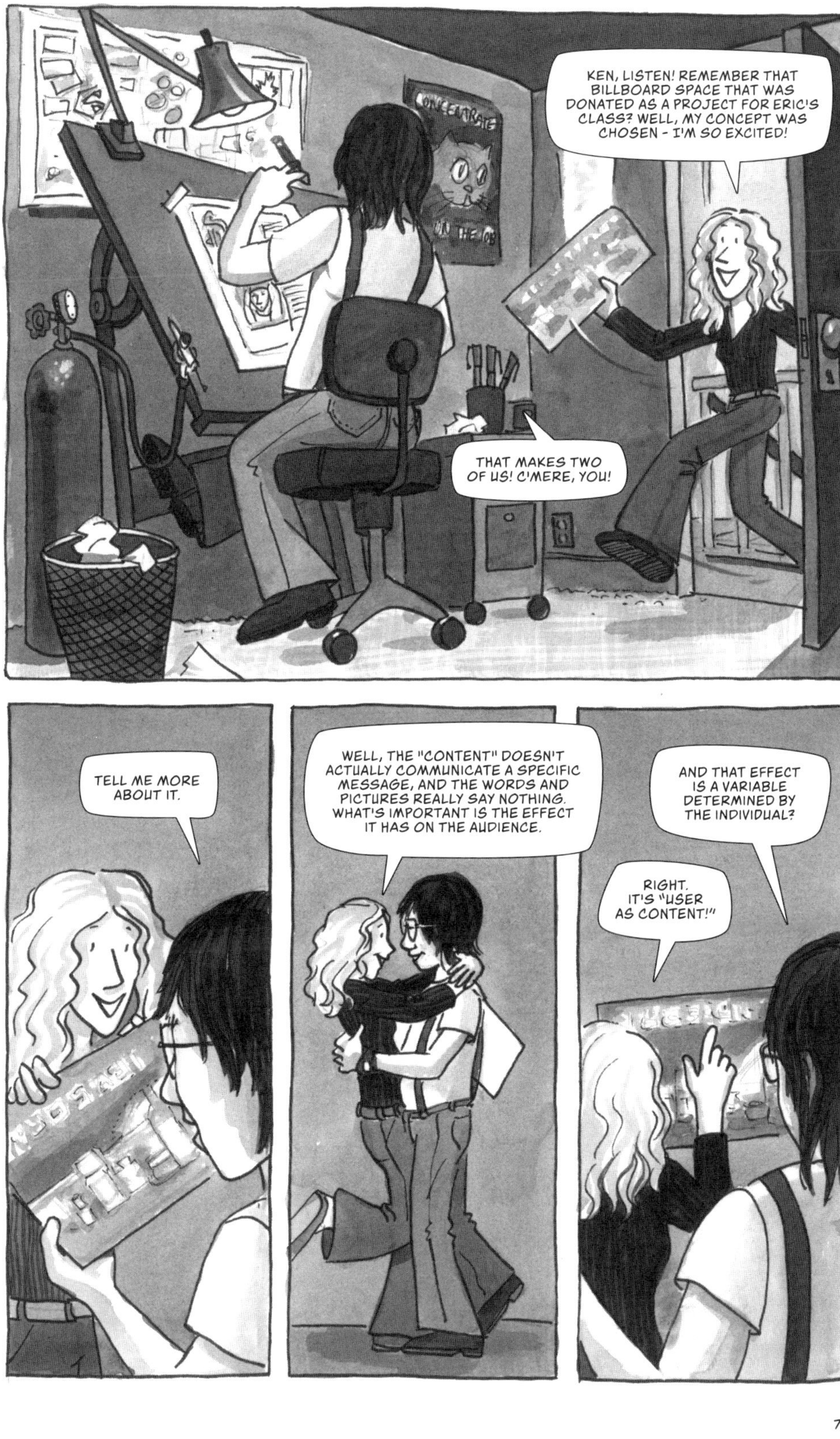
KEN, LISTEN! REMEMBER THAT BILLBOARD SPACE THAT WAS DONATED AS A PROJECT FOR ERIC'S CLASS? WELL, MY CONCEPT WAS CHOSEN - I'M SO EXCITED!
THAT MAKES TWO OF US! C'MERE, YOU!
TELL ME MORE ABOUT IT.
WELL, THE "CONTENT" DOESN'T ACTUALLY COMMUNICATE A SPECIFIC MESSAGE, AND THE WORDS AND PICTURES REALLY SAY NOTHING. WHAT'S IMPORTANT IS THE EFFECT IT HAS ON THE AUDIENCE.
AND THAT EFFECT IS A VARIABLE DETERMINED BY THE INDIVIDUAL?
RIGHT. IT'S "USER AS CONTENT!"

LOOKING GOOD – THAT REMINDS ME OF THE PRIEST WHO SNEEZED DURING HIS SERMON, AND SAID, "LET US SPRAY!"

GROAN...!

WOW, THAT WAS A CLOSE ONE – AT LEAST HE WAS PAYING ATTENTION. THE ONES THAT DRIVE OR WALK BY ARE REAL ZOMBIES.

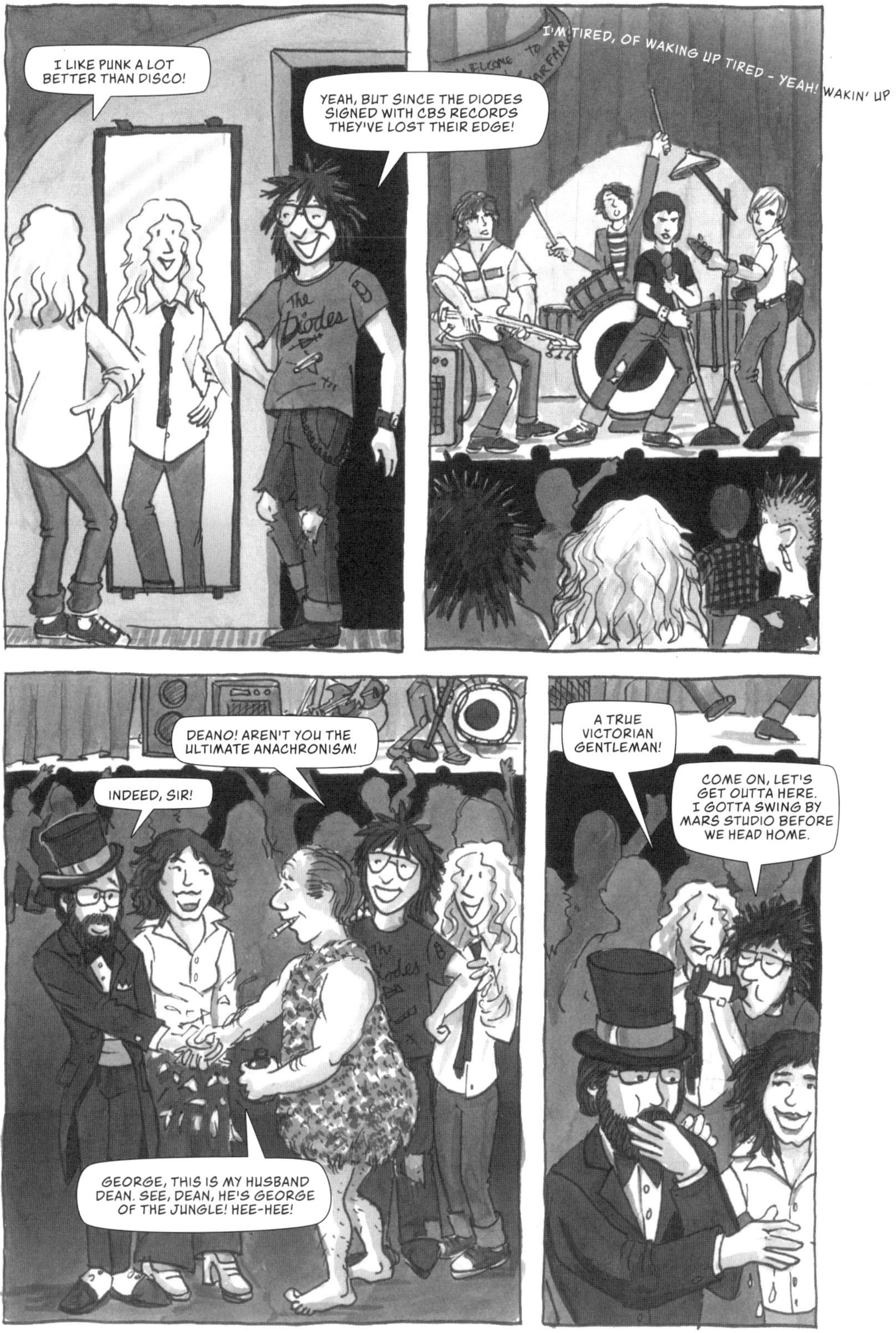
I LIKE PUNK A LOT BETTER THAN DISCO!
YEAH, BUT SINCE THE DIODES SIGNED WITH CBS RECORDS THEY'VE LOST THEIR EDGE!
The Diodes
I'M TIRED, OF WAKING UP TIRED - YEAH! WAKIN' UP
DEANO! AREN'T YOU THE ULTIMATE ANACHRONISM!
INDEED, SIR!
GEORGE, THIS IS MY HUSBAND DEAN. SEE, DEAN, HE'S GEORGE OF THE JUNGLE! HEE-HEE!
A TRUE VICTORIAN GENTLEMAN!
COME ON, LET'S GET OUTTA HERE. I GOTTA SWING BY MARS STUDIO BEFORE WE HEAD HOME.

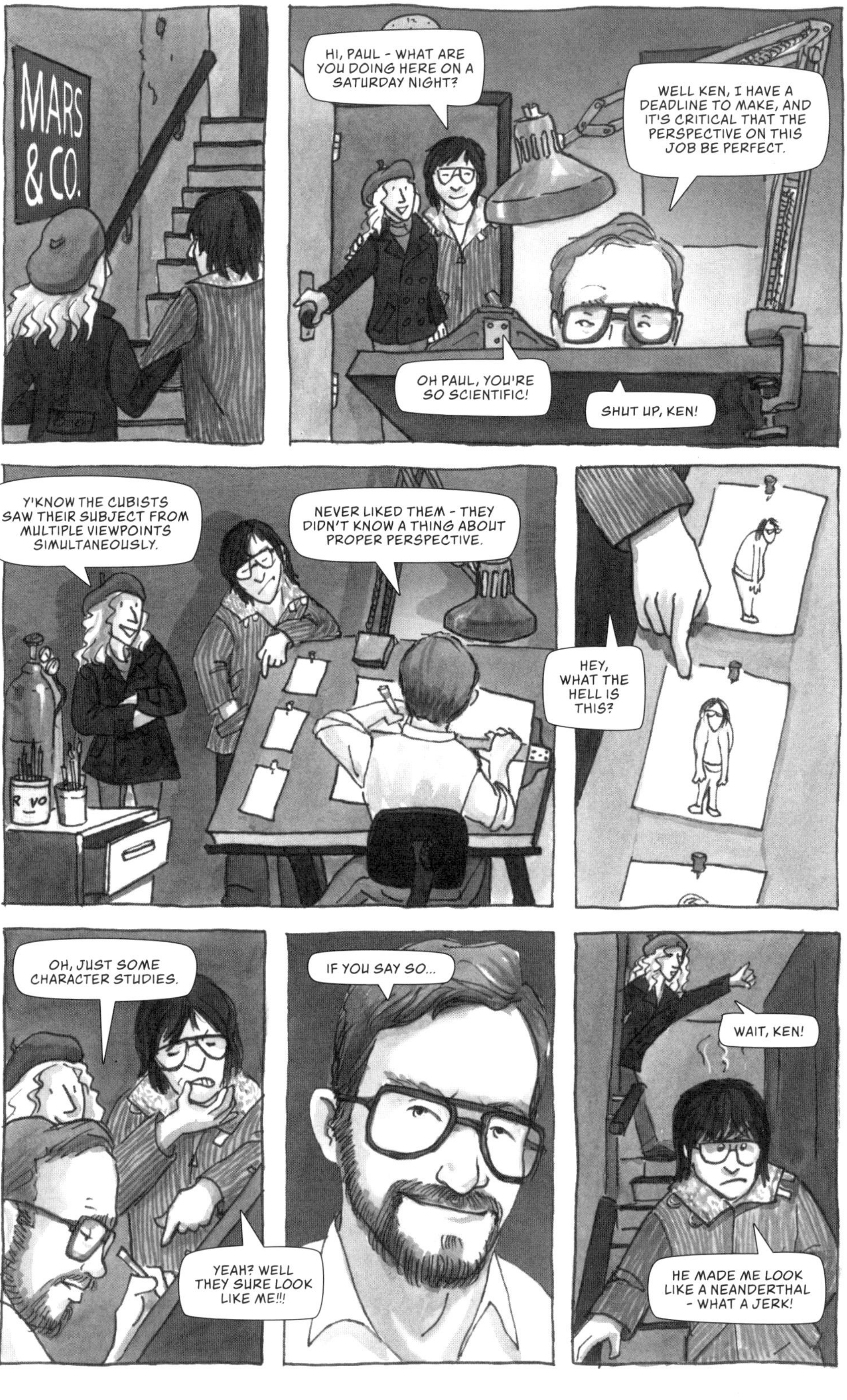
MARS & CO.
HI, PAUL - WHAT ARE YOU DOING HERE ON A SATURDAY NIGHT?
WELL KEN, I HAVE A DEADLINE TO MAKE, AND IT'S CRITICAL THAT THE PERSPECTIVE ON THIS JOB BE PERFECT.
OH PAUL, YOU'RE SO SCIENTIFIC!
SHUT UP, KEN!
Y'KNOW THE CUBISTS SAW THEIR SUBJECT FROM MULTIPLE VIEWPOINTS SIMULTANEOUSLY.
NEVER LIKED THEM - THEY DIDN'T KNOW A THING ABOUT PROPER PERSPECTIVE.
HEY, WHAT THE HELL IS THIS?
OH, JUST SOME CHARACTER STUDIES.
YEAH? WELL THEY SURE LOOK LIKE ME!!!
IF YOU SAY SO...
WAIT, KEN!
HE MADE ME LOOK LIKE A NEANDERTHAL - WHAT A JERK!

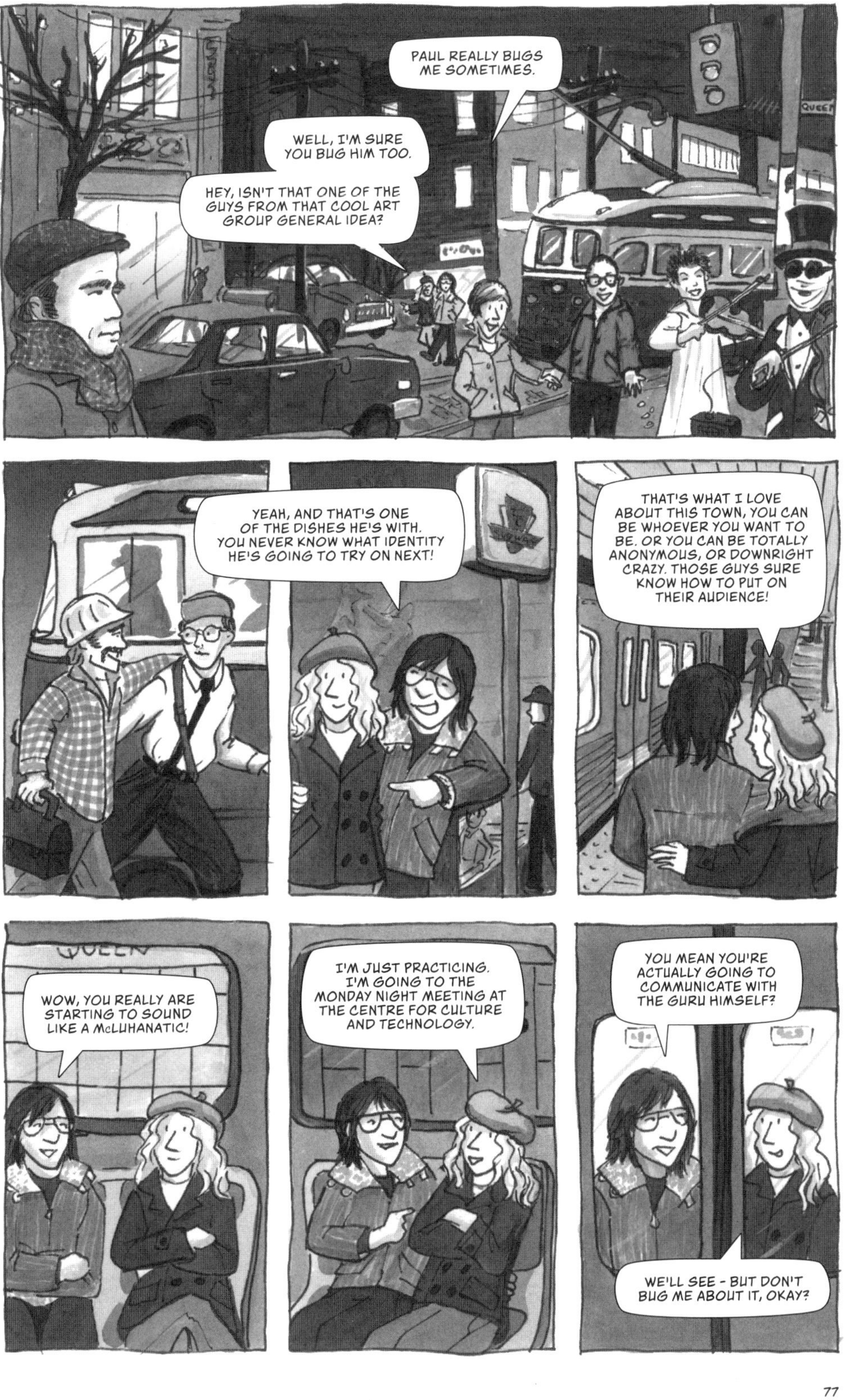
PAUL REALLY BUGS ME SOMETIMES.
WELL, I'M SURE YOU BUG HIM TOO.
HEY, ISN'T THAT ONE OF THE GUYS FROM THAT COOL ART GROUP GENERAL IDEA?
YEAH, AND THAT'S ONE OF THE DISHES HE'S WITH. YOU NEVER KNOW WHAT IDENTITY HE'S GOING TO TRY ON NEXT!
THAT'S WHAT I LOVE ABOUT THIS TOWN, YOU CAN BE WHOEVER YOU WANT TO BE. OR YOU CAN BE TOTALLY ANONYMOUS, OR DOWNRIGHT CRAZY. THOSE GUYS SURE KNOW HOW TO PUT ON THEIR AUDIENCE!
WOW, YOU REALLY ARE STARTING TO SOUND LIKE A McLUHANATIC!
I'M JUST PRACTICING. I'M GOING TO THE MONDAY NIGHT MEETING AT THE CENTRE FOR CULTURE AND TECHNOLOGY.
YOU MEAN YOU'RE ACTUALLY GOING TO COMMUNICATE WITH THE GURU HIMSELF?
WE'LL SEE - BUT DON'T BUG ME ABOUT IT, OKAY?

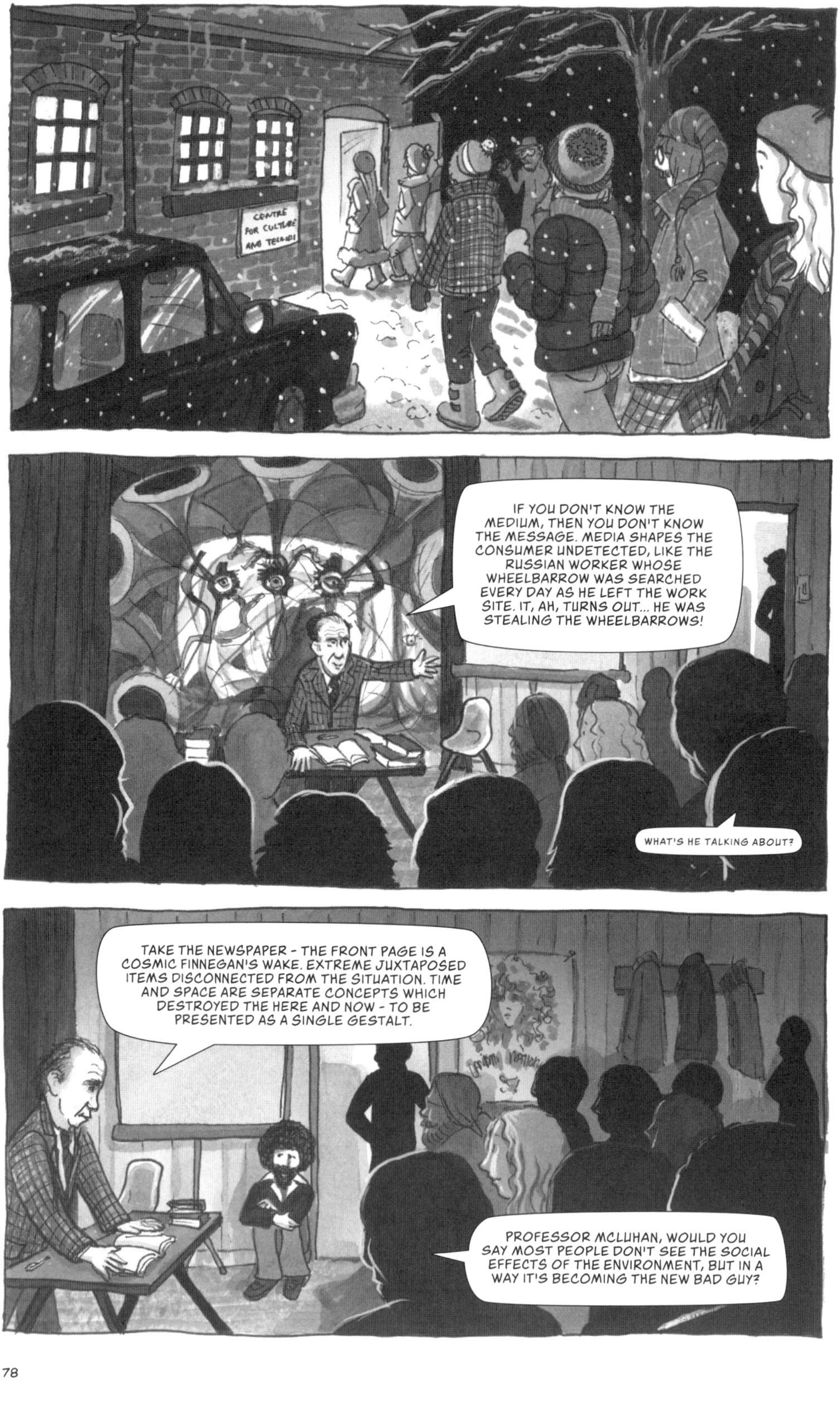
CENTRE FOR CULTURE
IF YOU DON'T KNOW THE MEDIUM, THEN YOU DON'T KNOW THE MESSAGE. MEDIA SHAPES THE CONSUMER UNDETECTED, LIKE THE RUSSIAN WORKER WHOSE WHEELBARROW WAS SEARCHED EVERY DAY AS HE LEFT THE WORK SITE. IT, AH, TURNS OUT... HE WAS STEALING THE WHEELBARROWS!
WHAT'S HE TALKING ABOUT?
TAKE THE NEWSPAPER - THE FRONT PAGE IS A COSMIC FINNEGAN'S WAKE. EXTREME JUXTAPOSED ITEMS DISCONNECTED FROM THE SITUATION. TIME AND SPACE ARE SEPARATE CONCEPTS WHICH DESTROYED THE HERE AND NOW - TO BE PRESENTED AS A SINGLE GESTALT.
PROFESSOR MCLUHAN, WOULD YOU SAY MOST PEOPLE DON'T SEE THE SOCIAL EFFECTS OF THE ENVIRONMENT, BUT IN A WAY IT'S BECOMING THE NEW BAD GUY?

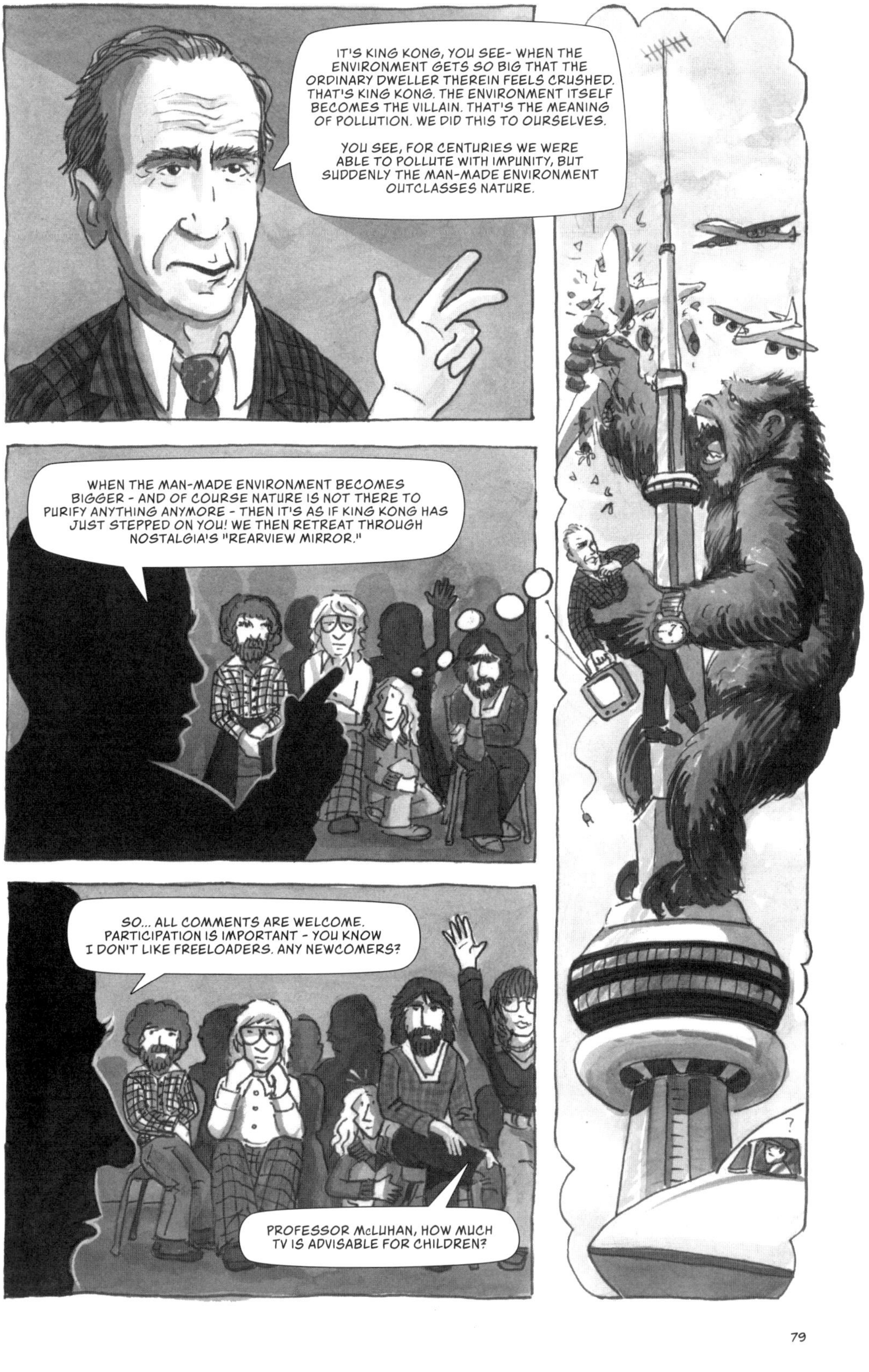
IT'S KING KONG, YOU SEE- WHEN THE ENVIRONMENT GETS SO BIG THAT THE ORDINARY DWELLER THEREIN FEELS CRUSHED. THAT'S KING KONG. THE ENVIRONMENT ITSELF BECOMES THE VILLAIN. THAT'S THE MEANING OF POLLUTION. WE DID THIS TO OURSELVES.
YOU SEE, FOR CENTURIES WE WERE ABLE TO POLLUTE WITH IMPUNITY, BUT SUDDENLY THE MAN-MADE ENVIRONMENT OUTCLASSES NATURE.
WHEN THE MAN-MADE ENVIRONMENT BECOMES BIGGER - AND OF COURSE NATURE IS NOT THERE TO PURIFY ANYTHING ANYMORE - THEN IT'S AS IF KING KONG HAS JUST STEPPED ON YOU! WE THEN RETREAT THROUGH NOSTALGIA'S "REARVIEW MIRROR."
SO... ALL COMMENTS ARE WELCOME. PARTICIPATION IS IMPORTANT - YOU KNOW I DON'T LIKE FREELOADERS. ANY NEWCOMERS?
PROFESSOR McLUHAN, HOW MUCH TV IS ADVISABLE FOR CHILDREN?
?

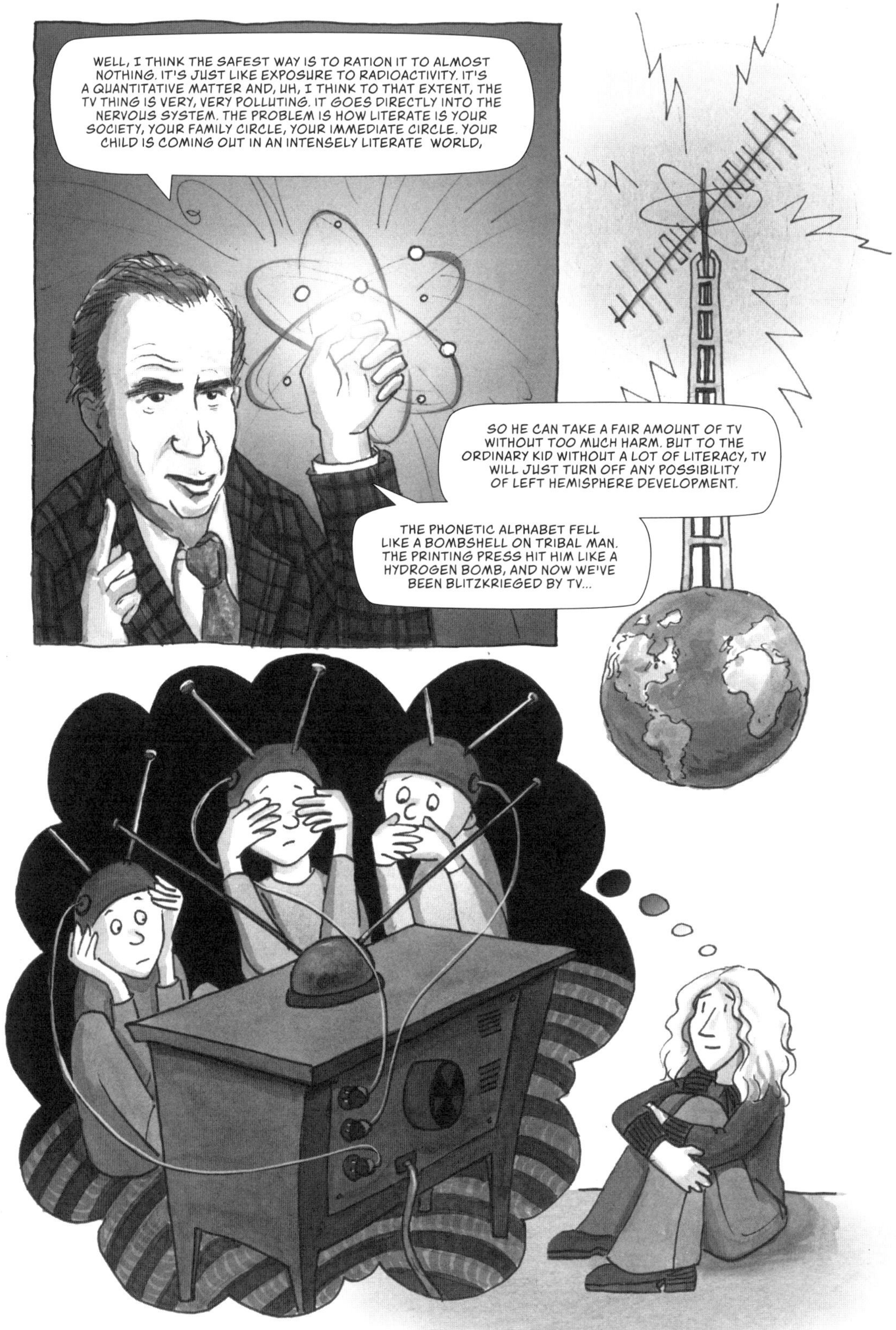
WELL, I THINK THE SAFEST WAY IS TO RATION IT TO ALMOST NOTHING. IT'S JUST LIKE EXPOSURE TO RADIOACTIVITY. IT'S A QUANTITATIVE MATTER AND, UH, I THINK TO THAT EXTENT, THE TV THING IS VERY, VERY POLLUTING. IT GOES DIRECTLY INTO THE NERVOUS SYSTEM. THE PROBLEM IS HOW LITERATE IS YOUR SOCIETY, YOUR FAMILY CIRCLE, YOUR IMMEDIATE CIRCLE. YOUR CHILD IS COMING OUT IN AN INTENSELY LITERATE WORLD,
SO HE CAN TAKE A FAIR AMOUNT OF TV WITHOUT TOO MUCH HARM. BUT TO THE ORDINARY KID WITHOUT A LOT OF LITERACY, TV WILL JUST TURN OFF ANY POSSIBILITY OF LEFT HEMISPHERE DEVELOPMENT.
THE PHONETIC ALPHABET FELL LIKE A BOMBSHELL ON TRIBAL MAN. THE PRINTING PRESS HIT HIM LIKE A HYDROGEN BOMB, AND NOW WE'VE BEEN BLITZKRIEGED BY TV...

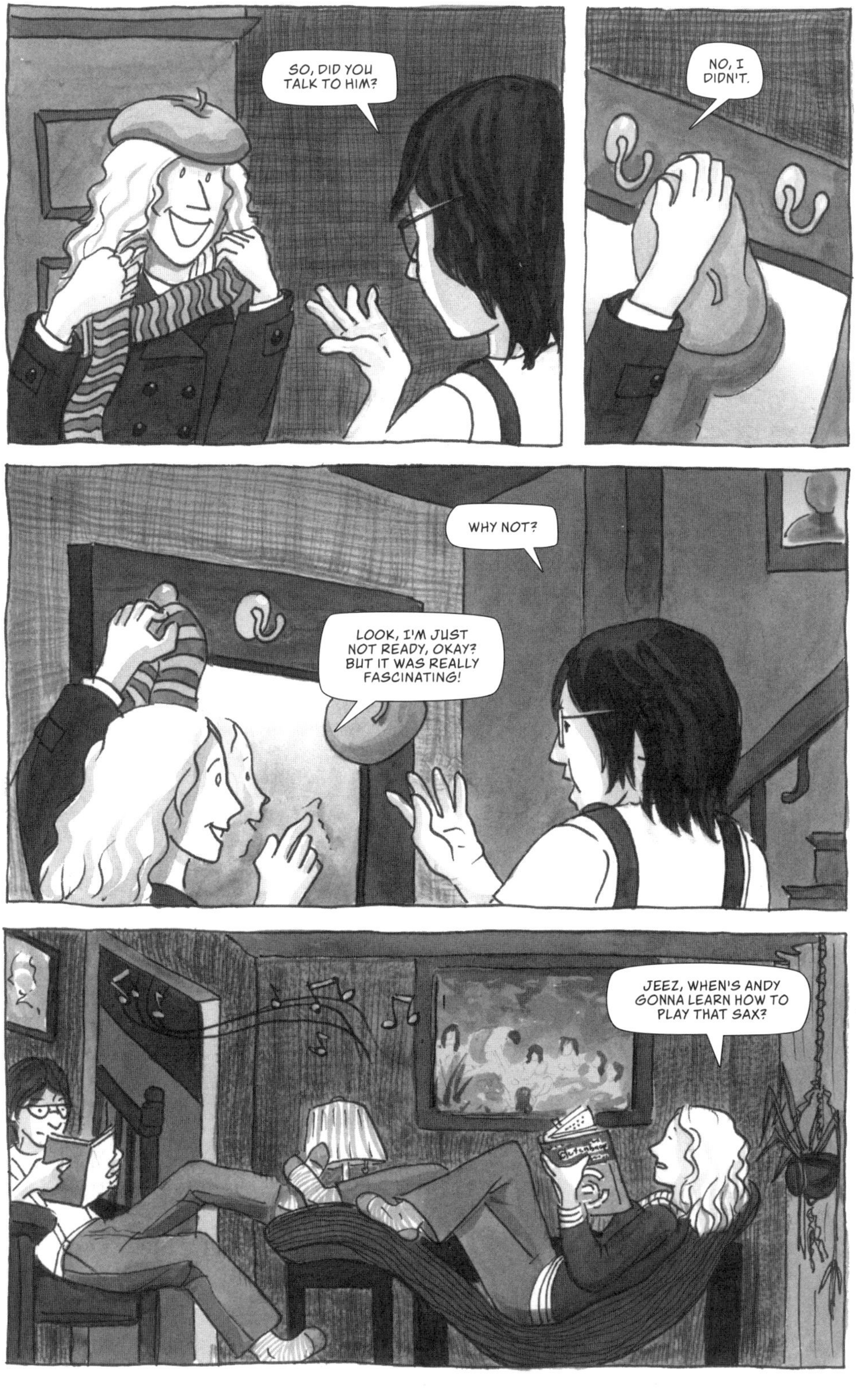
SO, DID YOU TALK TO HIM?
NO, I DIDN'T.
WHY NOT?
LOOK, I'M JUST NOT READY, OKAY? BUT IT WAS REALLY FASCINATING!
JEEZ, WHEN'S ANDY GONNA LEARN HOW TO PLAY THAT SAX?

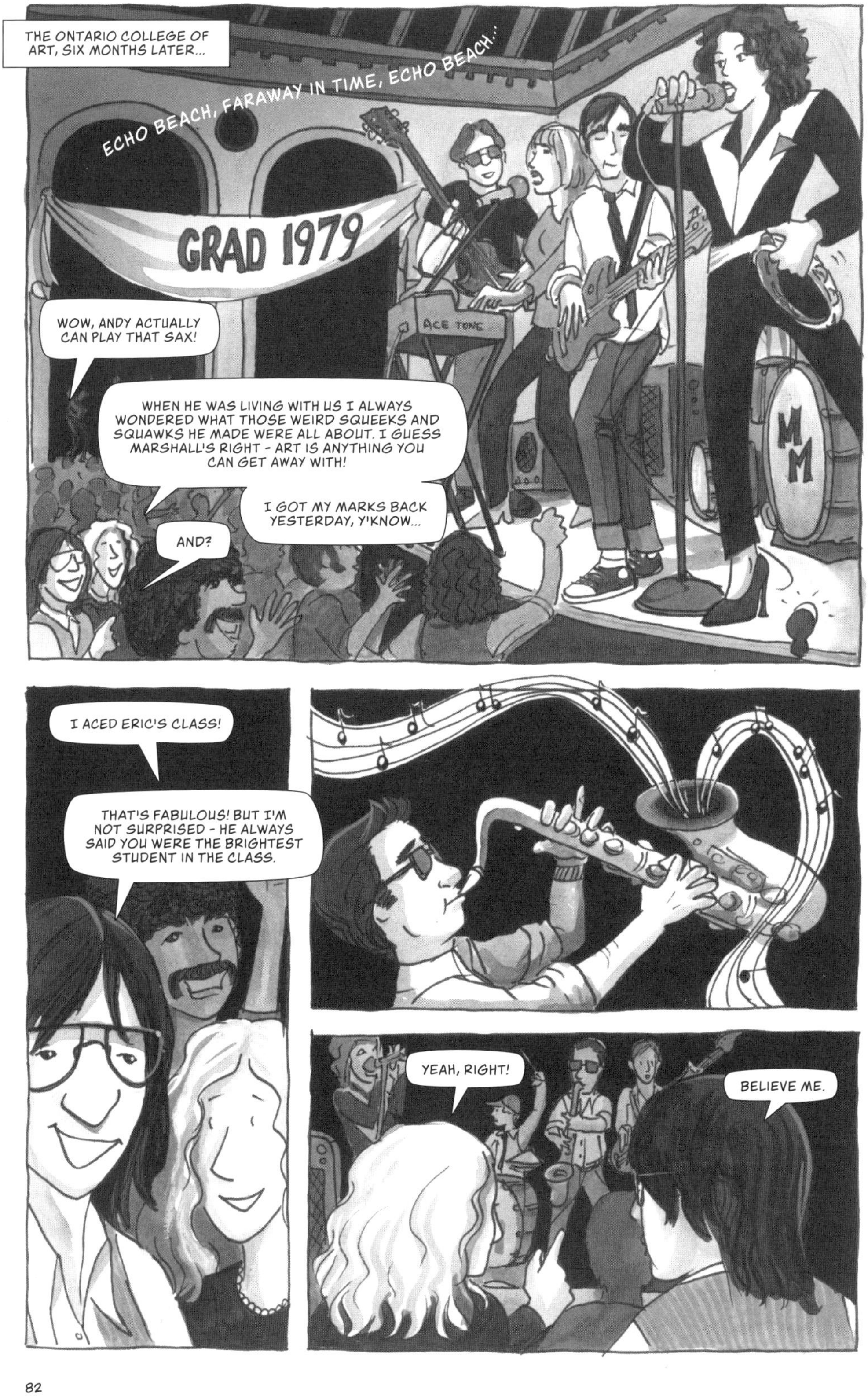
THE ONTARIO COLLEGE OF ART, SIX MONTHS LATER...
ECHO BEACH, FARAWAY IN TIME, ECHO BEACH...
GRAD 1979
ACE TONE
WOW, ANDY ACTUALLY CAN PLAY THAT SAX!
WHEN HE WAS LIVING WITH US I ALWAYS WONDERED WHAT THOSE WEIRD SQUEEKS AND SQUAWKS HE MADE WERE ALL ABOUT. I GUESS MARSHALL'S RIGHT - ART IS ANYTHING YOU CAN GET AWAY WITH!
I GOT MY MARKS BACK YESTERDAY, Y'KNOW...
AND?
I ACED ERIC'S CLASS!
THAT'S FABULOUS! BUT I'M NOT SURPRISED - HE ALWAYS SAID YOU WERE THE BRIGHTEST STUDENT IN THE CLASS.
YEAH, RIGHT!
BELIEVE ME.

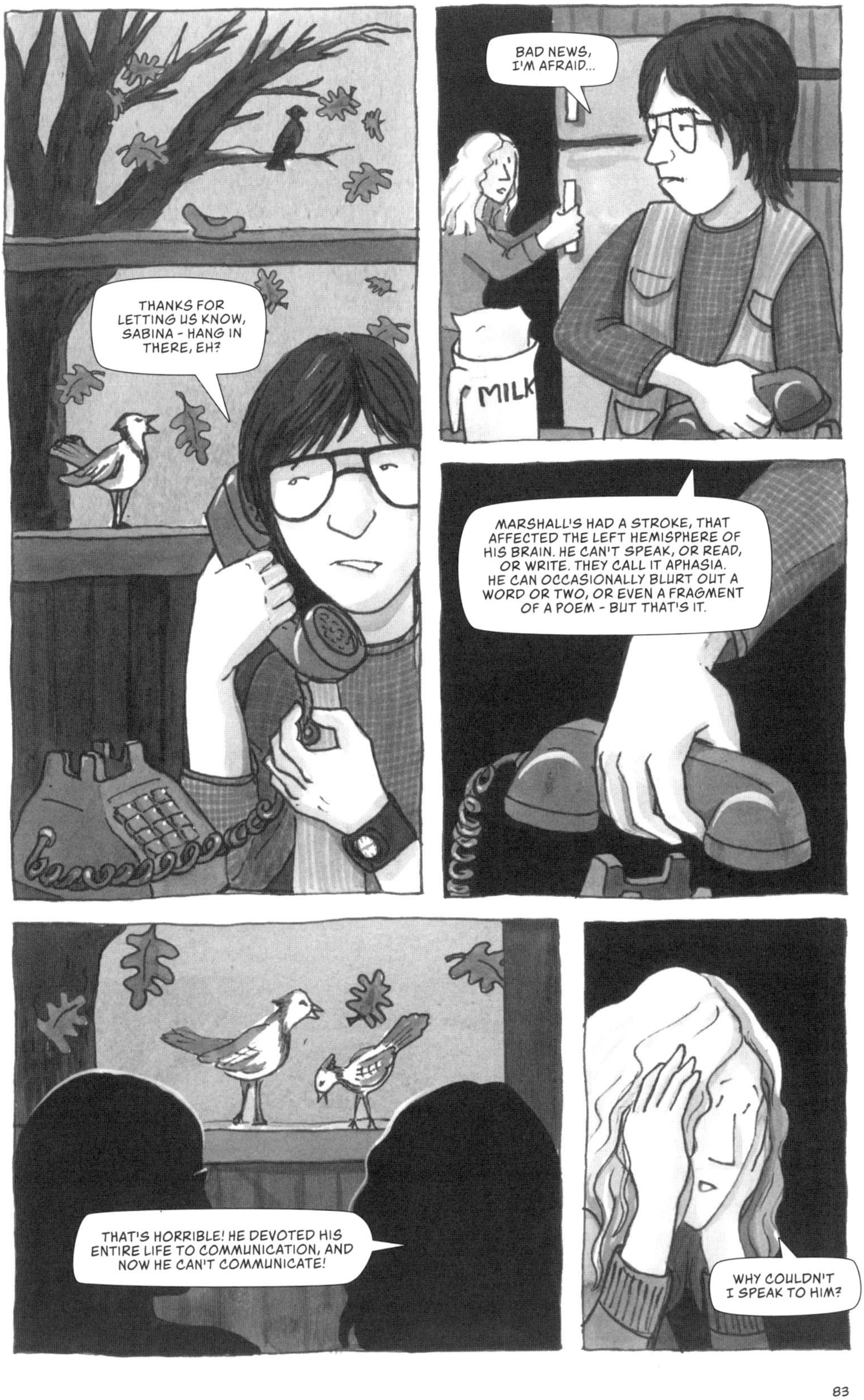
THANKS FOR LETTING US KNOW, SABINA - HANG IN THERE, EH?
BAD NEWS, I'M AFRAID...
MILK
MARSHALL'S HAD A STROKE, THAT AFFECTED THE LEFT HEMISPHERE OF HIS BRAIN. HE CAN'T SPEAK, OR READ, OR WRITE. THEY CALL IT APHASIA. HE CAN OCCASIONALLY BLURT OUT A WORD OR TWO, OR EVEN A FRAGMENT OF A POEM - BUT THAT'S IT.
THAT'S HORRIBLE! HE DEVOTED HIS ENTIRE LIFE TO COMMUNICATION, AND NOW HE CAN'T COMMUNICATE!
WHY COULDN'T I SPEAK TO HIM?

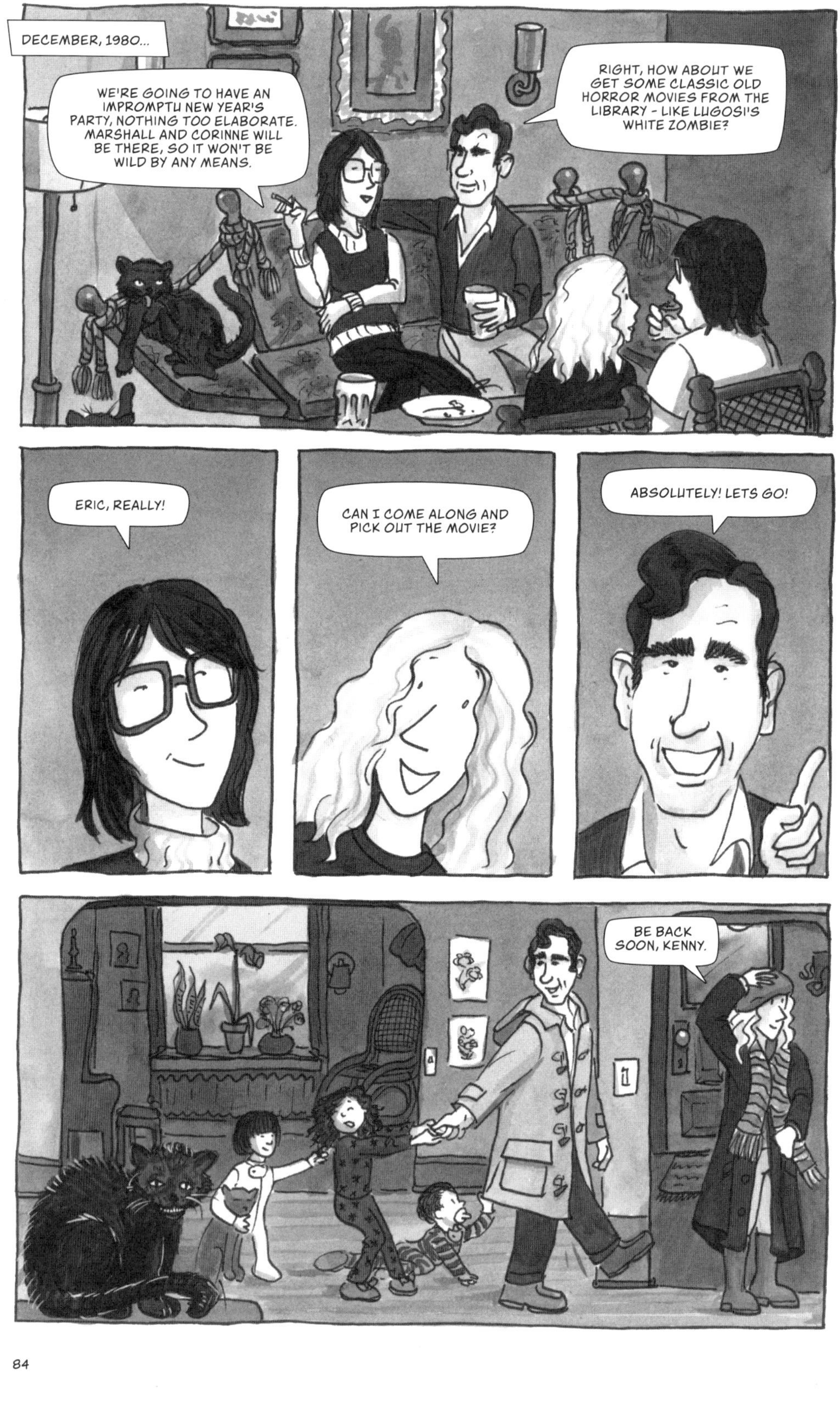
DECEMBER, 1980...
WE'RE GOING TO HAVE AN IMPROMPTU NEW YEAR'S PARTY, NOTHING TOO ELABORATE. MARSHALL AND CORINNE WILL BE THERE, SO IT WON'T BE WILD BY ANY MEANS.
RIGHT, HOW ABOUT WE GET SOME CLASSIC OLD HORROR MOVIES FROM THE LIBRARY - LIKE LUGOSI'S WHITE ZOMBIE?
ERIC, REALLY!
CAN I COME ALONG AND PICK OUT THE MOVIE?
ABSOLUTELY! LETS GO!
BE BACK SOON, KENNY.

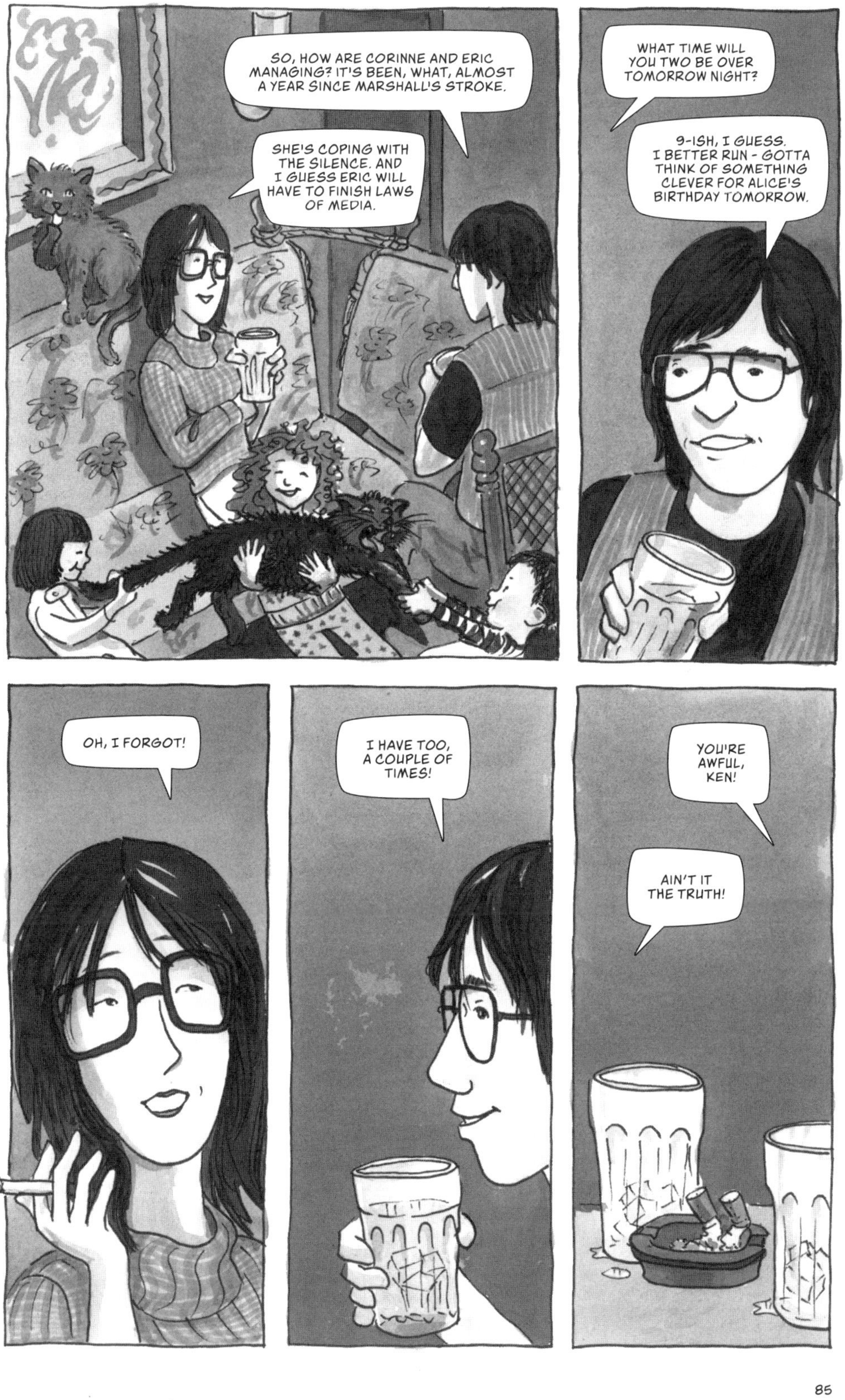
SO, HOW ARE CORINNE AND ERIC MANAGING? IT'S BEEN, WHAT, ALMOST A YEAR SINCE MARSHALL'S STROKE.
SHE'S COPING WITH THE SILENCE. AND I GUESS ERIC WILL HAVE TO FINISH LAWS OF MEDIA.
WHAT TIME WILL YOU TWO BE OVER TOMORROW NIGHT?
9-ISH, I GUESS. I BETTER RUN - GOTTA THINK OF SOMETHING CLEVER FOR ALICE'S BIRTHDAY TOMORROW.
OH, I FORGOT!
I HAVE TOO, A COUPLE OF TIMES!
YOU'RE AWFUL, KEN!
AIN'T IT THE TRUTH!

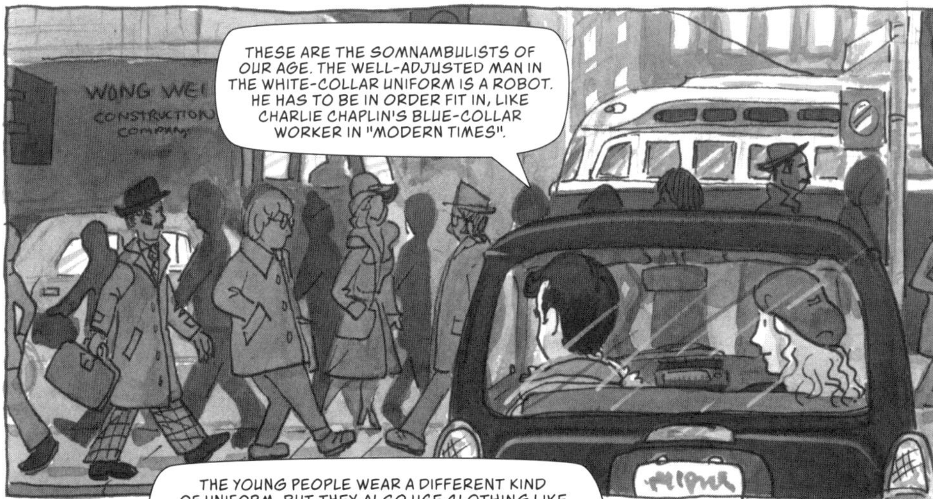
THESE ARE THE SOMNAMBULISTS OF OUR AGE. THE WELL-ADJUSTED MAN IN THE WHITE-COLLAR UNIFORM IS A ROBOT. HE HAS TO BE IN ORDER FIT IN, LIKE CHARLIE CHAPLIN'S BLUE-COLLAR WORKER IN "MODERN TIMES".
WONG WEI
CONSTRUCTION
COMPANY

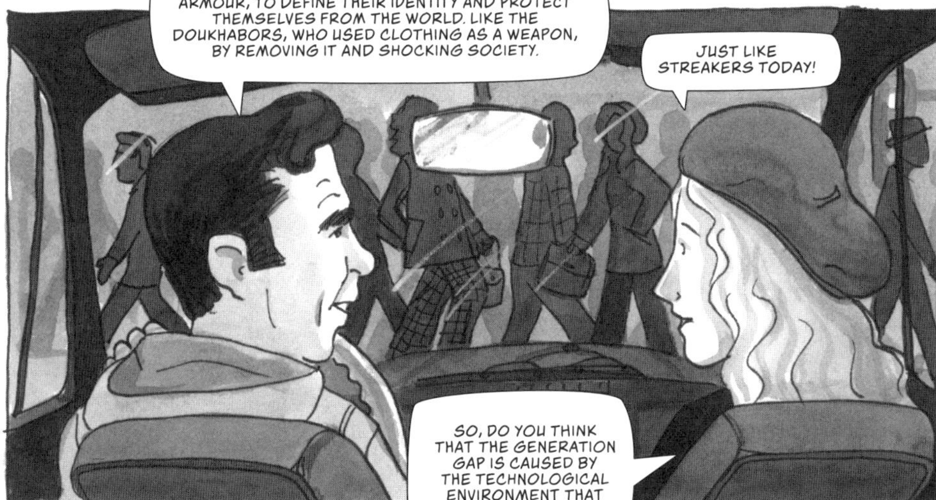
THE YOUNG PEOPLE WEAR A DIFFERENT KIND OF UNIFORM, BUT THEY ALSO USE CLOTHING LIKE ARMOUR, TO DEFINE THEIR IDENTITY AND PROTECT THEMSELVES FROM THE WORLD. LIKE THE DOUKHABORS, WHO USED CLOTHING AS A WEAPON, BY REMOVING IT AND SHOCKING SOCIETY.
JUST LIKE STREAKERS TODAY!
SO, DO YOU THINK THAT THE GENERATION GAP IS CAUSED BY THE TECHNOLOGICAL ENVIRONMENT THAT KIDS HAVE BEEN RAISED IN?

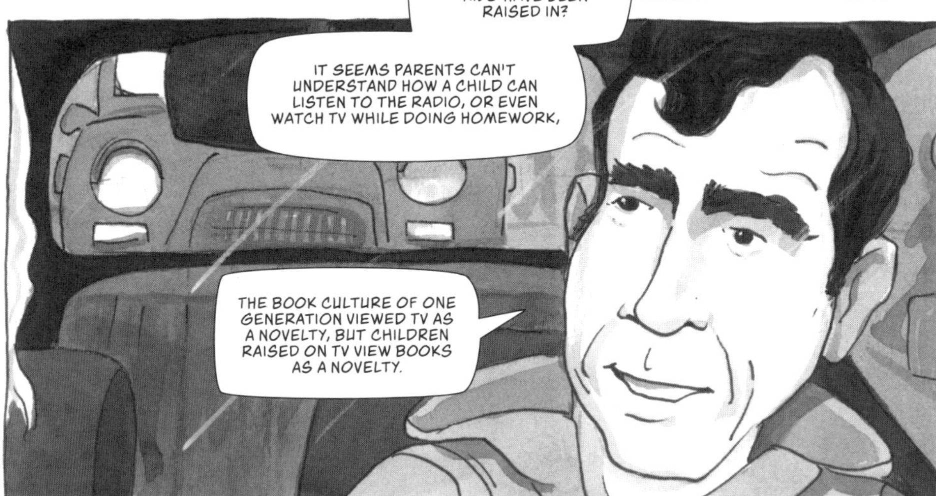
IT SEEMS PARENTS CAN'T UNDERSTAND HOW A CHILD CAN LISTEN TO THE RADIO, OR EVEN WATCH TV WHILE DOING HOMEWORK,
THE BOOK CULTURE OF ONE GENERATION VIEWED TV AS A NOVELTY, BUT CHILDREN RAISED ON TV VIEW BOOKS AS A NOVELTY.

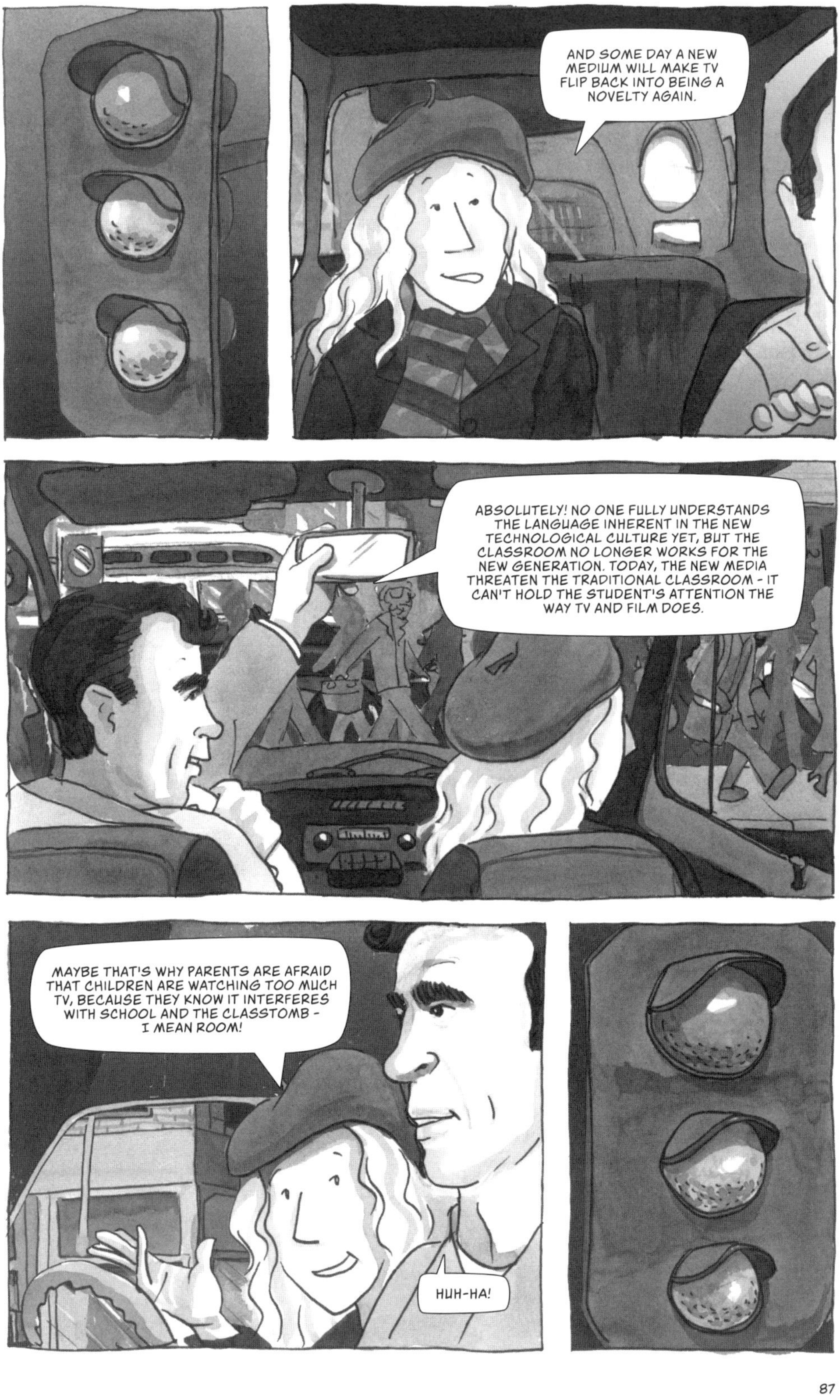
AND SOME DAY A NEW MEDIUM WILL MAKE TV FLIP BACK INTO BEING A NOVELTY AGAIN.
ABSOLUTELY! NO ONE FULLY UNDERSTANDS THE LANGUAGE INHERENT IN THE NEW TECHNOLOGICAL CULTURE YET, BUT THE CLASSROOM NO LONGER WORKS FOR THE NEW GENERATION. TODAY, THE NEW MEDIA THREATEN THE TRADITIONAL CLASSROOM - IT CAN'T HOLD THE STUDENT'S ATTENTION THE WAY TV AND FILM DOES.
MAYBE THAT'S WHY PARENTS ARE AFRAID THAT CHILDREN ARE WATCHING TOO MUCH TV, BECAUSE THEY KNOW IT INTERFERES WITH SCHOOL AND THE CLASSTOMB - I MEAN ROOM!
HUH-HA!

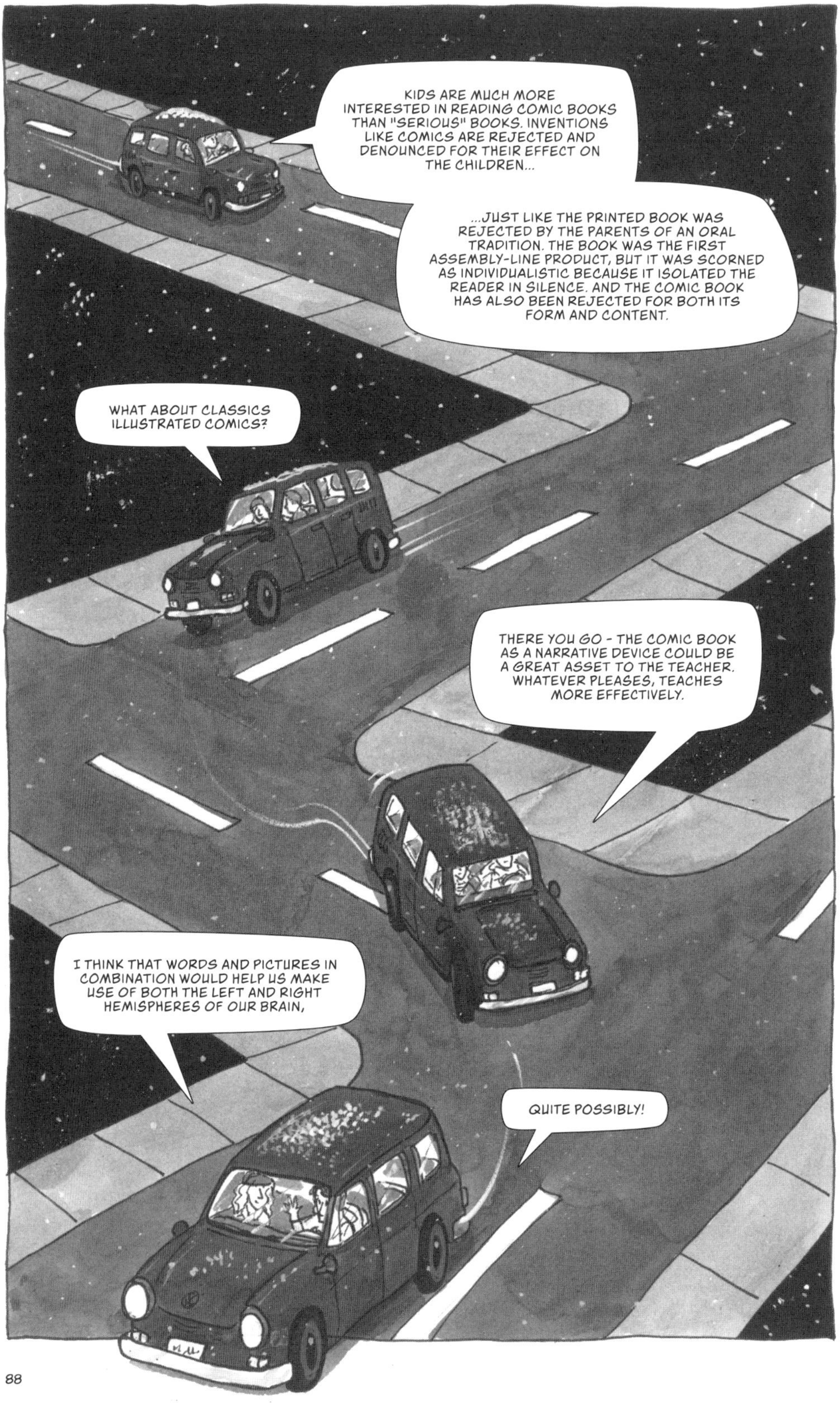
KIDS ARE MUCH MORE INTERESTED IN READING COMIC BOOKS THAN "SERIOUS" BOOKS. INVENTIONS LIKE COMICS ARE REJECTED AND DENOUNCED FOR THEIR EFFECT ON THE CHILDREN...
...JUST LIKE THE PRINTED BOOK WAS REJECTED BY THE PARENTS OF AN ORAL TRADITION. THE BOOK WAS THE FIRST ASSEMBLY-LINE PRODUCT, BUT IT WAS SCORNED AS INDIVIDUALISTIC BECAUSE IT ISOLATED THE READER IN SILENCE. AND THE COMIC BOOK HAS ALSO BEEN REJECTED FOR BOTH ITS FORM AND CONTENT.
WHAT ABOUT CLASSICS ILLUSTRATED COMICS?
THERE YOU GO - THE COMIC BOOK AS A NARRATIVE DEVICE COULD BE A GREAT ASSET TO THE TEACHER. WHATEVER PLEASES, TEACHES MORE EFFECTIVELY.
I THINK THAT WORDS AND PICTURES IN COMBINATION WOULD HELP US MAKE USE OF BOTH THE LEFT AND RIGHT HEMISPHERES OF OUR BRAIN,
QUITE POSSIBLY!

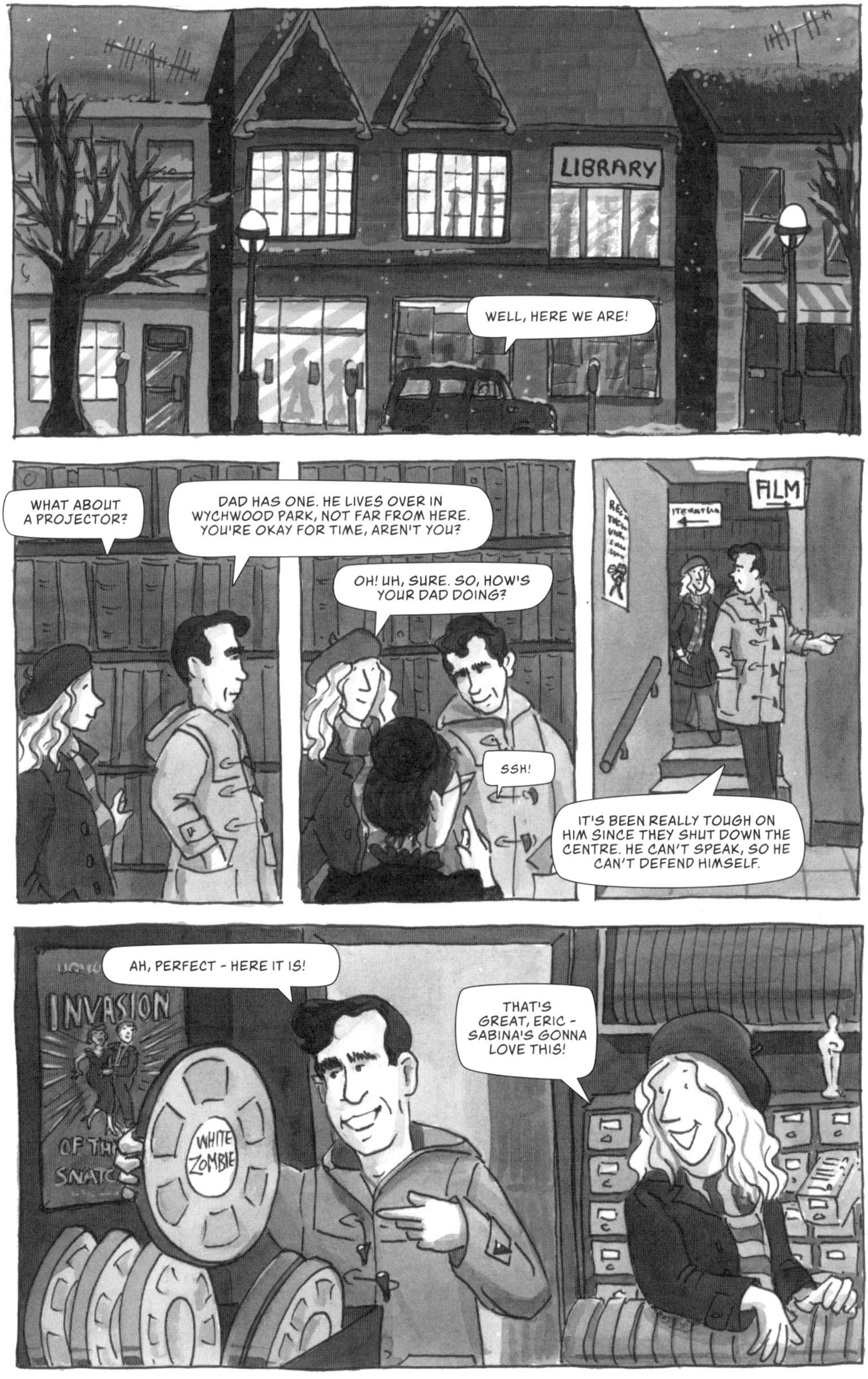

LIBRARY
WELL, HERE WE ARE!
WHAT ABOUT A PROJECTOR?
DAD HAS ONE. HE LIVES OVER IN WYCHWOOD PARK, NOT FAR FROM HERE. YOU'RE OKAY FOR TIME, AREN'T YOU?
OH! UH, SURE. SO, HOW'S YOUR DAD DOING?
SSH!
FILM
IT'S BEEN REALLY TOUGH ON HIM SINCE THEY SHUT DOWN THE CENTRE. HE CAN'T SPEAK, SO HE CAN'T DEFEND HIMSELF.
AH, PERFECT - HERE IT IS!
INVASION
WHITE ZOMBIE
THAT'S GREAT, ERIC - SABINA'S GONNA LOVE THIS!

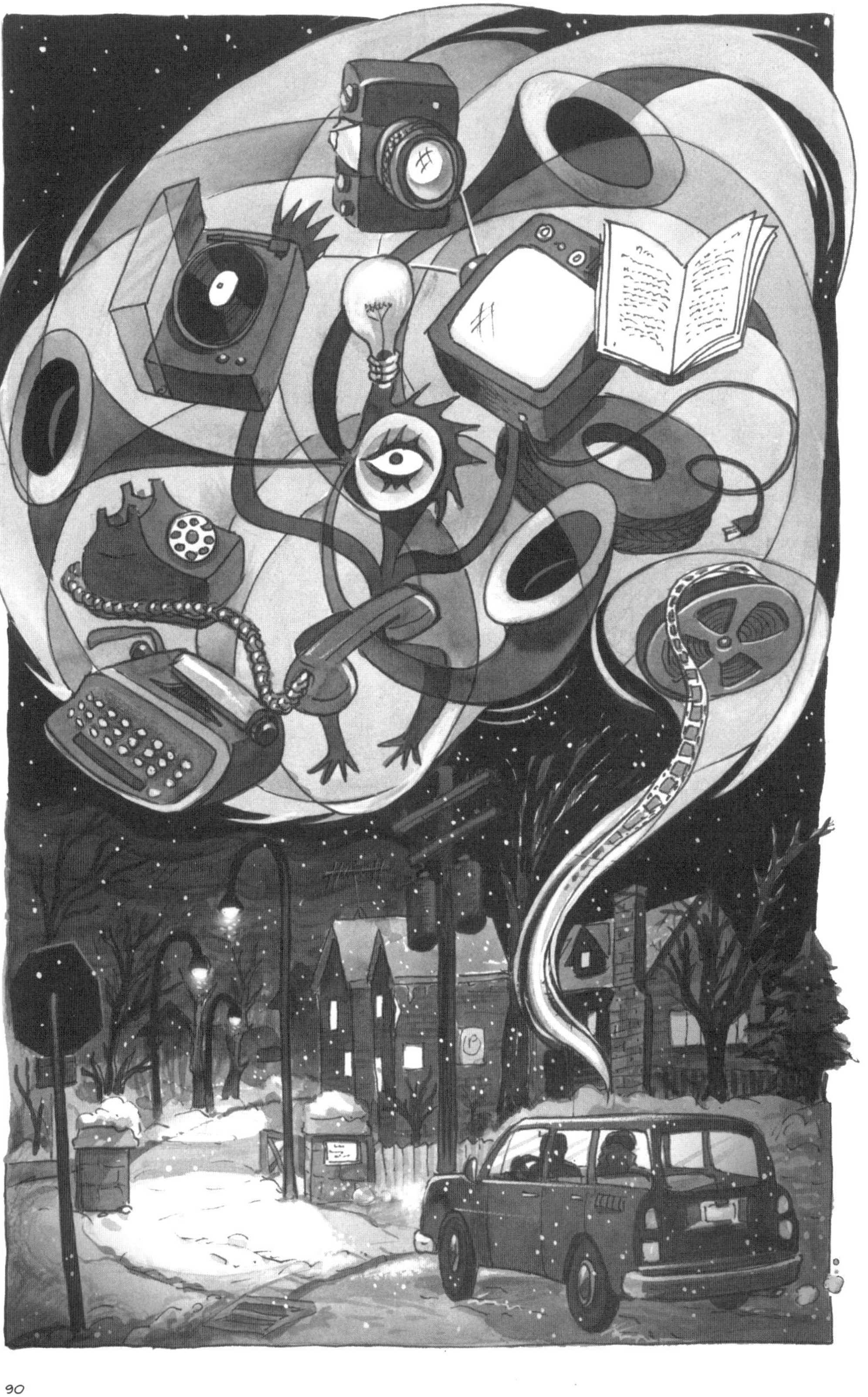
#1

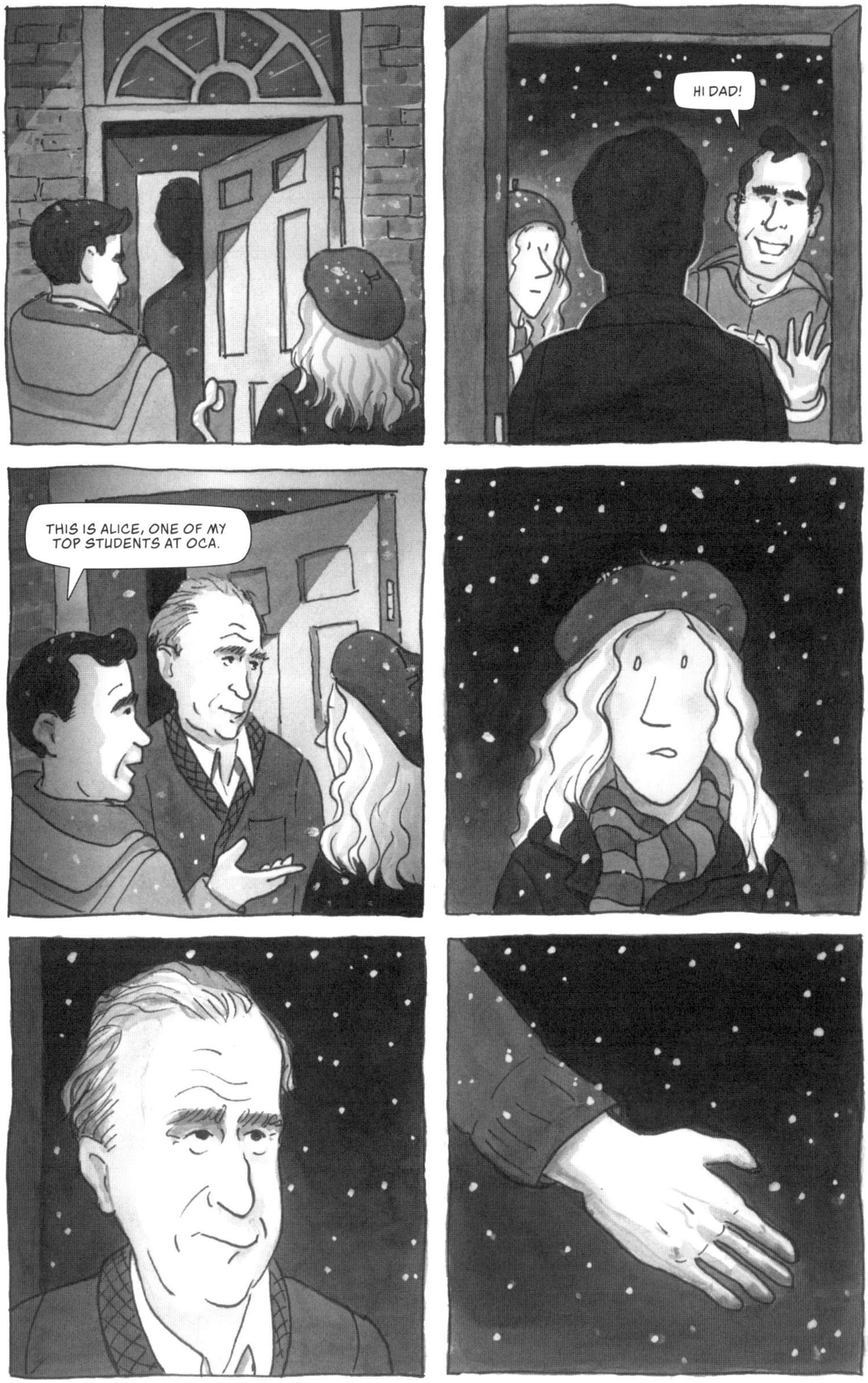
HI DAD!
THIS IS ALICE, ONE OF MY TOP STUDENTS AT OCA.

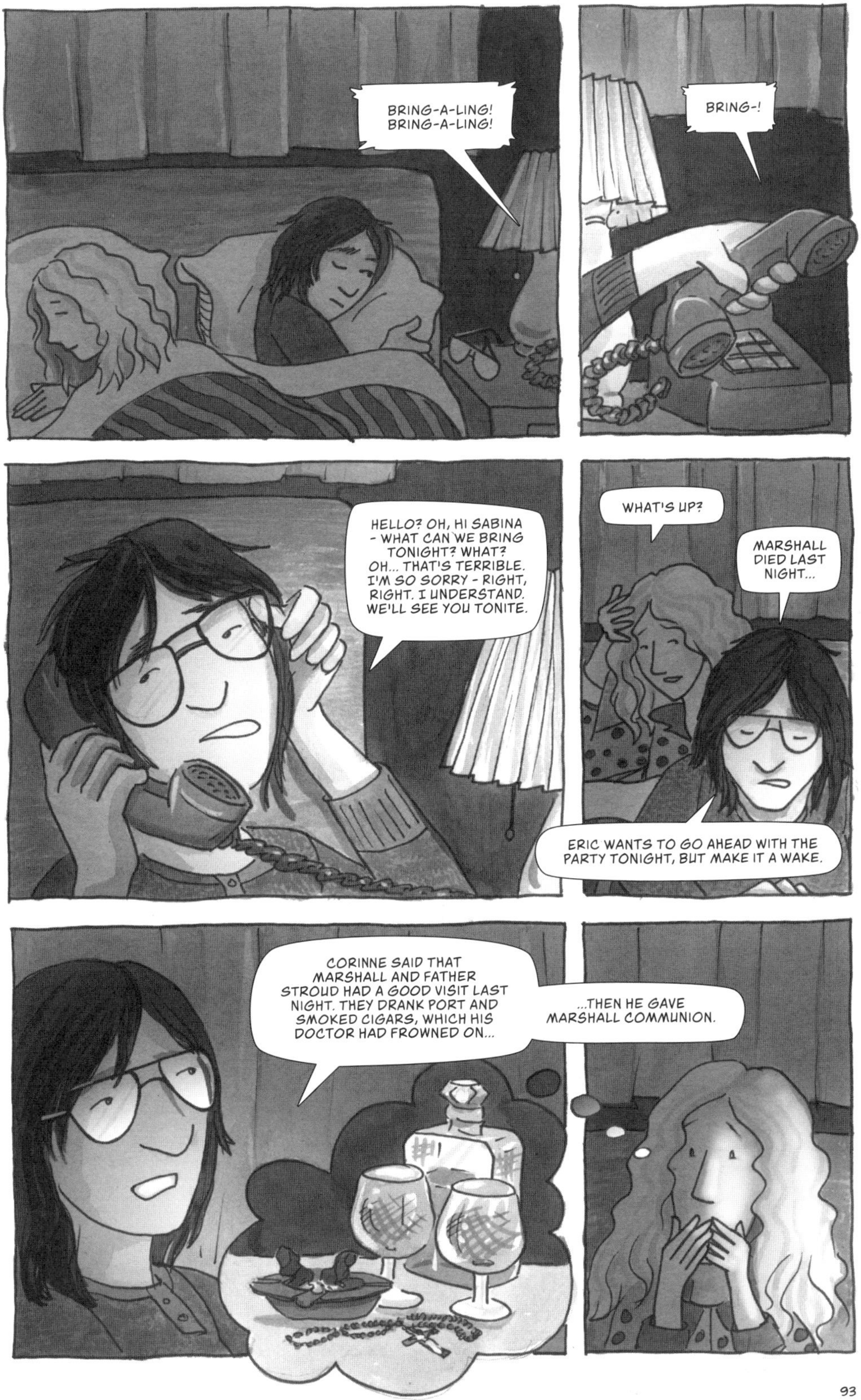

BRING-A-LING!
BRING-A-LING!
BRING-!
HELLO? OH, HI SABINA - WHAT CAN WE BRING TONIGHT? WHAT? OH... THAT'S TERRIBLE. I'M SO SORRY - RIGHT, RIGHT. I UNDERSTAND. WE'LL SEE YOU TONITE.
WHAT'S UP?
MARSHALL DIED LAST NIGHT...
ERIC WANTS TO GO AHEAD WITH THE PARTY TONIGHT, BUT MAKE IT A WAKE.
CORINNE SAID THAT MARSHALL AND FATHER STROUD HAD A GOOD VISIT LAST NIGHT. THEY DRANK PORT AND SMOKED CIGARS, WHICH HIS DOCTOR HAD FROWNED ON...
...THEN HE GAVE MARSHALL COMMUNION.

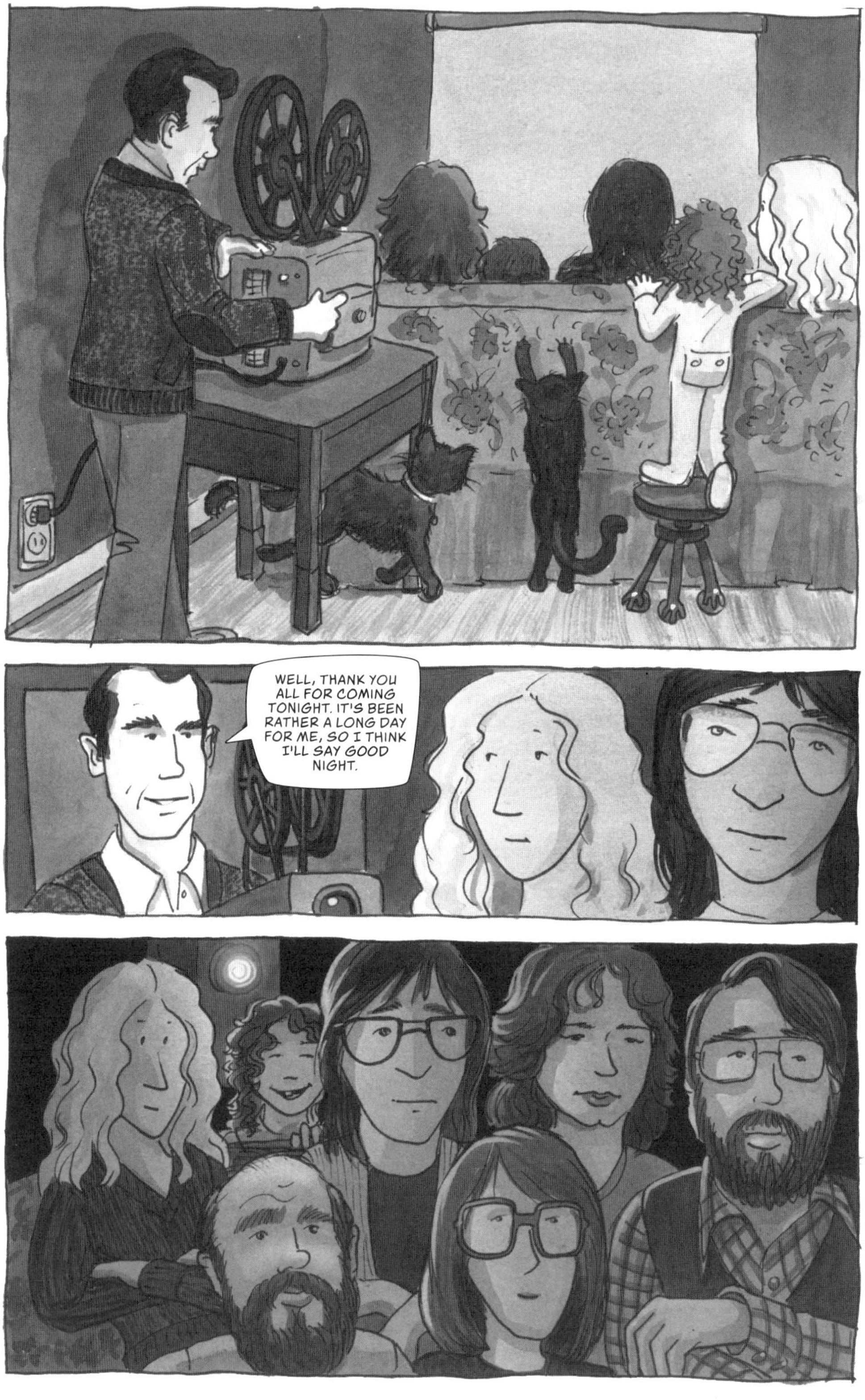
WELL, THANK YOU ALL FOR COMING TONIGHT. IT'S BEEN RATHER A LONG DAY FOR ME, SO I THINK I'LL SAY GOOD NIGHT.

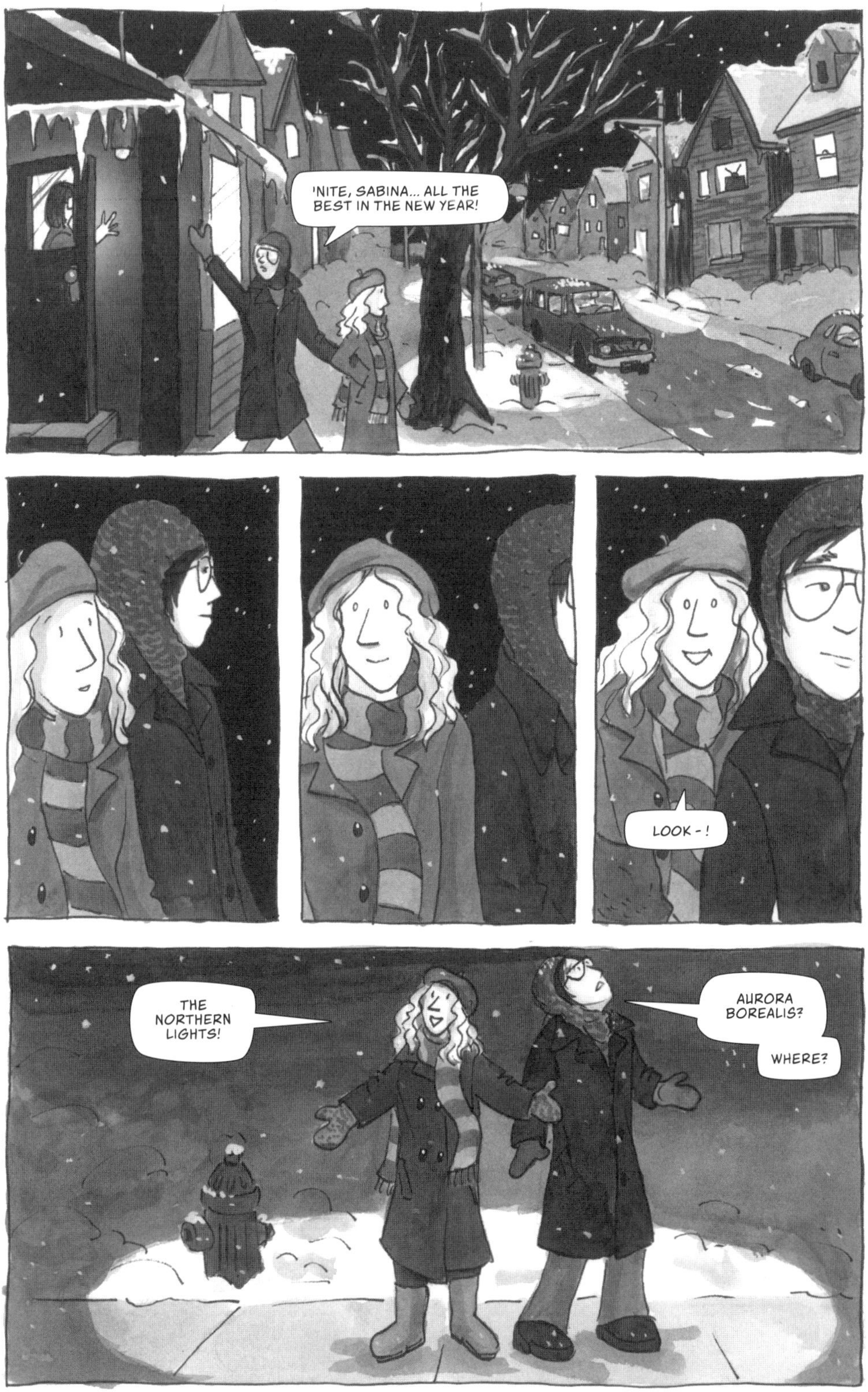
'NITE, SABINA... ALL THE BEST IN THE NEW YEAR!
LOOK - !
THE NORTHERN LIGHTS!
AURORA BOREALIS?
WHERE?

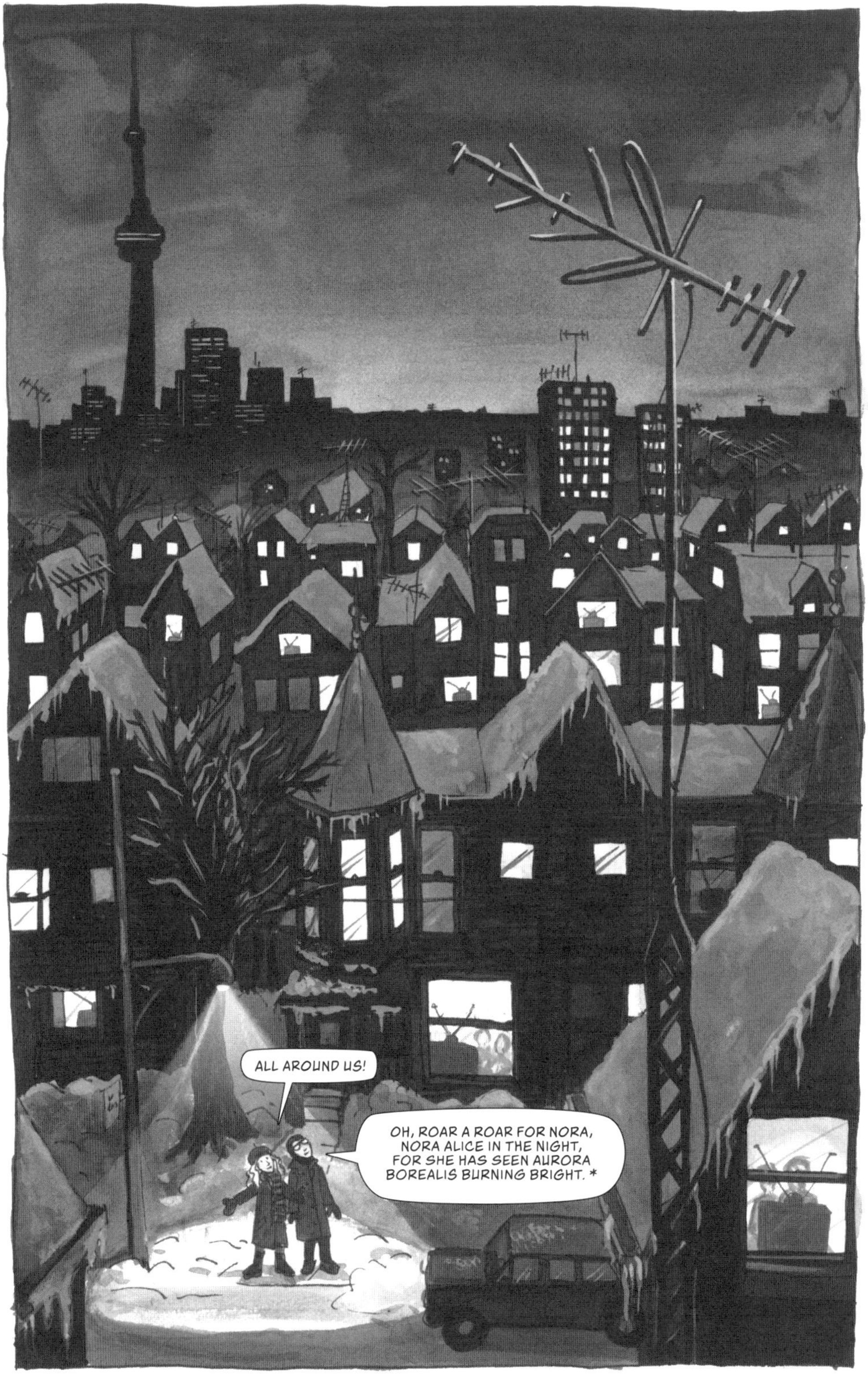
ALL AROUND US!
OH, ROAR A ROAR FOR NORA, NORA ALICE IN THE NIGHT, FOR SHE HAS SEEN AURORA BOREALIS BURNING BRIGHT. *

* *NORTHERN LIGHTS* BY WALT KELLY

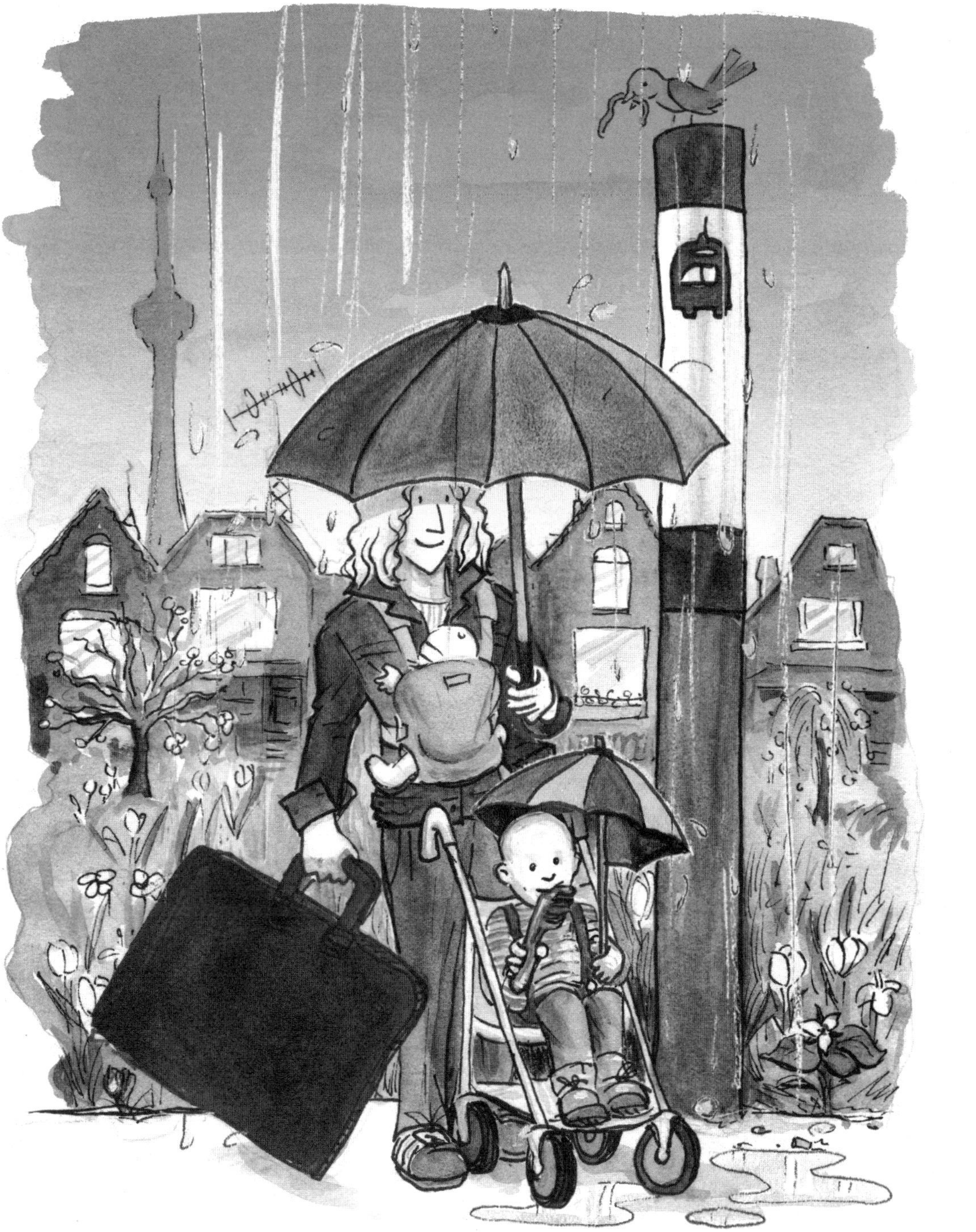

CHAPTER 2

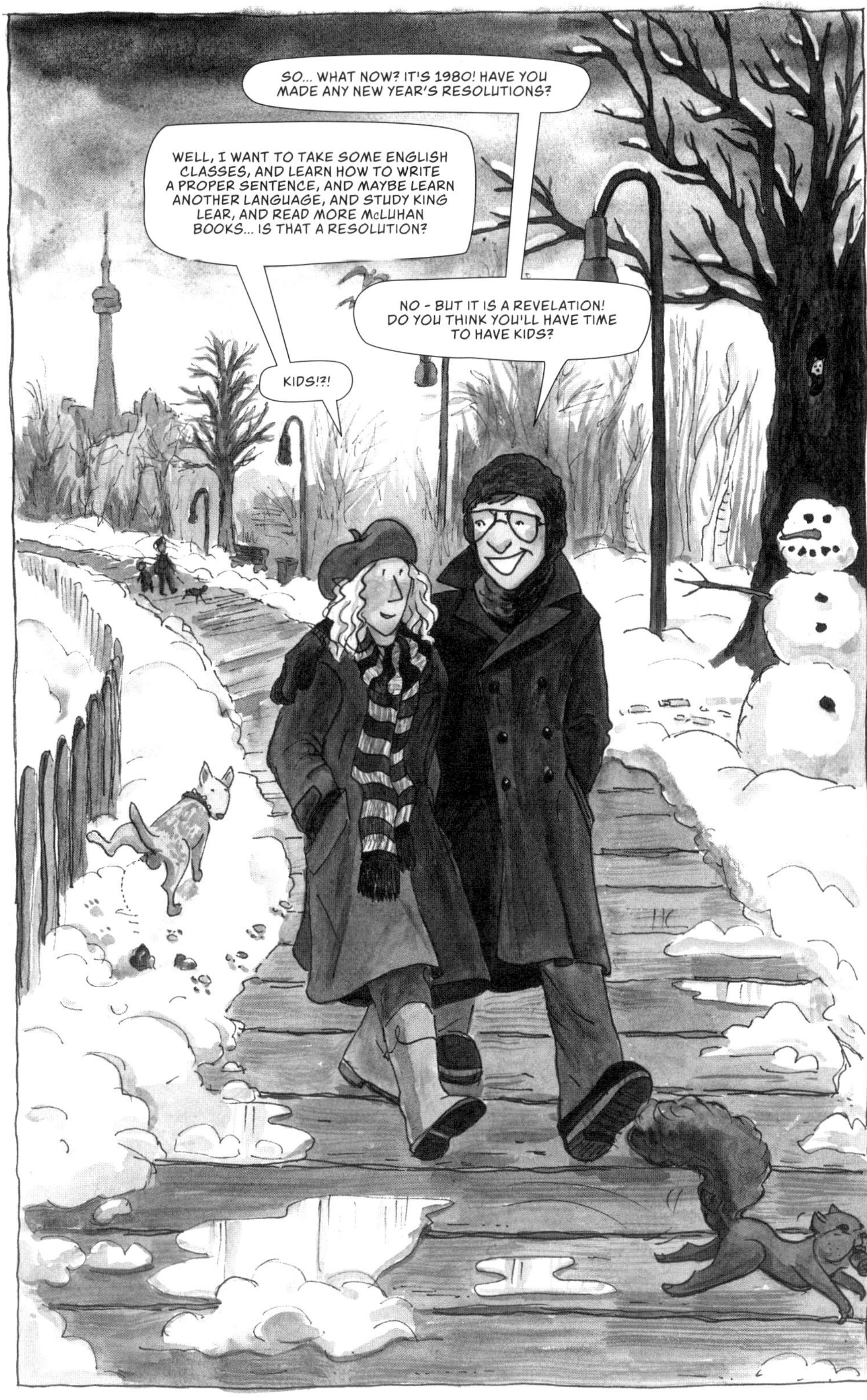
SO... WHAT NOW? IT'S 1980! HAVE YOU MADE ANY NEW YEAR'S RESOLUTIONS?
WELL, I WANT TO TAKE SOME ENGLISH CLASSES, AND LEARN HOW TO WRITE A PROPER SENTENCE, AND MAYBE LEARN ANOTHER LANGUAGE, AND STUDY KING LEAR, AND READ MORE McLUHAN BOOKS... IS THAT A RESOLUTION?
NO - BUT IT IS A REVELATION! DO YOU THINK YOU'LL HAVE TIME TO HAVE KIDS?
KIDS!?!

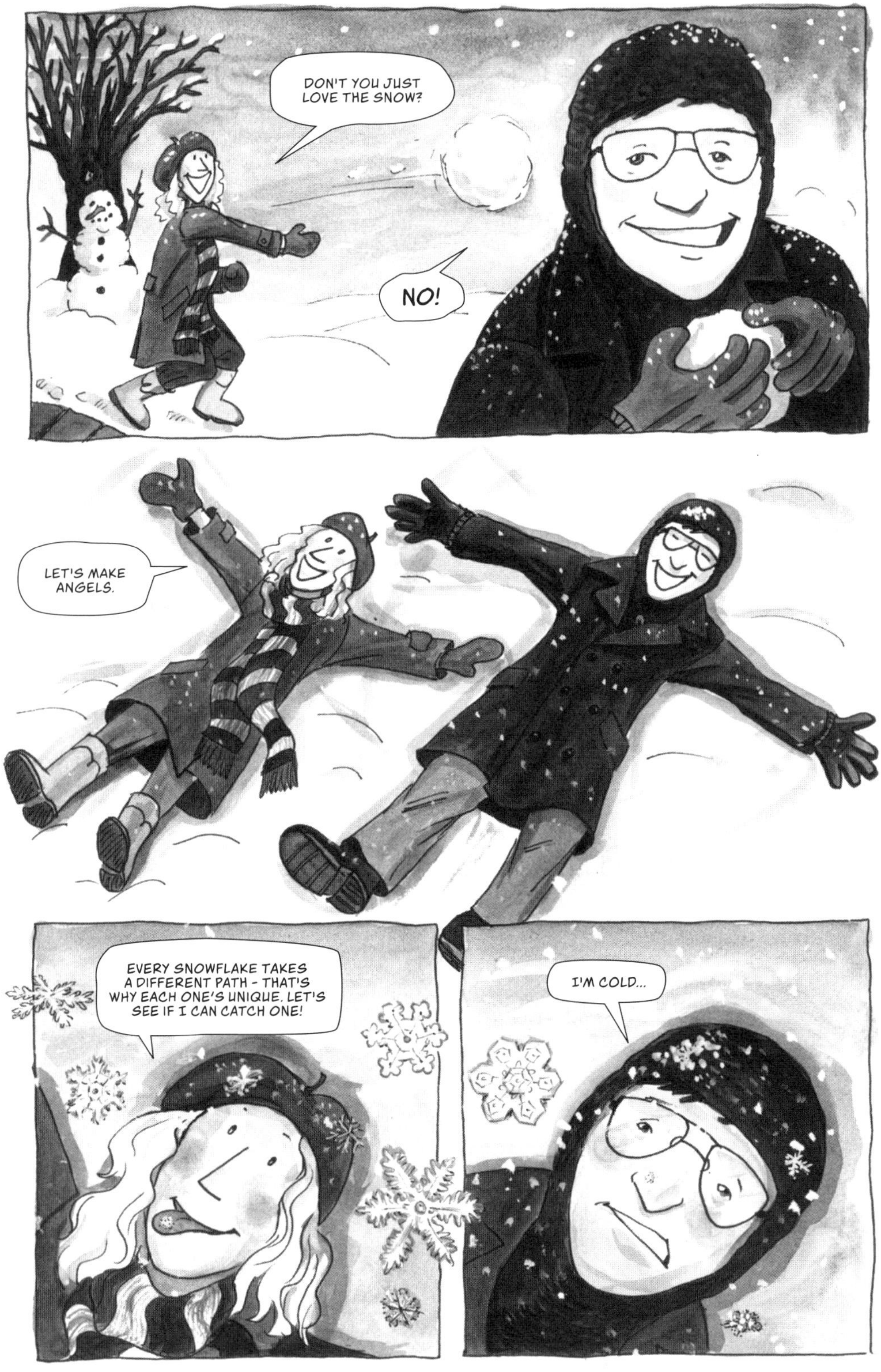
DON'T YOU JUST LOVE THE SNOW?
NO!
LET'S MAKE ANGELS.
EVERY SNOWFLAKE TAKES A DIFFERENT PATH - THAT'S WHY EACH ONE'S UNIQUE. LET'S SEE IF I CAN CATCH ONE!
I'M COLD...

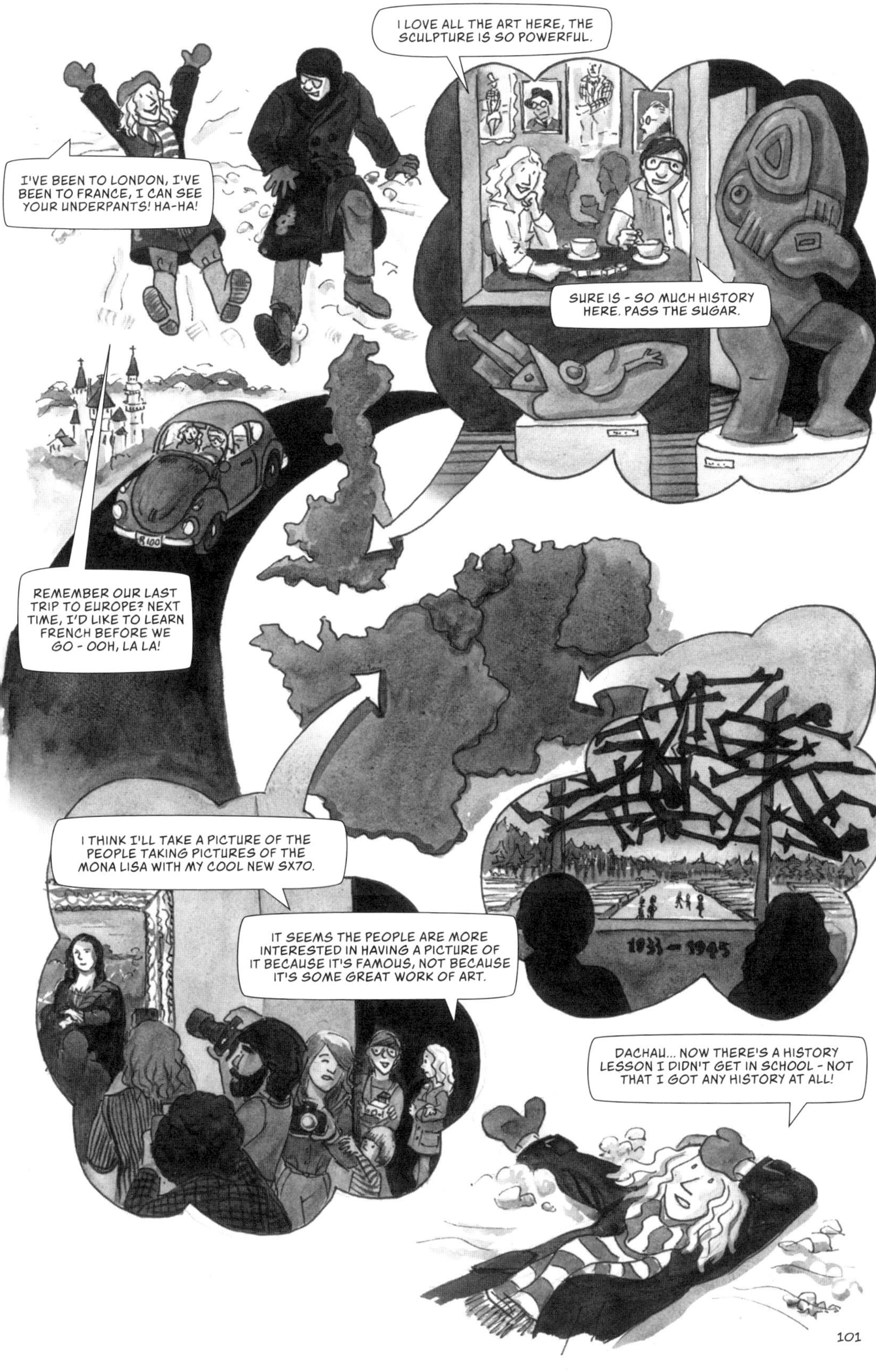
I'VE BEEN TO LONDON, I'VE BEEN TO FRANCE, I CAN SEE YOUR UNDERPANTS! HA-HA!
I LOVE ALL THE ART HERE, THE SCULPTURE IS SO POWERFUL.
SURE IS - SO MUCH HISTORY HERE. PASS THE SUGAR.
REMEMBER OUR LAST TRIP TO EUROPE? NEXT TIME, I'D LIKE TO LEARN FRENCH BEFORE WE GO - OOH, LA LA!
I THINK I'LL TAKE A PICTURE OF THE PEOPLE TAKING PICTURES OF THE MONA LISA WITH MY COOL NEW SX70.
IT SEEMS THE PEOPLE ARE MORE INTERESTED IN HAVING A PICTURE OF IT BECAUSE IT'S FAMOUS, NOT BECAUSE IT'S SOME GREAT WORK OF ART.
1933 - 1945
DACHAU... NOW THERE'S A HISTORY LESSON I DIDN'T GET IN SCHOOL - NOT THAT I GOT ANY HISTORY AT ALL!

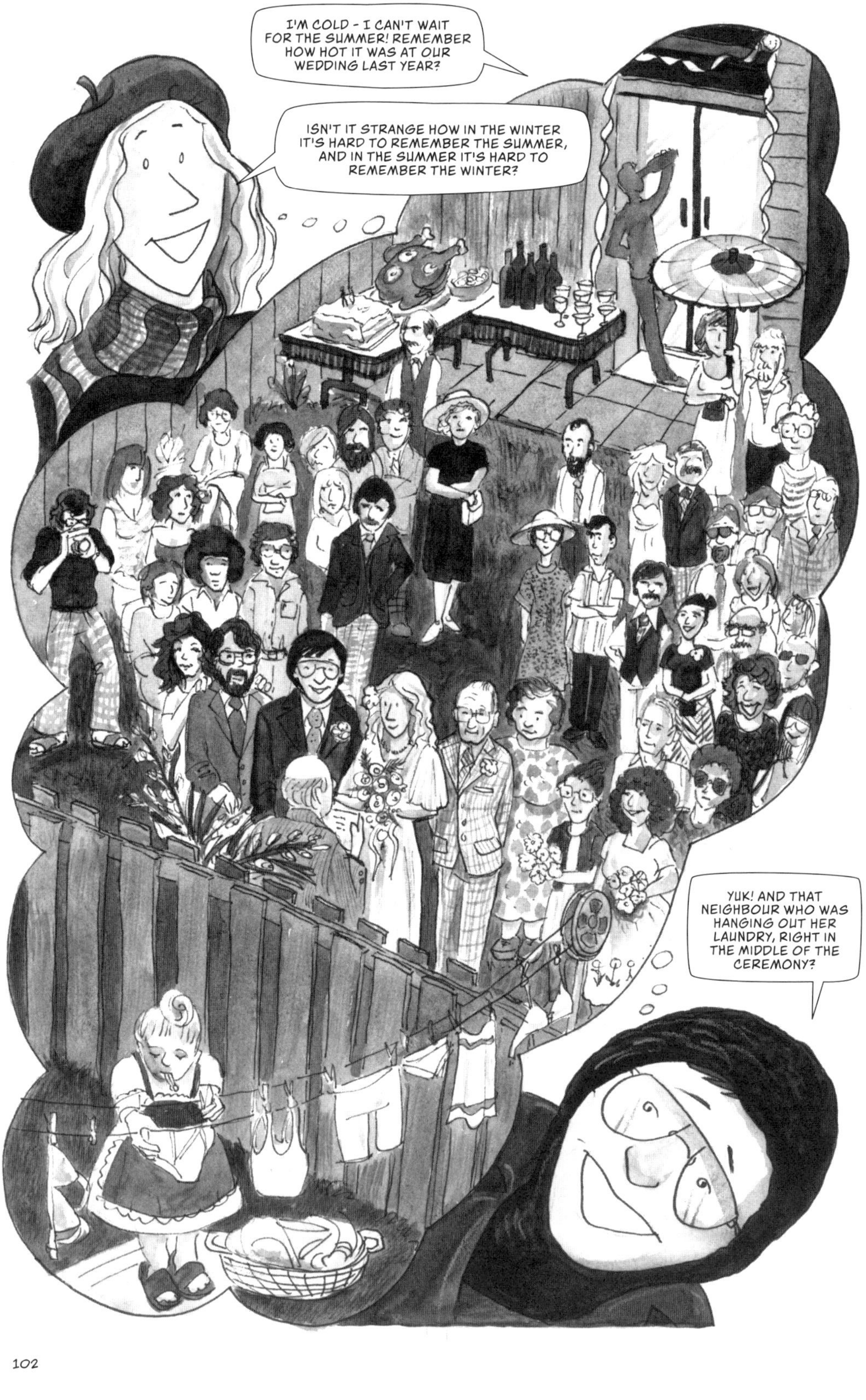
I'M COLD - I CAN'T WAIT FOR THE SUMMER! REMEMBER HOW HOT IT WAS AT OUR WEDDING LAST YEAR?
ISN'T IT STRANGE HOW IN THE WINTER IT'S HARD TO REMEMBER THE SUMMER, AND IN THE SUMMER IT'S HARD TO REMEMBER THE WINTER?
YUK! AND THAT NEIGHBOUR WHO WAS HANGING OUT HER LAUNDRY, RIGHT IN THE MIDDLE OF THE CEREMONY?

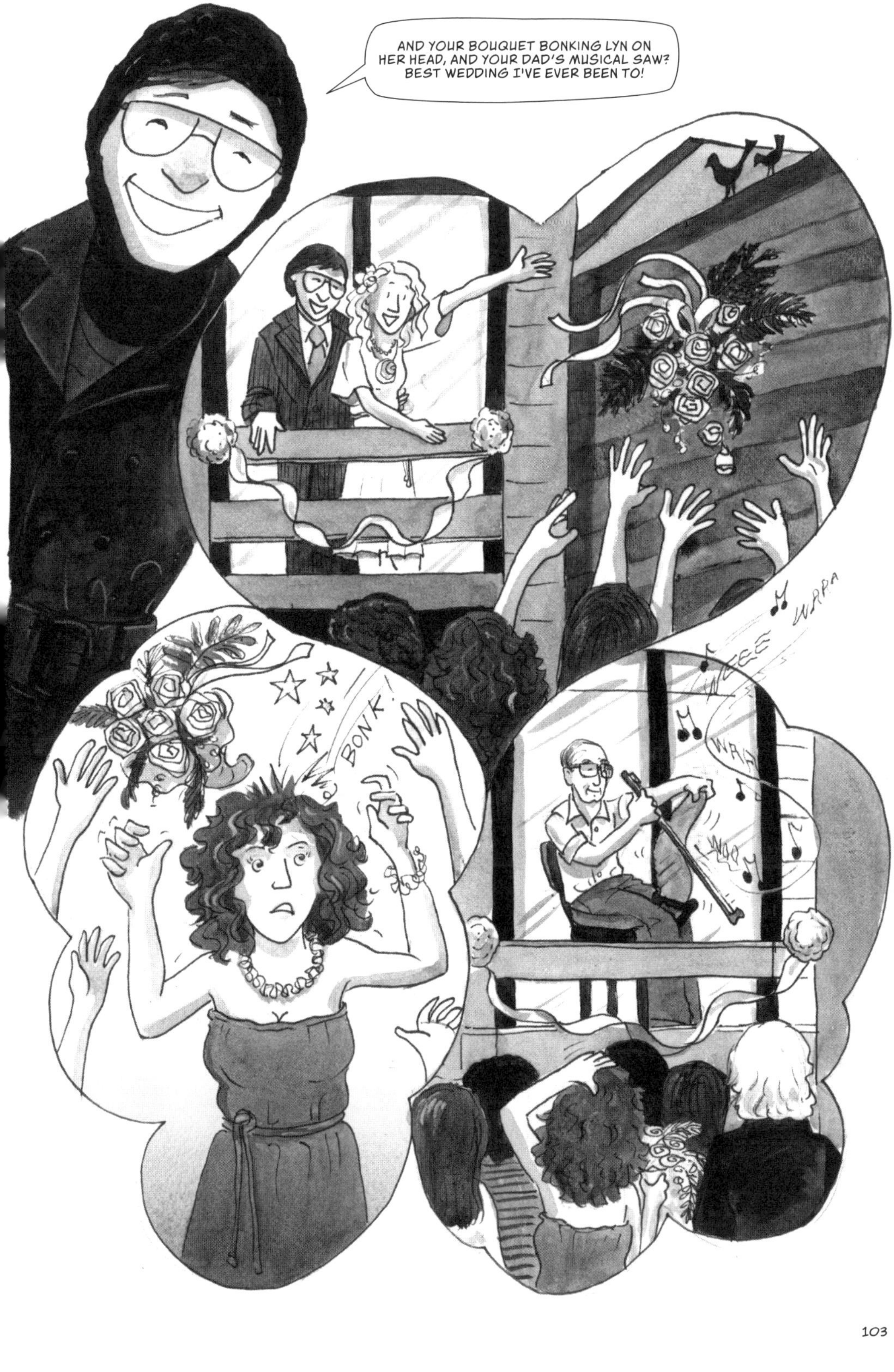
AND YOUR BOUQUET BONKING LYN ON HER HEAD, AND YOUR DAD'S MUSICAL SAW? BEST WEDDING I'VE EVER BEEN TO!
BONK!
WAA

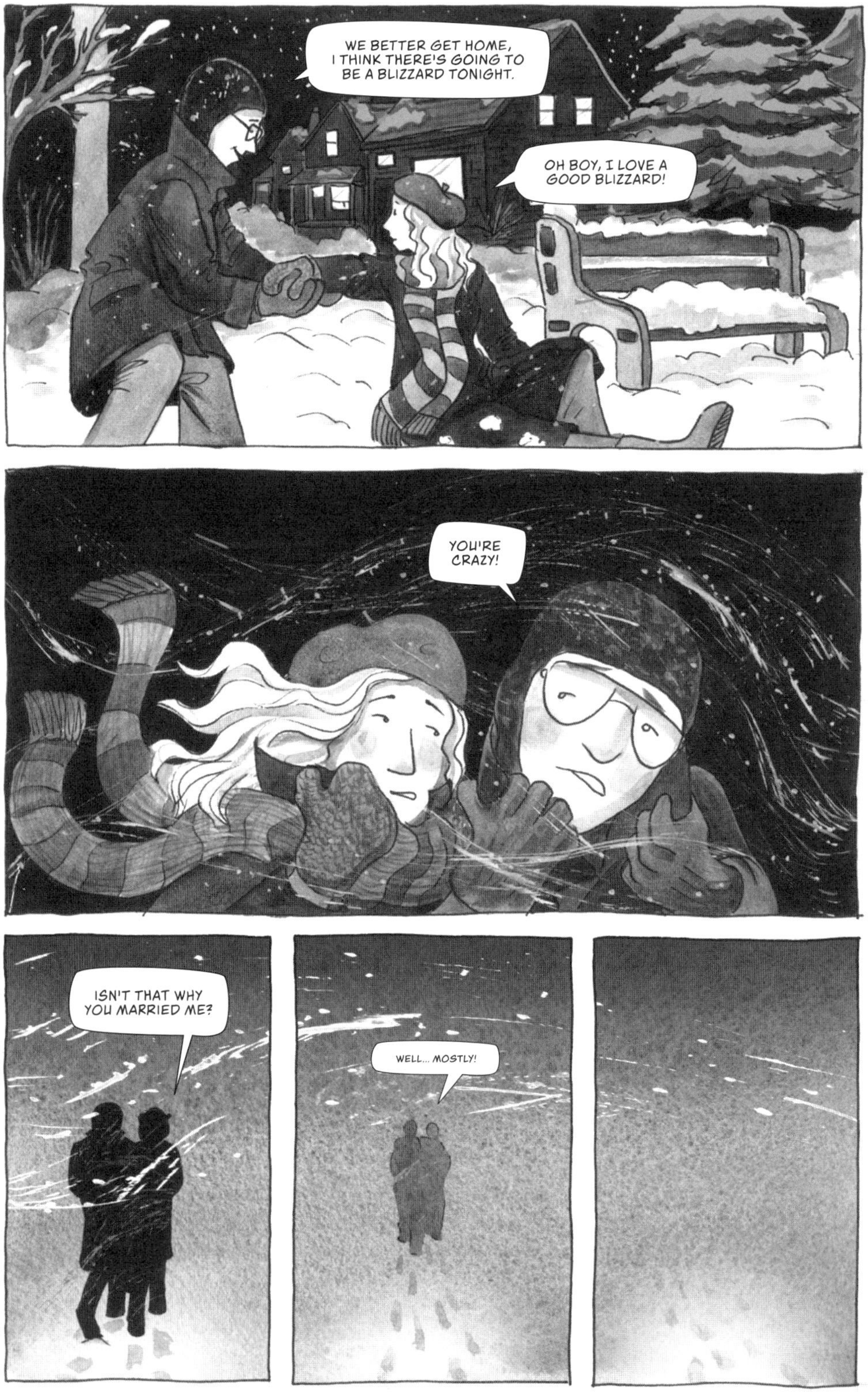
WE BETTER GET HOME, I THINK THERE'S GOING TO BE A BLIZZARD TONIGHT.
OH BOY, I LOVE A GOOD BLIZZARD!
YOU'RE CRAZY!
ISN'T THAT WHY YOU MARRIED ME?
WELL... MOSTLY!

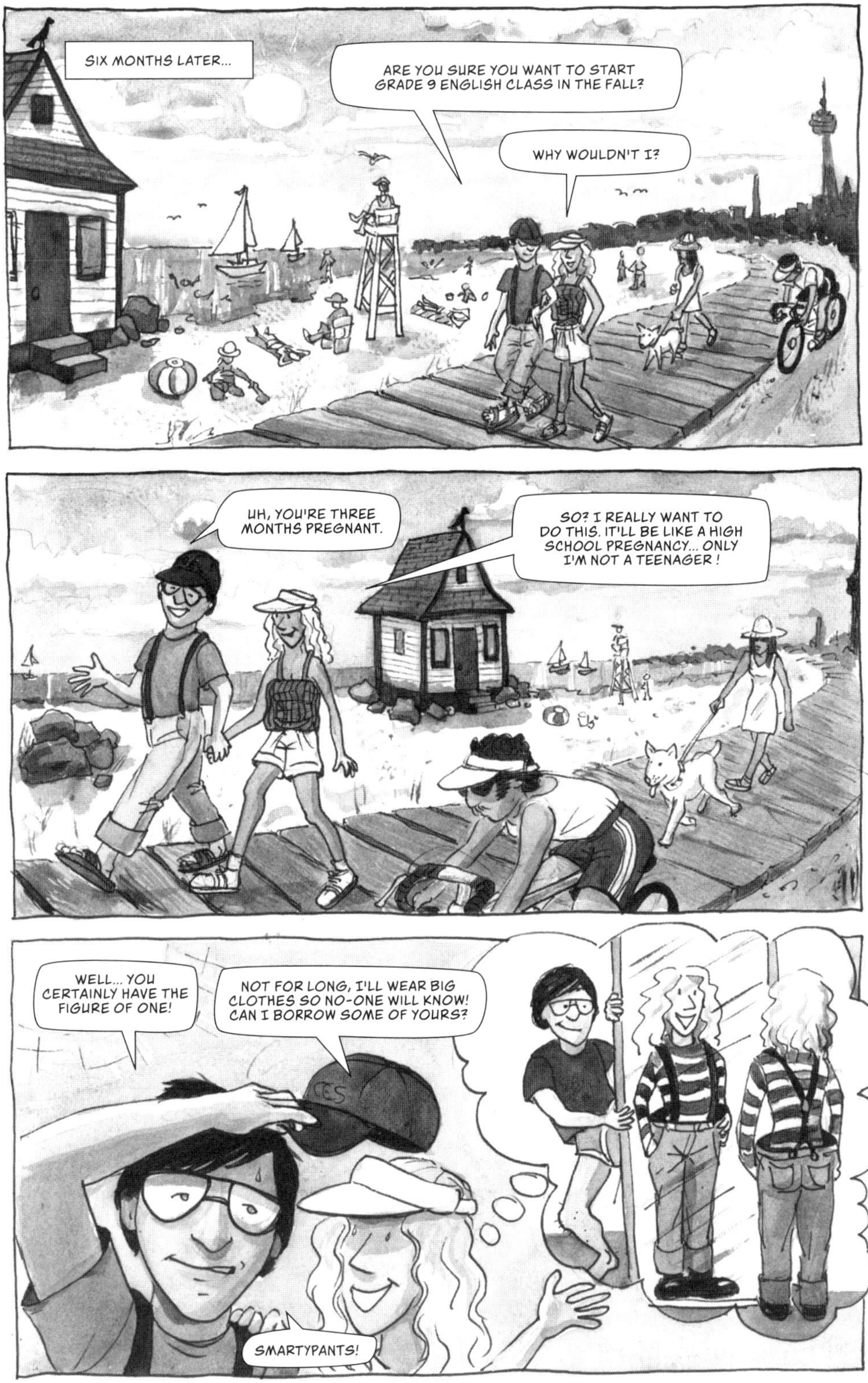
SIX MONTHS LATER...
ARE YOU SURE YOU WANT TO START GRADE 9 ENGLISH CLASS IN THE FALL?
WHY WOULDN'T I?
UH, YOU'RE THREE MONTHS PREGNANT.
SO? I REALLY WANT TO DO THIS. IT'LL BE LIKE A HIGH SCHOOL PREGNANCY... ONLY I'M NOT A TEENAGER !
WELL... YOU CERTAINLY HAVE THE FIGURE OF ONE!
NOT FOR LONG, I'LL WEAR BIG CLOTHES SO NO-ONE WILL KNOW! CAN I BORROW SOME OF YOURS?
CES
SMARTYPANTS!

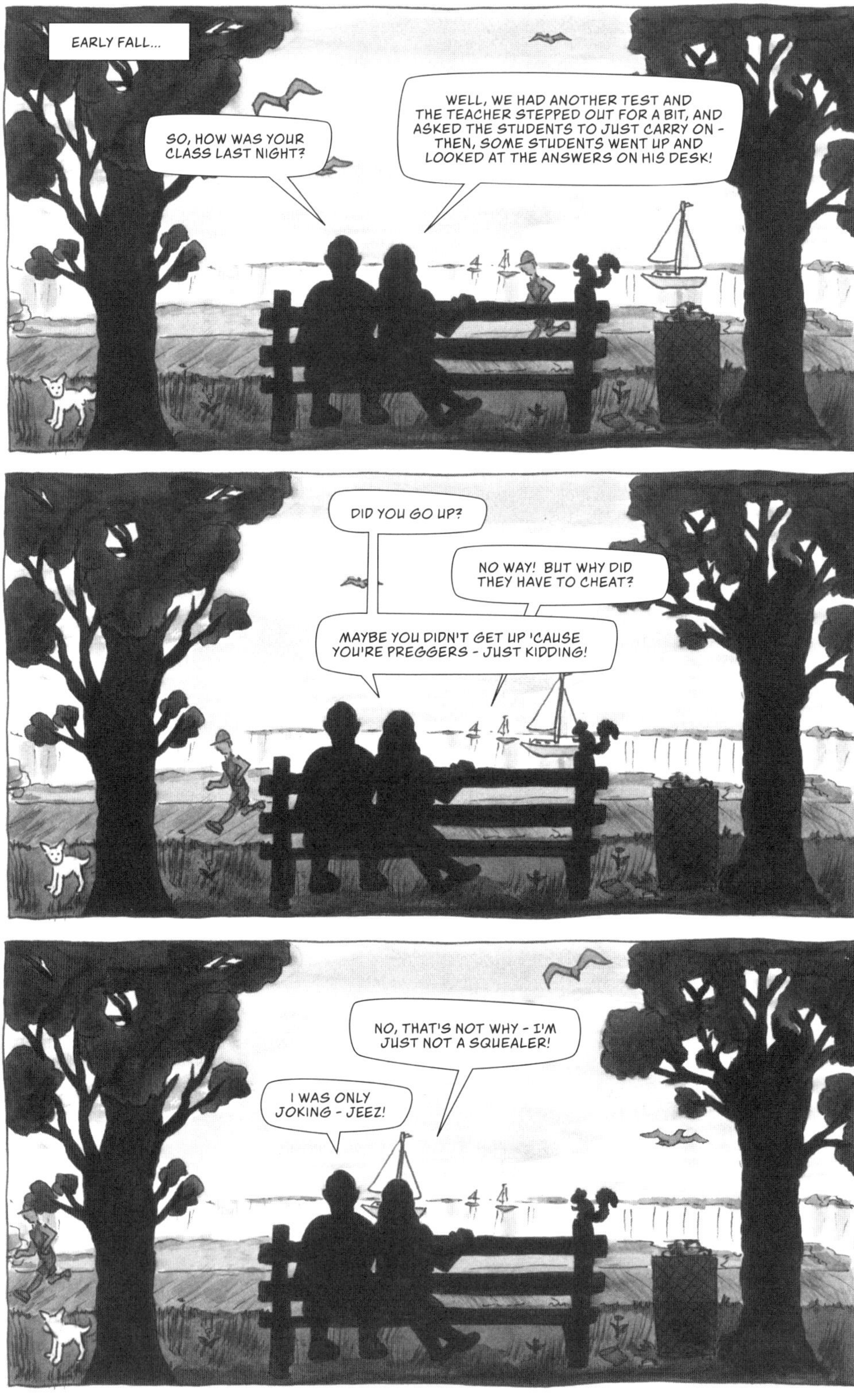
EARLY FALL...
SO, HOW WAS YOUR CLASS LAST NIGHT?
WELL, WE HAD ANOTHER TEST AND THE TEACHER STEPPED OUT FOR A BIT, AND ASKED THE STUDENTS TO JUST CARRY ON - THEN, SOME STUDENTS WENT UP AND LOOKED AT THE ANSWERS ON HIS DESK!
DID YOU GO UP?
NO WAY! BUT WHY DID THEY HAVE TO CHEAT?
MAYBE YOU DIDN'T GET UP 'CAUSE YOU'RE PREGGERS - JUST KIDDING!
NO, THAT'S NOT WHY - I'M JUST NOT A SQUEALER!
I WAS ONLY JOKING - JEEZ!

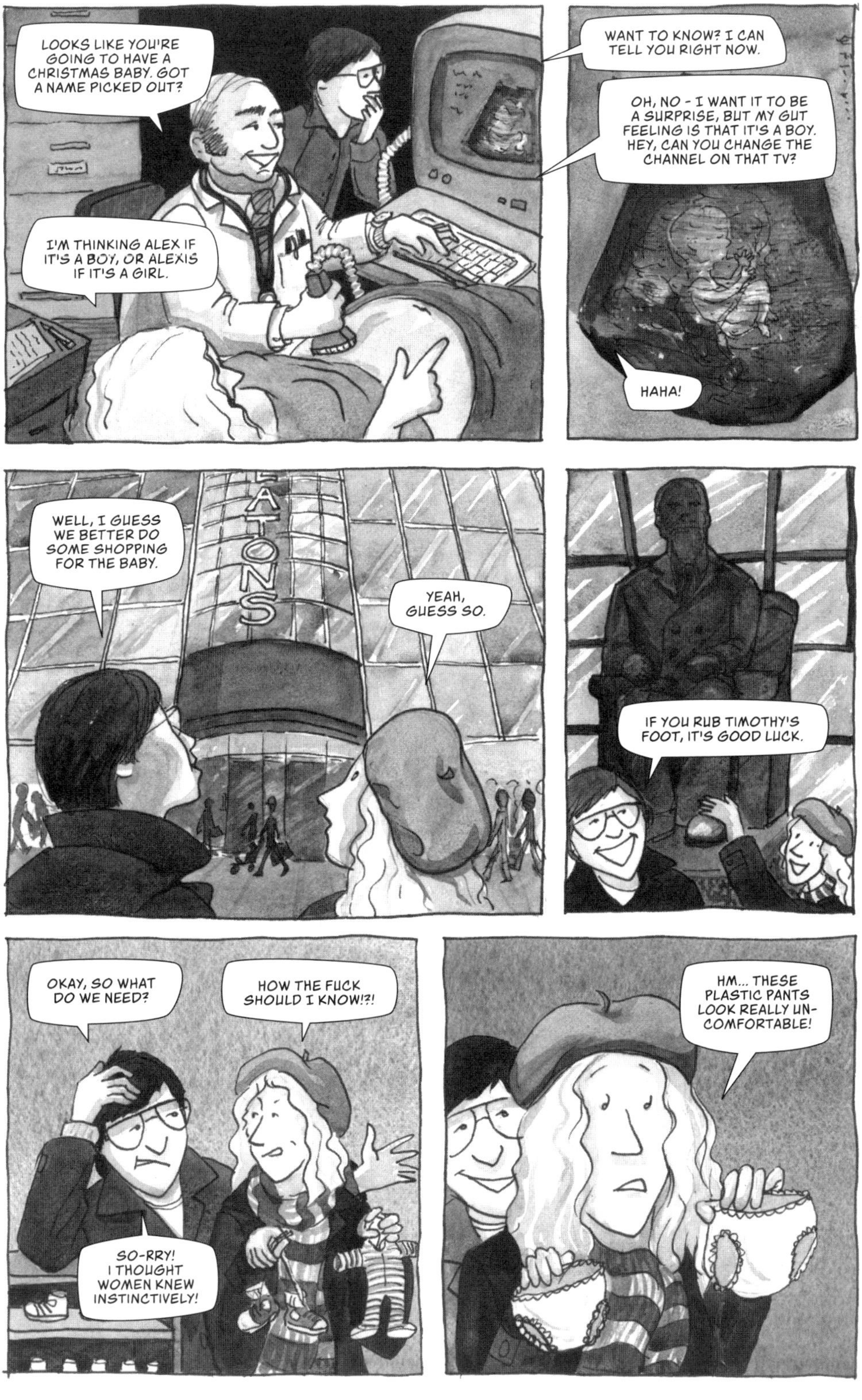
LOOKS LIKE YOU'RE GOING TO HAVE A CHRISTMAS BABY. GOT A NAME PICKED OUT?
I'M THINKING ALEX IF IT'S A BOY, OR ALEXIS IF IT'S A GIRL.
WANT TO KNOW? I CAN TELL YOU RIGHT NOW.
OH, NO - I WANT IT TO BE A SURPRISE, BUT MY GUT FEELING IS THAT IT'S A BOY. HEY, CAN YOU CHANGE THE CHANNEL ON THAT TV?
HAHA!
WELL, I GUESS WE BETTER DO SOME SHOPPING FOR THE BABY.
YEAH, GUESS SO.
IF YOU RUB TIMOTHY'S FOOT, IT'S GOOD LUCK.
OKAY, SO WHAT DO WE NEED?
HOW THE FUCK SHOULD I KNOW!?!
SO-RRY! I THOUGHT WOMEN KNEW INSTINCTIVELY!
HM... THESE PLASTIC PANTS LOOK REALLY UN-COMFORTABLE!

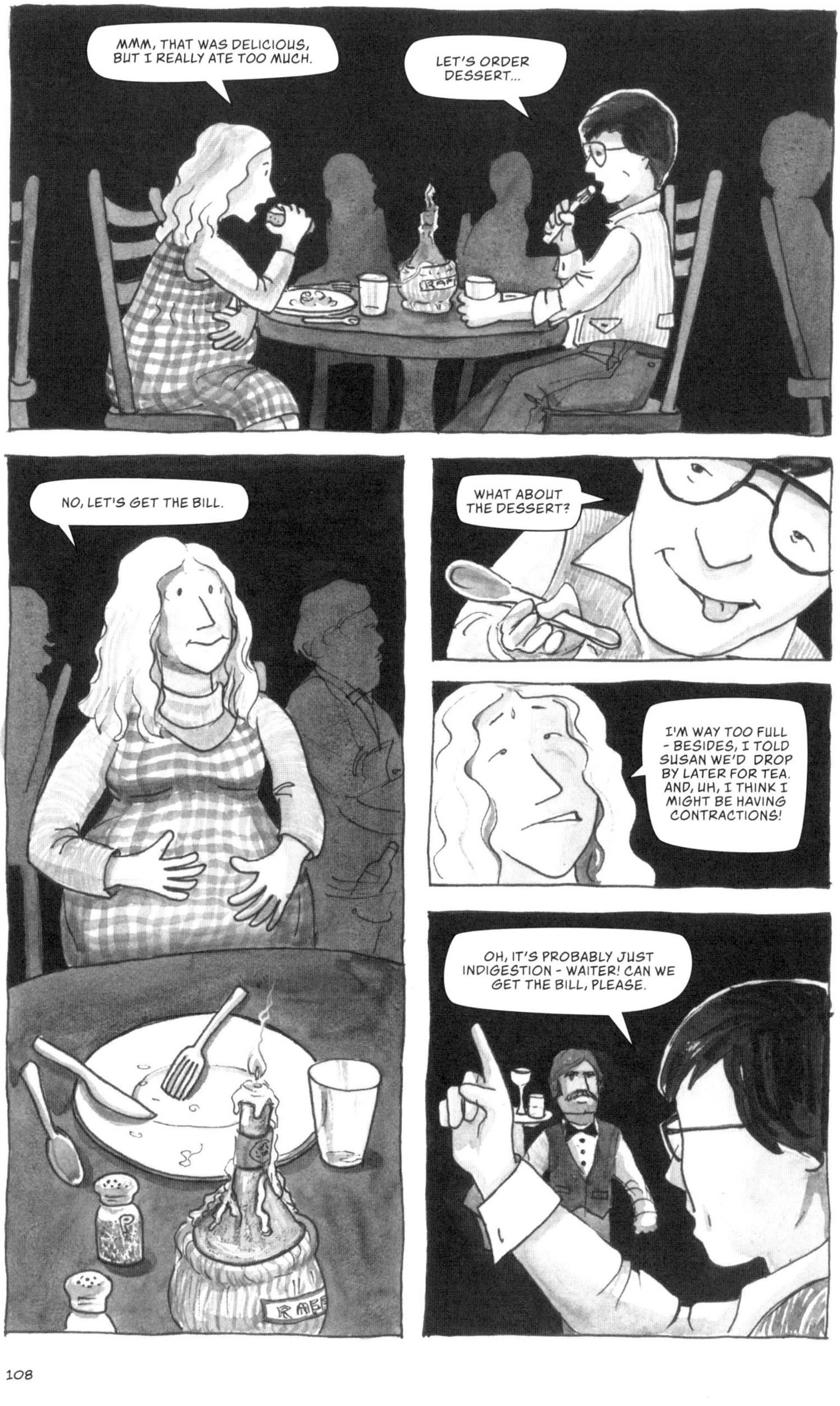
MMM, THAT WAS DELICIOUS, BUT I REALLY ATE TOO MUCH.
LET'S ORDER DESSERT...
NO, LET'S GET THE BILL.
WHAT ABOUT THE DESSERT?
I'M WAY TOO FULL - BESIDES, I TOLD SUSAN WE'D DROP BY LATER FOR TEA. AND, UH, I THINK I MIGHT BE HAVING CONTRACTIONS!
OH, IT'S PROBABLY JUST INDIGESTION - WAITER! CAN WE GET THE BILL, PLEASE.

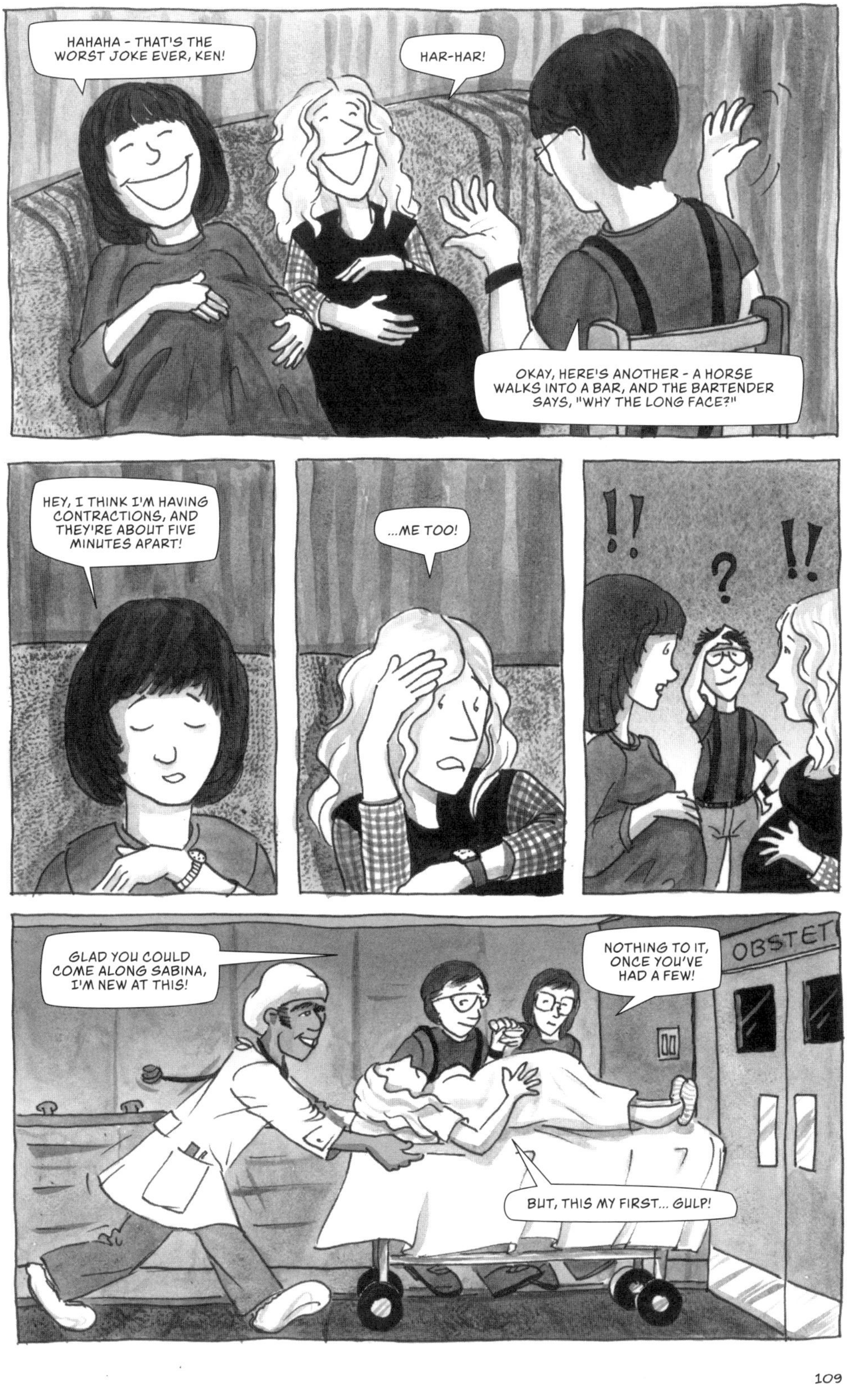
HAHAHA - THAT'S THE WORST JOKE EVER, KEN!
HAR-HAR!
OKAY, HERE'S ANOTHER - A HORSE WALKS INTO A BAR, AND THE BARTENDER SAYS, "WHY THE LONG FACE?"
HEY, I THINK I'M HAVING CONTRACTIONS, AND THEY'RE ABOUT FIVE MINUTES APART!
...ME TOO!
!!
?
!!
GLAD YOU COULD COME ALONG SABINA, I'M NEW AT THIS!
NOTHING TO IT, ONCE YOU'VE HAD A FEW!
BUT, THIS MY FIRST... GULP!
OBSTET

SHALLOW BREATHS, IT'LL BE ALL OVER SOON.

IT'S BEEN 16 HOURS!!!

WHERE'S THAT DAMN ANAESTHETIST?!

ARRRRGH! -AAAAAH!

SHIT, FUCK, PISS - YOU ASSHOLE!

WAH! WAH! WAAAAAAAAAAAHHH!

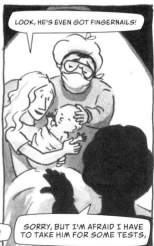

LOOK, HE'S EVEN GOT FINGERNAILS!

SORRY, BUT I'M AFRAID I HAVE TO TAKE HIM FOR SOME TESTS,

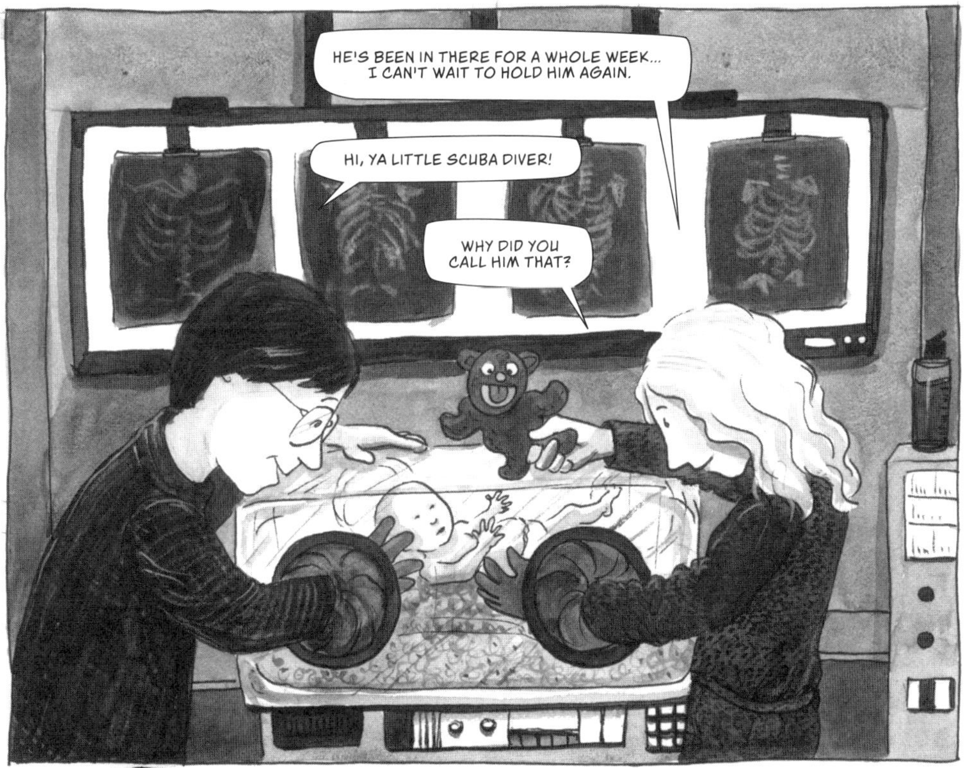
HE'S BEEN IN THERE FOR A WHOLE WEEK... I CAN'T WAIT TO HOLD HIM AGAIN.
HI, YA LITTLE SCUBA DIVER!
WHY DID YOU CALL HIM THAT?

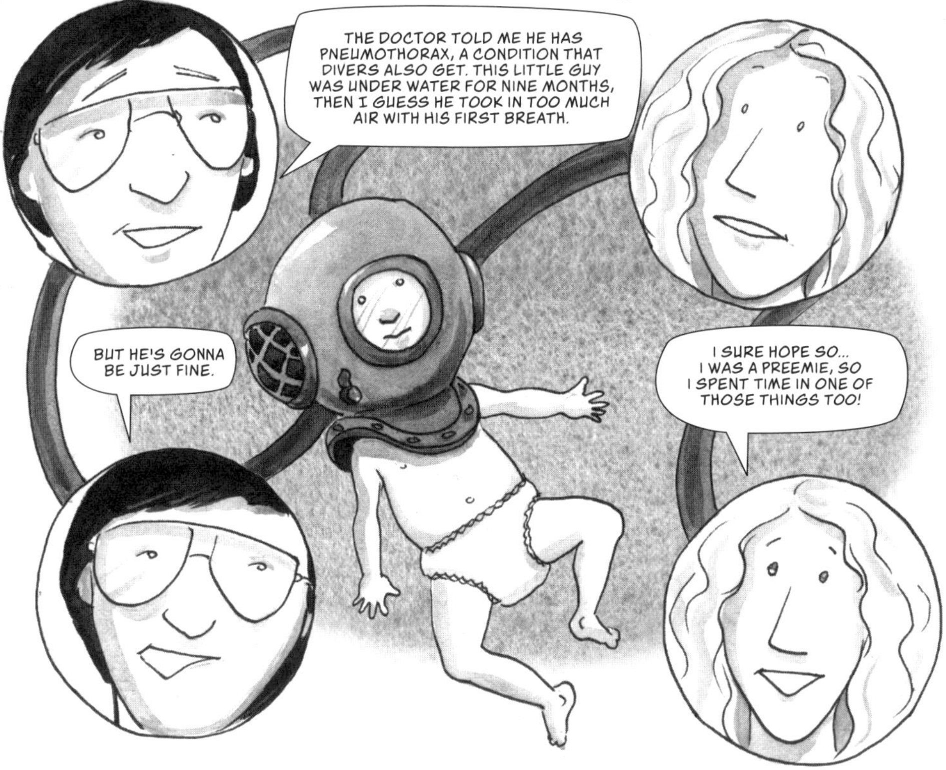
THE DOCTOR TOLD ME HE HAS PNEUMOTHORAX, A CONDITION THAT DIVERS ALSO GET. THIS LITTLE GUY WAS UNDER WATER FOR NINE MONTHS, THEN I GUESS HE TOOK IN TOO MUCH AIR WITH HIS FIRST BREATH.
BUT HE'S GONNA BE JUST FINE.
I SURE HOPE SO... I WAS A PREEMIE, SO I SPENT TIME IN ONE OF THOSE THINGS TOO!

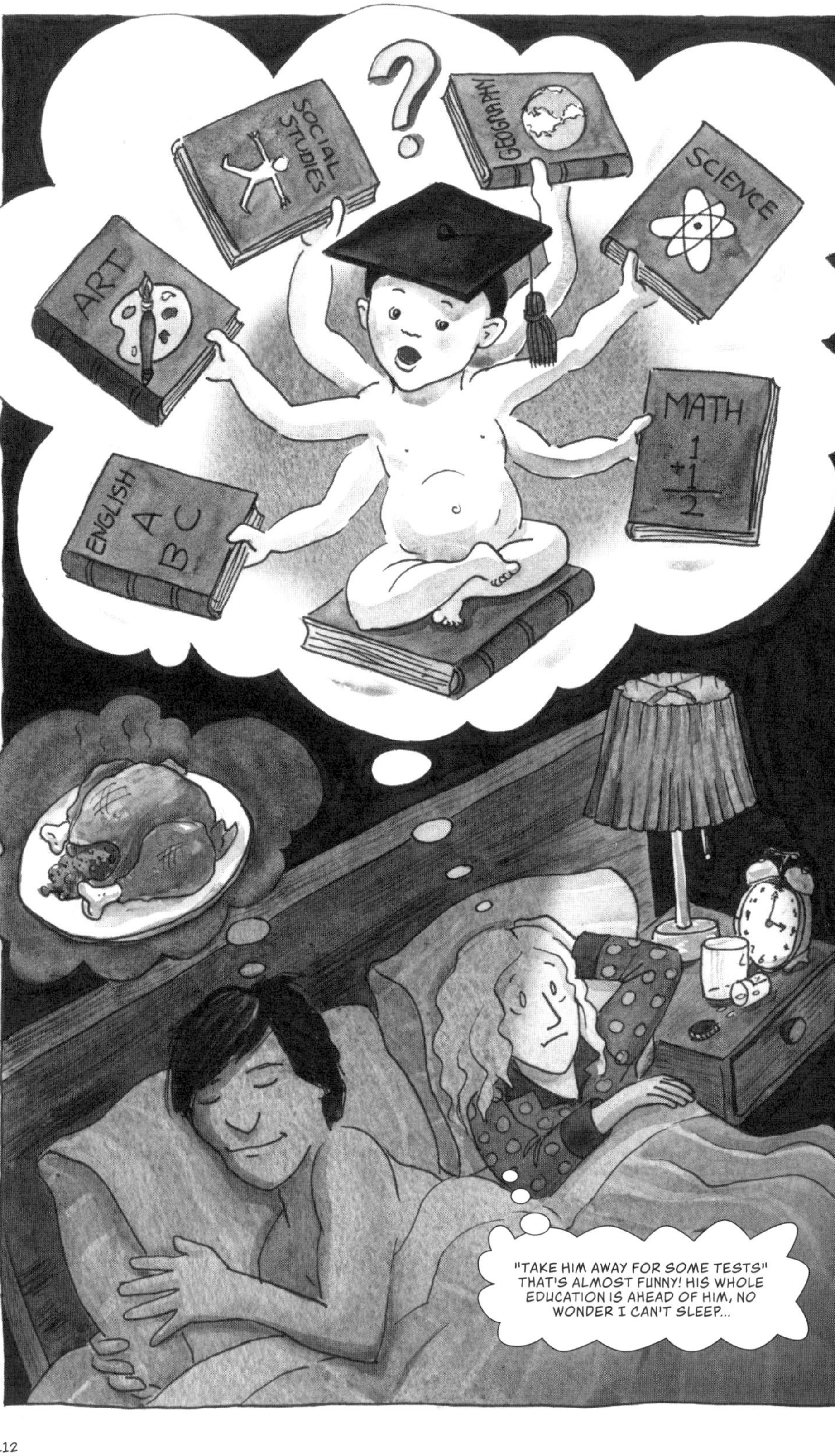
SOCIAL STUDIES
GEOGRAPHY
SCIENCE
ART
MATH
1
+1
2
ENGLISH
A
B C
"TAKE HIM AWAY FOR SOME TESTS" THAT'S ALMOST FUNNY! HIS WHOLE EDUCATION IS AHEAD OF HIM, NO WONDER I CAN'T SLEEP...

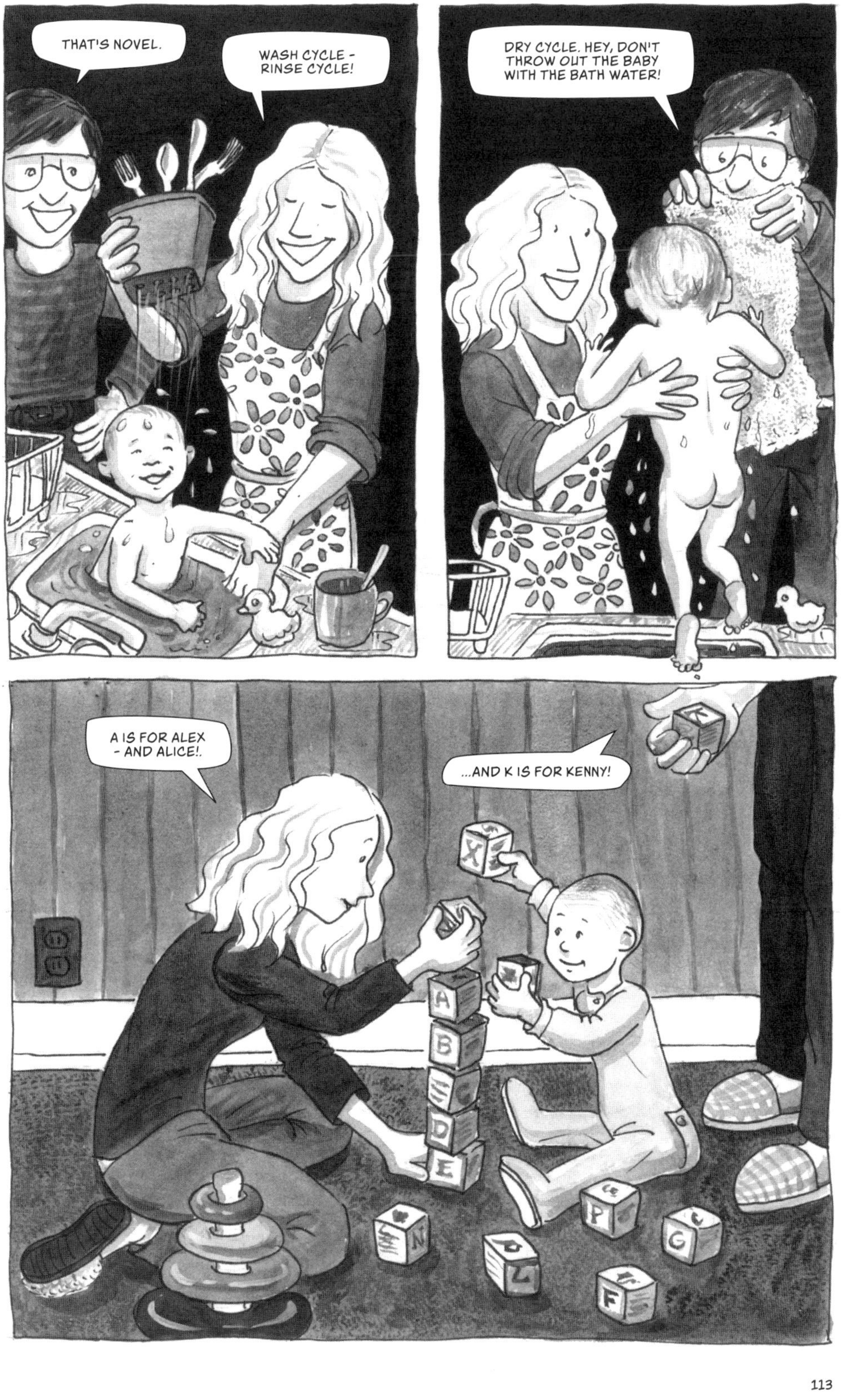
THAT'S NOVEL.
WASH CYCLE - RINSE CYCLE!
DRY CYCLE. HEY, DON'T THROW OUT THE BABY WITH THE BATH WATER!
A IS FOR ALEX - AND ALICE!.
...AND K IS FOR KENNY!

C D B, D B S A
B-Z B, S N T?
UH-OH!
UH-OH!
TAKE OFF, YOU HOSER!
WHAT'RE YA READING NOW?
THE GUTENBERG GALAXY. I WANT TO KNOW WHAT McLUHAN SAYS ABOUT KING LEAR. I HAVE AN ESSAY TO WRITE, AND I'M NOT SURE WHAT ANGLE TO TAKE.
I CAN HELP WITH THE GRAMMAR. WHEN DO YOU HAVE TIME TO STUDY?
WHEN ALEX NAPS.
LISTEN TO THIS; A PRINCIPLE THEME OF KING LEAR, NAMELY, THE ISOLATION OF THE VISUAL SENSE, IS A KIND OF BLINDNESS.

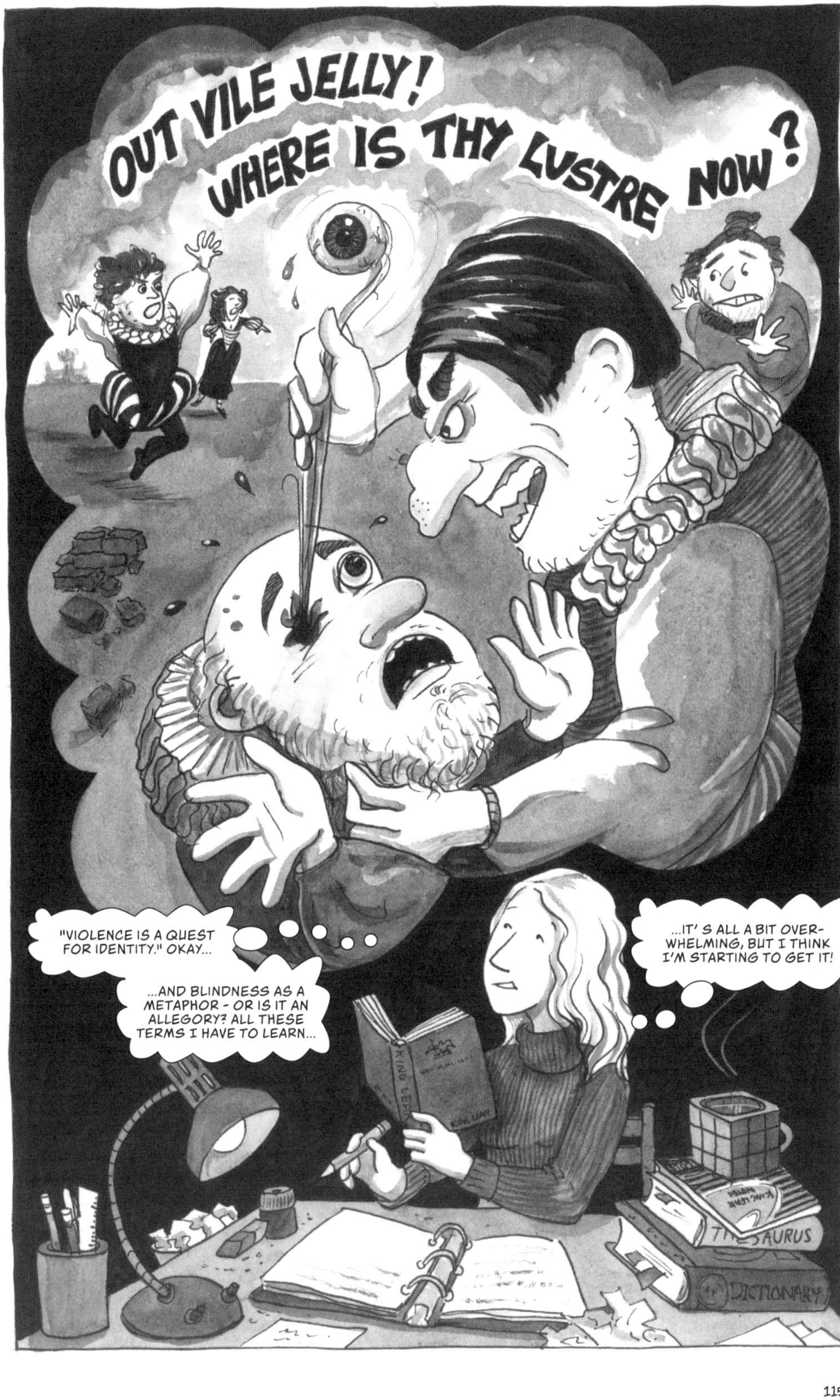
OUT VILE JELLY! WHERE IS THY LUSTRE NOW?
"VIOLENCE IS A QUEST FOR IDENTITY." OKAY...
...AND BLINDNESS AS A METAPHOR - OR IS IT AN ALLEGORY? ALL THESE TERMS I HAVE TO LEARN...
...IT' S ALL A BIT OVER-WHELMING, BUT I THINK I'M STARTING TO GET IT!
KING LEAR
THESAURUS
DICTIONARY

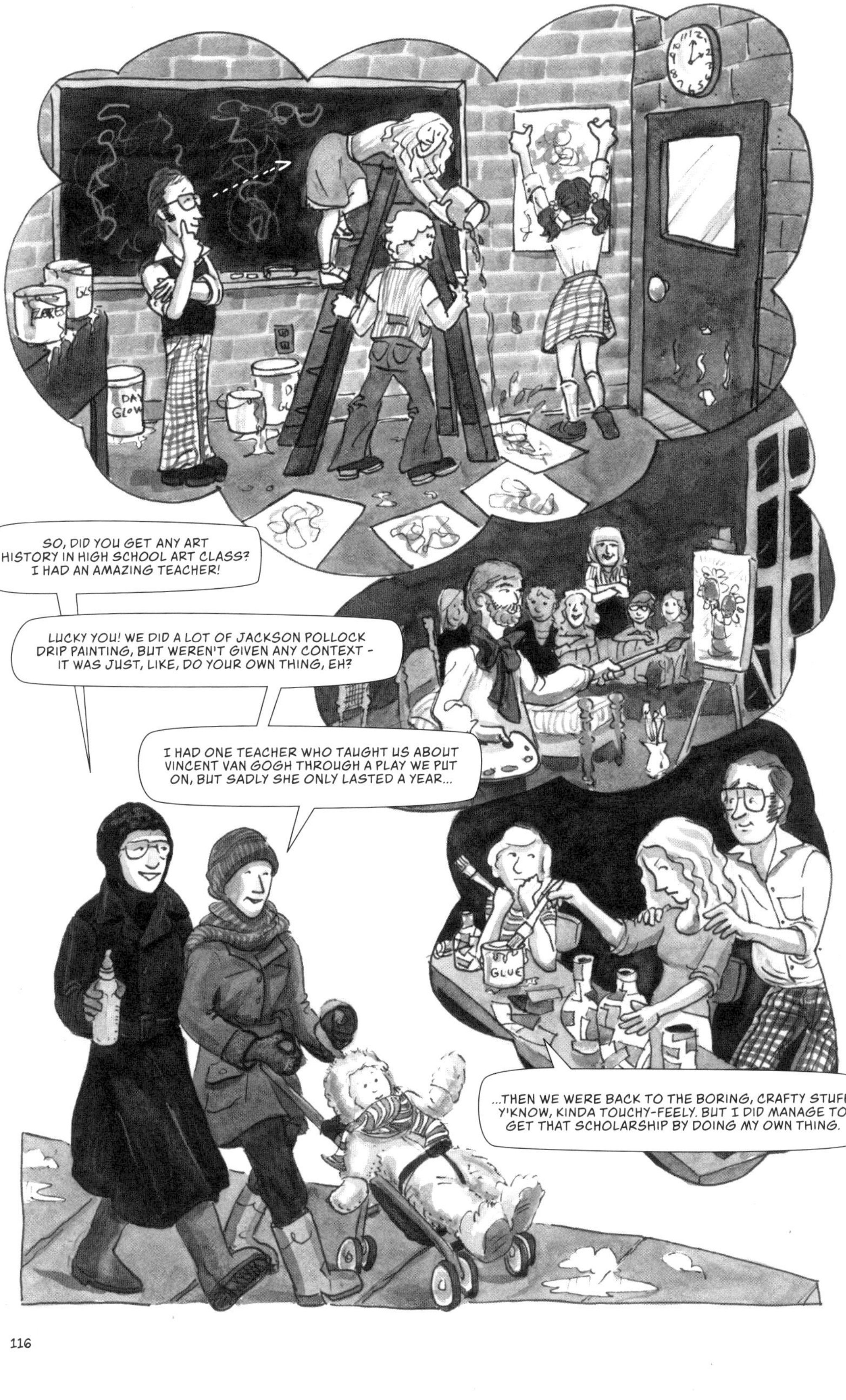

DAY GLOW
DAY GLOW
GLUE
SO, DID YOU GET ANY ART HISTORY IN HIGH SCHOOL ART CLASS? I HAD AN AMAZING TEACHER!
LUCKY YOU! WE DID A LOT OF JACKSON POLLOCK DRIP PAINTING, BUT WEREN'T GIVEN ANY CONTEXT - IT WAS JUST, LIKE, DO YOUR OWN THING, EH?
I HAD ONE TEACHER WHO TAUGHT US ABOUT VINCENT VAN GOGH THROUGH A PLAY WE PUT ON, BUT SADLY SHE ONLY LASTED A YEAR...
...THEN WE WERE BACK TO THE BORING, CRAFTY STUFF, Y'KNOW, KINDA TOUCHY-FEELY. BUT I DID MANAGE TO GET THAT SCHOLARSHIP BY DOING MY OWN THING.

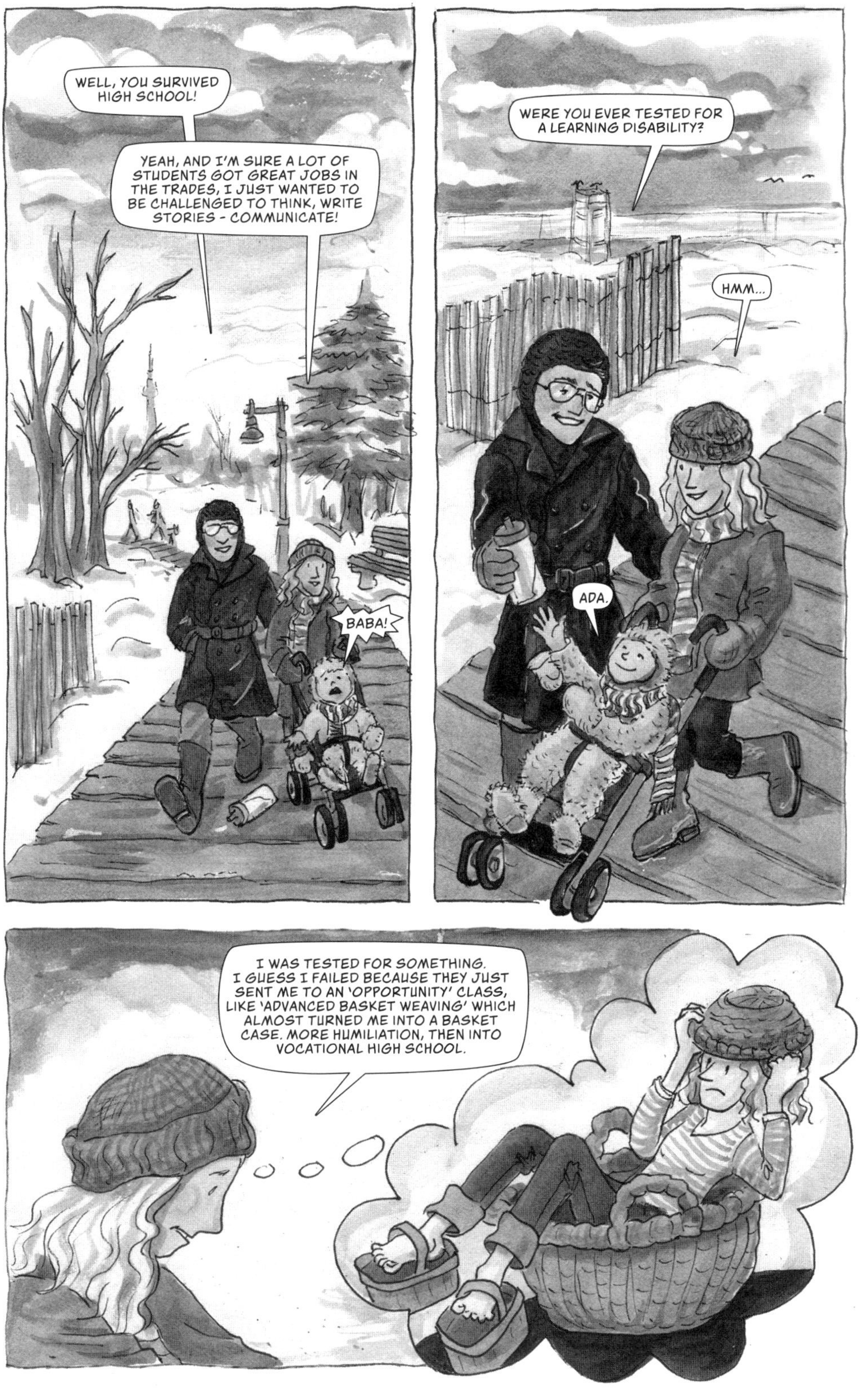
WELL, YOU SURVIVED HIGH SCHOOL!
YEAH, AND I'M SURE A LOT OF STUDENTS GOT GREAT JOBS IN THE TRADES, I JUST WANTED TO BE CHALLENGED TO THINK, WRITE STORIES - COMMUNICATE!
BABA!
WERE YOU EVER TESTED FOR A LEARNING DISABILITY?
HMM...
ADA.
I WAS TESTED FOR SOMETHING. I GUESS I FAILED BECAUSE THEY JUST SENT ME TO AN 'OPPORTUNITY' CLASS, LIKE 'ADVANCED BASKET WEAVING' WHICH ALMOST TURNED ME INTO A BASKET CASE. MORE HUMILIATION, THEN INTO VOCATIONAL HIGH SCHOOL.

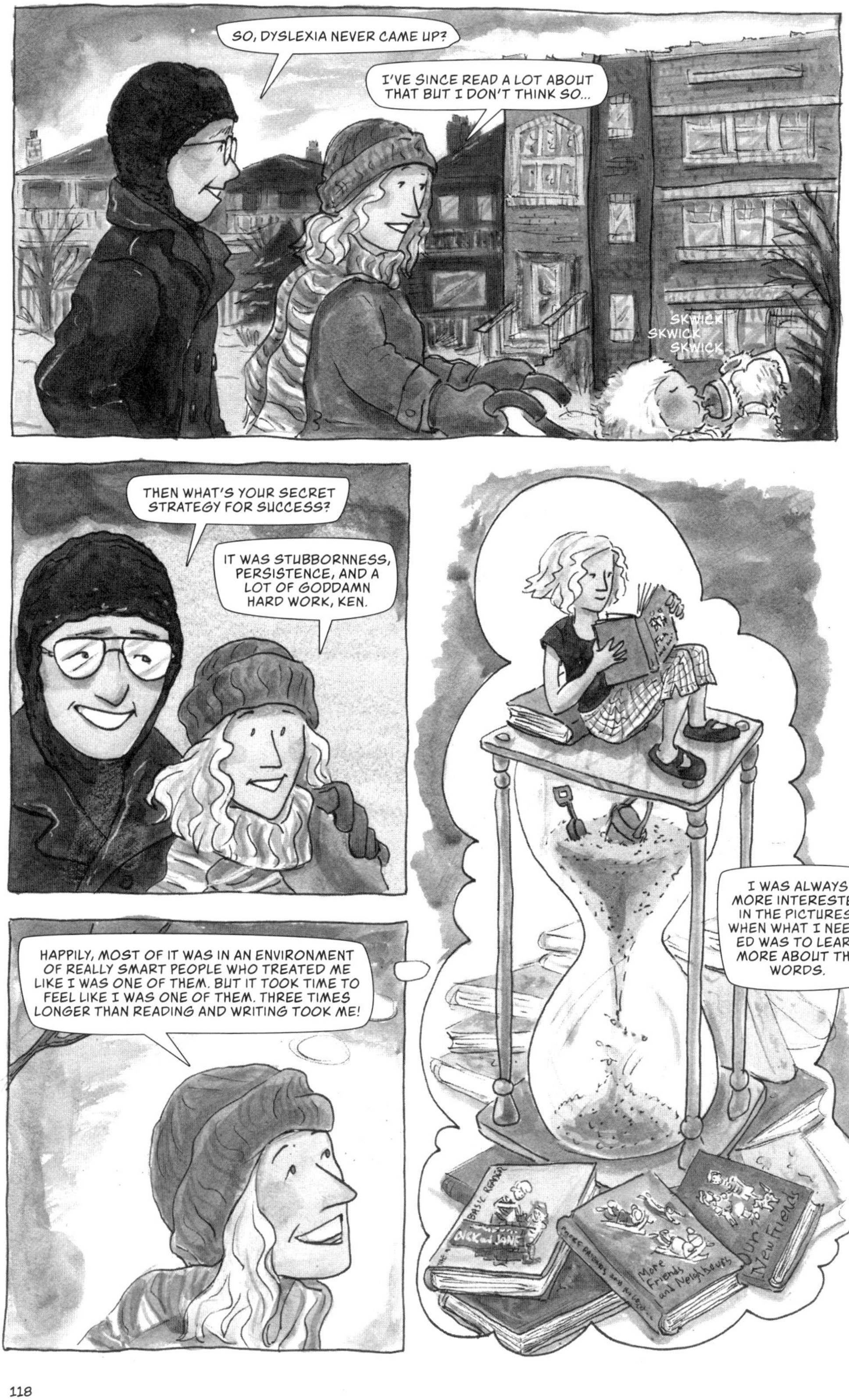
SO, DYSLEXIA NEVER CAME UP?
I'VE SINCE READ A LOT ABOUT THAT BUT I DON'T THINK SO...
SKWICK SKWICK SKWICK
THEN WHAT'S YOUR SECRET STRATEGY FOR SUCCESS?
IT WAS STUBBORNNESS, PERSISTENCE, AND A LOT OF GODDAMN HARD WORK, KEN.
I WAS ALWAYS MORE INTERESTED IN THE PICTURES, WHEN WHAT I NEEDED WAS TO LEARN MORE ABOUT THE WORDS.
Dick and Jane
More Friends and Neighbors
Our New Friends
HAPPILY, MOST OF IT WAS IN AN ENVIRONMENT OF REALLY SMART PEOPLE WHO TREATED ME LIKE I WAS ONE OF THEM. BUT IT TOOK TIME TO FEEL LIKE I WAS ONE OF THEM. THREE TIMES LONGER THAN READING AND WRITING TOOK ME!

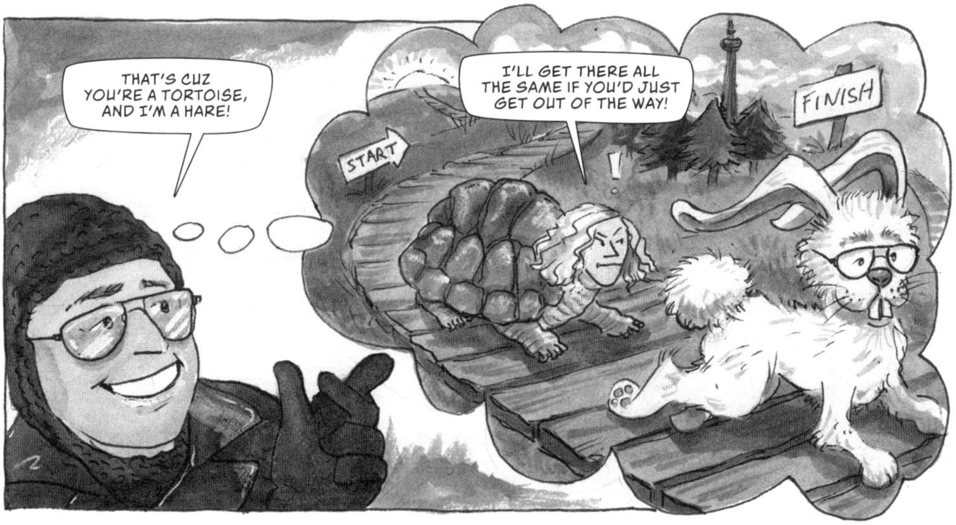
THAT'S CUZ YOU'RE A TORTOISE, AND I'M A HARE!
I'LL GET THERE ALL THE SAME IF YOU'D JUST GET OUT OF THE WAY!
START
FINISH
!

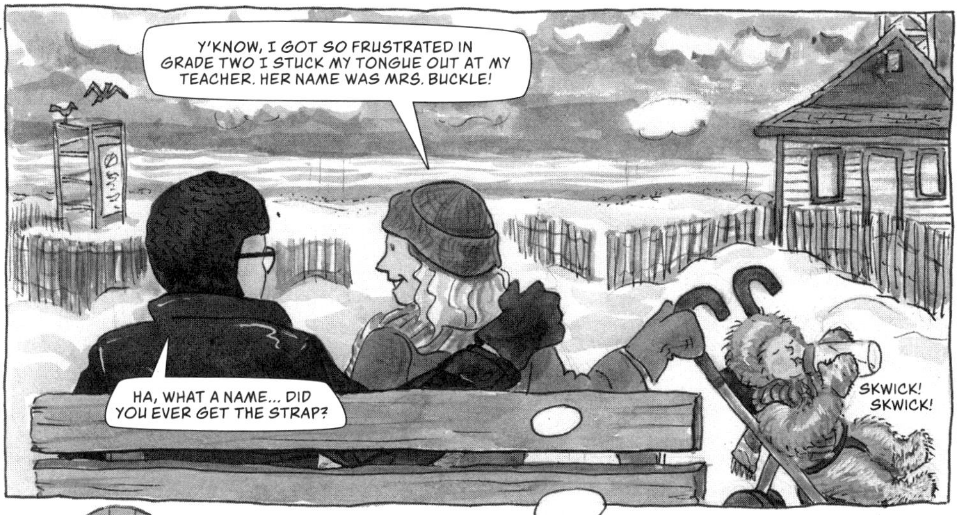
Y'KNOW, I GOT SO FRUSTRATED IN GRADE TWO I STUCK MY TONGUE OUT AT MY TEACHER. HER NAME WAS MRS. BUCKLE!
HA, WHAT A NAME... DID YOU EVER GET THE STRAP?
SKWICK! SKWICK!

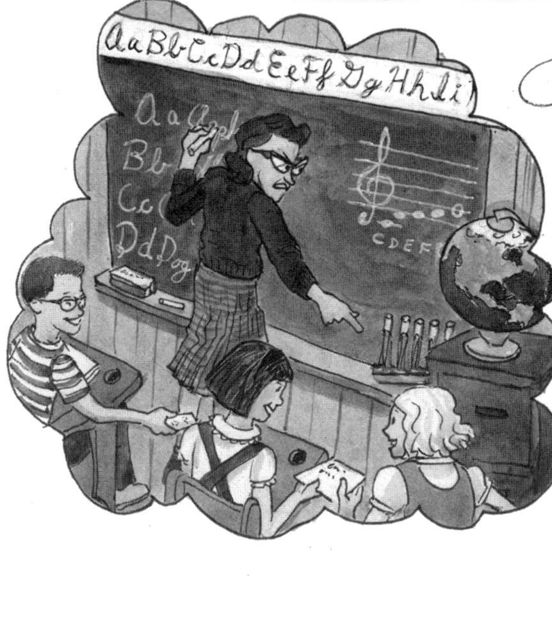
Aa Bb Cc Dd Ee Ff Gg Hh Ii
CDEF

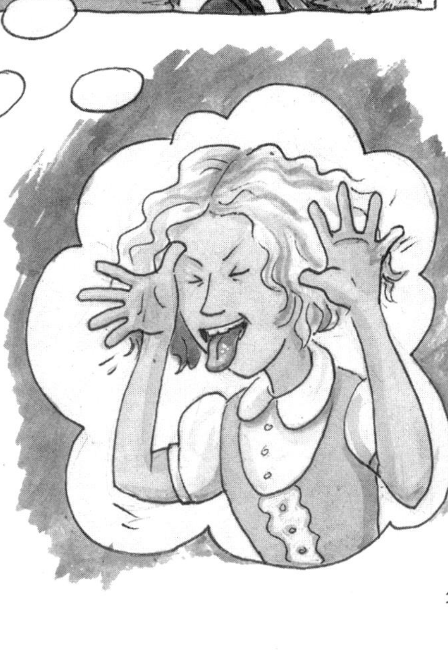

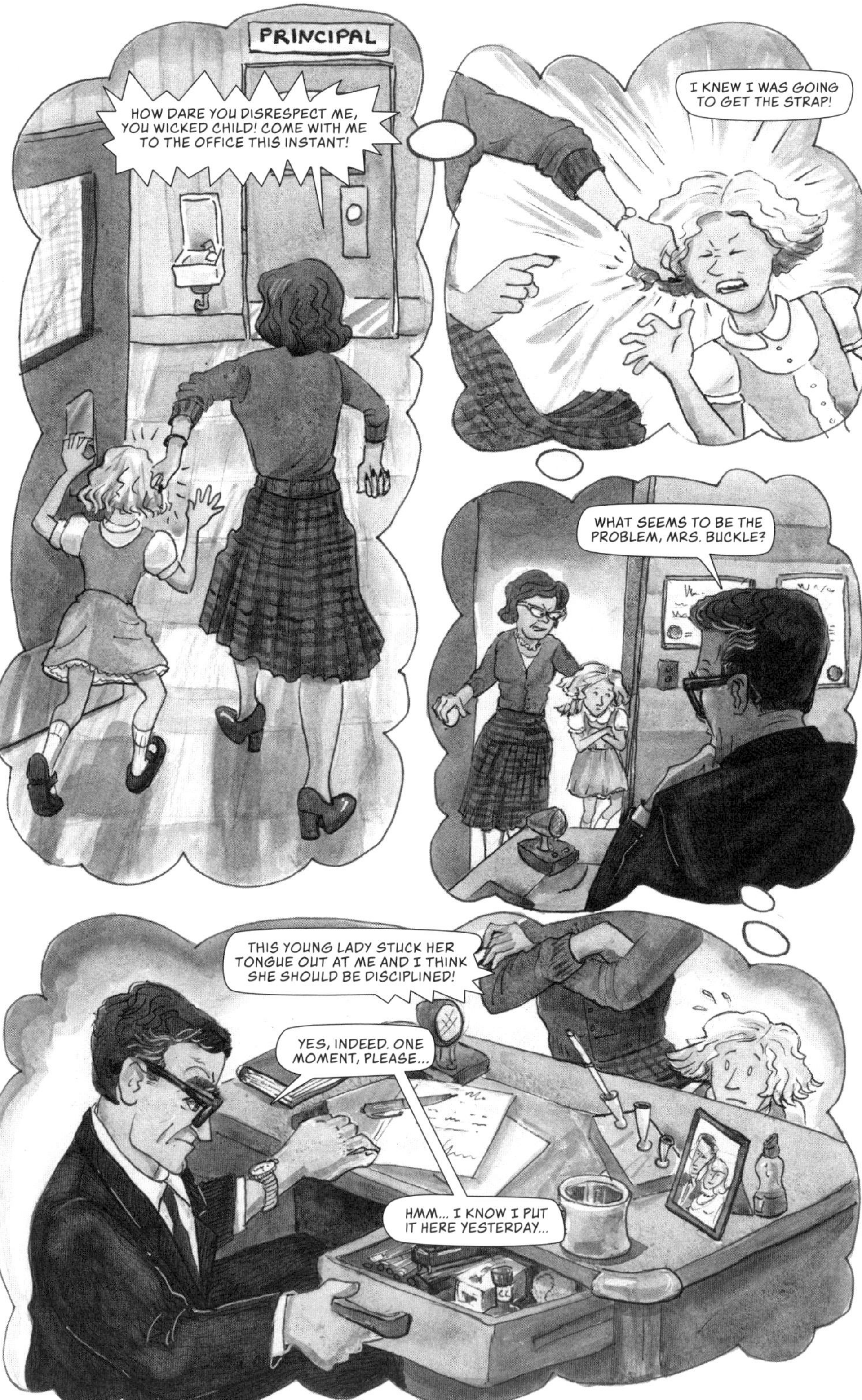
PRINCIPAL
HOW DARE YOU DISRESPECT ME, YOU WICKED CHILD! COME WITH ME TO THE OFFICE THIS INSTANT!
I KNEW I WAS GOING TO GET THE STRAP!
WHAT SEEMS TO BE THE PROBLEM, MRS. BUCKLE?
THIS YOUNG LADY STUCK HER TONGUE OUT AT ME AND I THINK SHE SHOULD BE DISCIPLINED!
YES, INDEED. ONE MOMENT, PLEASE...
HMM... I KNOW I PUT IT HERE YESTERDAY...

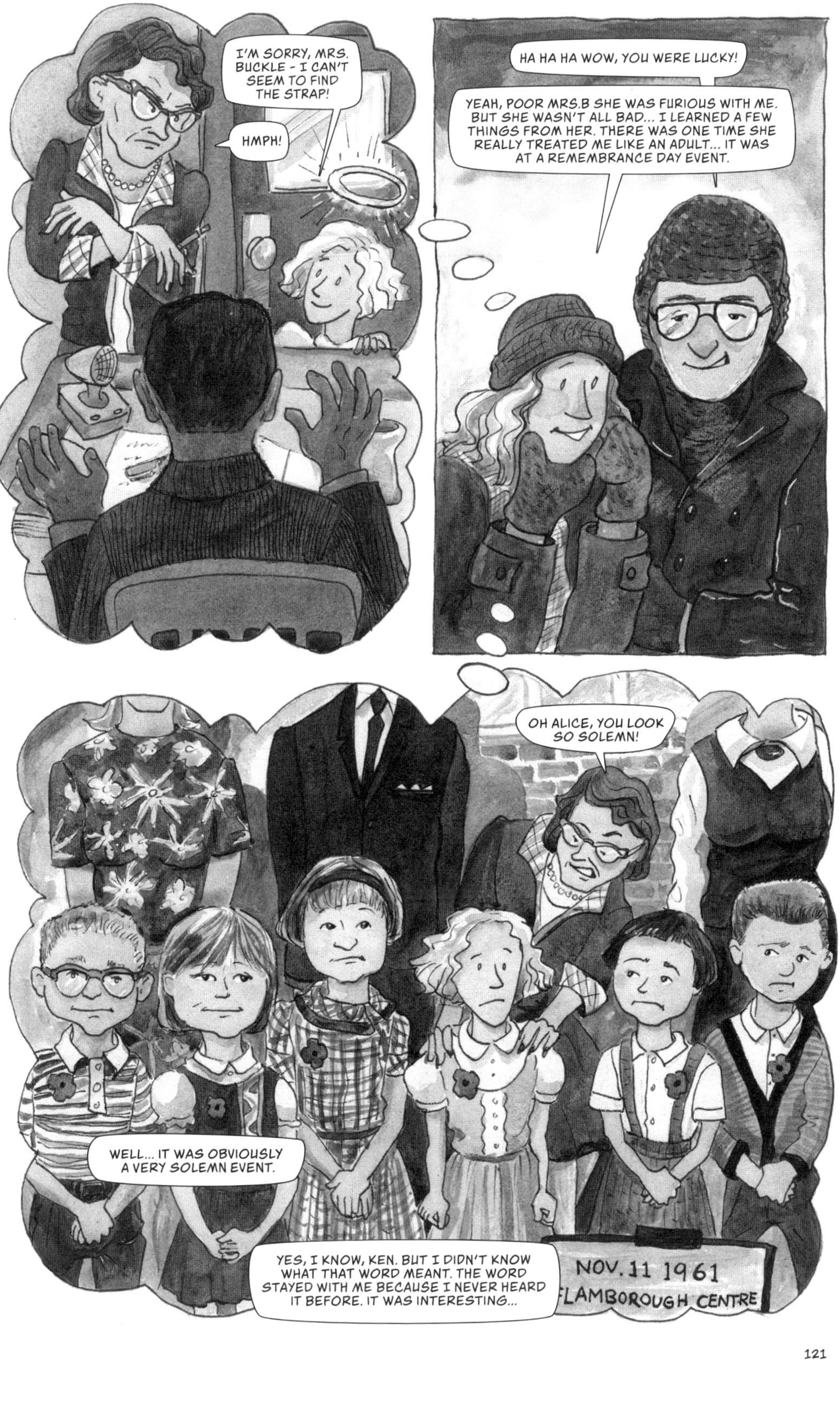
I'M SORRY, MRS. BUCKLE - I CAN'T SEEM TO FIND THE STRAP!
HMPH!
HA HA HA WOW, YOU WERE LUCKY!
YEAH, POOR MRS.B SHE WAS FURIOUS WITH ME. BUT SHE WASN'T ALL BAD... I LEARNED A FEW THINGS FROM HER. THERE WAS ONE TIME SHE REALLY TREATED ME LIKE AN ADULT... IT WAS AT A REMEMBRANCE DAY EVENT.
OH ALICE, YOU LOOK SO SOLEMN!
WELL... IT WAS OBVIOUSLY A VERY SOLEMN EVENT.
YES, I KNOW, KEN. BUT I DIDN'T KNOW WHAT THAT WORD MEANT. THE WORD STAYED WITH ME BECAUSE I NEVER HEARD IT BEFORE. IT WAS INTERESTING...
NOV. 11 1961
FLAMBOROUGH CENTRE

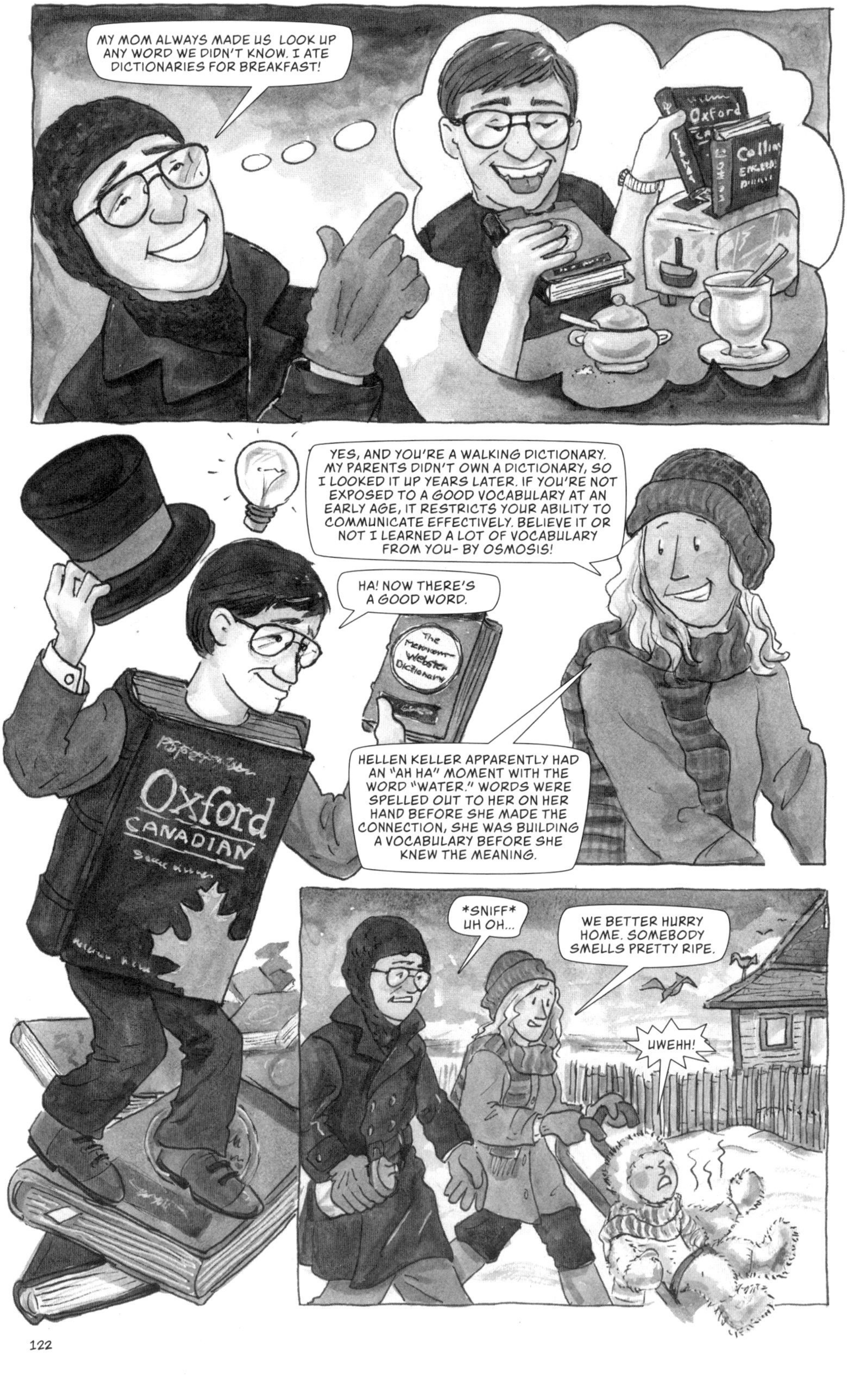
MY MOM ALWAYS MADE US LOOK UP ANY WORD WE DIDN'T KNOW. I ATE DICTIONARIES FOR BREAKFAST!
Oxford
Collins
YES, AND YOU'RE A WALKING DICTIONARY. MY PARENTS DIDN'T OWN A DICTIONARY, SO I LOOKED IT UP YEARS LATER. IF YOU'RE NOT EXPOSED TO A GOOD VOCABULARY AT AN EARLY AGE, IT RESTRICTS YOUR ABILITY TO COMMUNICATE EFFECTIVELY. BELIEVE IT OR NOT I LEARNED A LOT OF VOCABULARY FROM YOU- BY OSMOSIS!
HA! NOW THERE'S A GOOD WORD.
The Merriam-Webster Dictionary
Oxford CANADIAN
HELLEN KELLER APPARENTLY HAD AN "AH HA" MOMENT WITH THE WORD "WATER." WORDS WERE SPELLED OUT TO HER ON HER HAND BEFORE SHE MADE THE CONNECTION, SHE WAS BUILDING A VOCABULARY BEFORE SHE KNEW THE MEANING.
SNIFF UH OH...
WE BETTER HURRY HOME. SOMEBODY SMELLS PRETTY RIPE.
UWEHH!

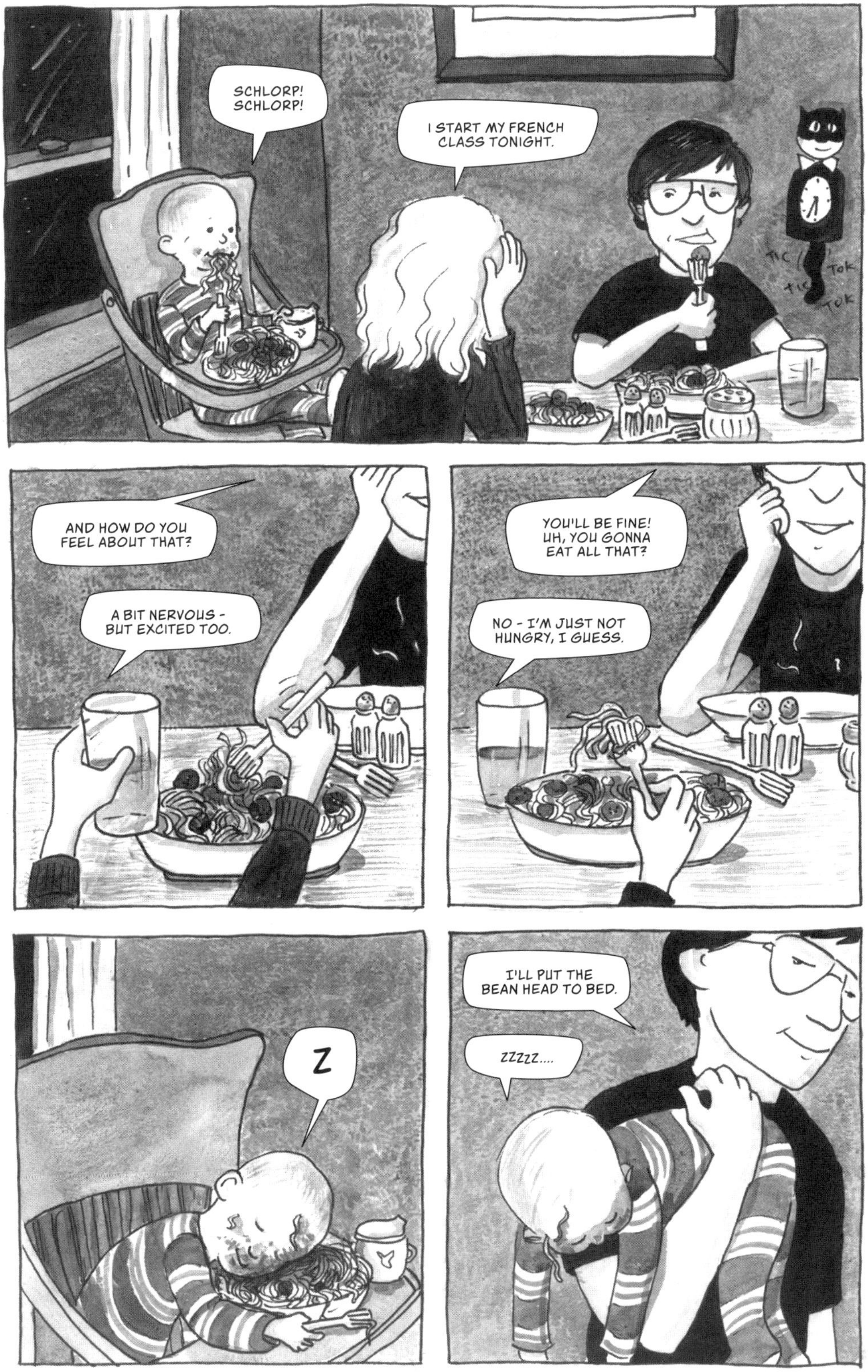
SCHLORP! SCHLORP!
I START MY FRENCH CLASS TONIGHT.
TIC TOK TIC TOK
AND HOW DO YOU FEEL ABOUT THAT?
A BIT NERVOUS - BUT EXCITED TOO.
YOU'LL BE FINE! UH, YOU GONNA EAT ALL THAT?
NO - I'M JUST NOT HUNGRY, I GUESS.
Z
I'LL PUT THE BEAN HEAD TO BED.
ZZZZZ....

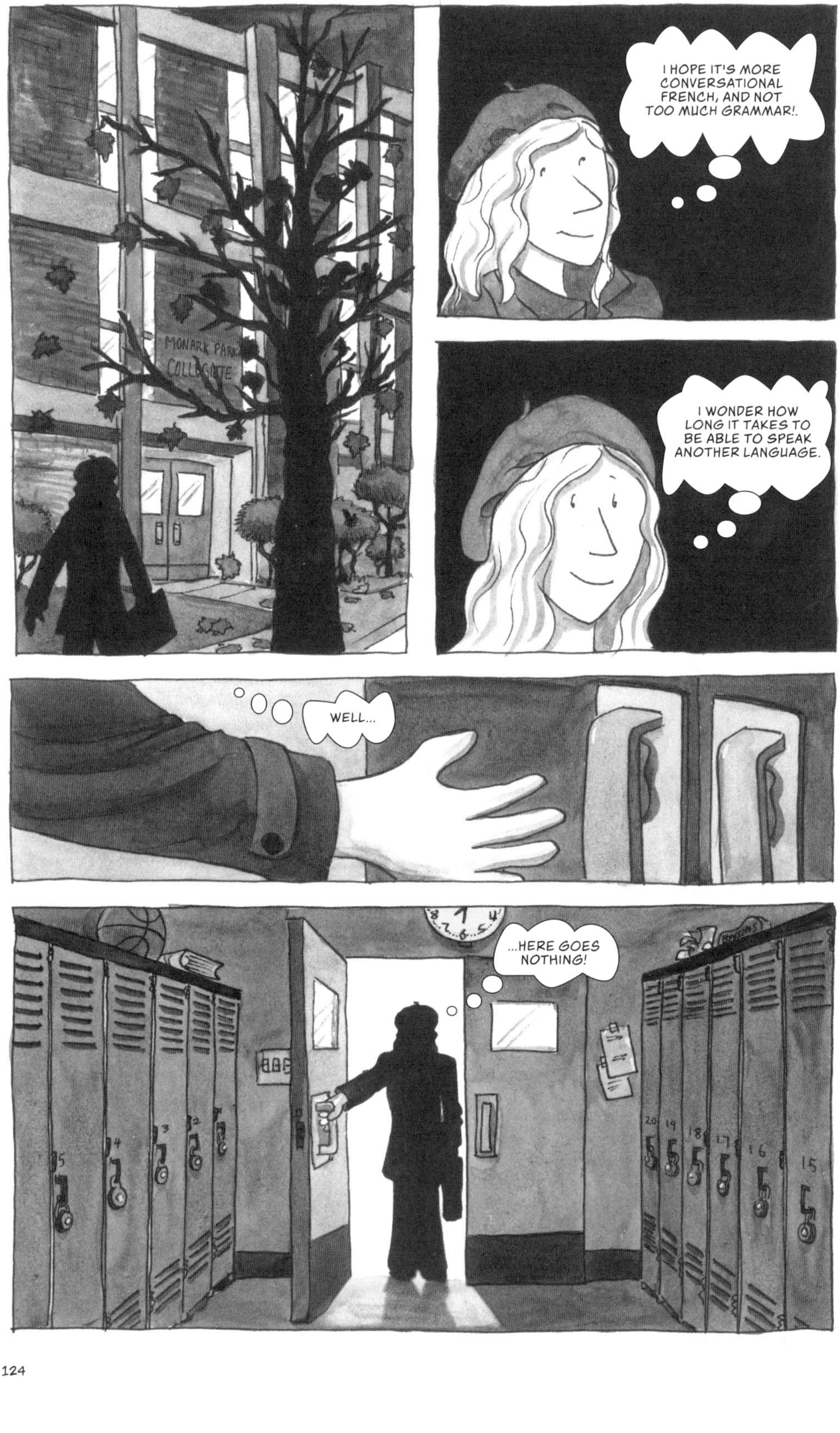
I HOPE IT'S MORE CONVERSATIONAL FRENCH, AND NOT TOO MUCH GRAMMAR!.
I WONDER HOW LONG IT TAKES TO BE ABLE TO SPEAK ANOTHER LANGUAGE.
WELL...
...HERE GOES NOTHING!

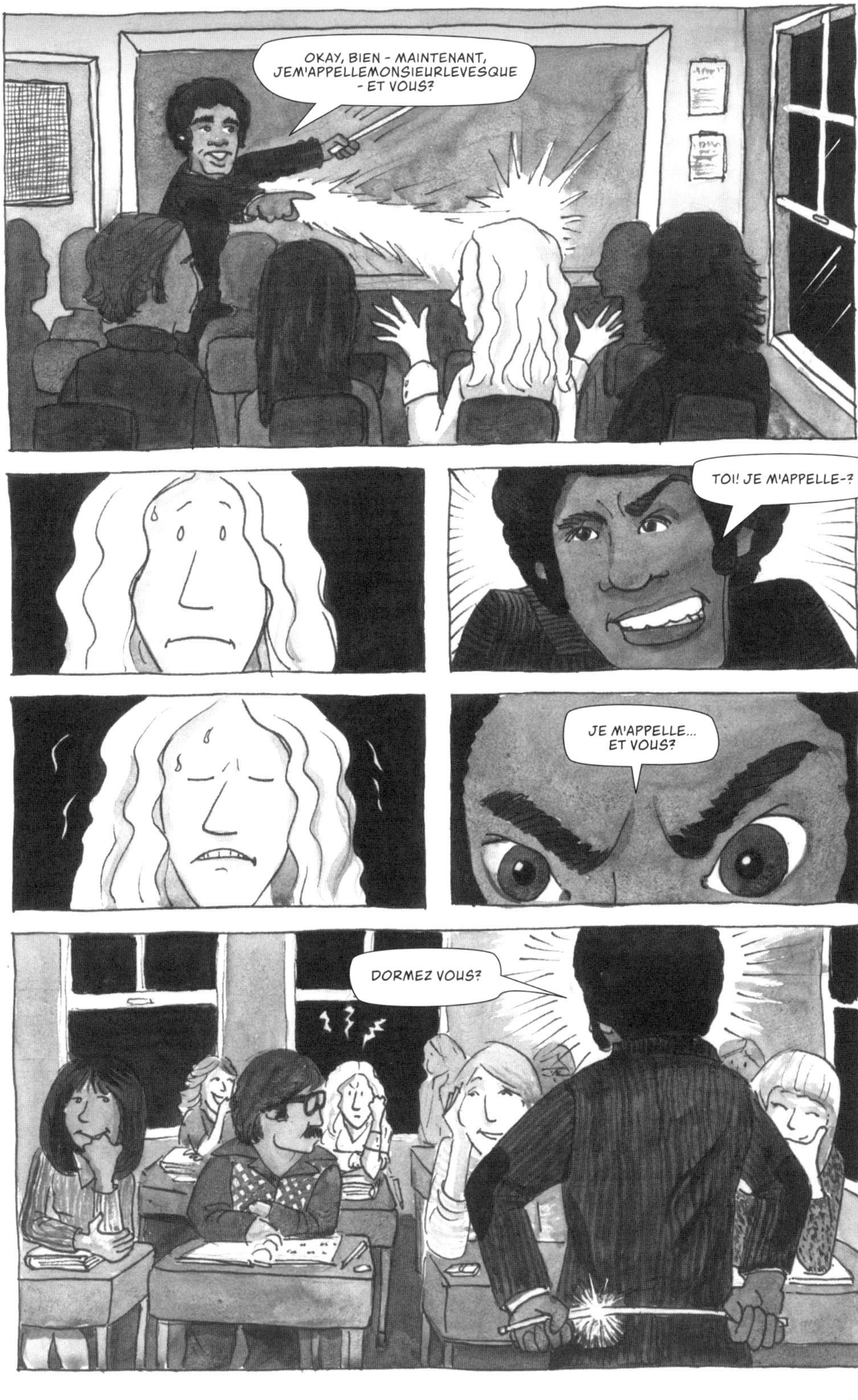

OKAY, BIEN - MAINTENANT, JEM'APPELLEMONSIEURLEVESQUE - ET VOUS?
TOI! JE M'APPELLE-?
JE M'APPELLE... ET VOUS?
DORMEZ VOUS?

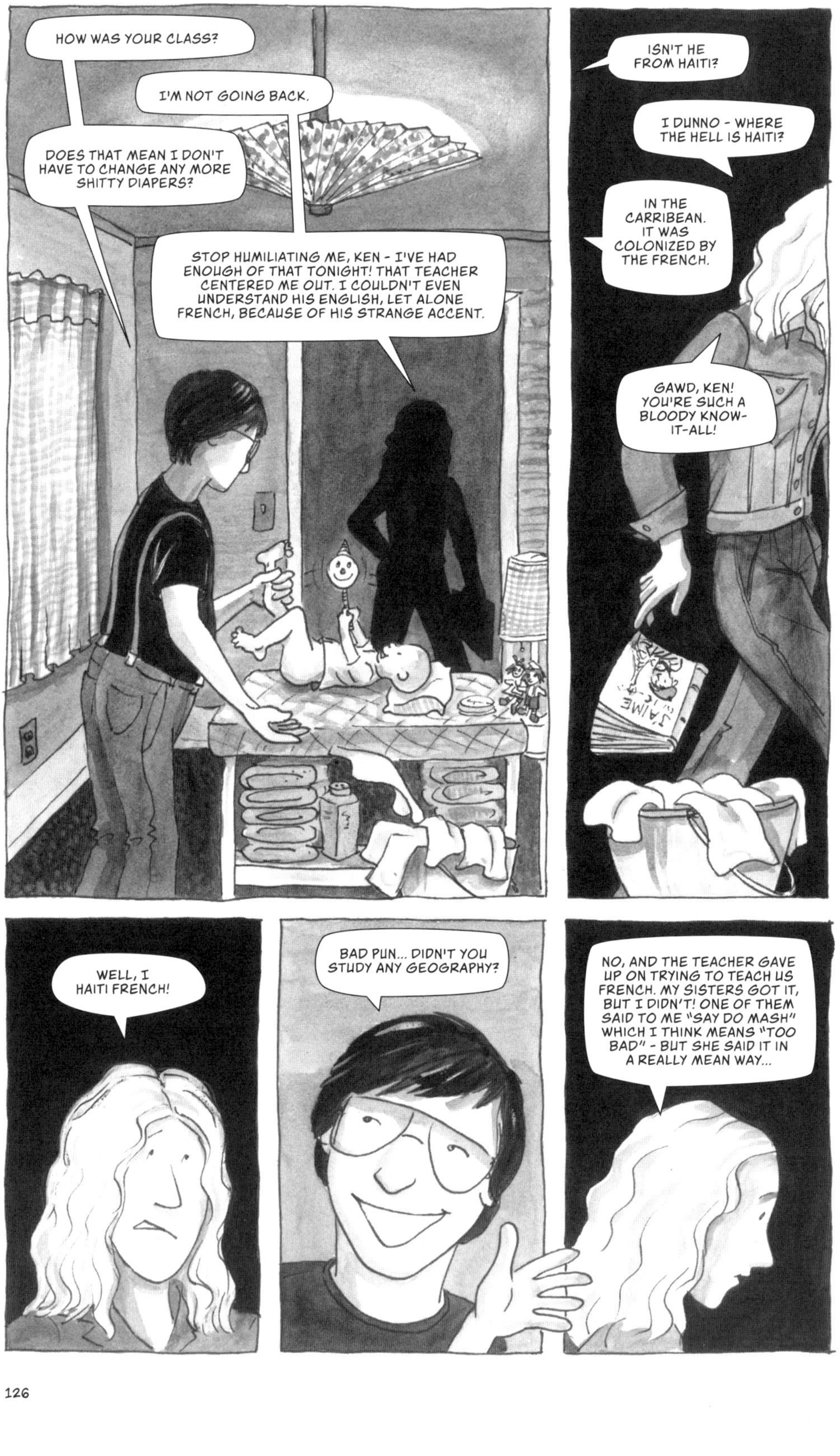
HOW WAS YOUR CLASS?
I'M NOT GOING BACK.
DOES THAT MEAN I DON'T HAVE TO CHANGE ANY MORE SHITTY DIAPERS?
STOP HUMILIATING ME, KEN - I'VE HAD ENOUGH OF THAT TONIGHT! THAT TEACHER CENTERED ME OUT. I COULDN'T EVEN UNDERSTAND HIS ENGLISH, LET ALONE FRENCH, BECAUSE OF HIS STRANGE ACCENT.
ISN'T HE FROM HAITI?
I DUNNO - WHERE THE HELL IS HAITI?
IN THE CARRIBEAN. IT WAS COLONIZED BY THE FRENCH.
GAWD, KEN! YOU'RE SUCH A BLOODY KNOW-IT-ALL!
WELL, I HAITI FRENCH!
BAD PUN... DIDN'T YOU STUDY ANY GEOGRAPHY?
NO, AND THE TEACHER GAVE UP ON TRYING TO TEACH US FRENCH. MY SISTERS GOT IT, BUT I DIDN'T! ONE OF THEM SAID TO ME "SAY DO MASH" WHICH I THINK MEANS "TOO BAD" - BUT SHE SAID IT IN A REALLY MEAN WAY...

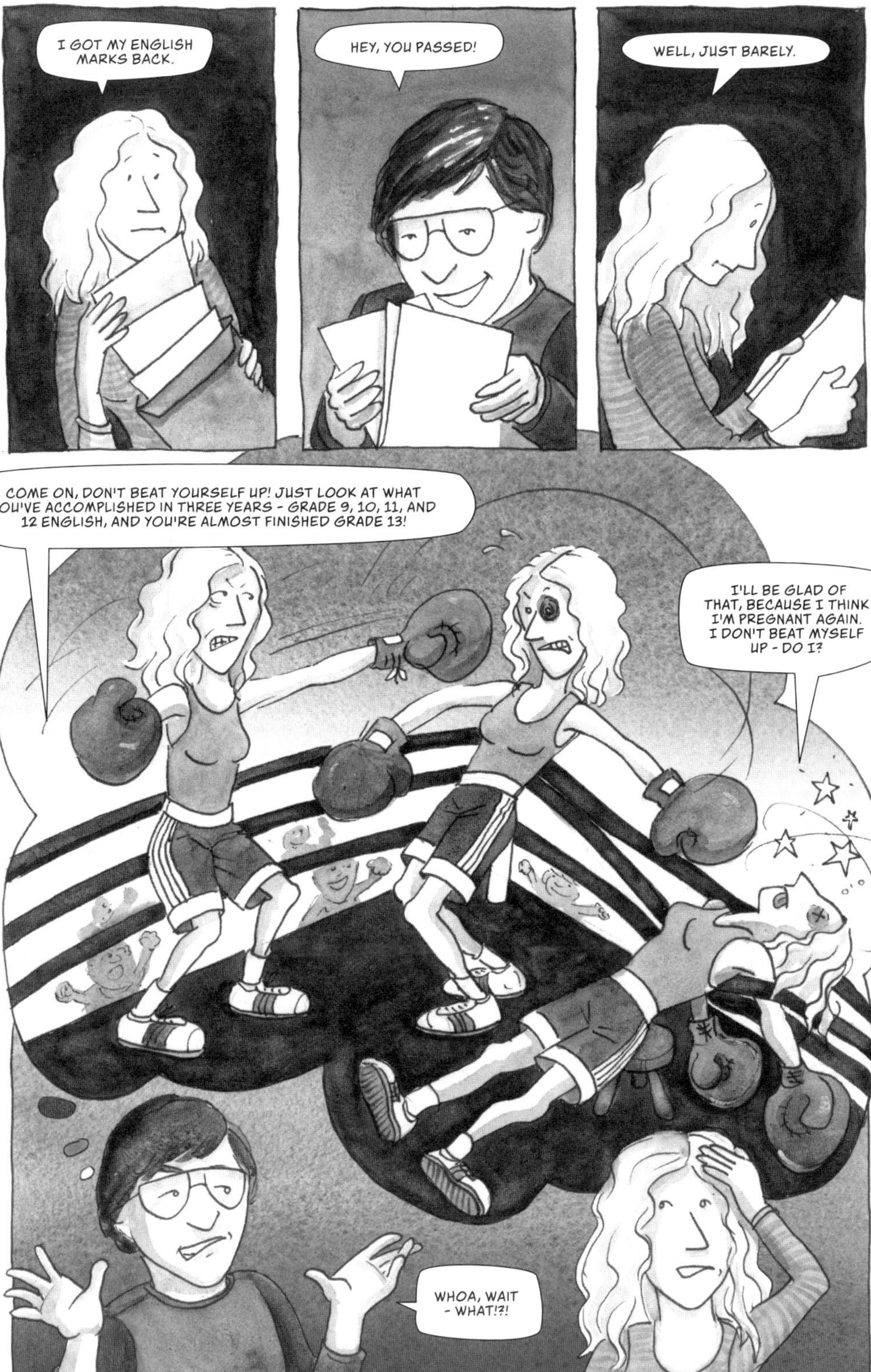
I GOT MY ENGLISH MARKS BACK.
HEY, YOU PASSED!
WELL, JUST BARELY.
COME ON, DON'T BEAT YOURSELF UP! JUST LOOK AT WHAT YOU'VE ACCOMPLISHED IN THREE YEARS - GRADE 9, 10, 11, AND 12 ENGLISH, AND YOU'RE ALMOST FINISHED GRADE 13!
I'LL BE GLAD OF THAT, BECAUSE I THINK I'M PREGNANT AGAIN. I DON'T BEAT MYSELF UP - DO I?
WHOA, WAIT - WHAT!?!

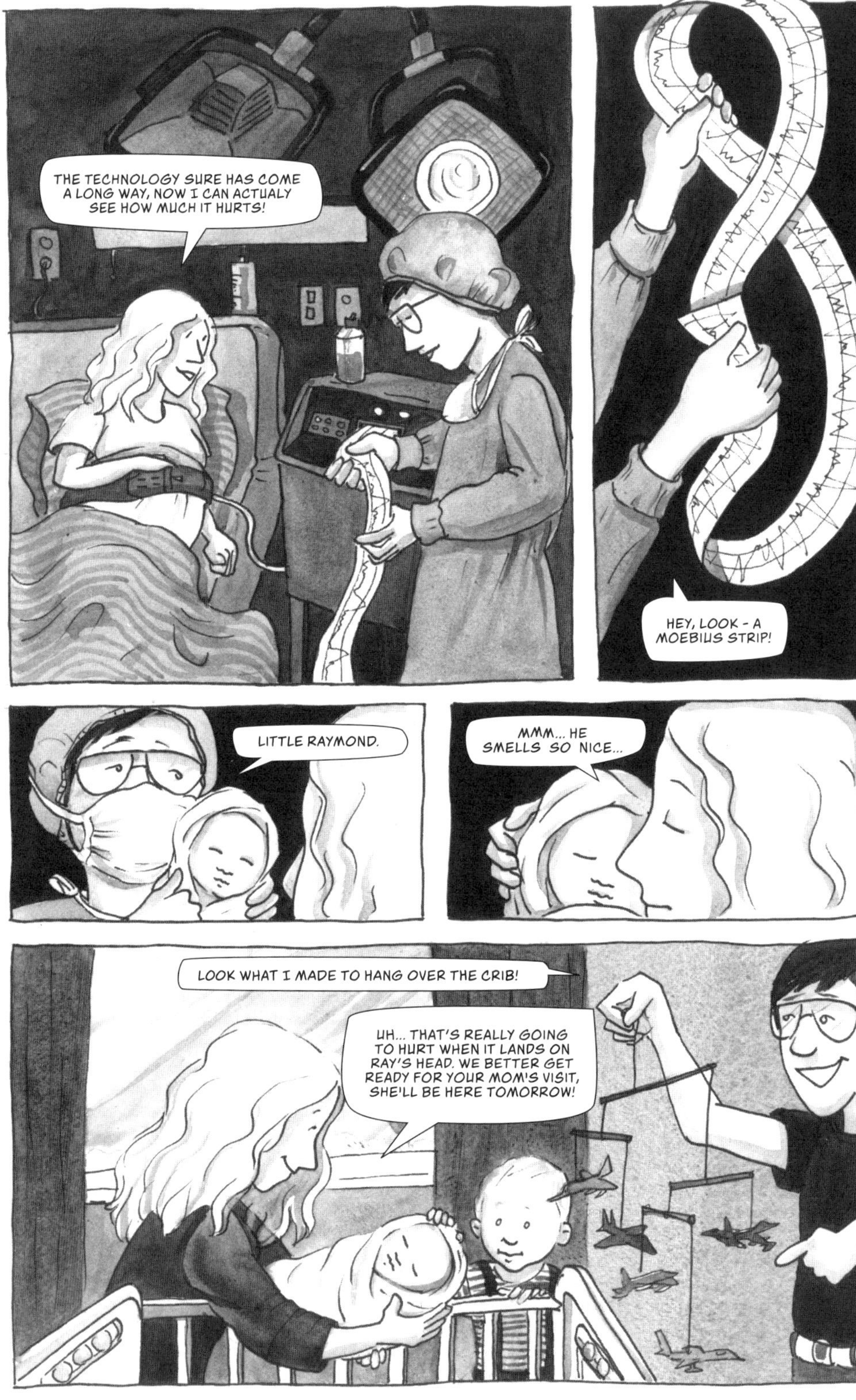
THE TECHNOLOGY SURE HAS COME A LONG WAY, NOW I CAN ACTUALY SEE HOW MUCH IT HURTS!
HEY, LOOK - A MOEBIUS STRIP!
LITTLE RAYMOND.
MMM... HE SMELLS SO NICE...
LOOK WHAT I MADE TO HANG OVER THE CRIB!
UH... THAT'S REALLY GOING TO HURT WHEN IT LANDS ON RAY'S HEAD. WE BETTER GET READY FOR YOUR MOM'S VISIT, SHE'LL BE HERE TOMORROW!

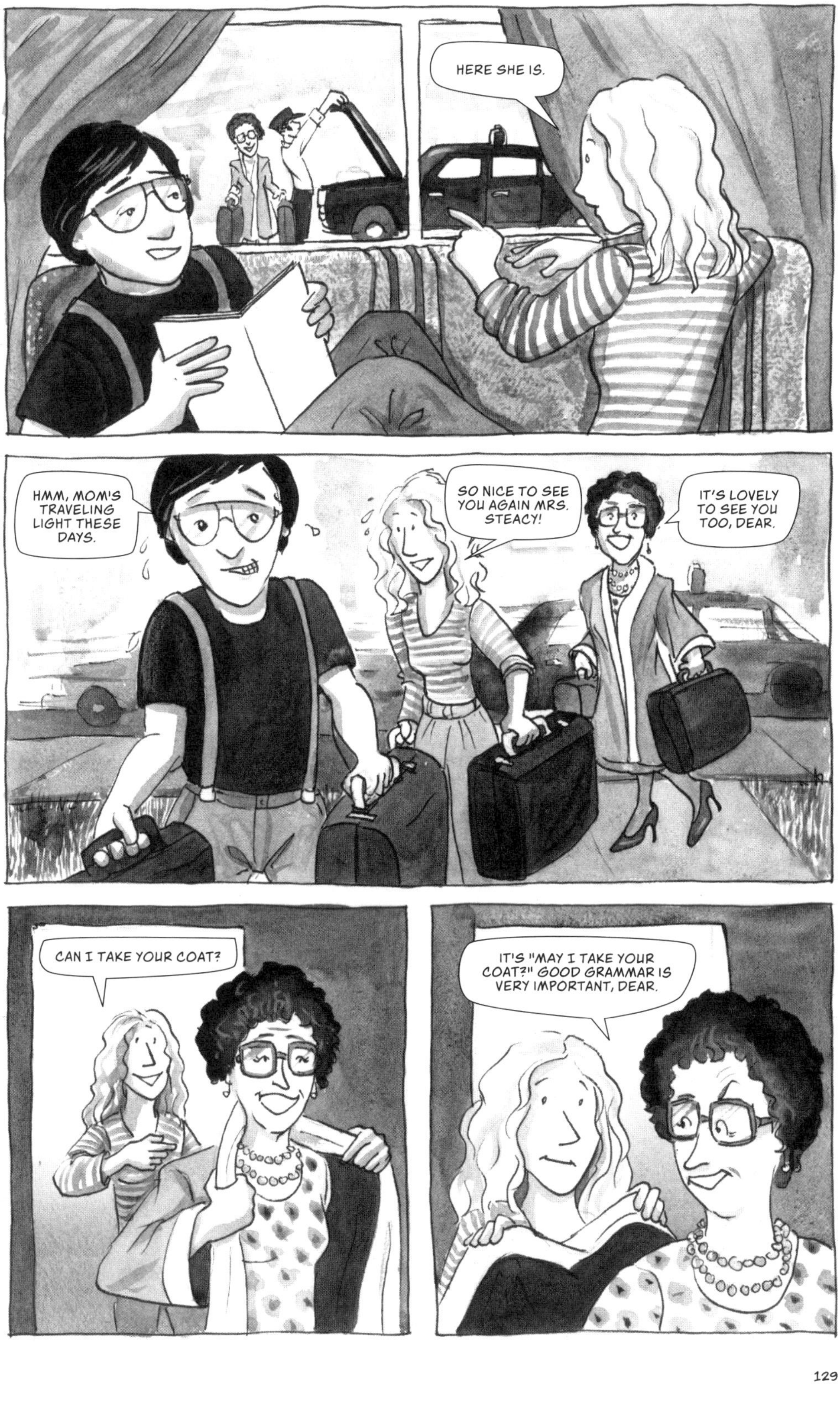
HERE SHE IS.
HMM, MOM'S TRAVELING LIGHT THESE DAYS.
SO NICE TO SEE YOU AGAIN MRS. STEACY!
IT'S LOVELY TO SEE YOU TOO, DEAR.
CAN I TAKE YOUR COAT?
IT'S "MAY I TAKE YOUR COAT?" GOOD GRAMMAR IS VERY IMPORTANT, DEAR.

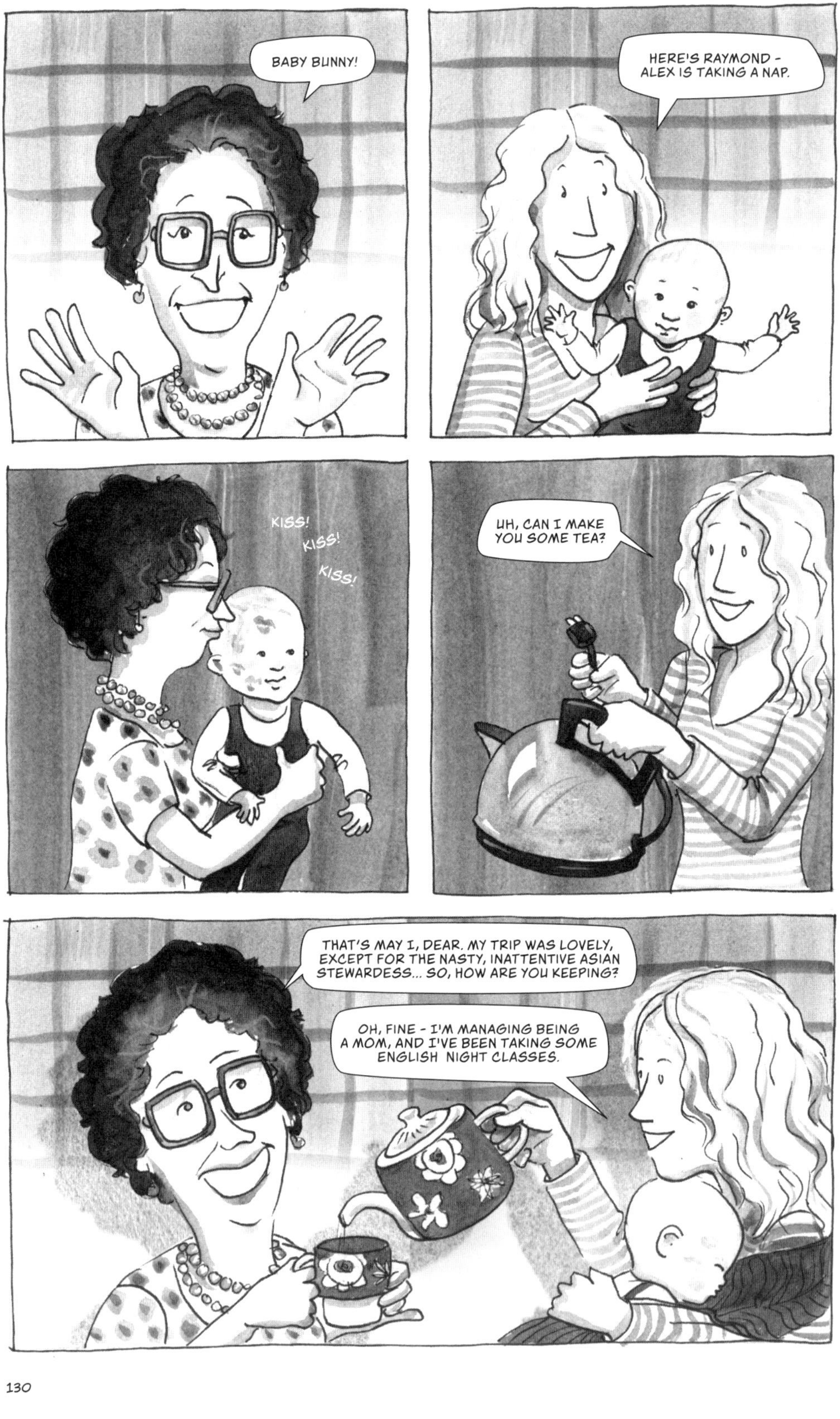
BABY BUNNY!
HERE'S RAYMOND - ALEX IS TAKING A NAP.
KISS! KISS! KISS!
UH, CAN I MAKE YOU SOME TEA?
THAT'S MAY I, DEAR. MY TRIP WAS LOVELY, EXCEPT FOR THE NASTY, INATTENTIVE ASIAN STEWARDESS... SO, HOW ARE YOU KEEPING?
OH, FINE - I'M MANAGING BEING A MOM, AND I'VE BEEN TAKING SOME ENGLISH NIGHT CLASSES.

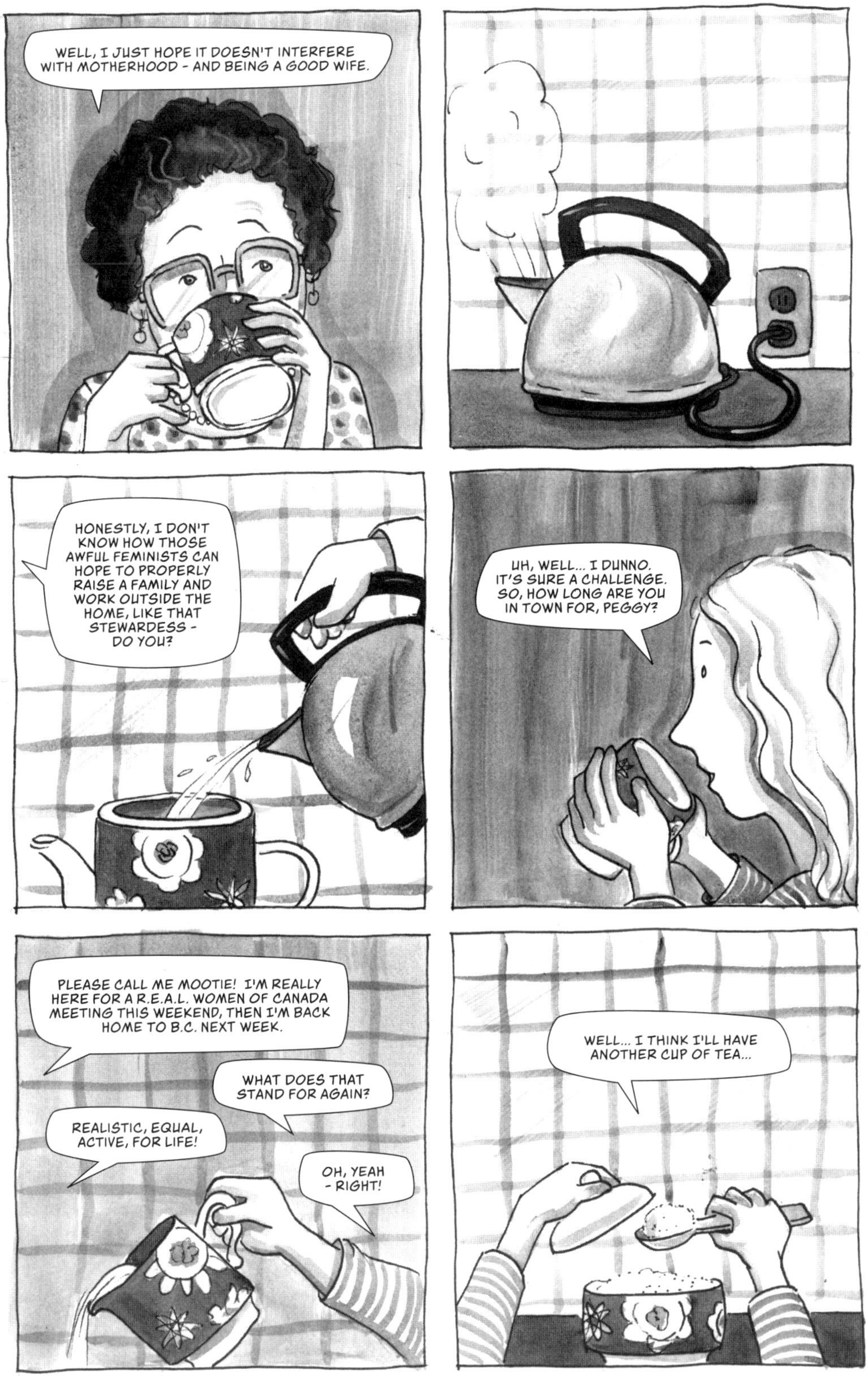
WELL, I JUST HOPE IT DOESN'T INTERFERE WITH MOTHERHOOD - AND BEING A GOOD WIFE.
HONESTLY, I DON'T KNOW HOW THOSE AWFUL FEMINISTS CAN HOPE TO PROPERLY RAISE A FAMILY AND WORK OUTSIDE THE HOME, LIKE THAT STEWARDESS - DO YOU?
UH, WELL... I DUNNO. IT'S SURE A CHALLENGE. SO, HOW LONG ARE YOU IN TOWN FOR, PEGGY?
PLEASE CALL ME MOOTIE! I'M REALLY HERE FOR A R.E.A.L. WOMEN OF CANADA MEETING THIS WEEKEND, THEN I'M BACK HOME TO B.C. NEXT WEEK.
WHAT DOES THAT STAND FOR AGAIN?
REALISTIC, EQUAL, ACTIVE, FOR LIFE!
OH, YEAH - RIGHT!
WELL... I THINK I'LL HAVE ANOTHER CUP OF TEA...

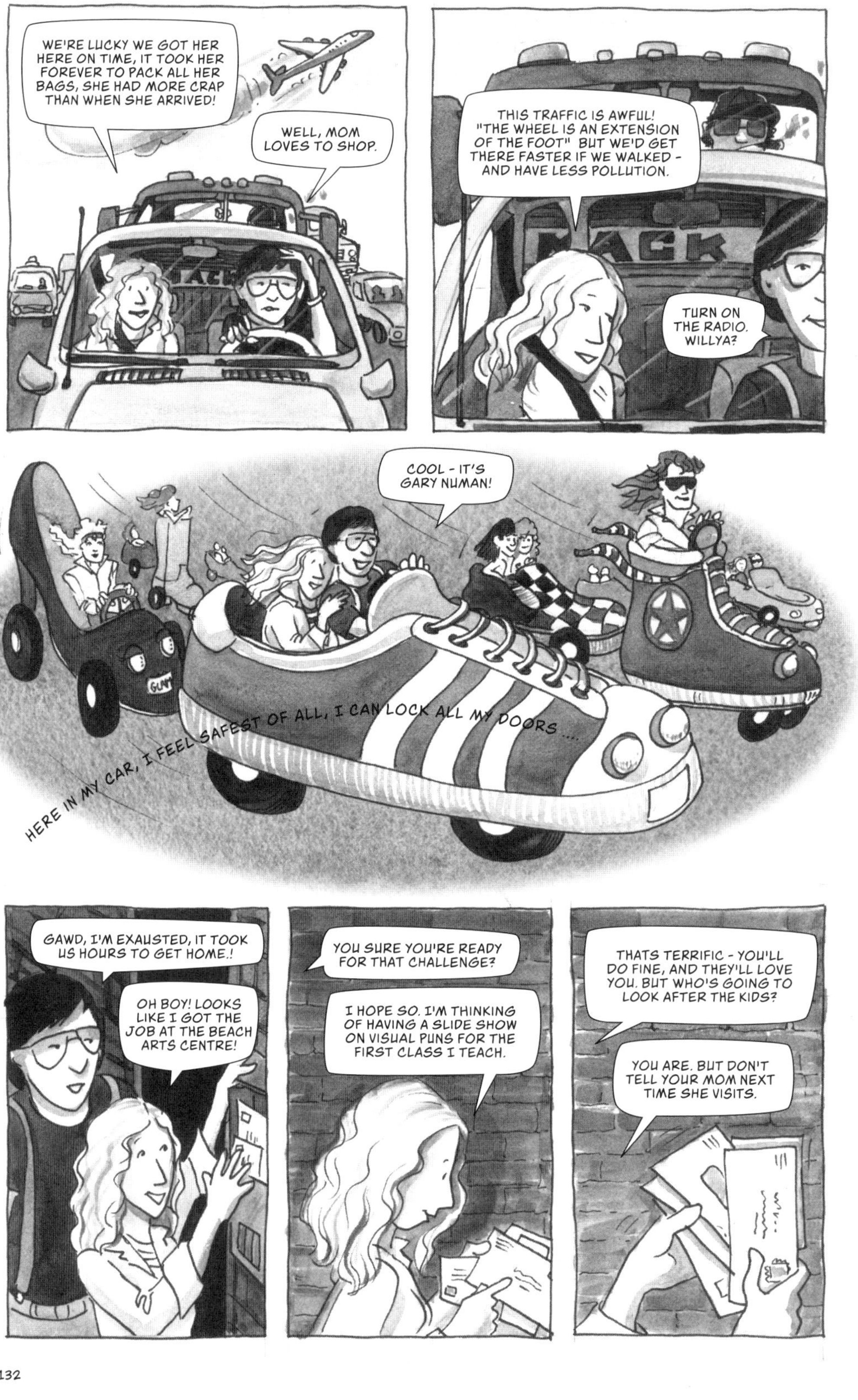

WE'RE LUCKY WE GOT HER HERE ON TIME, IT TOOK HER FOREVER TO PACK ALL HER BAGS, SHE HAD MORE CRAP THAN WHEN SHE ARRIVED!
WELL, MOM LOVES TO SHOP.
THIS TRAFFIC IS AWFUL! "THE WHEEL IS AN EXTENSION OF THE FOOT" BUT WE'D GET THERE FASTER IF WE WALKED - AND HAVE LESS POLLUTION.
TURN ON THE RADIO. WILLYA?
COOL - IT'S GARY NUMAN!
HERE IN MY CAR, I FEEL SAFEST OF ALL, I CAN LOCK ALL MY DOORS ....
GAWD, I'M EXAUSTED, IT TOOK US HOURS TO GET HOME.!
OH BOY! LOOKS LIKE I GOT THE JOB AT THE BEACH ARTS CENTRE!
YOU SURE YOU'RE READY FOR THAT CHALLENGE?
I HOPE SO. I'M THINKING OF HAVING A SLIDE SHOW ON VISUAL PUNS FOR THE FIRST CLASS I TEACH.
THATS TERRIFIC - YOU'LL DO FINE, AND THEY'LL LOVE YOU. BUT WHO'S GOING TO LOOK AFTER THE KIDS?
YOU ARE. BUT DON'T TELL YOUR MOM NEXT TIME SHE VISITS.

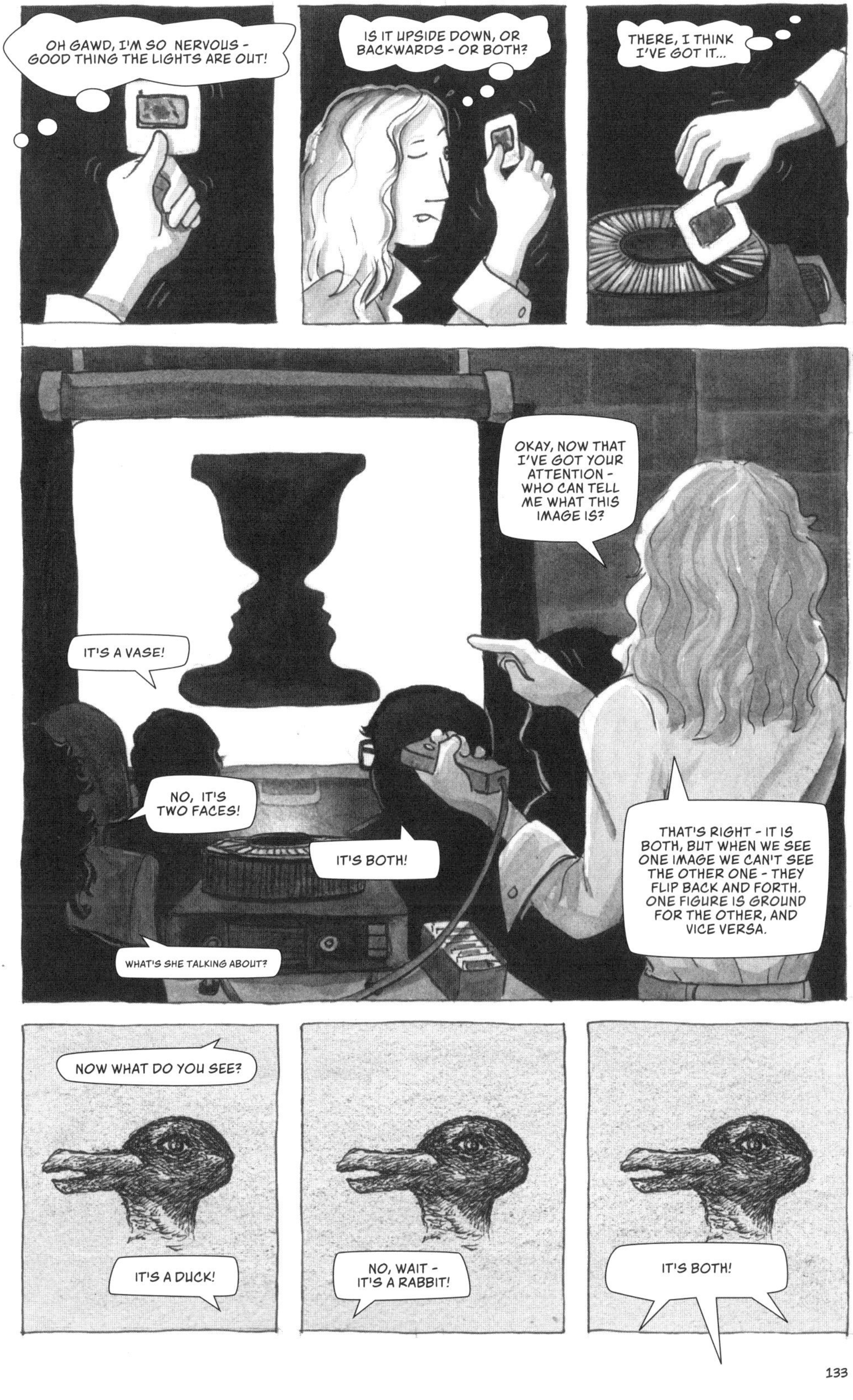
OH GAWD, I'M SO NERVOUS - GOOD THING THE LIGHTS ARE OUT!
IS IT UPSIDE DOWN, OR BACKWARDS - OR BOTH?
THERE, I THINK I'VE GOT IT...
OKAY, NOW THAT I'VE GOT YOUR ATTENTION - WHO CAN TELL ME WHAT THIS IMAGE IS?
IT'S A VASE!
NO, IT'S TWO FACES!
IT'S BOTH!
THAT'S RIGHT - IT IS BOTH, BUT WHEN WE SEE ONE IMAGE WE CAN'T SEE THE OTHER ONE - THEY FLIP BACK AND FORTH. ONE FIGURE IS GROUND FOR THE OTHER, AND VICE VERSA.
WHAT'S SHE TALKING ABOUT?
NOW WHAT DO YOU SEE?
IT'S A DUCK!
NO, WAIT - IT'S A RABBIT!
IT'S BOTH!

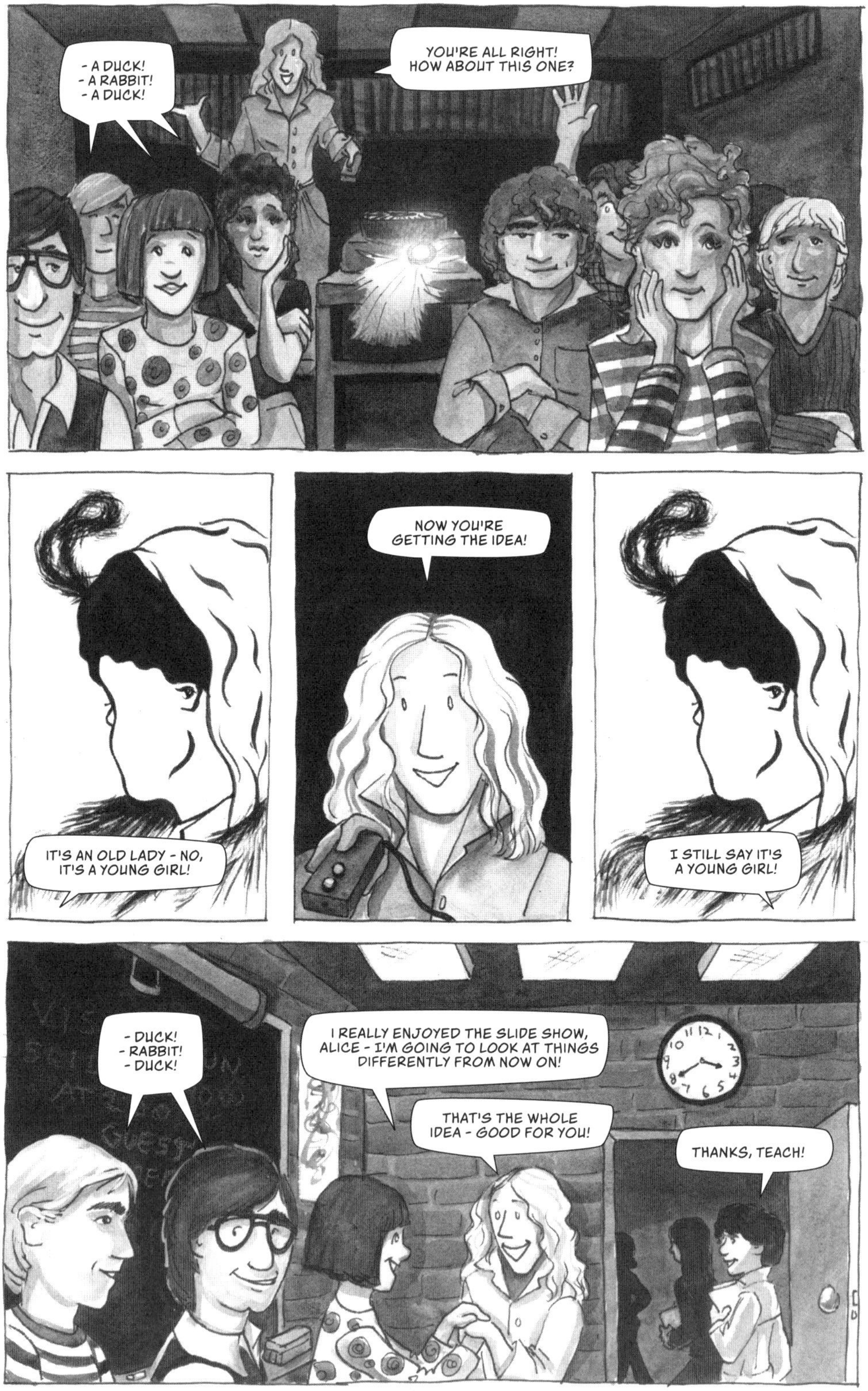
- A DUCK!
- A RABBIT!
- A DUCK!
YOU'RE ALL RIGHT! HOW ABOUT THIS ONE?
IT'S AN OLD LADY - NO, IT'S A YOUNG GIRL!
NOW YOU'RE GETTING THE IDEA!
I STILL SAY IT'S A YOUNG GIRL!
- DUCK!
- RABBIT!
- DUCK!
I REALLY ENJOYED THE SLIDE SHOW, ALICE - I'M GOING TO LOOK AT THINGS DIFFERENTLY FROM NOW ON!
THAT'S THE WHOLE IDEA - GOOD FOR YOU!
THANKS, TEACH!

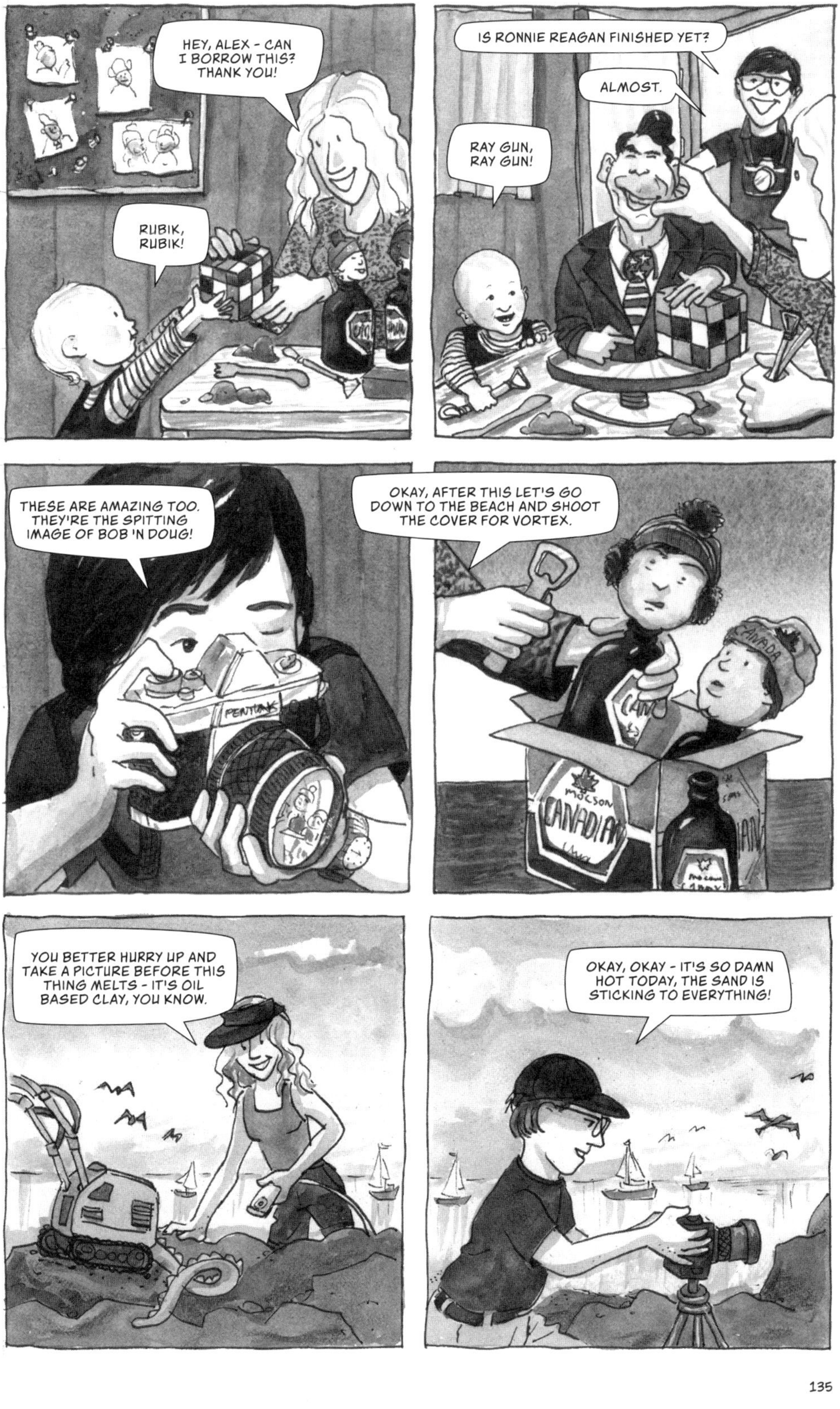
HEY, ALEX - CAN I BORROW THIS? THANK YOU!
RUBIK, RUBIK!
IS RONNIE REAGAN FINISHED YET?
ALMOST.
RAY GUN, RAY GUN!
THESE ARE AMAZING TOO. THEY'RE THE SPITTING IMAGE OF BOB 'N DOUG!
OKAY, AFTER THIS LET'S GO DOWN TO THE BEACH AND SHOOT THE COVER FOR VORTEX.
CANADA
YOU BETTER HURRY UP AND TAKE A PICTURE BEFORE THIS THING MELTS - IT'S OIL BASED CLAY, YOU KNOW.
OKAY, OKAY - IT'S SO DAMN HOT TODAY, THE SAND IS STICKING TO EVERYTHING!

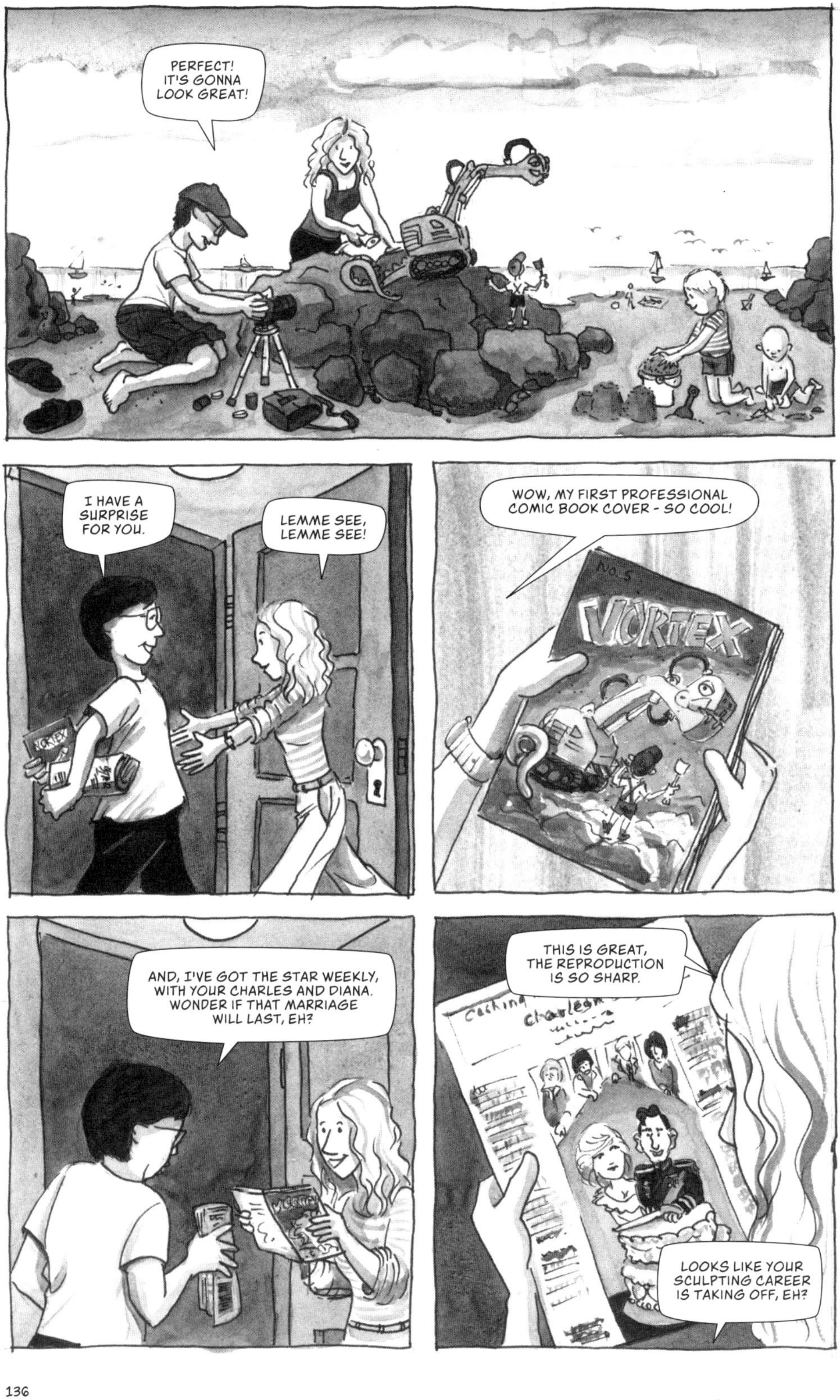
PERFECT! IT'S GONNA LOOK GREAT!
I HAVE A SURPRISE FOR YOU.
LEMME SEE, LEMME SEE!
WOW, MY FIRST PROFESSIONAL COMIC BOOK COVER - SO COOL!
VORTEX
AND, I'VE GOT THE STAR WEEKLY, WITH YOUR CHARLES AND DIANA. WONDER IF THAT MARRIAGE WILL LAST, EH?
THIS IS GREAT, THE REPRODUCTION IS SO SHARP.
LOOKS LIKE YOUR SCULPTING CAREER IS TAKING OFF, EH?

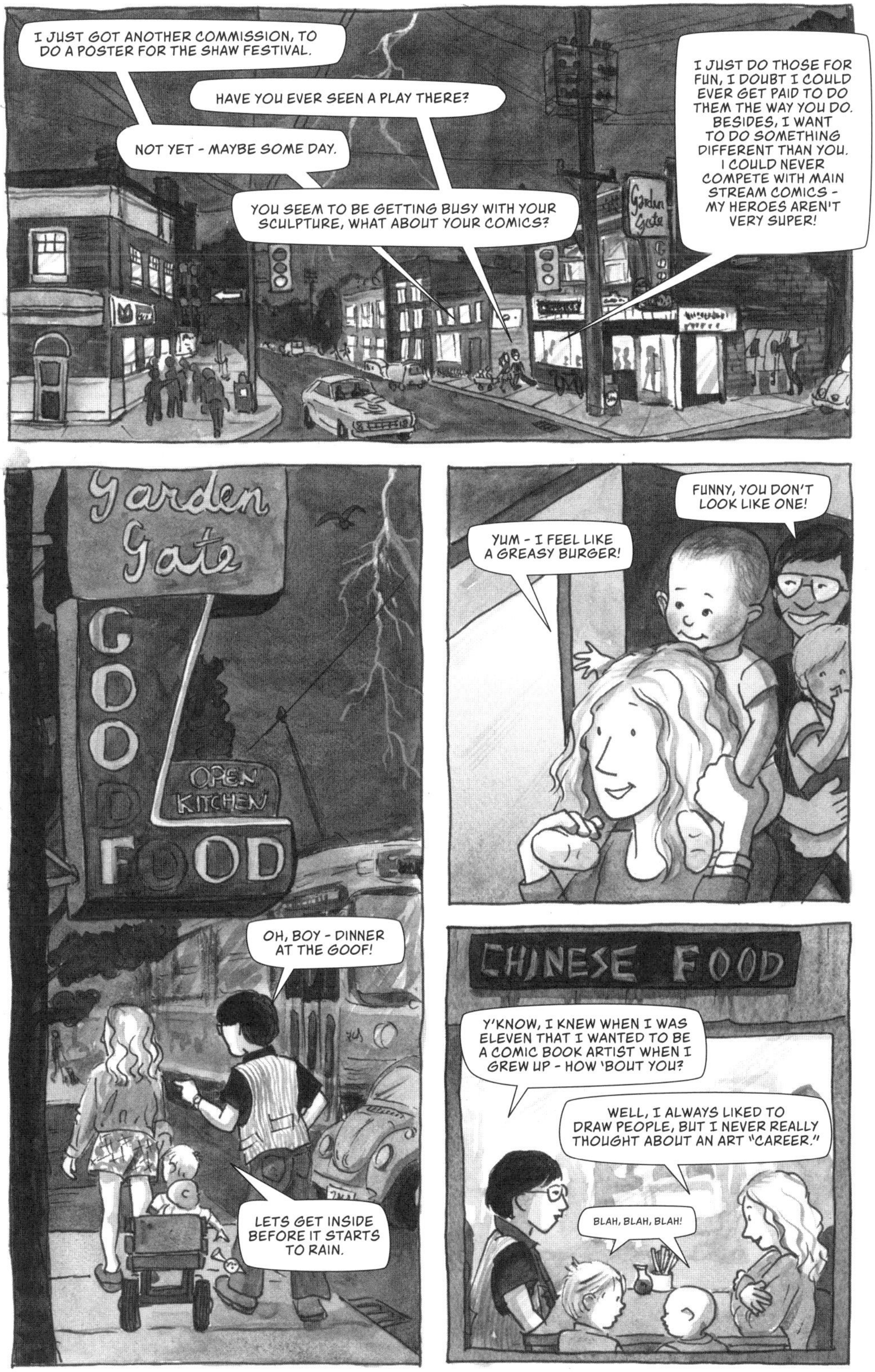
I JUST GOT ANOTHER COMMISSION, TO DO A POSTER FOR THE SHAW FESTIVAL.
HAVE YOU EVER SEEN A PLAY THERE?
NOT YET - MAYBE SOME DAY.
YOU SEEM TO BE GETTING BUSY WITH YOUR SCULPTURE, WHAT ABOUT YOUR COMICS?
I JUST DO THOSE FOR FUN, I DOUBT I COULD EVER GET PAID TO DO THEM THE WAY YOU DO. BESIDES, I WANT TO DO SOMETHING DIFFERENT THAN YOU. I COULD NEVER COMPETE WITH MAIN STREAM COMICS - MY HEROES AREN'T VERY SUPER!
Garden Gate
GOOD FOOD
OPEN KITCHEN
OH, BOY - DINNER AT THE GOOF!
LETS GET INSIDE BEFORE IT STARTS TO RAIN.
YUM - I FEEL LIKE A GREASY BURGER!
FUNNY, YOU DON'T LOOK LIKE ONE!
CHINESE FOOD
Y'KNOW, I KNEW WHEN I WAS ELEVEN THAT I WANTED TO BE A COMIC BOOK ARTIST WHEN I GREW UP - HOW 'BOUT YOU?
WELL, I ALWAYS LIKED TO DRAW PEOPLE, BUT I NEVER REALLY THOUGHT ABOUT AN ART "CAREER."
BLAH, BLAH, BLAH!

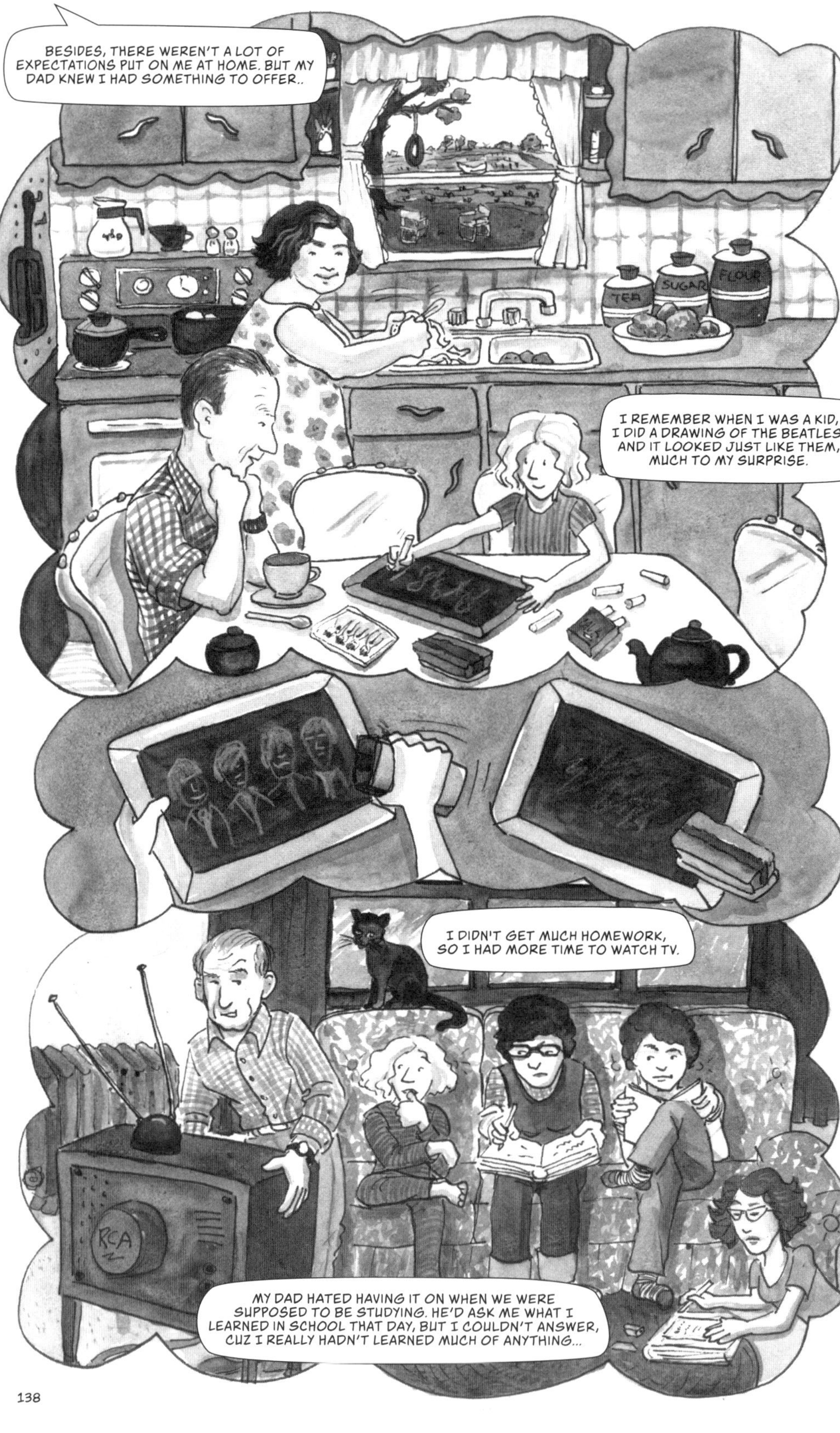
BESIDES, THERE WEREN'T A LOT OF EXPECTATIONS PUT ON ME AT HOME. BUT MY DAD KNEW I HAD SOMETHING TO OFFER..
TEA
SUGAR
FLOUR
I REMEMBER WHEN I WAS A KID, I DID A DRAWING OF THE BEATLES, AND IT LOOKED JUST LIKE THEM, MUCH TO MY SURPRISE.
I DIDN'T GET MUCH HOMEWORK, SO I HAD MORE TIME TO WATCH TV.
RCA
MY DAD HATED HAVING IT ON WHEN WE WERE SUPPOSED TO BE STUDYING. HE'D ASK ME WHAT I LEARNED IN SCHOOL THAT DAY, BUT I COULDN'T ANSWER, CUZ I REALLY HADN'T LEARNED MUCH OF ANYTHING...

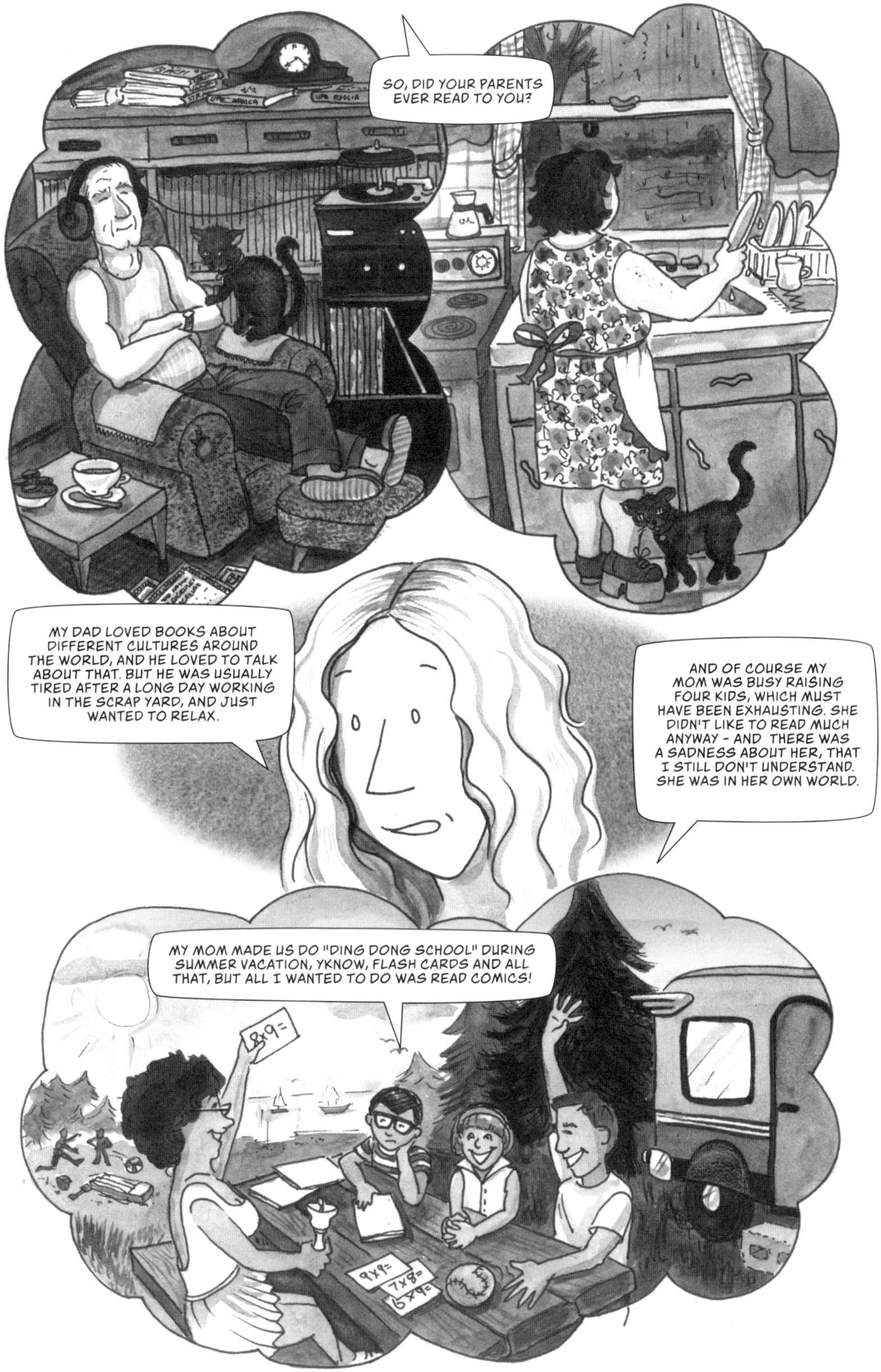
SO, DID YOUR PARENTS EVER READ TO YOU?
MY DAD LOVED BOOKS ABOUT DIFFERENT CULTURES AROUND THE WORLD, AND HE LOVED TO TALK ABOUT THAT. BUT HE WAS USUALLY TIRED AFTER A LONG DAY WORKING IN THE SCRAP YARD, AND JUST WANTED TO RELAX.
AND OF COURSE MY MOM WAS BUSY RAISING FOUR KIDS, WHICH MUST HAVE BEEN EXHAUSTING. SHE DIDN'T LIKE TO READ MUCH ANYWAY - AND THERE WAS A SADNESS ABOUT HER, THAT I STILL DON'T UNDERSTAND. SHE WAS IN HER OWN WORLD.
MY MOM MADE US DO "DING DONG SCHOOL" DURING SUMMER VACATION, YKNOW, FLASH CARDS AND ALL THAT, BUT ALL I WANTED TO DO WAS READ COMICS!
8x9=
9x9=
7x8=
6x9=

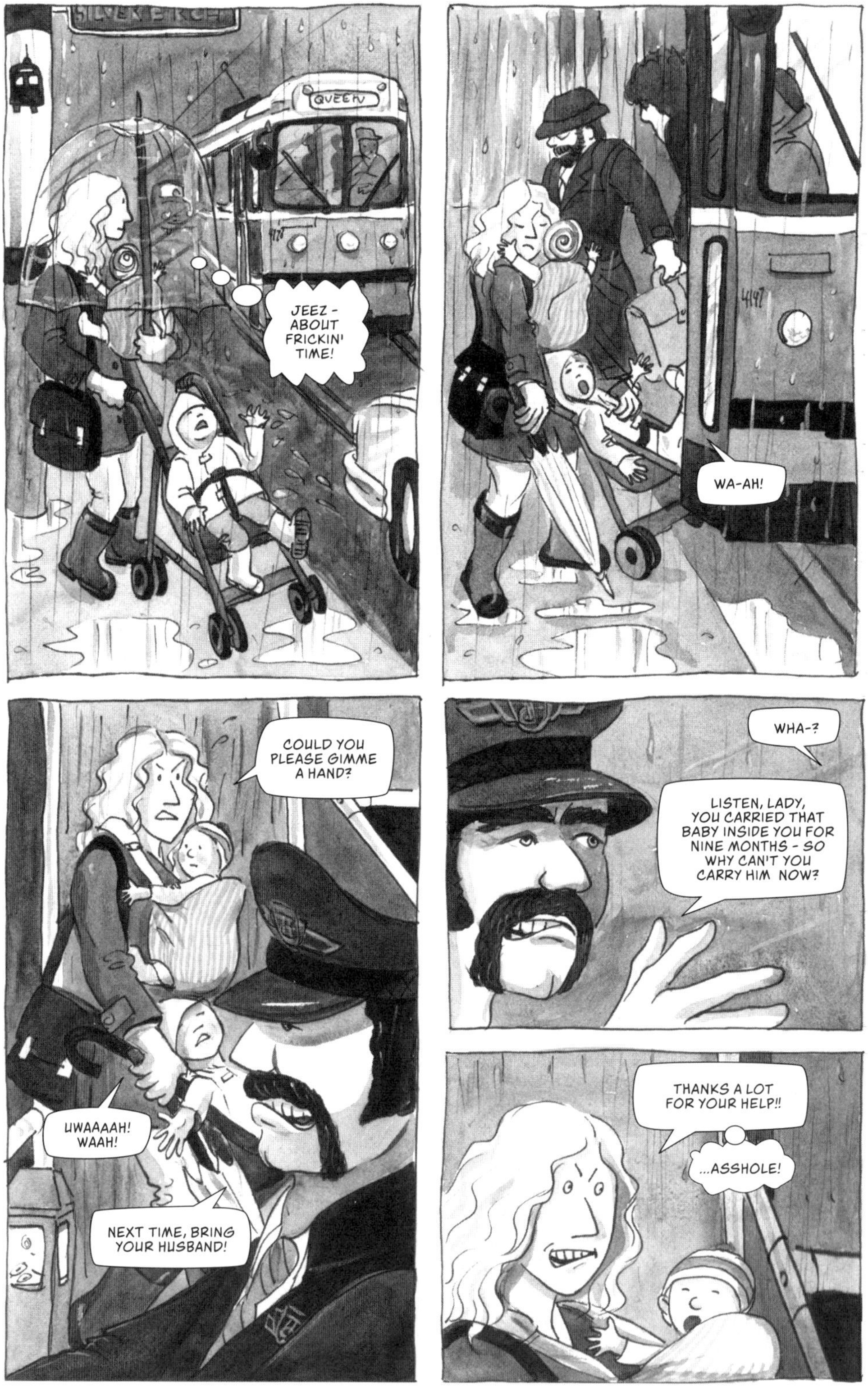
SILVER BIRCH
QUEEN
JEEZ - ABOUT FRICKIN' TIME!
WA-AH!
COULD YOU PLEASE GIMME A HAND?
UWAAAAH! WAAH!
NEXT TIME, BRING YOUR HUSBAND!
WHA-?
LISTEN, LADY, YOU CARRIED THAT BABY INSIDE YOU FOR NINE MONTHS - SO WHY CAN'T YOU CARRY HIM NOW?
THANKS A LOT FOR YOUR HELP!!
...ASSHOLE!

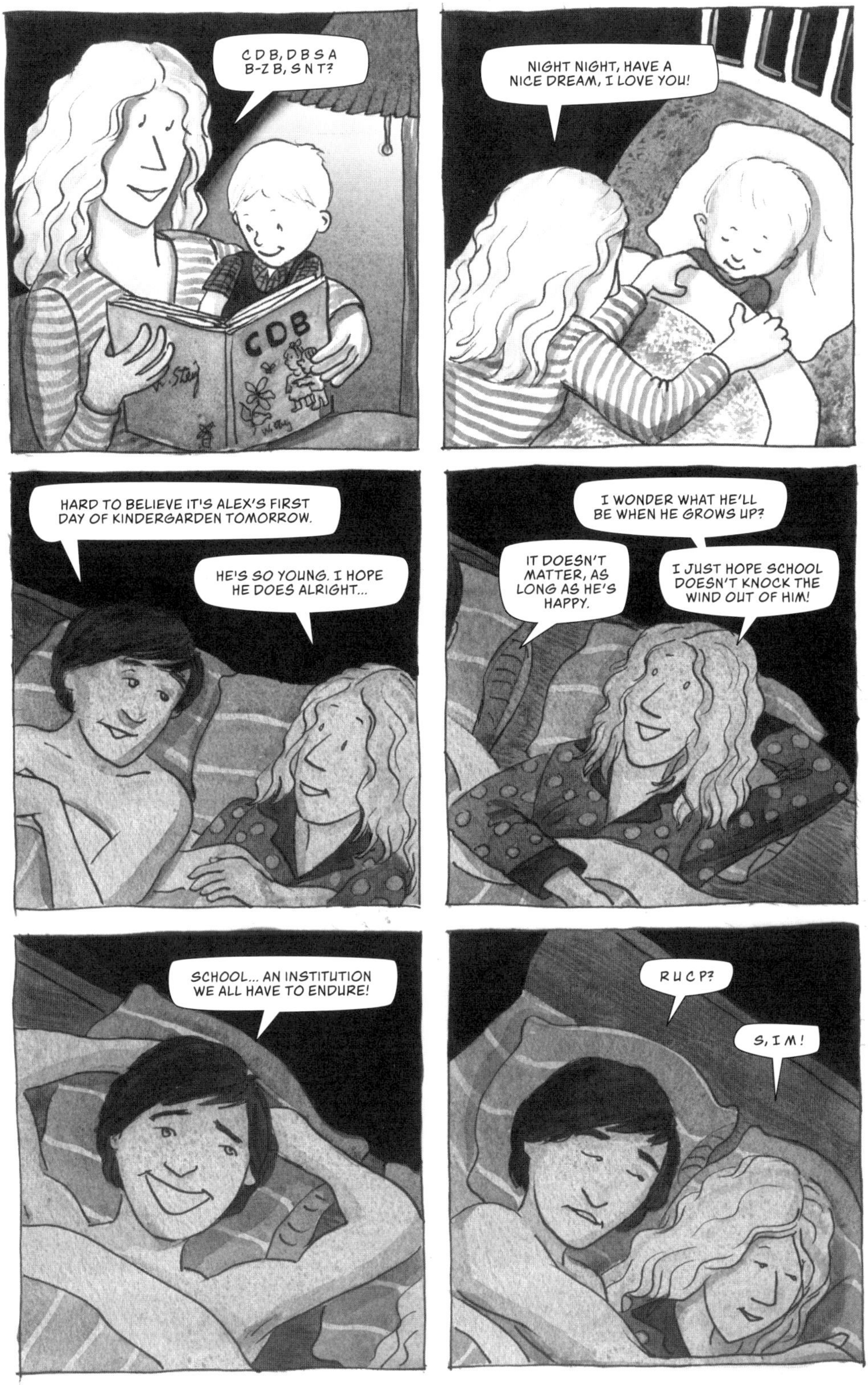
C D B, D B S A
B-Z B, S N T?
NIGHT NIGHT, HAVE A NICE DREAM, I LOVE YOU!
HARD TO BELIEVE IT'S ALEX'S FIRST DAY OF KINDERGARDEN TOMORROW.
HE'S SO YOUNG. I HOPE HE DOES ALRIGHT...
I WONDER WHAT HE'LL BE WHEN HE GROWS UP?
IT DOESN'T MATTER, AS LONG AS HE'S HAPPY.
I JUST HOPE SCHOOL DOESN'T KNOCK THE WIND OUT OF HIM!
SCHOOL... AN INSTITUTION WE ALL HAVE TO ENDURE!
R U C P?
S, I M!

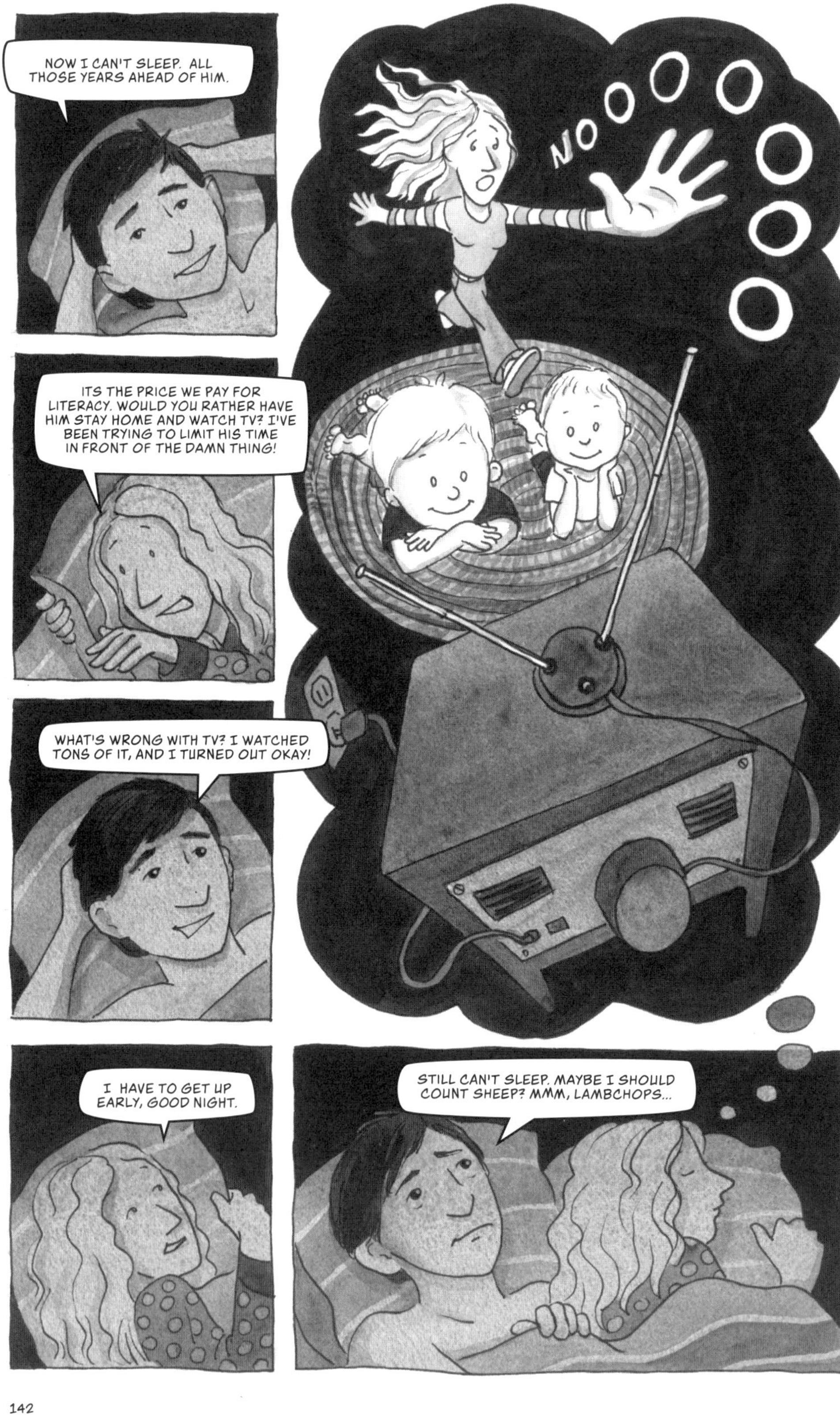
NOW I CAN'T SLEEP. ALL THOSE YEARS AHEAD OF HIM.
NOOOOOOOO
ITS THE PRICE WE PAY FOR LITERACY. WOULD YOU RATHER HAVE HIM STAY HOME AND WATCH TV? I'VE BEEN TRYING TO LIMIT HIS TIME IN FRONT OF THE DAMN THING!
WHAT'S WRONG WITH TV? I WATCHED TONS OF IT, AND I TURNED OUT OKAY!
I HAVE TO GET UP EARLY, GOOD NIGHT.
STILL CAN'T SLEEP. MAYBE I SHOULD COUNT SHEEP? MMM, LAMBCHOPS...

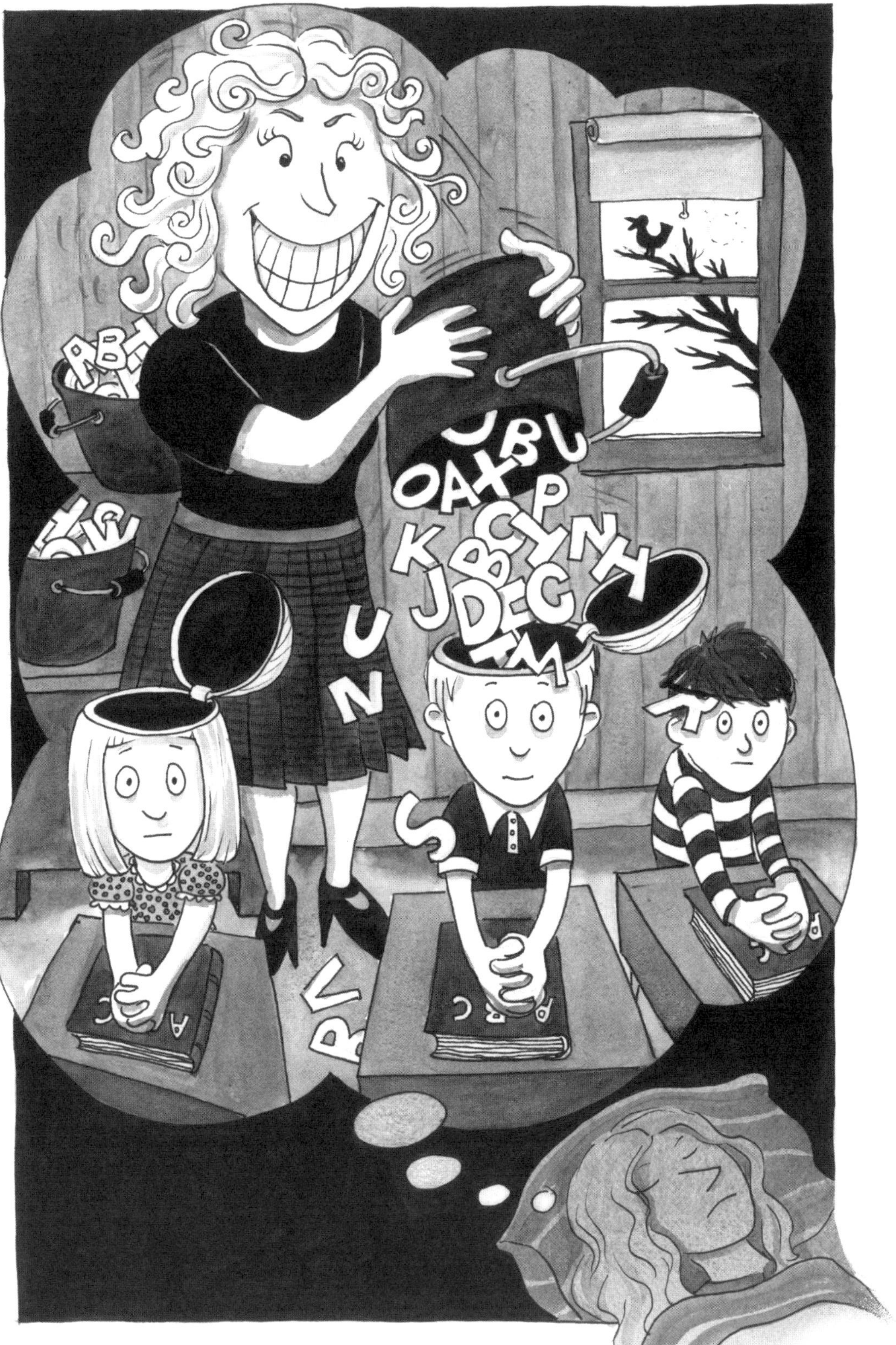

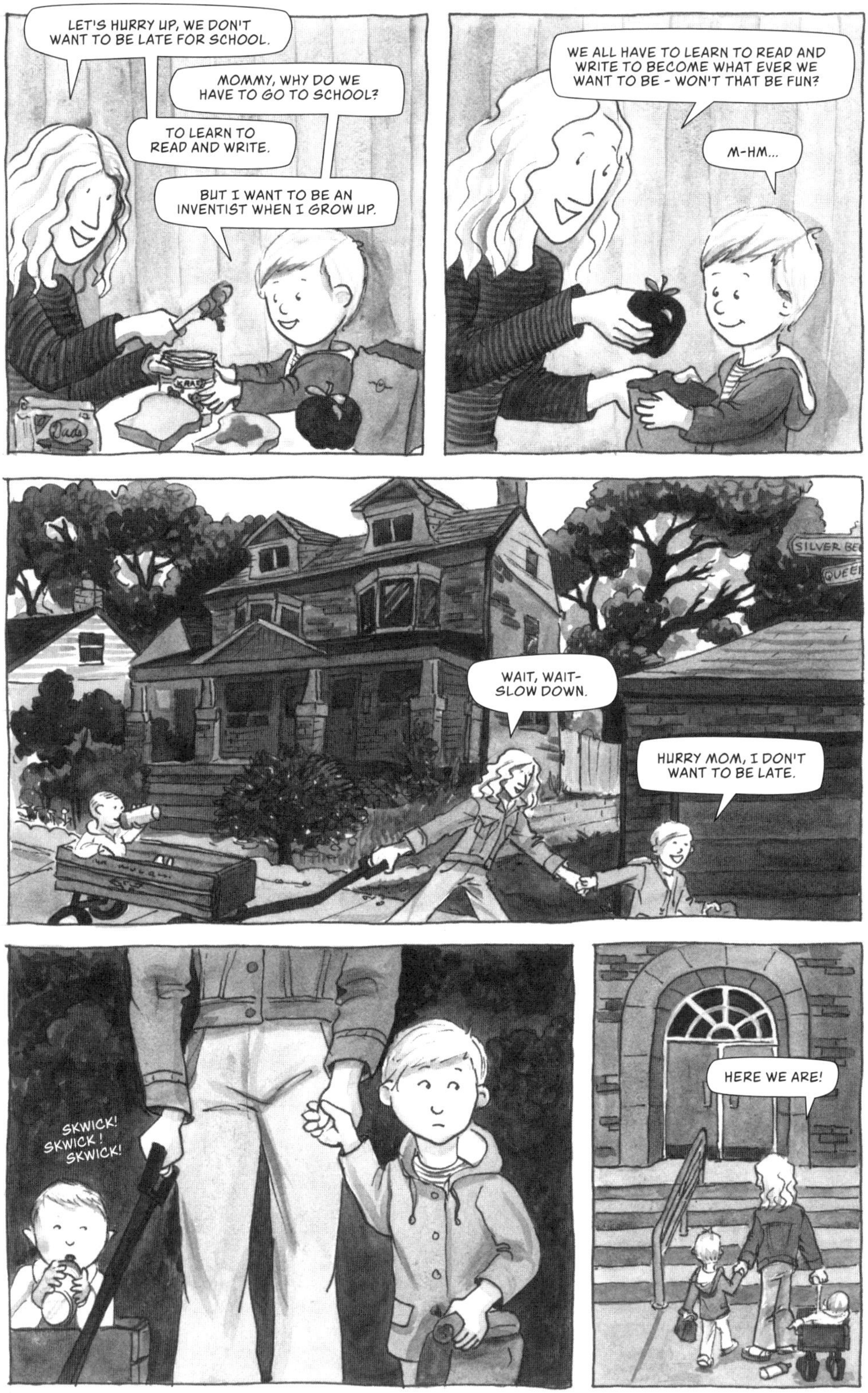
LET'S HURRY UP, WE DON'T WANT TO BE LATE FOR SCHOOL.
MOMMY, WHY DO WE HAVE TO GO TO SCHOOL?
TO LEARN TO READ AND WRITE.
BUT I WANT TO BE AN INVENTIST WHEN I GROW UP.
WE ALL HAVE TO LEARN TO READ AND WRITE TO BECOME WHAT EVER WE WANT TO BE - WON'T THAT BE FUN?
M-HM...
WAIT, WAIT- SLOW DOWN.
HURRY MOM, I DON'T WANT TO BE LATE.
SKWICK! SKWICK! SKWICK!
HERE WE ARE!

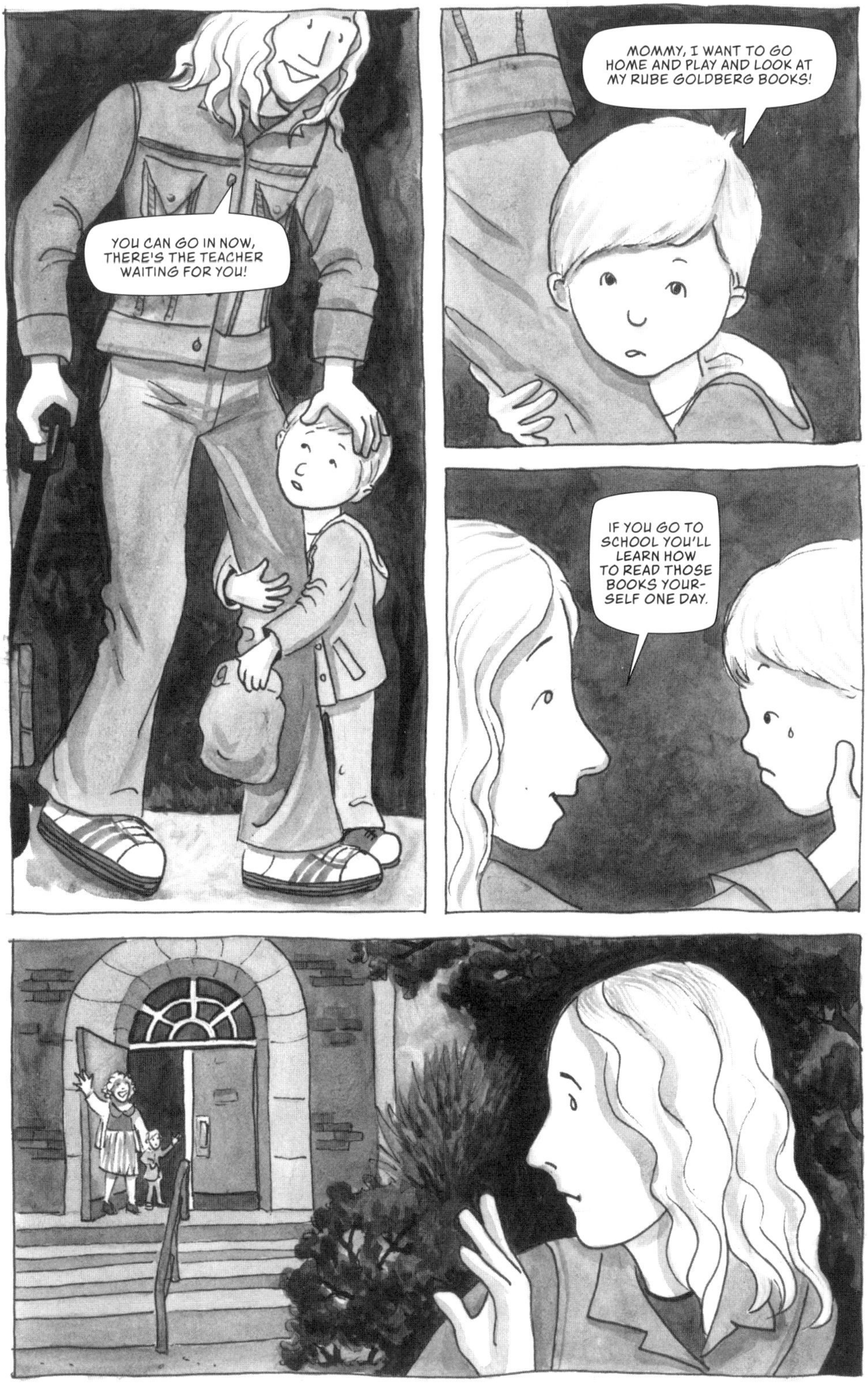
YOU CAN GO IN NOW, THERE'S THE TEACHER WAITING FOR YOU!
MOMMY, I WANT TO GO HOME AND PLAY AND LOOK AT MY RUBE GOLDBERG BOOKS!
IF YOU GO TO SCHOOL YOU'LL LEARN HOW TO READ THOSE BOOKS YOUR-SELF ONE DAY.

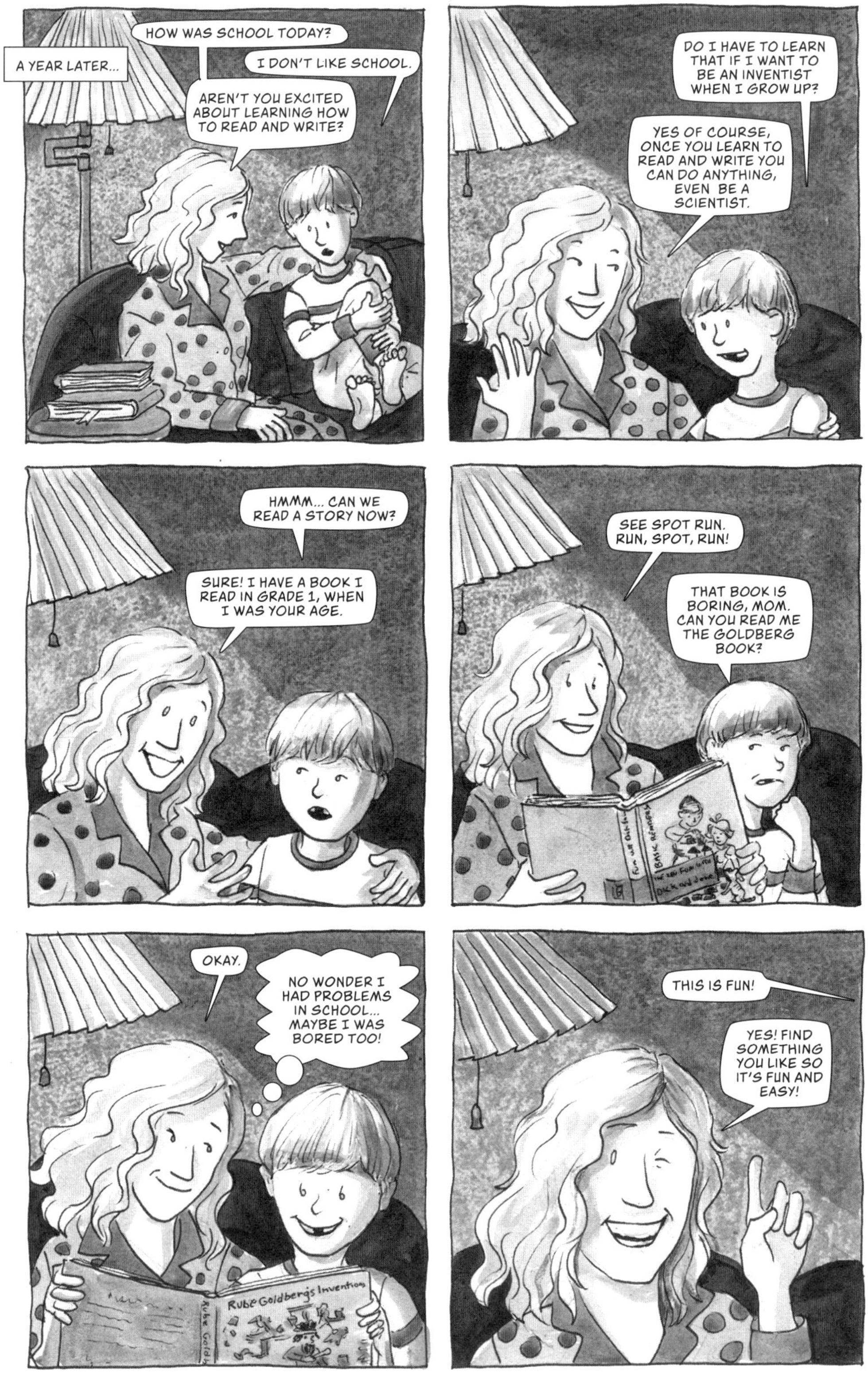

A YEAR LATER...
HOW WAS SCHOOL TODAY?
I DON'T LIKE SCHOOL.
AREN'T YOU EXCITED ABOUT LEARNING HOW TO READ AND WRITE?
DO I HAVE TO LEARN THAT IF I WANT TO BE AN INVENTIST WHEN I GROW UP?
YES OF COURSE, ONCE YOU LEARN TO READ AND WRITE YOU CAN DO ANYTHING, EVEN BE A SCIENTIST.
HMMM... CAN WE READ A STORY NOW?
SURE! I HAVE A BOOK I READ IN GRADE 1, WHEN I WAS YOUR AGE.
SEE SPOT RUN. RUN, SPOT, RUN!
THAT BOOK IS BORING, MOM. CAN YOU READ ME THE GOLDBERG BOOK?
OKAY.
NO WONDER I HAD PROBLEMS IN SCHOOL... MAYBE I WAS BORED TOO!
Rube Goldberg's Inventions
THIS IS FUN!
YES! FIND SOMETHING YOU LIKE SO IT'S FUN AND EASY!

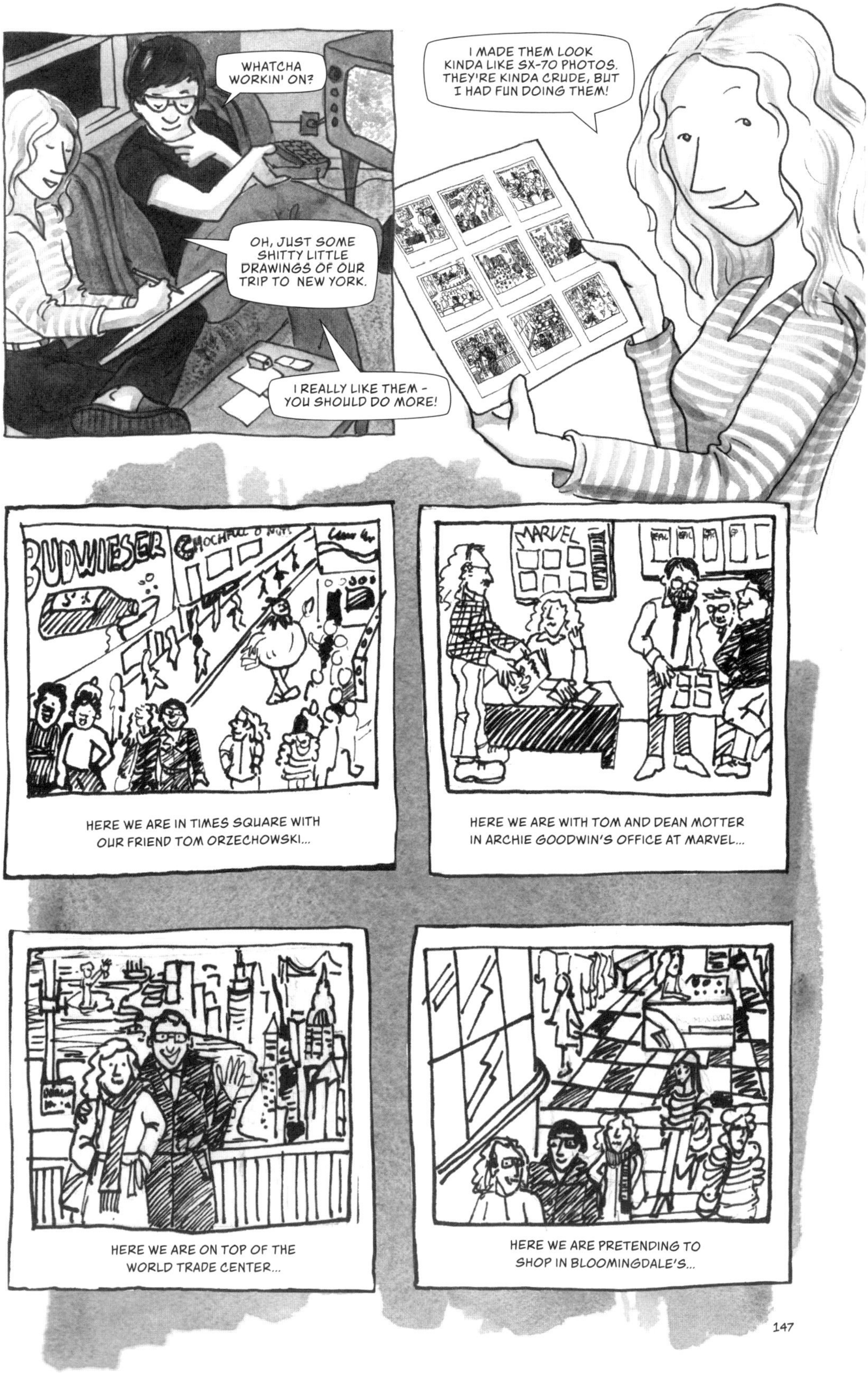
WHATCHA WORKIN' ON?
OH, JUST SOME SHITTY LITTLE DRAWINGS OF OUR TRIP TO NEW YORK.
I REALLY LIKE THEM - YOU SHOULD DO MORE!
I MADE THEM LOOK KINDA LIKE SX-70 PHOTOS. THEY'RE KINDA CRUDE, BUT I HAD FUN DOING THEM!
BUDWIESER
HERE WE ARE IN TIMES SQUARE WITH OUR FRIEND TOM ORZECHOWSKI...
MARVEL
HERE WE ARE WITH TOM AND DEAN MOTTER IN ARCHIE GOODWIN'S OFFICE AT MARVEL...
HERE WE ARE ON TOP OF THE WORLD TRADE CENTER...
HERE WE ARE PRETENDING TO SHOP IN BLOOMINGDALE'S...

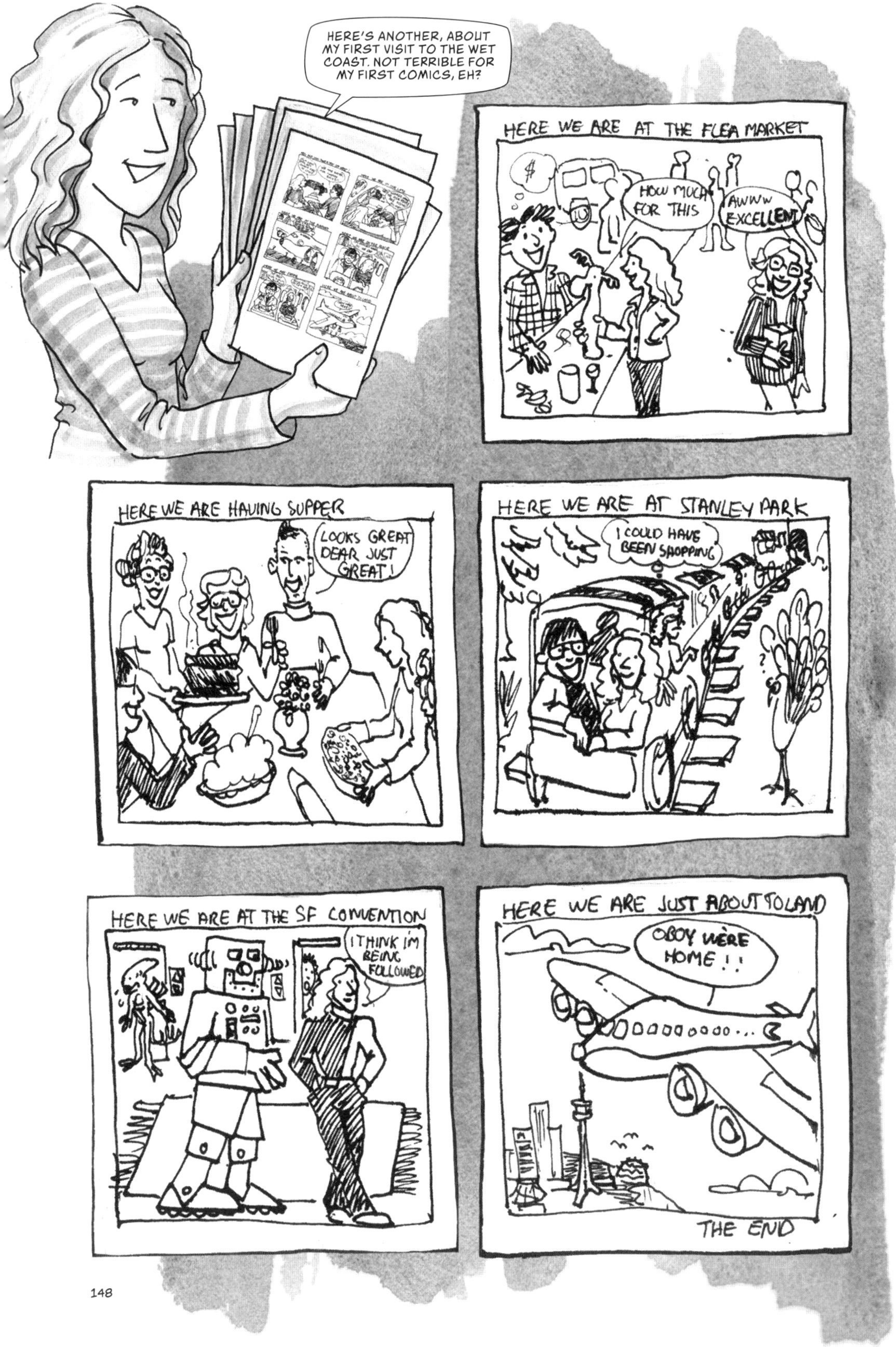
HERE'S ANOTHER, ABOUT MY FIRST VISIT TO THE WET COAST. NOT TERRIBLE FOR MY FIRST COMICS, EH?
HERE WE ARE AT THE FLEA MARKET
$
HOW MUCH FOR THIS
AWWW EXCELLENT
HERE WE ARE HAVING SUPPER
LOOKS GREAT DEAR JUST GREAT!
HERE WE ARE AT STANLEY PARK
I COULD HAVE BEEN SHOPPING
HERE WE ARE AT THE SF CONVENTION
I THINK I'M BEING FOLLOWED
HERE WE ARE JUST ABOUT TO LAND
OBOY WE'RE HOME!!
THE END

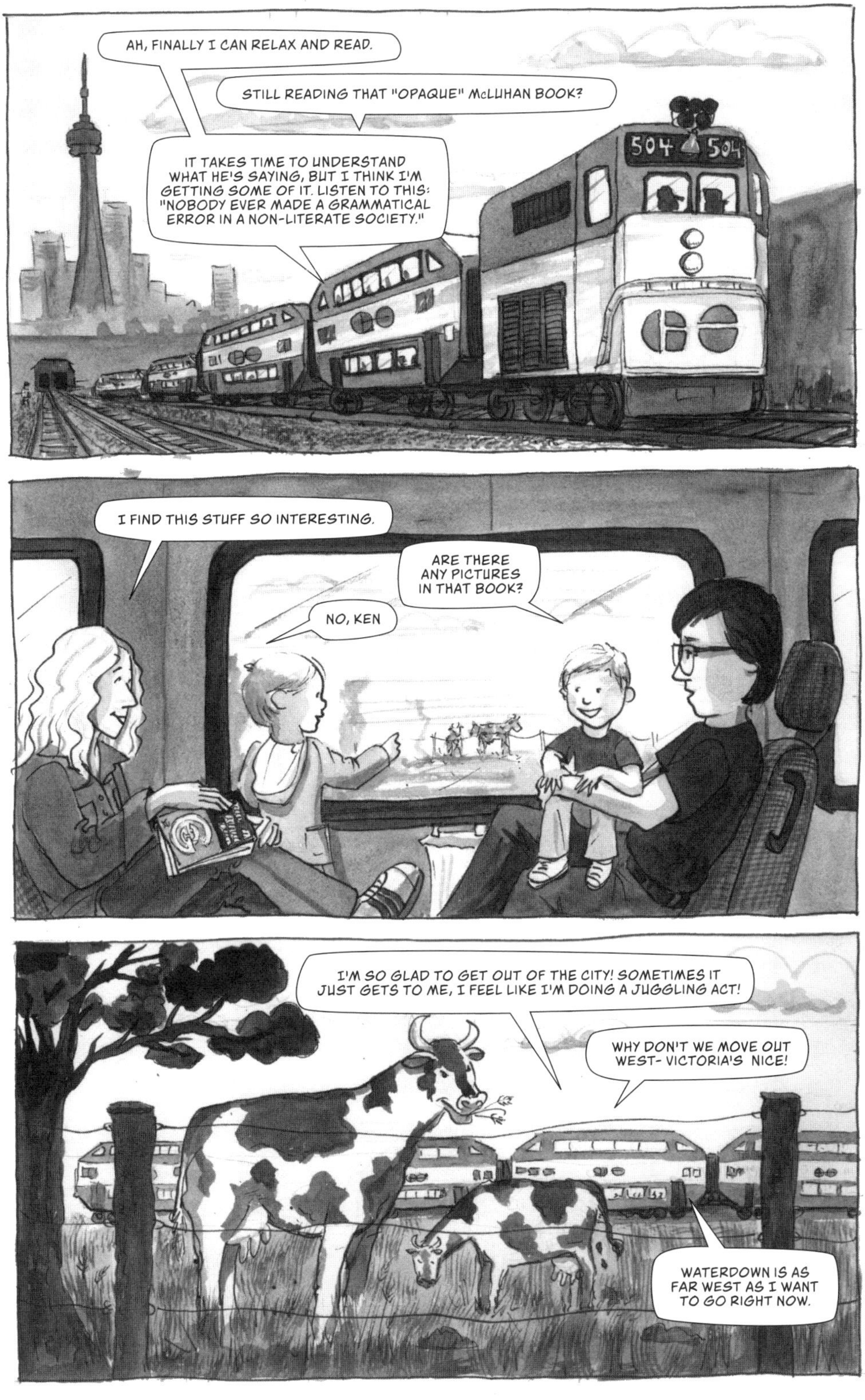
AH, FINALLY I CAN RELAX AND READ.
STILL READING THAT "OPAQUE" McLUHAN BOOK?
IT TAKES TIME TO UNDERSTAND WHAT HE'S SAYING, BUT I THINK I'M GETTING SOME OF IT. LISTEN TO THIS: "NOBODY EVER MADE A GRAMMATICAL ERROR IN A NON-LITERATE SOCIETY."
504
504
I FIND THIS STUFF SO INTERESTING.
ARE THERE ANY PICTURES IN THAT BOOK?
NO, KEN
I'M SO GLAD TO GET OUT OF THE CITY! SOMETIMES IT JUST GETS TO ME, I FEEL LIKE I'M DOING A JUGGLING ACT!
WHY DON'T WE MOVE OUT WEST- VICTORIA'S NICE!
WATERDOWN IS AS FAR WEST AS I WANT TO GO RIGHT NOW.

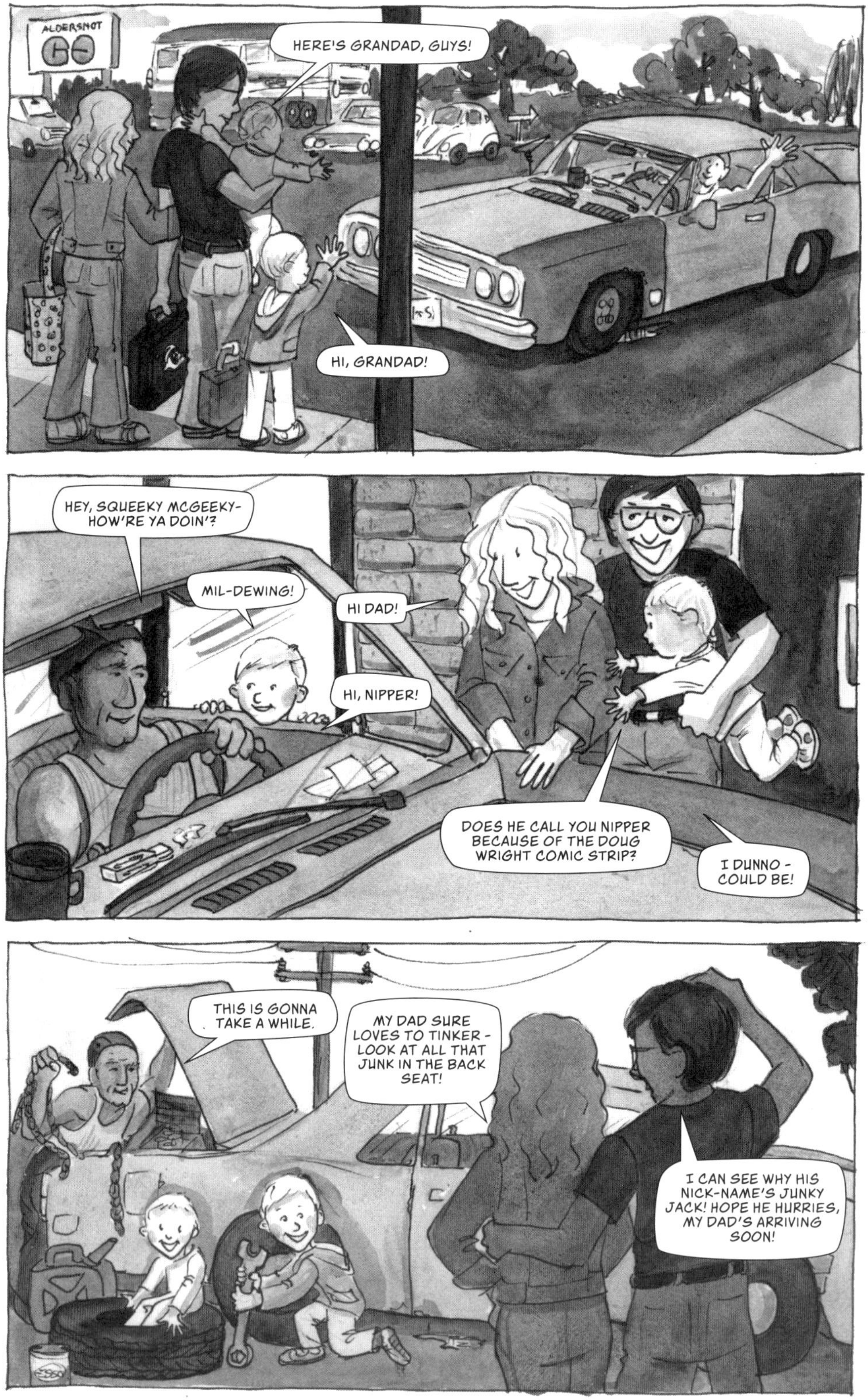
ALDERSHOT
GO
HERE'S GRANDAD, GUYS!
HI, GRANDAD!
HEY, SQUEEKY MCGEEKY-HOW'RE YA DOIN'?
MIL-DEWING!
HI DAD!
HI, NIPPER!
DOES HE CALL YOU NIPPER BECAUSE OF THE DOUG WRIGHT COMIC STRIP?
I DUNNO - COULD BE!
THIS IS GONNA TAKE A WHILE.
MY DAD SURE LOVES TO TINKER - LOOK AT ALL THAT JUNK IN THE BACK SEAT!
I CAN SEE WHY HIS NICK-NAME'S JUNKY JACK! HOPE HE HURRIES, MY DAD'S ARRIVING SOON!

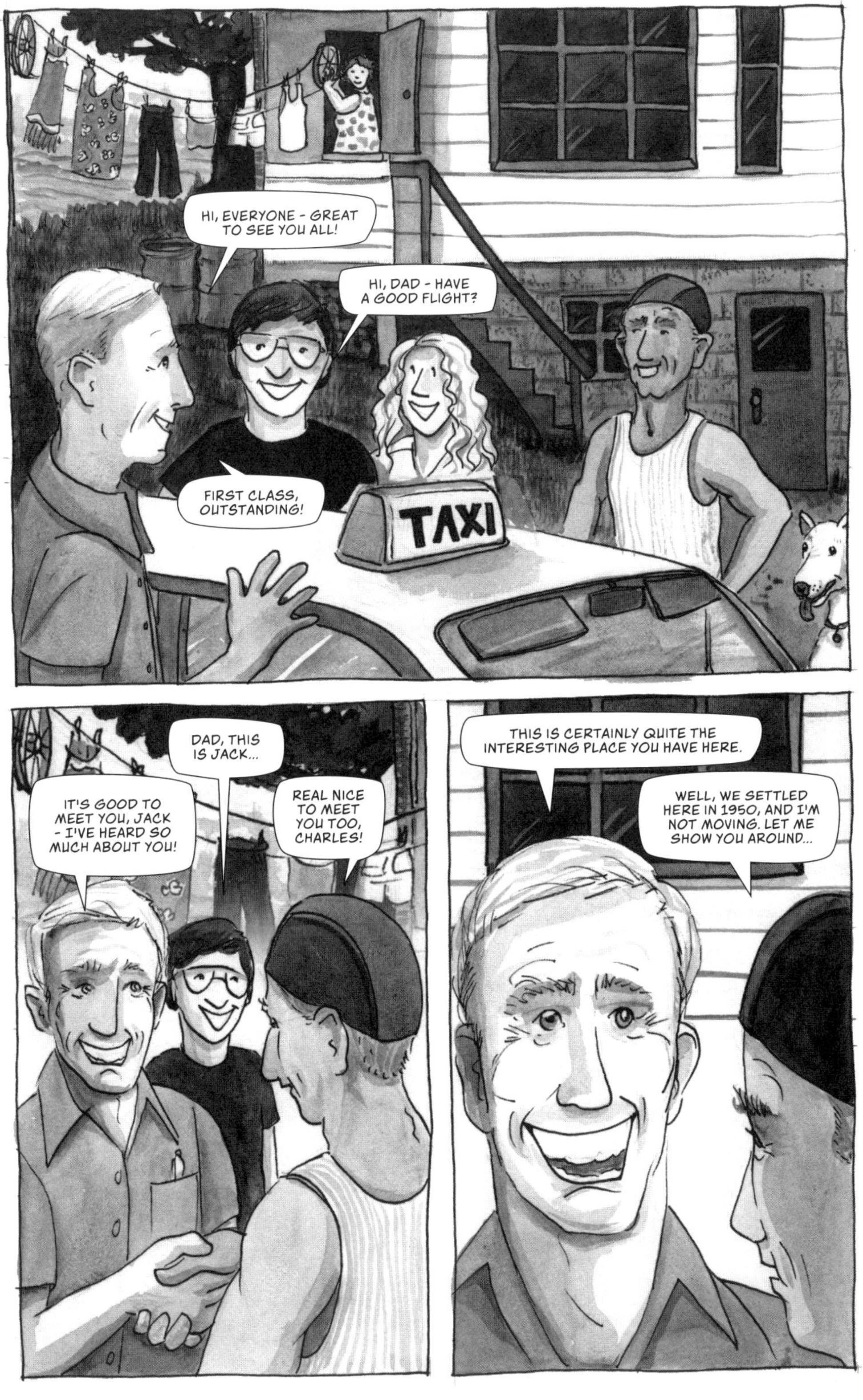
HI, EVERYONE - GREAT TO SEE YOU ALL!
HI, DAD - HAVE A GOOD FLIGHT?
FIRST CLASS, OUTSTANDING!
TAXI
DAD, THIS IS JACK...
IT'S GOOD TO MEET YOU, JACK - I'VE HEARD SO MUCH ABOUT YOU!
REAL NICE TO MEET YOU TOO, CHARLES!
THIS IS CERTAINLY QUITE THE INTERESTING PLACE YOU HAVE HERE.
WELL, WE SETTLED HERE IN 1950, AND I'M NOT MOVING. LET ME SHOW YOU AROUND...

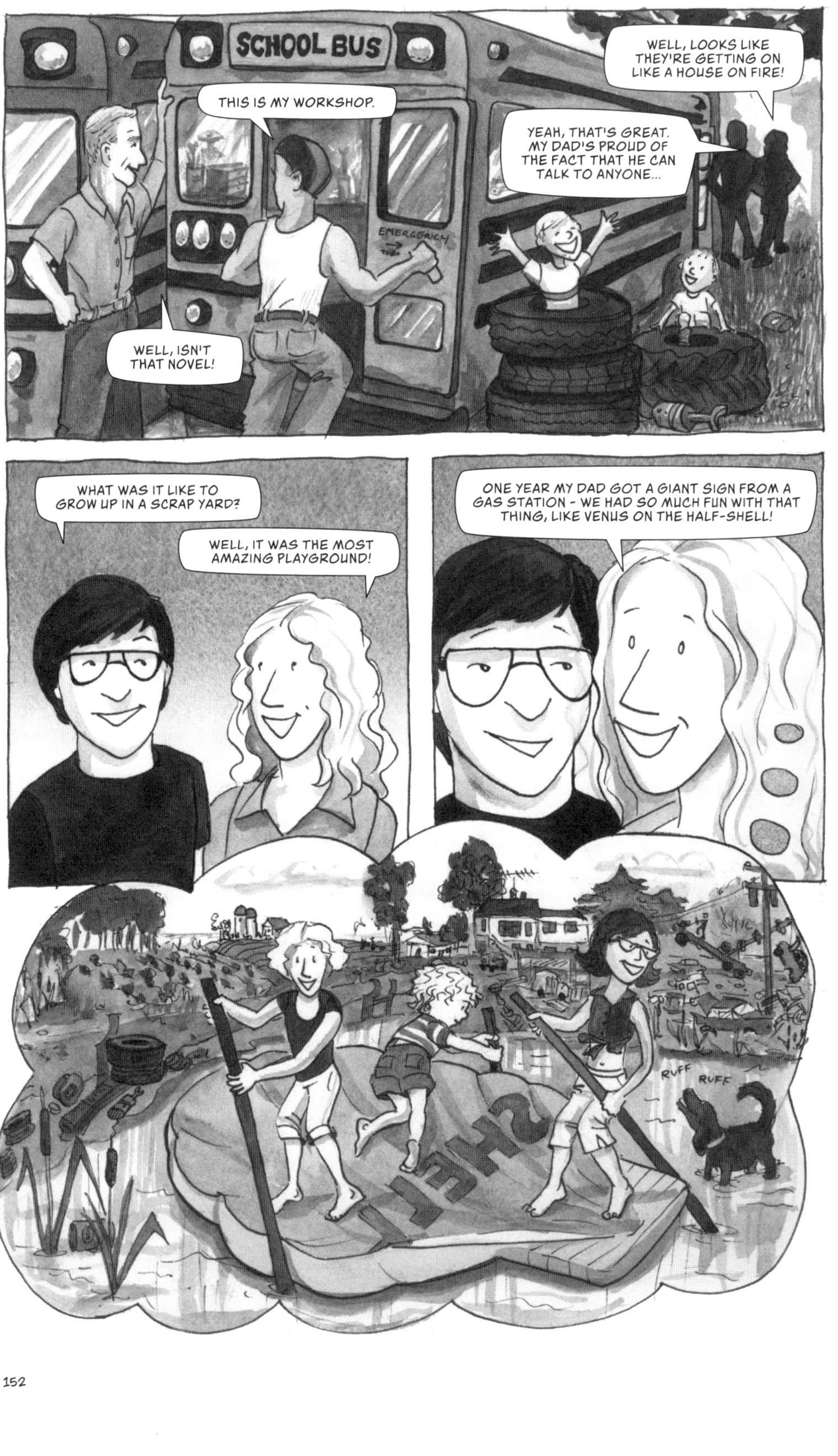
SCHOOL BUS
THIS IS MY WORKSHOP.
WELL, ISN'T THAT NOVEL!
WELL, LOOKS LIKE THEY'RE GETTING ON LIKE A HOUSE ON FIRE!
YEAH, THAT'S GREAT. MY DAD'S PROUD OF THE FACT THAT HE CAN TALK TO ANYONE...
WHAT WAS IT LIKE TO GROW UP IN A SCRAP YARD?
WELL, IT WAS THE MOST AMAZING PLAYGROUND!
ONE YEAR MY DAD GOT A GIANT SIGN FROM A GAS STATION - WE HAD SO MUCH FUN WITH THAT THING, LIKE VENUS ON THE HALF-SHELL!
RUFF
RUFF

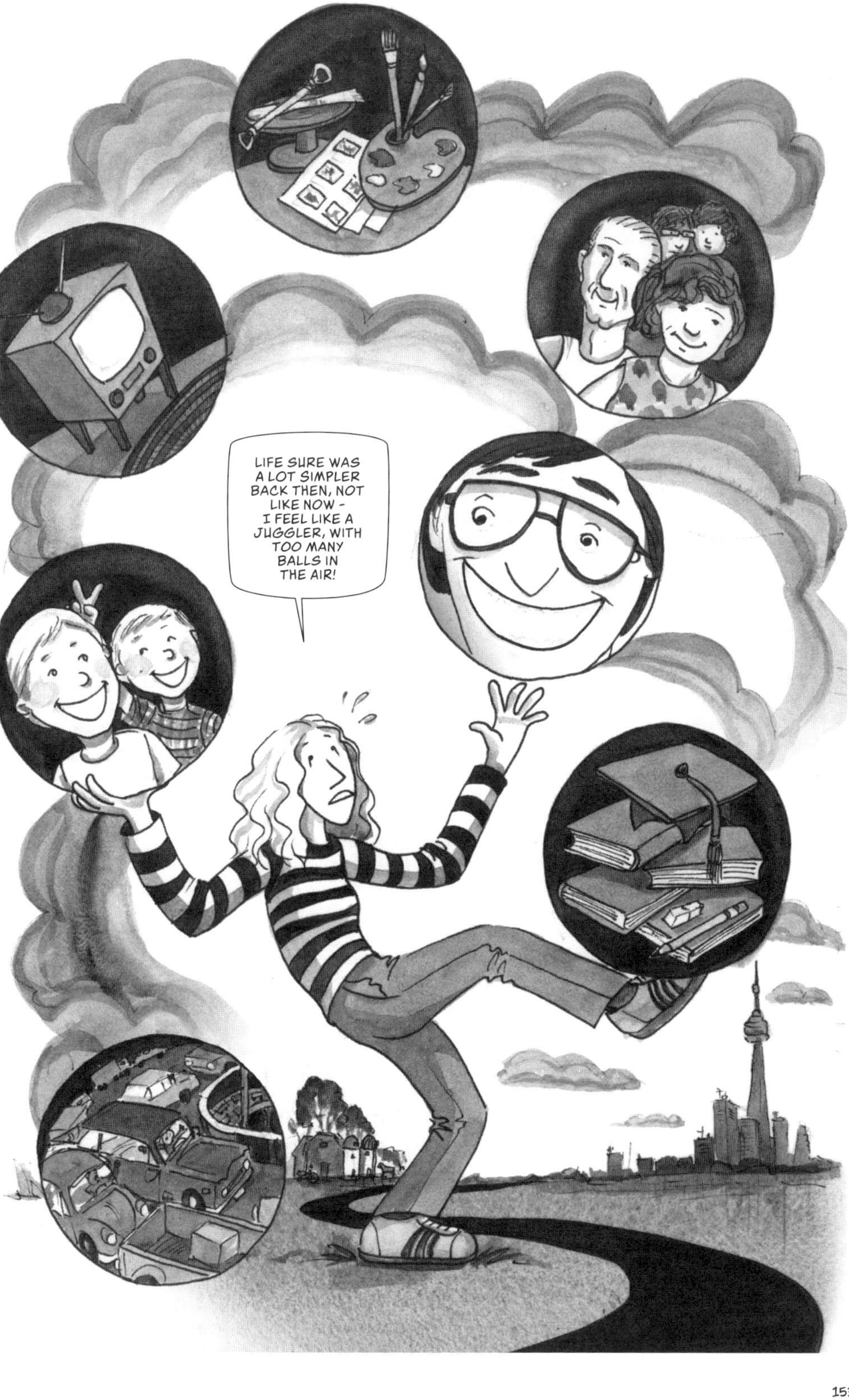
LIFE SURE WAS A LOT SIMPLER BACK THEN, NOT LIKE NOW - I FEEL LIKE A JUGGLER, WITH TOO MANY BALLS IN THE AIR!

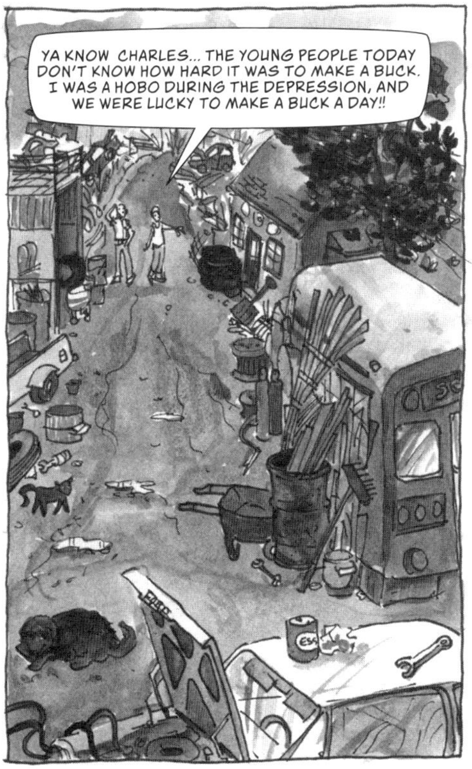
YA KNOW CHARLES... THE YOUNG PEOPLE TODAY DON'T KNOW HOW HARD IT WAS TO MAKE A BUCK. I WAS A HOBO DURING THE DEPRESSION, AND WE WERE LUCKY TO MAKE A BUCK A DAY!!

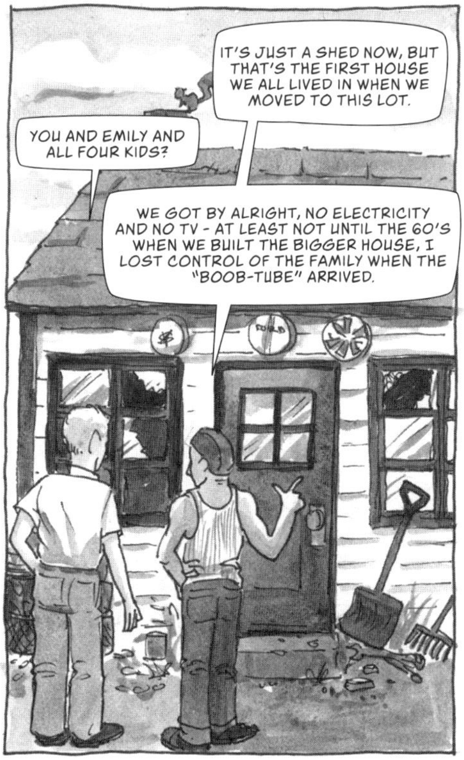
IT'S JUST A SHED NOW, BUT THAT'S THE FIRST HOUSE WE ALL LIVED IN WHEN WE MOVED TO THIS LOT.
YOU AND EMILY AND ALL FOUR KIDS?
WE GOT BY ALRIGHT, NO ELECTRICITY AND NO TV - AT LEAST NOT UNTIL THE 60'S WHEN WE BUILT THE BIGGER HOUSE, I LOST CONTROL OF THE FAMILY WHEN THE "BOOB-TUBE" ARRIVED.

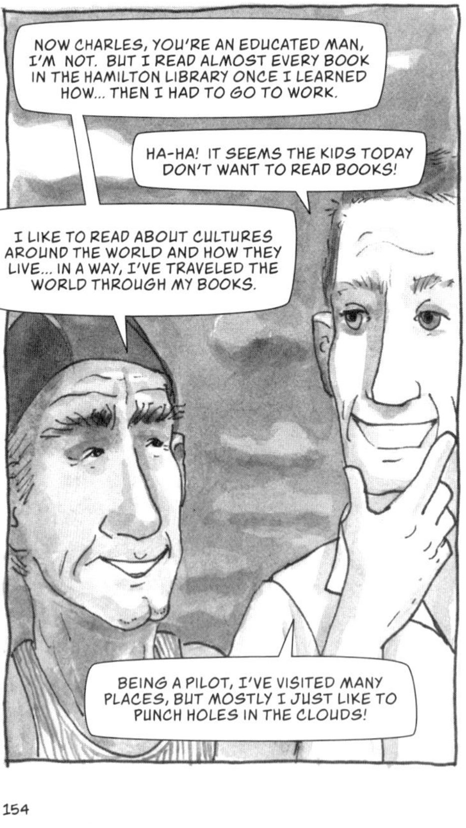
NOW CHARLES, YOU'RE AN EDUCATED MAN, I'M NOT. BUT I READ ALMOST EVERY BOOK IN THE HAMILTON LIBRARY ONCE I LEARNED HOW... THEN I HAD TO GO TO WORK.
HA-HA! IT SEEMS THE KIDS TODAY DON'T WANT TO READ BOOKS!
I LIKE TO READ ABOUT CULTURES AROUND THE WORLD AND HOW THEY LIVE... IN A WAY, I'VE TRAVELED THE WORLD THROUGH MY BOOKS.
BEING A PILOT, I'VE VISITED MANY PLACES, BUT MOSTLY I JUST LIKE TO PUNCH HOLES IN THE CLOUDS!

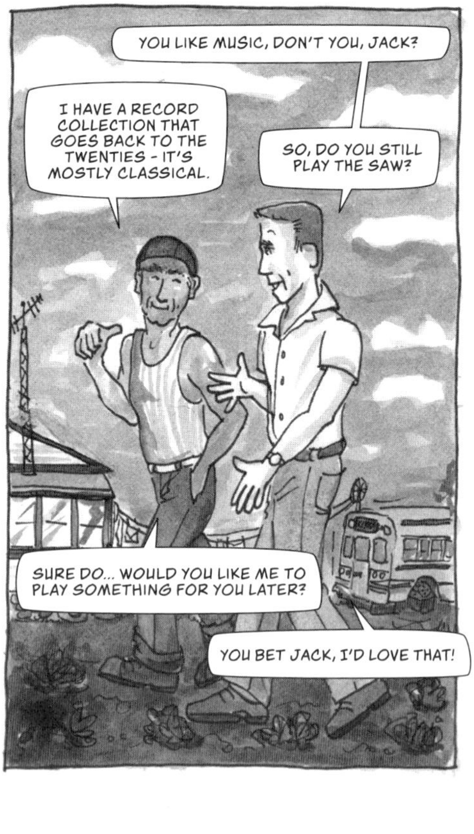
YOU LIKE MUSIC, DON'T YOU, JACK?
I HAVE A RECORD COLLECTION THAT GOES BACK TO THE TWENTIES - IT'S MOSTLY CLASSICAL.
SO, DO YOU STILL PLAY THE SAW?
SURE DO... WOULD YOU LIKE ME TO PLAY SOMETHING FOR YOU LATER?
YOU BET JACK, I'D LOVE THAT!

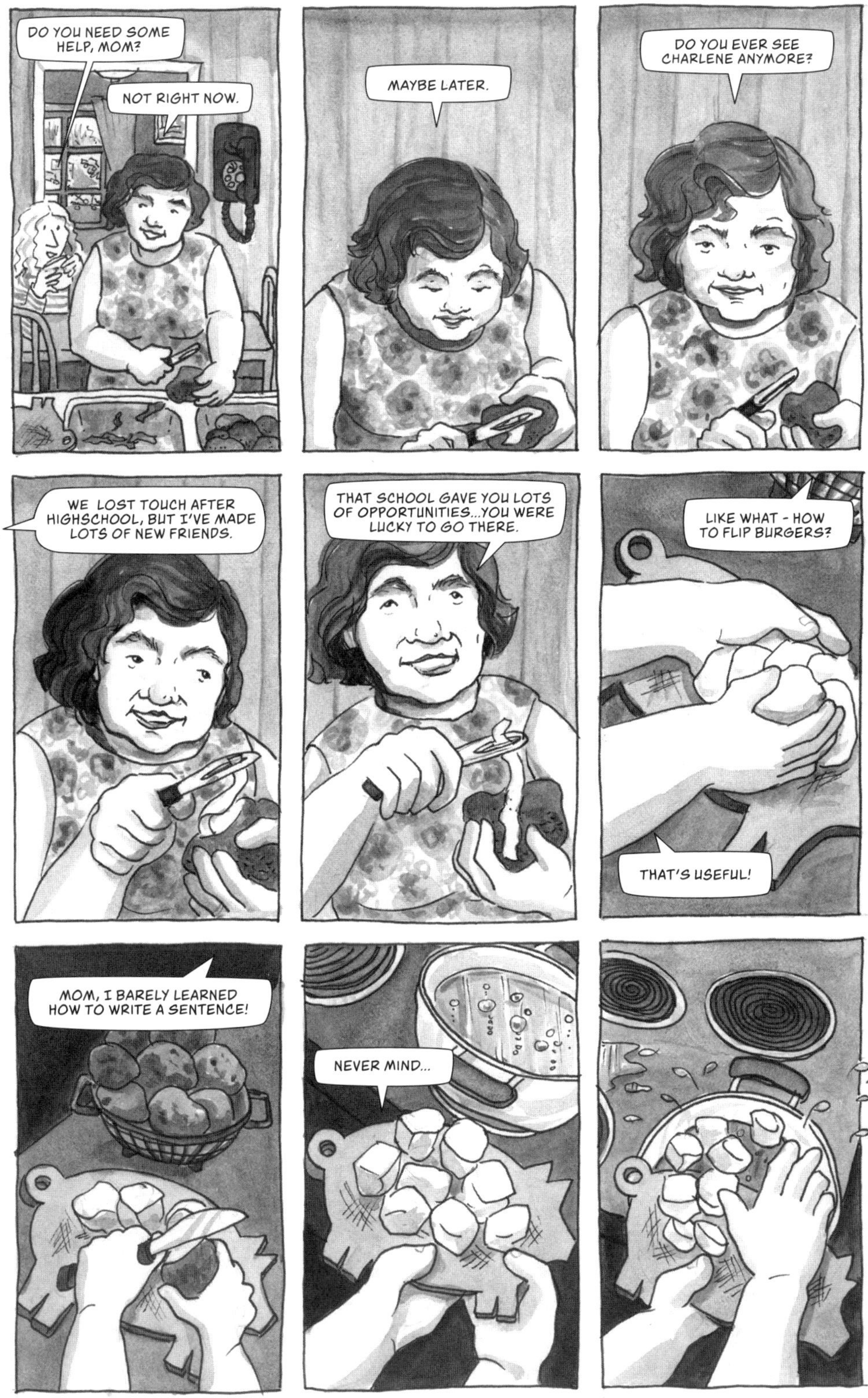
DO YOU NEED SOME HELP, MOM?
NOT RIGHT NOW.
MAYBE LATER.
DO YOU EVER SEE CHARLENE ANYMORE?
WE LOST TOUCH AFTER HIGHSCHOOL, BUT I'VE MADE LOTS OF NEW FRIENDS.
THAT SCHOOL GAVE YOU LOTS OF OPPORTUNITIES...YOU WERE LUCKY TO GO THERE.
LIKE WHAT - HOW TO FLIP BURGERS?
THAT'S USEFUL!
MOM, I BARELY LEARNED HOW TO WRITE A SENTENCE!
NEVER MIND...

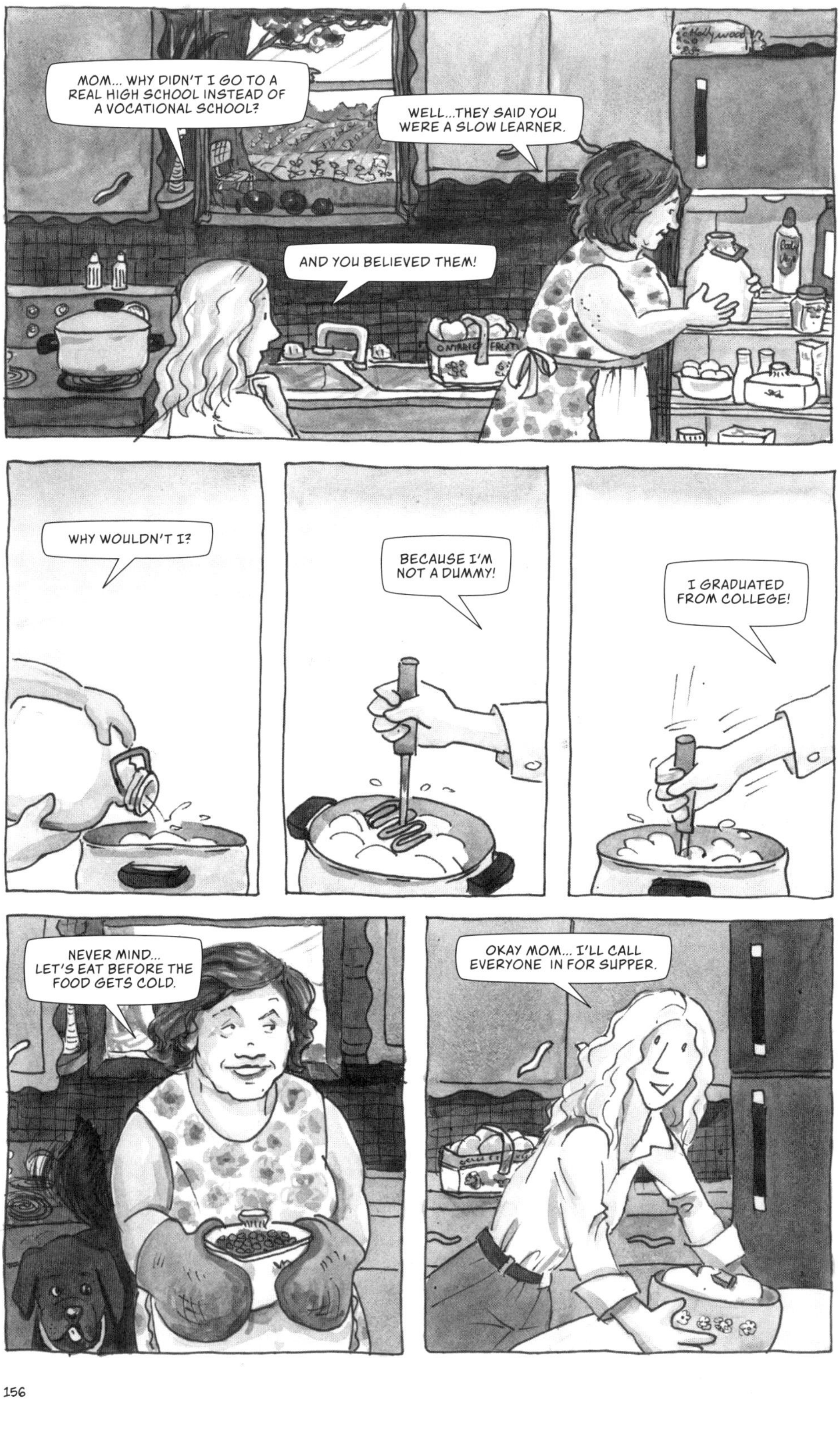

MOM... WHY DIDN'T I GO TO A REAL HIGH SCHOOL INSTEAD OF A VOCATIONAL SCHOOL?
WELL...THEY SAID YOU WERE A SLOW LEARNER.
AND YOU BELIEVED THEM!
ONTARIO FRUIT
WHY WOULDN'T I?
BECAUSE I'M NOT A DUMMY!
I GRADUATED FROM COLLEGE!
NEVER MIND... LET'S EAT BEFORE THE FOOD GETS COLD.
OKAY MOM... I'LL CALL EVERYONE IN FOR SUPPER.

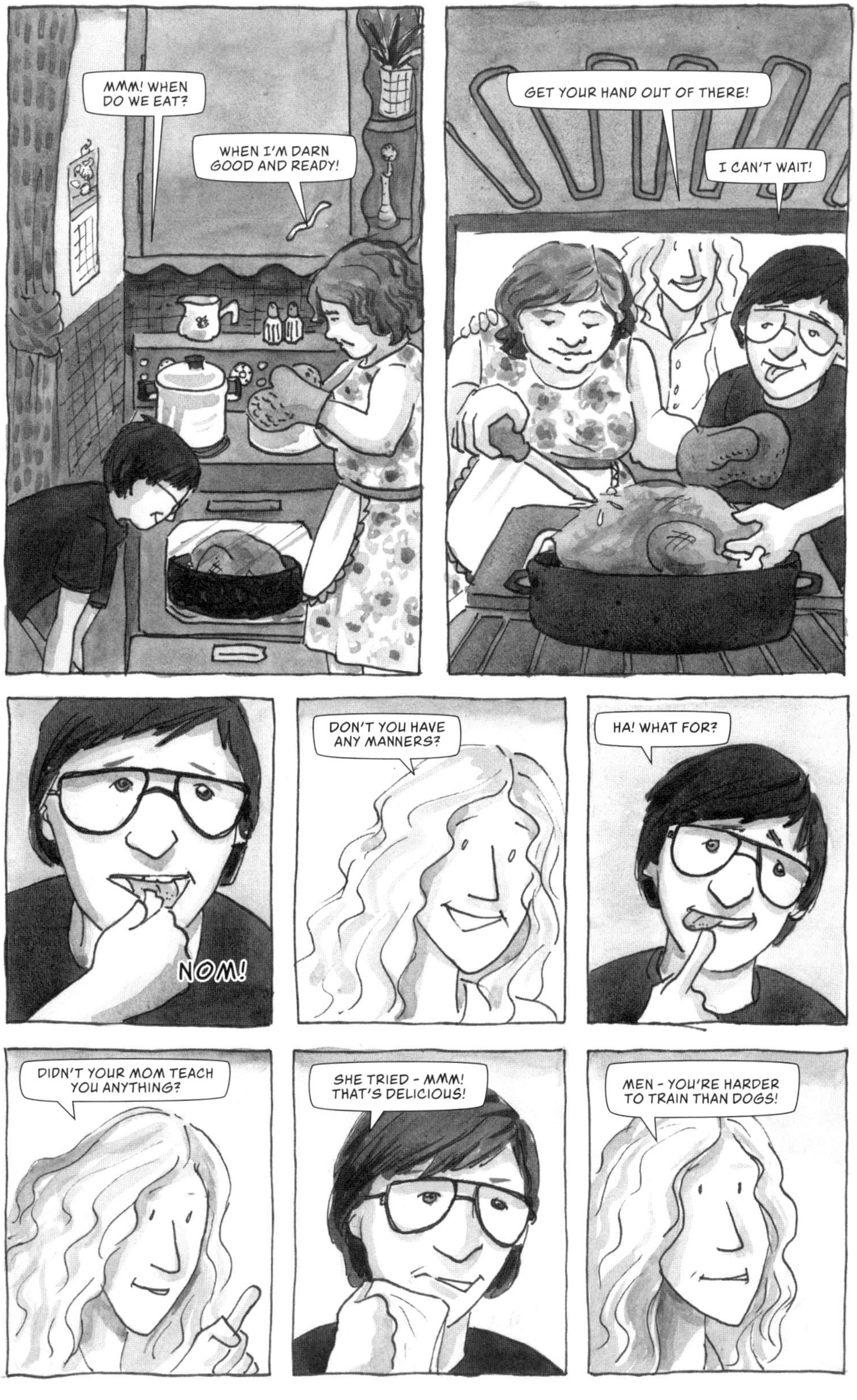
MMM! WHEN DO WE EAT?
WHEN I'M DARN GOOD AND READY!
GET YOUR HAND OUT OF THERE!
I CAN'T WAIT!
NOM!
DON'T YOU HAVE ANY MANNERS?
HA! WHAT FOR?
DIDN'T YOUR MOM TEACH YOU ANYTHING?
SHE TRIED - MMM! THAT'S DELICIOUS!
MEN - YOU'RE HARDER TO TRAIN THAN DOGS!

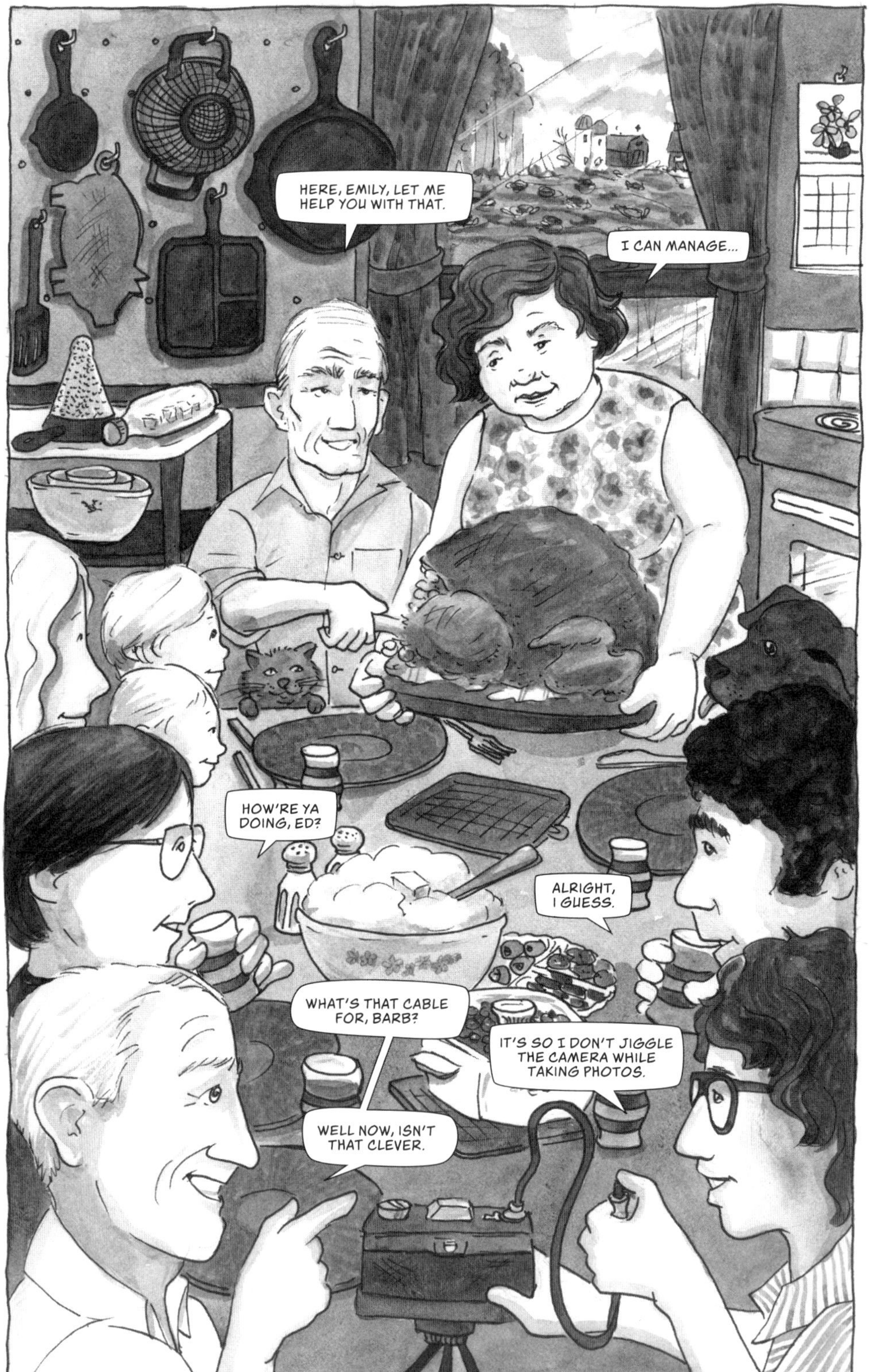
HERE, EMILY, LET ME HELP YOU WITH THAT.
I CAN MANAGE...
HOW'RE YA DOING, ED?
ALRIGHT, I GUESS.
WHAT'S THAT CABLE FOR, BARB?
IT'S SO I DON'T JIGGLE THE CAMERA WHILE TAKING PHOTOS.
WELL NOW, ISN'T THAT CLEVER.

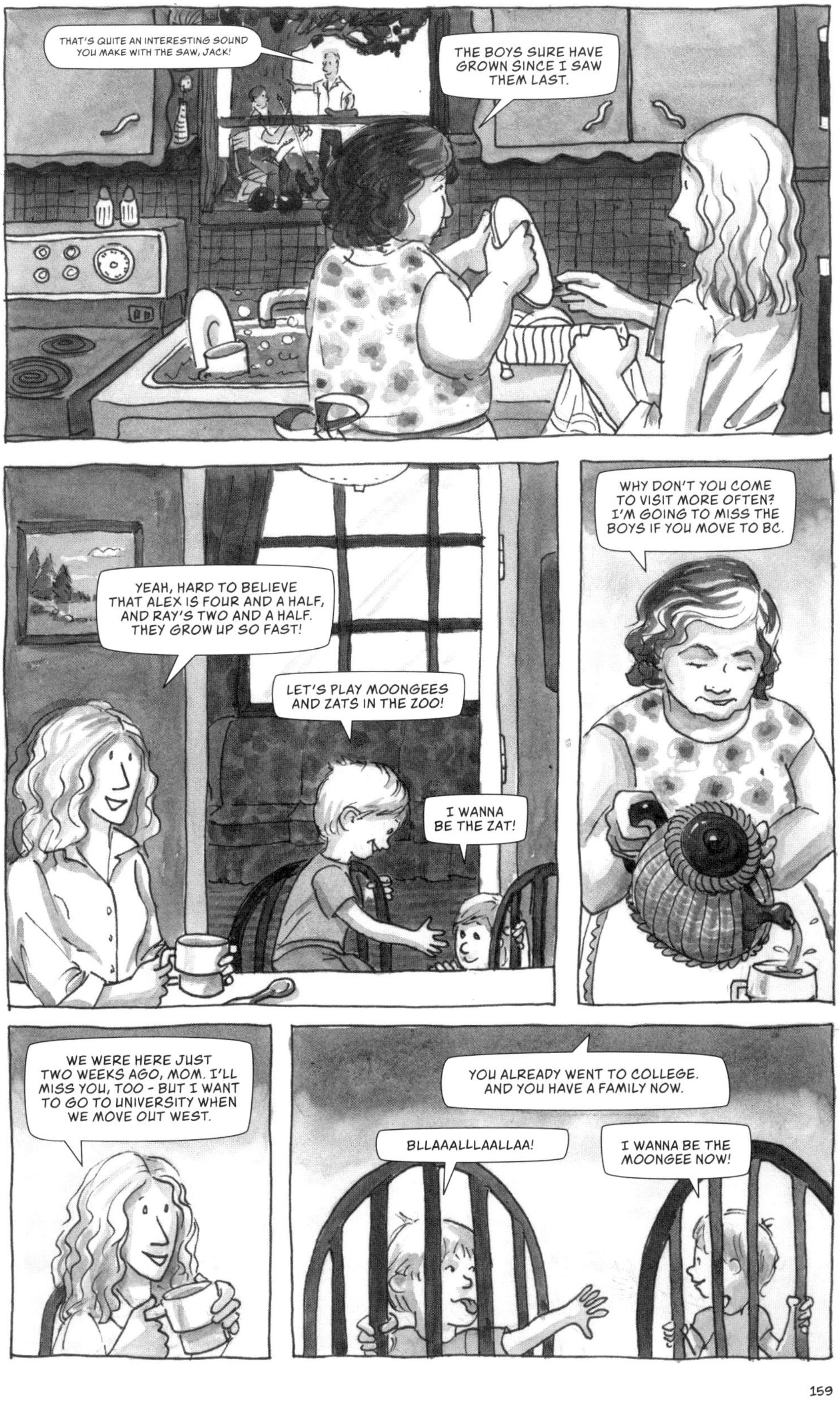

THAT'S QUITE AN INTERESTING SOUND YOU MAKE WITH THE SAW, JACK!
THE BOYS SURE HAVE GROWN SINCE I SAW THEM LAST.
YEAH, HARD TO BELIEVE THAT ALEX IS FOUR AND A HALF, AND RAY'S TWO AND A HALF. THEY GROW UP SO FAST!
LET'S PLAY MOONGEES AND ZATS IN THE ZOO!
I WANNA BE THE ZAT!
WHY DON'T YOU COME TO VISIT MORE OFTEN? I'M GOING TO MISS THE BOYS IF YOU MOVE TO BC.
WE WERE HERE JUST TWO WEEKS AGO, MOM. I'LL MISS YOU, TOO - BUT I WANT TO GO TO UNIVERSITY WHEN WE MOVE OUT WEST.
YOU ALREADY WENT TO COLLEGE. AND YOU HAVE A FAMILY NOW.
BLLAAALLLAALLAA!
I WANNA BE THE MOONGEE NOW!

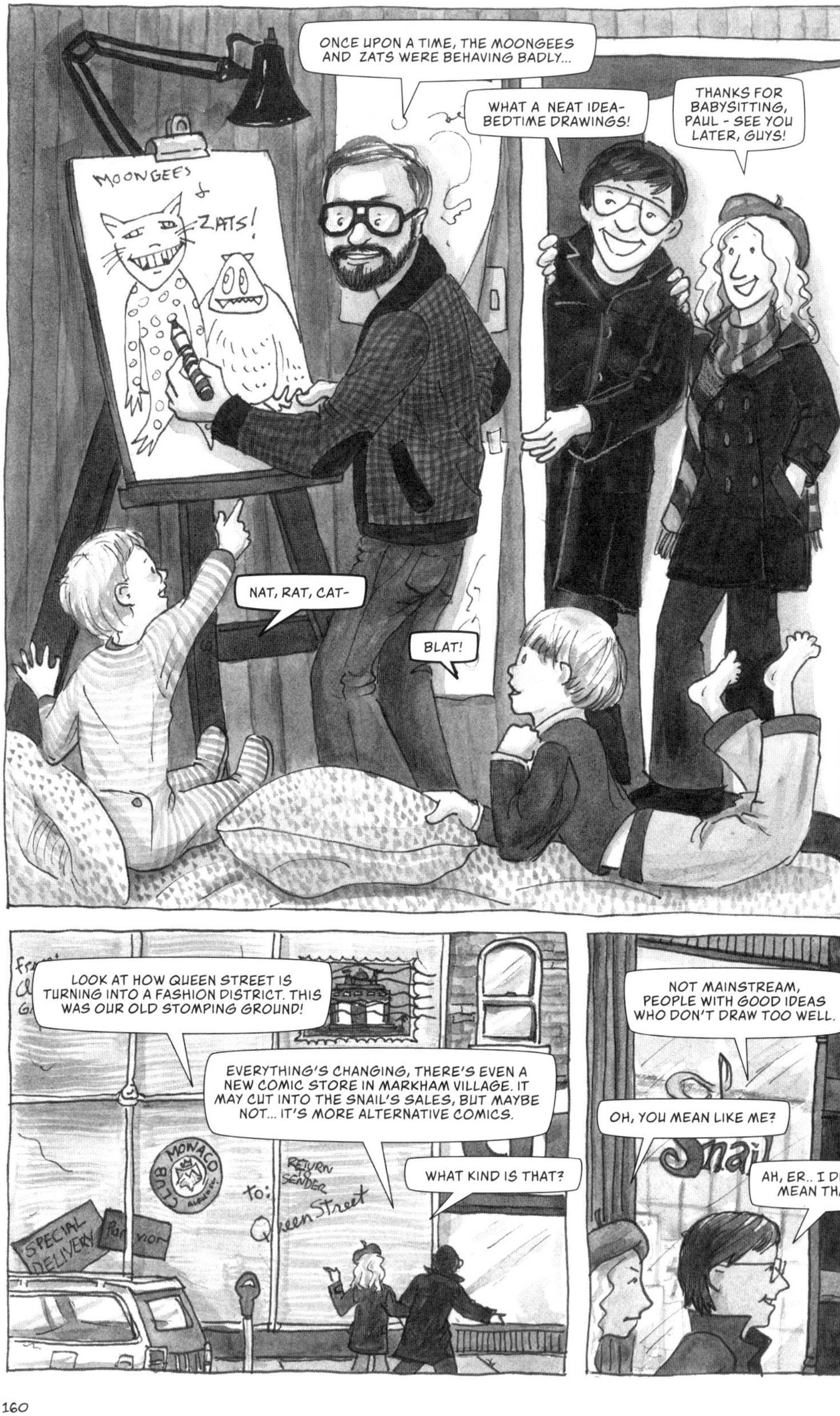

MOONGEES
ZATS!
ONCE UPON A TIME, THE MOONGEES AND ZATS WERE BEHAVING BADLY...
WHAT A NEAT IDEA- BEDTIME DRAWINGS!
THANKS FOR BABYSITTING, PAUL - SEE YOU LATER, GUYS!
NAT, RAT, CAT-
BLAT!
LOOK AT HOW QUEEN STREET IS TURNING INTO A FASHION DISTRICT. THIS WAS OUR OLD STOMPING GROUND!
EVERYTHING'S CHANGING, THERE'S EVEN A NEW COMIC STORE IN MARKHAM VILLAGE. IT MAY CUT INTO THE SNAIL'S SALES, BUT MAYBE NOT... IT'S MORE ALTERNATIVE COMICS.
WHAT KIND IS THAT?
CLUB MONACO
RETURN TO SENDER
to: Queen Street
SPECIAL DELIVERY
NOT MAINSTREAM, PEOPLE WITH GOOD IDEAS WHO DON'T DRAW TOO WELL.
OH, YOU MEAN LIKE ME?
AH, ER.. I DIDN'T MEAN THAT!

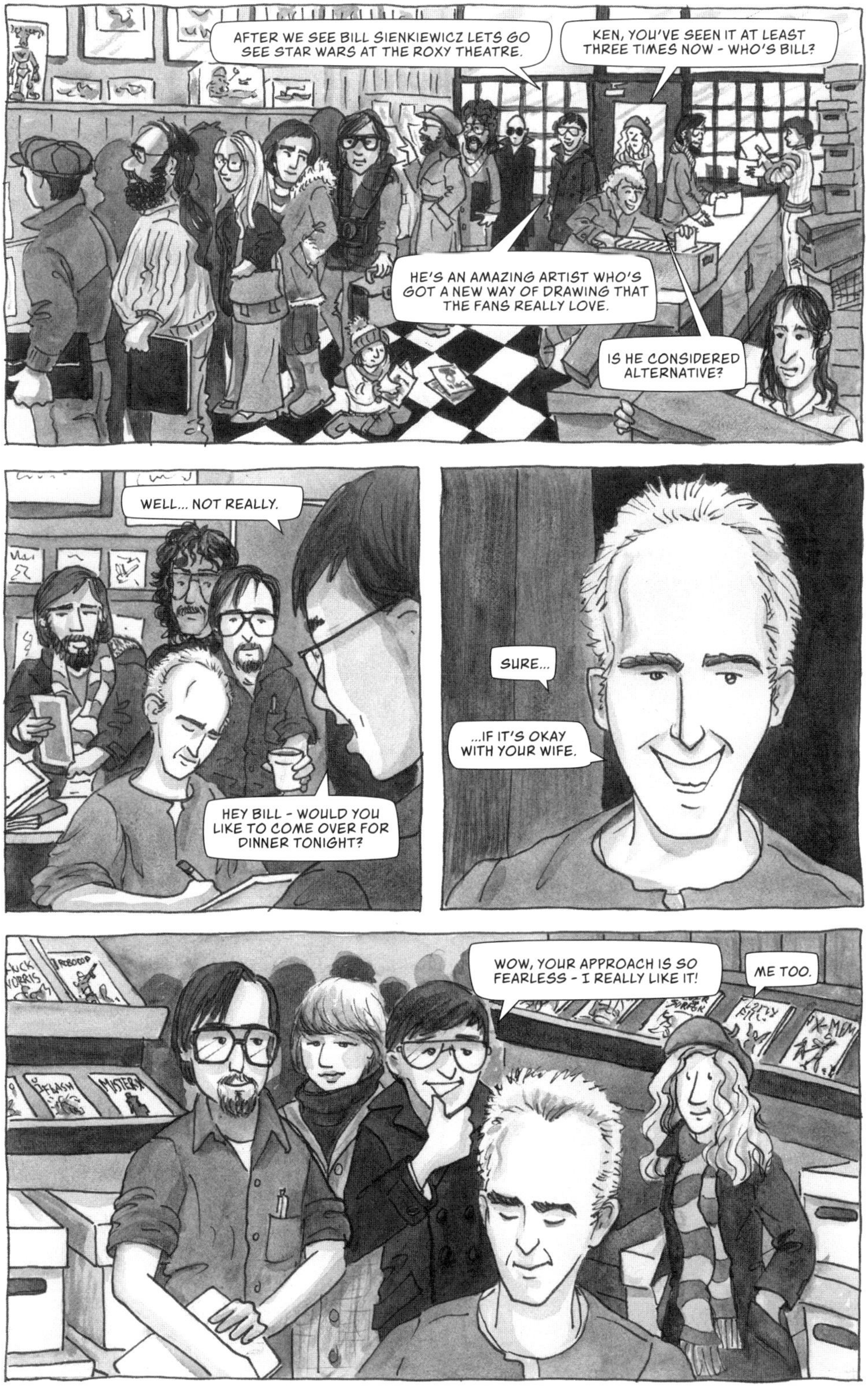
AFTER WE SEE BILL SIENKIEWICZ LETS GO SEE STAR WARS AT THE ROXY THEATRE.
KEN, YOU'VE SEEN IT AT LEAST THREE TIMES NOW - WHO'S BILL?
HE'S AN AMAZING ARTIST WHO'S GOT A NEW WAY OF DRAWING THAT THE FANS REALLY LOVE.
IS HE CONSIDERED ALTERNATIVE?
WELL... NOT REALLY.
HEY BILL - WOULD YOU LIKE TO COME OVER FOR DINNER TONIGHT?
SURE...
...IF IT'S OKAY WITH YOUR WIFE.
WOW, YOUR APPROACH IS SO FEARLESS - I REALLY LIKE IT!
ME TOO.

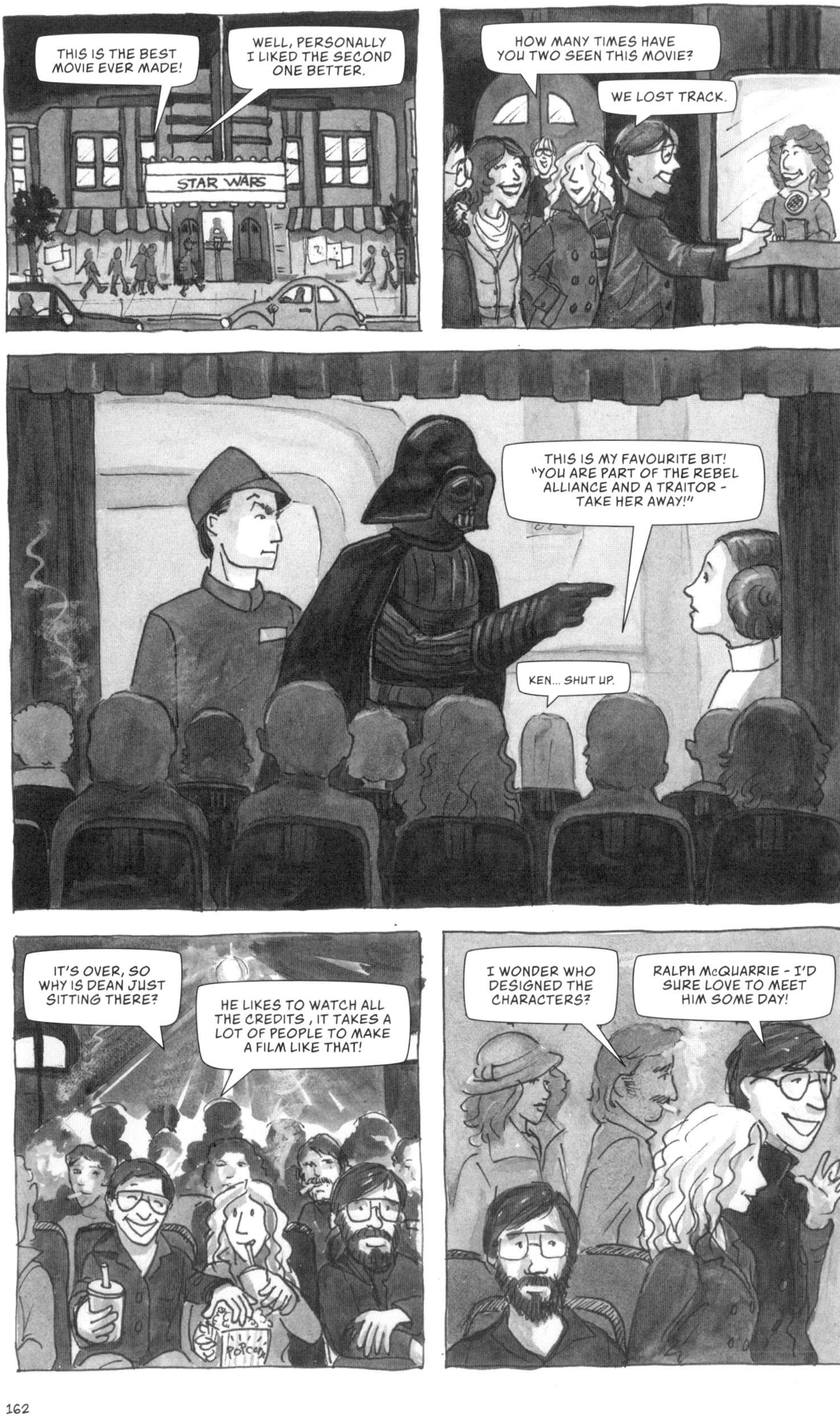
THIS IS THE BEST MOVIE EVER MADE!
WELL, PERSONALLY I LIKED THE SECOND ONE BETTER.
STAR WARS
HOW MANY TIMES HAVE YOU TWO SEEN THIS MOVIE?
WE LOST TRACK.
THIS IS MY FAVOURITE BIT! "YOU ARE PART OF THE REBEL ALLIANCE AND A TRAITOR - TAKE HER AWAY!"
KEN... SHUT UP.
IT'S OVER, SO WHY IS DEAN JUST SITTING THERE?
HE LIKES TO WATCH ALL THE CREDITS , IT TAKES A LOT OF PEOPLE TO MAKE A FILM LIKE THAT!
I WONDER WHO DESIGNED THE CHARACTERS?
RALPH McQUARRIE - I'D SURE LOVE TO MEET HIM SOME DAY!

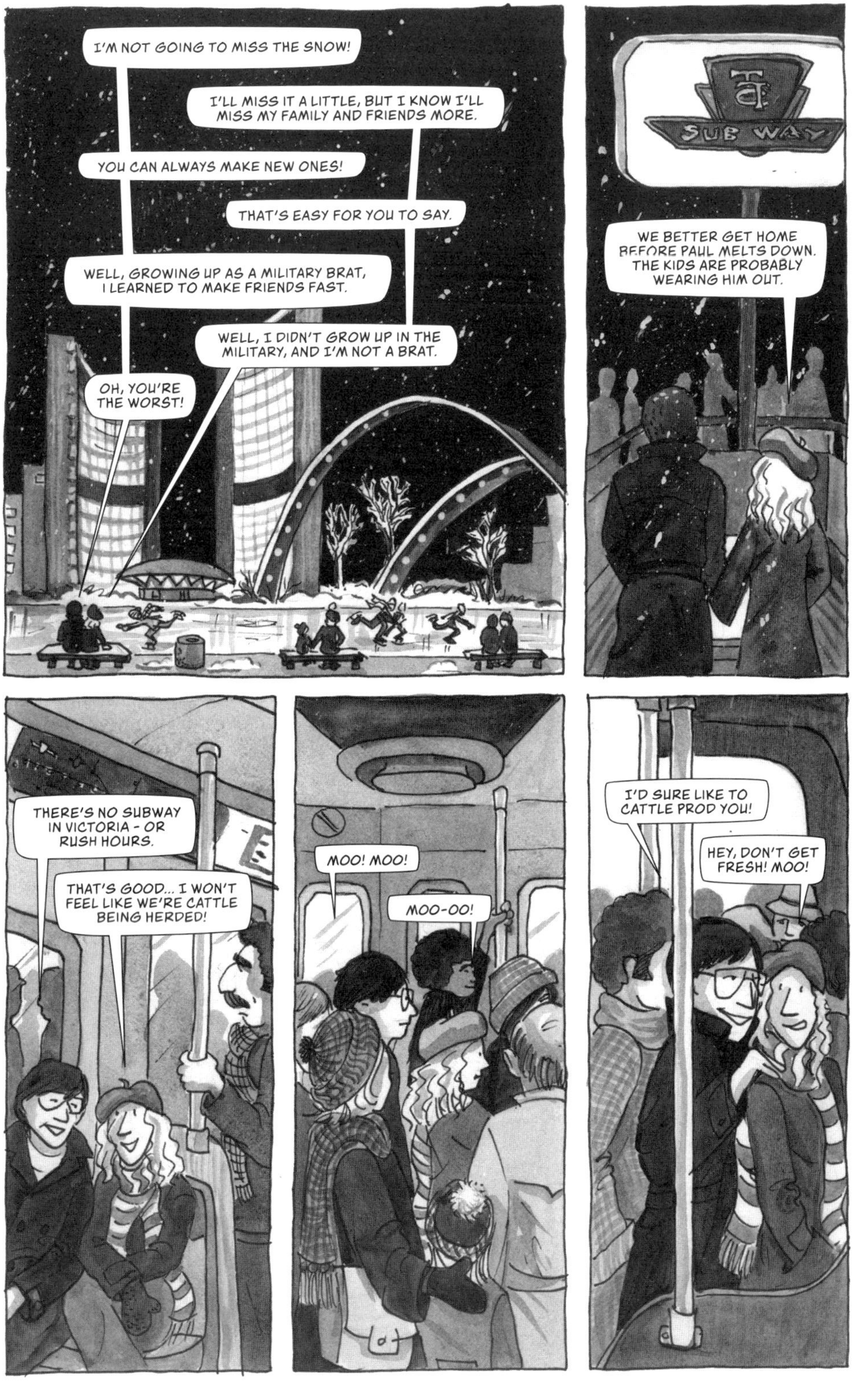
I'M NOT GOING TO MISS THE SNOW!
I'LL MISS IT A LITTLE, BUT I KNOW I'LL MISS MY FAMILY AND FRIENDS MORE.
YOU CAN ALWAYS MAKE NEW ONES!
THAT'S EASY FOR YOU TO SAY.
WELL, GROWING UP AS A MILITARY BRAT, I LEARNED TO MAKE FRIENDS FAST.
WELL, I DIDN'T GROW UP IN THE MILITARY, AND I'M NOT A BRAT.
OH, YOU'RE THE WORST!
SUB WAY
WE BETTER GET HOME BEFORE PAUL MELTS DOWN. THE KIDS ARE PROBABLY WEARING HIM OUT.
THERE'S NO SUBWAY IN VICTORIA - OR RUSH HOURS.
THAT'S GOOD... I WON'T FEEL LIKE WE'RE CATTLE BEING HERDED!
MOO! MOO!
MOO-OO!
I'D SURE LIKE TO CATTLE PROD YOU!
HEY, DON'T GET FRESH! MOO!

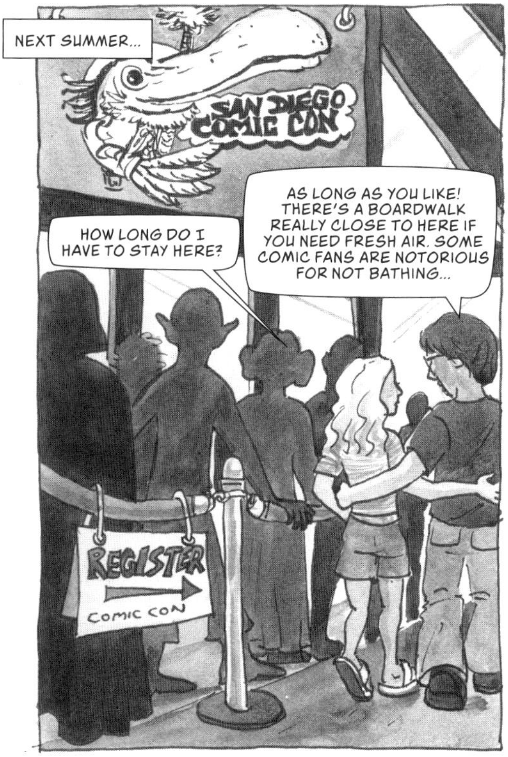
NEXT SUMMER...
SAN DIEGO COMIC CON
HOW LONG DO I HAVE TO STAY HERE?
AS LONG AS YOU LIKE! THERE'S A BOARDWALK REALLY CLOSE TO HERE IF YOU NEED FRESH AIR. SOME COMIC FANS ARE NOTORIOUS FOR NOT BATHING...
REGISTER
COMIC CON

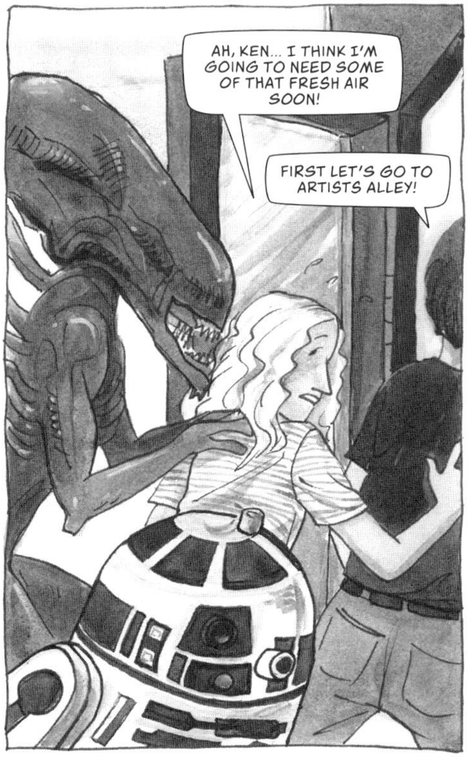
AH, KEN... I THINK I'M GOING TO NEED SOME OF THAT FRESH AIR SOON!
FIRST LET'S GO TO ARTISTS ALLEY!

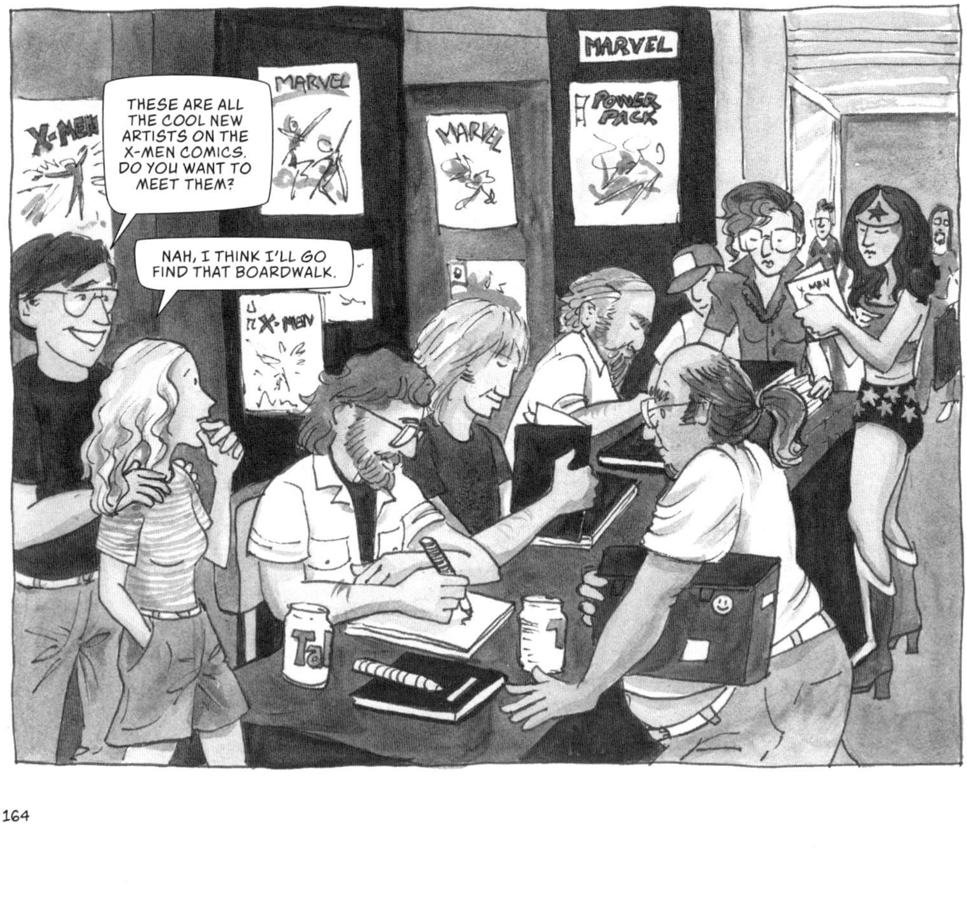
X-MEN
MARVEL
MARVEL
MARVEL
POWER PACK
X-MEN
THESE ARE ALL THE COOL NEW ARTISTS ON THE X-MEN COMICS. DO YOU WANT TO MEET THEM?
NAH, I THINK I'LL GO FIND THAT BOARDWALK.

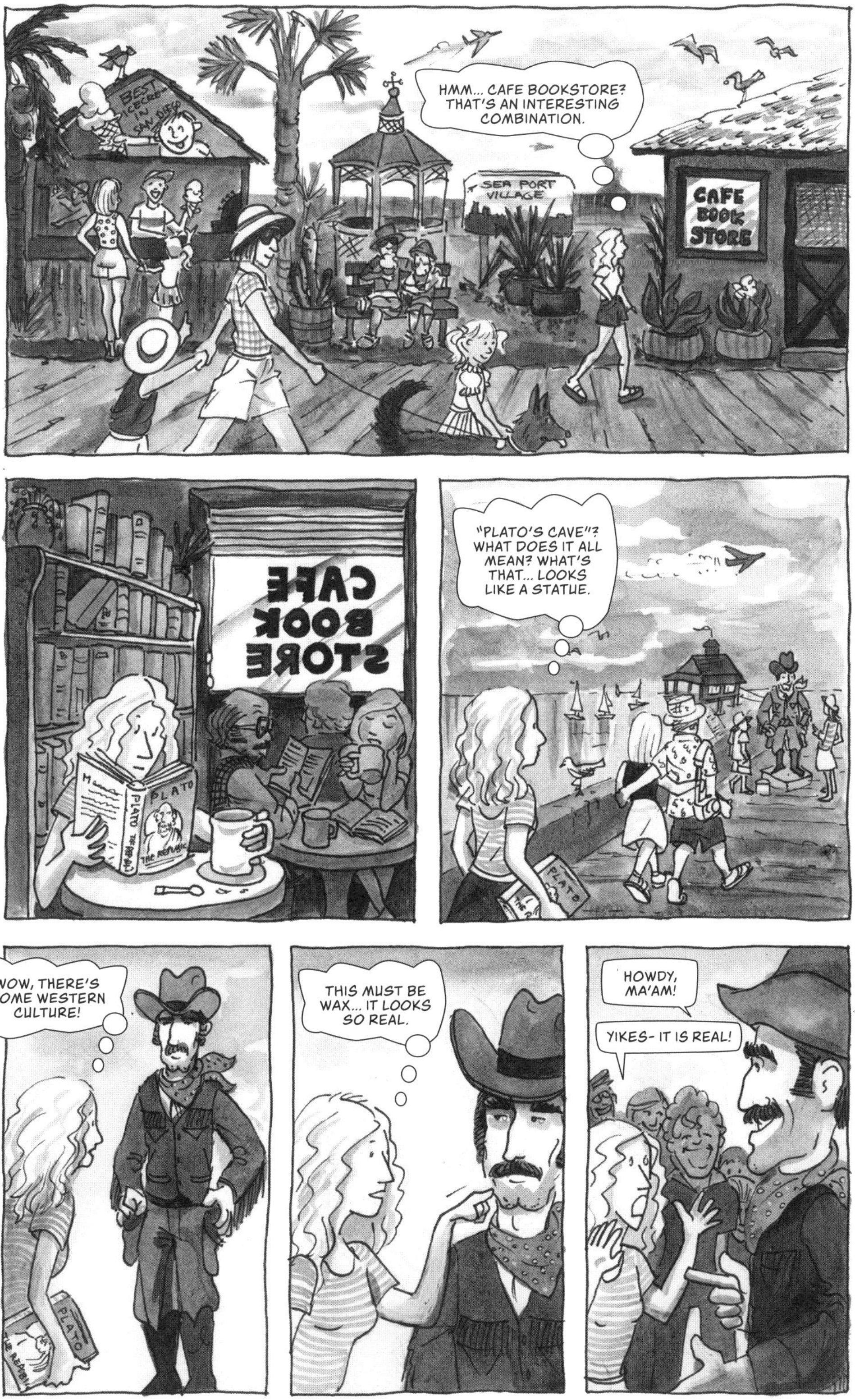
BEST ICECRE IN SAN DIEGO
HMM... CAFE BOOKSTORE? THAT'S AN INTERESTING COMBINATION.
SEA PORT VILLAGE
CAFE BOOK STORE
CAFE BOOK STORE
PLATO
THE REPUBLIC
"PLATO'S CAVE"? WHAT DOES IT ALL MEAN? WHAT'S THAT... LOOKS LIKE A STATUE.
PLATO
WOW, THERE'S SOME WESTERN CULTURE!
PLATO
THIS MUST BE WAX... IT LOOKS SO REAL.
HOWDY, MA'AM!
YIKES- IT IS REAL!

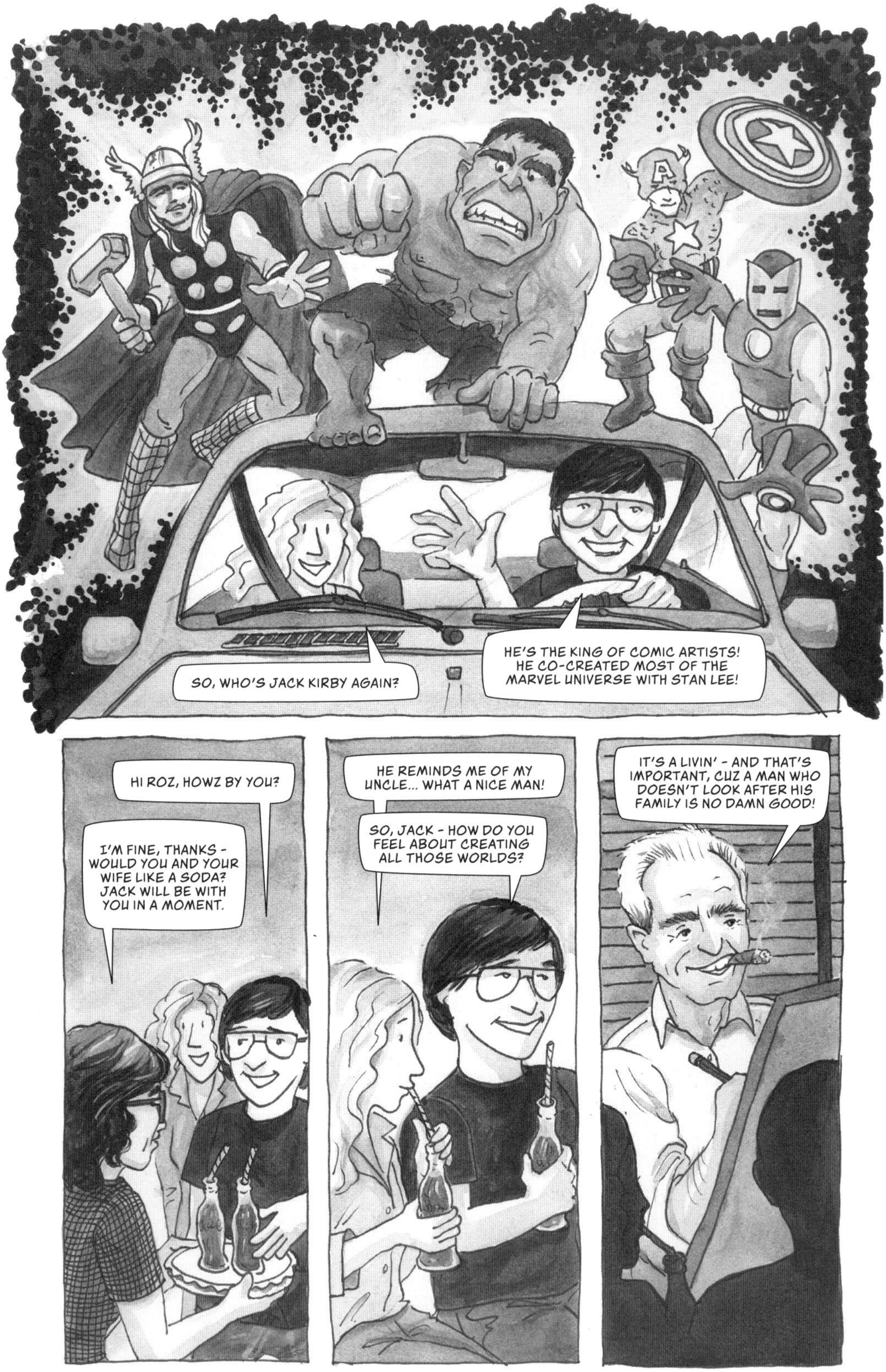
SO, WHO'S JACK KIRBY AGAIN?
HE'S THE KING OF COMIC ARTISTS! HE CO-CREATED MOST OF THE MARVEL UNIVERSE WITH STAN LEE!
HI ROZ, HOWZ BY YOU?
I'M FINE, THANKS - WOULD YOU AND YOUR WIFE LIKE A SODA? JACK WILL BE WITH YOU IN A MOMENT.
HE REMINDS ME OF MY UNCLE... WHAT A NICE MAN!
SO, JACK - HOW DO YOU FEEL ABOUT CREATING ALL THOSE WORLDS?
IT'S A LIVIN' - AND THAT'S IMPORTANT, CUZ A MAN WHO DOESN'T LOOK AFTER HIS FAMILY IS NO DAMN GOOD!

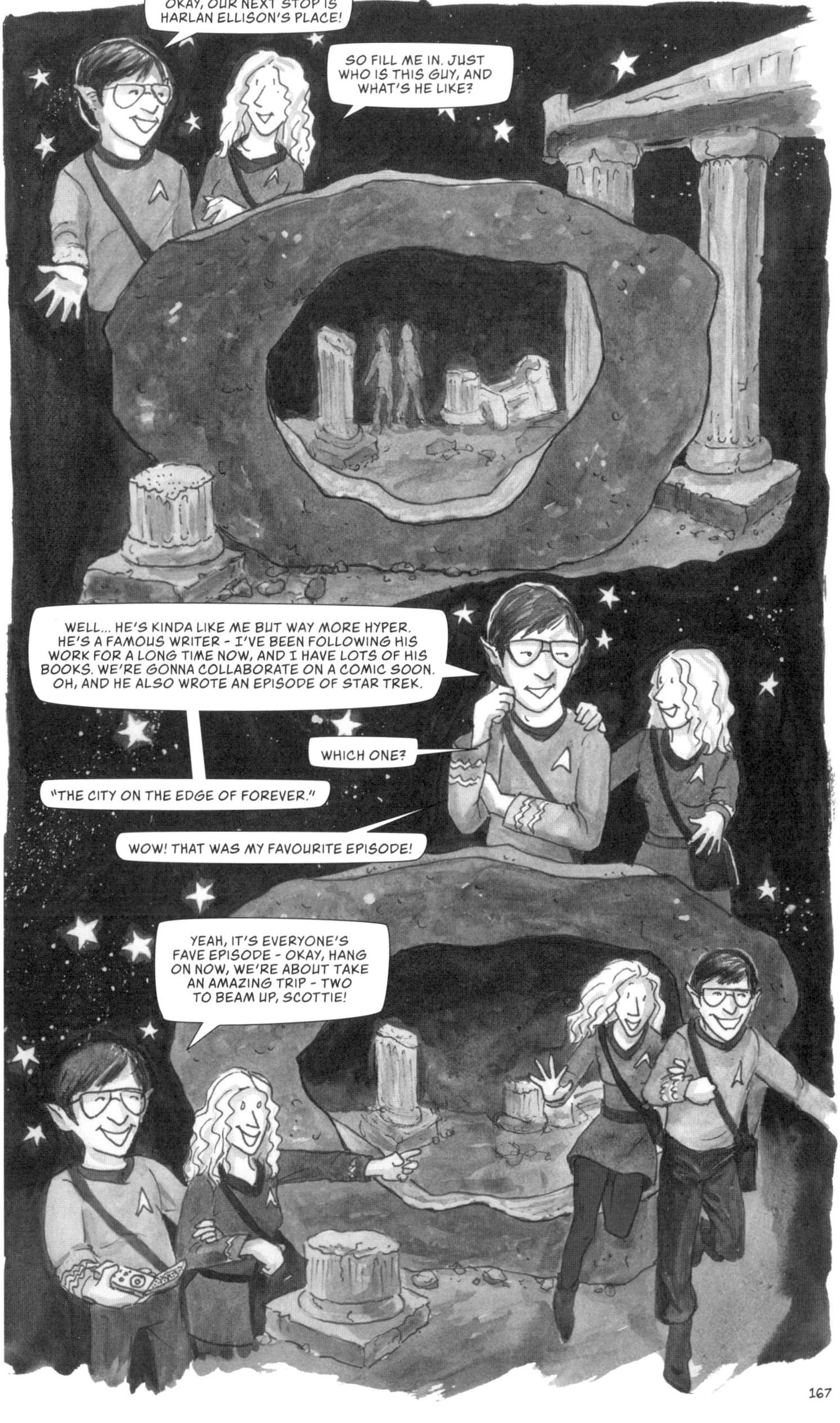
OKAY, OUR NEXT STOP IS HARLAN ELLISON'S PLACE!
SO FILL ME IN. JUST WHO IS THIS GUY, AND WHAT'S HE LIKE?
WELL... HE'S KINDA LIKE ME BUT WAY MORE HYPER. HE'S A FAMOUS WRITER - I'VE BEEN FOLLOWING HIS WORK FOR A LONG TIME NOW, AND I HAVE LOTS OF HIS BOOKS. WE'RE GONNA COLLABORATE ON A COMIC SOON. OH, AND HE ALSO WROTE AN EPISODE OF STAR TREK.
WHICH ONE?
"THE CITY ON THE EDGE OF FOREVER."
WOW! THAT WAS MY FAVOURITE EPISODE!
YEAH, IT'S EVERYONE'S FAVE EPISODE - OKAY, HANG ON NOW, WE'RE ABOUT TAKE AN AMAZING TRIP - TWO TO BEAM UP, SCOTTIE!

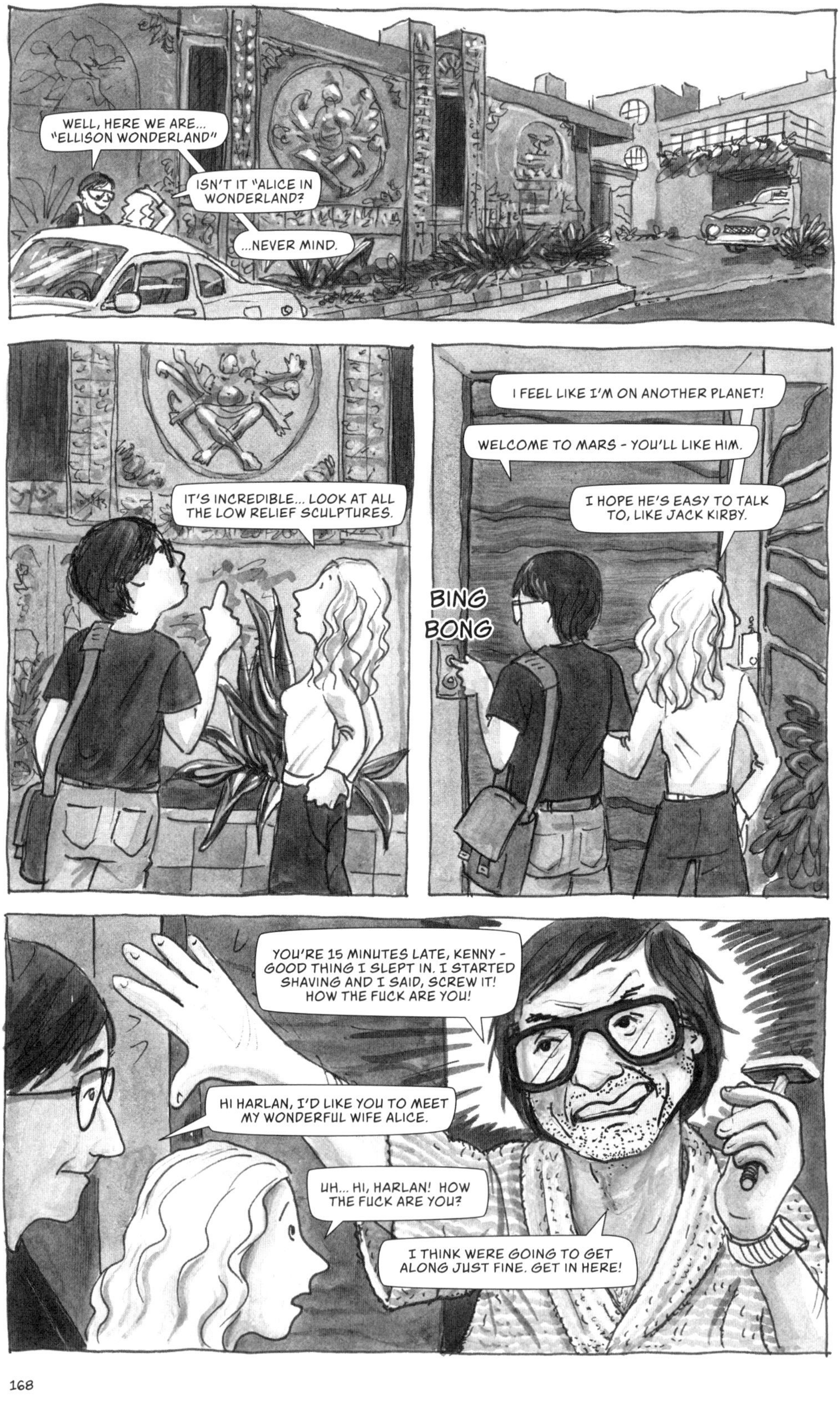
WELL, HERE WE ARE... "ELLISON WONDERLAND"
ISN'T IT "ALICE IN WONDERLAND?
...NEVER MIND.
IT'S INCREDIBLE... LOOK AT ALL THE LOW RELIEF SCULPTURES.
I FEEL LIKE I'M ON ANOTHER PLANET!
WELCOME TO MARS - YOU'LL LIKE HIM.
I HOPE HE'S EASY TO TALK TO, LIKE JACK KIRBY.
BING BONG
YOU'RE 15 MINUTES LATE, KENNY - GOOD THING I SLEPT IN. I STARTED SHAVING AND I SAID, SCREW IT! HOW THE FUCK ARE YOU!
HI HARLAN, I'D LIKE YOU TO MEET MY WONDERFUL WIFE ALICE.
UH... HI, HARLAN! HOW THE FUCK ARE YOU?
I THINK WERE GOING TO GET ALONG JUST FINE. GET IN HERE!

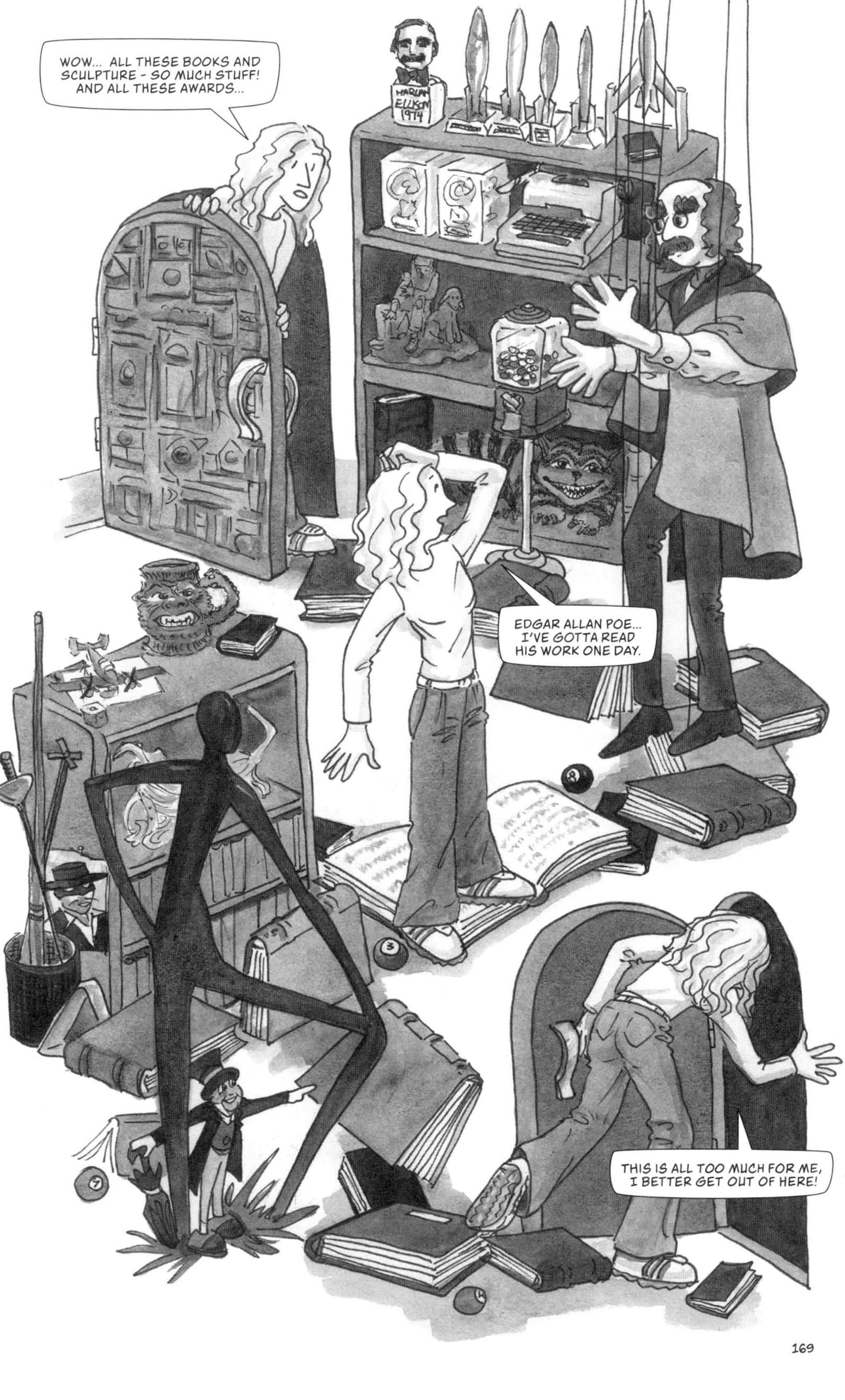
WOW... ALL THESE BOOKS AND SCULPTURE - SO MUCH STUFF! AND ALL THESE AWARDS...
EDGAR ALLAN POE... I'VE GOTTA READ HIS WORK ONE DAY.
THIS IS ALL TOO MUCH FOR ME, I BETTER GET OUT OF HERE!

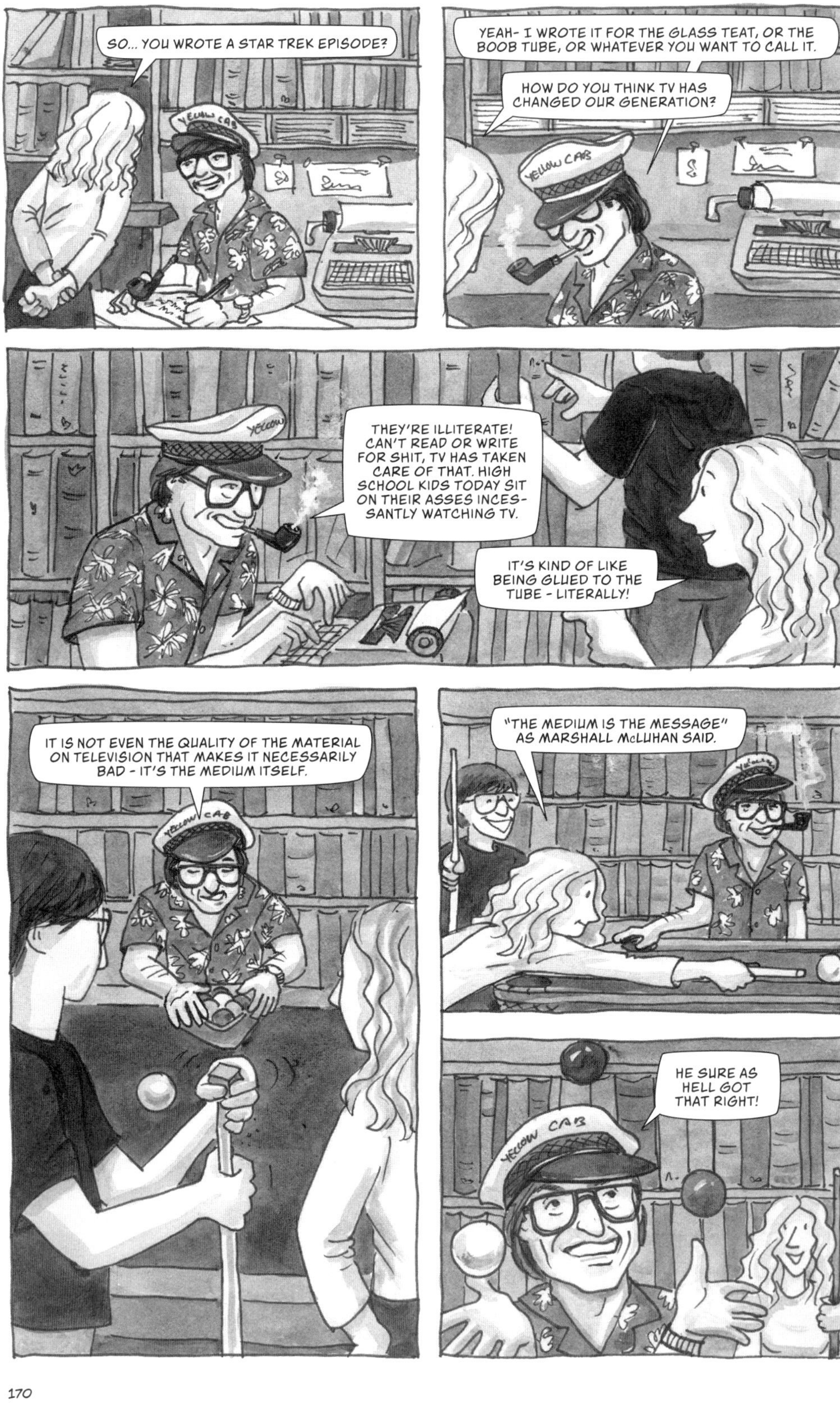
SO... YOU WROTE A STAR TREK EPISODE?
YEAH- I WROTE IT FOR THE GLASS TEAT, OR THE BOOB TUBE, OR WHATEVER YOU WANT TO CALL IT.
HOW DO YOU THINK TV HAS CHANGED OUR GENERATION?
THEY'RE ILLITERATE! CAN'T READ OR WRITE FOR SHIT, TV HAS TAKEN CARE OF THAT. HIGH SCHOOL KIDS TODAY SIT ON THEIR ASSES INCES-SANTLY WATCHING TV.
IT'S KIND OF LIKE BEING GLUED TO THE TUBE - LITERALLY!
IT IS NOT EVEN THE QUALITY OF THE MATERIAL ON TELEVISION THAT MAKES IT NECESSARILY BAD - IT'S THE MEDIUM ITSELF.
"THE MEDIUM IS THE MESSAGE" AS MARSHALL McLUHAN SAID.
HE SURE AS HELL GOT THAT RIGHT!

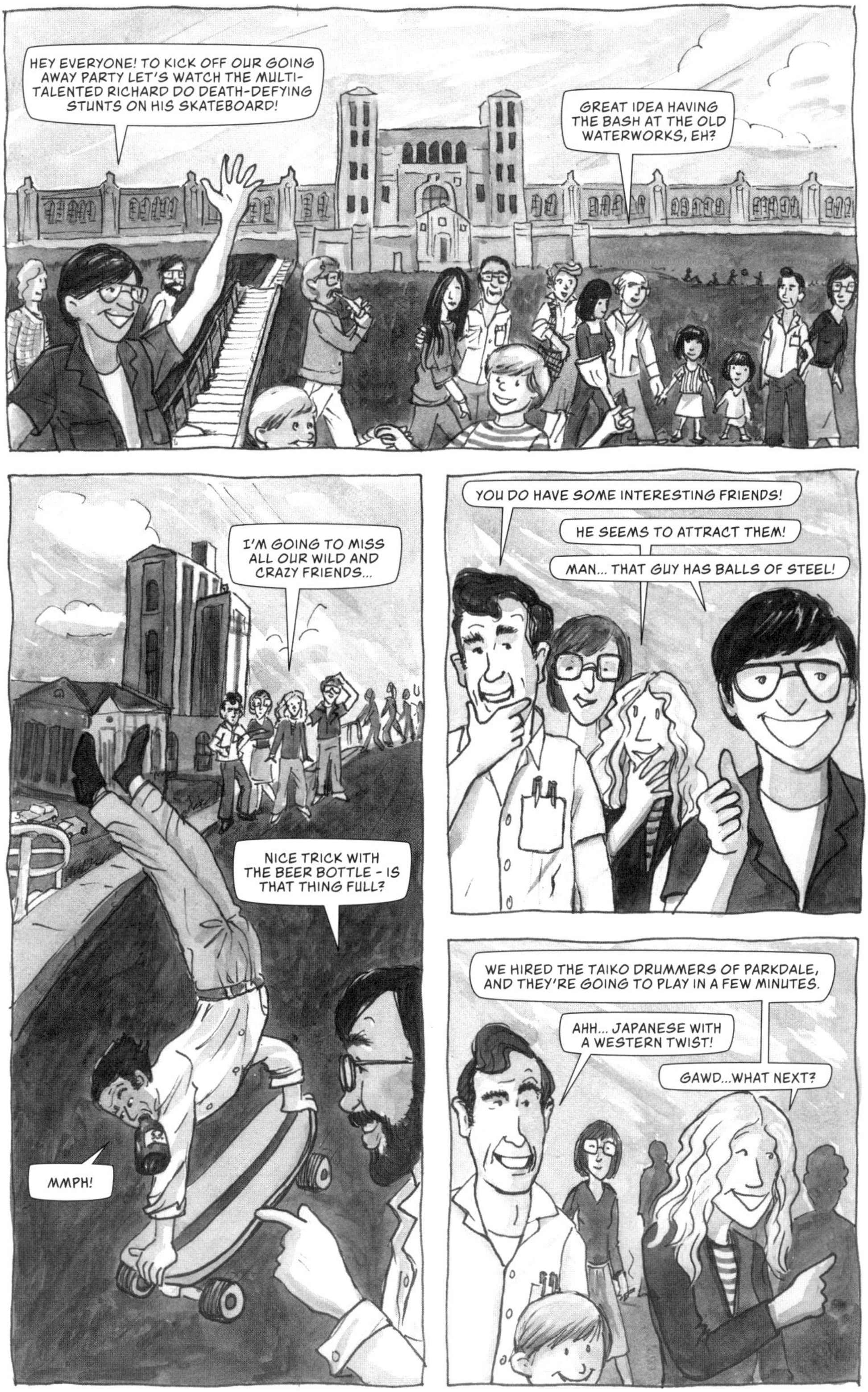
HEY EVERYONE! TO KICK OFF OUR GOING AWAY PARTY LET'S WATCH THE MULTI-TALENTED RICHARD DO DEATH-DEFYING STUNTS ON HIS SKATEBOARD!
GREAT IDEA HAVING THE BASH AT THE OLD WATERWORKS, EH?
I'M GOING TO MISS ALL OUR WILD AND CRAZY FRIENDS...
NICE TRICK WITH THE BEER BOTTLE - IS THAT THING FULL?
MMPH!
YOU DO HAVE SOME INTERESTING FRIENDS!
HE SEEMS TO ATTRACT THEM!
MAN... THAT GUY HAS BALLS OF STEEL!
WE HIRED THE TAIKO DRUMMERS OF PARKDALE, AND THEY'RE GOING TO PLAY IN A FEW MINUTES.
AHH... JAPANESE WITH A WESTERN TWIST!
GAWD...WHAT NEXT?

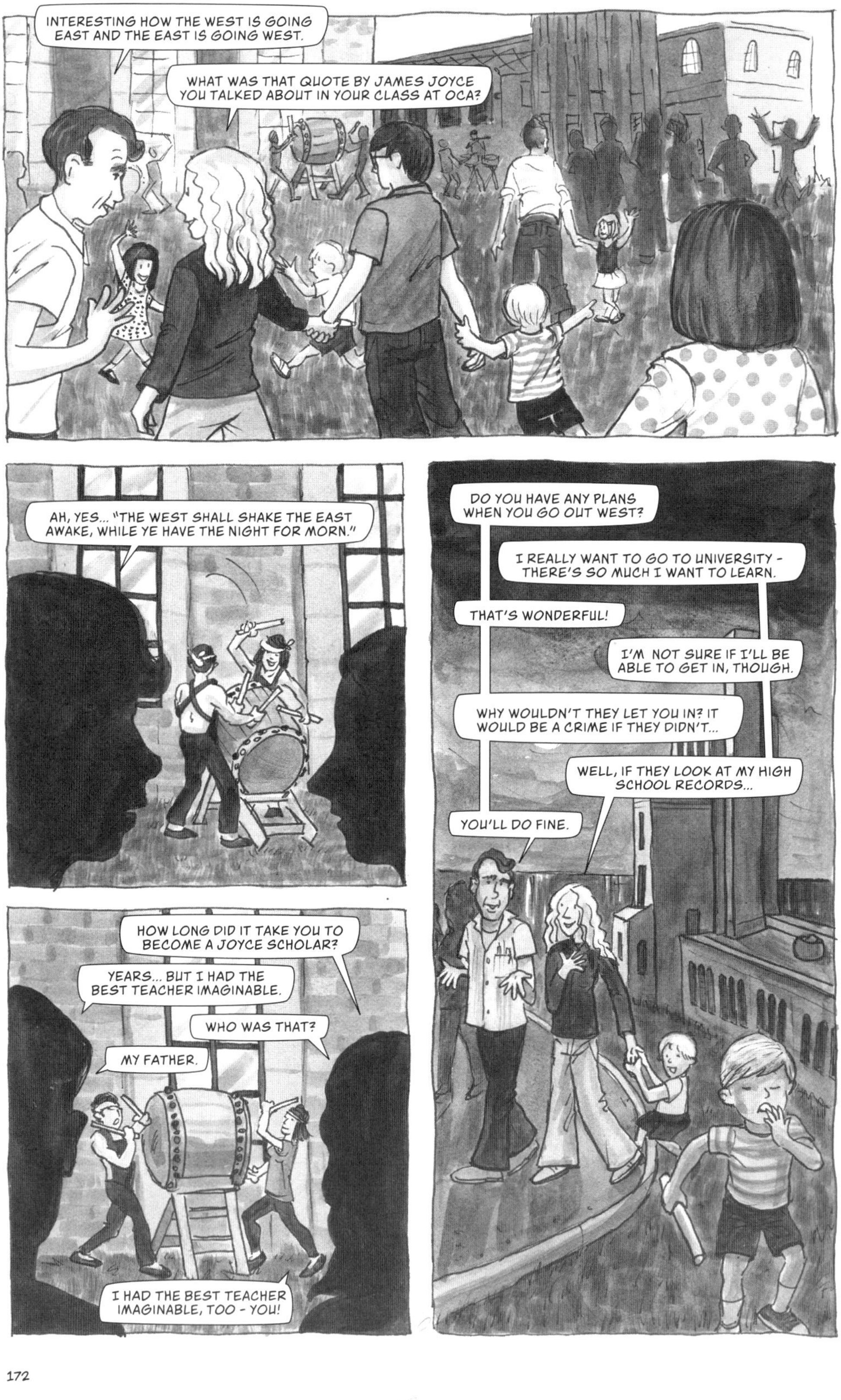
INTERESTING HOW THE WEST IS GOING EAST AND THE EAST IS GOING WEST.
WHAT WAS THAT QUOTE BY JAMES JOYCE YOU TALKED ABOUT IN YOUR CLASS AT OCA?
AH, YES... "THE WEST SHALL SHAKE THE EAST AWAKE, WHILE YE HAVE THE NIGHT FOR MORN."
HOW LONG DID IT TAKE YOU TO BECOME A JOYCE SCHOLAR?
YEARS... BUT I HAD THE BEST TEACHER IMAGINABLE.
WHO WAS THAT?
MY FATHER.
I HAD THE BEST TEACHER IMAGINABLE, TOO - YOU!
DO YOU HAVE ANY PLANS WHEN YOU GO OUT WEST?
I REALLY WANT TO GO TO UNIVERSITY - THERE'S SO MUCH I WANT TO LEARN.
THAT'S WONDERFUL!
I'M NOT SURE IF I'LL BE ABLE TO GET IN, THOUGH.
WHY WOULDN'T THEY LET YOU IN? IT WOULD BE A CRIME IF THEY DIDN'T...
WELL, IF THEY LOOK AT MY HIGH SCHOOL RECORDS...
YOU'LL DO FINE.

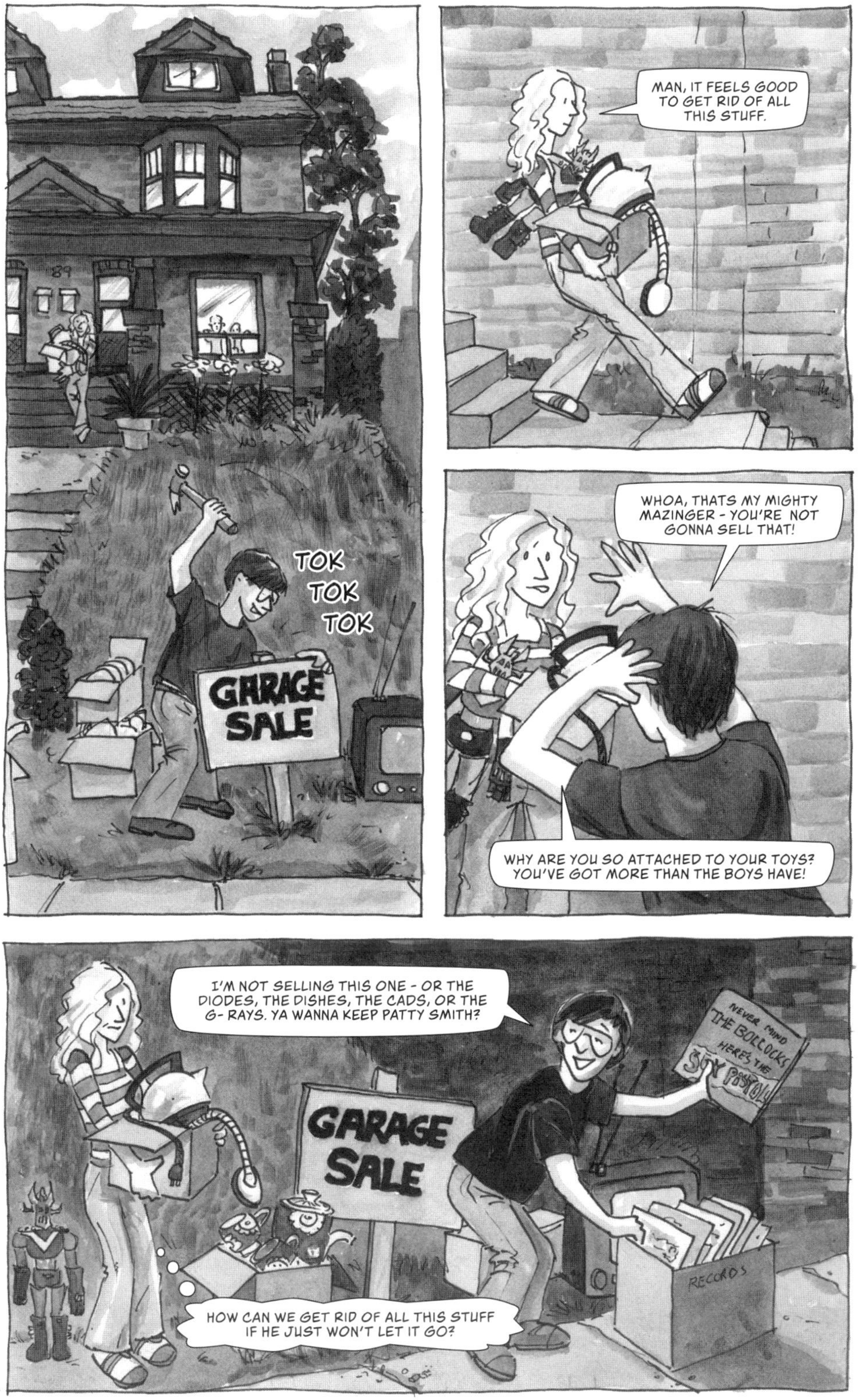
89
MAN, IT FEELS GOOD TO GET RID OF ALL THIS STUFF.
TOK TOK TOK
GARAGE SALE
WHOA, THATS MY MIGHTY MAZINGER - YOU'RE NOT GONNA SELL THAT!
WHY ARE YOU SO ATTACHED TO YOUR TOYS? YOU'VE GOT MORE THAN THE BOYS HAVE!
I'M NOT SELLING THIS ONE - OR THE DIODES, THE DISHES, THE CADS, OR THE G- RAYS. YA WANNA KEEP PATTY SMITH?
NEVER MIND THE BOLLOCKS HERES THE
GARAGE SALE
RECORDS
HOW CAN WE GET RID OF ALL THIS STUFF IF HE JUST WON'T LET IT GO?

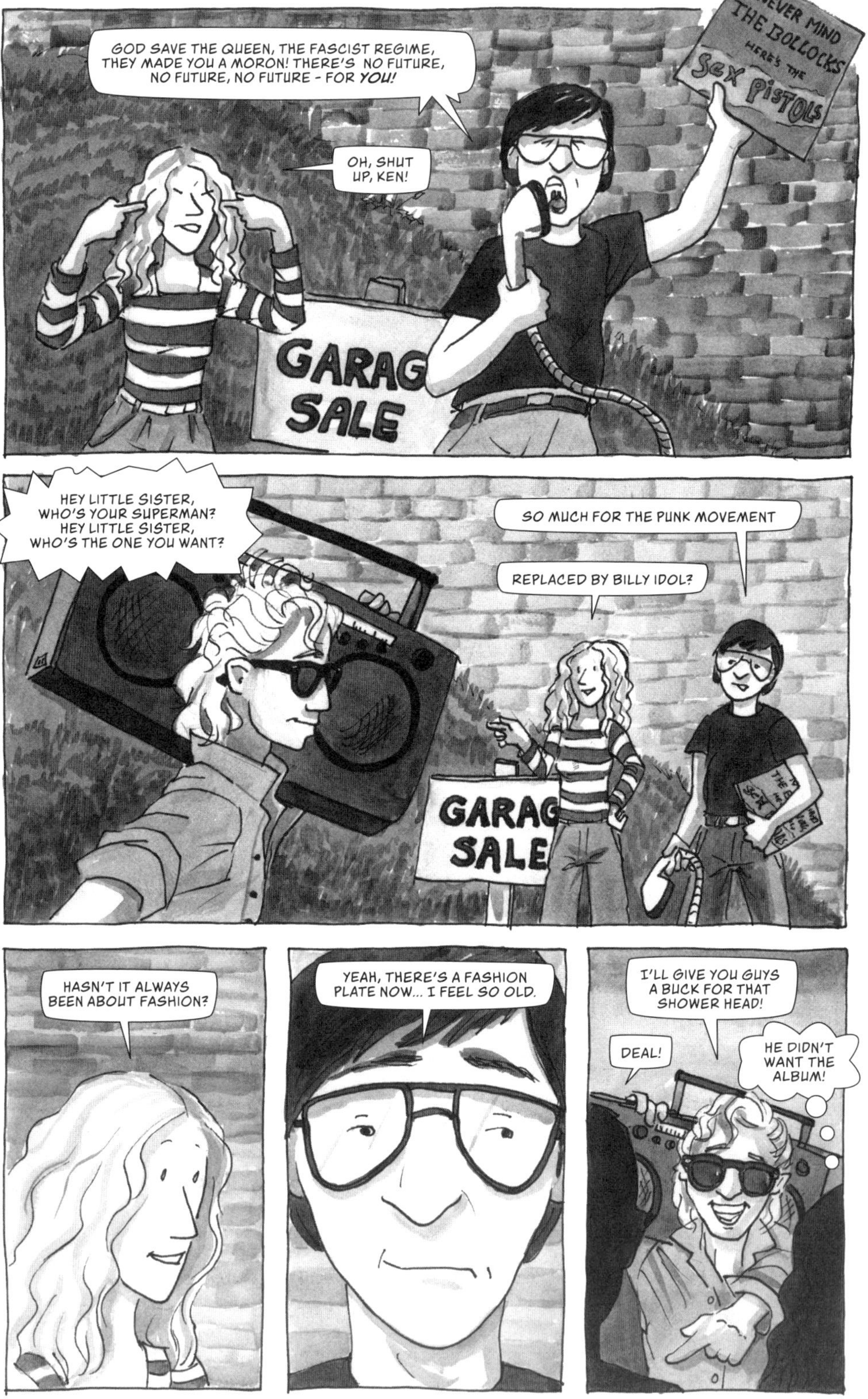
GOD SAVE THE QUEEN, THE FASCIST REGIME, THEY MADE YOU A MORON! THERE'S NO FUTURE, NO FUTURE, NO FUTURE - FOR *YOU!*
OH, SHUT UP, KEN!
NEVER MIND THE BOLLOCKS HERE'S THE SEX PISTOLS
GARAG SALE
HEY LITTLE SISTER, WHO'S YOUR SUPERMAN? HEY LITTLE SISTER, WHO'S THE ONE YOU WANT?
SO MUCH FOR THE PUNK MOVEMENT
REPLACED BY BILLY IDOL?
GARAG SALE
HASN'T IT ALWAYS BEEN ABOUT FASHION?
YEAH, THERE'S A FASHION PLATE NOW... I FEEL SO OLD.
I'LL GIVE YOU GUYS A BUCK FOR THAT SHOWER HEAD!
DEAL!
HE DIDN'T WANT THE ALBUM!

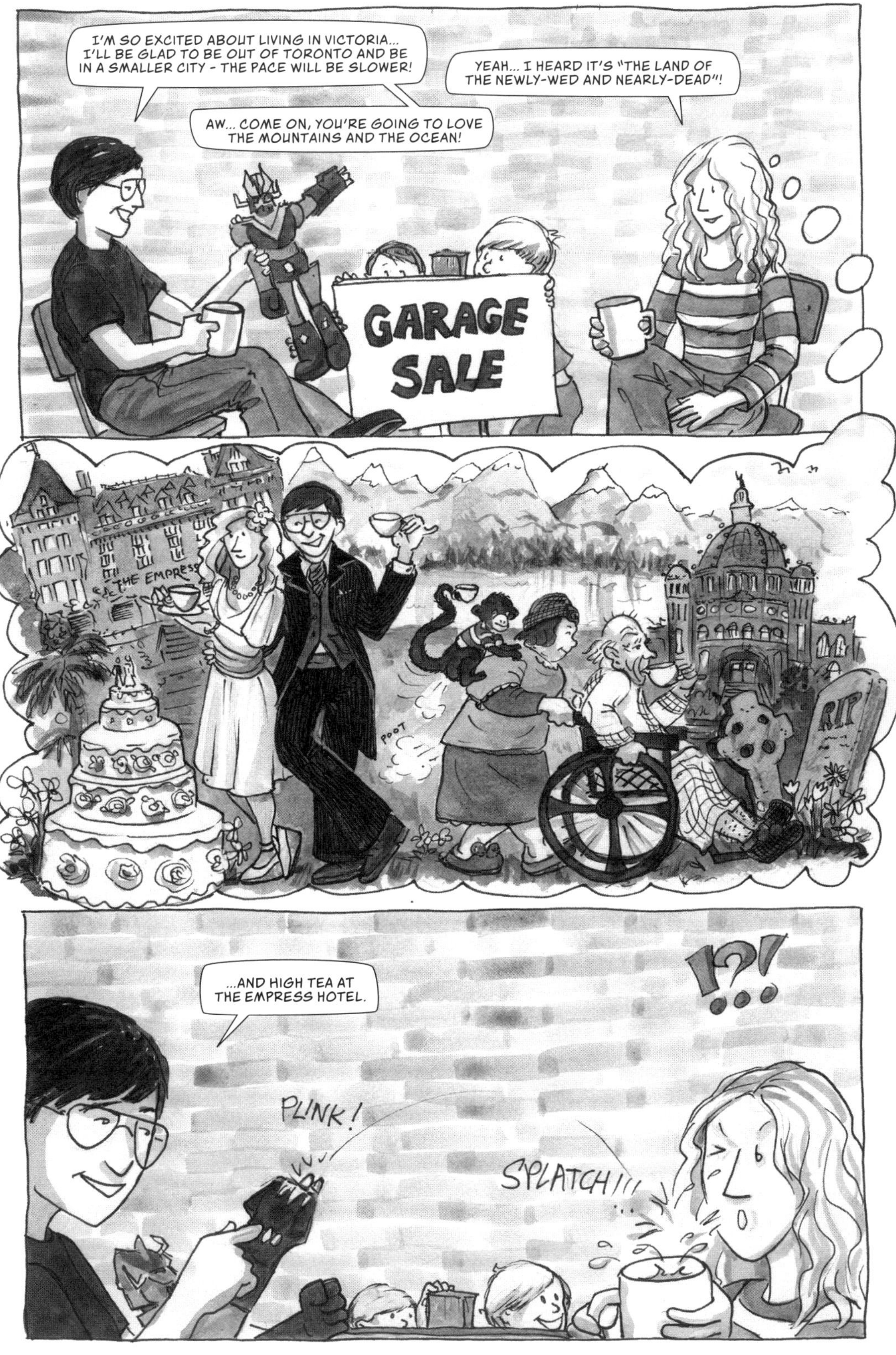
I'M SO EXCITED ABOUT LIVING IN VICTORIA... I'LL BE GLAD TO BE OUT OF TORONTO AND BE IN A SMALLER CITY - THE PACE WILL BE SLOWER!
AW... COME ON, YOU'RE GOING TO LOVE THE MOUNTAINS AND THE OCEAN!
YEAH... I HEARD IT'S "THE LAND OF THE NEWLY-WED AND NEARLY-DEAD"!
GARAGE SALE
THE EMPRESS
POOT
RIP
...AND HIGH TEA AT THE EMPRESS HOTEL.
!?!
PLINK!
SPLATCH!!!

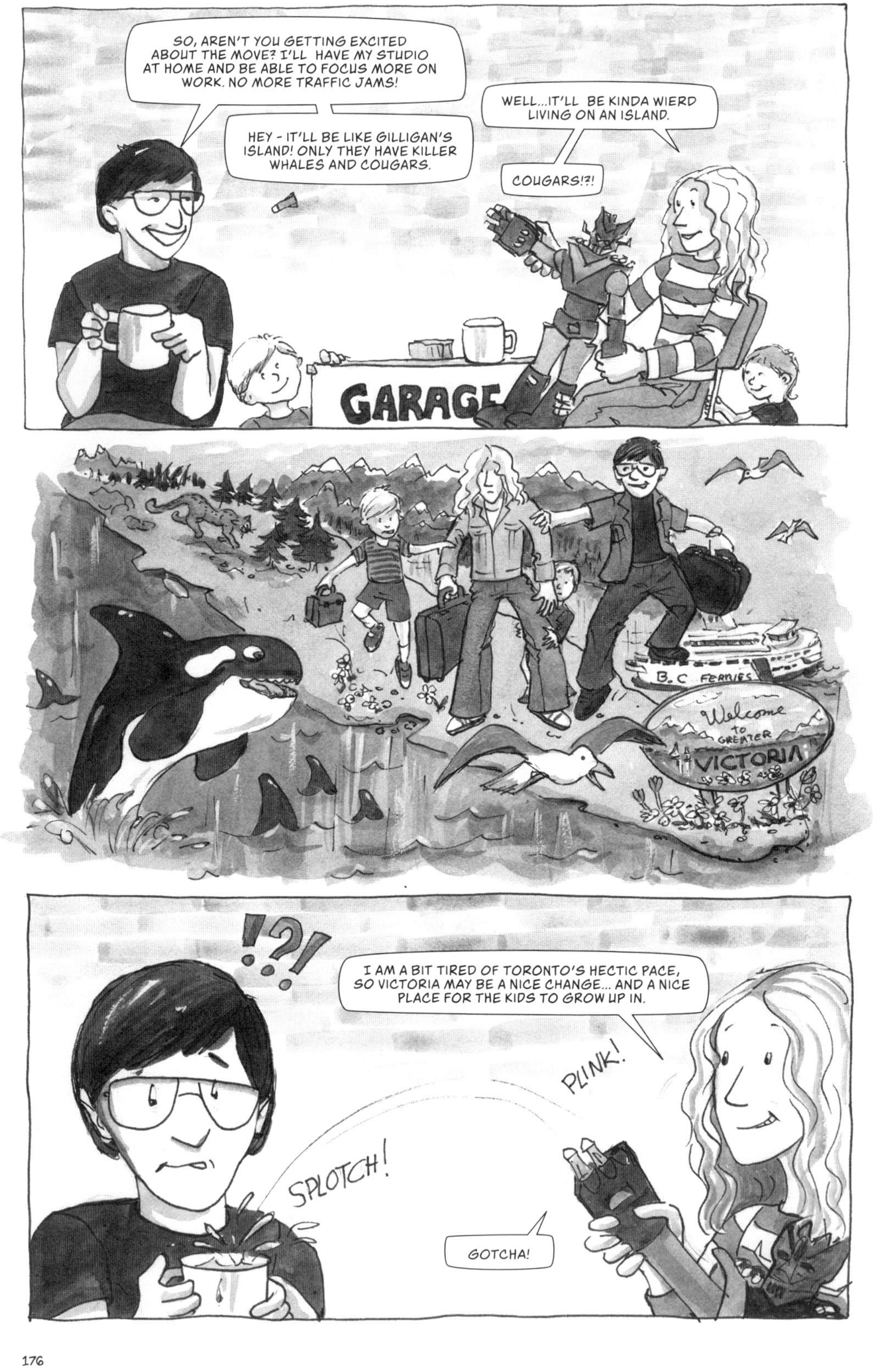
SO, AREN'T YOU GETTING EXCITED ABOUT THE MOVE? I'LL HAVE MY STUDIO AT HOME AND BE ABLE TO FOCUS MORE ON WORK. NO MORE TRAFFIC JAMS!
HEY - IT'LL BE LIKE GILLIGAN'S ISLAND! ONLY THEY HAVE KILLER WHALES AND COUGARS.
WELL...IT'LL BE KINDA WIERD LIVING ON AN ISLAND.
COUGARS!?!
GARAGE
B.C FERRIES
Welcome TO GREATER VICTORIA
!?!
I AM A BIT TIRED OF TORONTO'S HECTIC PACE, SO VICTORIA MAY BE A NICE CHANGE... AND A NICE PLACE FOR THE KIDS TO GROW UP IN.
PLINK!
SPLOTCH!
GOTCHA!

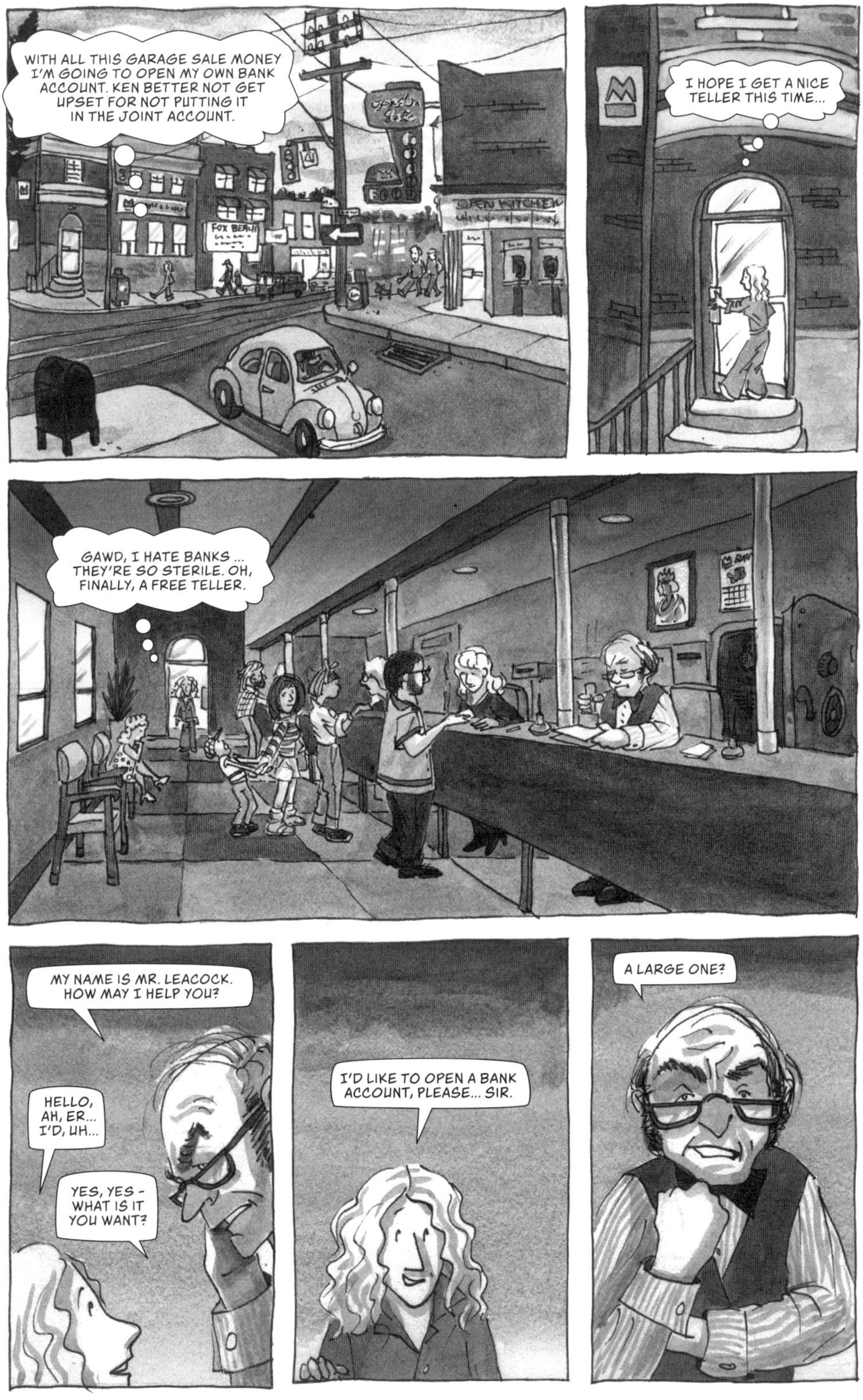
WITH ALL THIS GARAGE SALE MONEY I'M GOING TO OPEN MY OWN BANK ACCOUNT. KEN BETTER NOT GET UPSET FOR NOT PUTTING IT IN THE JOINT ACCOUNT.
I HOPE I GET A NICE TELLER THIS TIME...
GAWD, I HATE BANKS ... THEY'RE SO STERILE. OH, FINALLY, A FREE TELLER.
MY NAME IS MR. LEACOCK. HOW MAY I HELP YOU?
HELLO, AH, ER... I'D, UH...
YES, YES - WHAT IS IT YOU WANT?
I'D LIKE TO OPEN A BANK ACCOUNT, PLEASE... SIR.
A LARGE ONE?

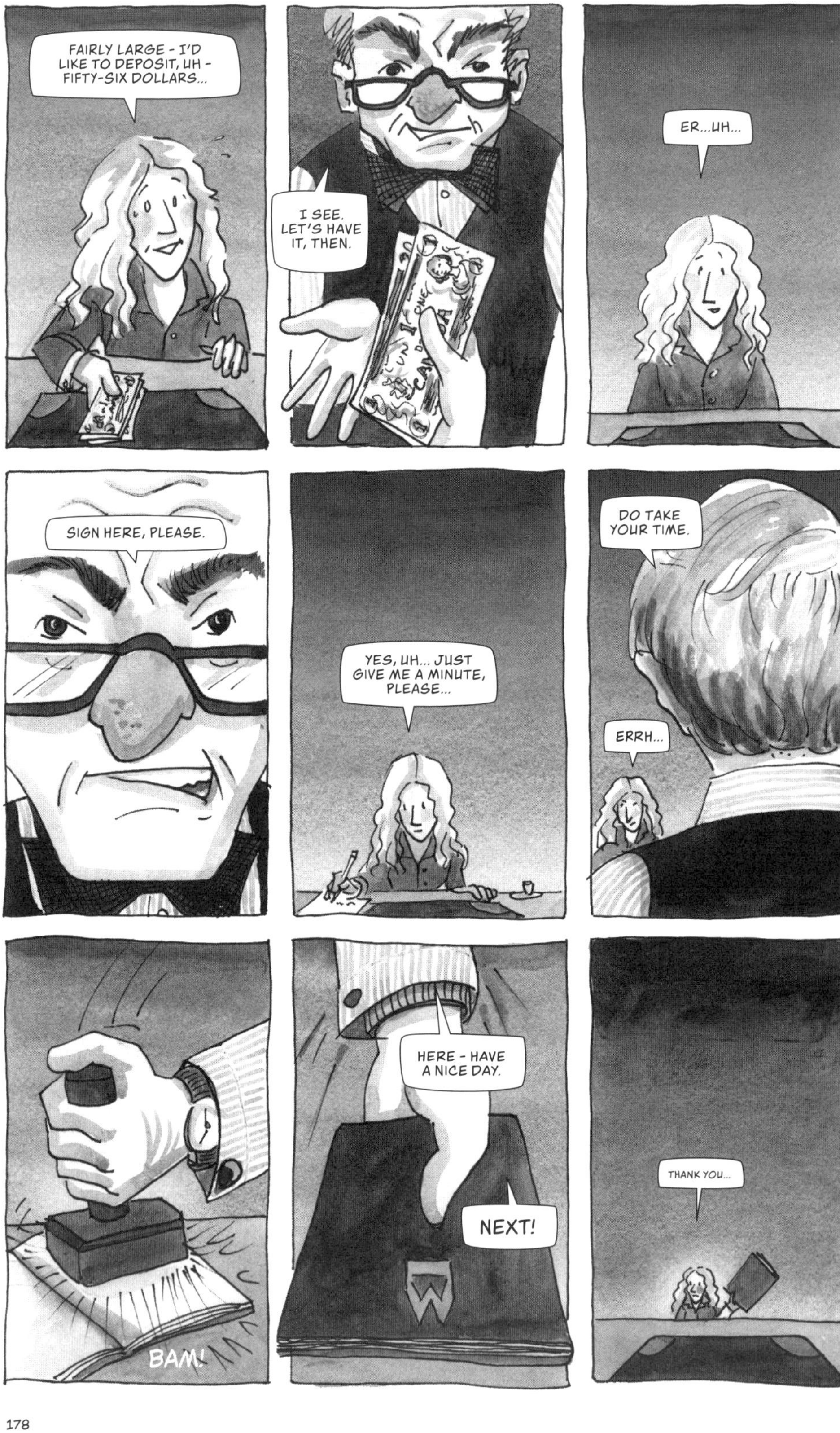
FAIRLY LARGE - I'D LIKE TO DEPOSIT, UH - FIFTY-SIX DOLLARS...
I SEE. LET'S HAVE IT, THEN.
ER...UH...
SIGN HERE, PLEASE.
YES, UH... JUST GIVE ME A MINUTE, PLEASE...
DO TAKE YOUR TIME.
ERRH...
BAM!
HERE - HAVE A NICE DAY.
NEXT!
THANK YOU...

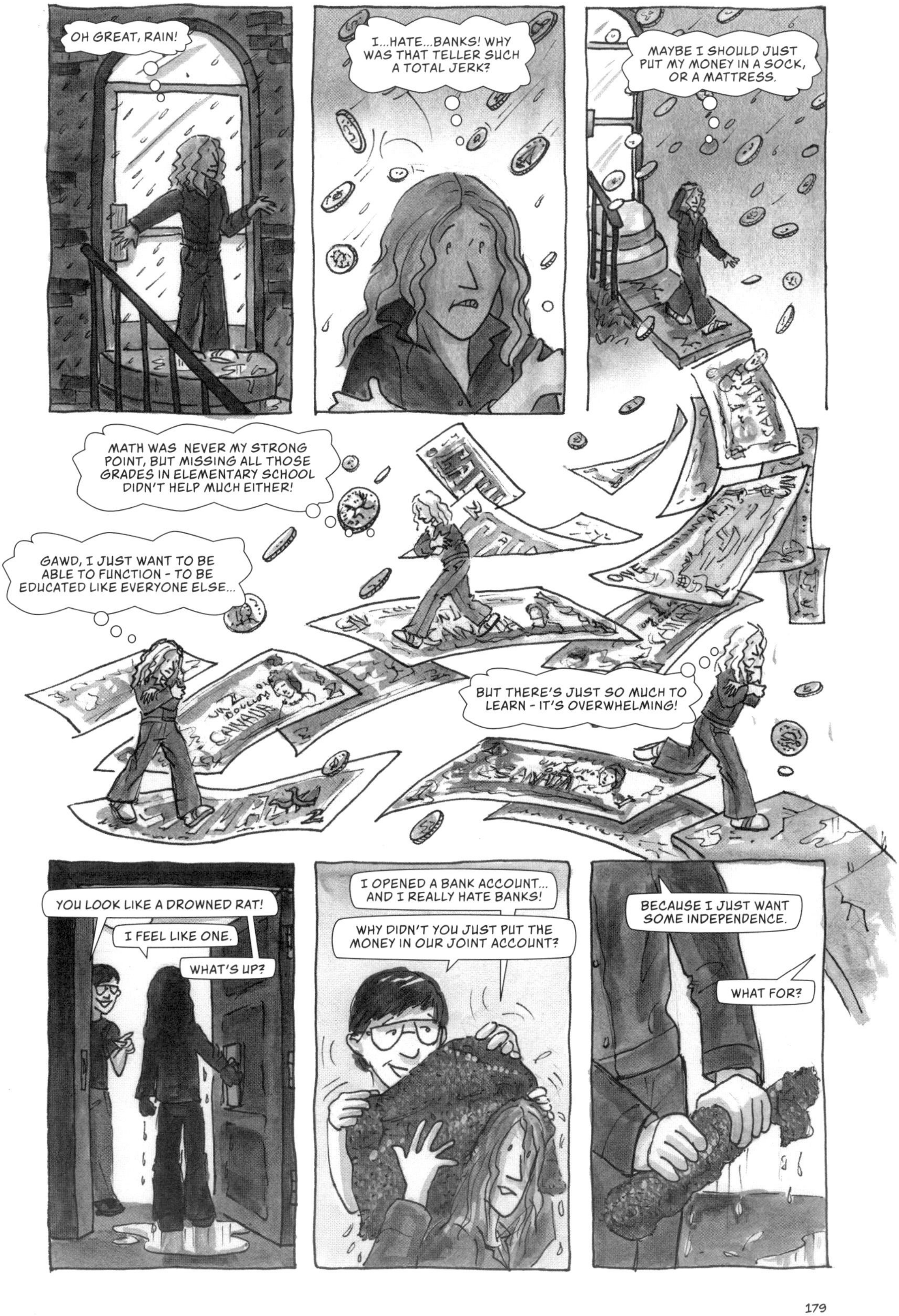

OH GREAT, RAIN!
I...HATE...BANKS! WHY WAS THAT TELLER SUCH A TOTAL JERK?
MAYBE I SHOULD JUST PUT MY MONEY IN A SOCK, OR A MATTRESS.
MATH WAS NEVER MY STRONG POINT, BUT MISSING ALL THOSE GRADES IN ELEMENTARY SCHOOL DIDN'T HELP MUCH EITHER!
GAWD, I JUST WANT TO BE ABLE TO FUNCTION - TO BE EDUCATED LIKE EVERYONE ELSE...
BUT THERE'S JUST SO MUCH TO LEARN - IT'S OVERWHELMING!
YOU LOOK LIKE A DROWNED RAT!
I FEEL LIKE ONE.
WHAT'S UP?
I OPENED A BANK ACCOUNT... AND I REALLY HATE BANKS!
WHY DIDN'T YOU JUST PUT THE MONEY IN OUR JOINT ACCOUNT?
BECAUSE I JUST WANT SOME INDEPENDENCE.
WHAT FOR?

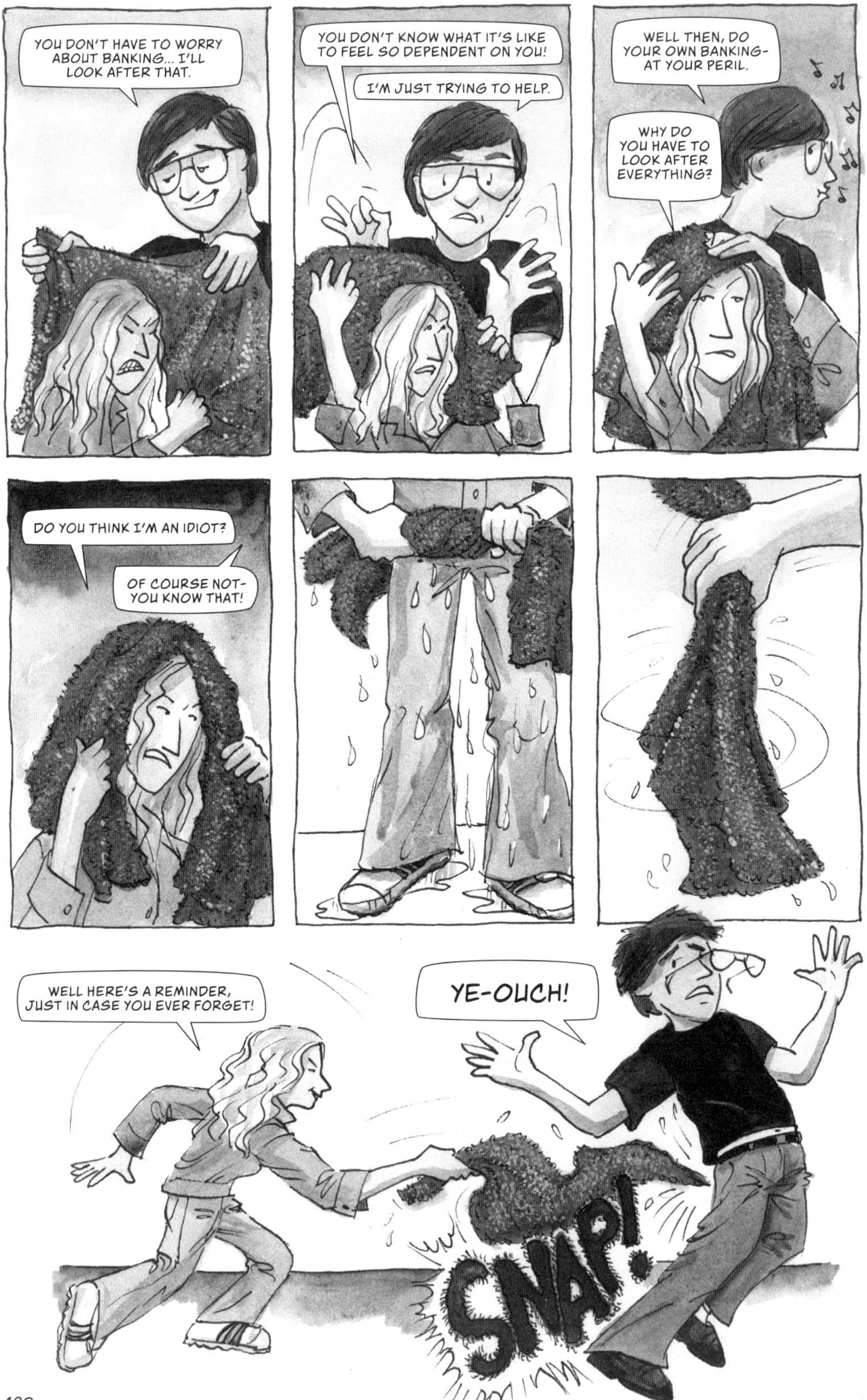
YOU DON'T HAVE TO WORRY ABOUT BANKING... I'LL LOOK AFTER THAT.
YOU DON'T KNOW WHAT IT'S LIKE TO FEEL SO DEPENDENT ON YOU!
I'M JUST TRYING TO HELP.
WELL THEN, DO YOUR OWN BANKING- AT YOUR PERIL.
WHY DO YOU HAVE TO LOOK AFTER EVERYTHING?
DO YOU THINK I'M AN IDIOT?
OF COURSE NOT- YOU KNOW THAT!
WELL HERE'S A REMINDER, JUST IN CASE YOU EVER FORGET!
YE-OUCH!
SNAP!

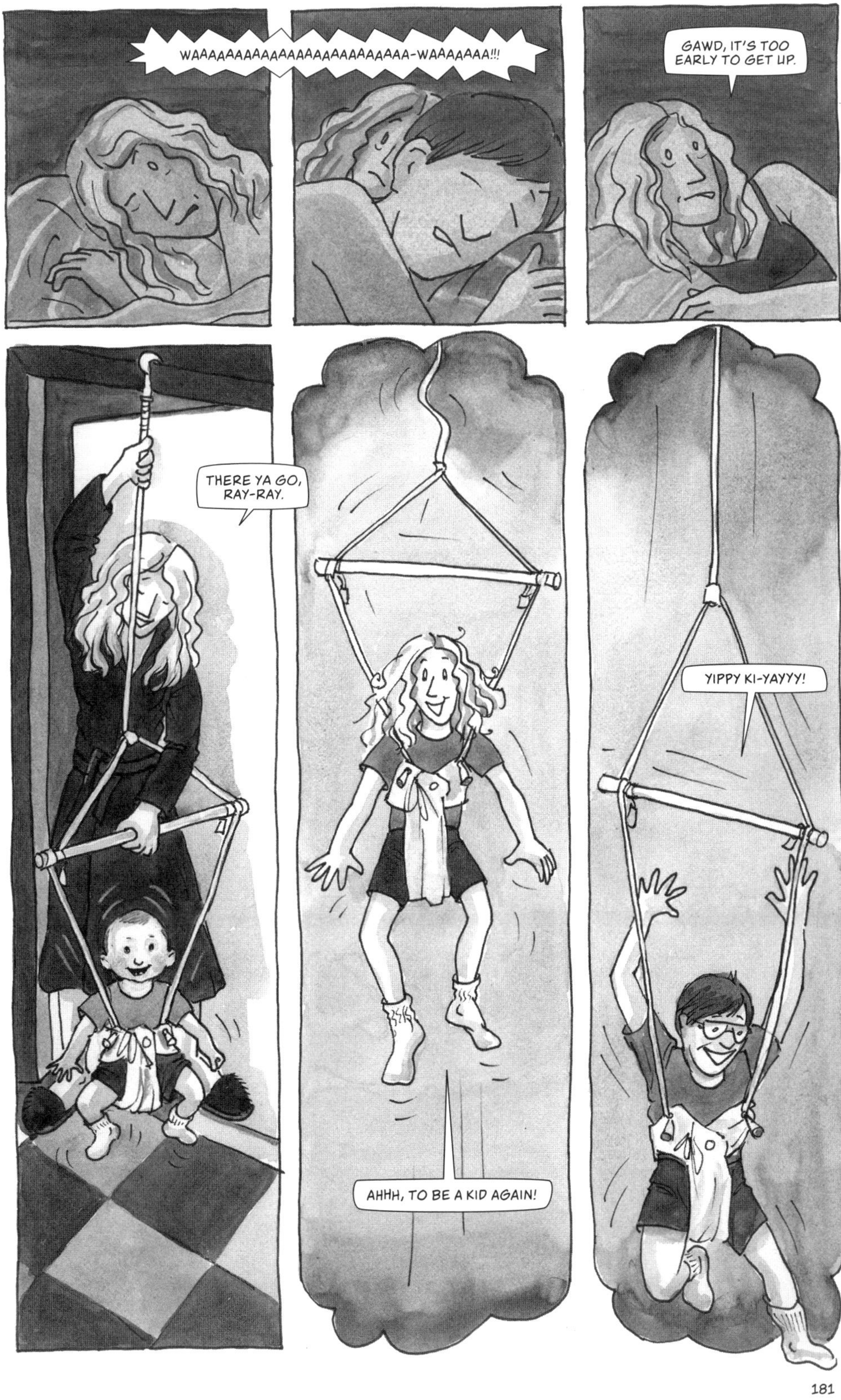
WAAAAAAAAAAAAAAAAAAAAAAAAA-WAAAAAAA!!!
GAWD, IT'S TOO EARLY TO GET UP.
THERE YA GO, RAY-RAY.
AHHH, TO BE A KID AGAIN!
YIPPY KI-YAYYY!

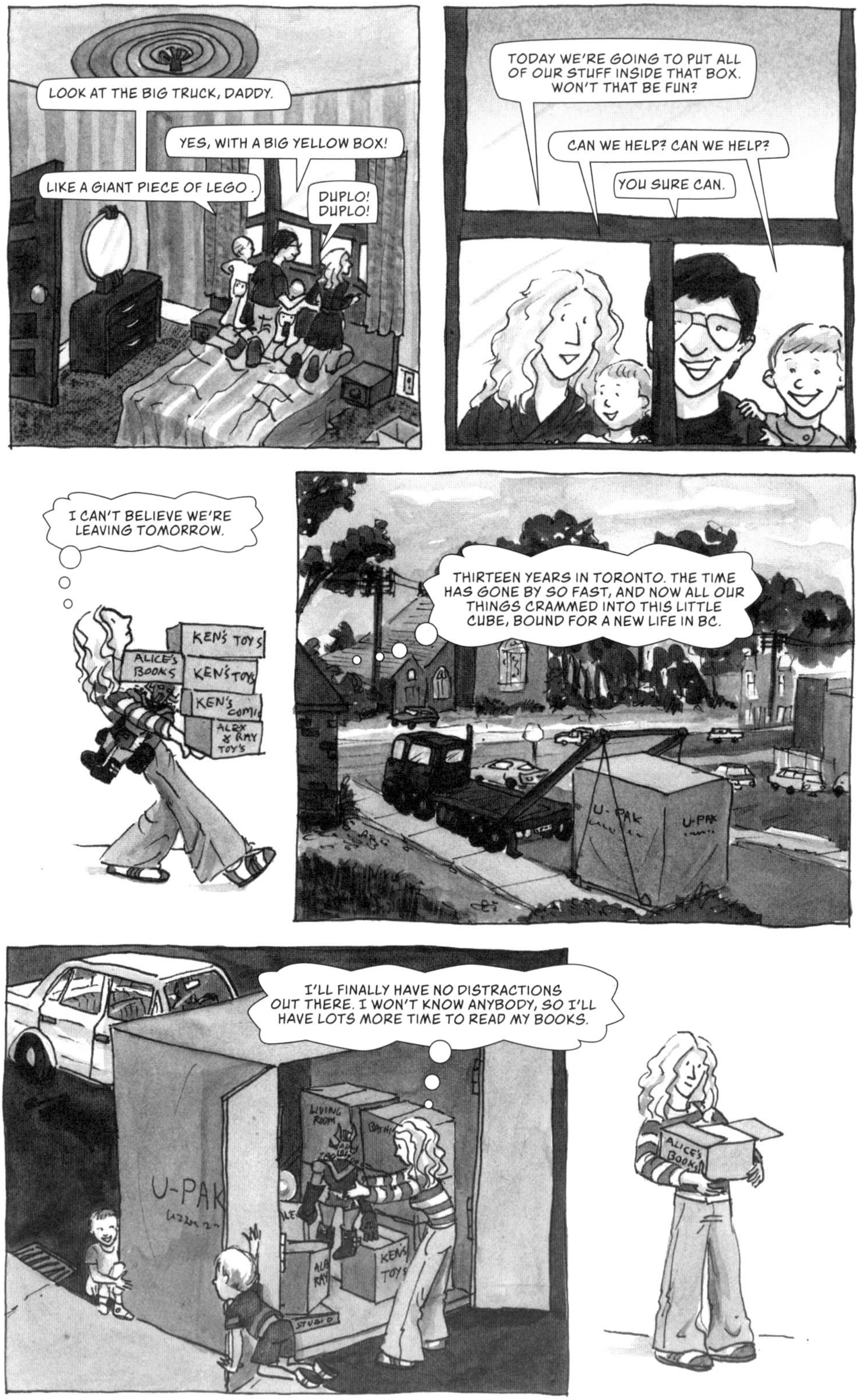
LOOK AT THE BIG TRUCK, DADDY.
YES, WITH A BIG YELLOW BOX!
LIKE A GIANT PIECE OF LEGO .
DUPLO! DUPLO!
TODAY WE'RE GOING TO PUT ALL OF OUR STUFF INSIDE THAT BOX. WON'T THAT BE FUN?
CAN WE HELP? CAN WE HELP?
YOU SURE CAN.
I CAN'T BELIEVE WE'RE LEAVING TOMORROW.
KEN'S TOYS
ALICE'S BOOKS
KEN'S TOYS
ALEX & RAY TOY'S
THIRTEEN YEARS IN TORONTO. THE TIME HAS GONE BY SO FAST, AND NOW ALL OUR THINGS CRAMMED INTO THIS LITTLE CUBE, BOUND FOR A NEW LIFE IN BC.
U-PAK
I'LL FINALLY HAVE NO DISTRACTIONS OUT THERE. I WON'T KNOW ANYBODY, SO I'LL HAVE LOTS MORE TIME TO READ MY BOOKS.
LIVING ROOM
U-PAK
KEN'S TOYS
ALICE'S BOOKS

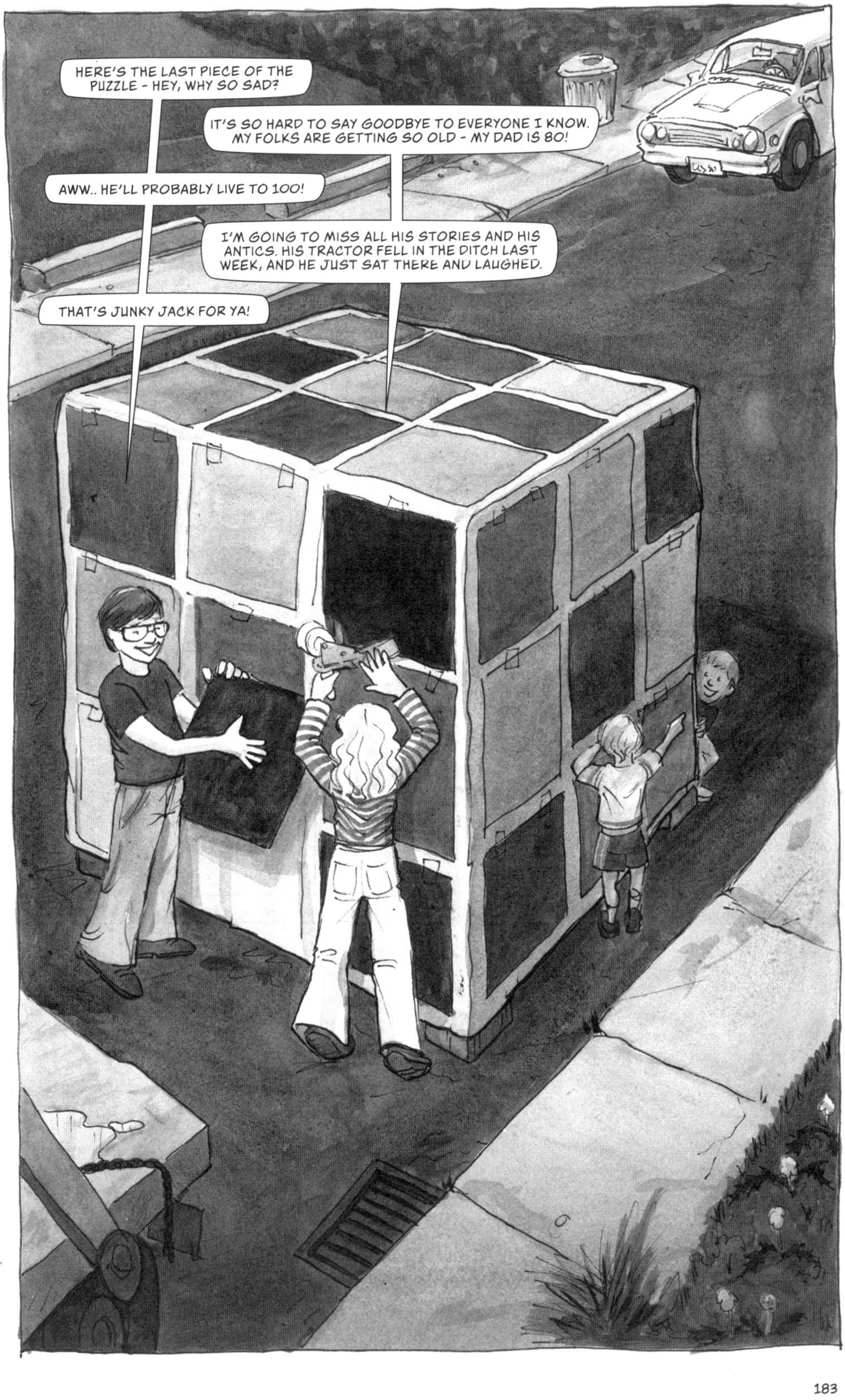
HERE'S THE LAST PIECE OF THE PUZZLE - HEY, WHY SO SAD?
IT'S SO HARD TO SAY GOODBYE TO EVERYONE I KNOW. MY FOLKS ARE GETTING SO OLD - MY DAD IS 80!
AWW.. HE'LL PROBABLY LIVE TO 100!
I'M GOING TO MISS ALL HIS STORIES AND HIS ANTICS. HIS TRACTOR FELL IN THE DITCH LAST WEEK, AND HE JUST SAT THERE AND LAUGHED.
THAT'S JUNKY JACK FOR YA!

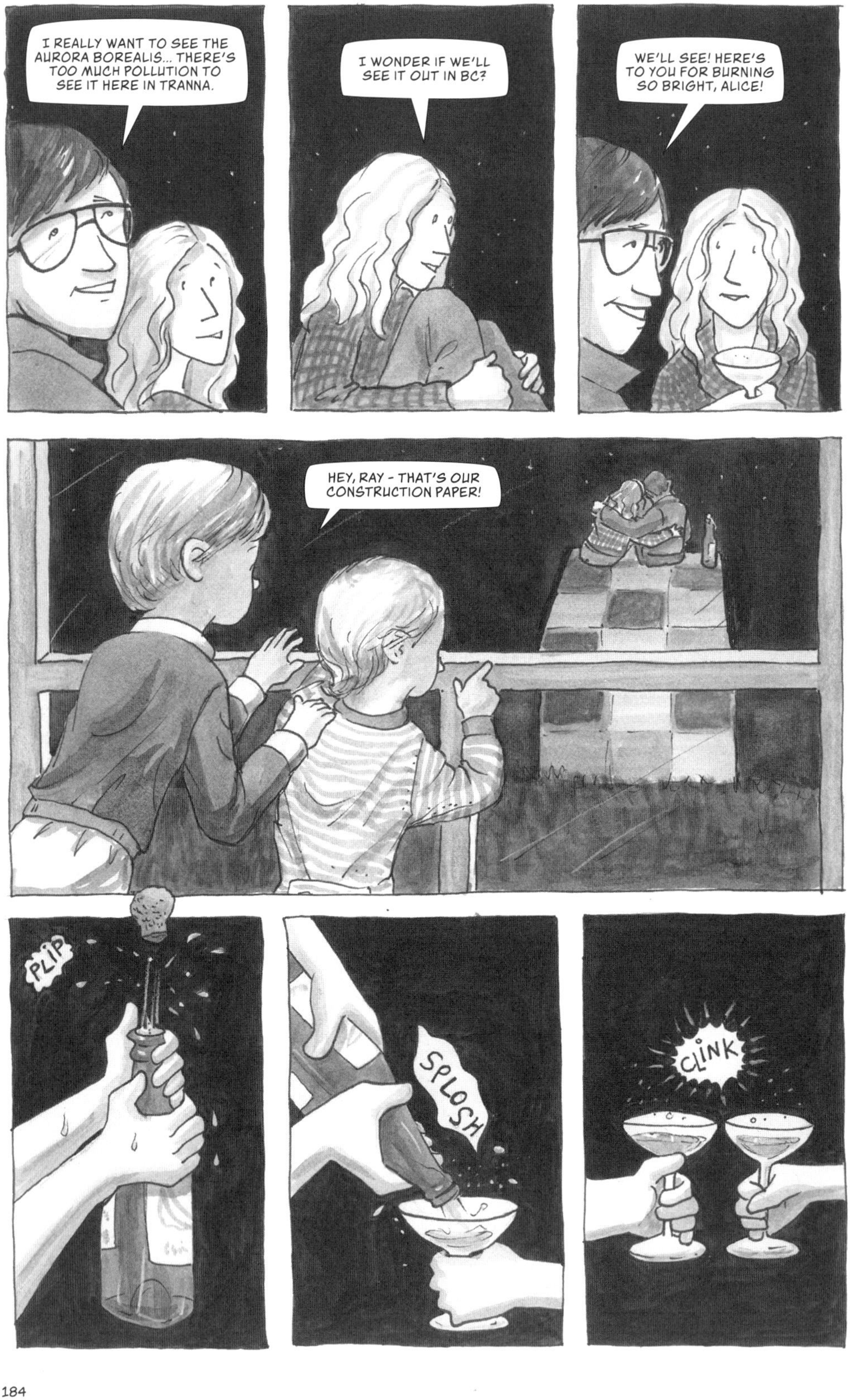
I REALLY WANT TO SEE THE AURORA BOREALIS... THERE'S TOO MUCH POLLUTION TO SEE IT HERE IN TRANNA.
I WONDER IF WE'LL SEE IT OUT IN BC?
WE'LL SEE! HERE'S TO YOU FOR BURNING SO BRIGHT, ALICE!
HEY, RAY - THAT'S OUR CONSTRUCTION PAPER!
PLIP
SPLOSH
CLINK

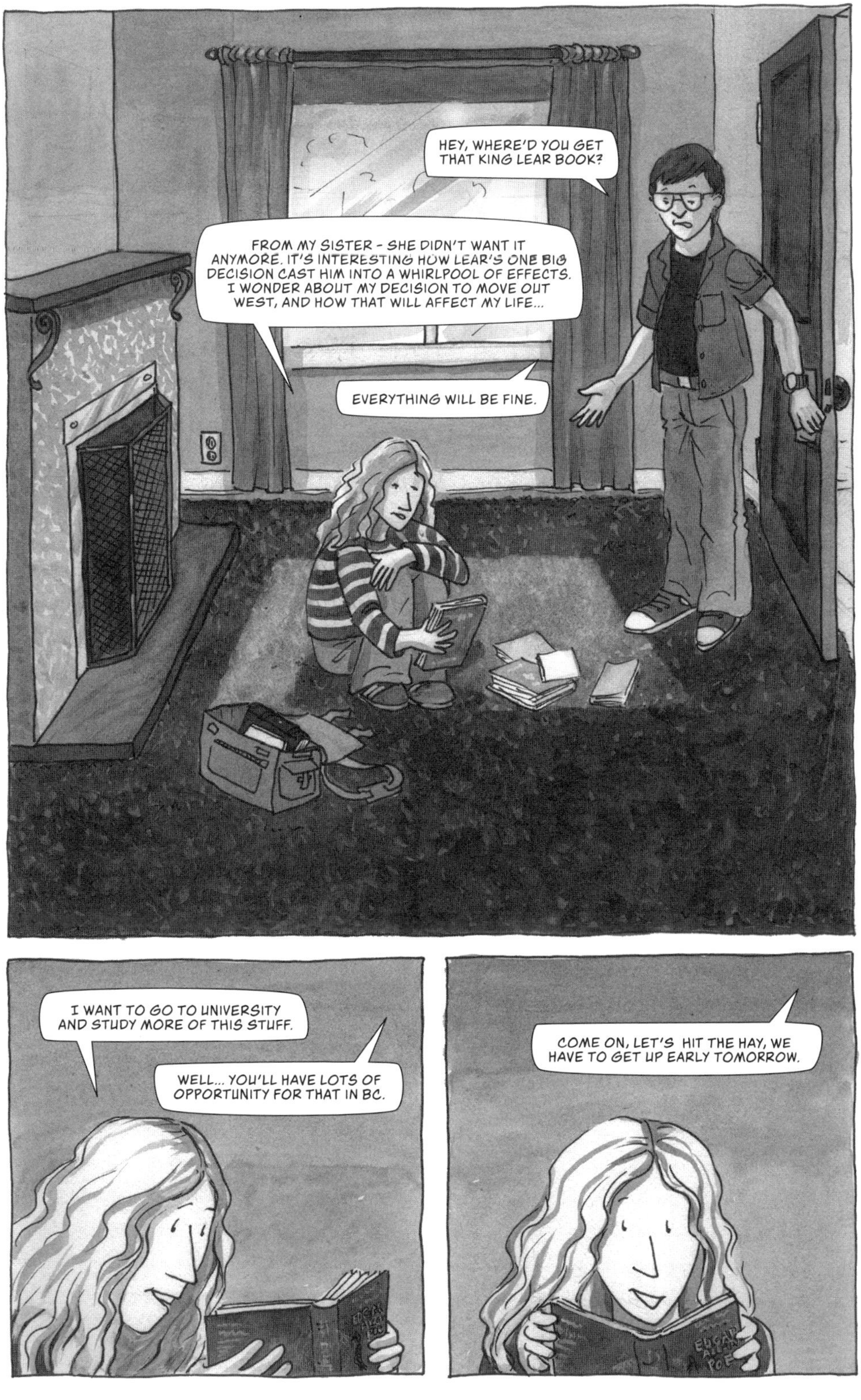
HEY, WHERE'D YOU GET THAT KING LEAR BOOK?
FROM MY SISTER - SHE DIDN'T WANT IT ANYMORE. IT'S INTERESTING HOW LEAR'S ONE BIG DECISION CAST HIM INTO A WHIRLPOOL OF EFFECTS. I WONDER ABOUT MY DECISION TO MOVE OUT WEST, AND HOW THAT WILL AFFECT MY LIFE...
EVERYTHING WILL BE FINE.
I WANT TO GO TO UNIVERSITY AND STUDY MORE OF THIS STUFF.
WELL... YOU'LL HAVE LOTS OF OPPORTUNITY FOR THAT IN BC.
COME ON, LET'S HIT THE HAY, WE HAVE TO GET UP EARLY TOMORROW.
EDGAR ALLAN POE

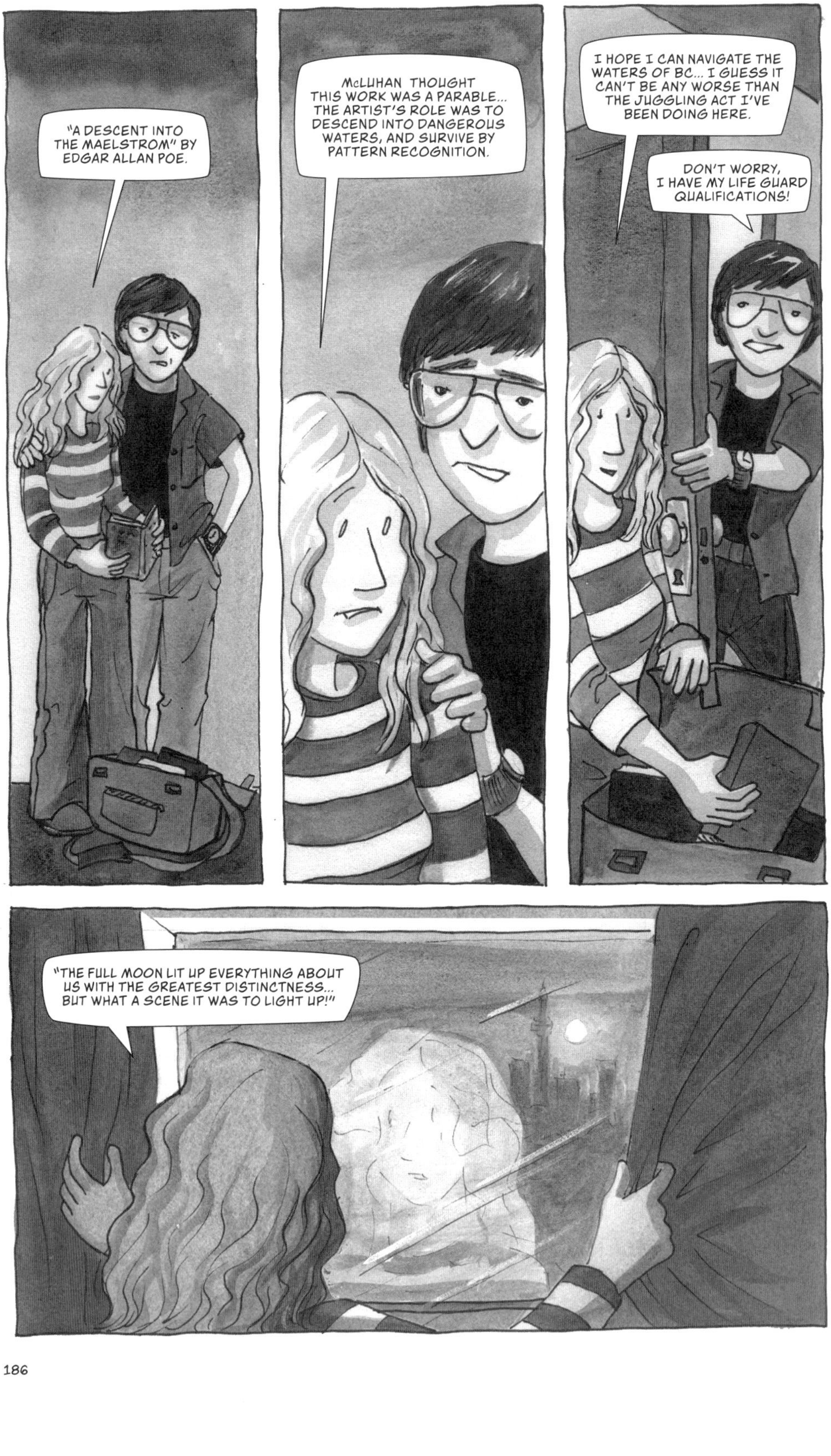
"A DESCENT INTO THE MAELSTROM" BY EDGAR ALLAN POE.
McLUHAN THOUGHT THIS WORK WAS A PARABLE... THE ARTIST'S ROLE WAS TO DESCEND INTO DANGEROUS WATERS, AND SURVIVE BY PATTERN RECOGNITION.
I HOPE I CAN NAVIGATE THE WATERS OF BC... I GUESS IT CAN'T BE ANY WORSE THAN THE JUGGLING ACT I'VE BEEN DOING HERE.
DON'T WORRY, I HAVE MY LIFE GUARD QUALIFICATIONS!
"THE FULL MOON LIT UP EVERYTHING ABOUT US WITH THE GREATEST DISTINCTNESS... BUT WHAT A SCENE IT WAS TO LIGHT UP!"

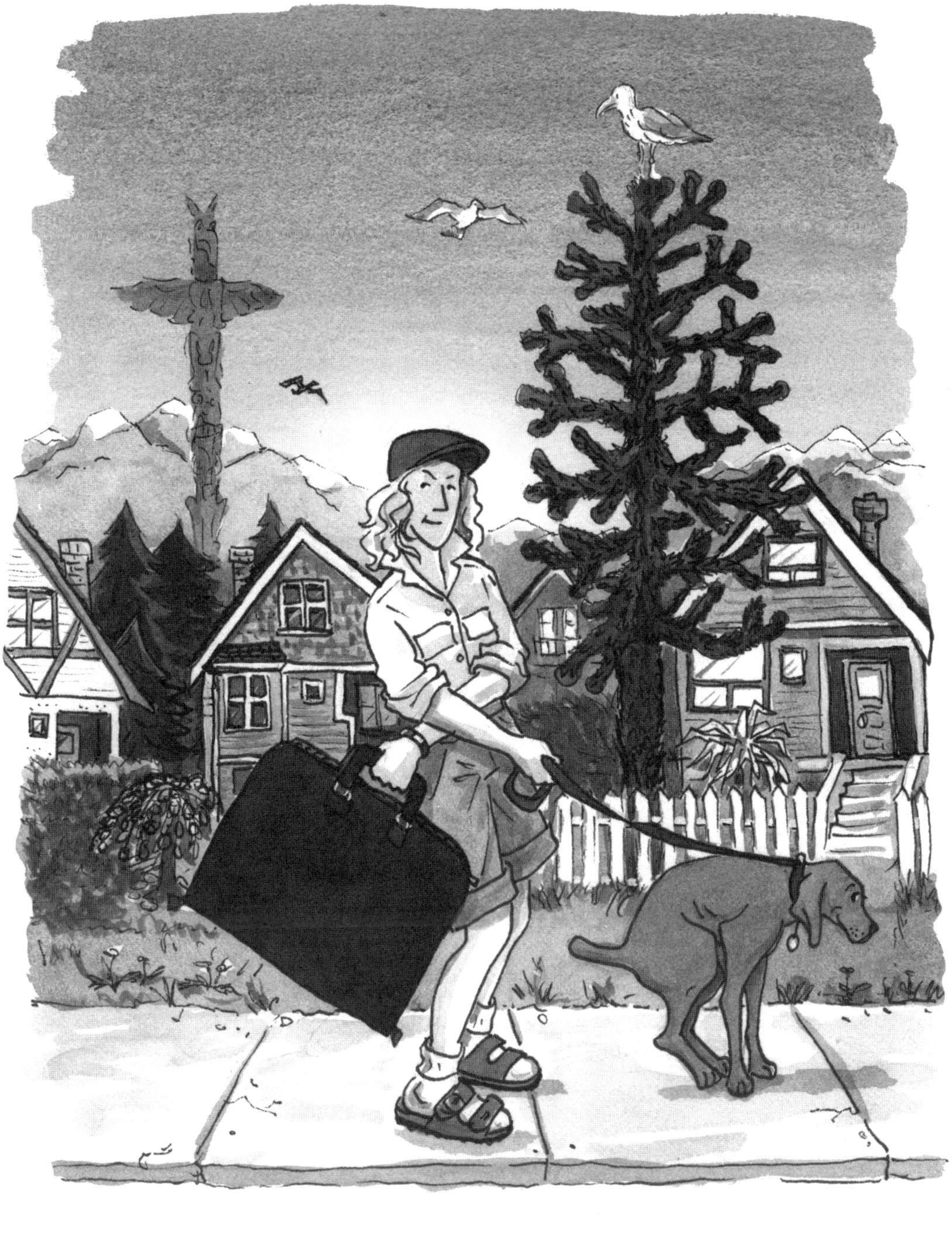

CHAPTER 3

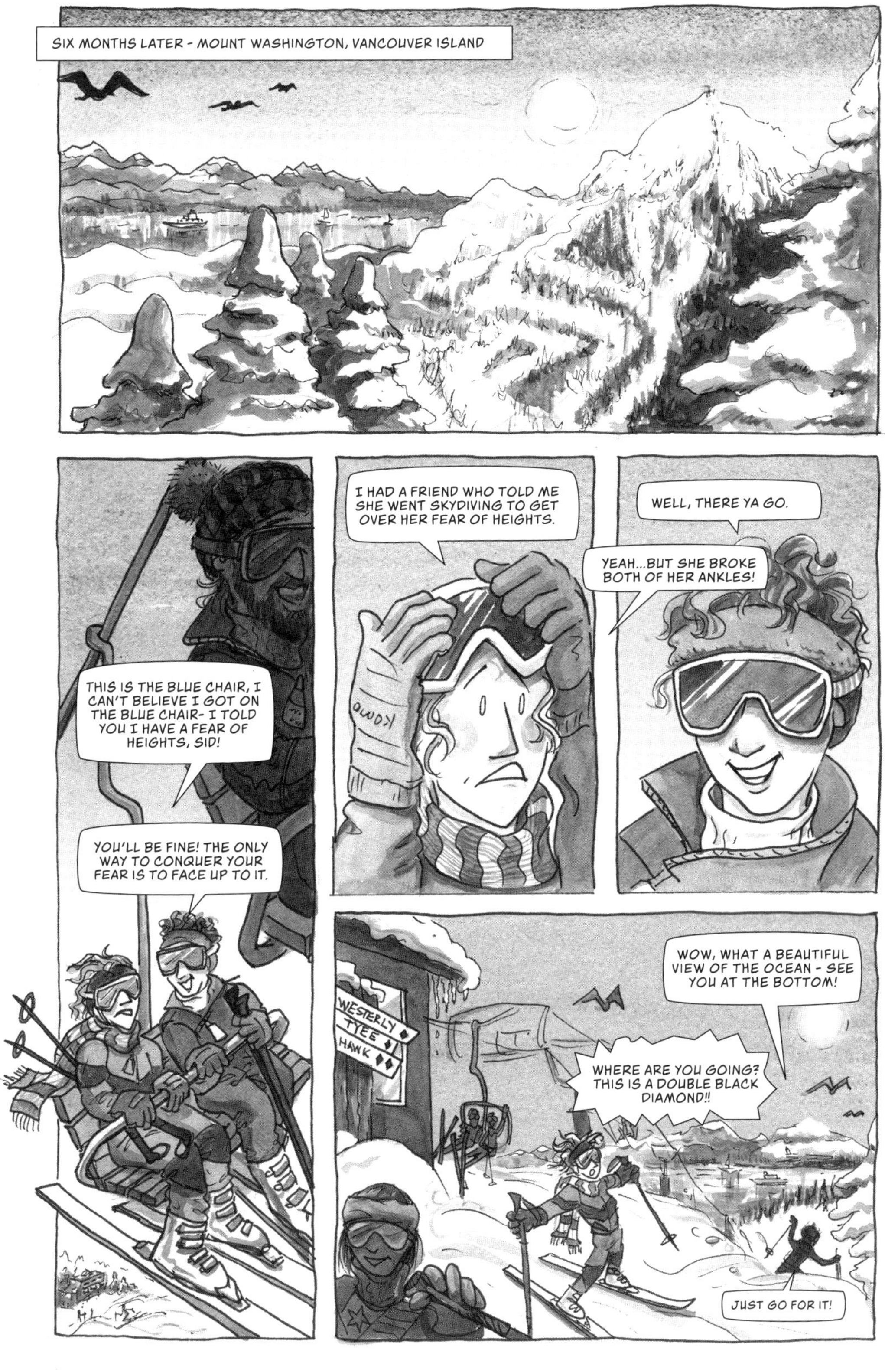
SIX MONTHS LATER - MOUNT WASHINGTON, VANCOUVER ISLAND
THIS IS THE BLUE CHAIR, I CAN'T BELIEVE I GOT ON THE BLUE CHAIR- I TOLD YOU I HAVE A FEAR OF HEIGHTS, SID!
YOU'LL BE FINE! THE ONLY WAY TO CONQUER YOUR FEAR IS TO FACE UP TO IT.
I HAD A FRIEND WHO TOLD ME SHE WENT SKYDIVING TO GET OVER HER FEAR OF HEIGHTS.
WELL, THERE YA GO.
YEAH...BUT SHE BROKE BOTH OF HER ANKLES!
WESTERLY
TYEE
HAWK
WOW, WHAT A BEAUTIFUL VIEW OF THE OCEAN - SEE YOU AT THE BOTTOM!
WHERE ARE YOU GOING? THIS IS A DOUBLE BLACK DIAMOND!!
JUST GO FOR IT!

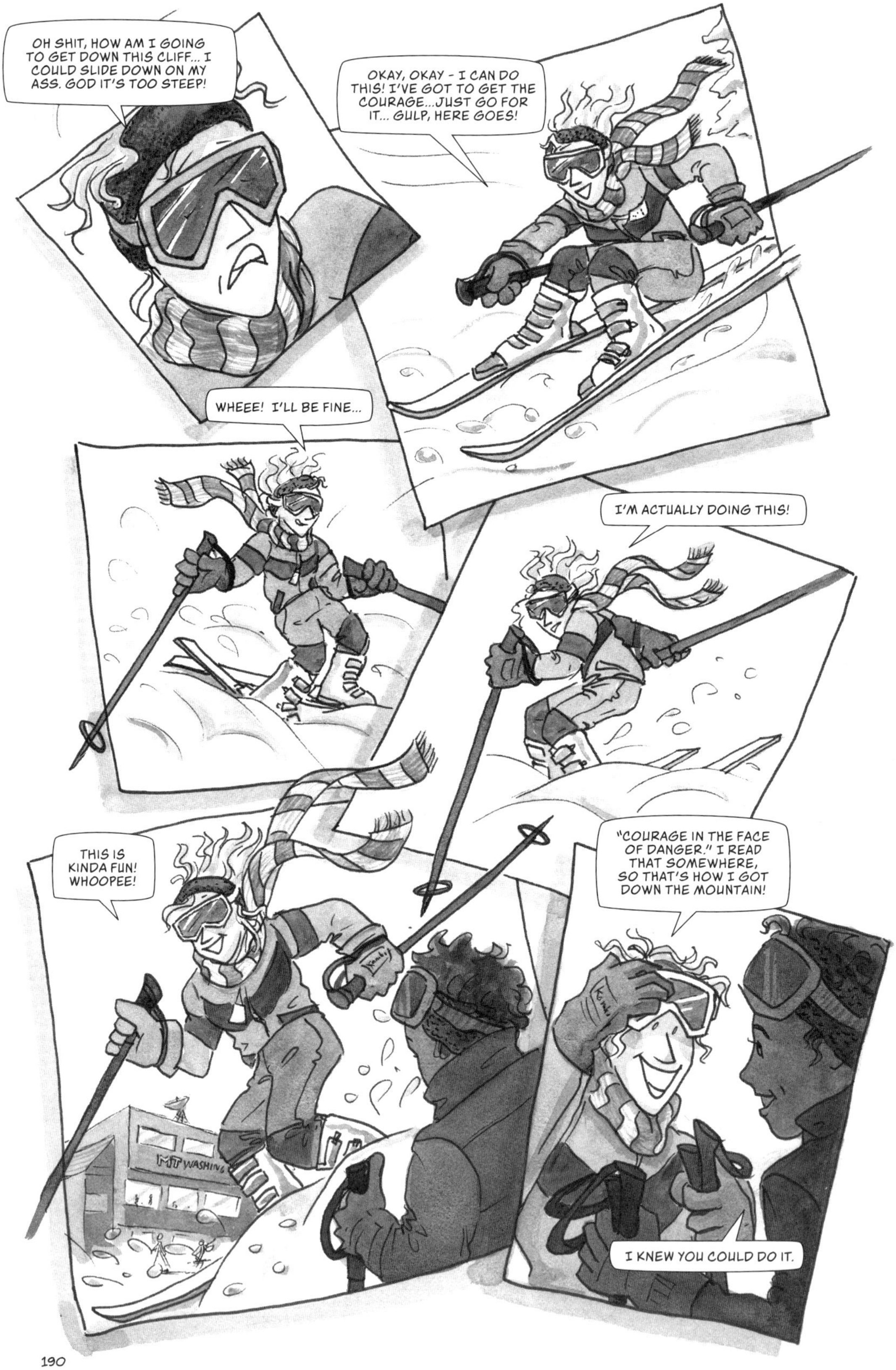

OH SHIT, HOW AM I GOING TO GET DOWN THIS CLIFF... I COULD SLIDE DOWN ON MY ASS. GOD IT'S TOO STEEP!
OKAY, OKAY - I CAN DO THIS! I'VE GOT TO GET THE COURAGE...JUST GO FOR IT... GULP, HERE GOES!
WHEEE! I'LL BE FINE...
I'M ACTUALLY DOING THIS!
THIS IS KINDA FUN! WHOOPEE!
MT WASHING
"COURAGE IN THE FACE OF DANGER." I READ THAT SOMEWHERE, SO THAT'S HOW I GOT DOWN THE MOUNTAIN!
I KNEW YOU COULD DO IT.

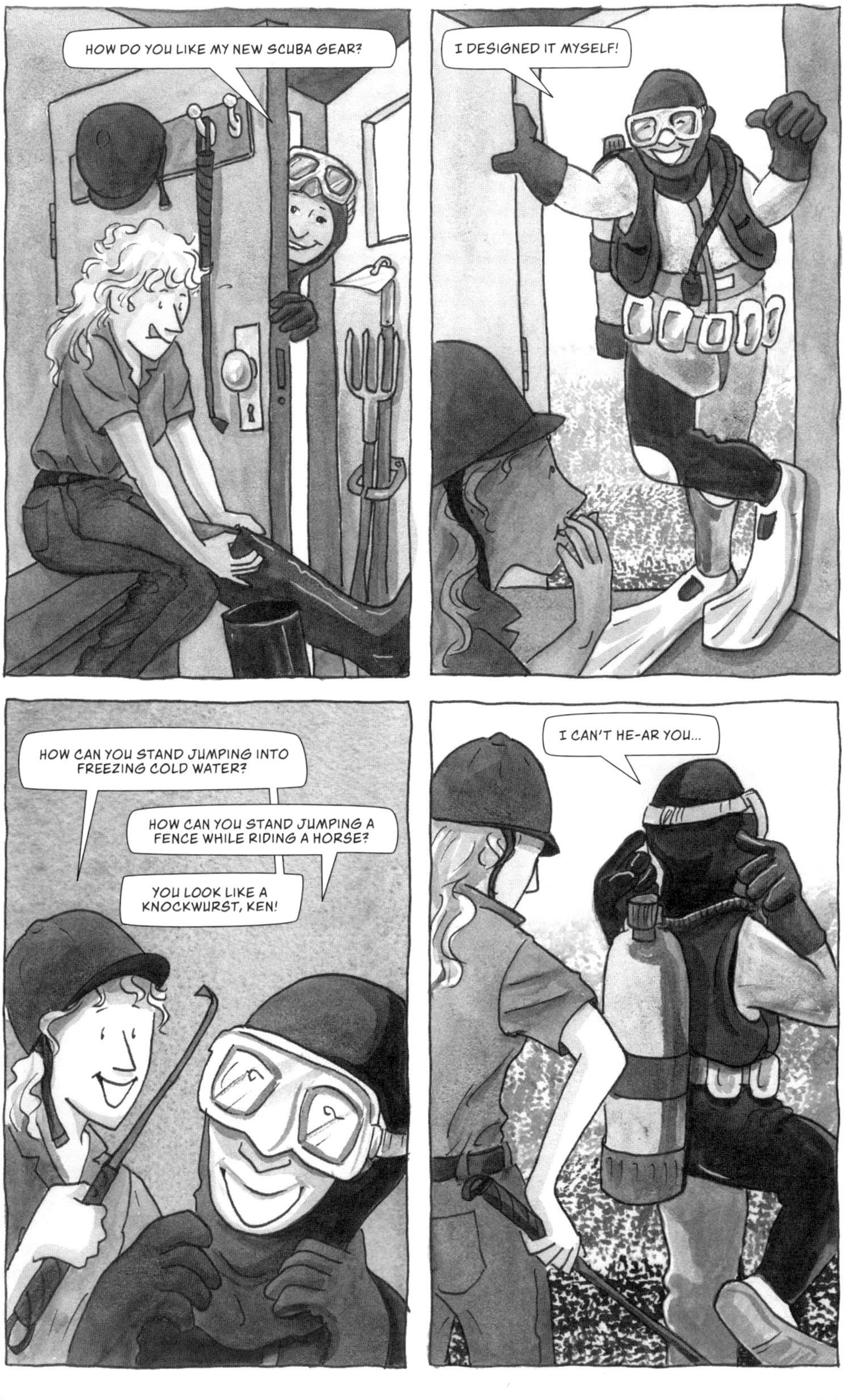
HOW DO YOU LIKE MY NEW SCUBA GEAR?
I DESIGNED IT MYSELF!
HOW CAN YOU STAND JUMPING INTO FREEZING COLD WATER?
HOW CAN YOU STAND JUMPING A FENCE WHILE RIDING A HORSE?
YOU LOOK LIKE A KNOCKWURST, KEN!
I CAN'T HE-AR YOU...

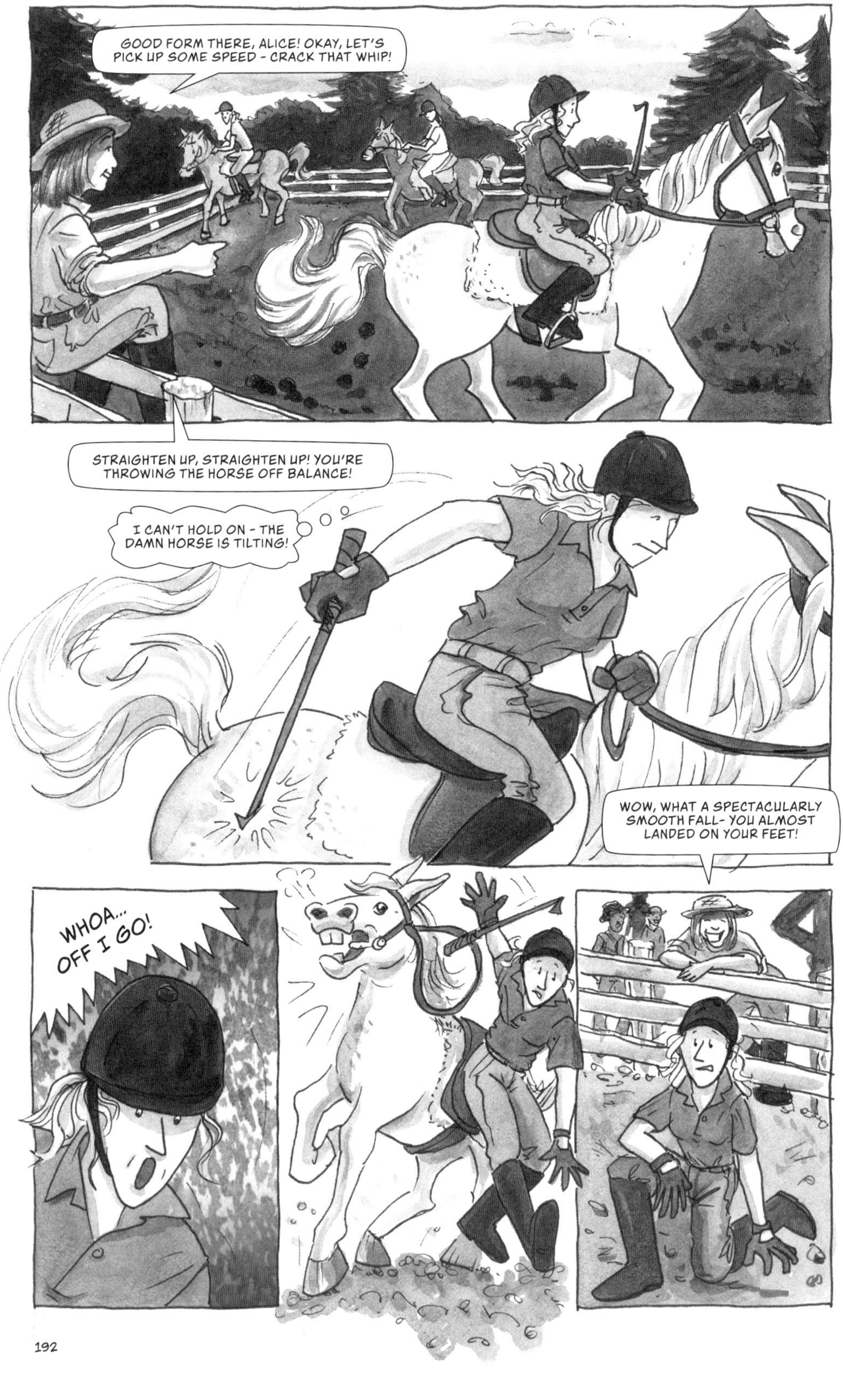

GOOD FORM THERE, ALICE! OKAY, LET'S PICK UP SOME SPEED - CRACK THAT WHIP!
STRAIGHTEN UP, STRAIGHTEN UP! YOU'RE THROWING THE HORSE OFF BALANCE!
I CAN'T HOLD ON - THE DAMN HORSE IS TILTING!
WHOA... OFF I GO!
WOW, WHAT A SPECTACULARLY SMOOTH FALL- YOU ALMOST LANDED ON YOUR FEET!

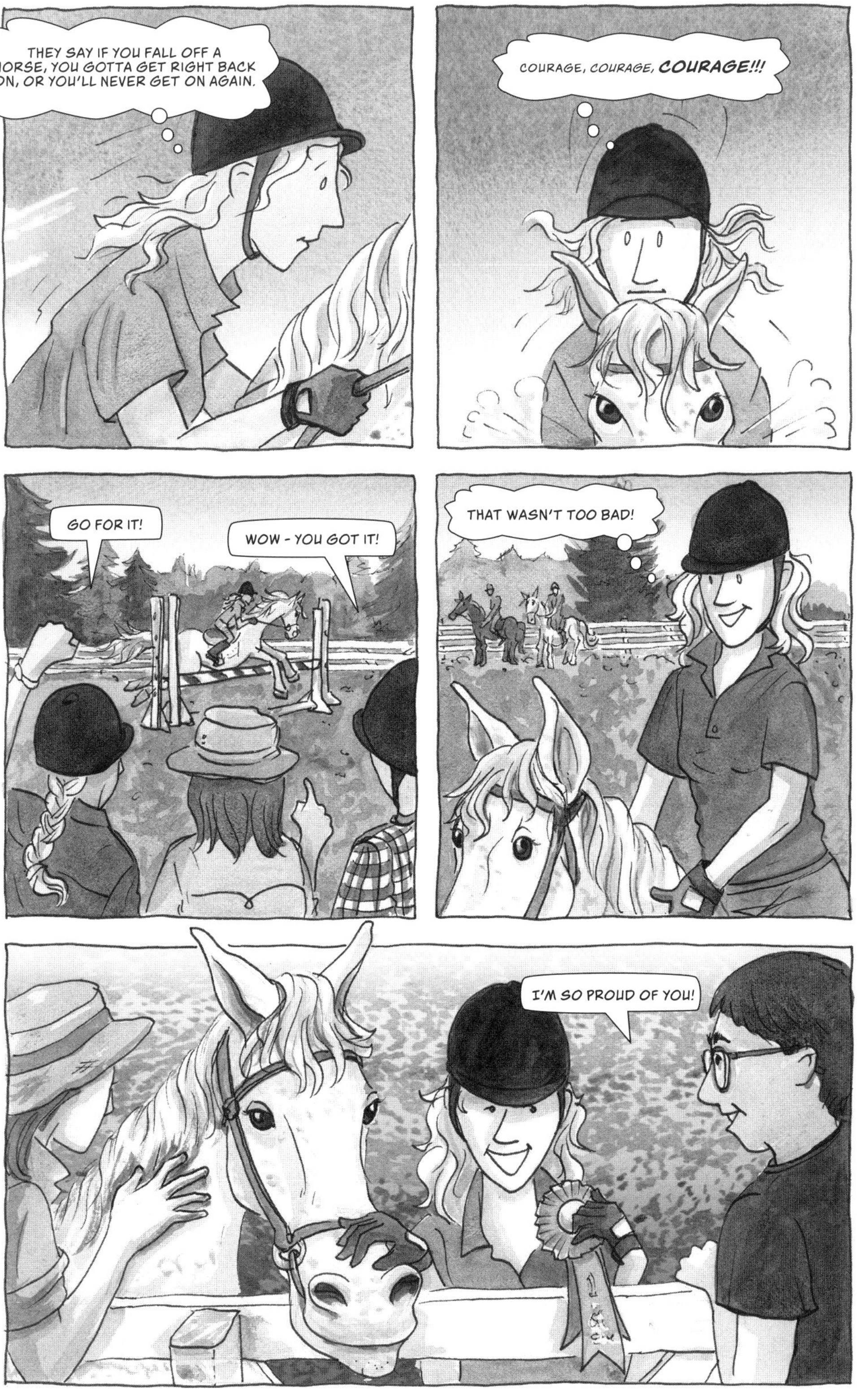
THEY SAY IF YOU FALL OFF A HORSE, YOU GOTTA GET RIGHT BACK ON, OR YOU'LL NEVER GET ON AGAIN.
COURAGE, COURAGE, **COURAGE!!!**
GO FOR IT!
WOW - YOU GOT IT!
THAT WASN'T TOO BAD!
I'M SO PROUD OF YOU!

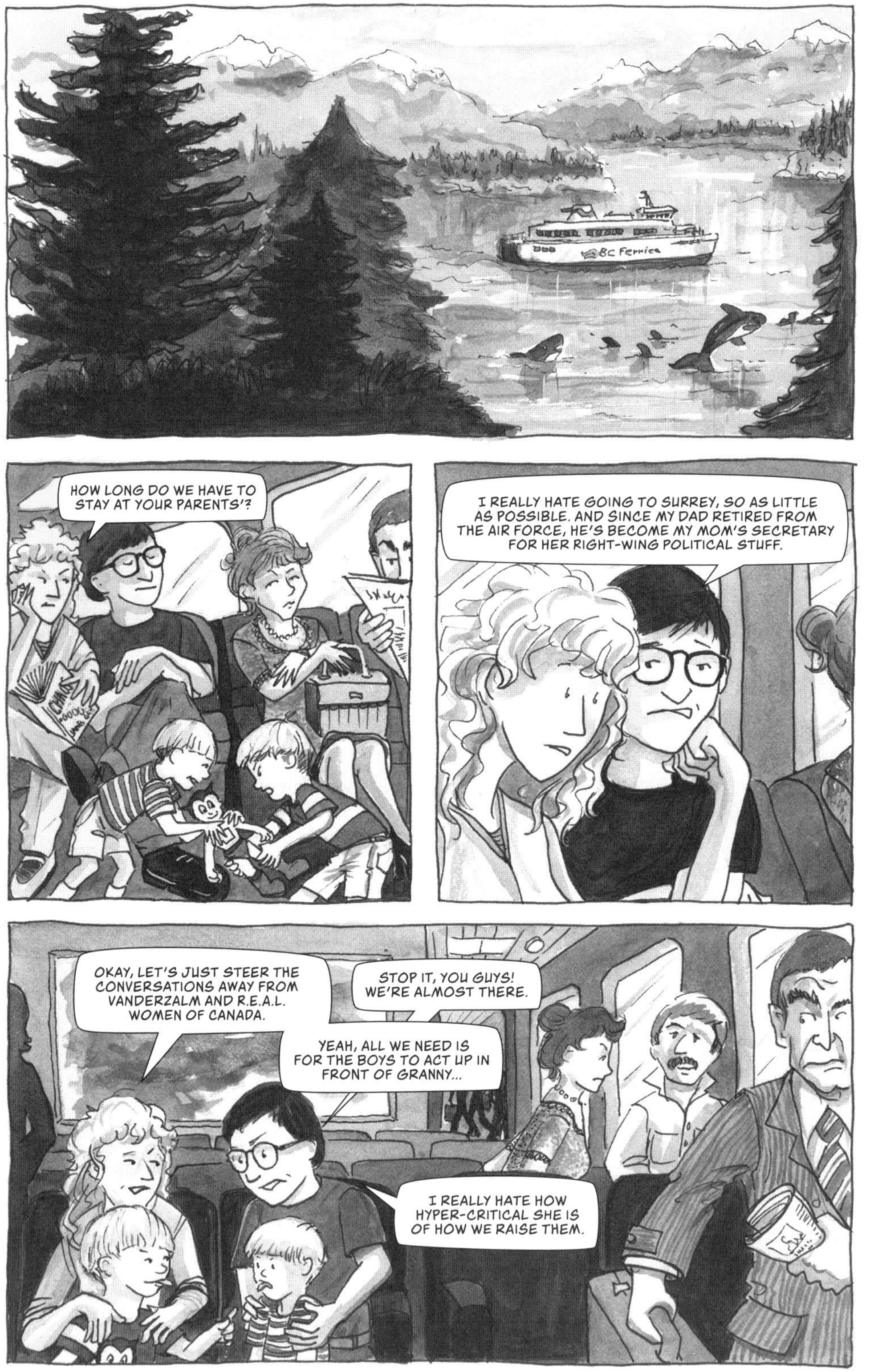
BC Ferries
HOW LONG DO WE HAVE TO STAY AT YOUR PARENTS'?
I REALLY HATE GOING TO SURREY, SO AS LITTLE AS POSSIBLE. AND SINCE MY DAD RETIRED FROM THE AIR FORCE, HE'S BECOME MY MOM'S SECRETARY FOR HER RIGHT-WING POLITICAL STUFF.
OKAY, LET'S JUST STEER THE CONVERSATIONS AWAY FROM VANDERZALM AND R.E.A.L. WOMEN OF CANADA.
STOP IT, YOU GUYS! WE'RE ALMOST THERE.
YEAH, ALL WE NEED IS FOR THE BOYS TO ACT UP IN FRONT OF GRANNY...
I REALLY HATE HOW HYPER-CRITICAL SHE IS OF HOW WE RAISE THEM.

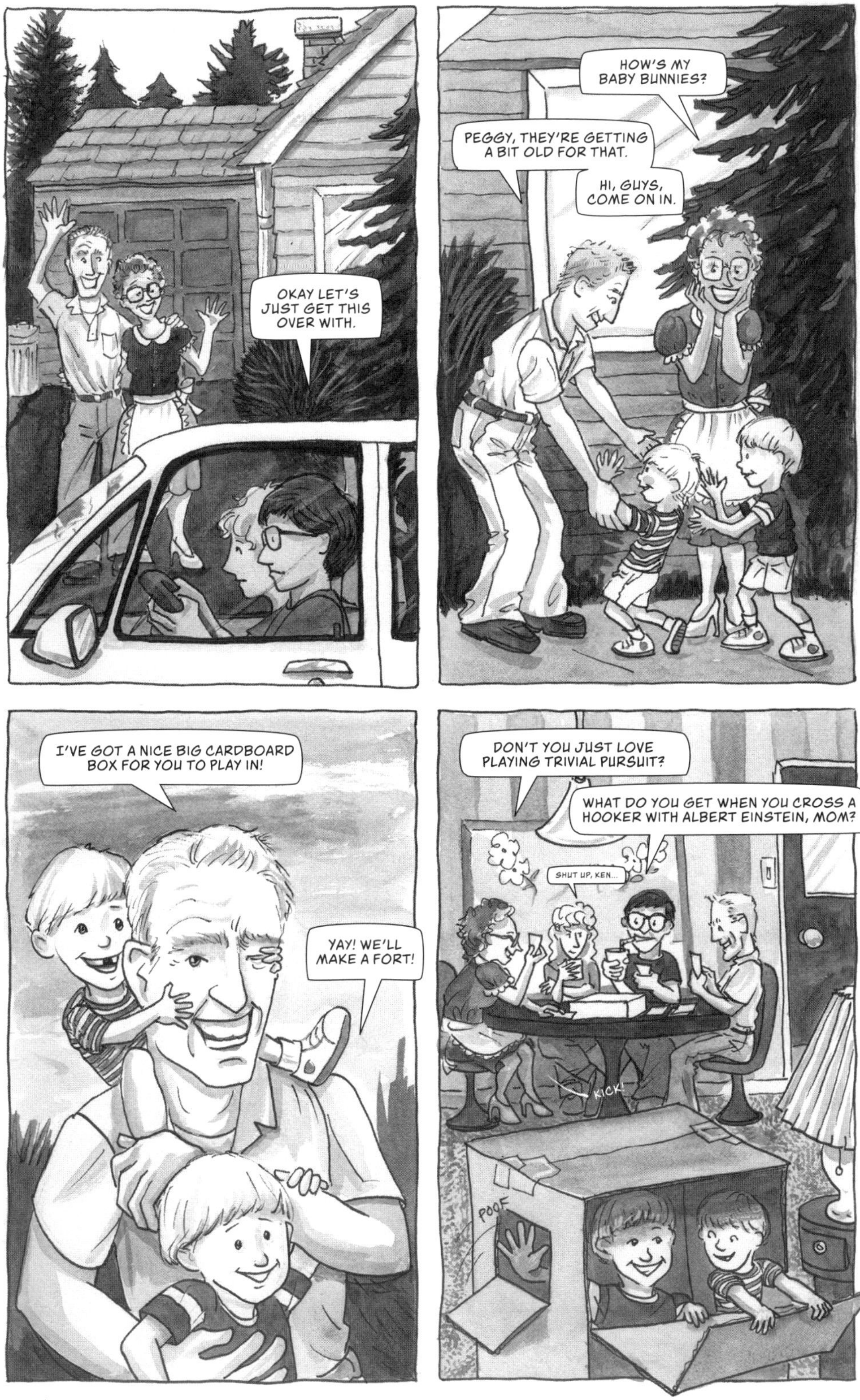
OKAY LET'S JUST GET THIS OVER WITH.
HOW'S MY BABY BUNNIES?
PEGGY, THEY'RE GETTING A BIT OLD FOR THAT.
HI, GUYS, COME ON IN.
I'VE GOT A NICE BIG CARDBOARD BOX FOR YOU TO PLAY IN!
YAY! WE'LL MAKE A FORT!
DON'T YOU JUST LOVE PLAYING TRIVIAL PURSUIT?
WHAT DO YOU GET WHEN YOU CROSS A HOOKER WITH ALBERT EINSTEIN, MOM?
SHUT UP, KEN...
KICK!
POOF

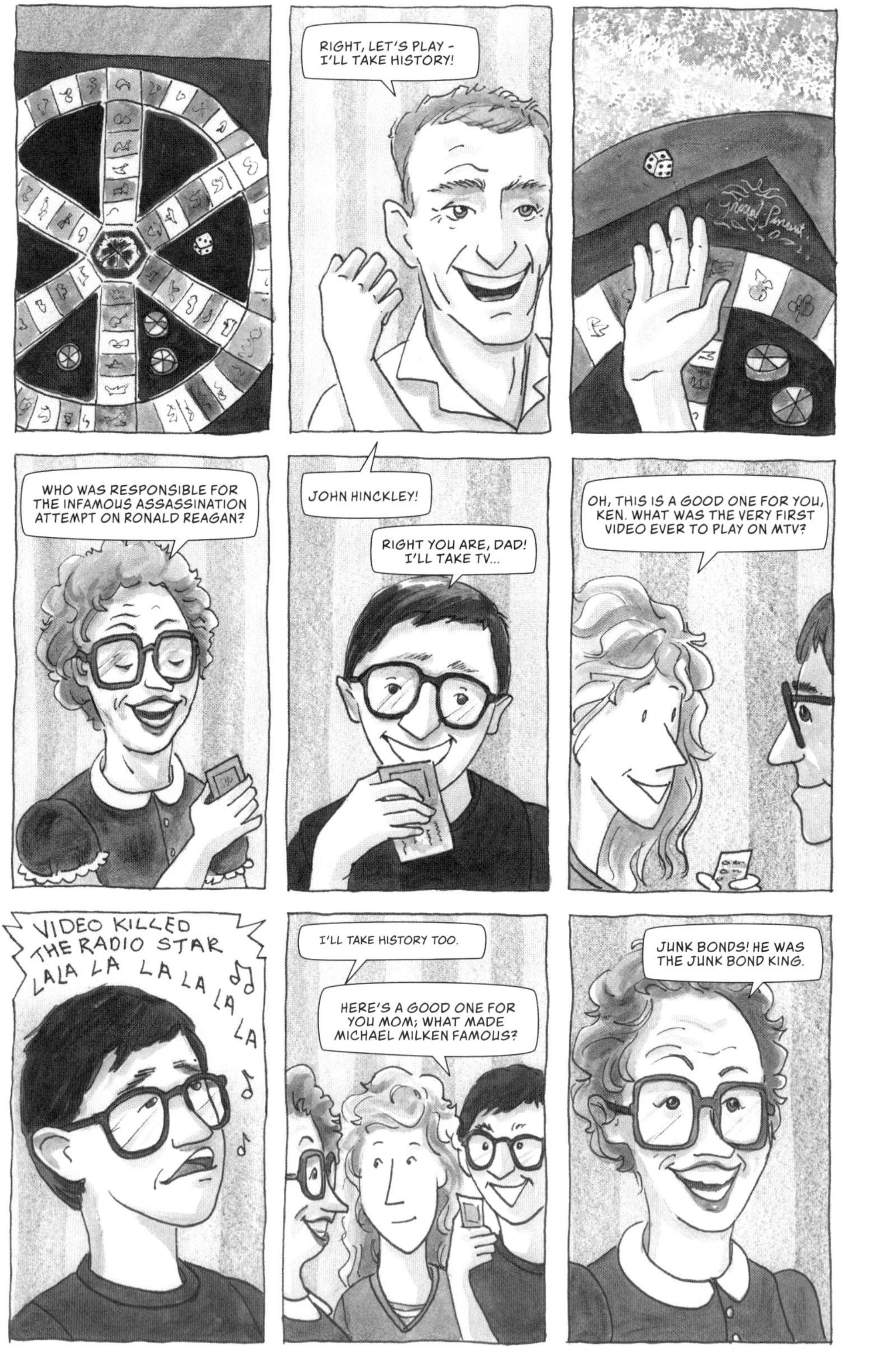

RIGHT, LET'S PLAY - I'LL TAKE HISTORY!
WHO WAS RESPONSIBLE FOR THE INFAMOUS ASSASSINATION ATTEMPT ON RONALD REAGAN?
JOHN HINCKLEY!
RIGHT YOU ARE, DAD! I'LL TAKE TV...
OH, THIS IS A GOOD ONE FOR YOU, KEN. WHAT WAS THE VERY FIRST VIDEO EVER TO PLAY ON MTV?
VIDEO KILLED THE RADIO STAR LALA LA LA LA LA LA LA
I'LL TAKE HISTORY TOO.
HERE'S A GOOD ONE FOR YOU MOM; WHAT MADE MICHAEL MILKEN FAMOUS?
JUNK BONDS! HE WAS THE JUNK BOND KING.

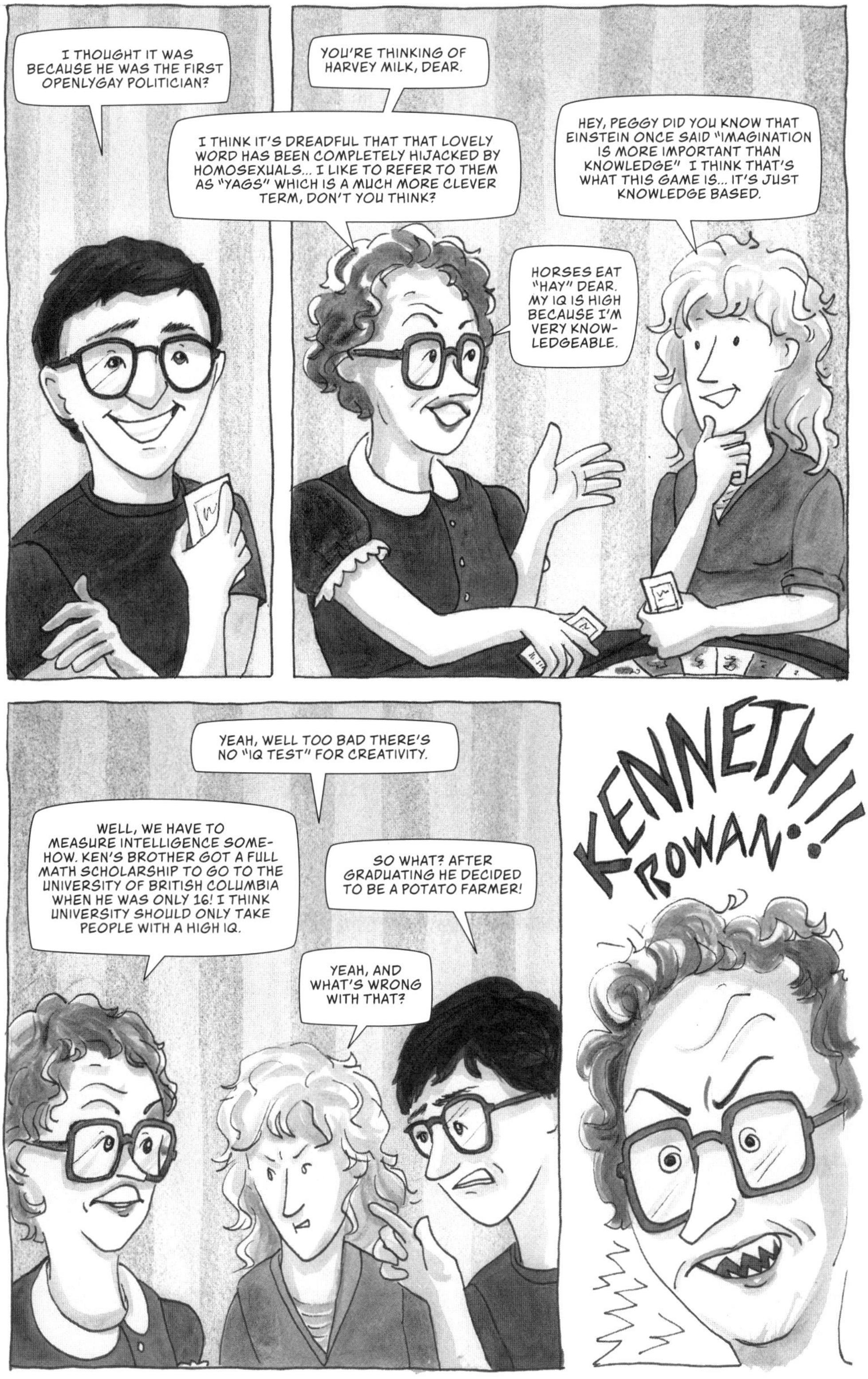
I THOUGHT IT WAS BECAUSE HE WAS THE FIRST OPENLYGAY POLITICIAN?
YOU'RE THINKING OF HARVEY MILK, DEAR.
I THINK IT'S DREADFUL THAT THAT LOVELY WORD HAS BEEN COMPLETELY HIJACKED BY HOMOSEXUALS... I LIKE TO REFER TO THEM AS "YAGS" WHICH IS A MUCH MORE CLEVER TERM, DON'T YOU THINK?
HEY, PEGGY DID YOU KNOW THAT EINSTEIN ONCE SAID "IMAGINATION IS MORE IMPORTANT THAN KNOWLEDGE" I THINK THAT'S WHAT THIS GAME IS... IT'S JUST KNOWLEDGE BASED.
HORSES EAT "HAY" DEAR. MY IQ IS HIGH BECAUSE I'M VERY KNOW-LEDGEABLE.
YEAH, WELL TOO BAD THERE'S NO "IQ TEST" FOR CREATIVITY.
WELL, WE HAVE TO MEASURE INTELLIGENCE SOME-HOW. KEN'S BROTHER GOT A FULL MATH SCHOLARSHIP TO GO TO THE UNIVERSITY OF BRITISH COLUMBIA WHEN HE WAS ONLY 16! I THINK UNIVERSITY SHOULD ONLY TAKE PEOPLE WITH A HIGH IQ.
SO WHAT? AFTER GRADUATING HE DECIDED TO BE A POTATO FARMER!
YEAH, AND WHAT'S WRONG WITH THAT?
KENNETH!!! ROWAN!!!

IF ONLY THERE WAS A REAL TEST FOR INTELLIGENCE. I THINK THE IQ TEST SHOULD BE ABOLISHED. THEY DO MORE HARM THAN GOOD, BECAUSE THEY'RE SO LEFT-HEMISPHERE BIASED.

WHAT'S ALL THIS RIGHT AND LEFT HEMISPHERE NONSENSE? ROBERT'S INTELLIGENCE QUOTIENT IS WHAT GOT HIM INTO UBC..

BUT WHAT ABOUT PEOPLE WHO THINK IN A DIFFERENT WAY?

I HARDLY THINK AN AUTHOR COULD WRITE BOOKS WITHOUT KNOWING PROPER GRAMMAR AND HOW TO SPELL.

ISN'T THAT THE EDITOR'S JOB? WHAT ABOUT IDEAS, AND CREATIVITY? SHOULD ARTISTS BE EXCLUDED FROM UNIVERSITY?

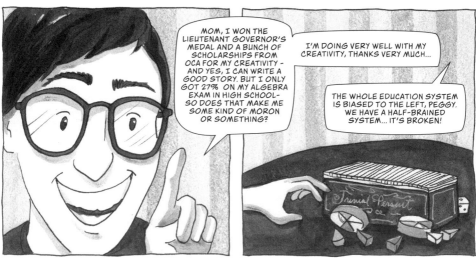

MOM, I WON THE LIEUTENANT GOVERNOR'S MEDAL AND A BUNCH OF SCHOLARSHIPS FROM OCA FOR MY CREATIVITY – AND YES, I CAN WRITE A GOOD STORY. BUT I ONLY GOT 27% ON MY ALGEBRA EXAM IN HIGH SCHOOL— SO DOES THAT MAKE ME SOME KIND OF MORON OR SOMETHING?

I'M DOING VERY WELL WITH MY CREATIVITY, THANKS VERY MUCH...

THE WHOLE EDUCATION SYSTEM IS BIASED TO THE LEFT, PEGGY. WE HAVE A HALF-BRAINED SYSTEM... IT'S BROKEN!

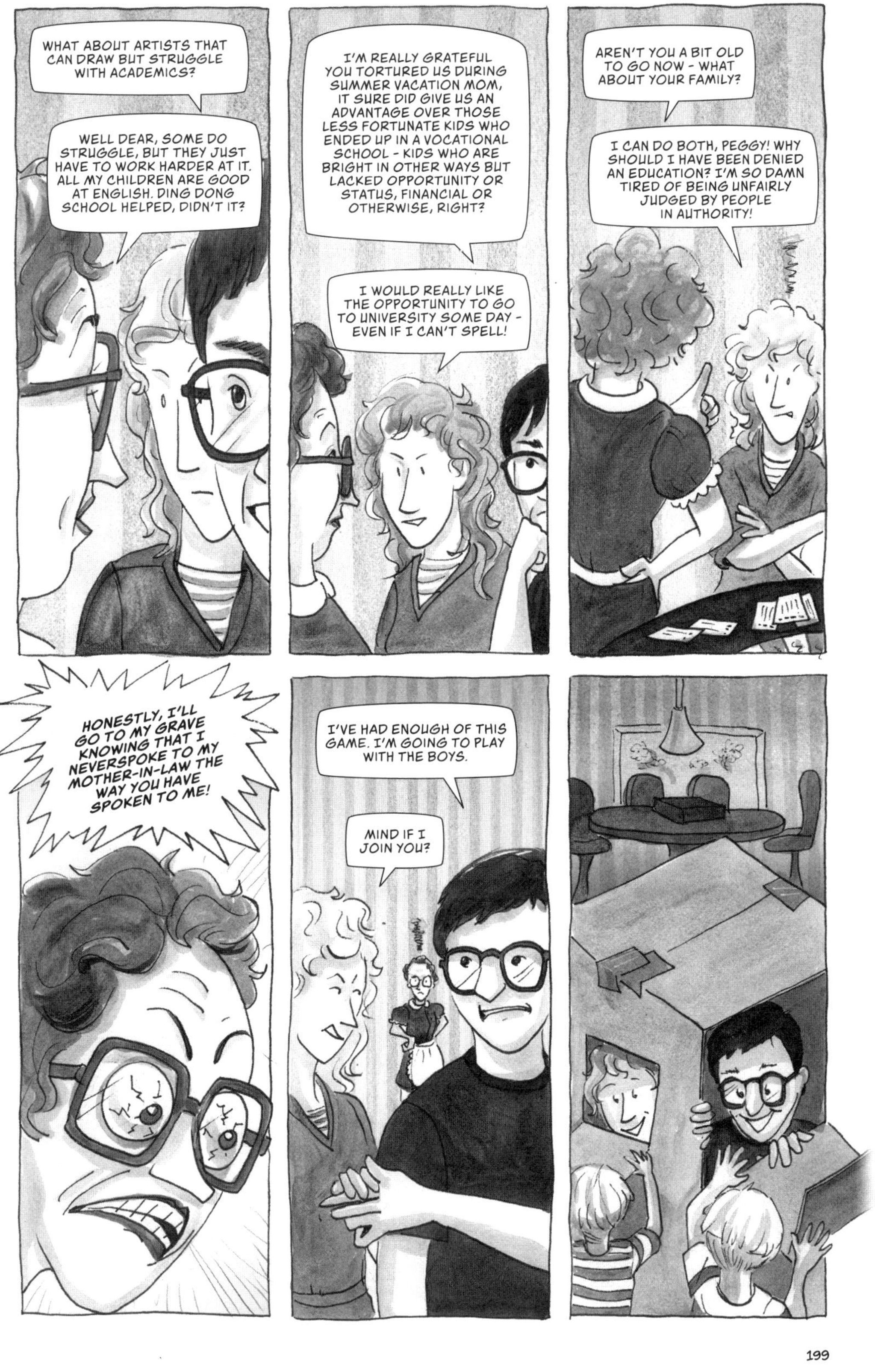

WHAT ABOUT ARTISTS THAT CAN DRAW BUT STRUGGLE WITH ACADEMICS?
WELL DEAR, SOME DO STRUGGLE, BUT THEY JUST HAVE TO WORK HARDER AT IT. ALL MY CHILDREN ARE GOOD AT ENGLISH. DING DONG SCHOOL HELPED, DIDN'T IT?
I'M REALLY GRATEFUL YOU TORTURED US DURING SUMMER VACATION MOM, IT SURE DID GIVE US AN ADVANTAGE OVER THOSE LESS FORTUNATE KIDS WHO ENDED UP IN A VOCATIONAL SCHOOL - KIDS WHO ARE BRIGHT IN OTHER WAYS BUT LACKED OPPORTUNITY OR STATUS, FINANCIAL OR OTHERWISE, RIGHT?
I WOULD REALLY LIKE THE OPPORTUNITY TO GO TO UNIVERSITY SOME DAY - EVEN IF I CAN'T SPELL!
AREN'T YOU A BIT OLD TO GO NOW - WHAT ABOUT YOUR FAMILY?
I CAN DO BOTH, PEGGY! WHY SHOULD I HAVE BEEN DENIED AN EDUCATION? I'M SO DAMN TIRED OF BEING UNFAIRLY JUDGED BY PEOPLE IN AUTHORITY!
HONESTLY, I'LL GO TO MY GRAVE KNOWING THAT I NEVERSPOKE TO MY MOTHER-IN-LAW THE WAY YOU HAVE SPOKEN TO ME!
I'VE HAD ENOUGH OF THIS GAME. I'M GOING TO PLAY WITH THE BOYS.
MIND IF I JOIN YOU?

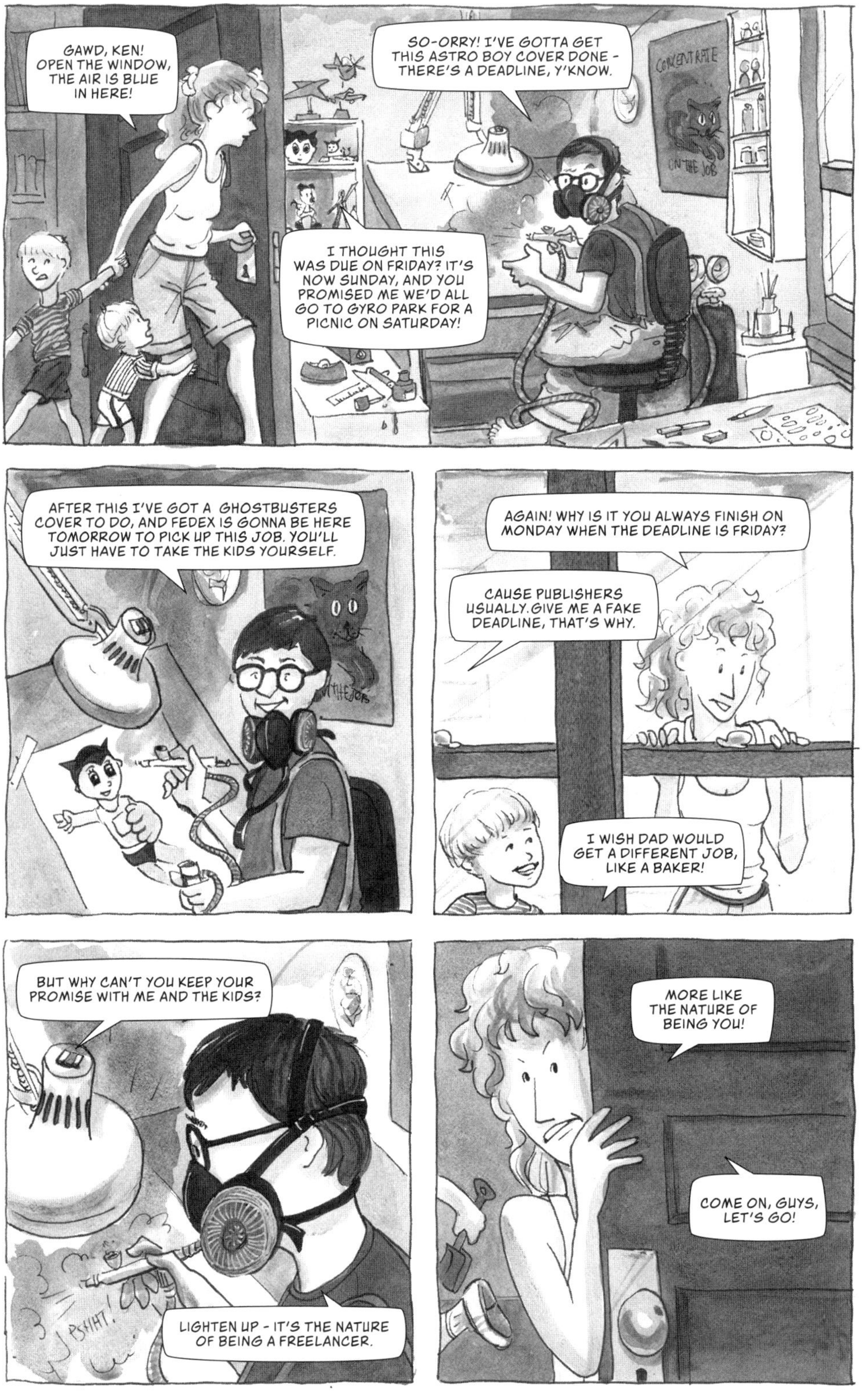
GAWD, KEN! OPEN THE WINDOW, THE AIR IS BLUE IN HERE!
SO-ORRY! I'VE GOTTA GET THIS ASTRO BOY COVER DONE - THERE'S A DEADLINE, Y'KNOW.
CONCENTRATE ON THE JOB
I THOUGHT THIS WAS DUE ON FRIDAY? IT'S NOW SUNDAY, AND YOU PROMISED ME WE'D ALL GO TO GYRO PARK FOR A PICNIC ON SATURDAY!
AFTER THIS I'VE GOT A GHOSTBUSTERS COVER TO DO, AND FEDEX IS GONNA BE HERE TOMORROW TO PICK UP THIS JOB. YOU'LL JUST HAVE TO TAKE THE KIDS YOURSELF.
AGAIN! WHY IS IT YOU ALWAYS FINISH ON MONDAY WHEN THE DEADLINE IS FRIDAY?
CAUSE PUBLISHERS USUALLY GIVE ME A FAKE DEADLINE, THAT'S WHY.
I WISH DAD WOULD GET A DIFFERENT JOB, LIKE A BAKER!
BUT WHY CAN'T YOU KEEP YOUR PROMISE WITH ME AND THE KIDS?
PSHHT!
LIGHTEN UP - IT'S THE NATURE OF BEING A FREELANCER.
MORE LIKE THE NATURE OF BEING YOU!
COME ON, GUYS, LET'S GO!

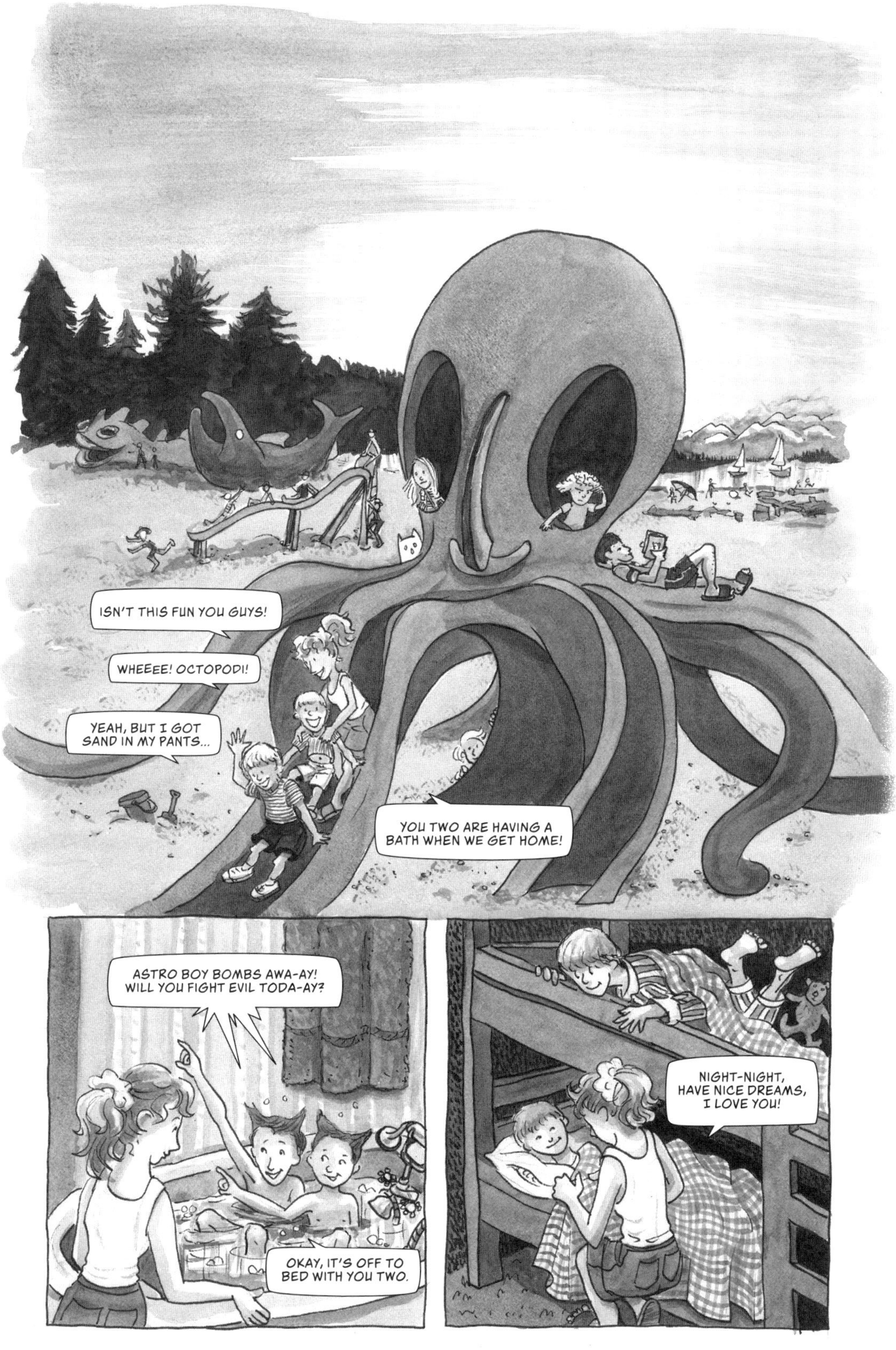
ISN'T THIS FUN YOU GUYS!
WHEEEE! OCTOPODI!
YEAH, BUT I GOT SAND IN MY PANTS...
YOU TWO ARE HAVING A BATH WHEN WE GET HOME!
ASTRO BOY BOMBS AWA-AY! WILL YOU FIGHT EVIL TODA-AY?
OKAY, IT'S OFF TO BED WITH YOU TWO.
NIGHT-NIGHT, HAVE NICE DREAMS, I LOVE YOU!

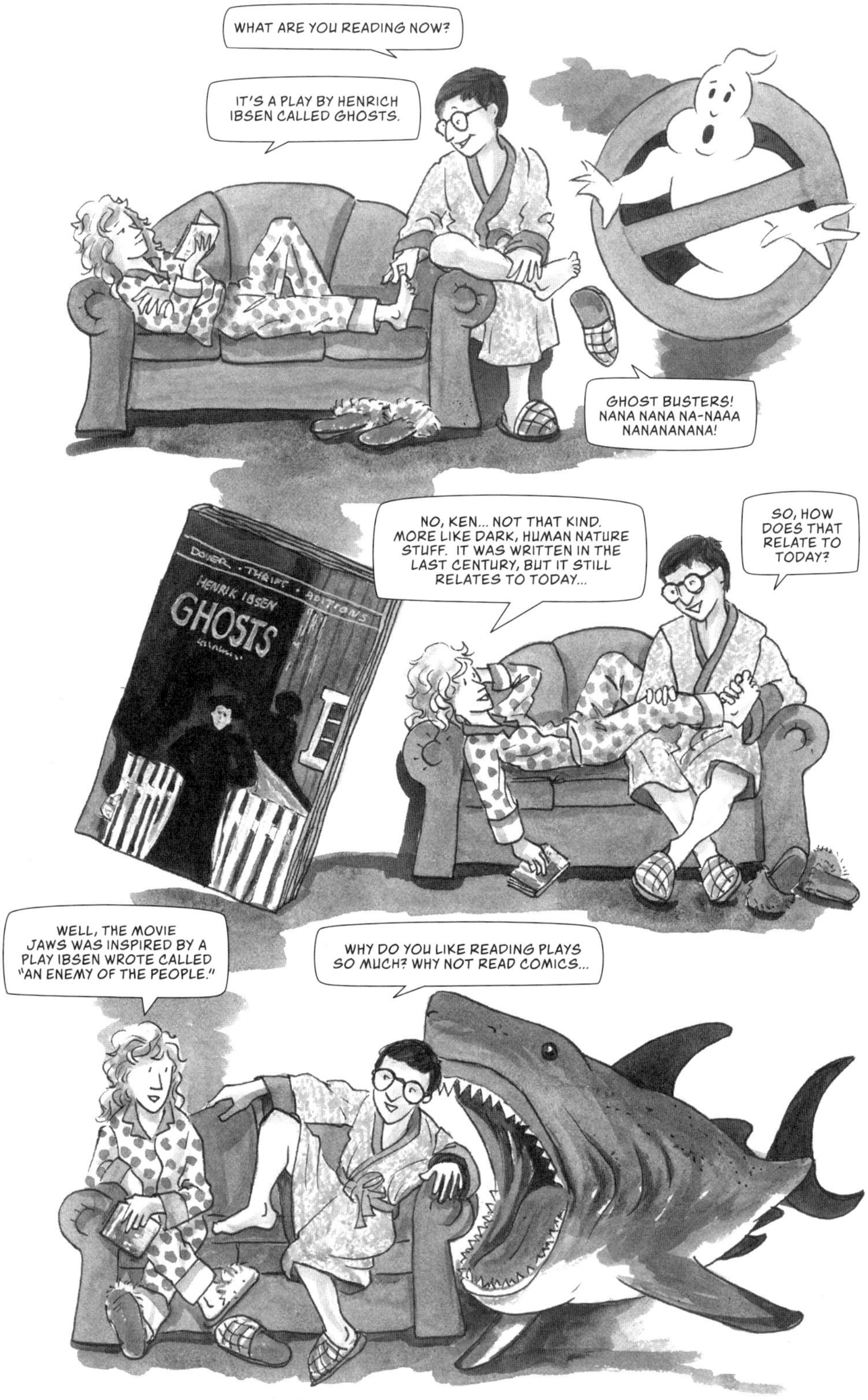
WHAT ARE YOU READING NOW?
IT'S A PLAY BY HENRICH IBSEN CALLED GHOSTS.
GHOST BUSTERS! NANA NANA NA-NAAA NANANANANA!
HENRIK IBSEN
GHOSTS
NO, KEN... NOT THAT KIND. MORE LIKE DARK, HUMAN NATURE STUFF. IT WAS WRITTEN IN THE LAST CENTURY, BUT IT STILL RELATES TO TODAY...
SO, HOW DOES THAT RELATE TO TODAY?
WELL, THE MOVIE JAWS WAS INSPIRED BY A PLAY IBSEN WROTE CALLED "AN ENEMY OF THE PEOPLE."
WHY DO YOU LIKE READING PLAYS SO MUCH? WHY NOT READ COMICS...

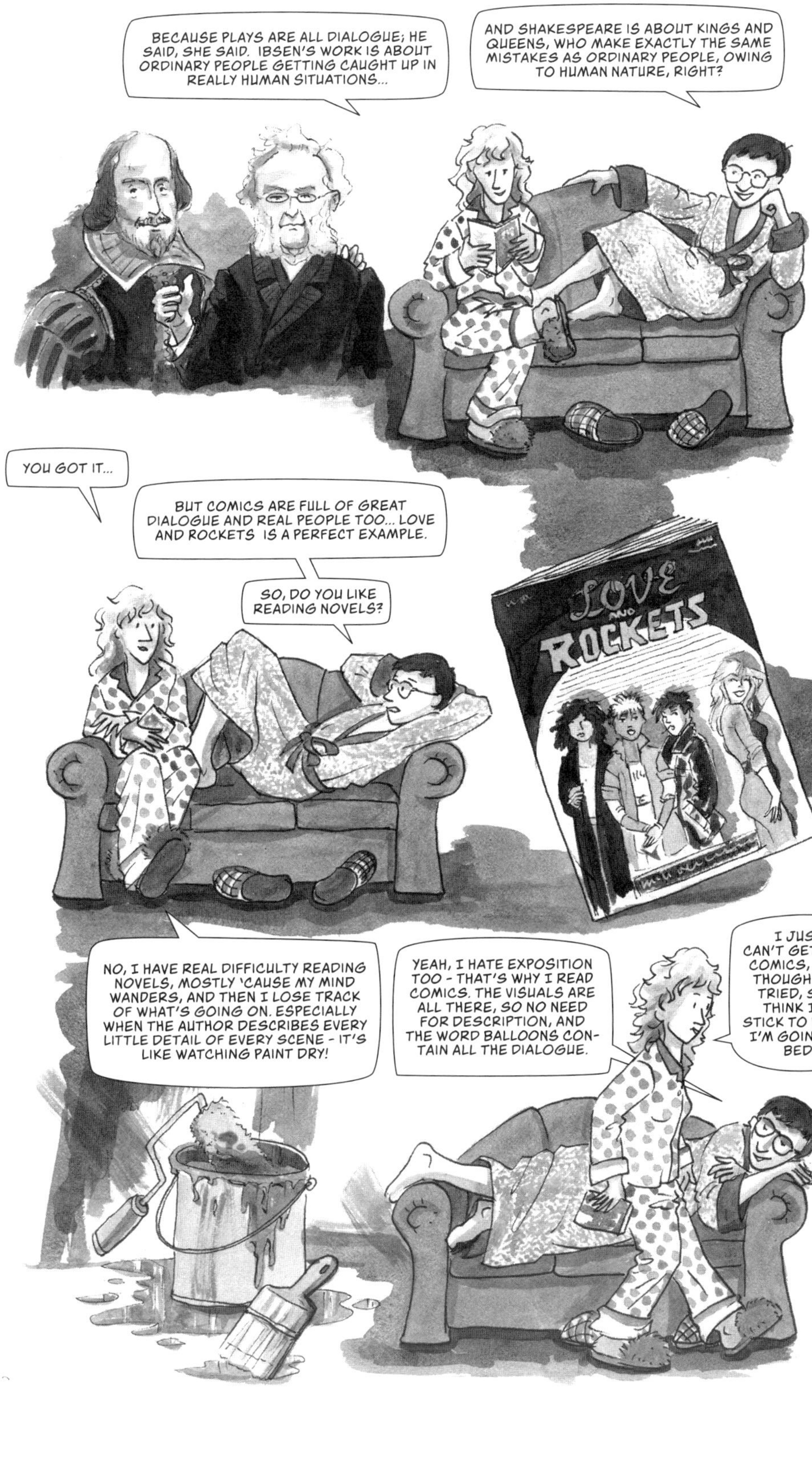

BECAUSE PLAYS ARE ALL DIALOGUE; HE SAID, SHE SAID. IBSEN'S WORK IS ABOUT ORDINARY PEOPLE GETTING CAUGHT UP IN REALLY HUMAN SITUATIONS...
AND SHAKESPEARE IS ABOUT KINGS AND QUEENS, WHO MAKE EXACTLY THE SAME MISTAKES AS ORDINARY PEOPLE, OWING TO HUMAN NATURE, RIGHT?
YOU GOT IT...
BUT COMICS ARE FULL OF GREAT DIALOGUE AND REAL PEOPLE TOO... LOVE AND ROCKETS IS A PERFECT EXAMPLE.
SO, DO YOU LIKE READING NOVELS?
LOVE AND ROCKETS
NO, I HAVE REAL DIFFICULTY READING NOVELS, MOSTLY 'CAUSE MY MIND WANDERS, AND THEN I LOSE TRACK OF WHAT'S GOING ON. ESPECIALLY WHEN THE AUTHOR DESCRIBES EVERY LITTLE DETAIL OF EVERY SCENE - IT'S LIKE WATCHING PAINT DRY!
YEAH, I HATE EXPOSITION TOO - THAT'S WHY I READ COMICS. THE VISUALS ARE ALL THERE, SO NO NEED FOR DESCRIPTION, AND THE WORD BALLOONS CONTAIN ALL THE DIALOGUE.
I JUST CAN'T GET INTO COMICS, EVEN THOUGH I'VE TRIED, SO I THINK I'LL STICK TO PLAYS. I'M GOING TO BED.

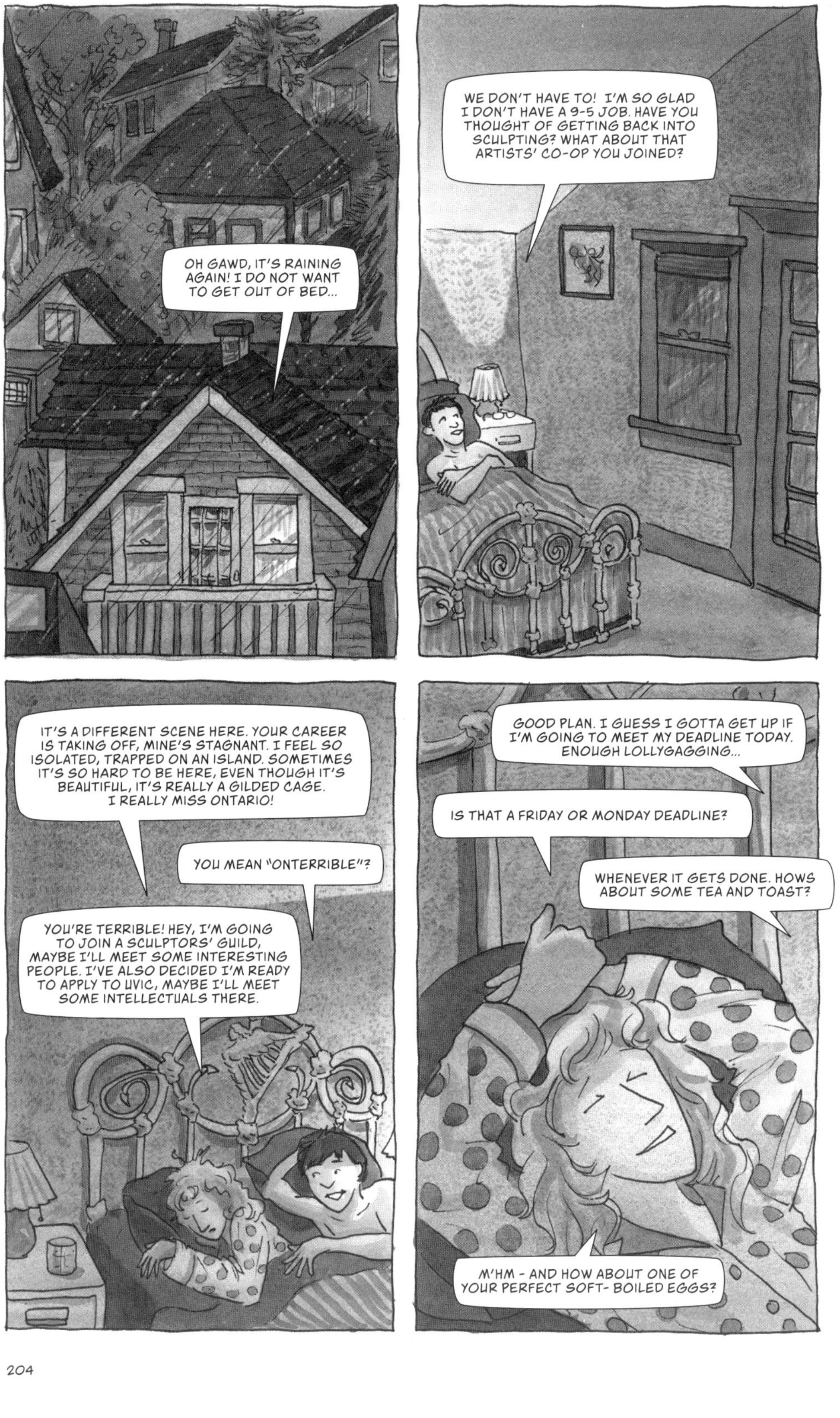
OH GAWD, IT'S RAINING AGAIN! I DO NOT WANT TO GET OUT OF BED...
WE DON'T HAVE TO! I'M SO GLAD I DON'T HAVE A 9-5 JOB. HAVE YOU THOUGHT OF GETTING BACK INTO SCULPTING? WHAT ABOUT THAT ARTISTS' CO-OP YOU JOINED?
IT'S A DIFFERENT SCENE HERE. YOUR CAREER IS TAKING OFF, MINE'S STAGNANT. I FEEL SO ISOLATED, TRAPPED ON AN ISLAND. SOMETIMES IT'S SO HARD TO BE HERE, EVEN THOUGH IT'S BEAUTIFUL, IT'S REALLY A GILDED CAGE. I REALLY MISS ONTARIO!
YOU MEAN "ONTERRIBLE"?
YOU'RE TERRIBLE! HEY, I'M GOING TO JOIN A SCULPTORS' GUILD, MAYBE I'LL MEET SOME INTERESTING PEOPLE. I'VE ALSO DECIDED I'M READY TO APPLY TO UVIC, MAYBE I'LL MEET SOME INTELLECTUALS THERE.
GOOD PLAN. I GUESS I GOTTA GET UP IF I'M GOING TO MEET MY DEADLINE TODAY. ENOUGH LOLLYGAGGING...
IS THAT A FRIDAY OR MONDAY DEADLINE?
WHENEVER IT GETS DONE. HOWS ABOUT SOME TEA AND TOAST?
M'HM - AND HOW ABOUT ONE OF YOUR PERFECT SOFT- BOILED EGGS?

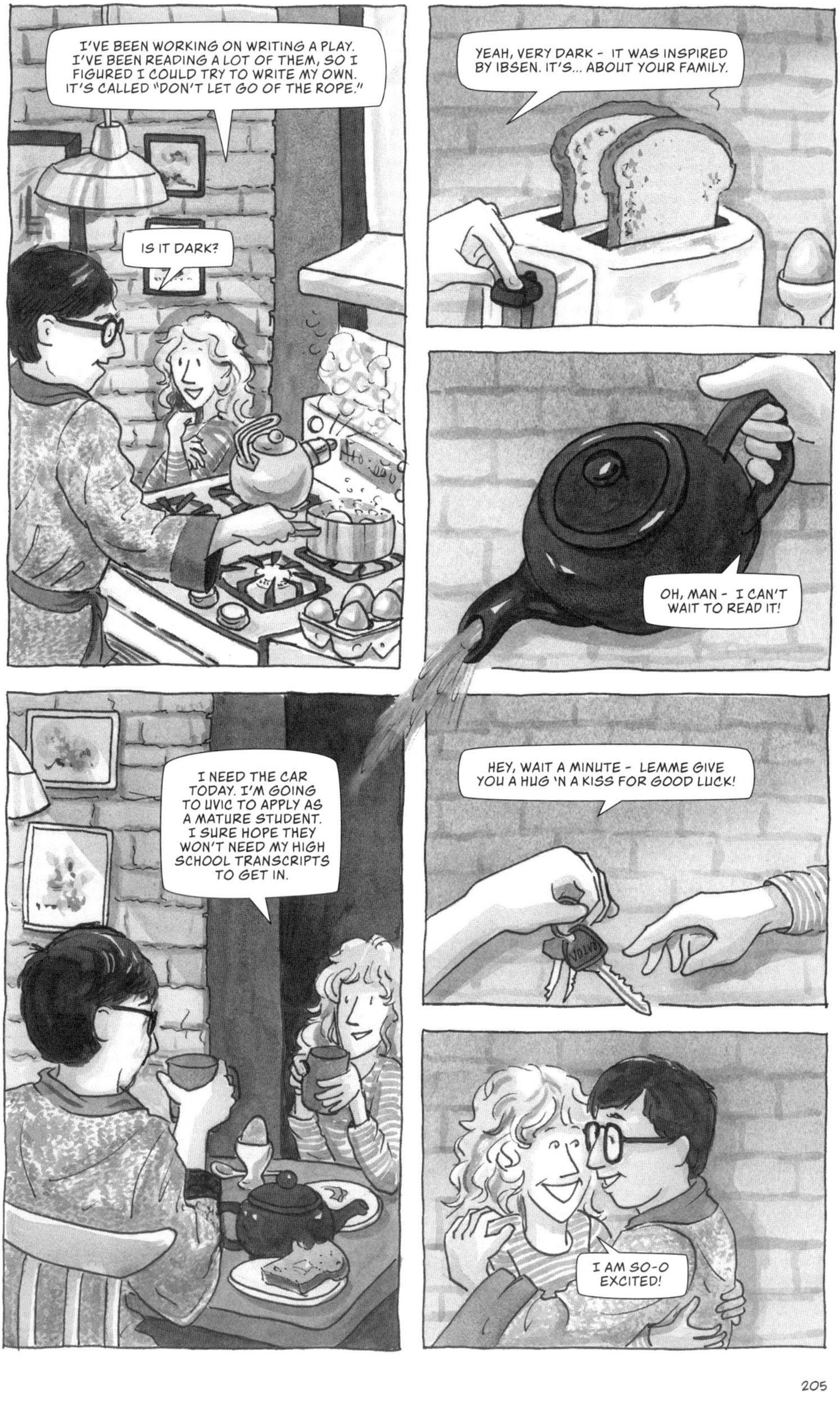
I'VE BEEN WORKING ON WRITING A PLAY. I'VE BEEN READING A LOT OF THEM, SO I FIGURED I COULD TRY TO WRITE MY OWN. IT'S CALLED "DON'T LET GO OF THE ROPE."
IS IT DARK?
YEAH, VERY DARK - IT WAS INSPIRED BY IBSEN. IT'S... ABOUT YOUR FAMILY.
OH, MAN - I CAN'T WAIT TO READ IT!
I NEED THE CAR TODAY. I'M GOING TO UVIC TO APPLY AS A MATURE STUDENT. I SURE HOPE THEY WON'T NEED MY HIGH SCHOOL TRANSCRIPTS TO GET IN.
HEY, WAIT A MINUTE - LEMME GIVE YOU A HUG 'N A KISS FOR GOOD LUCK!
I AM SO-O EXCITED!

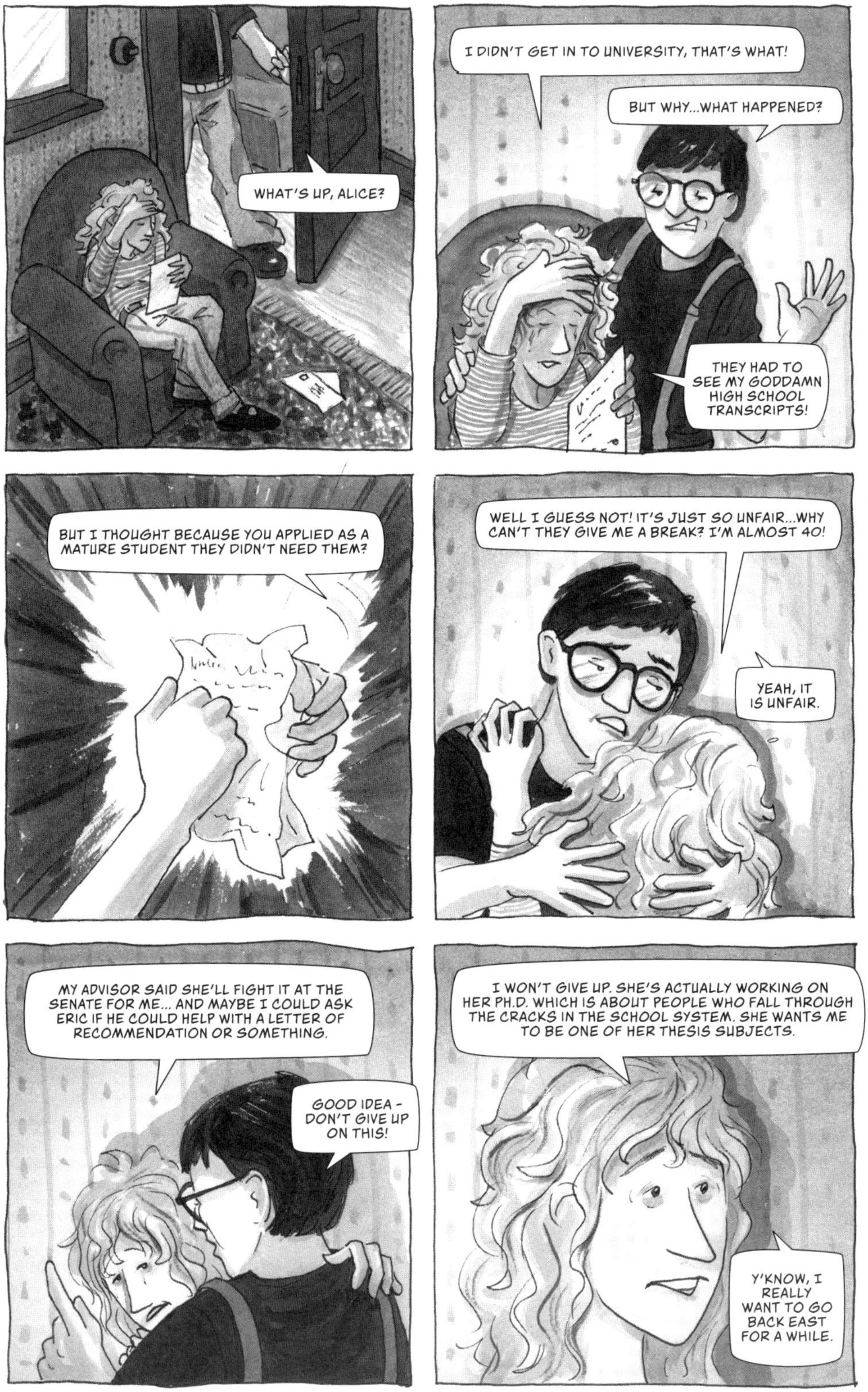
WHAT'S UP, ALICE?
I DIDN'T GET IN TO UNIVERSITY, THAT'S WHAT!
BUT WHY...WHAT HAPPENED?
THEY HAD TO SEE MY GODDAMN HIGH SCHOOL TRANSCRIPTS!
BUT I THOUGHT BECAUSE YOU APPLIED AS A MATURE STUDENT THEY DIDN'T NEED THEM?
WELL I GUESS NOT! IT'S JUST SO UNFAIR...WHY CAN'T THEY GIVE ME A BREAK? I'M ALMOST 40!
YEAH, IT IS UNFAIR.
MY ADVISOR SAID SHE'LL FIGHT IT AT THE SENATE FOR ME... AND MAYBE I COULD ASK ERIC IF HE COULD HELP WITH A LETTER OF RECOMMENDATION OR SOMETHING.
GOOD IDEA - DON'T GIVE UP ON THIS!
I WON'T GIVE UP. SHE'S ACTUALLY WORKING ON HER PH.D. WHICH IS ABOUT PEOPLE WHO FALL THROUGH THE CRACKS IN THE SCHOOL SYSTEM. SHE WANTS ME TO BE ONE OF HER THESIS SUBJECTS.
Y'KNOW, I REALLY WANT TO GO BACK EAST FOR A WHILE.

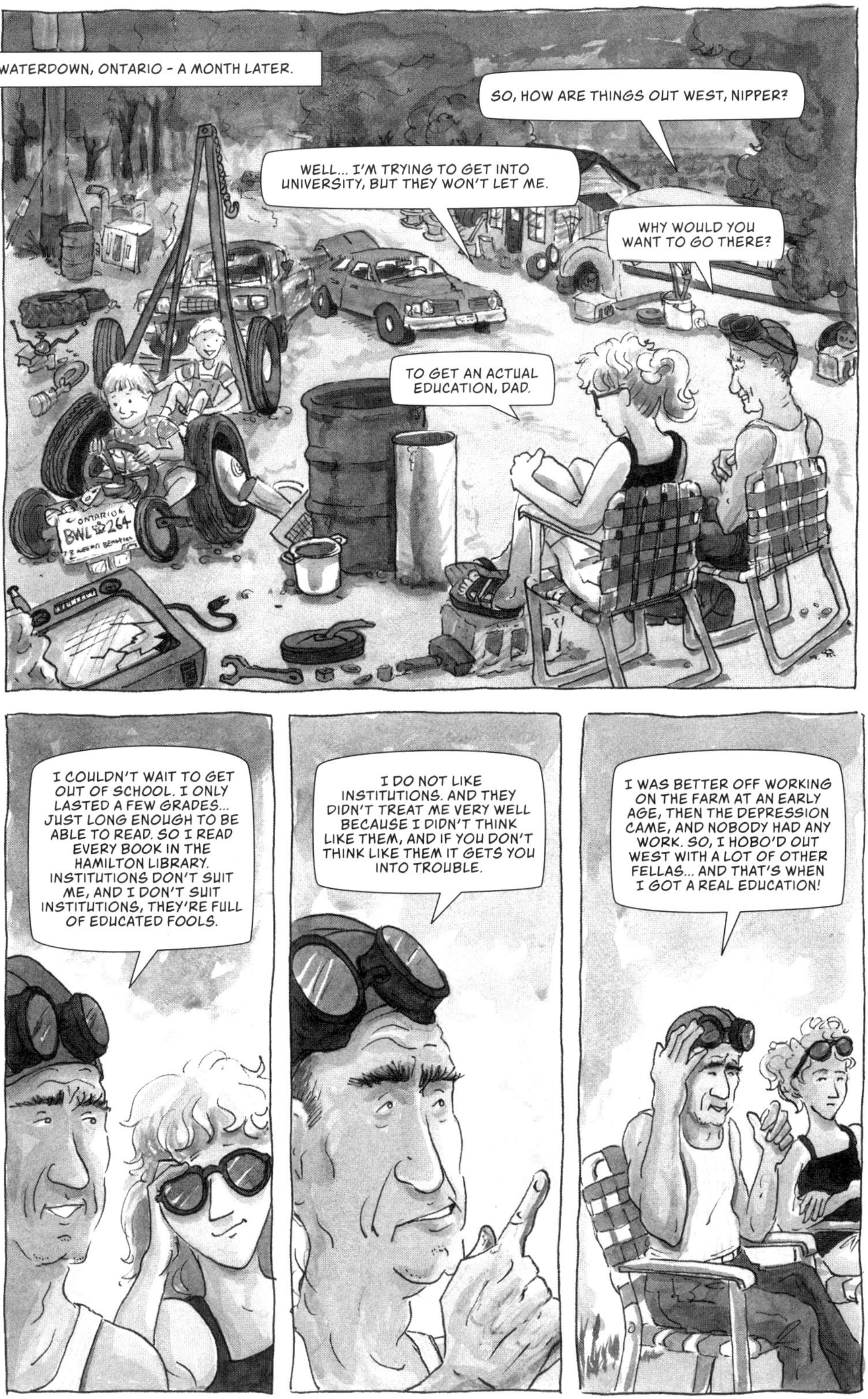
WATERDOWN, ONTARIO - A MONTH LATER.
SO, HOW ARE THINGS OUT WEST, NIPPER?
WELL... I'M TRYING TO GET INTO UNIVERSITY, BUT THEY WON'T LET ME.
WHY WOULD YOU WANT TO GO THERE?
TO GET AN ACTUAL EDUCATION, DAD.
ONTARIO
BWL 264
I COULDN'T WAIT TO GET OUT OF SCHOOL. I ONLY LASTED A FEW GRADES... JUST LONG ENOUGH TO BE ABLE TO READ. SO I READ EVERY BOOK IN THE HAMILTON LIBRARY. INSTITUTIONS DON'T SUIT ME, AND I DON'T SUIT INSTITUTIONS, THEY'RE FULL OF EDUCATED FOOLS.
I DO NOT LIKE INSTITUTIONS. AND THEY DIDN'T TREAT ME VERY WELL BECAUSE I DIDN'T THINK LIKE THEM, AND IF YOU DON'T THINK LIKE THEM IT GETS YOU INTO TROUBLE.
I WAS BETTER OFF WORKING ON THE FARM AT AN EARLY AGE, THEN THE DEPRESSION CAME, AND NOBODY HAD ANY WORK. SO, I HOBO'D OUT WEST WITH A LOT OF OTHER FELLAS... AND THAT'S WHEN I GOT A REAL EDUCATION!

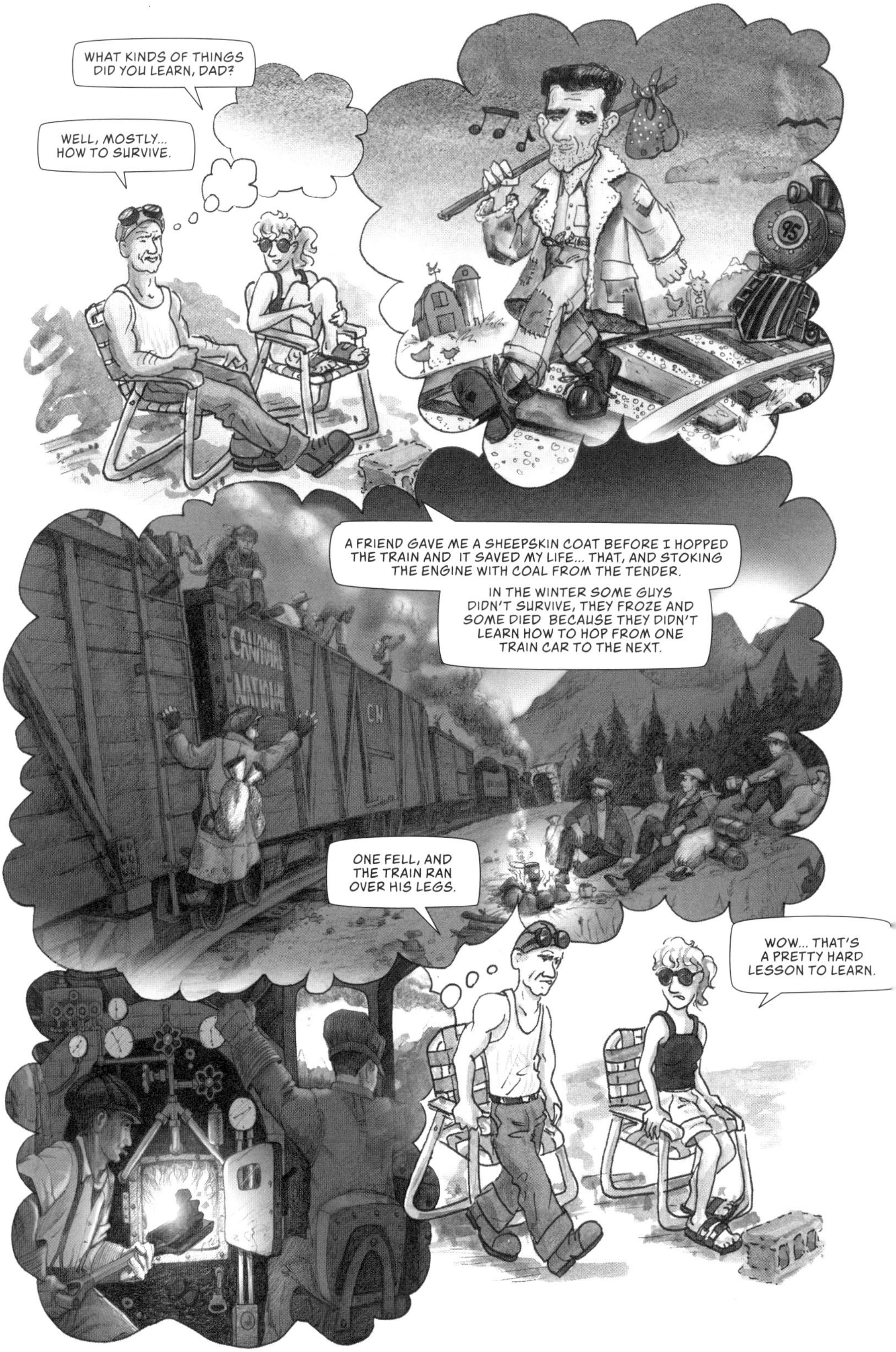
WHAT KINDS OF THINGS DID YOU LEARN, DAD?
WELL, MOSTLY... HOW TO SURVIVE.
95
A FRIEND GAVE ME A SHEEPSKIN COAT BEFORE I HOPPED THE TRAIN AND IT SAVED MY LIFE... THAT, AND STOKING THE ENGINE WITH COAL FROM THE TENDER.
IN THE WINTER SOME GUYS DIDN'T SURVIVE, THEY FROZE AND SOME DIED BECAUSE THEY DIDN'T LEARN HOW TO HOP FROM ONE TRAIN CAR TO THE NEXT.
CANADIAN NATIONAL
CN
ONE FELL, AND THE TRAIN RAN OVER HIS LEGS.
WOW... THAT'S A PRETTY HARD LESSON TO LEARN.

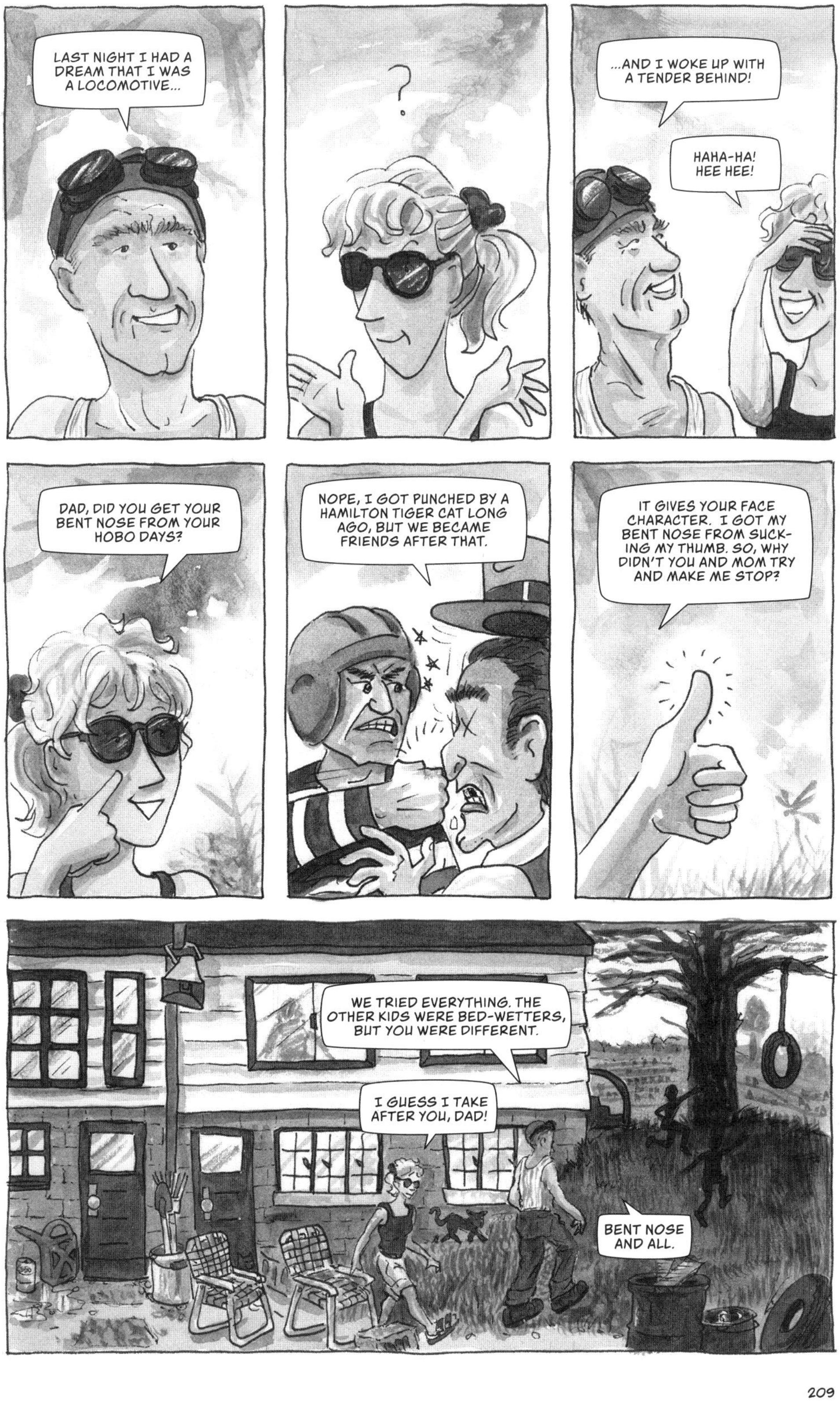
LAST NIGHT I HAD A DREAM THAT I WAS A LOCOMOTIVE...
?
...AND I WOKE UP WITH A TENDER BEHIND!
HAHA-HA! HEE HEE!
DAD, DID YOU GET YOUR BENT NOSE FROM YOUR HOBO DAYS?
NOPE, I GOT PUNCHED BY A HAMILTON TIGER CAT LONG AGO, BUT WE BECAME FRIENDS AFTER THAT.
IT GIVES YOUR FACE CHARACTER. I GOT MY BENT NOSE FROM SUCK-ING MY THUMB. SO, WHY DIDN'T YOU AND MOM TRY AND MAKE ME STOP?
WE TRIED EVERYTHING. THE OTHER KIDS WERE BED-WETTERS, BUT YOU WERE DIFFERENT.
I GUESS I TAKE AFTER YOU, DAD!
BENT NOSE AND ALL.

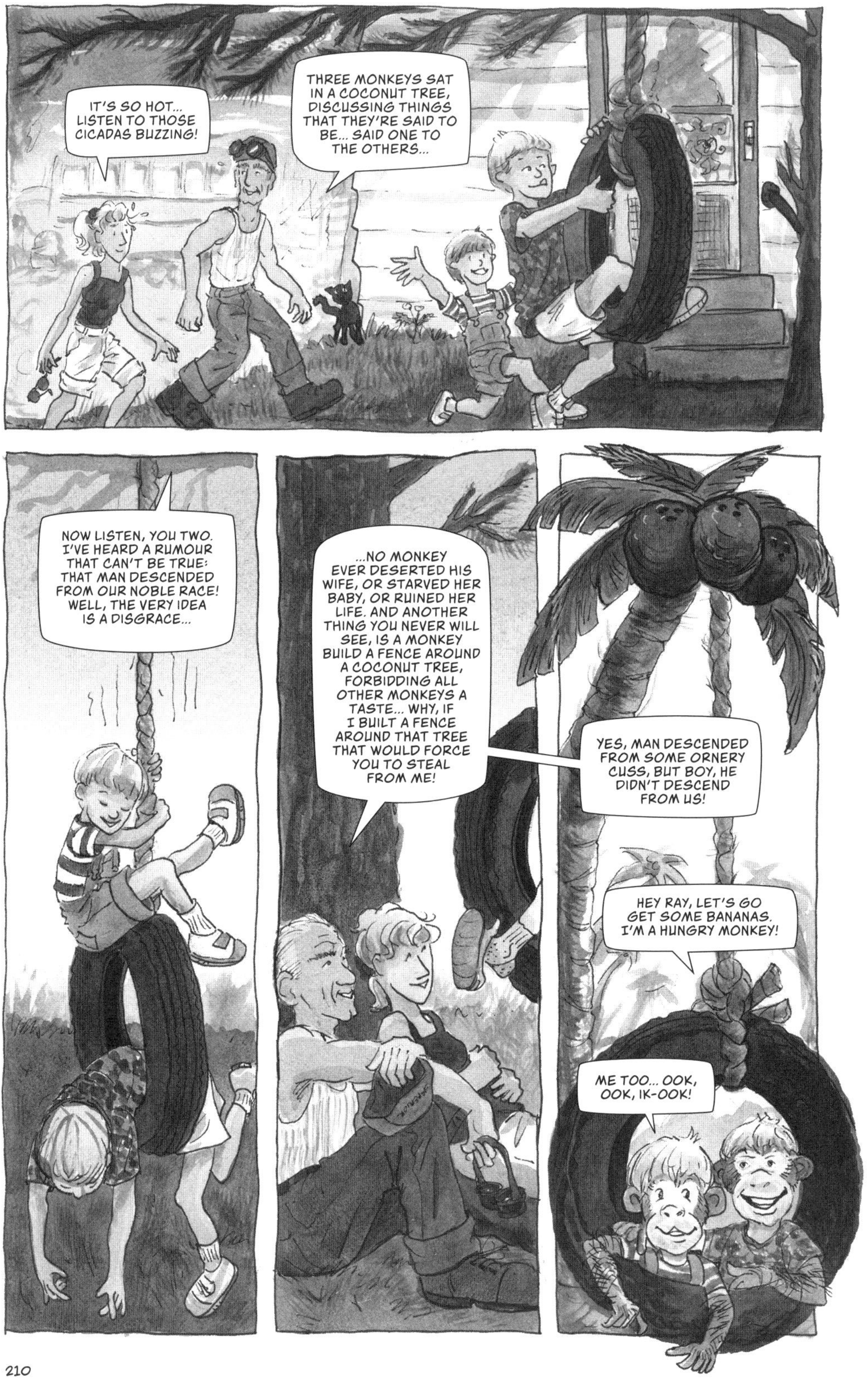
IT'S SO HOT... LISTEN TO THOSE CICADAS BUZZING!
THREE MONKEYS SAT IN A COCONUT TREE, DISCUSSING THINGS THAT THEY'RE SAID TO BE... SAID ONE TO THE OTHERS...
NOW LISTEN, YOU TWO. I'VE HEARD A RUMOUR THAT CAN'T BE TRUE: THAT MAN DESCENDED FROM OUR NOBLE RACE! WELL, THE VERY IDEA IS A DISGRACE...
...NO MONKEY EVER DESERTED HIS WIFE, OR STARVED HER BABY, OR RUINED HER LIFE. AND ANOTHER THING YOU NEVER WILL SEE, IS A MONKEY BUILD A FENCE AROUND A COCONUT TREE, FORBIDDING ALL OTHER MONKEYS A TASTE... WHY, IF I BUILT A FENCE AROUND THAT TREE THAT WOULD FORCE YOU TO STEAL FROM ME!
YES, MAN DESCENDED FROM SOME ORNERY CUSS, BUT BOY, HE DIDN'T DESCEND FROM US!
HEY RAY, LET'S GO GET SOME BANANAS. I'M A HUNGRY MONKEY!
ME TOO... OOK, OOK, IK-OOK!

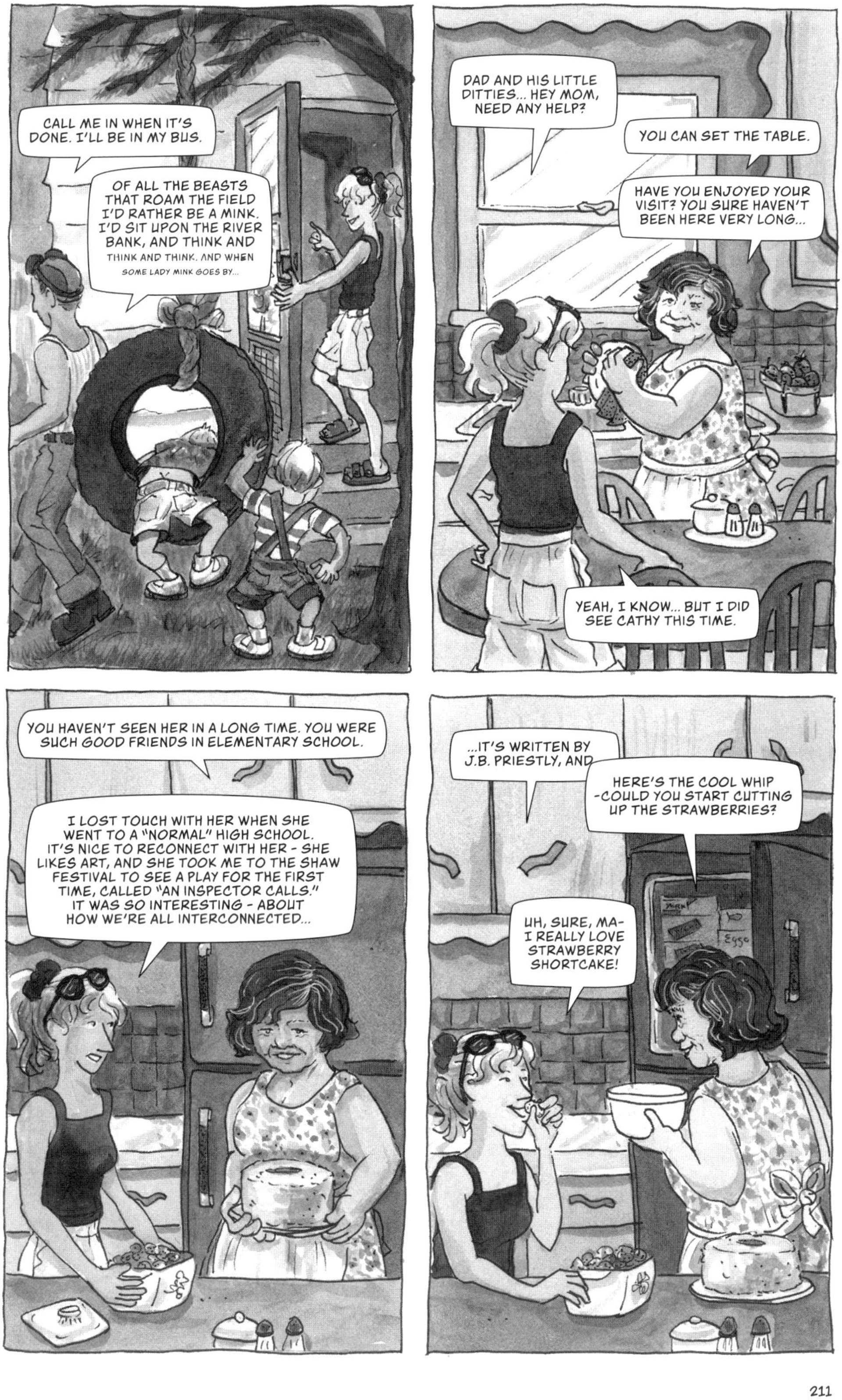
CALL ME IN WHEN IT'S DONE. I'LL BE IN MY BUS.
OF ALL THE BEASTS THAT ROAM THE FIELD I'D RATHER BE A MINK. I'D SIT UPON THE RIVER BANK, AND THINK AND THINK AND THINK. AND WHEN SOME LADY MINK GOES BY...
DAD AND HIS LITTLE DITTIES... HEY MOM, NEED ANY HELP?
YOU CAN SET THE TABLE.
HAVE YOU ENJOYED YOUR VISIT? YOU SURE HAVEN'T BEEN HERE VERY LONG...
YEAH, I KNOW... BUT I DID SEE CATHY THIS TIME.
YOU HAVEN'T SEEN HER IN A LONG TIME. YOU WERE SUCH GOOD FRIENDS IN ELEMENTARY SCHOOL.
I LOST TOUCH WITH HER WHEN SHE WENT TO A "NORMAL" HIGH SCHOOL. IT'S NICE TO RECONNECT WITH HER - SHE LIKES ART, AND SHE TOOK ME TO THE SHAW FESTIVAL TO SEE A PLAY FOR THE FIRST TIME, CALLED "AN INSPECTOR CALLS." IT WAS SO INTERESTING - ABOUT HOW WE'RE ALL INTERCONNECTED...
...IT'S WRITTEN BY J.B. PRIESTLY, AND
HERE'S THE COOL WHIP -COULD YOU START CUTTING UP THE STRAWBERRIES?
UH, SURE, MA- I REALLY LOVE STRAWBERRY SHORTCAKE!
Eggo

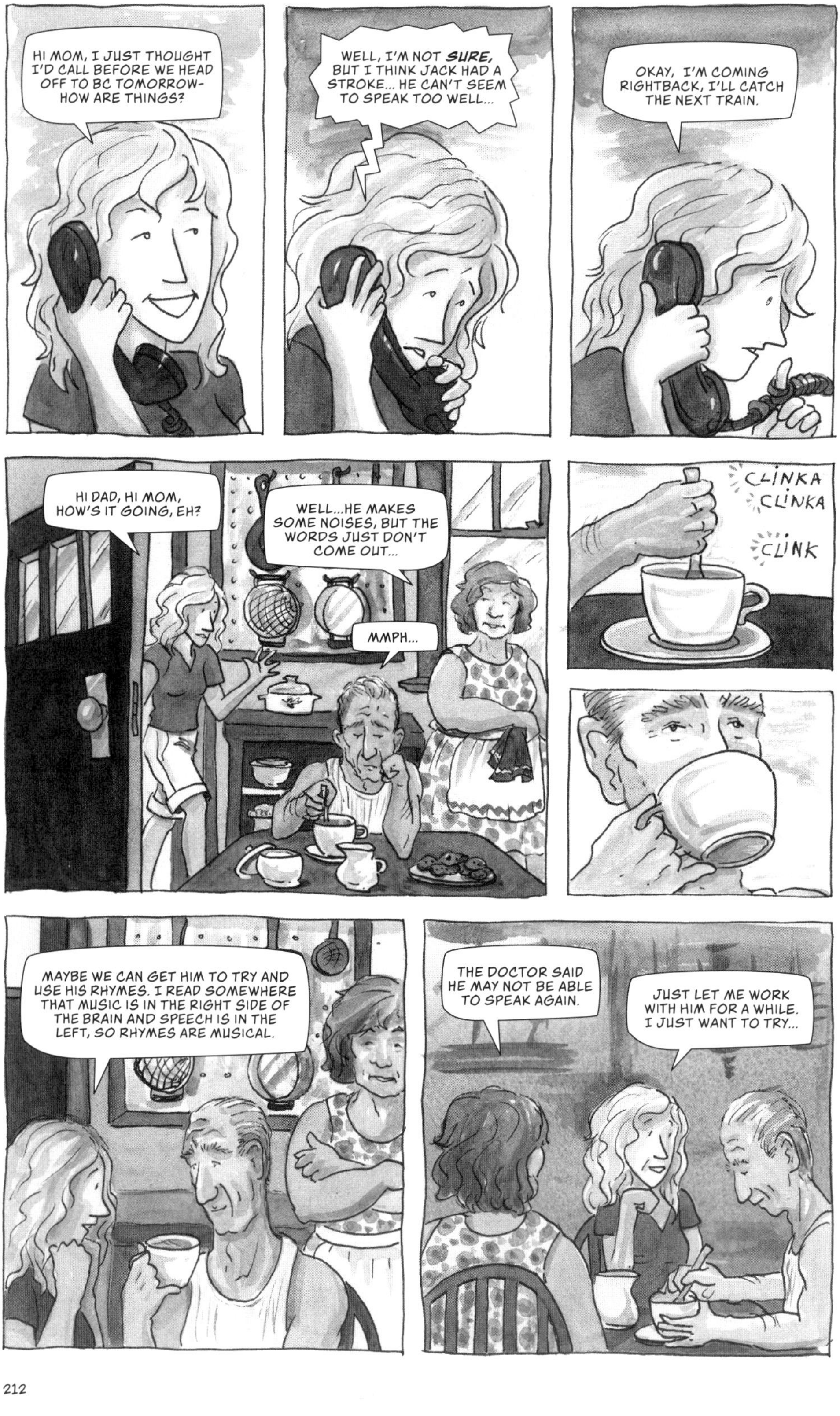
HI MOM, I JUST THOUGHT I'D CALL BEFORE WE HEAD OFF TO BC TOMORROW- HOW ARE THINGS?
WELL, I'M NOT SURE, BUT I THINK JACK HAD A STROKE... HE CAN'T SEEM TO SPEAK TOO WELL...
OKAY, I'M COMING RIGHTBACK, I'LL CATCH THE NEXT TRAIN.
HI DAD, HI MOM, HOW'S IT GOING, EH?
WELL...HE MAKES SOME NOISES, BUT THE WORDS JUST DON'T COME OUT...
MMPH...
CLINKA
CLINKA
CLINK
MAYBE WE CAN GET HIM TO TRY AND USE HIS RHYMES. I READ SOMEWHERE THAT MUSIC IS IN THE RIGHT SIDE OF THE BRAIN AND SPEECH IS IN THE LEFT, SO RHYMES ARE MUSICAL.
THE DOCTOR SAID HE MAY NOT BE ABLE TO SPEAK AGAIN.
JUST LET ME WORK WITH HIM FOR A WHILE. I JUST WANT TO TRY...

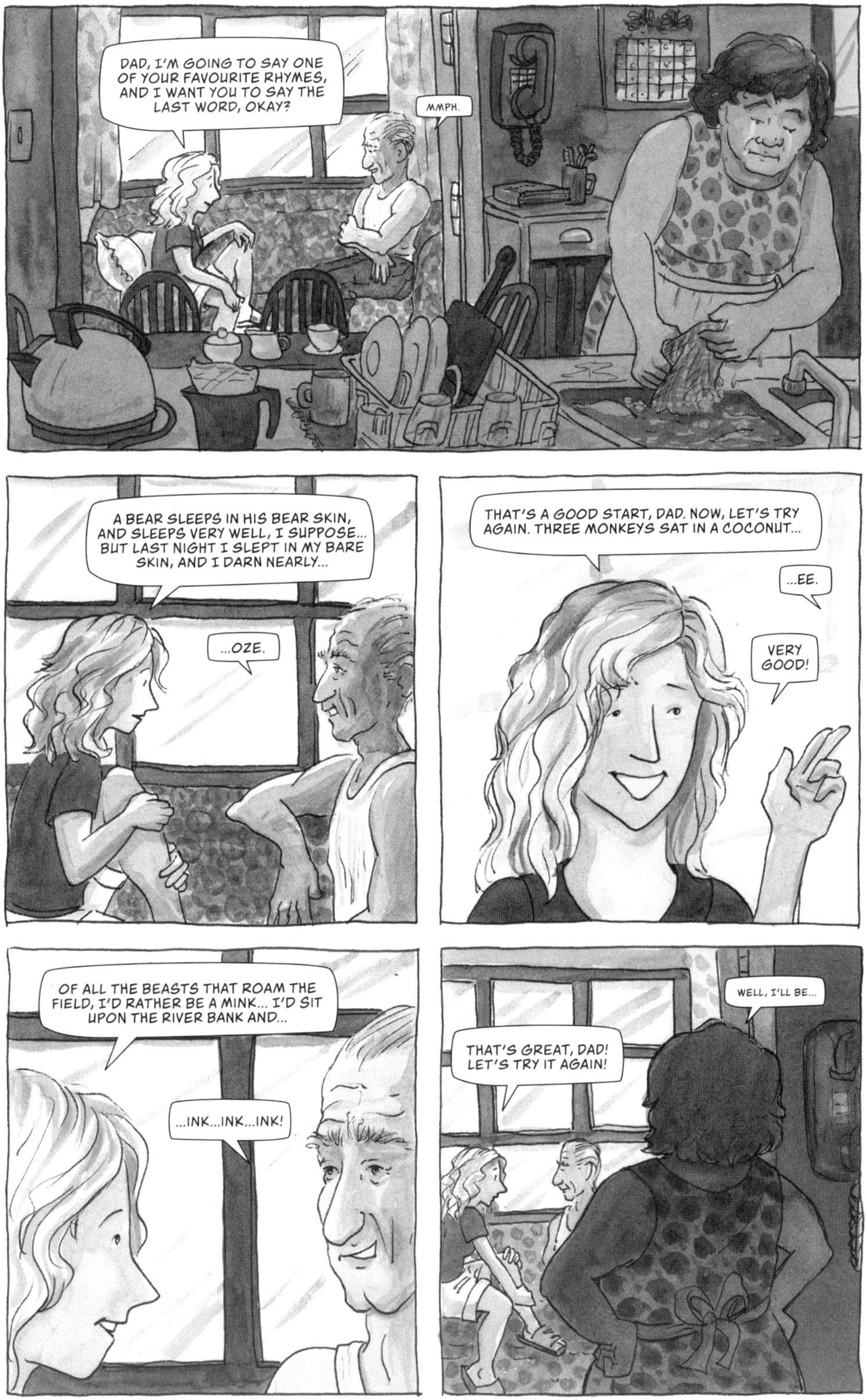
DAD, I'M GOING TO SAY ONE OF YOUR FAVOURITE RHYMES, AND I WANT YOU TO SAY THE LAST WORD, OKAY?
MMPH.
A BEAR SLEEPS IN HIS BEAR SKIN, AND SLEEPS VERY WELL, I SUPPOSE... BUT LAST NIGHT I SLEPT IN MY BARE SKIN, AND I DARN NEARLY...
...OZE.
THAT'S A GOOD START, DAD. NOW, LET'S TRY AGAIN. THREE MONKEYS SAT IN A COCONUT...
...EE.
VERY GOOD!
OF ALL THE BEASTS THAT ROAM THE FIELD, I'D RATHER BE A MINK... I'D SIT UPON THE RIVER BANK AND...
...INK...INK...INK!
WELL, I'LL BE...
THAT'S GREAT, DAD! LET'S TRY IT AGAIN!

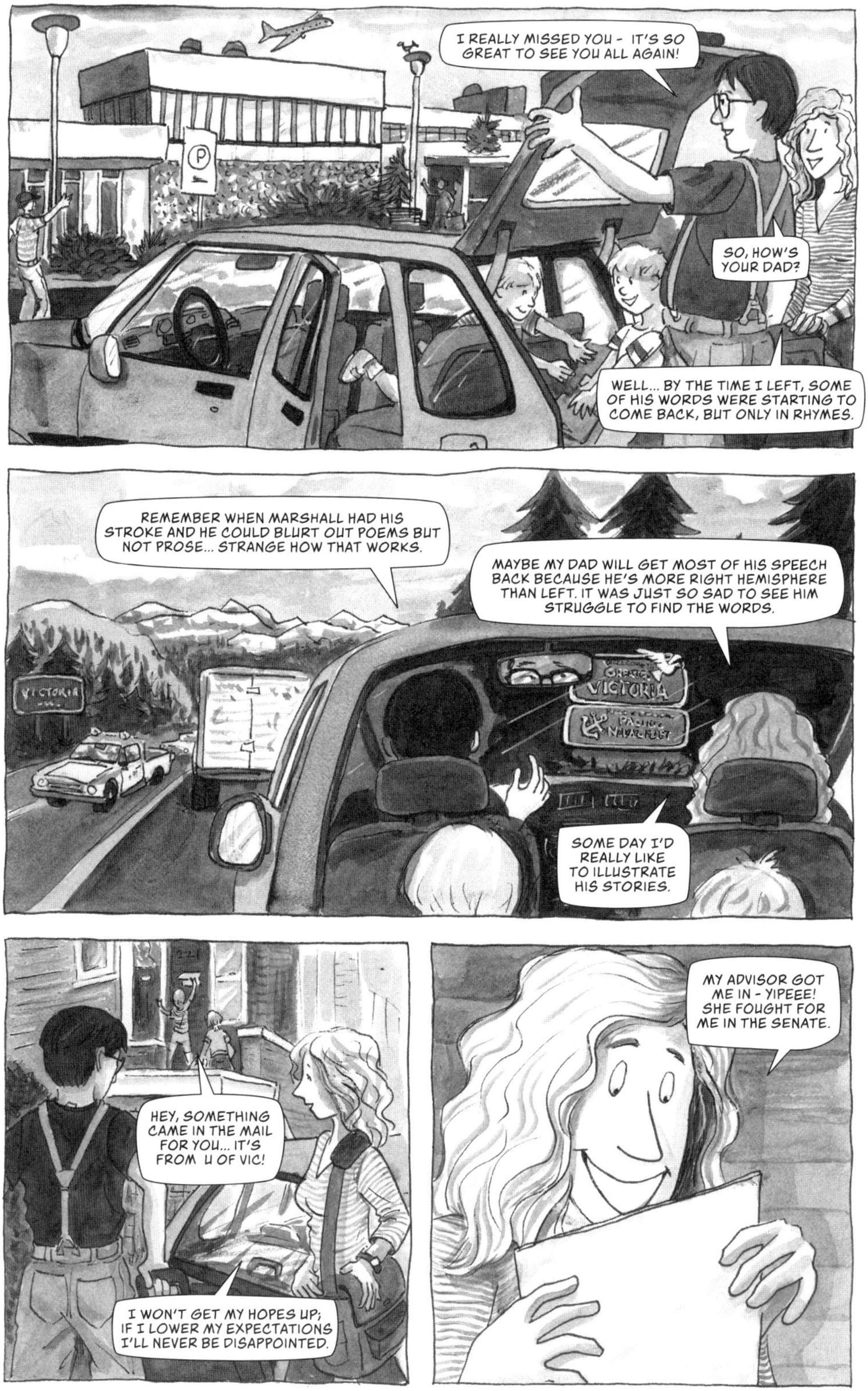
I REALLY MISSED YOU - IT'S SO GREAT TO SEE YOU ALL AGAIN!
SO, HOW'S YOUR DAD?
WELL... BY THE TIME I LEFT, SOME OF HIS WORDS WERE STARTING TO COME BACK, BUT ONLY IN RHYMES.
REMEMBER WHEN MARSHALL HAD HIS STROKE AND HE COULD BLURT OUT POEMS BUT NOT PROSE... STRANGE HOW THAT WORKS.
MAYBE MY DAD WILL GET MOST OF HIS SPEECH BACK BECAUSE HE'S MORE RIGHT HEMISPHERE THAN LEFT. IT WAS JUST SO SAD TO SEE HIM STRUGGLE TO FIND THE WORDS.
SOME DAY I'D REALLY LIKE TO ILLUSTRATE HIS STORIES.
HEY, SOMETHING CAME IN THE MAIL FOR YOU... IT'S FROM U OF VIC!
I WON'T GET MY HOPES UP; IF I LOWER MY EXPECTATIONS I'LL NEVER BE DISAPPOINTED.
MY ADVISOR GOT ME IN - YIPEEE! SHE FOUGHT FOR ME IN THE SENATE.

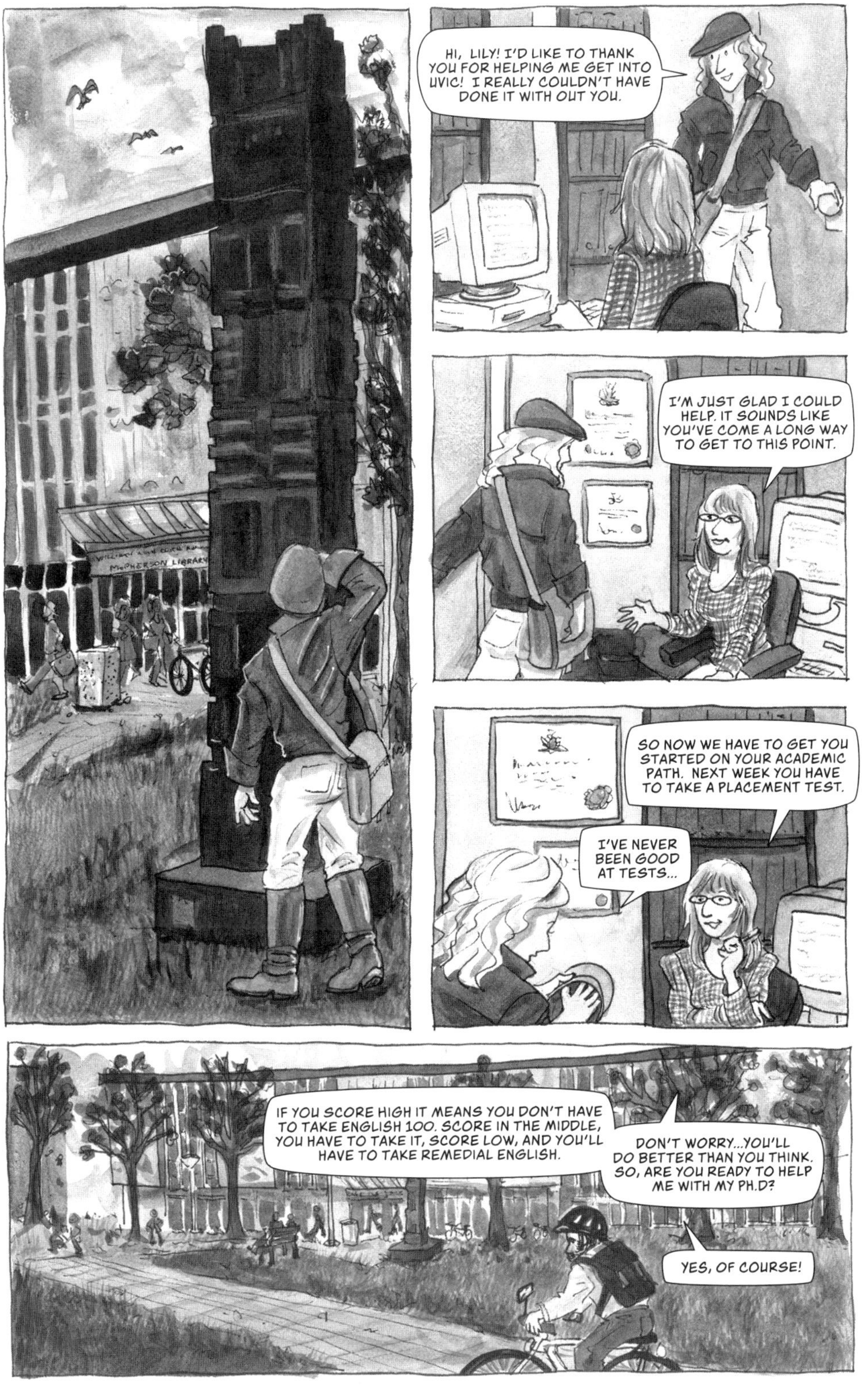
McPHERSON LIBRARY
HI, LILY! I'D LIKE TO THANK YOU FOR HELPING ME GET INTO UVIC! I REALLY COULDN'T HAVE DONE IT WITH OUT YOU.
I'M JUST GLAD I COULD HELP. IT SOUNDS LIKE YOU'VE COME A LONG WAY TO GET TO THIS POINT.
SO NOW WE HAVE TO GET YOU STARTED ON YOUR ACADEMIC PATH. NEXT WEEK YOU HAVE TO TAKE A PLACEMENT TEST.
I'VE NEVER BEEN GOOD AT TESTS...
IF YOU SCORE HIGH IT MEANS YOU DON'T HAVE TO TAKE ENGLISH 100. SCORE IN THE MIDDLE, YOU HAVE TO TAKE IT, SCORE LOW, AND YOU'LL HAVE TO TAKE REMEDIAL ENGLISH.
DON'T WORRY...YOU'LL DO BETTER THAN YOU THINK. SO, ARE YOU READY TO HELP ME WITH MY PH.D?
YES, OF COURSE!

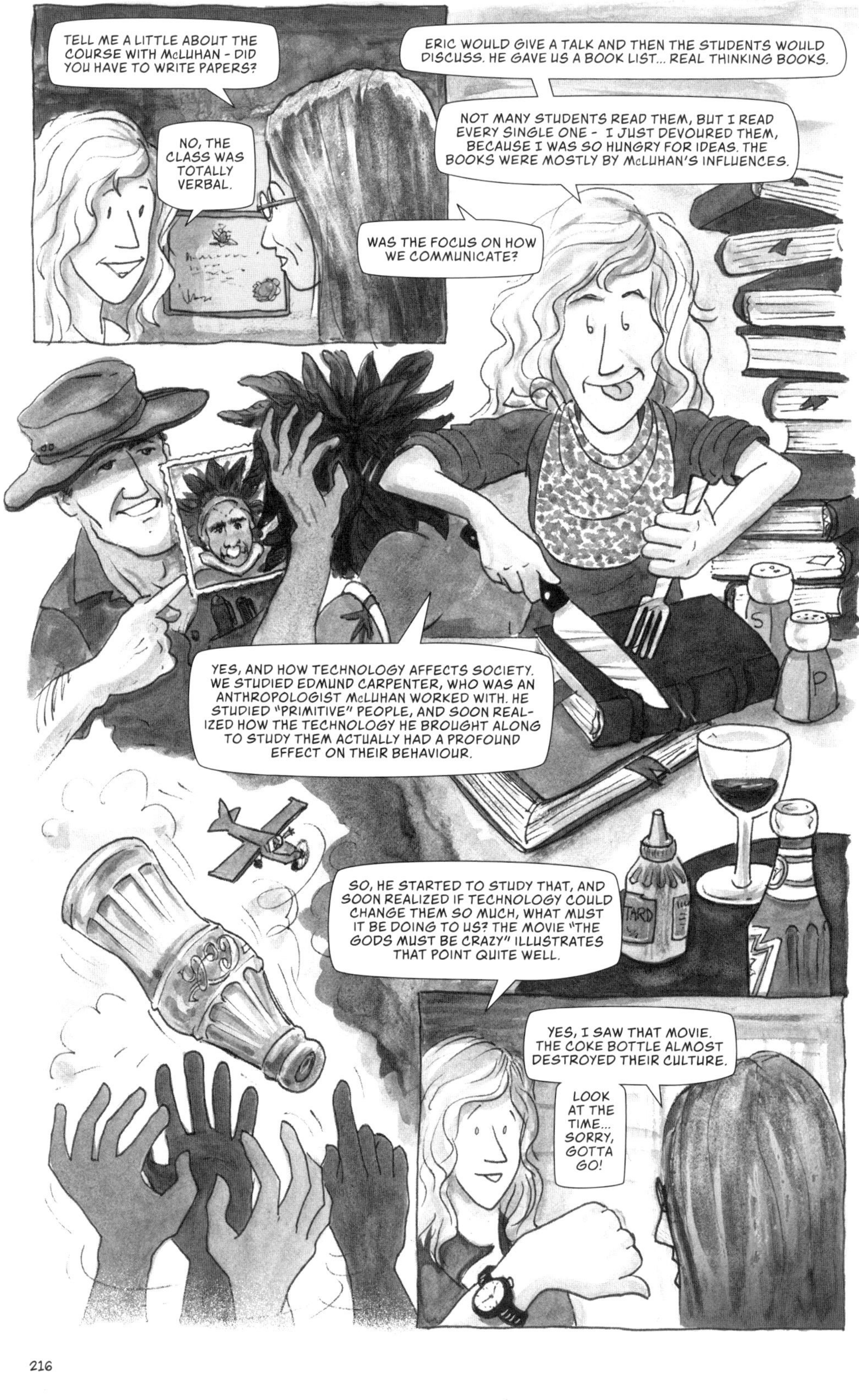
TELL ME A LITTLE ABOUT THE COURSE WITH McLUHAN - DID YOU HAVE TO WRITE PAPERS?
NO, THE CLASS WAS TOTALLY VERBAL.
ERIC WOULD GIVE A TALK AND THEN THE STUDENTS WOULD DISCUSS. HE GAVE US A BOOK LIST... REAL THINKING BOOKS.
NOT MANY STUDENTS READ THEM, BUT I READ EVERY SINGLE ONE - I JUST DEVOURED THEM, BECAUSE I WAS SO HUNGRY FOR IDEAS. THE BOOKS WERE MOSTLY BY McLUHAN'S INFLUENCES.
WAS THE FOCUS ON HOW WE COMMUNICATE?
YES, AND HOW TECHNOLOGY AFFECTS SOCIETY. WE STUDIED EDMUND CARPENTER, WHO WAS AN ANTHROPOLOGIST McLUHAN WORKED WITH. HE STUDIED "PRIMITIVE" PEOPLE, AND SOON REAL-IZED HOW THE TECHNOLOGY HE BROUGHT ALONG TO STUDY THEM ACTUALLY HAD A PROFOUND EFFECT ON THEIR BEHAVIOUR.
SO, HE STARTED TO STUDY THAT, AND SOON REALIZED IF TECHNOLOGY COULD CHANGE THEM SO MUCH, WHAT MUST IT BE DOING TO US? THE MOVIE "THE GODS MUST BE CRAZY" ILLUSTRATES THAT POINT QUITE WELL.
YES, I SAW THAT MOVIE. THE COKE BOTTLE ALMOST DESTROYED THEIR CULTURE.
LOOK AT THE TIME... SORRY, GOTTA GO!

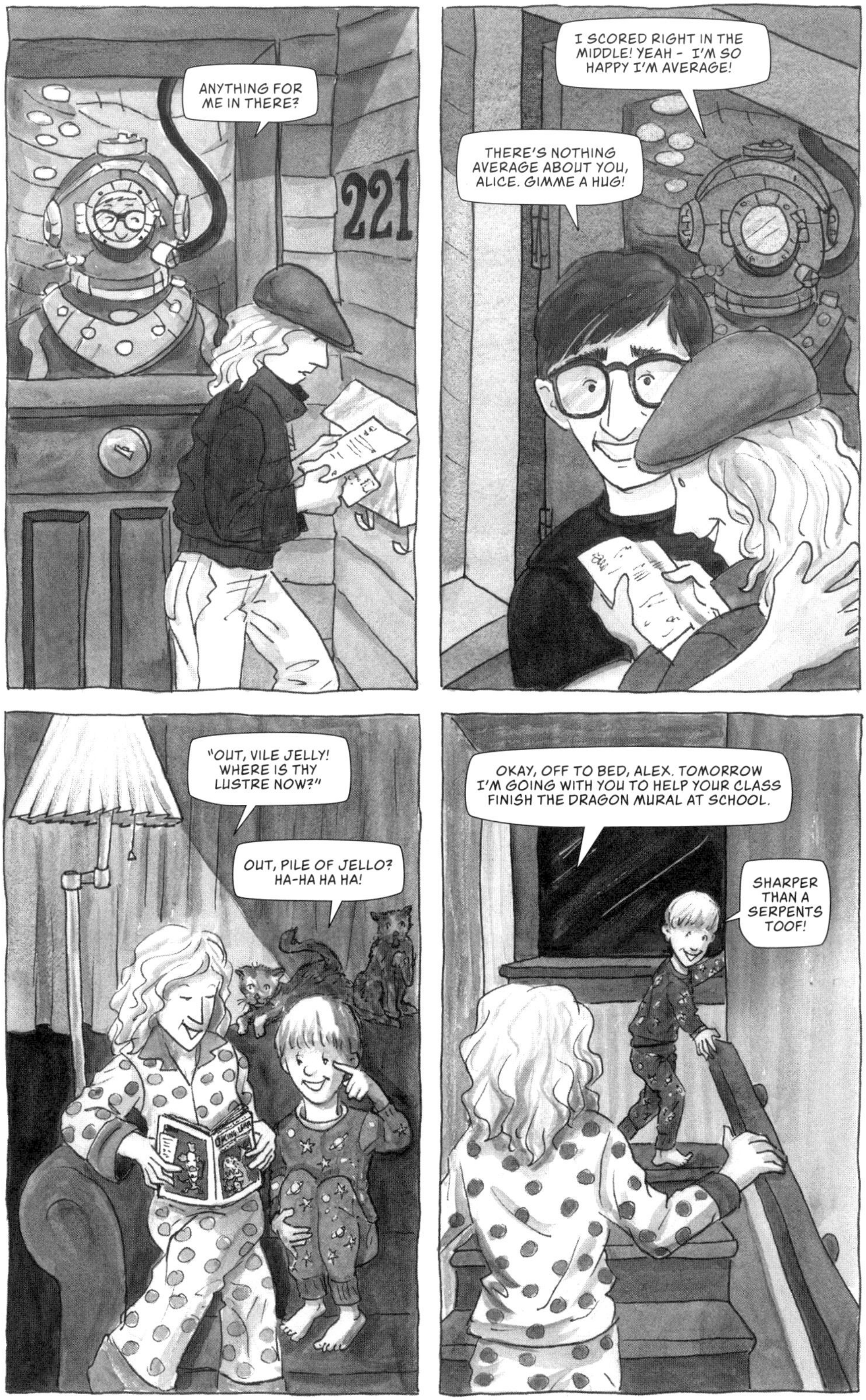
ANYTHING FOR ME IN THERE?
221
I SCORED RIGHT IN THE MIDDLE! YEAH - I'M SO HAPPY I'M AVERAGE!
THERE'S NOTHING AVERAGE ABOUT YOU, ALICE. GIMME A HUG!
"OUT, VILE JELLY! WHERE IS THY LUSTRE NOW?"
OUT, PILE OF JELLO? HA-HA HA HA!
OKAY, OFF TO BED, ALEX. TOMORROW I'M GOING WITH YOU TO HELP YOUR CLASS FINISH THE DRAGON MURAL AT SCHOOL.
SHARPER THAN A SERPENTS TOOF!

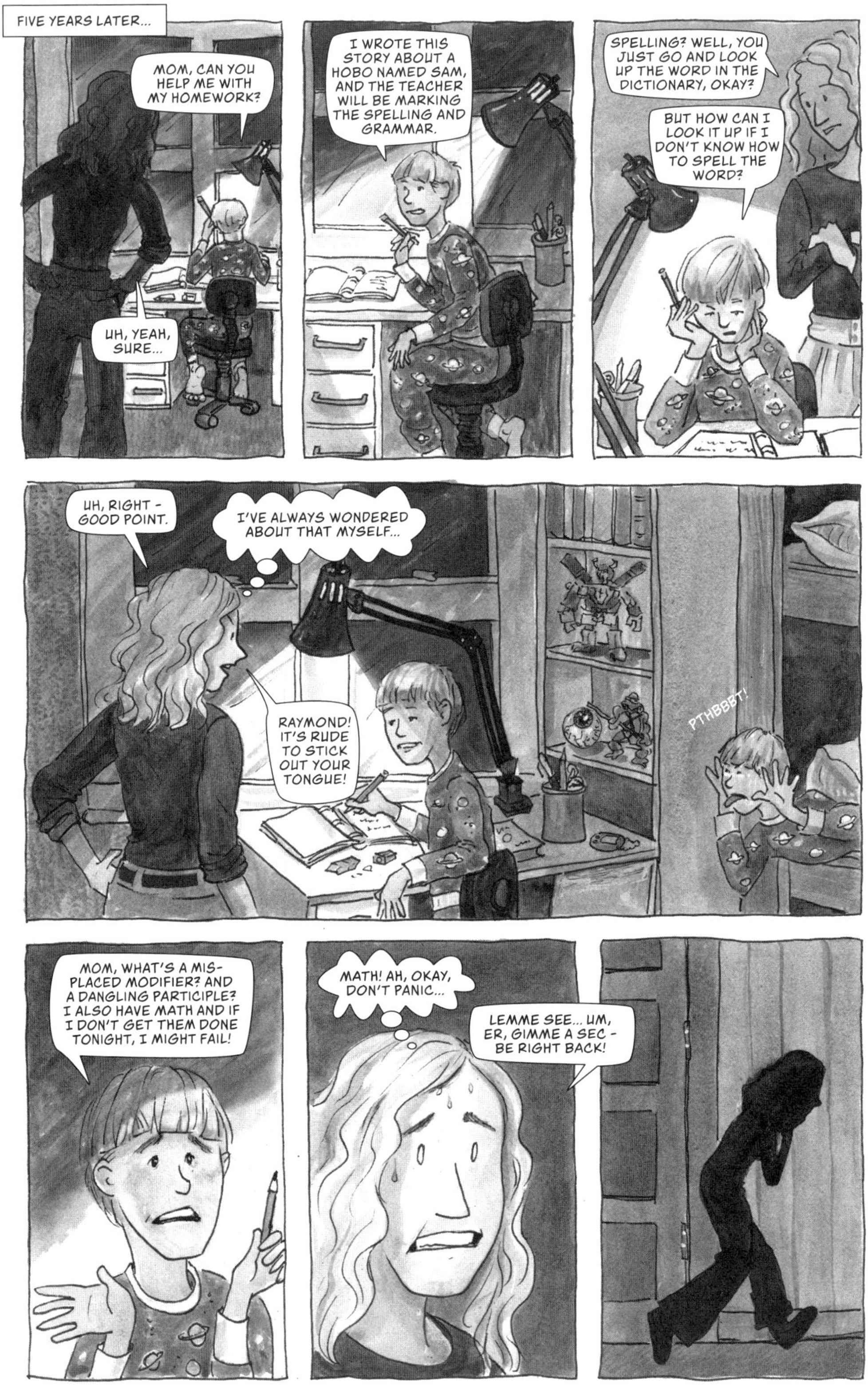
FIVE YEARS LATER...
MOM, CAN YOU HELP ME WITH MY HOMEWORK?
UH, YEAH, SURE...
I WROTE THIS STORY ABOUT A HOBO NAMED SAM, AND THE TEACHER WILL BE MARKING THE SPELLING AND GRAMMAR.
SPELLING? WELL, YOU JUST GO AND LOOK UP THE WORD IN THE DICTIONARY, OKAY?
BUT HOW CAN I LOOK IT UP IF I DON'T KNOW HOW TO SPELL THE WORD?
UH, RIGHT - GOOD POINT.
I'VE ALWAYS WONDERED ABOUT THAT MYSELF...
RAYMOND! IT'S RUDE TO STICK OUT YOUR TONGUE!
PTHBBBT!
MOM, WHAT'S A MIS-PLACED MODIFIER? AND A DANGLING PARTICIPLE? I ALSO HAVE MATH AND IF I DON'T GET THEM DONE TONIGHT, I MIGHT FAIL!
MATH! AH, OKAY, DON'T PANIC...
LEMME SEE... UM, ER, GIMME A SEC - BE RIGHT BACK!

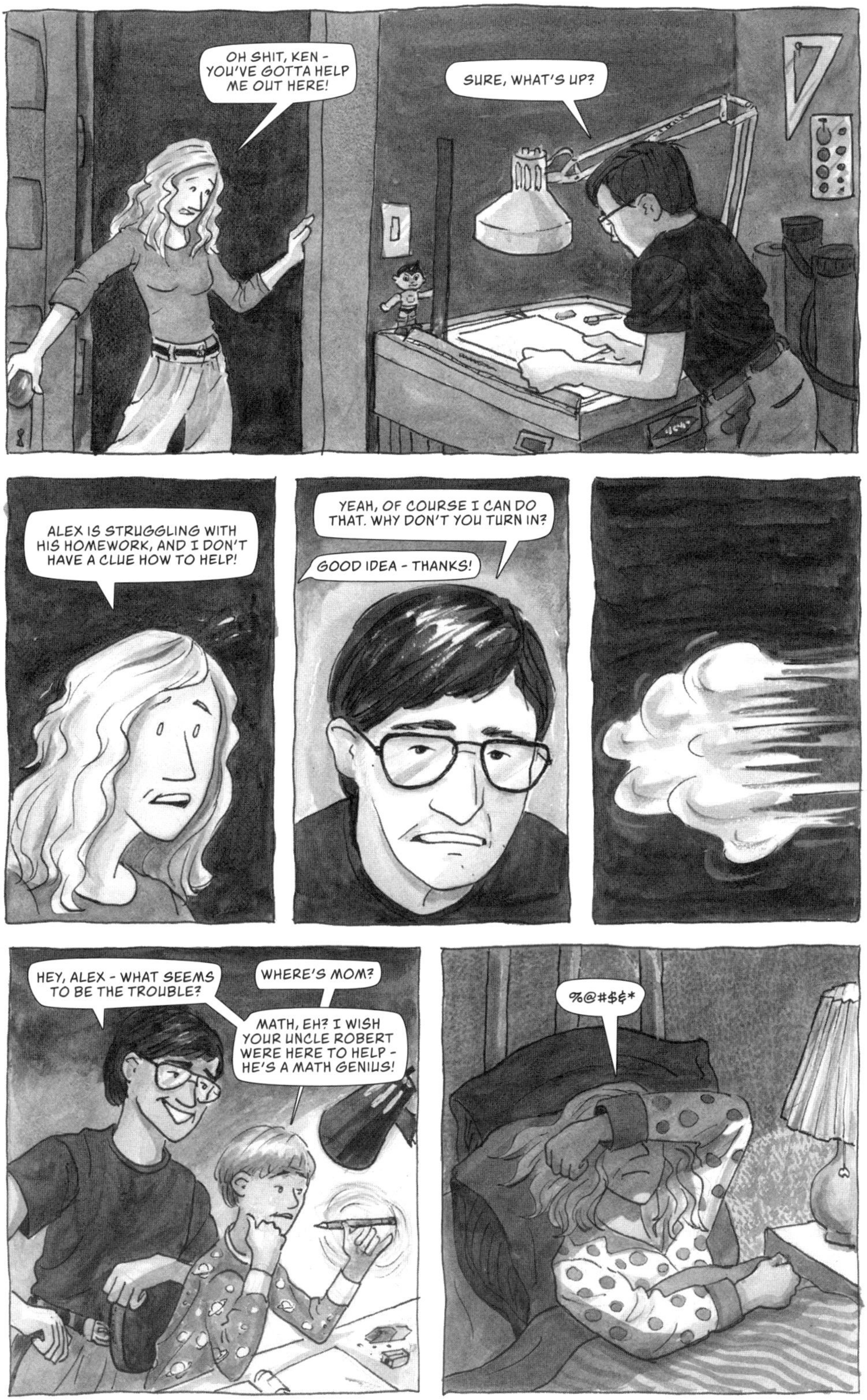
OH SHIT, KEN - YOU'VE GOTTA HELP ME OUT HERE!
SURE, WHAT'S UP?
ALEX IS STRUGGLING WITH HIS HOMEWORK, AND I DON'T HAVE A CLUE HOW TO HELP!
YEAH, OF COURSE I CAN DO THAT. WHY DON'T YOU TURN IN?
GOOD IDEA - THANKS!
HEY, ALEX - WHAT SEEMS TO BE THE TROUBLE?
WHERE'S MOM?
MATH, EH? I WISH YOUR UNCLE ROBERT WERE HERE TO HELP - HE'S A MATH GENIUS!
%@#$&*

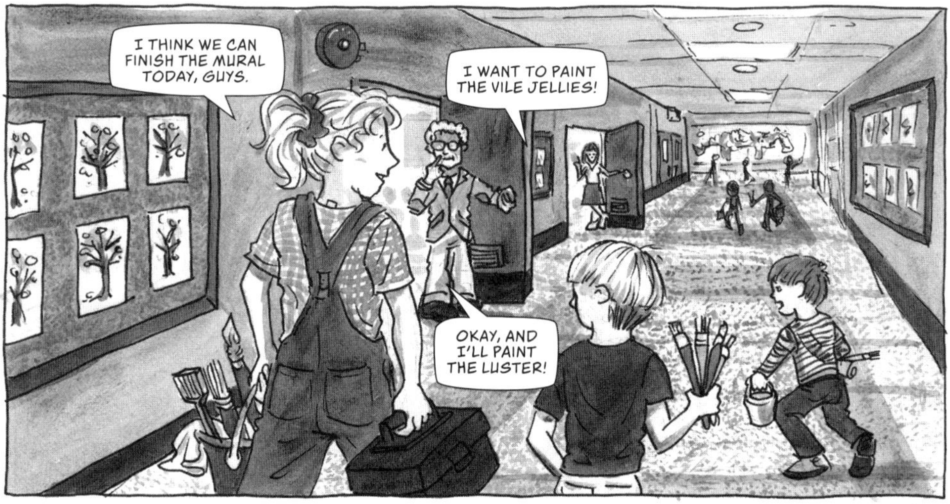
I THINK WE CAN FINISH THE MURAL TODAY, GUYS.
I WANT TO PAINT THE VILE JELLIES!
OKAY, AND I'LL PAINT THE LUSTER!

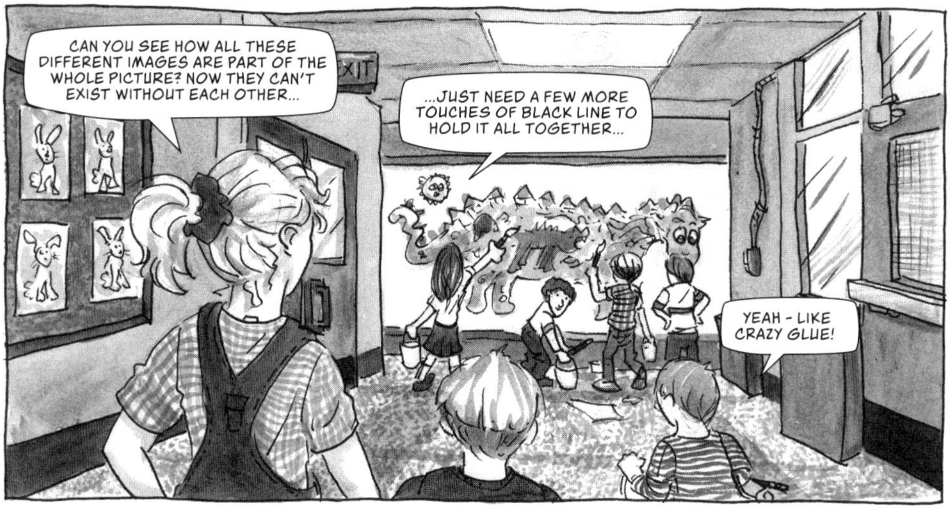
CAN YOU SEE HOW ALL THESE DIFFERENT IMAGES ARE PART OF THE WHOLE PICTURE? NOW THEY CAN'T EXIST WITHOUT EACH OTHER...
EXIT
...JUST NEED A FEW MORE TOUCHES OF BLACK LINE TO HOLD IT ALL TOGETHER...
YEAH - LIKE CRAZY GLUE!

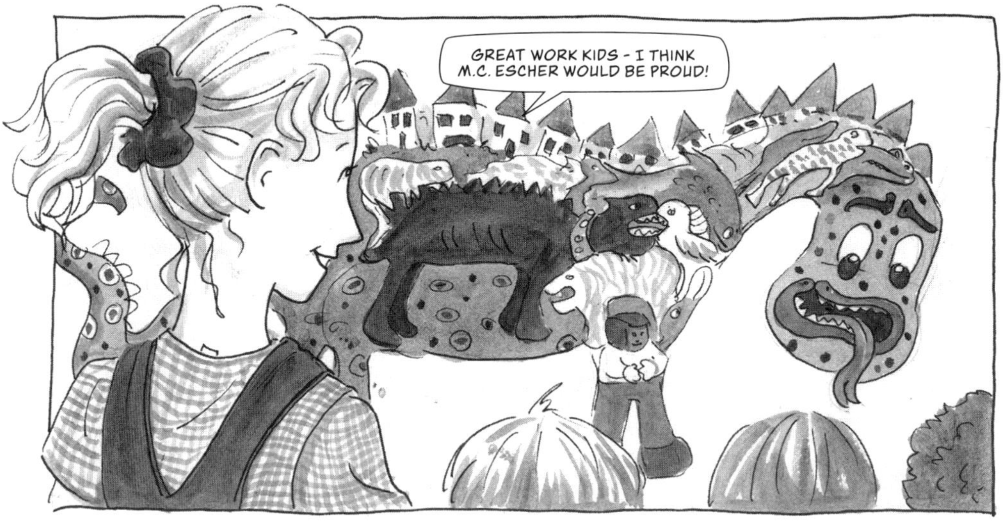
GREAT WORK KIDS - I THINK M.C. ESCHER WOULD BE PROUD!

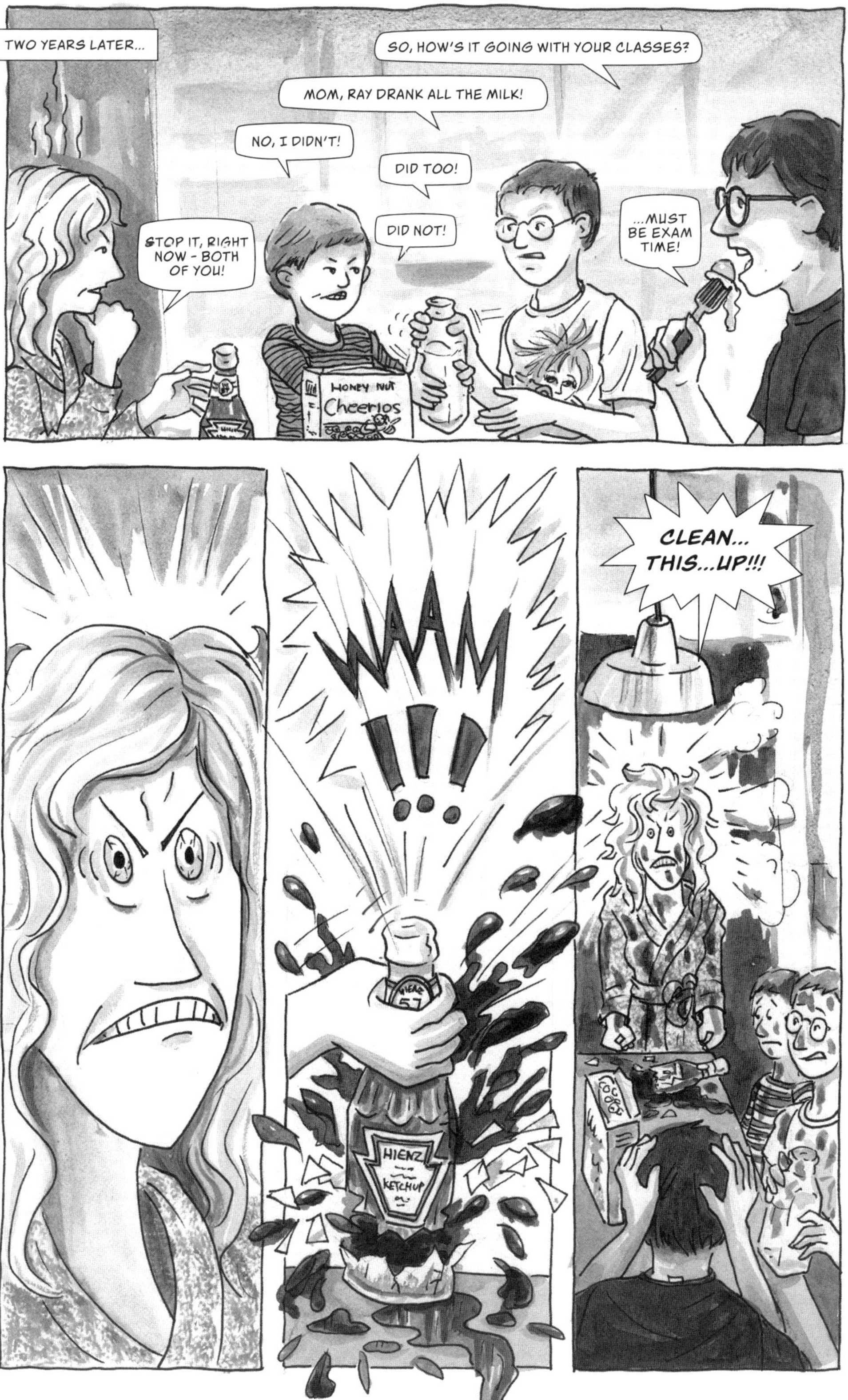
TWO YEARS LATER...
SO, HOW'S IT GOING WITH YOUR CLASSES?
MOM, RAY DRANK ALL THE MILK!
NO, I DIDN'T!
DID TOO!
DID NOT!
STOP IT, RIGHT NOW - BOTH OF YOU!
...MUST BE EXAM TIME!
HONEY NUT Cheerios
WAAM!!!...
HIENZ 57
HIENZ KETCHUP
CLEAN... THIS...UP!!!

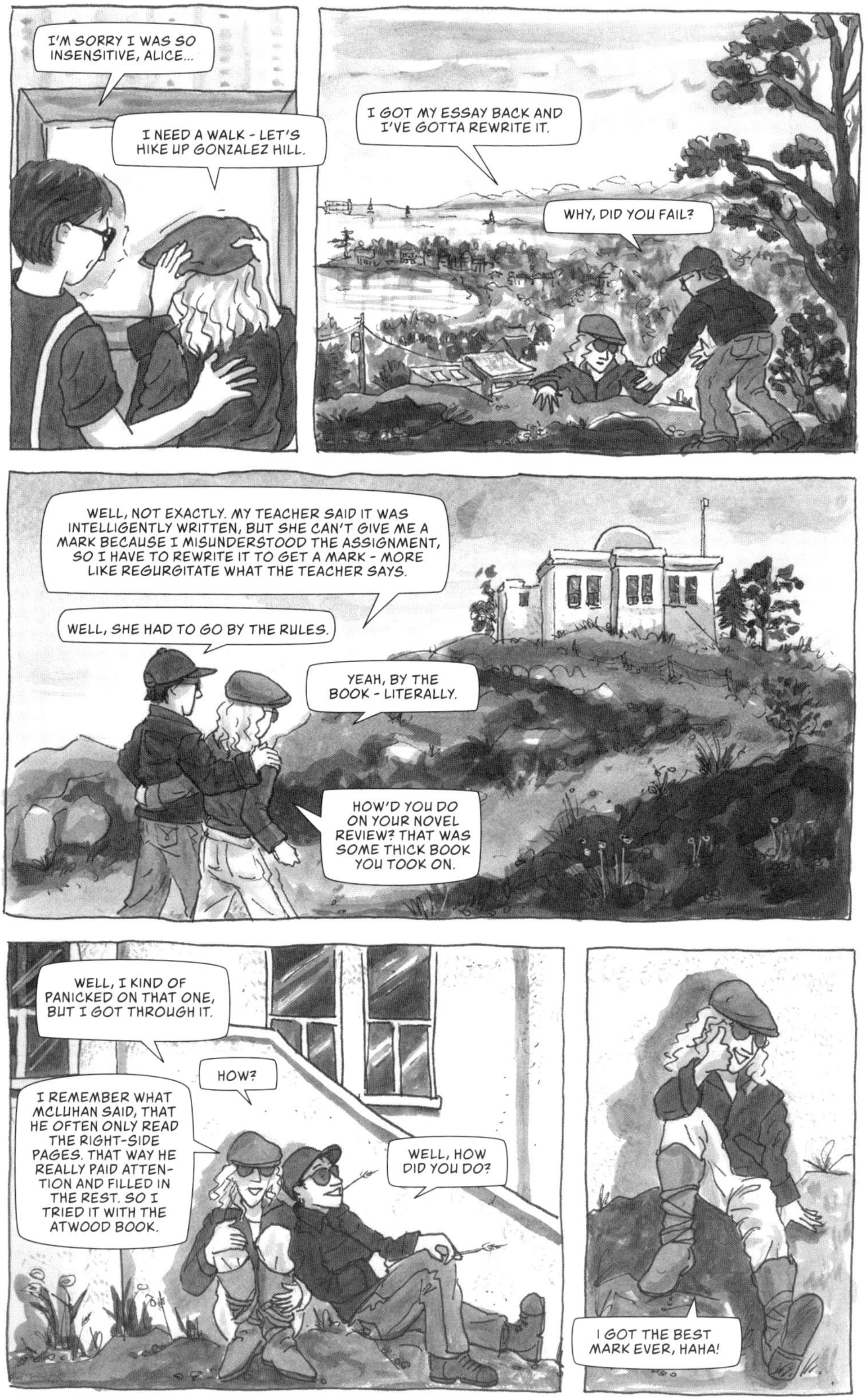

I'M SORRY I WAS SO INSENSITIVE, ALICE...
I NEED A WALK - LET'S HIKE UP GONZALEZ HILL.
I GOT MY ESSAY BACK AND I'VE GOTTA REWRITE IT.
WHY, DID YOU FAIL?
WELL, NOT EXACTLY. MY TEACHER SAID IT WAS INTELLIGENTLY WRITTEN, BUT SHE CAN'T GIVE ME A MARK BECAUSE I MISUNDERSTOOD THE ASSIGNMENT, SO I HAVE TO REWRITE IT TO GET A MARK - MORE LIKE REGURGITATE WHAT THE TEACHER SAYS.
WELL, SHE HAD TO GO BY THE RULES.
YEAH, BY THE BOOK - LITERALLY.
HOW'D YOU DO ON YOUR NOVEL REVIEW? THAT WAS SOME THICK BOOK YOU TOOK ON.
WELL, I KIND OF PANICKED ON THAT ONE, BUT I GOT THROUGH IT.
HOW?
I REMEMBER WHAT MCLUHAN SAID, THAT HE OFTEN ONLY READ THE RIGHT-SIDE PAGES. THAT WAY HE REALLY PAID ATTENTION AND FILLED IN THE REST. SO I TRIED IT WITH THE ATWOOD BOOK.
WELL, HOW DID YOU DO?
I GOT THE BEST MARK EVER, HAHA!

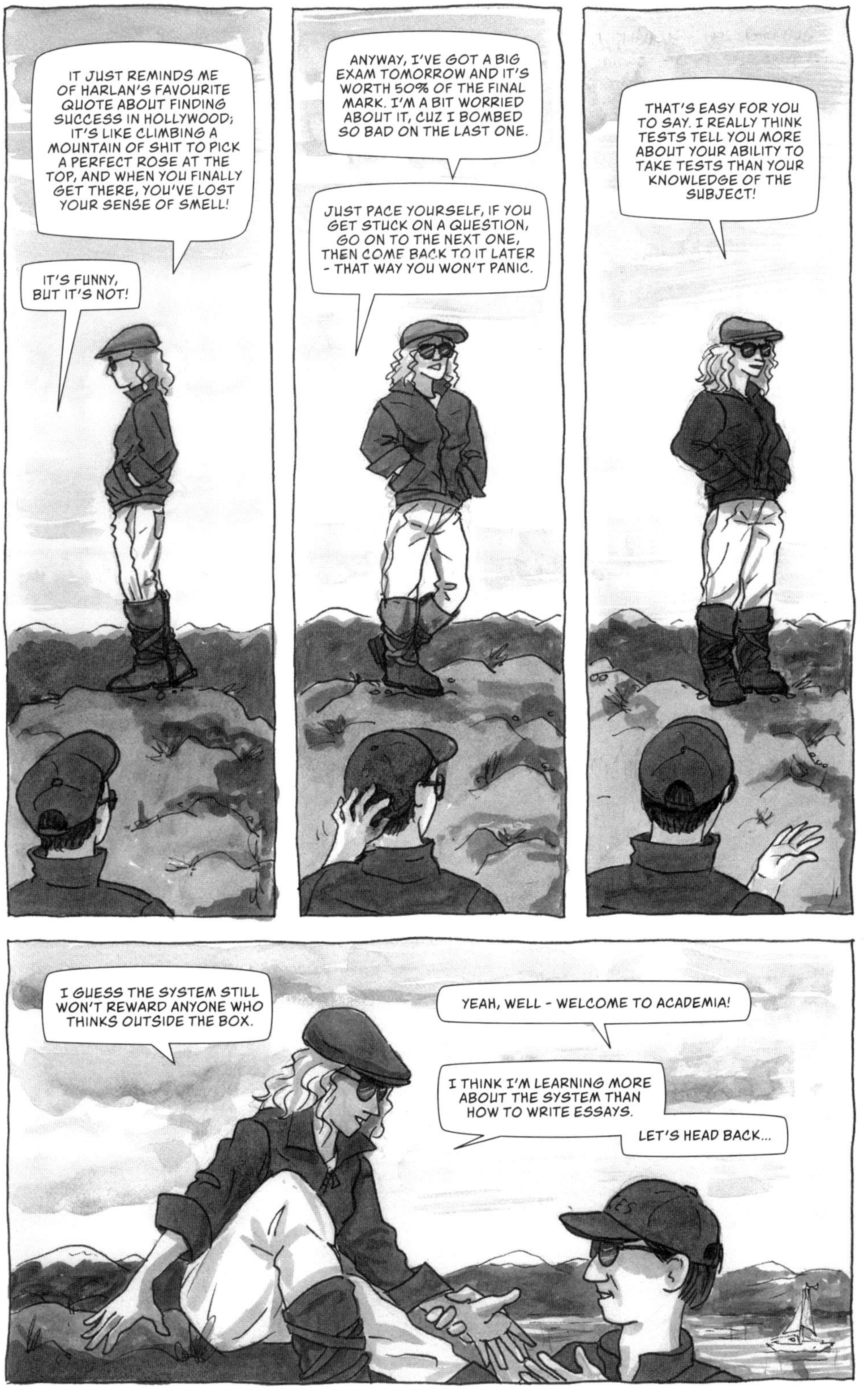
IT JUST REMINDS ME OF HARLAN'S FAVOURITE QUOTE ABOUT FINDING SUCCESS IN HOLLYWOOD; IT'S LIKE CLIMBING A MOUNTAIN OF SHIT TO PICK A PERFECT ROSE AT THE TOP, AND WHEN YOU FINALLY GET THERE, YOU'VE LOST YOUR SENSE OF SMELL!
IT'S FUNNY, BUT IT'S NOT!
ANYWAY, I'VE GOT A BIG EXAM TOMORROW AND IT'S WORTH 50% OF THE FINAL MARK. I'M A BIT WORRIED ABOUT IT, CUZ I BOMBED SO BAD ON THE LAST ONE.
JUST PACE YOURSELF, IF YOU GET STUCK ON A QUESTION, GO ON TO THE NEXT ONE, THEN COME BACK TO IT LATER - THAT WAY YOU WON'T PANIC.
THAT'S EASY FOR YOU TO SAY. I REALLY THINK TESTS TELL YOU MORE ABOUT YOUR ABILITY TO TAKE TESTS THAN YOUR KNOWLEDGE OF THE SUBJECT!
I GUESS THE SYSTEM STILL WON'T REWARD ANYONE WHO THINKS OUTSIDE THE BOX.
YEAH, WELL - WELCOME TO ACADEMIA!
I THINK I'M LEARNING MORE ABOUT THE SYSTEM THAN HOW TO WRITE ESSAYS.
LET'S HEAD BACK...

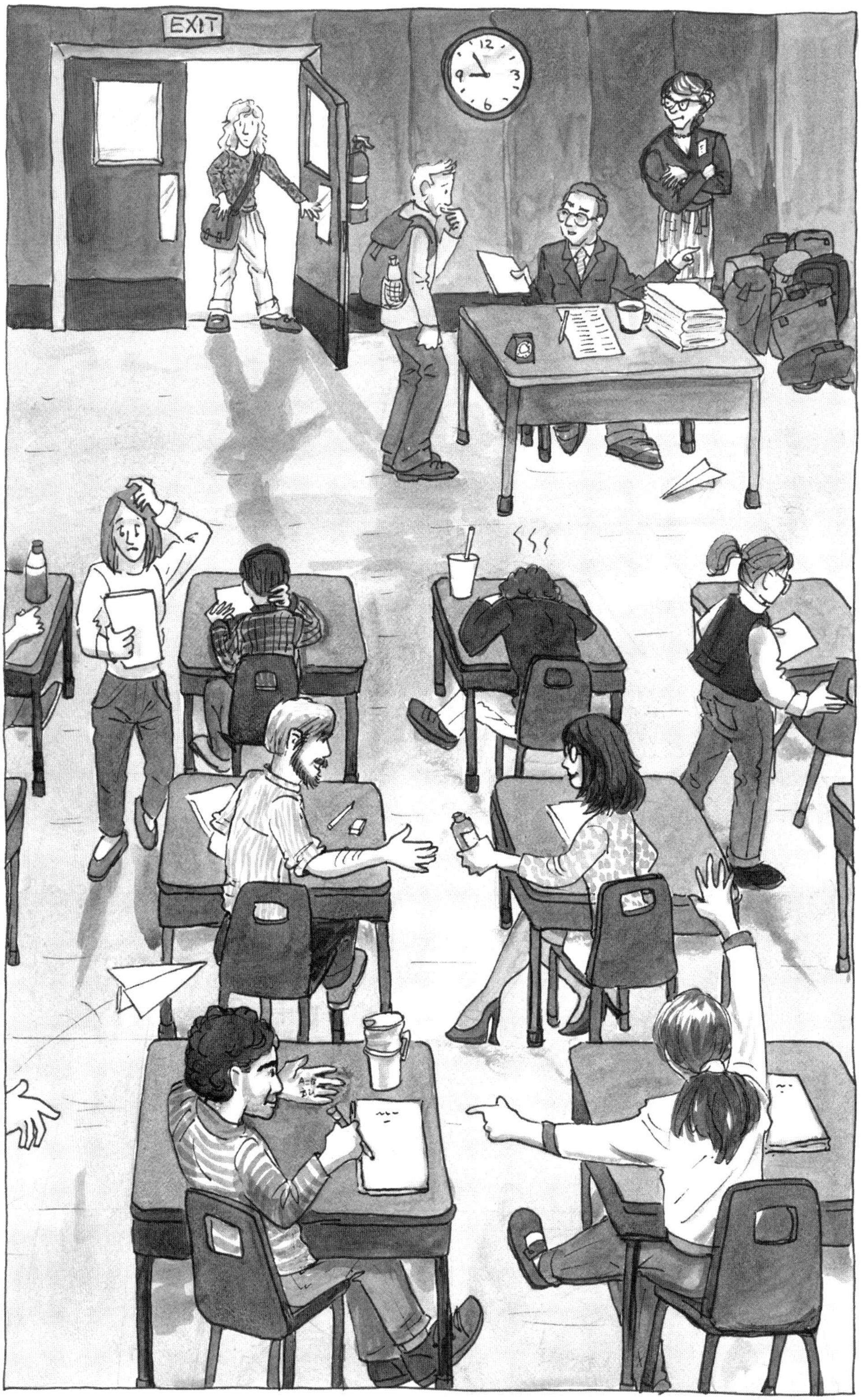
EXIT

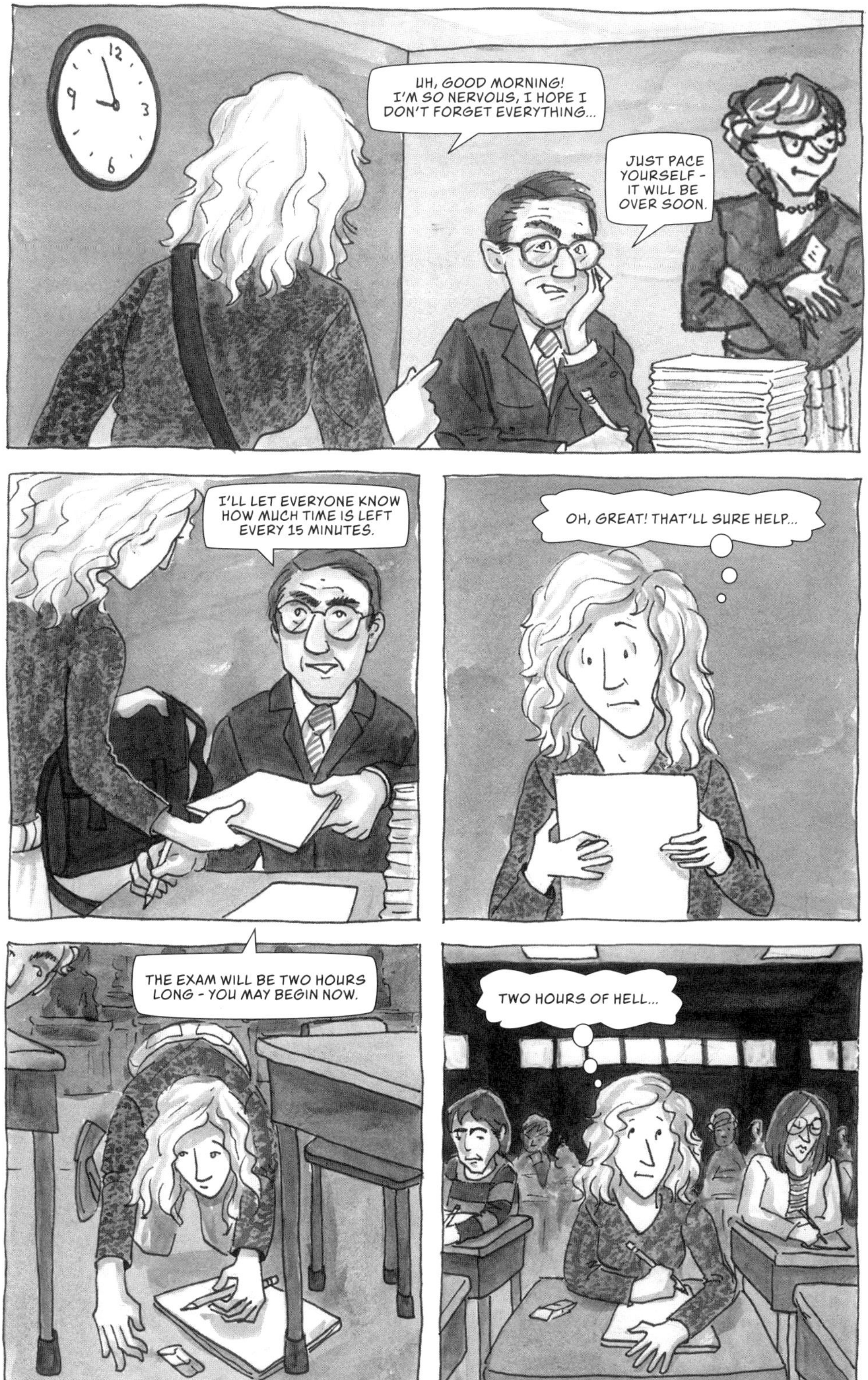
UH, GOOD MORNING! I'M SO NERVOUS, I HOPE I DON'T FORGET EVERYTHING...
JUST PACE YOURSELF - IT WILL BE OVER SOON.
I'LL LET EVERYONE KNOW HOW MUCH TIME IS LEFT EVERY 15 MINUTES.
OH, GREAT! THAT'LL SURE HELP...
THE EXAM WILL BE TWO HOURS LONG - YOU MAY BEGIN NOW.
TWO HOURS OF HELL...

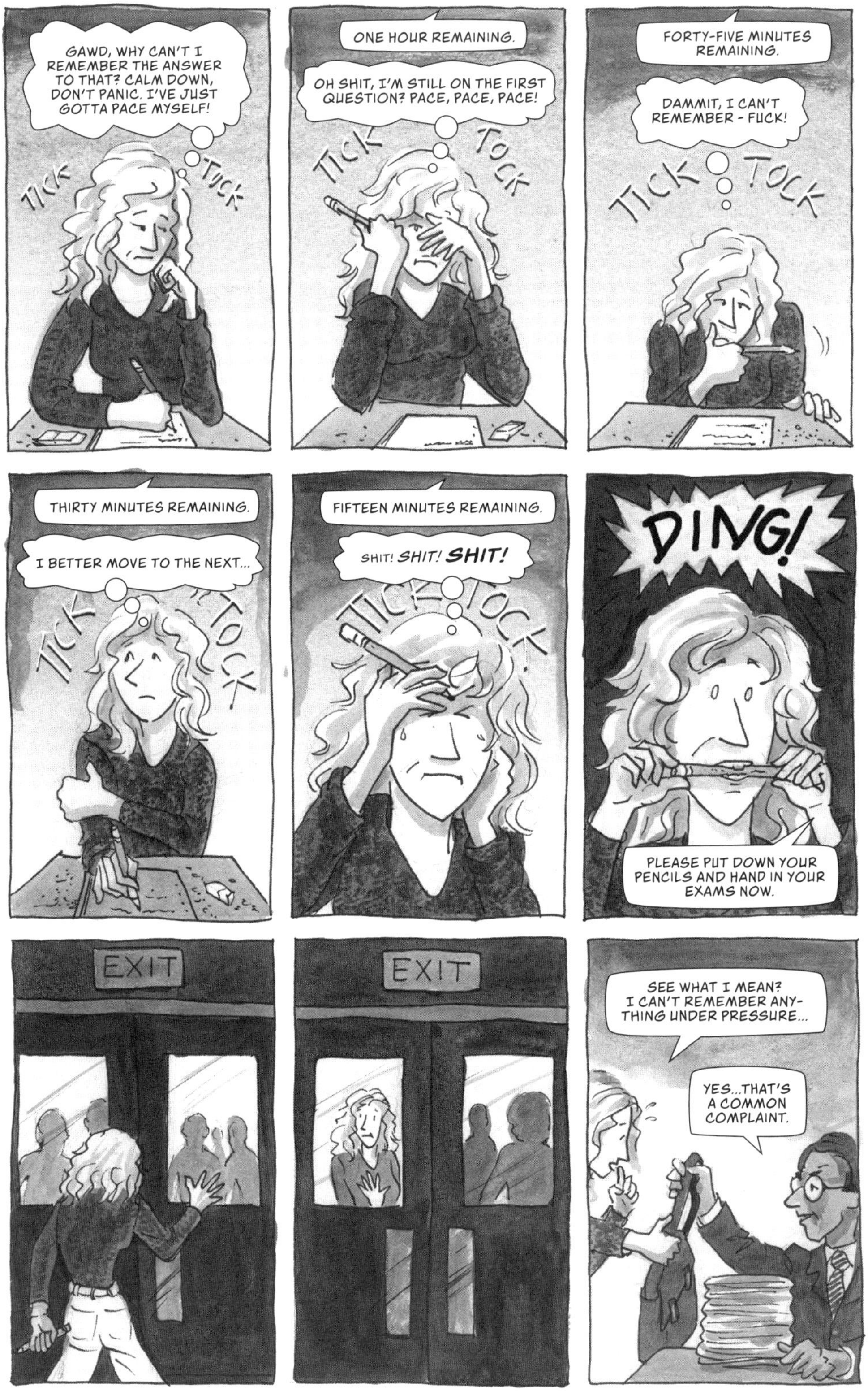
GAWD, WHY CAN'T I REMEMBER THE ANSWER TO THAT? CALM DOWN, DON'T PANIC. I'VE JUST GOTTA PACE MYSELF!
TICK TOCK
ONE HOUR REMAINING.
OH SHIT, I'M STILL ON THE FIRST QUESTION? PACE, PACE, PACE!
TICK TOCK
FORTY-FIVE MINUTES REMAINING.
DAMMIT, I CAN'T REMEMBER - FUCK!
TICK TOCK
THIRTY MINUTES REMAINING.
I BETTER MOVE TO THE NEXT...
TICK TOCK
FIFTEEN MINUTES REMAINING.
SHIT! SHIT! SHIT!
TICK TOCK
DING!
PLEASE PUT DOWN YOUR PENCILS AND HAND IN YOUR EXAMS NOW.
EXIT
EXIT
SEE WHAT I MEAN? I CAN'T REMEMBER ANY-THING UNDER PRESSURE...
YES...THAT'S A COMMON COMPLAINT.

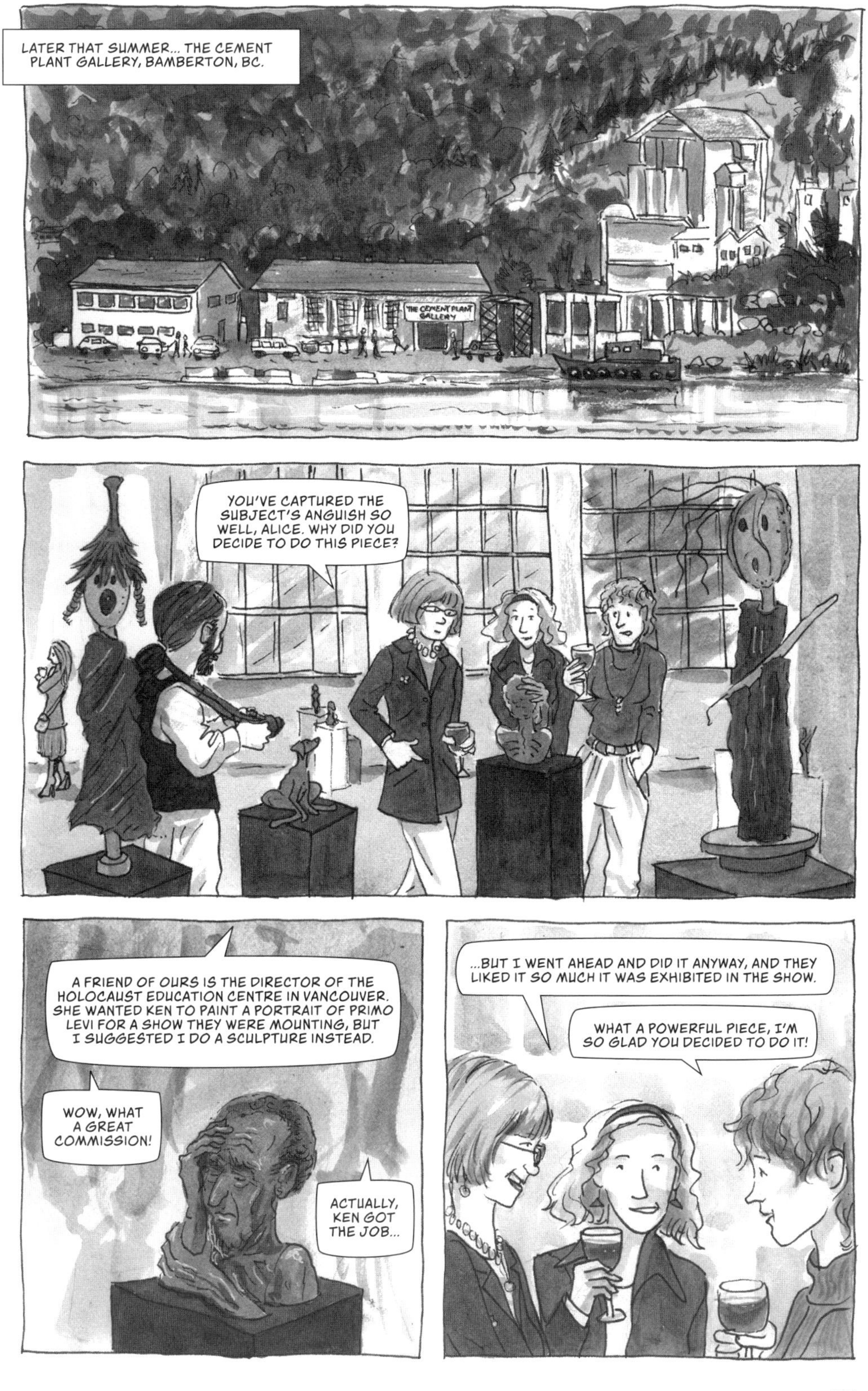
LATER THAT SUMMER... THE CEMENT PLANT GALLERY, BAMBERTON, BC.
THE CEMENT PLANT GALLERY
YOU'VE CAPTURED THE SUBJECT'S ANGUISH SO WELL, ALICE. WHY DID YOU DECIDE TO DO THIS PIECE?
A FRIEND OF OURS IS THE DIRECTOR OF THE HOLOCAUST EDUCATION CENTRE IN VANCOUVER. SHE WANTED KEN TO PAINT A PORTRAIT OF PRIMO LEVI FOR A SHOW THEY WERE MOUNTING, BUT I SUGGESTED I DO A SCULPTURE INSTEAD.
WOW, WHAT A GREAT COMMISSION!
ACTUALLY, KEN GOT THE JOB...
...BUT I WENT AHEAD AND DID IT ANYWAY, AND THEY LIKED IT SO MUCH IT WAS EXHIBITED IN THE SHOW.
WHAT A POWERFUL PIECE, I'M SO GLAD YOU DECIDED TO DO IT!

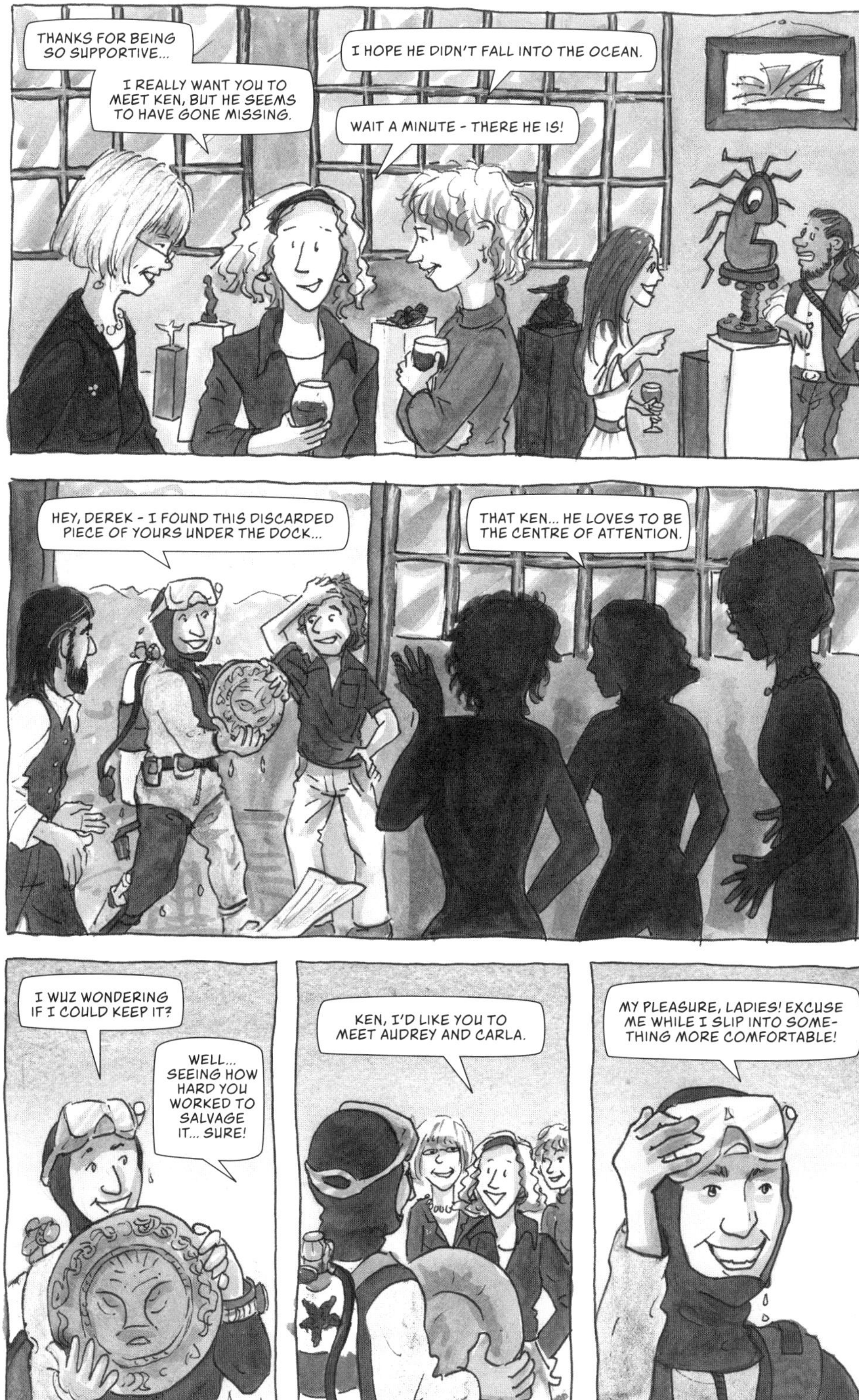
THANKS FOR BEING SO SUPPORTIVE...
I REALLY WANT YOU TO MEET KEN, BUT HE SEEMS TO HAVE GONE MISSING.
I HOPE HE DIDN'T FALL INTO THE OCEAN.
WAIT A MINUTE - THERE HE IS!
HEY, DEREK - I FOUND THIS DISCARDED PIECE OF YOURS UNDER THE DOCK...
THAT KEN... HE LOVES TO BE THE CENTRE OF ATTENTION.
I WUZ WONDERING IF I COULD KEEP IT?
WELL... SEEING HOW HARD YOU WORKED TO SALVAGE IT... SURE!
KEN, I'D LIKE YOU TO MEET AUDREY AND CARLA.
MY PLEASURE, LADIES! EXCUSE ME WHILE I SLIP INTO SOMETHING MORE COMFORTABLE!

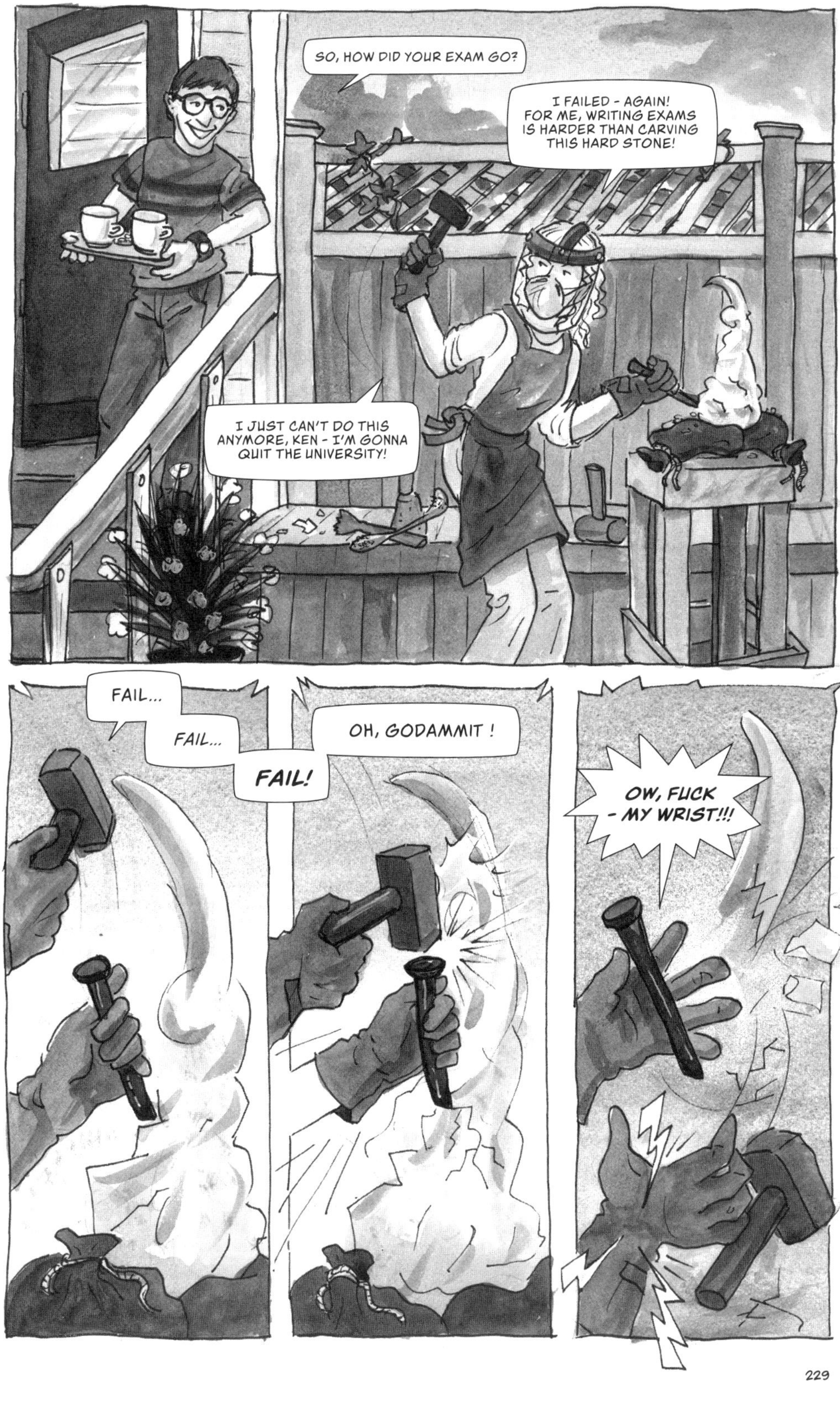

SO, HOW DID YOUR EXAM GO?
I FAILED - AGAIN! FOR ME, WRITING EXAMS IS HARDER THAN CARVING THIS HARD STONE!
I JUST CAN'T DO THIS ANYMORE, KEN - I'M GONNA QUIT THE UNIVERSITY!
FAIL...
FAIL...
FAIL!
OH, GODAMMIT !
OW, FUCK - MY WRIST!!!

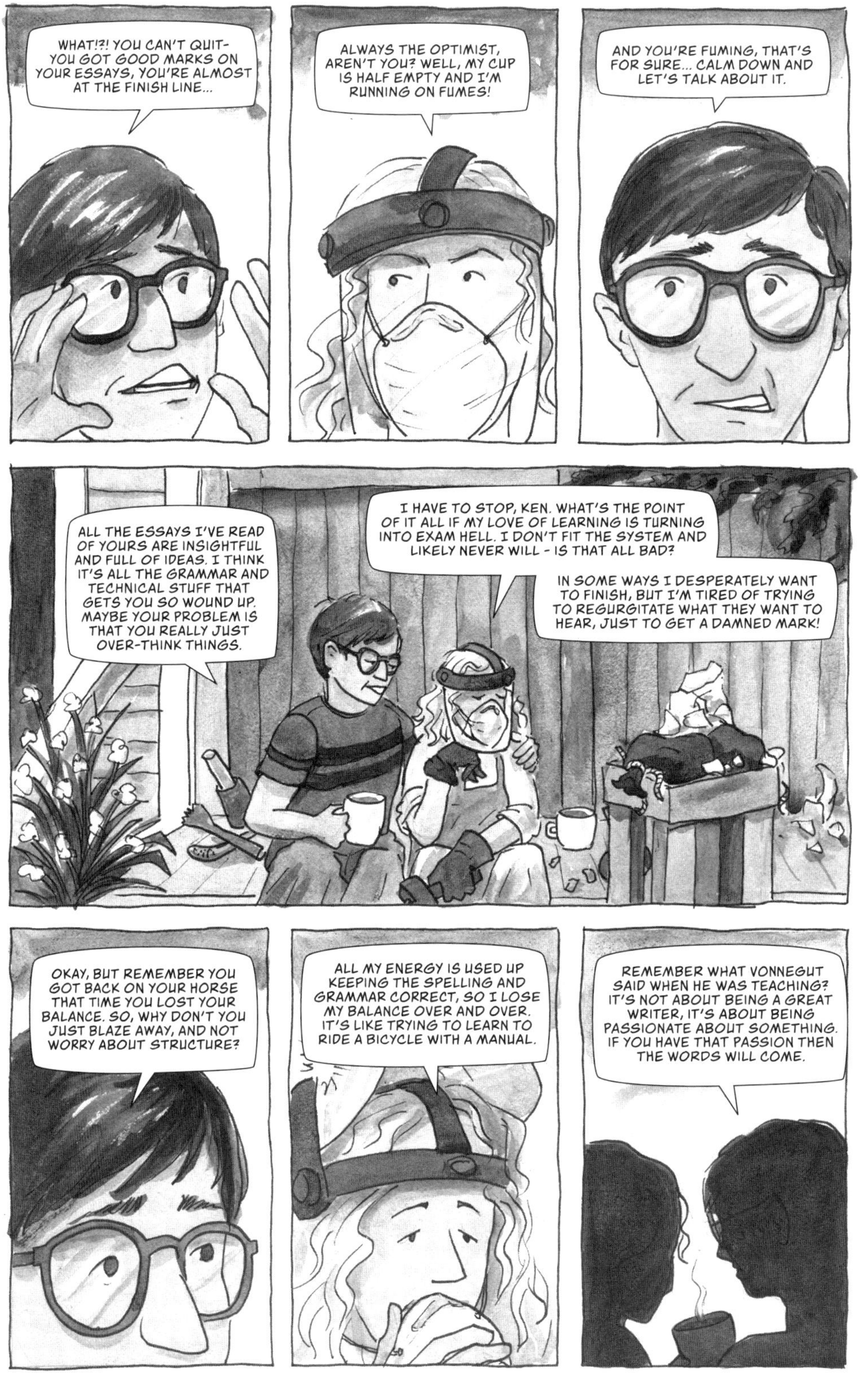
WHAT!?! YOU CAN'T QUIT- YOU GOT GOOD MARKS ON YOUR ESSAYS, YOU'RE ALMOST AT THE FINISH LINE...
ALWAYS THE OPTIMIST, AREN'T YOU? WELL, MY CUP IS HALF EMPTY AND I'M RUNNING ON FUMES!
AND YOU'RE FUMING, THAT'S FOR SURE... CALM DOWN AND LET'S TALK ABOUT IT.
ALL THE ESSAYS I'VE READ OF YOURS ARE INSIGHTFUL AND FULL OF IDEAS. I THINK IT'S ALL THE GRAMMAR AND TECHNICAL STUFF THAT GETS YOU SO WOUND UP. MAYBE YOUR PROBLEM IS THAT YOU REALLY JUST OVER-THINK THINGS.
I HAVE TO STOP, KEN. WHAT'S THE POINT OF IT ALL IF MY LOVE OF LEARNING IS TURNING INTO EXAM HELL. I DON'T FIT THE SYSTEM AND LIKELY NEVER WILL - IS THAT ALL BAD?
IN SOME WAYS I DESPERATELY WANT TO FINISH, BUT I'M TIRED OF TRYING TO REGURGITATE WHAT THEY WANT TO HEAR, JUST TO GET A DAMNED MARK!
OKAY, BUT REMEMBER YOU GOT BACK ON YOUR HORSE THAT TIME YOU LOST YOUR BALANCE. SO, WHY DON'T YOU JUST BLAZE AWAY, AND NOT WORRY ABOUT STRUCTURE?
ALL MY ENERGY IS USED UP KEEPING THE SPELLING AND GRAMMAR CORRECT, SO I LOSE MY BALANCE OVER AND OVER. IT'S LIKE TRYING TO LEARN TO RIDE A BICYCLE WITH A MANUAL.
REMEMBER WHAT VONNEGUT SAID WHEN HE WAS TEACHING? IT'S NOT ABOUT BEING A GREAT WRITER, IT'S ABOUT BEING PASSIONATE ABOUT SOMETHING. IF YOU HAVE THAT PASSION THEN THE WORDS WILL COME.

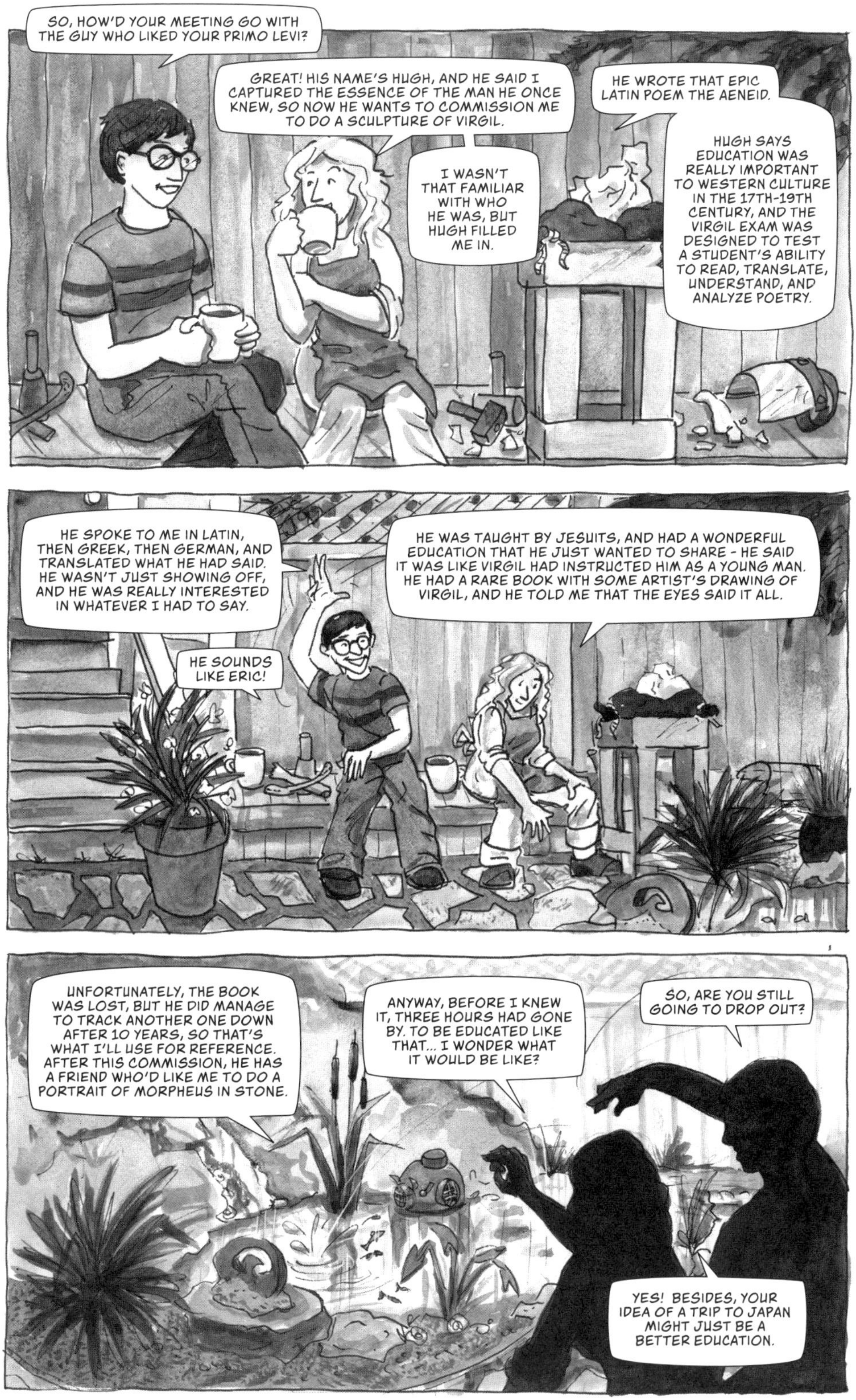
SO, HOW'D YOUR MEETING GO WITH THE GUY WHO LIKED YOUR PRIMO LEVI?
GREAT! HIS NAME'S HUGH, AND HE SAID I CAPTURED THE ESSENCE OF THE MAN HE ONCE KNEW, SO NOW HE WANTS TO COMMISSION ME TO DO A SCULPTURE OF VIRGIL.
I WASN'T THAT FAMILIAR WITH WHO HE WAS, BUT HUGH FILLED ME IN.
HE WROTE THAT EPIC LATIN POEM THE AENEID.
HUGH SAYS EDUCATION WAS REALLY IMPORTANT TO WESTERN CULTURE IN THE 17TH-19TH CENTURY, AND THE VIRGIL EXAM WAS DESIGNED TO TEST A STUDENT'S ABILITY TO READ, TRANSLATE, UNDERSTAND, AND ANALYZE POETRY.
HE SPOKE TO ME IN LATIN, THEN GREEK, THEN GERMAN, AND TRANSLATED WHAT HE HAD SAID. HE WASN'T JUST SHOWING OFF, AND HE WAS REALLY INTERESTED IN WHATEVER I HAD TO SAY.
HE WAS TAUGHT BY JESUITS, AND HAD A WONDERFUL EDUCATION THAT HE JUST WANTED TO SHARE - HE SAID IT WAS LIKE VIRGIL HAD INSTRUCTED HIM AS A YOUNG MAN. HE HAD A RARE BOOK WITH SOME ARTIST'S DRAWING OF VIRGIL, AND HE TOLD ME THAT THE EYES SAID IT ALL.
HE SOUNDS LIKE ERIC!
UNFORTUNATELY, THE BOOK WAS LOST, BUT HE DID MANAGE TO TRACK ANOTHER ONE DOWN AFTER 10 YEARS, SO THAT'S WHAT I'LL USE FOR REFERENCE. AFTER THIS COMMISSION, HE HAS A FRIEND WHO'D LIKE ME TO DO A PORTRAIT OF MORPHEUS IN STONE.
ANYWAY, BEFORE I KNEW IT, THREE HOURS HAD GONE BY. TO BE EDUCATED LIKE THAT... I WONDER WHAT IT WOULD BE LIKE?
SO, ARE YOU STILL GOING TO DROP OUT?
YES! BESIDES, YOUR IDEA OF A TRIP TO JAPAN MIGHT JUST BE A BETTER EDUCATION.

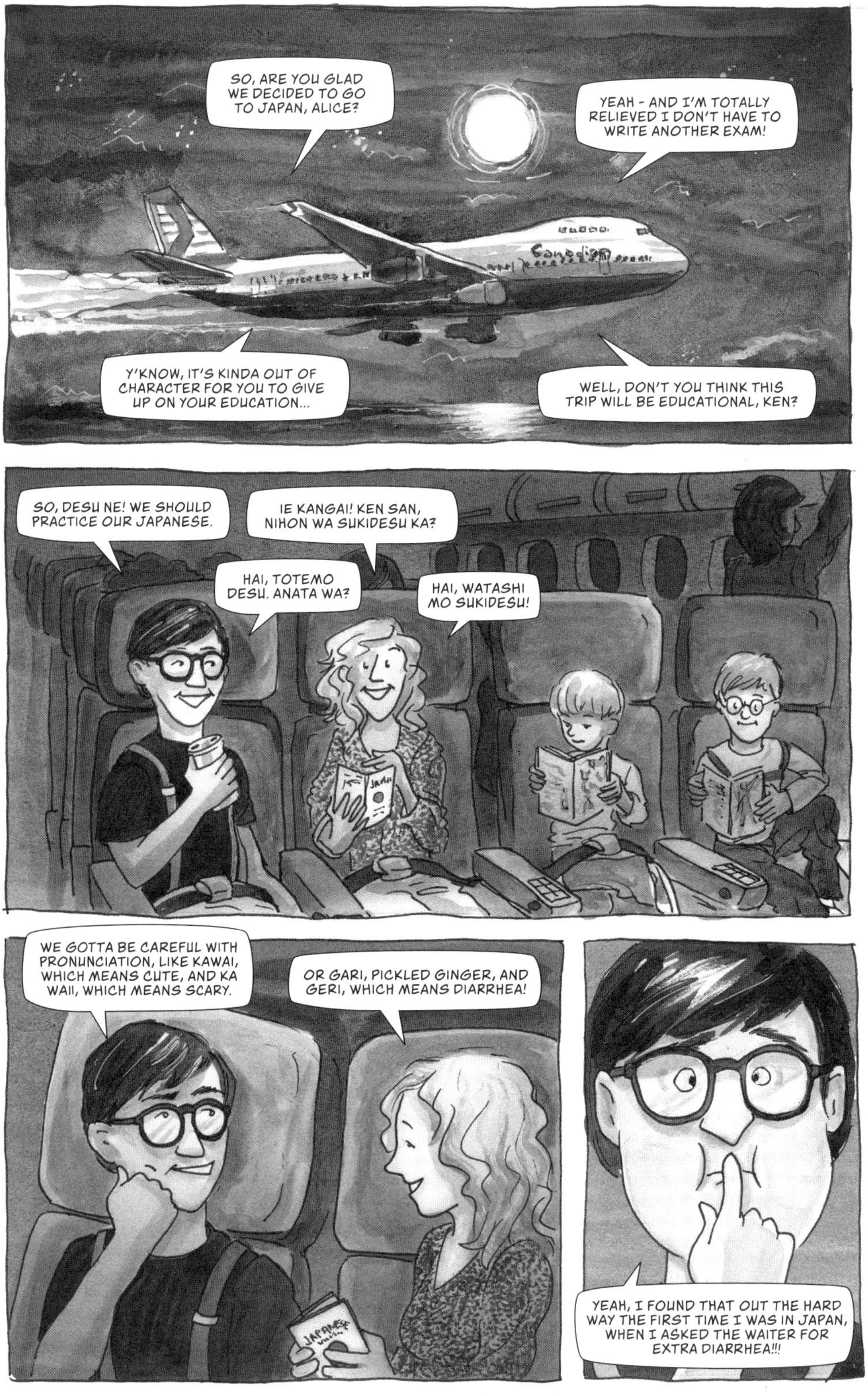
SO, ARE YOU GLAD WE DECIDED TO GO TO JAPAN, ALICE?
YEAH - AND I'M TOTALLY RELIEVED I DON'T HAVE TO WRITE ANOTHER EXAM!
Y'KNOW, IT'S KINDA OUT OF CHARACTER FOR YOU TO GIVE UP ON YOUR EDUCATION...
WELL, DON'T YOU THINK THIS TRIP WILL BE EDUCATIONAL, KEN?
SO, DESU NE! WE SHOULD PRACTICE OUR JAPANESE.
IE KANGAI! KEN SAN, NIHON WA SUKIDESU KA?
HAI, TOTEMO DESU. ANATA WA?
HAI, WATASHI MO SUKIDESU!
JAPAN
WE GOTTA BE CAREFUL WITH PRONUNCIATION, LIKE KAWAI, WHICH MEANS CUTE, AND KA WAII, WHICH MEANS SCARY.
OR GARI, PICKLED GINGER, AND GERI, WHICH MEANS DIARRHEA!
JAPANESE
YEAH, I FOUND THAT OUT THE HARD WAY THE FIRST TIME I WAS IN JAPAN, WHEN I ASKED THE WAITER FOR EXTRA DIARRHEA!!!

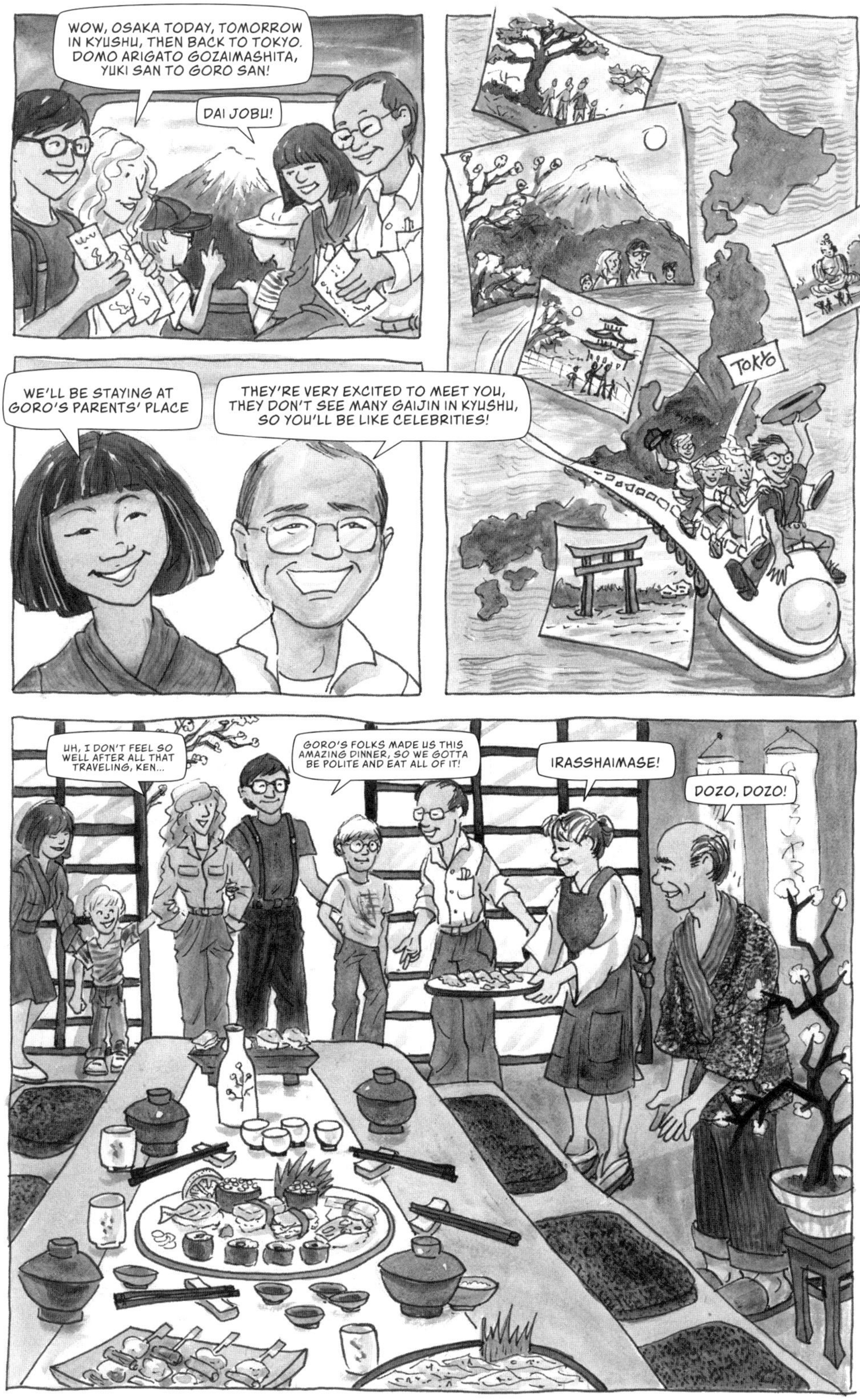
WOW, OSAKA TODAY, TOMORROW IN KYUSHU, THEN BACK TO TOKYO. DOMO ARIGATO GOZAIMASHITA, YUKI SAN TO GORO SAN!
DAI JOBU!
TOKYO
WE'LL BE STAYING AT GORO'S PARENTS' PLACE
THEY'RE VERY EXCITED TO MEET YOU, THEY DON'T SEE MANY GAIJIN IN KYUSHU, SO YOU'LL BE LIKE CELEBRITIES!
UH, I DON'T FEEL SO WELL AFTER ALL THAT TRAVELING, KEN...
GORO'S FOLKS MADE US THIS AMAZING DINNER, SO WE GOTTA BE POLITE AND EAT ALL OF IT!
IRASSHAIMASE!
DOZO, DOZO!

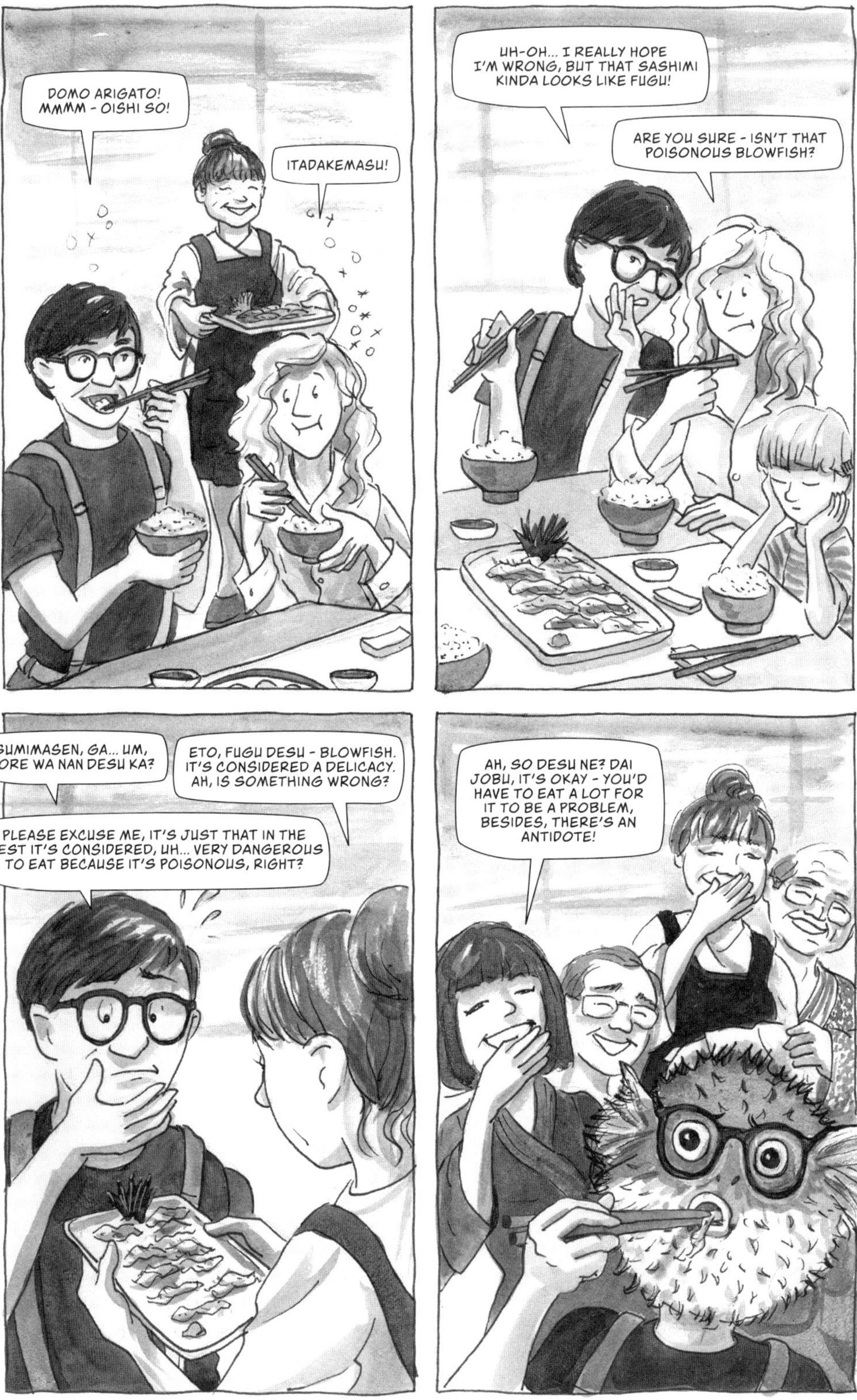
DOMO ARIGATO! MMMM - OISHI SO!
ITADAKEMASU!
UH-OH... I REALLY HOPE I'M WRONG, BUT THAT SASHIMI KINDA LOOKS LIKE FUGU!
ARE YOU SURE - ISN'T THAT POISONOUS BLOWFISH?
SUMIMASEN, GA... UM, SORE WA NAN DESU KA?
ETO, FUGU DESU - BLOWFISH. IT'S CONSIDERED A DELICACY. AH, IS SOMETHING WRONG?
PLEASE EXCUSE ME, IT'S JUST THAT IN THE WEST IT'S CONSIDERED, UH... VERY DANGEROUS TO EAT BECAUSE IT'S POISONOUS, RIGHT?
AH, SO DESU NE? DAI JOBU, IT'S OKAY - YOU'D HAVE TO EAT A LOT FOR IT TO BE A PROBLEM, BESIDES, THERE'S AN ANTIDOTE!

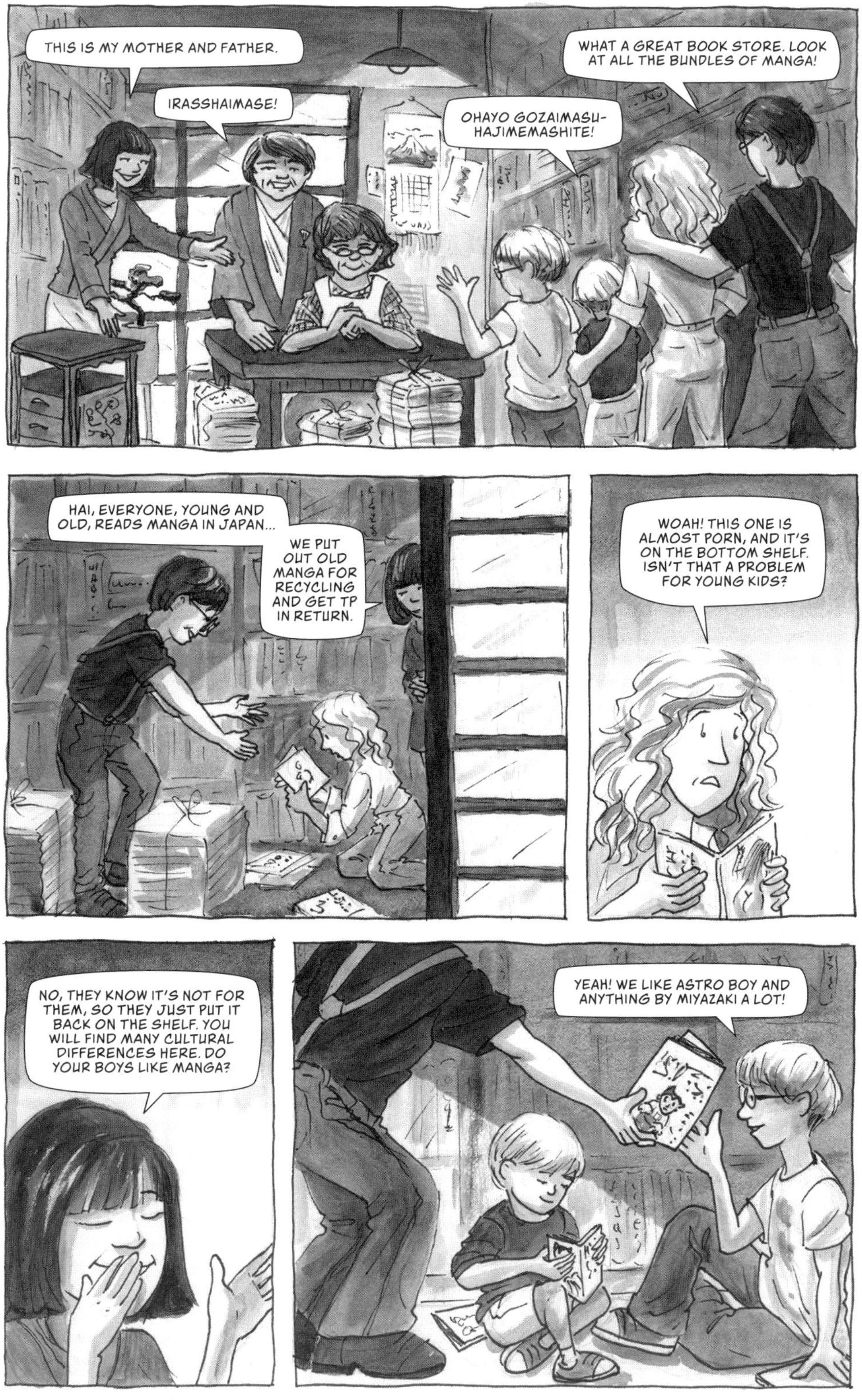
THIS IS MY MOTHER AND FATHER.
IRASSHAIMASE!
OHAYO GOZAIMASU-HAJIMEMASHITE!
WHAT A GREAT BOOK STORE. LOOK AT ALL THE BUNDLES OF MANGA!
HAI, EVERYONE, YOUNG AND OLD, READS MANGA IN JAPAN...
WE PUT OUT OLD MANGA FOR RECYCLING AND GET TP IN RETURN.
WOAH! THIS ONE IS ALMOST PORN, AND IT'S ON THE BOTTOM SHELF. ISN'T THAT A PROBLEM FOR YOUNG KIDS?
NO, THEY KNOW IT'S NOT FOR THEM, SO THEY JUST PUT IT BACK ON THE SHELF. YOU WILL FIND MANY CULTURAL DIFFERENCES HERE. DO YOUR BOYS LIKE MANGA?
YEAH! WE LIKE ASTRO BOY AND ANYTHING BY MIYAZAKI A LOT!

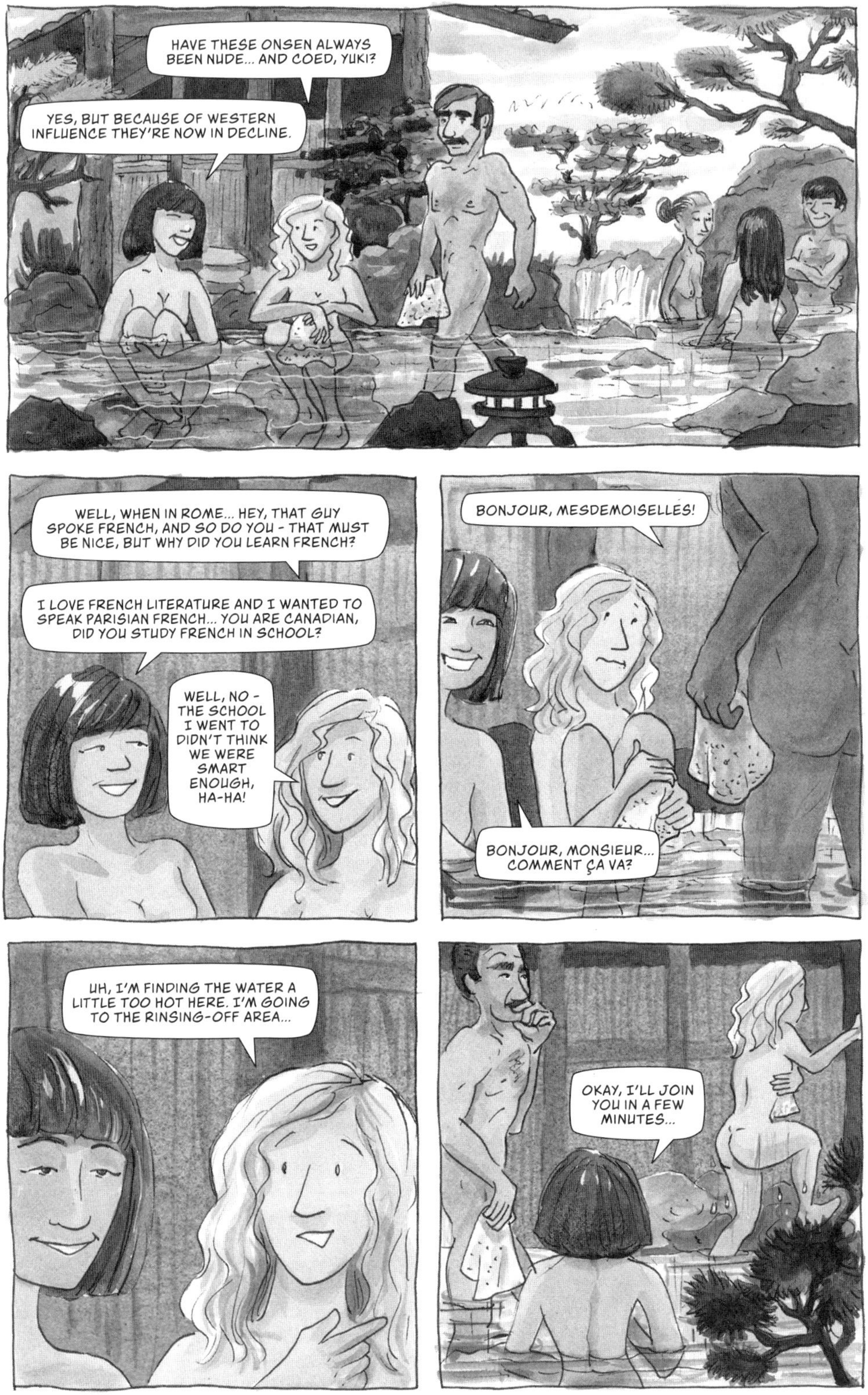
HAVE THESE ONSEN ALWAYS BEEN NUDE... AND COED, YUKI?
YES, BUT BECAUSE OF WESTERN INFLUENCE THEY'RE NOW IN DECLINE.
WELL, WHEN IN ROME... HEY, THAT GUY SPOKE FRENCH, AND SO DO YOU - THAT MUST BE NICE, BUT WHY DID YOU LEARN FRENCH?
I LOVE FRENCH LITERATURE AND I WANTED TO SPEAK PARISIAN FRENCH... YOU ARE CANADIAN, DID YOU STUDY FRENCH IN SCHOOL?
WELL, NO - THE SCHOOL I WENT TO DIDN'T THINK WE WERE SMART ENOUGH, HA-HA!
BONJOUR, MESDEMOISELLES!
BONJOUR, MONSIEUR... COMMENT ÇA VA?
UH, I'M FINDING THE WATER A LITTLE TOO HOT HERE. I'M GOING TO THE RINSING-OFF AREA...
OKAY, I'LL JOIN YOU IN A FEW MINUTES...

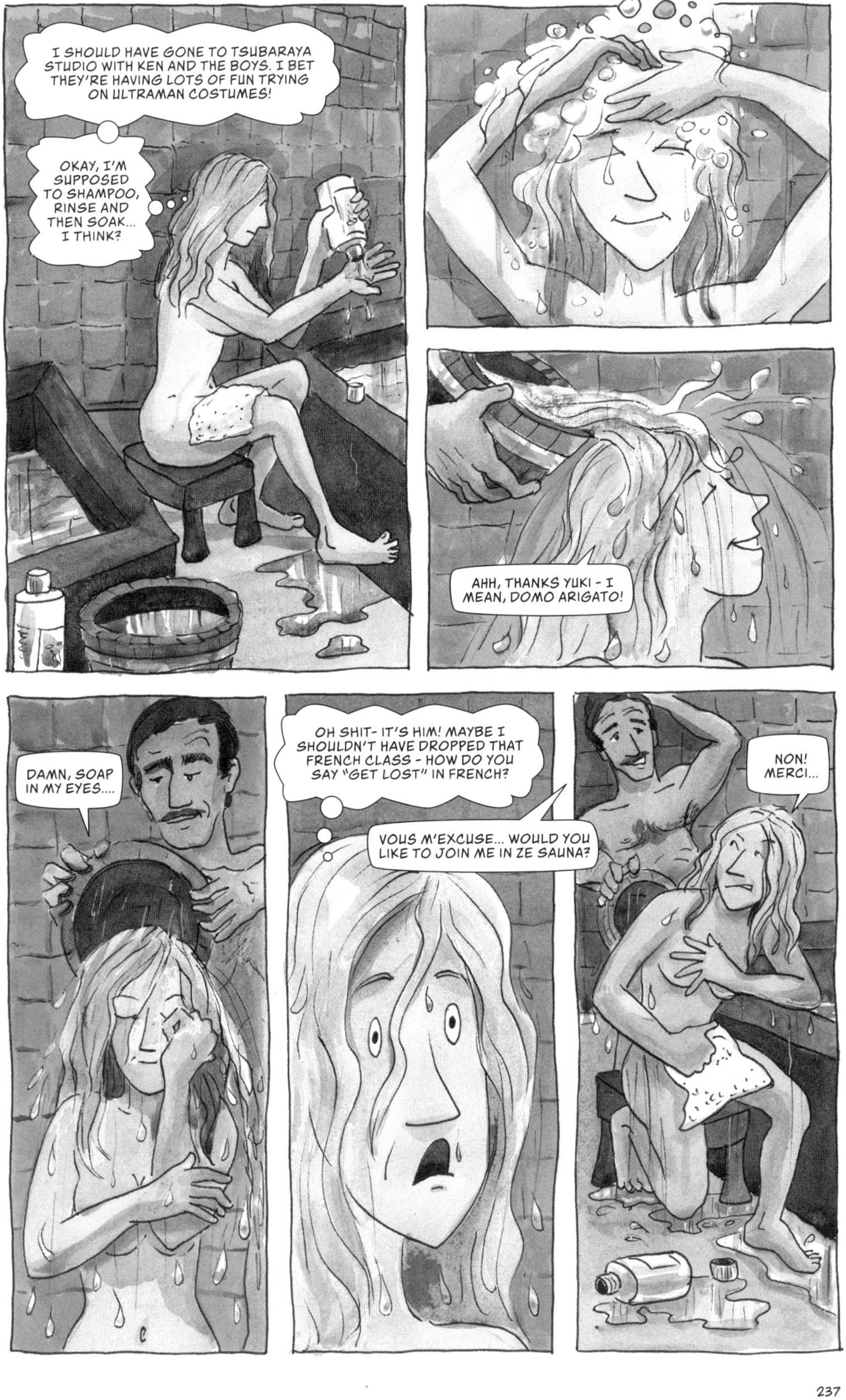
I SHOULD HAVE GONE TO TSUBARAYA STUDIO WITH KEN AND THE BOYS. I BET THEY'RE HAVING LOTS OF FUN TRYING ON ULTRAMAN COSTUMES!
OKAY, I'M SUPPOSED TO SHAMPOO, RINSE AND THEN SOAK... I THINK?
AHH, THANKS YUKI - I MEAN, DOMO ARIGATO!
DAMN, SOAP IN MY EYES....
OH SHIT- IT'S HIM! MAYBE I SHOULDN'T HAVE DROPPED THAT FRENCH CLASS - HOW DO YOU SAY "GET LOST" IN FRENCH?
VOUS M'EXCUSE... WOULD YOU LIKE TO JOIN ME IN ZE SAUNA?
NON! MERCI...

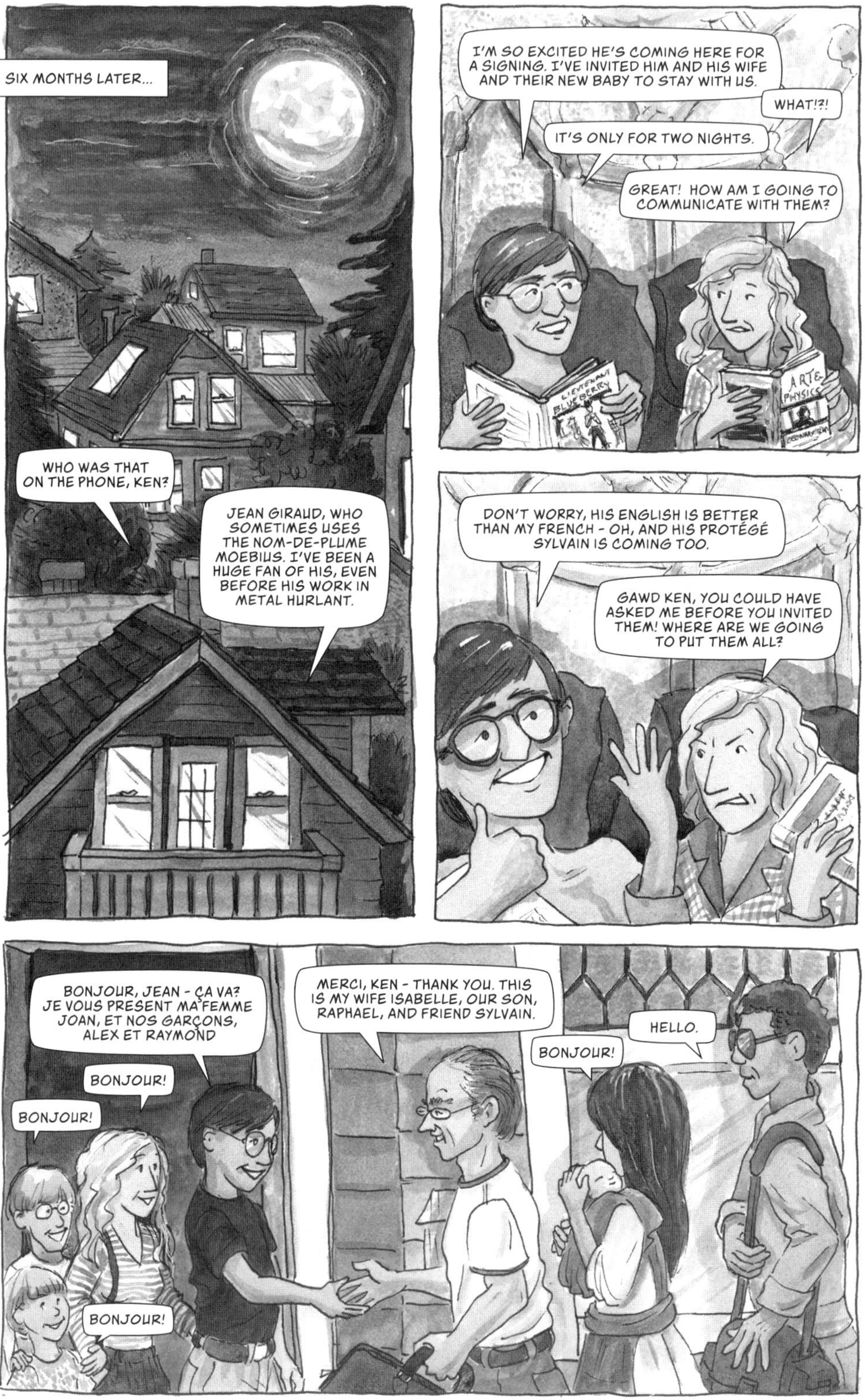
SIX MONTHS LATER...
WHO WAS THAT ON THE PHONE, KEN?
JEAN GIRAUD, WHO SOMETIMES USES THE NOM-DE-PLUME MOEBIUS. I'VE BEEN A HUGE FAN OF HIS, EVEN BEFORE HIS WORK IN METAL HURLANT.
I'M SO EXCITED HE'S COMING HERE FOR A SIGNING. I'VE INVITED HIM AND HIS WIFE AND THEIR NEW BABY TO STAY WITH US.
WHAT!?!
IT'S ONLY FOR TWO NIGHTS.
GREAT! HOW AM I GOING TO COMMUNICATE WITH THEM?
LIEUTENANT BLUEBERRY
ARTE PHYSICS
DON'T WORRY, HIS ENGLISH IS BETTER THAN MY FRENCH - OH, AND HIS PROTÉGÉ SYLVAIN IS COMING TOO.
GAWD KEN, YOU COULD HAVE ASKED ME BEFORE YOU INVITED THEM! WHERE ARE WE GOING TO PUT THEM ALL?
BONJOUR, JEAN - ÇA VA? JE VOUS PRESENT MA FEMME JOAN, ET NOS GARÇONS, ALEX ET RAYMOND
BONJOUR!
BONJOUR!
BONJOUR!
MERCI, KEN - THANK YOU. THIS IS MY WIFE ISABELLE, OUR SON, RAPHAEL, AND FRIEND SYLVAIN.
BONJOUR!
HELLO.

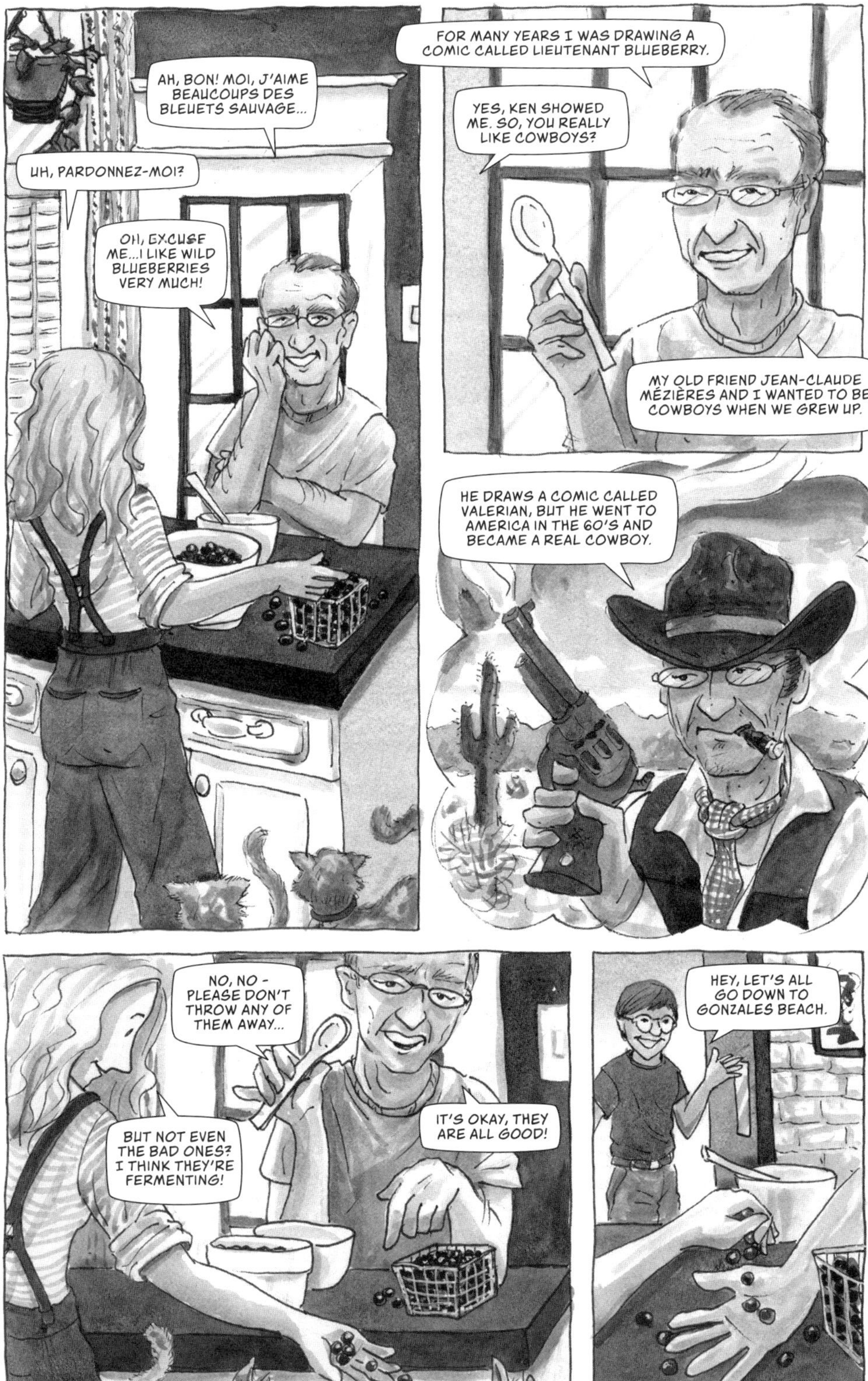
AH, BON! MOI, J'AIME BEAUCOUPS DES BLEUETS SAUVAGE...
UH, PARDONNEZ-MOI?
OH, EXCUSE ME...I LIKE WILD BLUEBERRIES VERY MUCH!
FOR MANY YEARS I WAS DRAWING A COMIC CALLED LIEUTENANT BLUEBERRY.
YES, KEN SHOWED ME. SO, YOU REALLY LIKE COWBOYS?
MY OLD FRIEND JEAN-CLAUDE MÉZIÈRES AND I WANTED TO BE COWBOYS WHEN WE GREW UP.
HE DRAWS A COMIC CALLED VALERIAN, BUT HE WENT TO AMERICA IN THE 60'S AND BECAME A REAL COWBOY.
NO, NO - PLEASE DON'T THROW ANY OF THEM AWAY...
BUT NOT EVEN THE BAD ONES? I THINK THEY'RE FERMENTING!
IT'S OKAY, THEY ARE ALL GOOD!
HEY, LET'S ALL GO DOWN TO GONZALES BEACH.

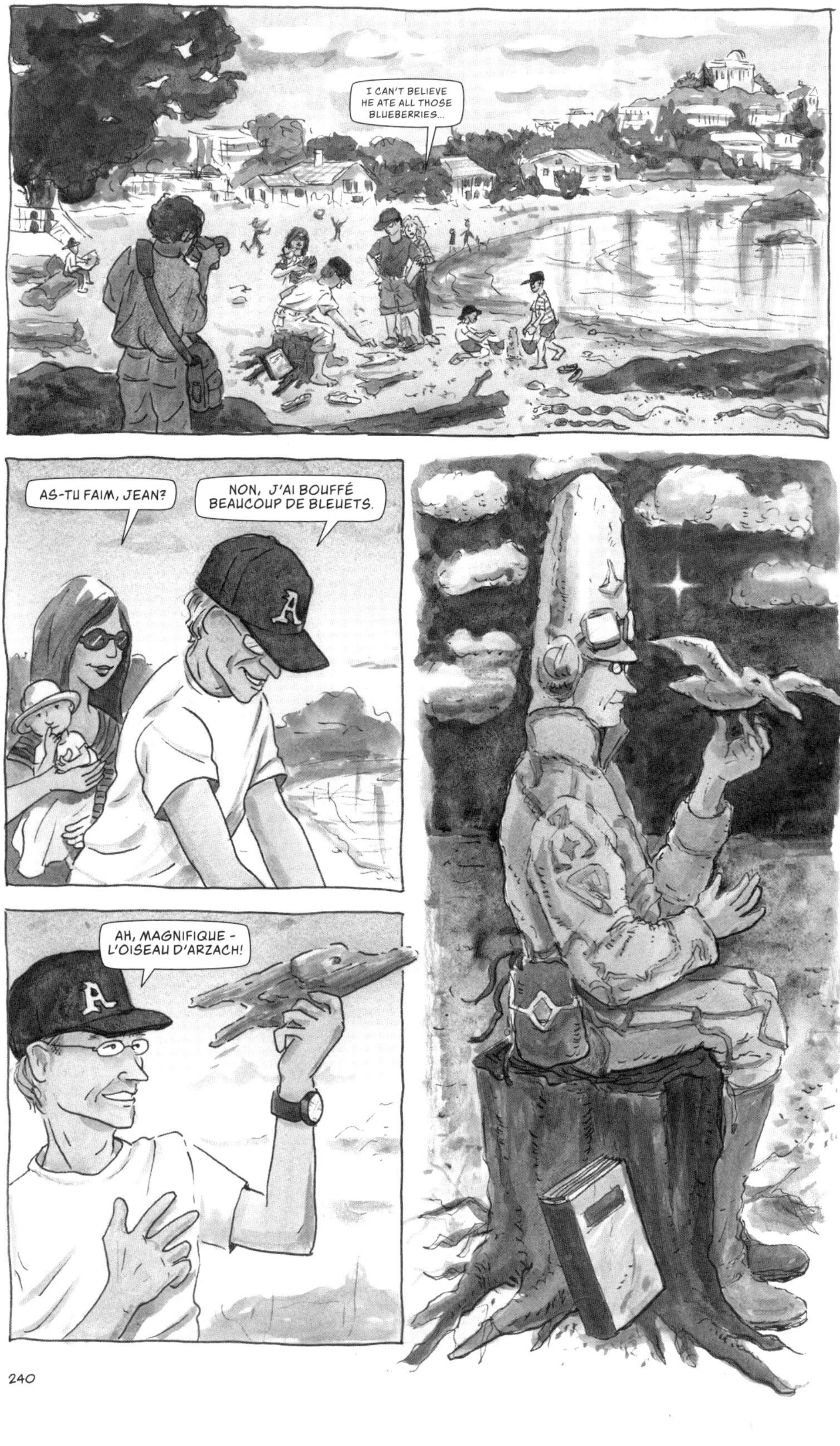
I CAN'T BELIEVE HE ATE ALL THOSE BLUEBERRIES...
AS-TU FAIM, JEAN?
NON, J'AI BOUFFÉ BEAUCOUP DE BLEUETS.
AH, MAGNIFIQUE - L'OISEAU D'ARZACH!

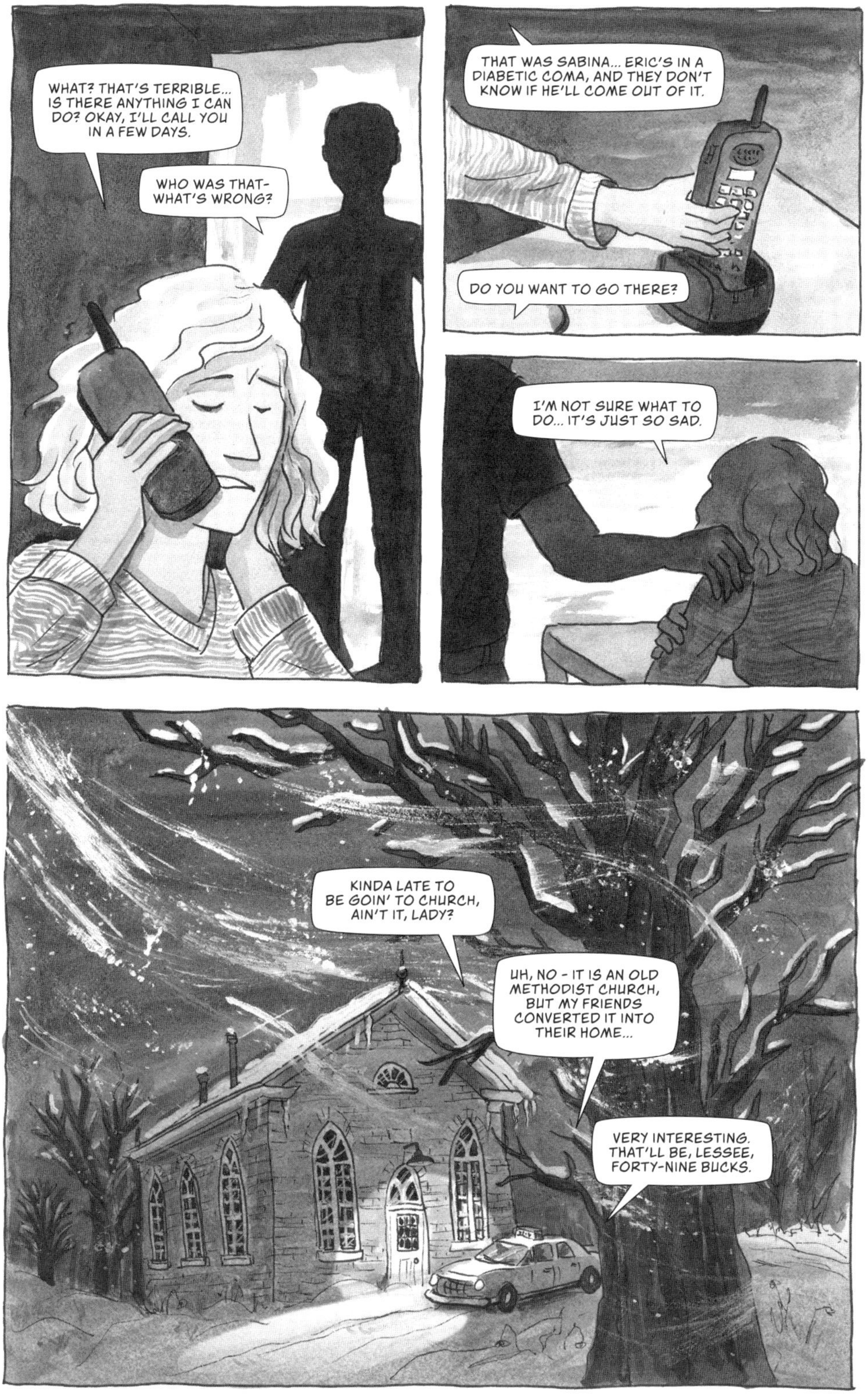
WHAT? THAT'S TERRIBLE... IS THERE ANYTHING I CAN DO? OKAY, I'LL CALL YOU IN A FEW DAYS.
WHO WAS THAT- WHAT'S WRONG?
THAT WAS SABINA... ERIC'S IN A DIABETIC COMA, AND THEY DON'T KNOW IF HE'LL COME OUT OF IT.
DO YOU WANT TO GO THERE?
I'M NOT SURE WHAT TO DO... IT'S JUST SO SAD.
KINDA LATE TO BE GOIN' TO CHURCH, AIN'T IT, LADY?
UH, NO - IT IS AN OLD METHODIST CHURCH, BUT MY FRIENDS CONVERTED IT INTO THEIR HOME...
VERY INTERESTING. THAT'LL BE, LESSEE, FORTY-NINE BUCKS.

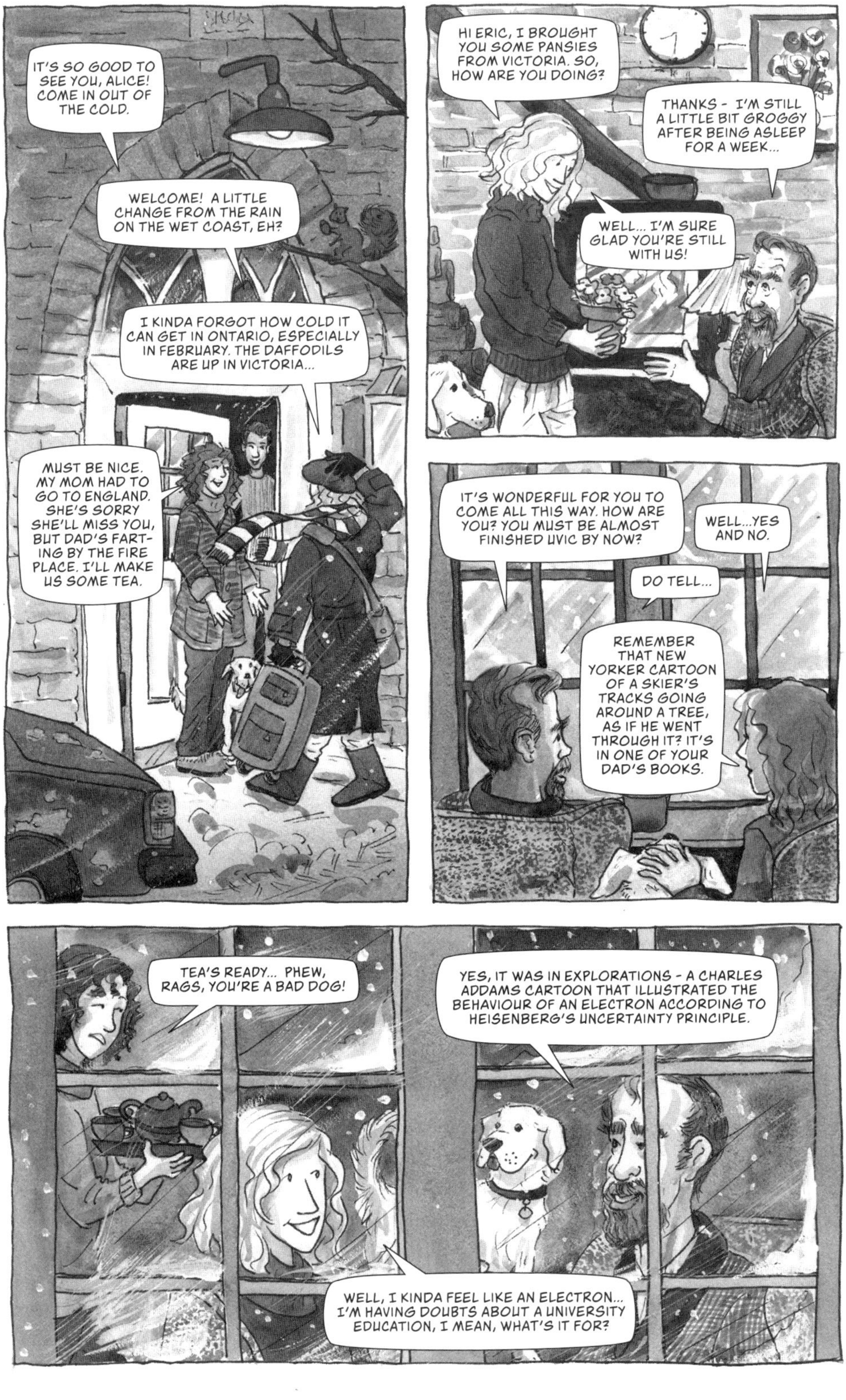
IT'S SO GOOD TO SEE YOU, ALICE! COME IN OUT OF THE COLD.
WELCOME! A LITTLE CHANGE FROM THE RAIN ON THE WET COAST, EH?
I KINDA FORGOT HOW COLD IT CAN GET IN ONTARIO, ESPECIALLY IN FEBRUARY. THE DAFFODILS ARE UP IN VICTORIA...
MUST BE NICE. MY MOM HAD TO GO TO ENGLAND. SHE'S SORRY SHE'LL MISS YOU, BUT DAD'S FARTING BY THE FIRE PLACE. I'LL MAKE US SOME TEA.
HI ERIC, I BROUGHT YOU SOME PANSIES FROM VICTORIA. SO, HOW ARE YOU DOING?
THANKS - I'M STILL A LITTLE BIT GROGGY AFTER BEING ASLEEP FOR A WEEK...
WELL... I'M SURE GLAD YOU'RE STILL WITH US!
IT'S WONDERFUL FOR YOU TO COME ALL THIS WAY. HOW ARE YOU? YOU MUST BE ALMOST FINISHED UVIC BY NOW?
WELL...YES AND NO.
DO TELL...
REMEMBER THAT NEW YORKER CARTOON OF A SKIER'S TRACKS GOING AROUND A TREE, AS IF HE WENT THROUGH IT? IT'S IN ONE OF YOUR DAD'S BOOKS.
TEA'S READY... PHEW, RAGS, YOU'RE A BAD DOG!
YES, IT WAS IN EXPLORATIONS - A CHARLES ADDAMS CARTOON THAT ILLUSTRATED THE BEHAVIOUR OF AN ELECTRON ACCORDING TO HEISENBERG'S UNCERTAINTY PRINCIPLE.
WELL, I KINDA FEEL LIKE AN ELECTRON... I'M HAVING DOUBTS ABOUT A UNIVERSITY EDUCATION, I MEAN, WHAT'S IT FOR?

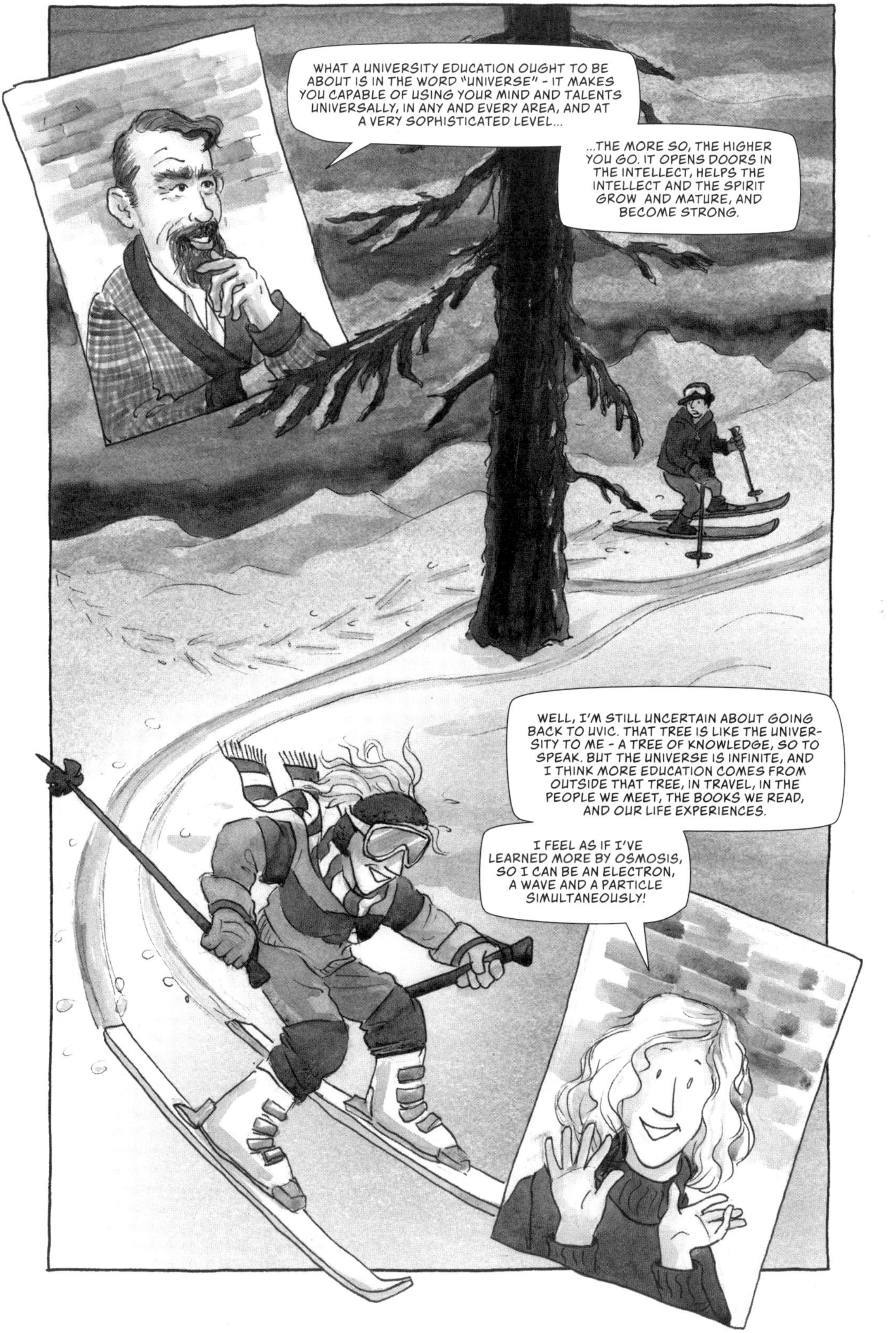
WHAT A UNIVERSITY EDUCATION OUGHT TO BE ABOUT IS IN THE WORD "UNIVERSE" - IT MAKES YOU CAPABLE OF USING YOUR MIND AND TALENTS UNIVERSALLY, IN ANY AND EVERY AREA, AND AT A VERY SOPHISTICATED LEVEL...
...THE MORE SO, THE HIGHER YOU GO. IT OPENS DOORS IN THE INTELLECT, HELPS THE INTELLECT AND THE SPIRIT GROW AND MATURE, AND BECOME STRONG.
WELL, I'M STILL UNCERTAIN ABOUT GOING BACK TO UVIC. THAT TREE IS LIKE THE UNIVERSITY TO ME - A TREE OF KNOWLEDGE, SO TO SPEAK. BUT THE UNIVERSE IS INFINITE, AND I THINK MORE EDUCATION COMES FROM OUTSIDE THAT TREE, IN TRAVEL, IN THE PEOPLE WE MEET, THE BOOKS WE READ, AND OUR LIFE EXPERIENCES.
I FEEL AS IF I'VE LEARNED MORE BY OSMOSIS, SO I CAN BE AN ELECTRON, A WAVE AND A PARTICLE SIMULTANEOUSLY!

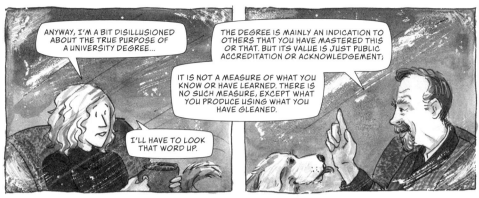

ANYWAY, I'M A BIT DISILLUSIONED ABOUT THE TRUE PURPOSE OF A UNIVERSITY DEGREE...

THE DEGREE IS MAINLY AN INDICATION TO OTHERS THAT YOU HAVE MASTERED THIS OR THAT. BUT ITS VALUE IS JUST PUBLIC ACCREDITATION OR ACKNOWLEDGEMENT;

IT IS NOT A MEASURE OF WHAT YOU KNOW OR HAVE LEARNED. THERE IS NO SUCH MEASURE, EXCEPT WHAT YOU PRODUCE USING WHAT YOU HAVE GLEANED.

I'LL HAVE TO LOOK THAT WORD UP.

I DID LEARN A LOT AT UVIC, BUT I LEARNED MORE IN THE ONE YEAR I TOOK FROM YOU, ERIC!

ANOTHER USE OF THE DEGREE IS THAT IT FORCES YOU TO EXAMINE IDEAS AND MATERIAL THAT YOU WOULD NOT OTHERWISE LOOK AT, THEREFORE IT BROADENS YOU.

EDUCATION COMES FROM MANY PLACES, AND OUR INSTITUTIONS ARE GREAT PLACES TO LEARN. IN THE PAST I KNOW I'VE SAID THAT SCHOOLS ARE OBSOLETE BUT I WAS SPEAKING METAPHORICALLY.

BUT IT'S NOT LIKE YOU TO DROP OUT - YOU HAVE SO MUCH TO OFFER, SO GO BACK AND GIVE IT ALL YOU'VE GOT!

BUT I FLUNKED ALL MY EXAMS!

EXAMS ARE GENERALLY NOT MUCH USE, JUST A WAY TO KEEP THOSE IN LINE WHO AREN'T WORKING ON ANYTHING FOR THEMSELVES. MOST OFTEN WHAT YOU REMEMBER FROM A COURSE YEARS LATER IS IN THE PAPERS YOU WROTE.

SO WRITE MORE PAPERS THAN THEY ASK FOR, AND MAYBE HAND THEM IN TO THE TEACHERS YOU RESPECT. AND READ EVERY BOOK ON THE READING LIST.

THANKS, ERIC - YOU KNOW, IN HIGH SCHOOL I WAS NEVER TAUGHT ABOUT METAPHORS, OR EVEN HEARD ANY LITERARY TERMS LIKE THAT.

I FOUND THAT THINKING OUTSIDE THE BOX WASN'T ENCOURAGED - NEITHER WAS CREATIVITY!

THAT'S A CRIME - BUT UNIVERSITY IS NOT HIGH SCHOOL.

MAN, RAGS IS GETTING RIPE - LET'S GO TO THE STUDY....

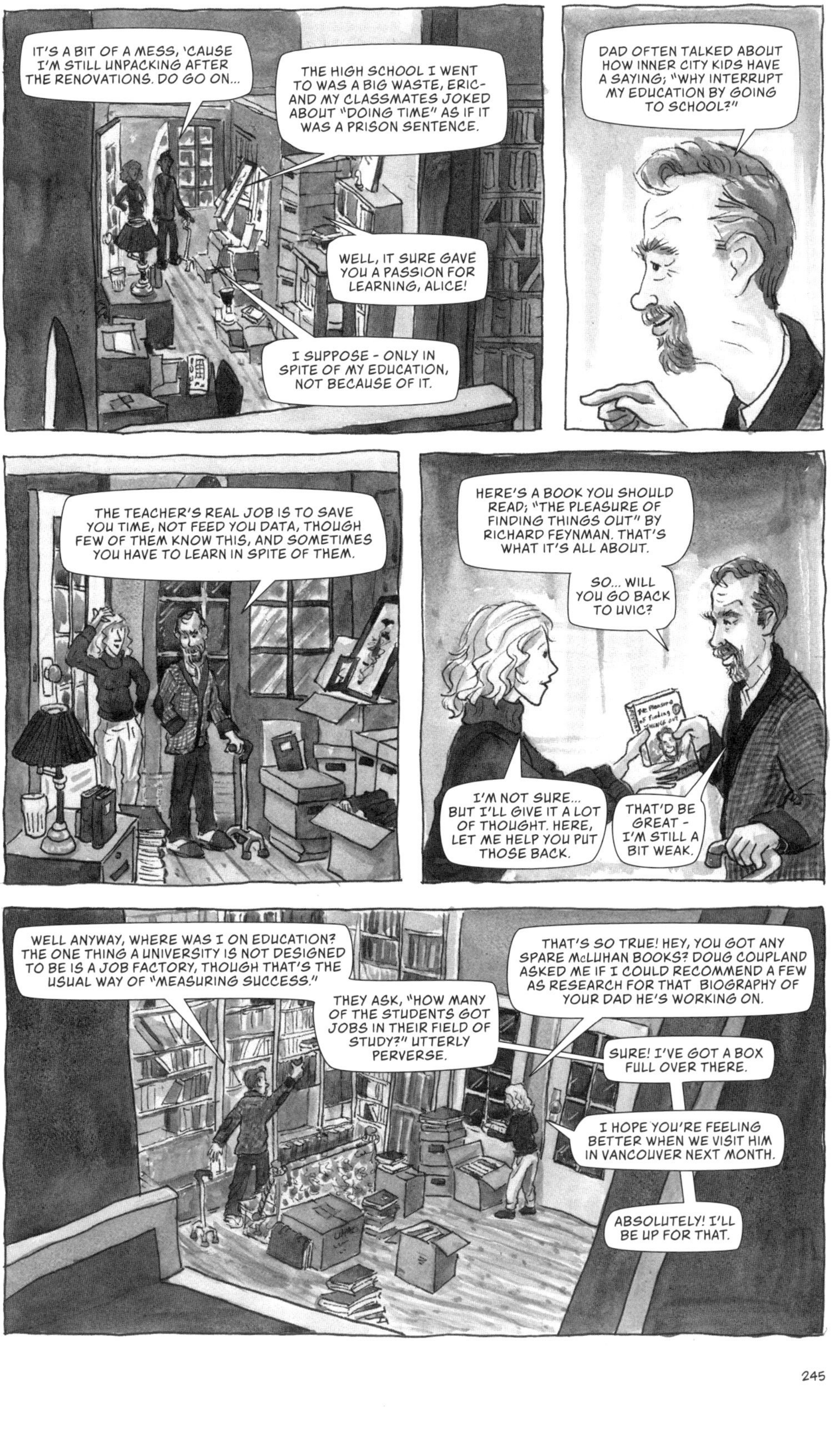
IT'S A BIT OF A MESS, 'CAUSE I'M STILL UNPACKING AFTER THE RENOVATIONS. DO GO ON...
THE HIGH SCHOOL I WENT TO WAS A BIG WASTE, ERIC- AND MY CLASSMATES JOKED ABOUT "DOING TIME" AS IF IT WAS A PRISON SENTENCE.
WELL, IT SURE GAVE YOU A PASSION FOR LEARNING, ALICE!
I SUPPOSE - ONLY IN SPITE OF MY EDUCATION, NOT BECAUSE OF IT.
DAD OFTEN TALKED ABOUT HOW INNER CITY KIDS HAVE A SAYING; "WHY INTERRUPT MY EDUCATION BY GOING TO SCHOOL?"
THE TEACHER'S REAL JOB IS TO SAVE YOU TIME, NOT FEED YOU DATA, THOUGH FEW OF THEM KNOW THIS, AND SOMETIMES YOU HAVE TO LEARN IN SPITE OF THEM.
HERE'S A BOOK YOU SHOULD READ; "THE PLEASURE OF FINDING THINGS OUT" BY RICHARD FEYNMAN. THAT'S WHAT IT'S ALL ABOUT.
SO... WILL YOU GO BACK TO UVIC?
I'M NOT SURE... BUT I'LL GIVE IT A LOT OF THOUGHT. HERE, LET ME HELP YOU PUT THOSE BACK.
THAT'D BE GREAT - I'M STILL A BIT WEAK.
WELL ANYWAY, WHERE WAS I ON EDUCATION? THE ONE THING A UNIVERSITY IS NOT DESIGNED TO BE IS A JOB FACTORY, THOUGH THAT'S THE USUAL WAY OF "MEASURING SUCCESS."
THEY ASK, "HOW MANY OF THE STUDENTS GOT JOBS IN THEIR FIELD OF STUDY?" UTTERLY PERVERSE.
THAT'S SO TRUE! HEY, YOU GOT ANY SPARE McLUHAN BOOKS? DOUG COUPLAND ASKED ME IF I COULD RECOMMEND A FEW AS RESEARCH FOR THAT BIOGRAPHY OF YOUR DAD HE'S WORKING ON.
SURE! I'VE GOT A BOX FULL OVER THERE.
I HOPE YOU'RE FEELING BETTER WHEN WE VISIT HIM IN VANCOUVER NEXT MONTH.
ABSOLUTELY! I'LL BE UP FOR THAT.

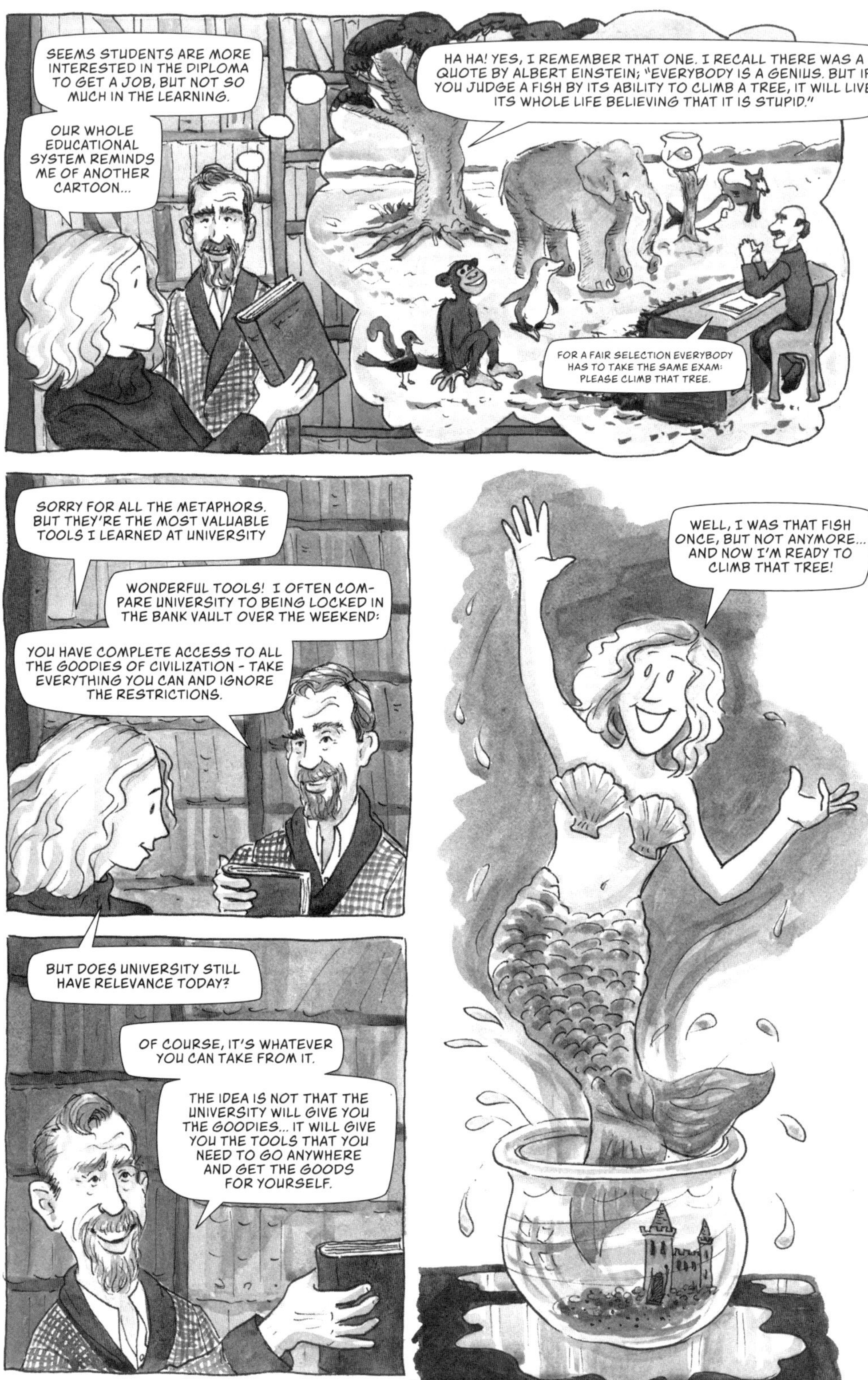
SEEMS STUDENTS ARE MORE INTERESTED IN THE DIPLOMA TO GET A JOB, BUT NOT SO MUCH IN THE LEARNING.
OUR WHOLE EDUCATIONAL SYSTEM REMINDS ME OF ANOTHER CARTOON...
HA HA! YES, I REMEMBER THAT ONE. I RECALL THERE WAS A QUOTE BY ALBERT EINSTEIN; "EVERYBODY IS A GENIUS. BUT IF YOU JUDGE A FISH BY ITS ABILITY TO CLIMB A TREE, IT WILL LIVE ITS WHOLE LIFE BELIEVING THAT IT IS STUPID."
FOR A FAIR SELECTION EVERYBODY HAS TO TAKE THE SAME EXAM: PLEASE CLIMB THAT TREE.
SORRY FOR ALL THE METAPHORS. BUT THEY'RE THE MOST VALUABLE TOOLS I LEARNED AT UNIVERSITY
WONDERFUL TOOLS! I OFTEN COMPARE UNIVERSITY TO BEING LOCKED IN THE BANK VAULT OVER THE WEEKEND:
YOU HAVE COMPLETE ACCESS TO ALL THE GOODIES OF CIVILIZATION - TAKE EVERYTHING YOU CAN AND IGNORE THE RESTRICTIONS.
BUT DOES UNIVERSITY STILL HAVE RELEVANCE TODAY?
OF COURSE, IT'S WHATEVER YOU CAN TAKE FROM IT.
THE IDEA IS NOT THAT THE UNIVERSITY WILL GIVE YOU THE GOODIES... IT WILL GIVE YOU THE TOOLS THAT YOU NEED TO GO ANYWHERE AND GET THE GOODS FOR YOURSELF.
WELL, I WAS THAT FISH ONCE, BUT NOT ANYMORE... AND NOW I'M READY TO CLIMB THAT TREE!

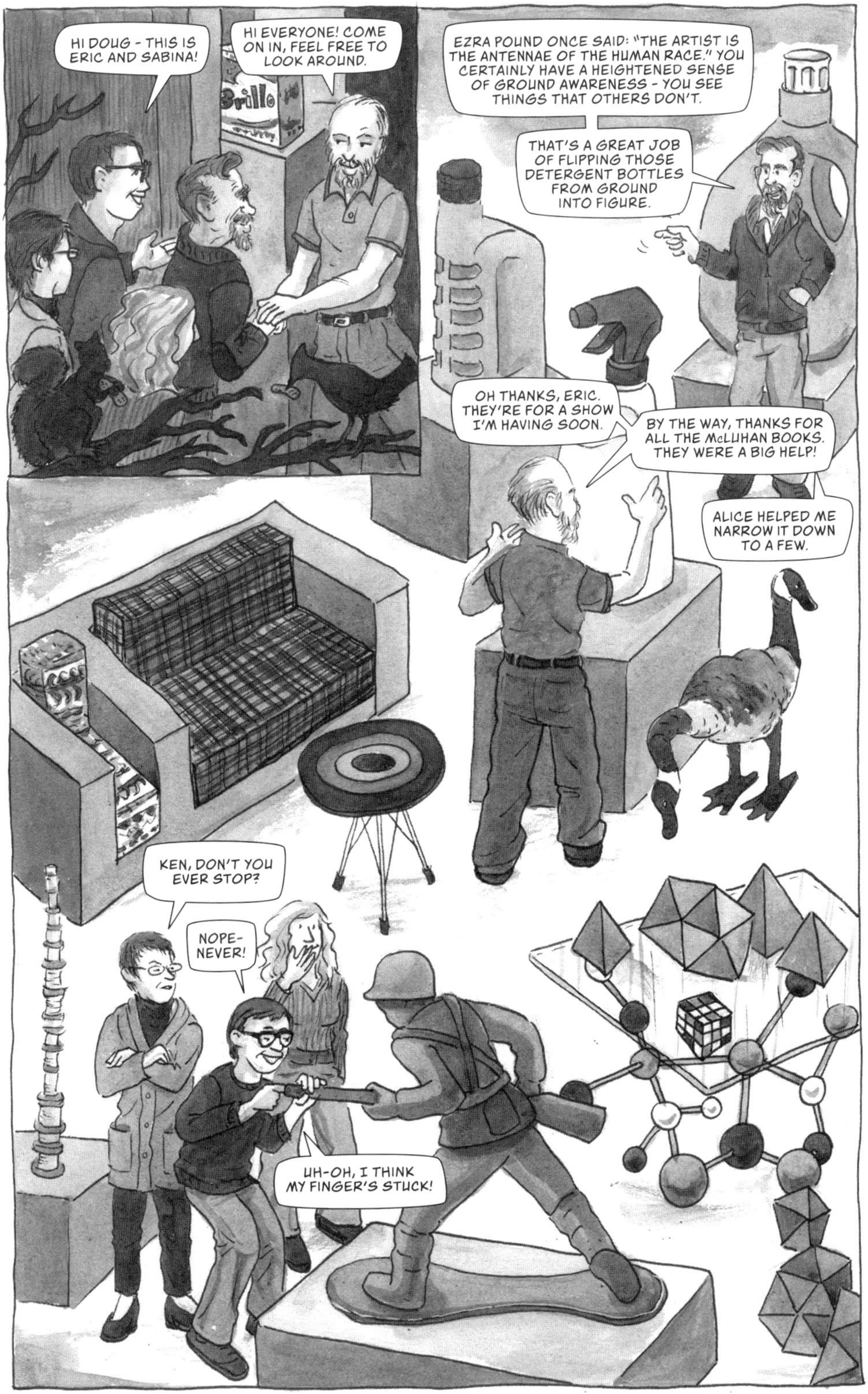
HI DOUG - THIS IS ERIC AND SABINA!
HI EVERYONE! COME ON IN, FEEL FREE TO LOOK AROUND.
Brillo
EZRA POUND ONCE SAID: "THE ARTIST IS THE ANTENNAE OF THE HUMAN RACE." YOU CERTAINLY HAVE A HEIGHTENED SENSE OF GROUND AWARENESS - YOU SEE THINGS THAT OTHERS DON'T.
THAT'S A GREAT JOB OF FLIPPING THOSE DETERGENT BOTTLES FROM GROUND INTO FIGURE.
OH THANKS, ERIC. THEY'RE FOR A SHOW I'M HAVING SOON.
BY THE WAY, THANKS FOR ALL THE McLUHAN BOOKS. THEY WERE A BIG HELP!
ALICE HELPED ME NARROW IT DOWN TO A FEW.
KEN, DON'T YOU EVER STOP?
NOPE-NEVER!
UH-OH, I THINK MY FINGER'S STUCK!

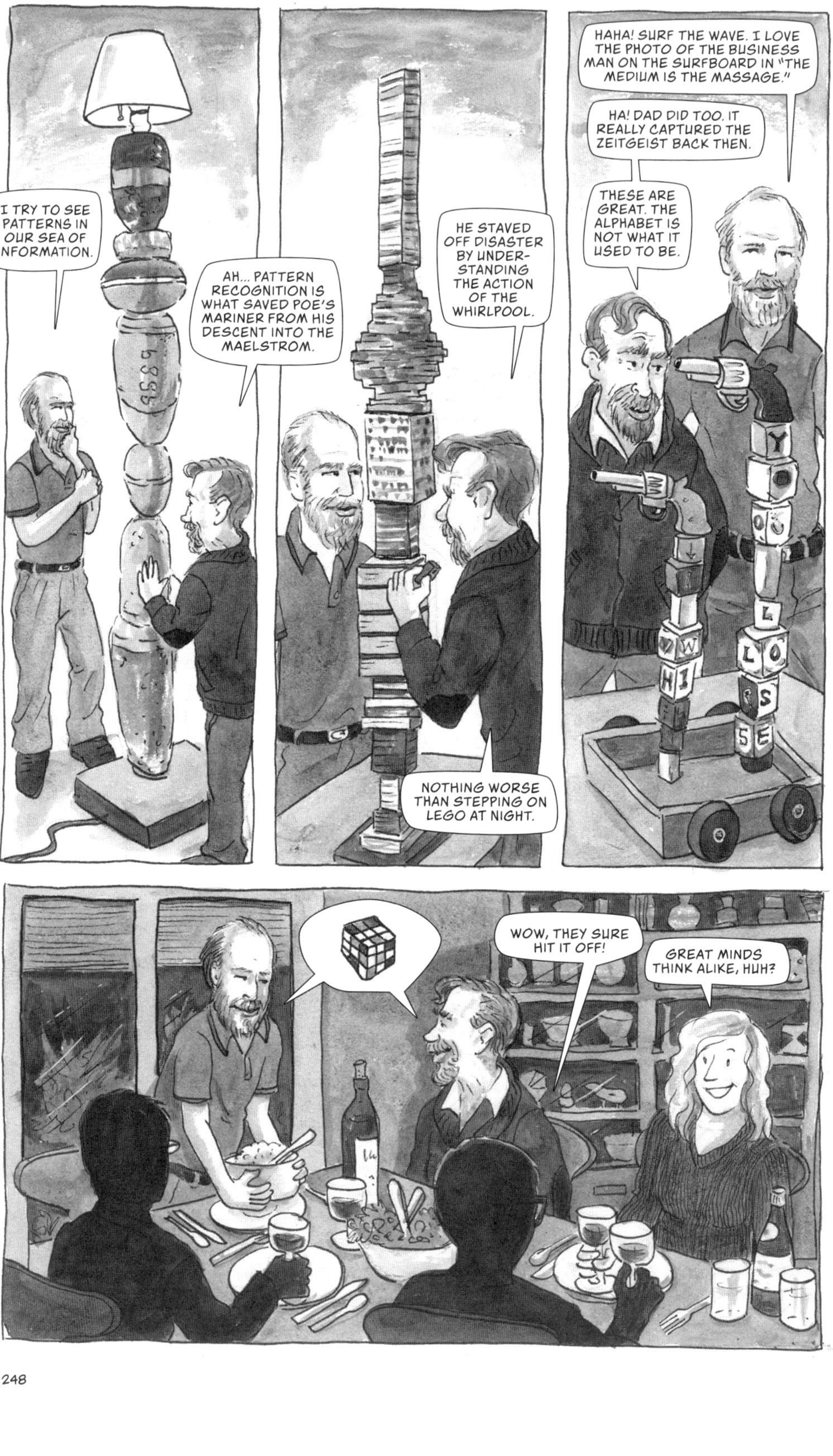
I TRY TO SEE PATTERNS IN OUR SEA OF INFORMATION.
AH... PATTERN RECOGNITION IS WHAT SAVED POE'S MARINER FROM HIS DESCENT INTO THE MAELSTROM.
HE STAVED OFF DISASTER BY UNDERSTANDING THE ACTION OF THE WHIRLPOOL.
NOTHING WORSE THAN STEPPING ON LEGO AT NIGHT.
HAHA! SURF THE WAVE. I LOVE THE PHOTO OF THE BUSINESS MAN ON THE SURFBOARD IN "THE MEDIUM IS THE MASSAGE."
HA! DAD DID TOO. IT REALLY CAPTURED THE ZEITGEIST BACK THEN.
THESE ARE GREAT. THE ALPHABET IS NOT WHAT IT USED TO BE.
WOW, THEY SURE HIT IT OFF!
GREAT MINDS THINK ALIKE, HUH?

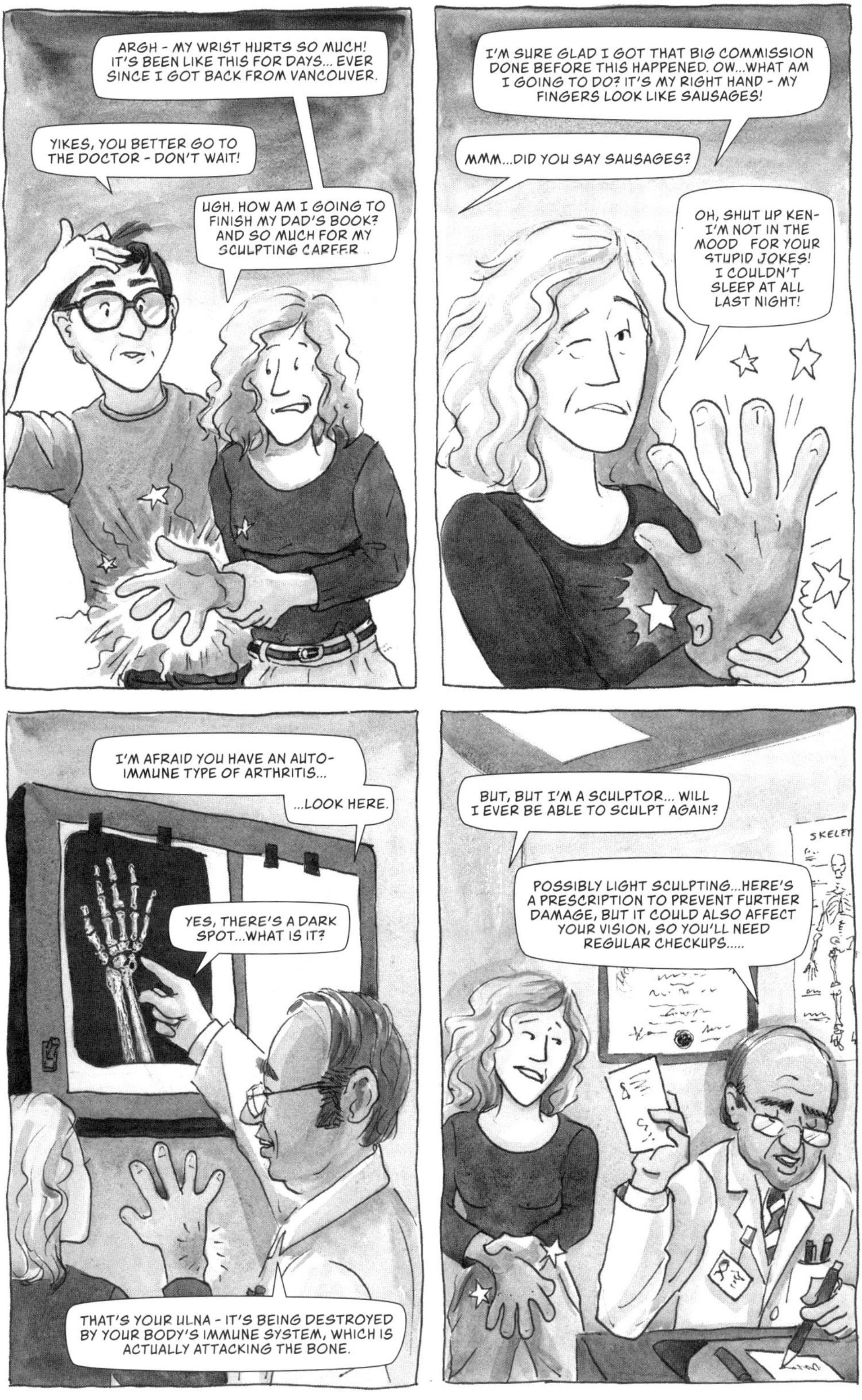
ARGH - MY WRIST HURTS SO MUCH! IT'S BEEN LIKE THIS FOR DAYS... EVER SINCE I GOT BACK FROM VANCOUVER.
YIKES, YOU BETTER GO TO THE DOCTOR - DON'T WAIT!
UGH. HOW AM I GOING TO FINISH MY DAD'S BOOK? AND SO MUCH FOR MY SCULPTING CAREER...
I'M SURE GLAD I GOT THAT BIG COMMISSION DONE BEFORE THIS HAPPENED. OW...WHAT AM I GOING TO DO? IT'S MY RIGHT HAND - MY FINGERS LOOK LIKE SAUSAGES!
MMM...DID YOU SAY SAUSAGES?
OH, SHUT UP KEN- I'M NOT IN THE MOOD FOR YOUR STUPID JOKES! I COULDN'T SLEEP AT ALL LAST NIGHT!
I'M AFRAID YOU HAVE AN AUTO-IMMUNE TYPE OF ARTHRITIS...
...LOOK HERE.
YES, THERE'S A DARK SPOT...WHAT IS IT?
THAT'S YOUR ULNA - IT'S BEING DESTROYED BY YOUR BODY'S IMMUNE SYSTEM, WHICH IS ACTUALLY ATTACKING THE BONE.
BUT, BUT I'M A SCULPTOR... WILL I EVER BE ABLE TO SCULPT AGAIN?
POSSIBLY LIGHT SCULPTING...HERE'S A PRESCRIPTION TO PREVENT FURTHER DAMAGE, BUT IT COULD ALSO AFFECT YOUR VISION, SO YOU'LL NEED REGULAR CHECKUPS.....

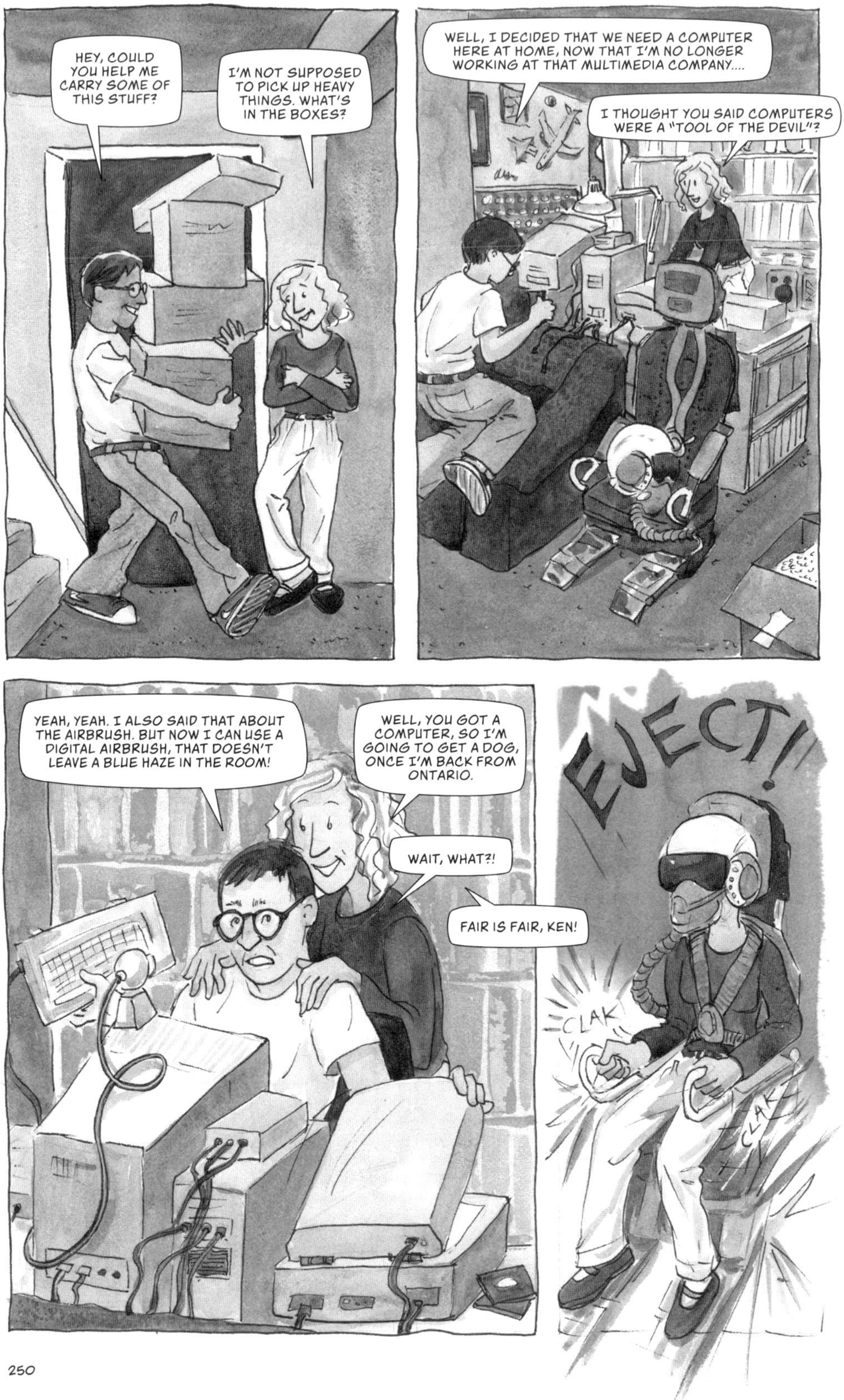
HEY, COULD YOU HELP ME CARRY SOME OF THIS STUFF?
I'M NOT SUPPOSED TO PICK UP HEAVY THINGS. WHAT'S IN THE BOXES?
WELL, I DECIDED THAT WE NEED A COMPUTER HERE AT HOME, NOW THAT I'M NO LONGER WORKING AT THAT MULTIMEDIA COMPANY....
I THOUGHT YOU SAID COMPUTERS WERE A "TOOL OF THE DEVIL"?
YEAH, YEAH. I ALSO SAID THAT ABOUT THE AIRBRUSH. BUT NOW I CAN USE A DIGITAL AIRBRUSH, THAT DOESN'T LEAVE A BLUE HAZE IN THE ROOM!
WELL, YOU GOT A COMPUTER, SO I'M GOING TO GET A DOG, ONCE I'M BACK FROM ONTARIO.
WAIT, WHAT?!
FAIR IS FAIR, KEN!
EJECT!
CLAK
CLAK

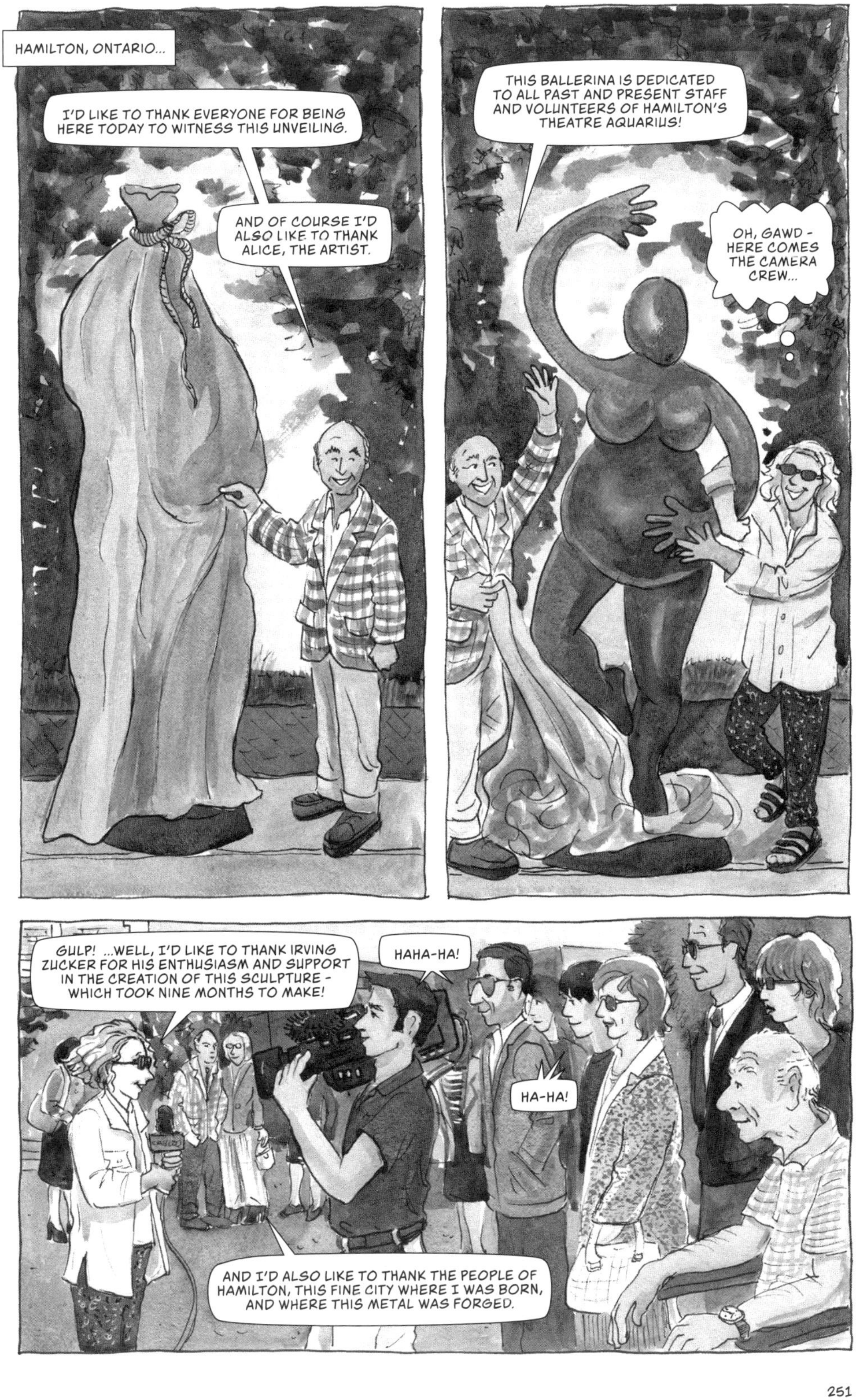
HAMILTON, ONTARIO...
I'D LIKE TO THANK EVERYONE FOR BEING HERE TODAY TO WITNESS THIS UNVEILING.
AND OF COURSE I'D ALSO LIKE TO THANK ALICE, THE ARTIST.
THIS BALLERINA IS DEDICATED TO ALL PAST AND PRESENT STAFF AND VOLUNTEERS OF HAMILTON'S THEATRE AQUARIUS!
OH, GAWD - HERE COMES THE CAMERA CREW...
GULP! ...WELL, I'D LIKE TO THANK IRVING ZUCKER FOR HIS ENTHUSIASM AND SUPPORT IN THE CREATION OF THIS SCULPTURE - WHICH TOOK NINE MONTHS TO MAKE!
HAHA-HA!
HA-HA!
AND I'D ALSO LIKE TO THANK THE PEOPLE OF HAMILTON, THIS FINE CITY WHERE I WAS BORN, AND WHERE THIS METAL WAS FORGED.

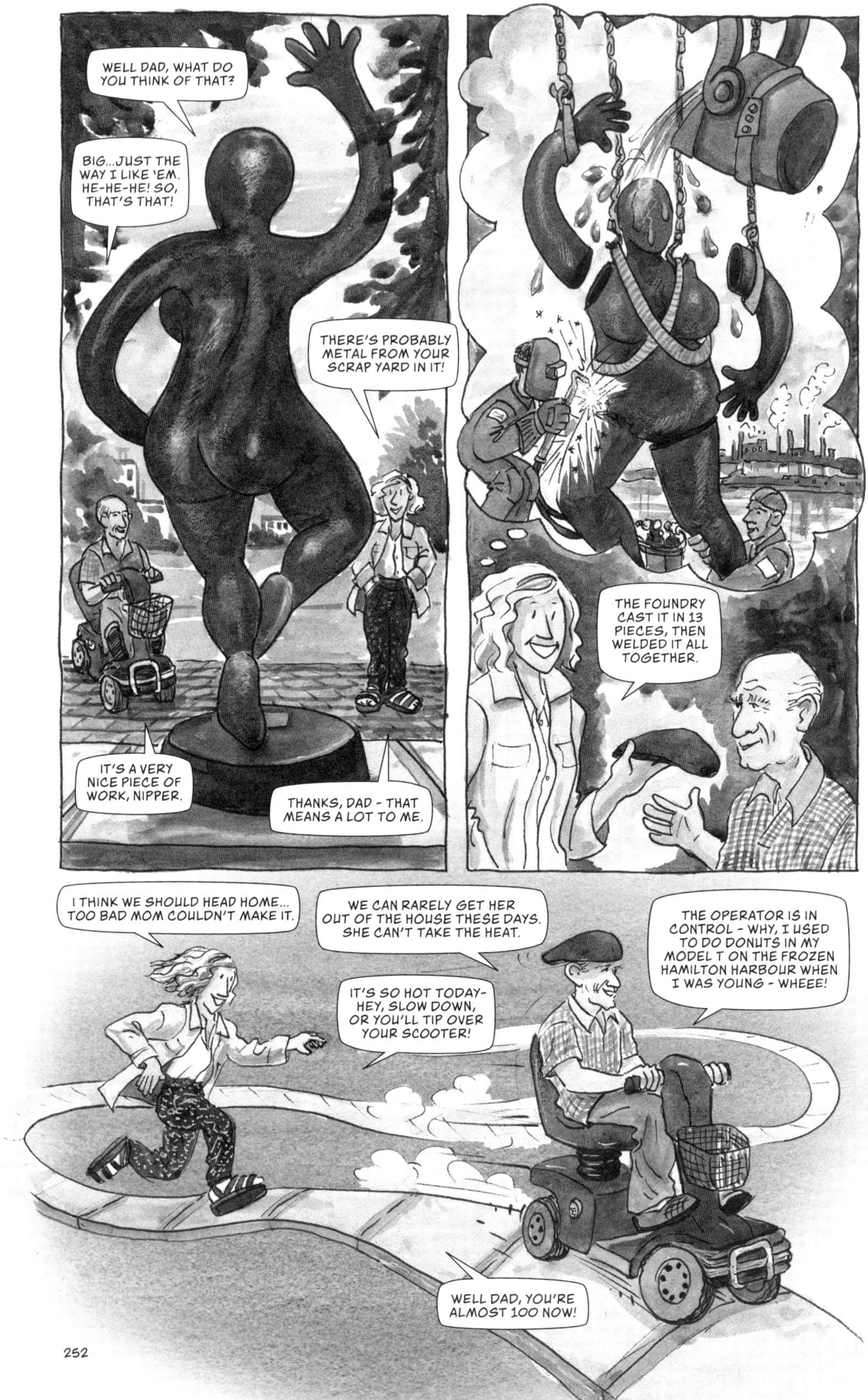
WELL DAD, WHAT DO YOU THINK OF THAT?
BIG...JUST THE WAY I LIKE 'EM. HE-HE-HE! SO, THAT'S THAT!
THERE'S PROBABLY METAL FROM YOUR SCRAP YARD IN IT!
IT'S A VERY NICE PIECE OF WORK, NIPPER.
THANKS, DAD - THAT MEANS A LOT TO ME.
THE FOUNDRY CAST IT IN 13 PIECES, THEN WELDED IT ALL TOGETHER.
I THINK WE SHOULD HEAD HOME... TOO BAD MOM COULDN'T MAKE IT.
WE CAN RARELY GET HER OUT OF THE HOUSE THESE DAYS. SHE CAN'T TAKE THE HEAT.
IT'S SO HOT TODAY- HEY, SLOW DOWN, OR YOU'LL TIP OVER YOUR SCOOTER!
THE OPERATOR IS IN CONTROL - WHY, I USED TO DO DONUTS IN MY MODEL T ON THE FROZEN HAMILTON HARBOUR WHEN I WAS YOUNG - WHEEE!
WELL DAD, YOU'RE ALMOST 100 NOW!

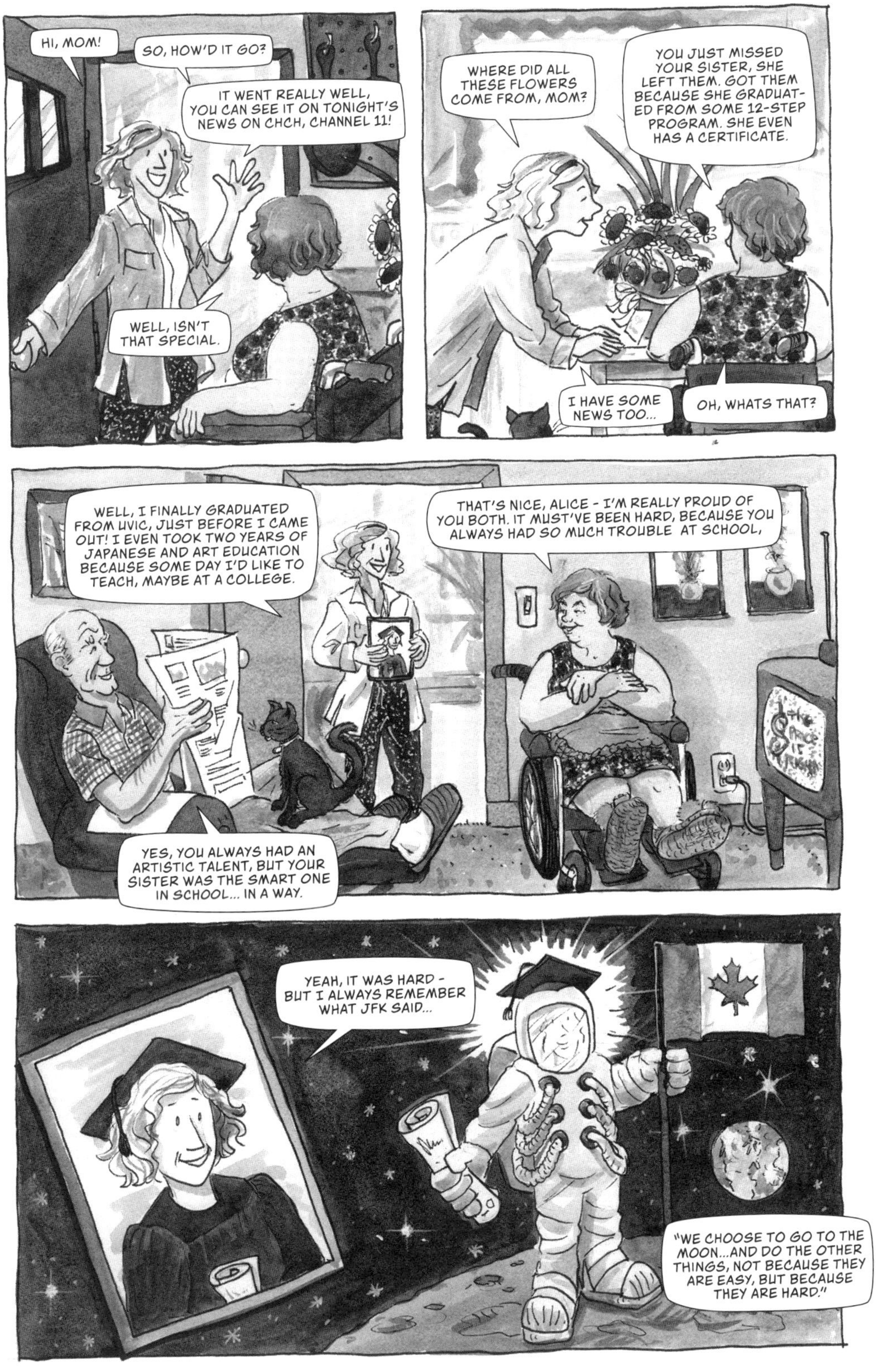
HI, MOM!
SO, HOW'D IT GO?
IT WENT REALLY WELL, YOU CAN SEE IT ON TONIGHT'S NEWS ON CHCH, CHANNEL 11!
WELL, ISN'T THAT SPECIAL.
WHERE DID ALL THESE FLOWERS COME FROM, MOM?
YOU JUST MISSED YOUR SISTER, SHE LEFT THEM. GOT THEM BECAUSE SHE GRADUATED FROM SOME 12-STEP PROGRAM. SHE EVEN HAS A CERTIFICATE.
I HAVE SOME NEWS TOO...
OH, WHATS THAT?
WELL, I FINALLY GRADUATED FROM UVIC, JUST BEFORE I CAME OUT! I EVEN TOOK TWO YEARS OF JAPANESE AND ART EDUCATION BECAUSE SOME DAY I'D LIKE TO TEACH, MAYBE AT A COLLEGE.
THAT'S NICE, ALICE - I'M REALLY PROUD OF YOU BOTH. IT MUST'VE BEEN HARD, BECAUSE YOU ALWAYS HAD SO MUCH TROUBLE AT SCHOOL,
YES, YOU ALWAYS HAD AN ARTISTIC TALENT, BUT YOUR SISTER WAS THE SMART ONE IN SCHOOL... IN A WAY.
YEAH, IT WAS HARD - BUT I ALWAYS REMEMBER WHAT JFK SAID...
"WE CHOOSE TO GO TO THE MOON...AND DO THE OTHER THINGS, NOT BECAUSE THEY ARE EASY, BUT BECAUSE THEY ARE HARD."

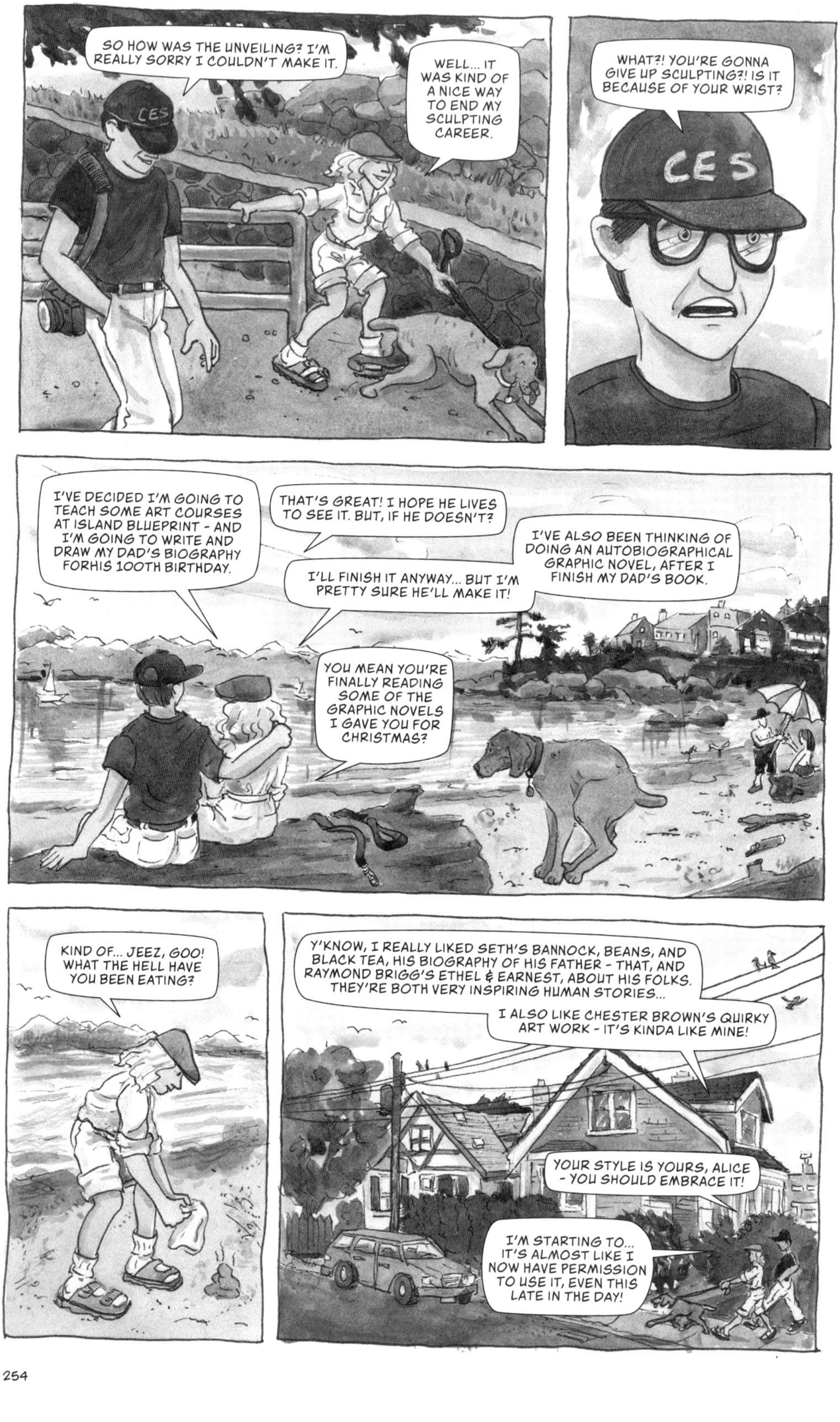
SO HOW WAS THE UNVEILING? I'M REALLY SORRY I COULDN'T MAKE IT.
WELL... IT WAS KIND OF A NICE WAY TO END MY SCULPTING CAREER.
CES
WHAT?! YOU'RE GONNA GIVE UP SCULPTING?! IS IT BECAUSE OF YOUR WRIST?
CES
I'VE DECIDED I'M GOING TO TEACH SOME ART COURSES AT ISLAND BLUEPRINT - AND I'M GOING TO WRITE AND DRAW MY DAD'S BIOGRAPHY FORHIS 100TH BIRTHDAY.
THAT'S GREAT! I HOPE HE LIVES TO SEE IT. BUT, IF HE DOESN'T?
I'LL FINISH IT ANYWAY... BUT I'M PRETTY SURE HE'LL MAKE IT!
I'VE ALSO BEEN THINKING OF DOING AN AUTOBIOGRAPHICAL GRAPHIC NOVEL, AFTER I FINISH MY DAD'S BOOK.
YOU MEAN YOU'RE FINALLY READING SOME OF THE GRAPHIC NOVELS I GAVE YOU FOR CHRISTMAS?
KIND OF... JEEZ, GOO! WHAT THE HELL HAVE YOU BEEN EATING?
Y'KNOW, I REALLY LIKED SETH'S BANNOCK, BEANS, AND BLACK TEA, HIS BIOGRAPHY OF HIS FATHER - THAT, AND RAYMOND BRIGG'S ETHEL & EARNEST, ABOUT HIS FOLKS. THEY'RE BOTH VERY INSPIRING HUMAN STORIES...
I ALSO LIKE CHESTER BROWN'S QUIRKY ART WORK - IT'S KINDA LIKE MINE!
YOUR STYLE IS YOURS, ALICE - YOU SHOULD EMBRACE IT!
I'M STARTING TO... IT'S ALMOST LIKE I NOW HAVE PERMISSION TO USE IT, EVEN THIS LATE IN THE DAY!

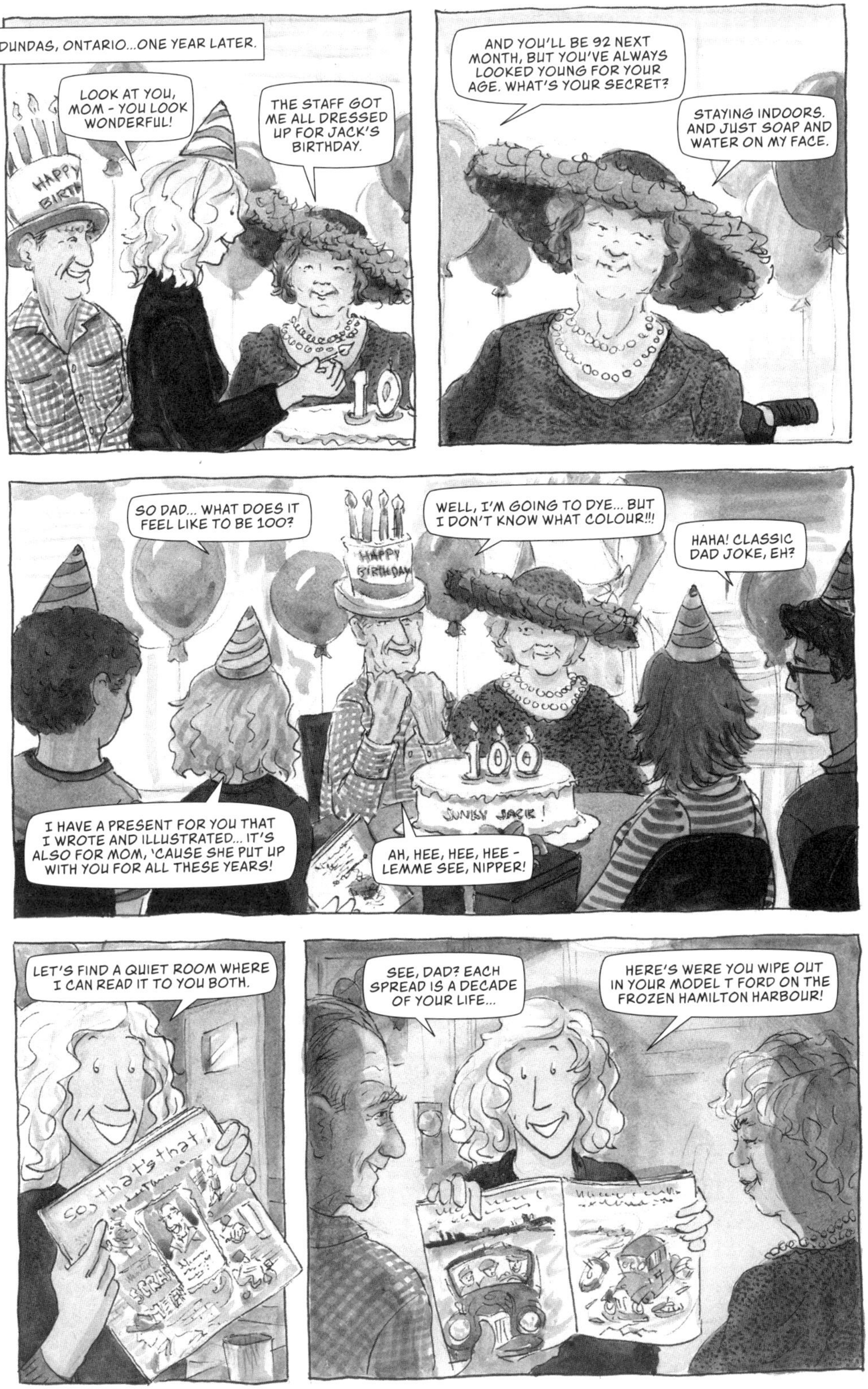
DUNDAS, ONTARIO...ONE YEAR LATER.
HAPPY BIRTH
LOOK AT YOU, MOM - YOU LOOK WONDERFUL!
THE STAFF GOT ME ALL DRESSED UP FOR JACK'S BIRTHDAY.
AND YOU'LL BE 92 NEXT MONTH, BUT YOU'VE ALWAYS LOOKED YOUNG FOR YOUR AGE. WHAT'S YOUR SECRET?
STAYING INDOORS. AND JUST SOAP AND WATER ON MY FACE.
SO DAD... WHAT DOES IT FEEL LIKE TO BE 100?
HAPPY BIRTHDAY
WELL, I'M GOING TO DYE... BUT I DON'T KNOW WHAT COLOUR!!!
HAHA! CLASSIC DAD JOKE, EH?
I HAVE A PRESENT FOR YOU THAT I WROTE AND ILLUSTRATED... IT'S ALSO FOR MOM, 'CAUSE SHE PUT UP WITH YOU FOR ALL THESE YEARS!
AH, HEE, HEE, HEE - LEMME SEE, NIPPER!
LET'S FIND A QUIET ROOM WHERE I CAN READ IT TO YOU BOTH.
so that's that!
SEE, DAD? EACH SPREAD IS A DECADE OF YOUR LIFE...
HERE'S WERE YOU WIPE OUT IN YOUR MODEL T FORD ON THE FROZEN HAMILTON HARBOUR!

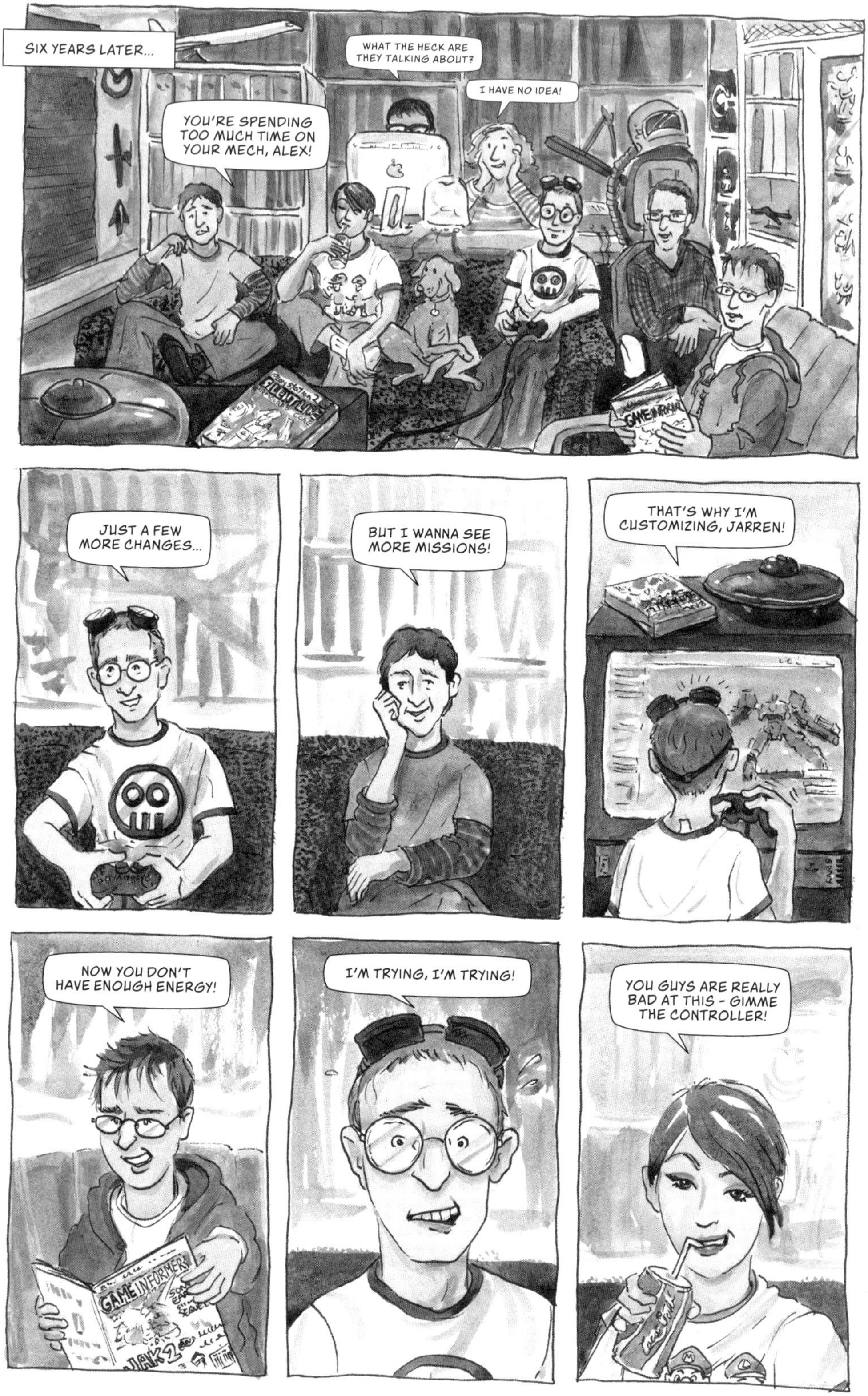
SIX YEARS LATER...
YOU'RE SPENDING TOO MUCH TIME ON YOUR MECH, ALEX!
WHAT THE HECK ARE THEY TALKING ABOUT?
I HAVE NO IDEA!
JUST A FEW MORE CHANGES...
BUT I WANNA SEE MORE MISSIONS!
THAT'S WHY I'M CUSTOMIZING, JARREN!
NOW YOU DON'T HAVE ENOUGH ENERGY!
I'M TRYING, I'M TRYING!
YOU GUYS ARE REALLY BAD AT THIS - GIMME THE CONTROLLER!

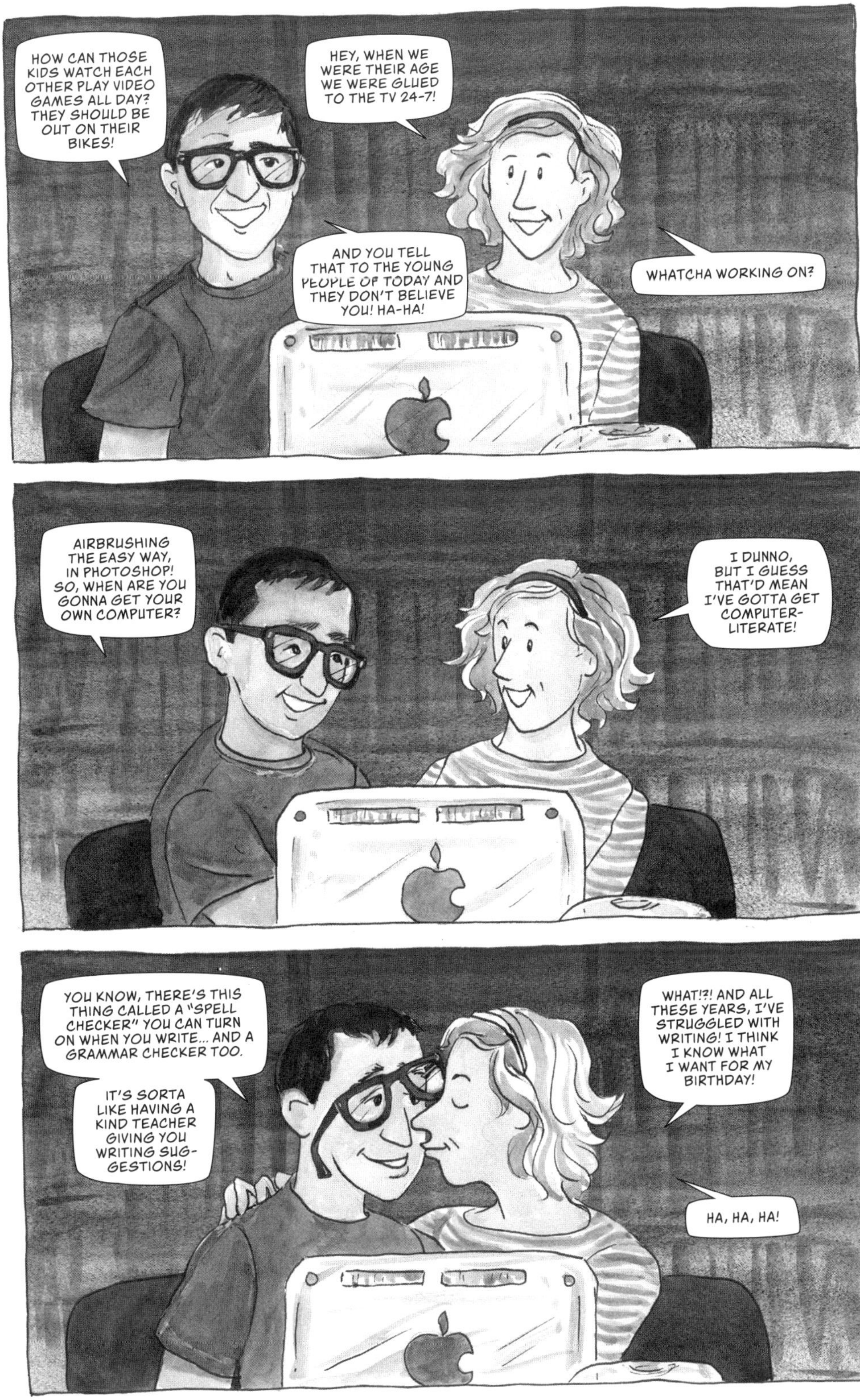
HOW CAN THOSE KIDS WATCH EACH OTHER PLAY VIDEO GAMES ALL DAY? THEY SHOULD BE OUT ON THEIR BIKES!
HEY, WHEN WE WERE THEIR AGE WE WERE GLUED TO THE TV 24-7!
AND YOU TELL THAT TO THE YOUNG PEOPLE OF TODAY AND THEY DON'T BELIEVE YOU! HA-HA!
WHATCHA WORKING ON?
AIRBRUSHING THE EASY WAY, IN PHOTOSHOP! SO, WHEN ARE YOU GONNA GET YOUR OWN COMPUTER?
I DUNNO, BUT I GUESS THAT'D MEAN I'VE GOTTA GET COMPUTER-LITERATE!
YOU KNOW, THERE'S THIS THING CALLED A "SPELL CHECKER" YOU CAN TURN ON WHEN YOU WRITE... AND A GRAMMAR CHECKER TOO.
IT'S SORTA LIKE HAVING A KIND TEACHER GIVING YOU WRITING SUG-GESTIONS!
WHAT!?! AND ALL THESE YEARS, I'VE STRUGGLED WITH WRITING! I THINK I KNOW WHAT I WANT FOR MY BIRTHDAY!
HA, HA, HA!

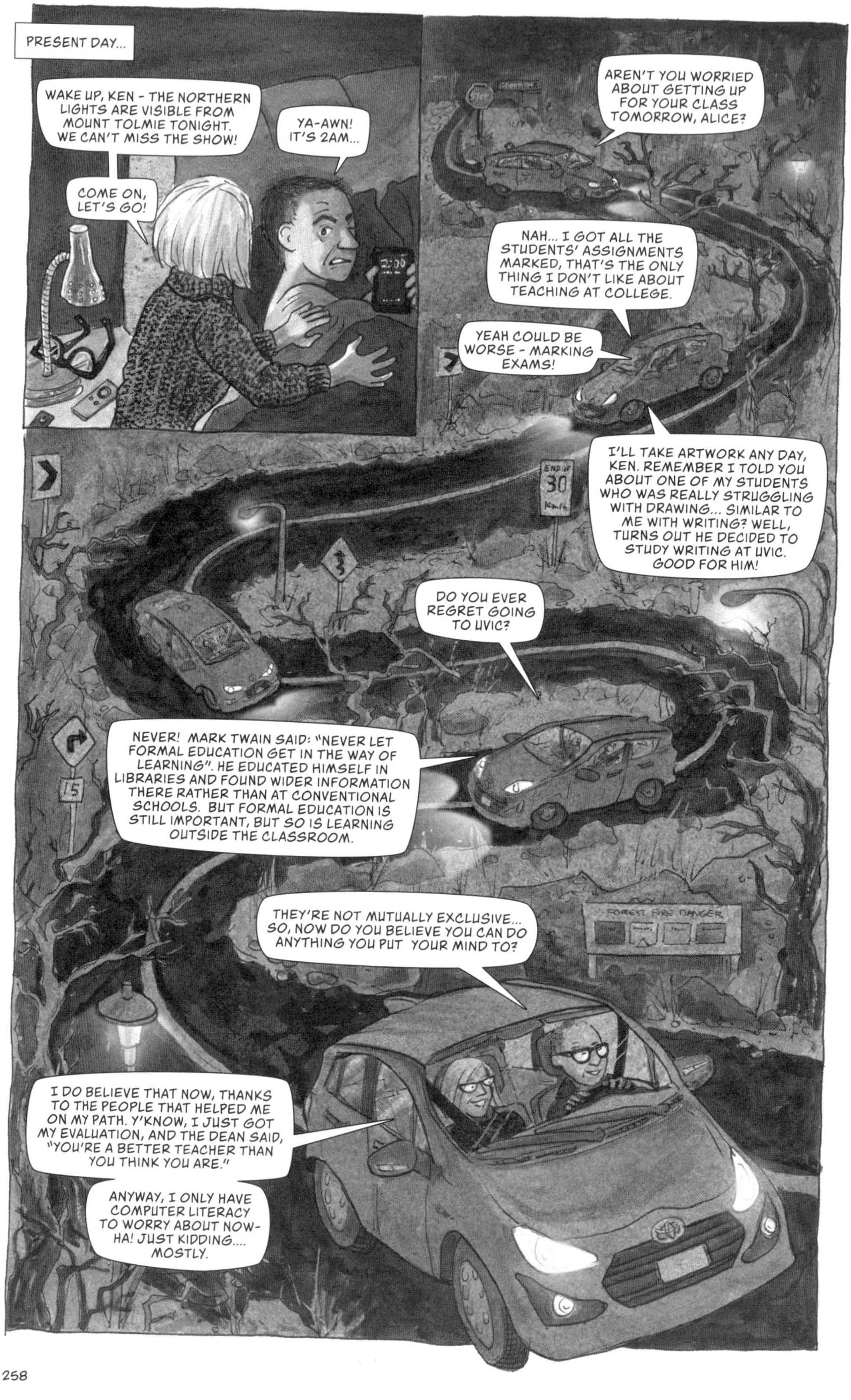
PRESENT DAY...
WAKE UP, KEN - THE NORTHERN LIGHTS ARE VISIBLE FROM MOUNT TOLMIE TONIGHT. WE CAN'T MISS THE SHOW!
YA-AWN! IT'S 2AM...
COME ON, LET'S GO!
AREN'T YOU WORRIED ABOUT GETTING UP FOR YOUR CLASS TOMORROW, ALICE?
NAH... I GOT ALL THE STUDENTS' ASSIGNMENTS MARKED, THAT'S THE ONLY THING I DON'T LIKE ABOUT TEACHING AT COLLEGE.
YEAH COULD BE WORSE - MARKING EXAMS!
I'LL TAKE ARTWORK ANY DAY, KEN. REMEMBER I TOLD YOU ABOUT ONE OF MY STUDENTS WHO WAS REALLY STRUGGLING WITH DRAWING... SIMILAR TO ME WITH WRITING? WELL, TURNS OUT HE DECIDED TO STUDY WRITING AT UVIC. GOOD FOR HIM!
DO YOU EVER REGRET GOING TO UVIC?
NEVER! MARK TWAIN SAID: "NEVER LET FORMAL EDUCATION GET IN THE WAY OF LEARNING". HE EDUCATED HIMSELF IN LIBRARIES AND FOUND WIDER INFORMATION THERE RATHER THAN AT CONVENTIONAL SCHOOLS. BUT FORMAL EDUCATION IS STILL IMPORTANT, BUT SO IS LEARNING OUTSIDE THE CLASSROOM.
THEY'RE NOT MUTUALLY EXCLUSIVE... SO, NOW DO YOU BELIEVE YOU CAN DO ANYTHING YOU PUT YOUR MIND TO?
I DO BELIEVE THAT NOW, THANKS TO THE PEOPLE THAT HELPED ME ON MY PATH. Y'KNOW, I JUST GOT MY EVALUATION, AND THE DEAN SAID, "YOU'RE A BETTER TEACHER THAN YOU THINK YOU ARE."
ANYWAY, I ONLY HAVE COMPUTER LITERACY TO WORRY ABOUT NOW- HA! JUST KIDDING.... MOSTLY.
FOREST FIRE DANGER

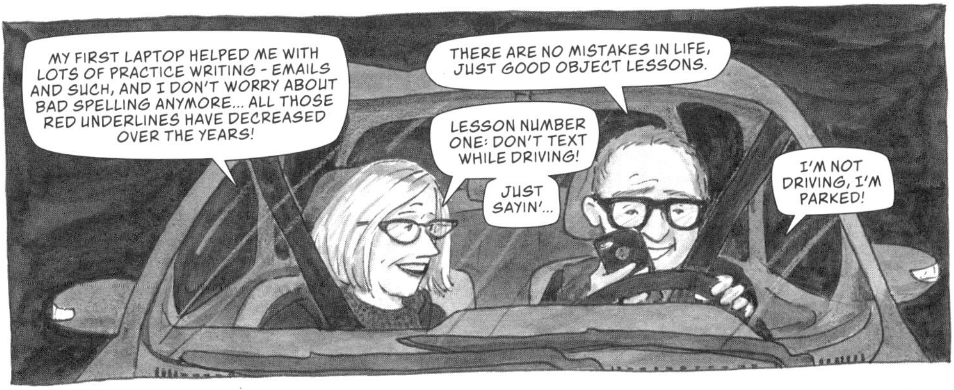
MY FIRST LAPTOP HELPED ME WITH LOTS OF PRACTICE WRITING - EMAILS AND SUCH, AND I DON'T WORRY ABOUT BAD SPELLING ANYMORE... ALL THOSE RED UNDERLINES HAVE DECREASED OVER THE YEARS!
THERE ARE NO MISTAKES IN LIFE, JUST GOOD OBJECT LESSONS.
LESSON NUMBER ONE: DON'T TEXT WHILE DRIVING!
JUST SAYIN'...
I'M NOT DRIVING, I'M PARKED!

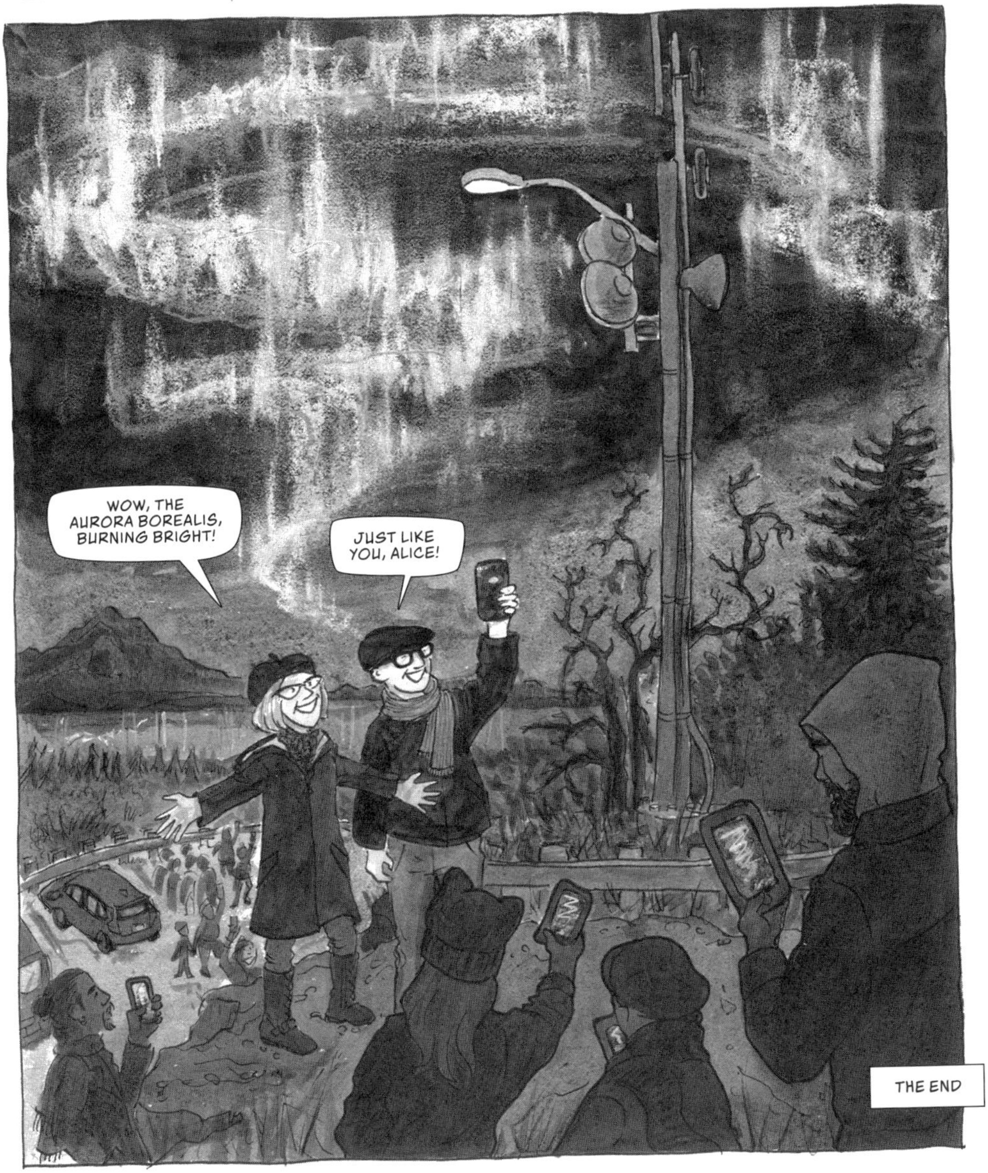
WOW, THE AURORA BOREALIS, BURNING BRIGHT!
JUST LIKE YOU, ALICE!
THE END

ABOUT THE VISUAL STORYTELLER

Joan Steacy grew up in southern Ontario, and is a graduate of Sheridan College, The Ontario College of Art & Design, and The University of Victoria. A visual artist who has worked in a variety of disciplines including sculpture, traditional illustration, and digital imaging, she wrote and illustrated *So, That's That!*, a storybook biography of her father who lived to be 100 years old. She currently teaches Comics & Graphic Novels at Camosun College in Victoria BC, a visual storytelling program she co-created with her husband, author/illustrator Ken Steacy.

www.joansteacy.blogspot.com

DEDICATION

This graphic novel is dedicated to Eric McLuhan Ph.D. 1942 - 2018

My friend Eric was a teacher and mentor who inspired me to believe that I could learn beyond my dreams. Likewise, to all the other educators who have made a lasting difference in their students' lives; thank you.

Thanks so much to everyone who helped with this book, especially:

My loving husband Ken, for his unwavering support throughout this project. His art direction, editorial, and technical help was invaluable.
Alex Steacy, for additional technical support, feedback, and for being there when I needed him.
Diana Schutz, for her greatly appreciated editorial input.
Trina Robbins, for her wonderful intro, and Paul Chadwick, Douglas Coupland, Gareth Gaudin, and Jeff Lemire, for their generous quotes.
Andy Brown, my publisher at Conundrum Press, for bringing my story into print, and for his sharp editorial eye.
All my students over the years, for accepting and forgiving my little foibles. I only hope that I too have made a difference in their lives.

My story is based on real life events, only my name is changed. Alice was my given first name, which I have chosen to use for my character in the book, so it is with that name that I sign:

Alice Joan Steacy